Handbook of Families and Work

Interdisciplinary Perspectives

Edited by
D. Russell Crane
E. Jeffrey Hill

UNIVERSITY PRESS OF AMERICA,® INC.
Lanham • Boulder • New York • Toronto • Plymouth, UK

Copyright © 2009 by
University Press of America,® Inc.
4501 Forbes Boulevard
Suite 200
Lanham, Maryland 20706
UPA Acquisitions Department (301) 459-3366

Estover Road
Plymouth PL6 7PY
United Kingdom

Library of Congress Control Number: 2008943821
ISBN: 978-0-7618-4435-8 (paperback : alk. paper)
eISBN: 978-0-7618-4436-5

∞™ The paper used in this publication meets the minimum
requirements of American National Standard for Information
Sciences—Permanence of Paper for Printed Library Materials,
ANSI Z39.48—1984

Contents

Foreword

by Robert Drago

Beginning in the 1960s, middle-class women in the United States began entering the labor force in large numbers, and the mothers among them eventually followed. Today, a solid majority of women and mothers are employed, and even a majority of mothers with infants under the age of one year are employed. The field of work and family research grew out of this phenomenon, as researchers sought to understand both the implications of simultaneous commitments to paid employment and unpaid care, and how resulting conflicts could be mitigated, ameliorated, or otherwise resolved. And the scope of these has expanded to include fathers as well as mothers, those with elder care needs, as well as those with any other personal needs. This *Handbook of Families and Work* documents our progress in this regard.

Given where we started, it is not surprising that much of the early research in the 1970s represented an attempt to return us to an earlier era—the *Leave It to Beaver* middle-class families of the 1950s. That research sought to demonstrate that employed mothers were damaging their children psychologically, emotionally, and in terms of their cognitive development. Women should therefore abandon employment.

Although this early research is covered in this book, the actual findings turned out to be complex. And it remains that employed mothers are a fact of both our present and our future, so perhaps a more appropriate question is how work and family can be successfully melded for the benefit of children, adults, parents, communities, employers, and society as a whole. The *Handbook of Families and Work* provides a wealth of knowledge in answer to that broader question. And a handbook is indeed needed because families and the economy have become far more diverse in recent decades.

To answer the broader question in today's context requires expanding our view to encompass not just employed mothers in America, but also fathers, single mothers, poor families, grandparents, a wide range of sometimes precarious jobs, an increasingly global economy, and governmental policies. To understand the combining of family and work in this context, some of the authors focus on resources as broadly defined, including the ability to put food on the table and provide access to health care, but also the ability to commute to a job, and the web of supports that allow or do not allow parents to respond to emergencies at work and at home.

Relationships matter as well, whether we consider the expanding involvement of American fathers in their children's lives, the role of grandparents in the provision of childcare, or the sympathetic recognition of dual commitments by others in the workplace and the home.

In addition to resources and relationships, much of the research here addresses norms, values, ideology, and beliefs regarding the appropriate roles of mothers, fathers, children, our schools and communities, and our government. Here we see both stability in the generally strong work ethic in our society and a belief in the value of parenting, but also shifts as many Americans have come to hold strong beliefs in gender equity and in the importance of life outside of work even as many Americans increasingly choose or need to work beyond the traditional age of retirement.

Finally, many of the chapters, and particularly the last one, turn the original question on its head. They ask how family and work can complement, support, and enrich our ability to make commitments to both. Answering that question casts a positive and proactive light on the overarching question of what we should be doing to help create a better society. The pages that follow provide an abundant source of solutions, and as such are a source of great hope for our future, and for future generations.

NOTE

Robert Drago, Ph.D., a professor of Labor Studies and Women's Studies at The Pennsylvania State University, is past president of the College and University Work-Family Association, and moderates the Workfam newsgroup on the internet. He holds a Ph.D. in Economics from the University of Massachusetts at Amherst, and was a Senior Fulbright Research Scholar. The author of four books and more than 70 articles, his most recent book is *Striking a Balance*, published by Dollars & Sense in 2007.

Chapter One

Editors' Introduction

by E. Jeffrey Hill and D. Russell Crane

This *Handbook of Families and Work: Interdisciplinary Perspectives* is intended to explore the most recent topics in research, practice, and policy related to the intersection of family life and work life, and how that intersection can be optimized for families. This handbook is truly interdisciplinary in nature, beginning with the collaboration of the co-authors, a marriage and family therapist and a corporate work-life researcher turned family life professor. The 44 other contributors represent scholars and practitioners from a wide range of disciplines including business, economics, family studies, home and family living, human development, leadership, management, marriage, medicine, psychology, public health, social work, sociology, statistics, and women's studies. The handbook is also international in scope, with contributors from Australia, Canada, Italy, and the Netherlands as well as the United States.

Most publications in this research domain use the terms *work and family* (indicating that variables pertaining to work are more present or more important or both than variables related to family) or *work and life* (indicating the intersection of work and all aspects of non-work life, not just family life). That the title of this handbook uses the words *families and work* sets it apart from other publications in several ways. First, the positioning of the word *families* in the title indicates that family variables are of primary interest, of greater importance than work in this publication. Second, the word *families* in the title is plural indicating the desire to examine various aspects and types of family life. Finally, the use of the word *families* in the title indicates a focused look at aspects of family life, and that other aspects of an individual's

1

non-work life are of secondary importance. It should also be noted that under the direction of Ellen Galinsky there is an excellent research establishment in New York City named the Families and Work Institute. This handbook has no connection with that institution, other than that Ellen Galinsky and Terry Bond are co-authors of one chapter in this book.

BACKGROUND OF THIS *HANDBOOK*

This *Handbook of Families and Work: Interdisciplinary Perspective* is a product of the Family Studies Center, the research division of the School of Family Life at Brigham Young University in Provo, Utah. The mission of the Family Studies Center is to strengthen families "by encouraging, sponsoring, coordinating, and disseminating the university's intellectual effort related to the family" (Family Studies Center, 2008). More than 75 faculty members are affiliated with the Family Studies Center and focus their research on family topics, such as marriage, parenting, home and family living, human development within the family context, family and consumer sciences, and families and work. This is considered to be the largest concentration of family scholars in the world (Family Studies Center, 2008). The Family Studies Center supports these scholars and disseminates the results of their research to families, educators, church and social organizations, family practitioners, government agencies, and the public. The sponsorship of this *Handbook* is an example of that dissemination.

Beginning in 2002 the Family Studies Center has sponsored a large, international, interdisciplinary conference, in which leading scholars in an important field are invited to present papers representing cutting-edge research about the state of that field in relation to families. The proceedings of the conferences provide the nucleus for a book published in handbook format. Following an extensive literature review and consultation with noted leaders in the field, additional scholars are invited to contribute to further broaden the perspective of the particular handbook.

In 2002 the Families and Health Conference was sponsored by the Family Studies Center and the *Handbook of Families and Health: Interdisciplinary Perspectives* (Crane & Marshall, 2005) was later published. This book presents state-of-the-art summaries of research related to couple, marital, and family influences on health. In 2004 the Families and Poverty Conference was sponsored and the *Handbook of Families and Poverty* (Crane & Heaton, 2007) was later published. This book presents insightful summaries of research involving poverty and its relationship to couple, marital, and family dynamics.

This *Handbook of Families and Work: Interdisciplinary Perspectives* began as an outgrowth of the 2006 Families and Work Conference, organized by D. Russell Crane, director of the Family Studies Center. The topic of families and work was selected in recognition of the coming of age of work-family research as a legitimate field of scholarly inquiry related to the family (Pitt-Catsouphes, Kossek, & Sweet, 2006b). The conference was held in Provo, Utah, March 20–22, 2006.

FAMILIES AND WORK AS A LEGITIMATE FIELD OF SCHOLARLY INQUIRY

Peer-reviewed scholarly research examining the intersection of work and personal/family life has existed for almost 100 years. The first peer-reviewed work-family article is thought to have been published in 1909 in the *American Journal of Sociology* (Weatherly, 1909). From the early 1900s through the 1970s there were infrequent articles in a variety of disciplinary journals that examined the intersection of work and personal/family life, but these were often isolated and not overtly coordinated. There simply was not an organized work-family field per se.

The genesis of today's work and family field of scholarly inquiry is often coupled with Rosabeth Moss Kanter's (1977) publication of *Work and Family in the United States: A Critical Review and Agenda for Research and Policy*. This publication helped energize numerous scholars to collaborate and to reach across disciplines to encourage work and family scholarly research. After that time there was more of a tendency to see work and family as its own multi-disciplinary field (Pitt-Catsouphes, Kossek, & Sweet, 2006a).

The success of this endeavor is reflected in the dramatic increase in the quantity of scholarly articles related to work and family since the 1970s. A scan of major scholarly databases between 1970 and 2000 revealed that the quantity of work and family articles increased three-fold in history, seven-fold in psychology, and twelve-fold in sociology (Pitt-Catsouphes, Kossek, & Sweet, 2006a). In an effort to identify the major quality publishing venues for work and family research, Drago and Kashian (2003) recently identified 49 scholarly journals that regularly published in the work and family field. The top ten included journals from family studies, business, psychology, and sociology: *Journal of Marriage and Family, Journal of Family Issues, Journal of Vocational Behavior, Journal of Organizational Behavior, Journal of Applied Psychology, Family Relations, Human Relations, Work and Occupations, Women in Management Review,* and *Monthly Labor Review.*

During the 1980s and 1990s work and family sections, panels, tracks, and focus groups began to spring up at the annual conferences of many disciplines. Just a few of these are the annual conferences of the American Psychological Association, the National Council on Family Relations, the National Academy of Management, and the Society for Industrial and Organizational Psychologists. Perhaps more important, several large-scale interdisciplinary work and family conferences have been sponsored by entities such as Brandeis University, the Sloan Foundation, the Business and Professional Women's Foundation, and the Family Studies Center at Brigham Young University.

That special issues of peer-reviewed scholarly journals have been devoted entirely to work-family issues is also evidence of the increasing importance of this dynamic, multi-disciplinary field. Some of the recent journals dedicating whole issues to the topic of work and family include *Human Resource Management* (Lobel, 1993), *Journal of Occupational Health Psychology* (Westman & Piotrkowski, 1999), *Qualitative Sociology* (Gerstel & Clawson, 2000), and *International Journal of Cross-Cultural Management* (Poelmans, 2003). In 1998 Suzan Lewis and Carolyn Kagan at Manchester Metropolitan University in the United Kingdom began publishing *Community, Work, and Family,* the first journal wholly dedicated to this multi-disciplinary field. It has also given impetus to work and family as an international scholarly field, publishing work and family research from every inhabited continent.

Finally, the growing recognition of work-family as a legitimate field of scholarly inquiry became further evident with the publishing in 2006 of the first full-length handbook in this domain (Pitt-Catsouphes, Kossek, & Sweet, 2006b). The *Work and Family Handbook: Multi-Disciplinary Perspectives and Approaches* is a valuable reference work emphasizing that work-family scholarship demands the use of multiple disciplinary perspectives. In this landmark handbook, Pitt-Catsouphes, Kossek, and Sweet brought together 63 work-family scholars in the fields of social work, psychology, sociology, organizational behavior, human resource management, and other disciplines. These work-family leaders contribute chapters explaining different disciplinary approaches and a variety of theoretical perspectives. In addition, they inform us about how numerous methodologies can be used to understand work and family. Finally, they examine models to advance work-family policy and organizational change.

Clearly work and family is a healthy, even burgeoning multi-disciplinary field of scholarly inquiry. However, it is young and will continue to benefit from projects to bring various work and family perspectives to together. This *Handbook* is an additional attempt to do that.

OUTLINE OF THIS *HANDBOOK*

In Part 1, we explore many facets of the work-family interface, with a focus on the impact of work on family. We examine the concept of work-family balance, look at job stress and its effects on the family, work-family facilitation (how work and family benefit one another), demands and resources, and work-family in a global context.

In Part 2, we focus on cutting-edge research concerning the relationship of flexible work arrangements to work and family outcomes. Many organizations are implementing flexibility in order to meet business goals with the underlying assumption that this flexibility will also benefit employees' personal and family lives. Researchers in this volume scrutinize that assumption and report interesting findings.

In Part 3, we examine work and family in a parental and multi-generational context. Chapters look at how fathers' work conditions affect the father-child relationship, maternal employment, maternal shift work, linkages between job conditions and working class parents, and the interaction of marital relationship and retirement.

Finally, in Part 4, we write about implications of work and family for family life. In this section we step back and look more philosophically about the work-family interface.

This *Families and Work Handbook: Interdisciplinary Perspectives* builds upon and extends the work of Pitt-Catsouphes, Kossek, and Sweet (2006b) and the ground work of other edited volumes, special issues, the journal *Community, Work, and Family,* and other thoughtful scholarly projects. However, no handbook can cover all of the important issues related to families and work. We recognize that this *Handbook of Families and Work* is no different. We believe its unique contribution is that it focuses more on family life and family relationships. In many edited volumes the emphasis is not as specific. In many the emphasis is on the interface of work with all facets of life. This volume zeros in more on the influence specifically on family life.

We did not require contributors to adhere to a standard format for the chapters. Instead, we encouraged authors to write in the way that best addressed their areas of expertise. We think this approach should enrich the ongoing interdisciplinary discussion of work and family.

AUDIENCE FOR THE WORK

This *Handbook of Families and Work* includes the perspectives of a broad range of disciplines. However, it is a compilation rather than an integration.

The handbook is intended for readers from all areas devoted to work and family. Just as we sought a wide range of scholars to create this book, we hope that readers from all disciplines may be enriched by the work. We expect that work-family researchers, managers, students, and others will find areas to entice their interests, provoke their thinking, and expand their practice.

REFERENCES

Crane, D. R., & Marshall, E. S. (Eds.). (2005). *Handbook of families and health: Interdisciplinary perspectives.* Thousand Oaks, CA: Sage.

Crane, D. R., & Heaton, T. B. (Eds.). (2007). *Handbook of families and poverty.* Thousand Oaks, CA: Sage.

Drago, R., & Kashian, R. (2003). Mapping the terrain of work/family journals. *Journal of Family Issues*, 24(4), 488–512.

Family Studies Center (2008). *Family Studies Center* [Electronic version]. Retrieved May 12, 2008, from http://familycenter.byu.edu.

Gerstel, N. & Clawson, D. (2000). Introduction to the special issue on work and families. *Qualitative Sociology*, 23(4), 375–378.

Kanter, R. (1977). *Work and family in the United States: A critical review and agenda for research and policy.* New York: Russell Sage Found.

Lobel, S. A. (1992) Editor's note: Introduction to special issue on work and family. *Human Resource Management, 31*(3), 153–155.

Pitt-Catsouphes, M., Kossek, E. E., & Sweet, S. (Eds.). (2006a). *The work and family handbook: Multi-disciplinary perspectives and approaches.* Mahwah, NJ: Lawrence Erlbaum Associates.

———. (2006b). Charting new territory: Advancing multi-disciplinary perspectives, methods, and approaches in the study of work and family. In. M. Pitt-Catsouphes, E. E. Kossek, & S. Sweet (Eds.), *The work and family handbook: Multi-disciplinary perspectives and approaches* (pp. 1–16). Mahwah, NJ: Lawrence Erlbaum Associates.

Poelmans, S. (2003). Editorial. The multi-level "fit" model of work and family (Editorial introduction to special issue on "Theoretical frameworks for cross-cultural research on work and family.") *International Journal of Cross-Cultural Management*, 3(3), 267–274.

Weatherly, U. G. (1909). How does the access of women to industrial occupations react on the family? *American Journal of Sociology, 14,* 740–765.

Westman, M., & Piotrkowski, C. S. (1999). Introduction to the special issue: Work-family research in occupational health psychology. *Journal of Occupational Health Psychology, 49*(4), 301–306.

Part 1

EXPLORING THE WORK-FAMILY INTERFACE

Chapter Two

Job Demands, Spousal Support, and Work-Family Balance: A Daily Analysis of the Work-Family Interface

by Adam B. Butler, Brenda L. Bass,
and Joseph G. Grzywacz

ABSTRACT

Although the concept of work-family balance has proved popular with the general public, there is little empirical research on the construct. Although most research on the intersection of work and family focuses on conflict between the two domains, there is a growing recognition that a balanced life implies something more than the absence of conflict. Yet, few studies have measured balance directly, as a construct distinct from work-family conflict. We surveyed 88 non-professional workers at the end of every day for two consecutive weeks about their work and family experiences. We found that greater job demands were related to decreased levels of work-family balance, and greater spousal support was related to increased levels of work-family balance. Moreover, work-to-family conflict and family-to-work enrichment, respectively, partially mediated these effects. Our results provide preliminary and partial support for conceptual models of balance proposed by Greenhaus and Allen and Voydanoff (2005a).

A search of the recent press reveals dozens of articles, personal interest stories, and business features on the topic of work-family balance. Such popular interest suggests that the concept of balance is one way, if not the primary way, in which people evaluate their success in meeting daily work and family responsibilities. Yet, research on the topic of work-family balance is minimal, and there is little in the way of theoretical or model development. This lack of research constrains our knowledge of the work-family interface, and also prevents an understanding of how individuals, organizations, and families might better promote balance. In this chapter, we begin addressing this shortcoming by examining the putative antecedents of work-family balance and by partially testing conceptual models of balance proposed by Voydanoff (2005a) and Greenhaus and Allen. We also evaluate these associations using daily diary data to better capture the ebb and flow of adults' work and family lives.

Work-family balance is typically defined in the literature as the absence of work-family conflict (e.g., Hill, Hawkins, Ferris, & Weitzman, 2001; Lambert, Kass, Piotrowski, & Vodanovich, 2006). Likewise, recommendations to improve balance have focused principally on reducing conflicts between work and family (Quick, Henley, & Quick, 2004). A secondary definition of work-family balance follows from recent theorizing and research suggesting that, in addition to conflicting with one another, work and family may benefit each other (Greenhaus & Powell, 2006; Grzywacz, Carlson, Kacmar, & Wayne, in press; Grzywacz & Marks, 2000). Consistent with this theorizing, work-family balance has been defined as the absence of conflict coupled with the presence of enrichment between work and family (e.g., Aryee, Srinivas, & Tan, 2005; Frone, 2003; Grzywacz, Butler, & Almeida, 2008). One problem with defining work-family balance in terms of conflict and enrichment is that these constructs describe the impact of one role on another, whereas balance suggests an overall sense that work and family roles are in a homeostatic state (Greenhaus, Collins, & Shaw, 2003). Likewise, conflict and enrichment are deficient in capturing the evaluative process we believe inherent to the balance concept. Given these distinctions, both conflict and enrichment are probably better conceived as antecedents to balance rather than as balance per se (Greenhaus & Allen; Voydanoff, in press).

There is no agreed-upon definition of work-family balance (Grzywacz & Butler, 2007), and the differing definitions of the construct in two chapters in this volume are evidence of this lack of consensus. Greenhaus and Allen define *balance* as "the extent to which an individual's effectiveness and satisfaction in work and family roles are compatible with the individual's life role priorities at a given point in time." By emphasizing role effectiveness and satisfaction, Greenhaus and Allen suggest that balance derives from the consequences of role engagement. In contrast, Voydanoff (in press) emphasizes that balance emerges from the adequacy of resources antecedent to role engagement. She defines *balance* as "a form of inter-role congruence in which work and family resources are sufficient to meet work and family demands such that participation is effective in both domains." Both definitions describe the conditions that create balance, but they do not provide a clear indication of what it means to feel balance. We focus on the subjective meaning of a balanced state by defining it as the extent to which an individual is engaged in both work and family and the two domains are perceived as well-integrated (Grzywacz & Butler, 2007). We believe that balance is a summative judgment that the allocation of one's resources (e.g., time, effort) across work and family domains is consistent with one's values. Our definition is similar to that proffered by Voydanoff (2005a), who defined *balance* as "an overall appraisal of the extent of harmony, equilibrium, and integration of work and family life" (p. 825). In addition, our focus on an evaluation of an optimal work and family life implicitly recognizes the role of values (cf., Greenhaus & Allen). One practical implication of our definition is that relevant measures of work-family balance ought to reflect the overall nature of the evaluation that one's work and family life are in balance, an operational definition that we employ in the present study.

A MODEL OF WORK-FAMILY BALANCE

We test a simplified model of work-family balance that is based on more elaborate models of the antecedents of balance proposed by Greenhaus and Allen and Voydanoff (2005a). Both of these more elaborate models hypothesize that characteristics of work and family are antecedent to the experience of work-family balance. Voydanoff as well as Greenhaus and Allen further classify work and family role characteristics as either demands or resources. Voydanoff (2004) defines *demands* as role requirements that necessitate physical or mental exertion, and *resources* as role-based assets that facilitate performance or reduce demands. The model also hypothesizes interrole mechanisms through which role characteristics influence balance. The interrole mechanism in the Voydanoff model is cross-domain demands-resources fit, whereas work-family conflict and enrichment are the interrole mechanisms in the Greenhaus and Allen model. Finally, both models postulate processes that intervene between the interrole mechanisms (i.e., fit, conflict, enrichment) and balance. In the Voydanoff model, these consist of behavioral strategies to reduce demands or enhance resources, and in the Greenhaus and Allen model they consist of role performance and attitudes. The model we test in this chapter, presented in Figure 2.1 and described in detail, is an amalgamation and partial test of these two models.

The literature is full of studies of the antecedents of work-family conflict (for recent reviews see Bellavia & Frone, 2005; Eby, Casper, Lockwood, Bordeaux, & Brinley, 2005; Grzywacz & Butler, in press), but we believe there is added value in exploring the antecedents of work-family balance. First, as

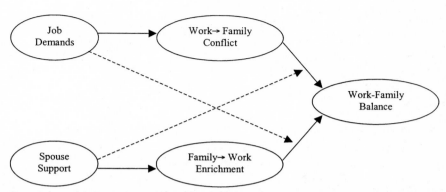

Figure 2.1.   Moderated mediation model of work-family balance. Note: Hypothesized relationships are represented by solid lines, and research questions are represented by dotted lines.

an overall appraisal of the degree to which one is living optimally with regard to work and family, balance may be more strongly related to outcomes of interest such as health and well-being than more narrowly defined constructs such as work-family conflict. Second, given that working parents readily identify with the feeling evoked by the term *balance* (as evidenced by its popularity), understanding factors that promote or hinder balance may translate more directly into the development of policies or programs that improve life quality. Likewise, identifying resources that protect against or buffer negative influences on balance is critical to help people who face persistent, negative pressures that undermine balance (Voydanoff, in press). Finally, such models are important from a research perspective because they inform debates about the distinctiveness and relative merits of different work-family constructs (Voydanoff, in press).

Our conceptual model includes one work-role characteristic, job demands, that we propose undermines work-family balance. The concept of demand is at the center of the work-family literature. Role theory, the dominant theoretical framework underlying work-family research, essentially argues that structural and psychological aspects of role occupancy place demands on role occupants' finite resources (Kahn, Wolfe, Quinn, Snoek, & Rosenthal, 1964). Although we are not aware of published research relating job demands to balance, job demands are included as a work-role characteristic indirectly related to balance in Voydanoff's (2005a) model. In addition, Keene and Quadango (2004) found that longer work hours were associated with reduced balance. We similarly believe that, to the extent that job demands drain resources necessary for meeting family responsibilities, job demands should reduce feelings of work-family balance.

Hypothesis 1. Greater daily job demands are associated with lower daily work-family balance. Consistent with the model of work-family balance proposed by Greenhaus and Allen, our model also predicts that job demands are indirectly related to work-family balance through their association with work-to-family conflict (WFC). Greenhaus and Beutell (1985) defined work-family conflict as an incompatibility between work and family role pressures. Although work-family conflict is often conceptualized bidirectionally, from work-to-family and vice versa, we only examine conflict stemming from work because previous research suggests that demands at work are more likely to be related to conflict stemming from work (see Bellavia & Frone, 2005; Eby et al., 2005; Mesmer-Magnus & Viswesvaran, 2005).

For WFC to function as a mediator in our model, two conditions must minimally be met. First, job demands must predict WFC, and second, WFC must predict work-family balance (Baron & Kenny, 1986). Consistent with the first requirement, there is a substantial body of research linking job demands with greater WFC (e.g., Butler, Grzywacz, Bass, & Linney, 2005a; Frone, Yardley, & Markel, 1997; Grzywacz & Butler, 2005; Janssen, Peeters, de Jonge, Houkes, & Tummers, 2004). Although not as voluminous, there is also some research supporting an association between WFC and balance. Keene and Quadango (2004) found that some types of negative spillover from work-to-family (e.g., missing a family event) were associated with decreased balance. In a previous study, we found that greater daily WFC was associated with lower daily work-family balance (Butler, Grzywacz, Bass, & Linney, 2005b). Finally, Hill, Hawkins, Martinson, and Ferris (2003) found that WFC partially mediated the relationship between workload and work-family fit, a construct similar to balance. Based on these findings, we believe that WFC will mediate the relationship between job demands and work-family balance.

Hypothesis 2. Work-to-family conflict mediates the negative relationship between job demands and work-family balance. Our model also includes one family role characteristic, spousal support, that we believe should be positively related to balance. Although we are not aware of research explicitly linking spousal support to balance, Voydanoff (2005a) lists spousal support as a family resource that may impact balance. One small sample study found that greater social support at work was associated with greater perceived work-family balance (Haddock, Zimmerman, Schindler, Ziemba, & Lyness, 2006), and it is reasonable to expect that a similar effect may arise from social support in the family domain.

Hypothesis 3. Greater daily spousal support is associated with greater daily work-family balance. Consistent with the Greenhaus and Allen model of work-family balance, we believe that the mechanism linking spousal support to work-family balance is family-to-work enrichment (FWE). Following

Greenhaus and Powell (2006), we define FWE as an improvement in the quality of the work role due to involvement with the family role. As with work-family conflict, enrichment can be conceptualized bidirectionally, but research generally shows that family experiences are better predictors of family-to-work enrichment than work-to-family enrichment (e.g., Grzywacz & Marks, 2000). Thus, our analysis focuses on enrichment that flows from family.

Again, to show that FWE is a mediator between spousal support and work-family balance, we must demonstrate that spousal support is related to FWE and that FWE is related to balance. Despite the newness of the enrichment construct, several studies have shown that greater spousal support is related to greater FWE (Aryee et al., 2005; Grzywacz & Marks, 2000; Voydanoff, 2005b; Wayne, Randel, & Stevens, 2006). However, we are aware of only one study linking FWE to work-family balance. In a previous study, we found that greater daily levels of FWE were associated with greater daily work-family balance (Butler et al., 2005b). Although there are no studies examining FWE as a mediator of relationships between family resources and work-family balance, based on the Greenhaus and Allen model and the limited research to date, we predict that FWE will mediate the relationship between spousal support and balance.

Hypothesis 4. Family-to-work enrichment mediates the positive relationship between spousal support and work-family balance. Finally, we also examine whether job demands or family resources serve as moderators of the indirect relationships shown in Figure 2.1. Voydanoff (2005a) includes behavioral strategies as a moderator between work-family fit and balance in her model, and Hill et al. (2003) found that a work resource, flextime, ameliorated the negative relationship between work-to-family conflict and work-family fit. We are particularly interested in whether spousal support moderates the negative relationship between job demands and work-family balance. However, past research on social support as a moderator of relationships with work-family conflict has yielded mixed results (e.g., Carlson & Perrewe, 1999; Martins, Eddleston, & Veiga, 2002). Although less important from a practical standpoint, we are also interested in whether job demands moderate the positive relationship between spousal support and work-family balance. Given the lack of research on these relationships, we formed research questions about potential moderation rather than hypotheses.

Research question 1. Does spousal support moderate the indirect effect (see hypothesis 2) of job demands on work-family balance?

Research question 2. Do job demands moderate the indirect effect (see hypothesis 4) of spousal support on work-family balance?

We are not aware of any previously published studies examining within-person relationships involving work-family balance. Despite calls for an increase in the use of longitudinal designs (e.g., Casper, Eby, Bordeaux, Lock-wood, & Lambert, 2007), the vast majority of work-family research uses be-tween-person designs, capturing work and family experiences at a single point in time. There are two limitations associated with the use of between-person designs. First, recognizing that responsibilities at work and in the fam-ily are dynamic (Morehead, 2001), it is reasonable to expect individuals' judgments of successes in balancing work and family to vary, perhaps sub-stantially, from day to day (cf., Butler et al., 2005a). Second, between-person comparisons are frequently used to make inferences at the within-person level, yet evidence indicates that a relationship observed between persons may not be congruent with the relationship observed within persons (Kenny, Bolger, & Kashy, 2002). Thus, research explicitly examining within-person covariation between work and family demands and resources and work-fam-ily balance is necessary to understand the dynamic nature of work-family ex-periences as well as to better inform practice and policy.

METHOD

Participants

The sample consists of 43 non-professional, dual-earner couples, plus two ad-ditional people whose partner had missing data which precluded his or her in-clusion in the study. Thus, the total sample size for the analyses reported be-low is 88. All participants lived in a Midwestern U.S. state, had dependent children living at home, and were married to or cohabiting with their partners. The average age of respondents was 34 years ($SD = 6.1$), 91% were white, and 96% were married to their partners. Slightly more than 66% of respon-dents had completed at least a technical or trade school (e.g., community col-lege) degree, and 63% of respondents reported family earnings of less than $60,000 (U.S.) per year. Slightly more than 80% of the participants were paid hourly. The participants had an average of two children living at home ($SD = 0.8$); the average age of the youngest child was six ($SD = 4.8$) and the aver-age of the oldest was 10 ($SD = 6.0$).

Procedure

Participants were recruited through posters and announcements at organiza-tions employing large numbers of non-professional workers in the region. Potential participants called a number and were screened to meet our inclu-sion criteria, which were that they and a partner or spouse were employed full-time in non-professional occupations and had dependent children at home. Qualified and interested couples met in their homes or at a public location with a research assistant who obtained informed consent and gave the couple personal digital assistants (PDAs) running the Experience Sampling Program (Barrett & Barrett, n.d.) for the purpose of collecting daily data. Each partner was given his or her own PDA, clearly marked "male" and "female," and participants practiced on a "tester" PDA to learn how the diary operated. Participants were instructed to complete the diary in private for 14 consecutive days at the end of their day, just prior to going to sleep. This method differs from experience sampling in that respondents are not signaled to respond at multiple intervals throughout the day; instead, their responses reflect their overall impression of their experiences that day. Upon completion of the study, participants were compensated $50. We obtained participants from 12 different organizations, but the nature of our recruitment did not permit an analysis of response rate. Data indicated excellent compliance with the protocol, and participants quickly became familiar with and enjoyed using the PDA (Bass, Linney, Butler, & Grzywacz, 2007).

Measures

All of the items comprising the scales reported below were measured using a 5-point response scale from *Strongly Disagree* (1) to *Strongly Agree* (5). A sixth response option was included for respondents to indicate if they did not work on any given day.

Personal covariates. Self-reported gender and number of dependent children under the age of 18 living at home were included as personal covariates in the models.

Job demands. Job demands were measured using a single item, "I had too many demands on me at work today." The item was developed for this study but was based on those included in the Job Content Questionnaire (Karasek & Theorell, 1990).

Spousal support. Spousal support was measured with two items: "I felt supported by my spouse today," and "I felt appreciated by my spouse today." The items were developed for this study.

Work-to-family conflict. Work-to-family conflict was measured with three items developed for this study, although the wording of items is similar to that in other measures (e.g., Carlson, Kacmar, & Williams, 2000). The items tapped cognitive, affective, and behavioral conflict. They read, "Something that happened at work made me unhappy at home today," "I couldn't do some things I wanted to do at home today because of work," and "Even though I wanted to, I couldn't get work off my mind when I got home."

Family-to-work enrichment. Family-to-work enrichment was measured with three items developed for this study. The items largely tapped affective and efficiency dimensions of enrichment (cf., Carlson, Kacmar, Wayne, & Grzywacz, 2005). They were, "My attitude at work today was better because of things that happened at home," "Experiences at home made me happier at work today," and "The mood I was in when I left home made me a better employee today."

Work-family balance. Work-family balance was measured with a single item developed for this study. The item reflected an overall appraisal of balance and read, "I was successful in balancing work and family demands today."

RESULTS

Analyses

Daily data were analyzed using the mixed procedure in SAS for multilevel models (Singer, 1998). In these models, responses to the daily measures are conceptualized as level-one variables that are nested within individual participants who serve as level-two variables. Only days in which participants reported working and interacting with a spouse were analyzed, resulting in analyses based on 523 observations. We tested a random intercepts model with slope coefficients estimated as fixed effects. To control for temporal dependencies in daily data (West & Hepworth, 1991), we included a one-day lagged measure of the dependent variable in all models. We also reduced collinearity by person-centering the level-one predictors on each individual's average across his or her diary period (Kreft, de Leeuw, & Aiken, 1995). Significant interactions were explored using procedures detailed in Aiken and West (1991).

We tested the moderated mediation model presented in Figure 2.1 using procedures outlined by Muller, Judd, and Yzerbyt (2005). The specified model is consistent with typical moderated mediation models where there is a significant, non-moderated main effect of the exogenous variables, job demands and spousal support, on the outcome work-family balance. However, the partial effect of the mediator on the outcome may be moderated. In this case, we examine whether spousal support moderates the indirect effect of job demands on balance through work-to-family conflict, as well as whether job demands moderate the indirect effect of spousal support on work-family balance through family-to-work enrichment.

Following Muller et al. (2005), we tested the conceptual model in Figure 2.1 using a series of models. In the first model, we examined the direct effect of job demands and spousal support and the interaction between demands and support in relationship to work-family balance:

Equation 2.1. Direct Effect of Job Demands and Spousal Support:

$$\text{W-F BALANCE}_{it} = b_i + b_{It-1} \text{ (WFB PREVIOUS DAY)}$$
$$+ b_{2t} \text{ (JOB DEMANDS)} + b_{3t} \text{ (SPOUSAL SUPPORT)}$$
$$+ b_{4t} \text{ (DEMANDS} \times \text{SUPPORT)} + e_{it} \quad (1)$$

Interaction Between Demands and Support in Relation to Work-Family Balance where W-F Balance is the reported level of work-family balance for person i on day t, b_i is the predicted level of balance when person i experiences average levels of the other predictors on day t, b_{It-1} is the person's previous day's level of work-family balance and controls for autocorrelation, b_{2-3t} are the within-person slopes for job demands and spousal support on day t, respectively, b_{5t} is the within-person cross-product showing moderation of job demands by spousal support on day t, and e_{it} is a random residual. Results would be consistent with the model shown in Figure 2.1 if the b_{2-3t} terms are significant and the moderator term b_{5t} is non-significant.

The second and third models we tested are similar to the first, except that the hypothesized mediators, work-to-family conflict and family-to-work enrichment, are substitute criteria for work-family balance, and the previous day's level of those criteria is substituted for previous day's level of balance. With the substitute criteria and predictors, tests of these models are consistent with the model in Figure 2.1 if b_{2t} is a significant predictor of work-to-family conflict and if b_{3t} is a significant predictor of family-to-work enrichment. Results would also be consistent with the moderated mediation shown in Figure 2.1 (dotted lines) if the b_{4t} term is a significant predictor of conflict and enrichment.

The fourth model, shown in Equation 2.2, tests the partial effect of job demands and spousal support, the partial effect of the mediator work-to-family conflict (WFC), as well as moderation of the indirect effect of work-family conflict by spousal support on work-family balance.

Equation 2.2: Partial effect of job demands and spousal support; moderation of mediator work-to-family conflict (WFC); moderation of the indirect effect of work-family conflict by spousal support on work-family balance:

$$\text{W-F BALANCE}_{it} = b_i + b_{2It-1} \text{ (WFB PREVIOUS DAY)}$$
$$+ b_{22t} \text{ (JOB DEMANDS)} + b_{23t} \text{ (SPOUSAL SUPPORT)}$$
$$+ b_{24t} \text{ (DEMANDS x SUPPORT)} + b_{25t} \text{ (WFC)}$$
$$+ b_{26t} \text{ (WFC x SUPPORT)} + e_{it} \quad (2)$$

where W-F Balance is the reported level of work-family balance for person i on day t, and b_i and b_{2It-1} are as defined for Equation 2.1, b_{22-4t} are the within-person effects as defined for Equation 2.1 after partialling out the effect of the mediator WFC, b_{25t} is the within-person effect of the mediator work-to-family conflict on day t, b_{26t} is the within-person cross-product showing moderation of work-to-family conflict by spousal support on day t, and e_{it} is a random residual. Results would be consistent with the model in Figure 2.1 if the b_{22t} term is no longer significant (as compared to Equation 2.1) and the b_{25t} term is significant. Results would also be consistent with the moderated mediation shown in Figure 2.1 (dotted lines) if the b_{26t} term is significant.

The fifth and final model, shown in Equation 2.3, is similar to the fourth model, except we instead test the partial effect of the mediator family-to-work enrichment (FWE), as well as moderation of family-to-work enrichment by job demands.

Equation 2.3. Partial effect of mediator family-to-work enrichment; moderator of family to-work enrichment by job demands:

$$\text{W-F BALANCE}_{it} = b_i + b_{3lt-1} \text{ (WFB PREVIOUS DAY)}$$
$$+ b_{32t} \text{ (JOB DEMANDS)} + b_{33t} \text{ (SPOUSAL SUPPORT)}$$
$$+ b_{34t} \text{ (DEMANDS x SUPPORT)} + b_{35t} \text{ (FWE)}$$
$$+ b_{36t} \text{ (FWE x DEMANDS)} + e_{it} \text{ (3)}$$

Whereby W-F Balance is the reported level of work-family balance for person i on day t, and b_i and b_{3lt-1} are as defined for Equation 2.1, b_{32-4t} are the within-person effects as defined in Equation 2.1 after partialling out the effect of the mediator FEW, b_{35t} is the within-person effect of the mediator family-to-work enrichment on day t, b_{46t} is the within-person cross-product showing moderation of family-to-work enrichment by job demands on day t, and e_{it} is a random residual. Results would be consistent with the model in Figure 2.1 if the b_{33t} term is no longer significant (as compared to Equation 2.1) and the b_{35t} term is significant. Results would also be consistent with the moderated mediation shown in Figure 2.1 (dotted lines) if the b_{46t} term is significant.

Daily Measure Validity

As part of the larger research study from which these data come, participants completed an extensive baseline measure that contained longer and validated measures or both of many of the constructs included in the daily survey. Here we report the correlation between the daily measure of a construct and its respective baseline measure. All of the correlations were significant, providing evidence of convergent validity for the daily measures. The correlation between the daily measure of WFC and the baseline measure (Gutek, Serle, & Klepa, 1991) was 36. The correlation between the daily measure of FWE and the baseline measure (Grzywacz & Marks, 2000) was .24. The correlation between the daily measure of work-family balance and a four-item baseline measure that we developed was .28. The correlation between the daily measure of job demands and the baseline measure (Karasek & Theorell, 1990) was .30. Finally, the correlation between the daily measure of spousal support and the baseline measure (Grzywacz & Marks, 2000) was .32.

Correlations

Although not directly relevant to the model tests, there are a couple of correlations worth noting. First, there is no relationship between WFC and FWE, suggesting that both may independently mediate relationships with work-family balance as shown in Figure 2.1. Likewise, the correlation between job demands and spousal support is zero, indicating that job demands do not engender support so there is no need to model that relationship. Correlation coefficients are presented in Table 2.1.

Model Tests

As a first step in testing our broader model, we tested the model presented in Equation 2.1, and these results are presented in Table 2.2. We found that the previous day's work-family balance was unrelated to daily levels of work-family balance. Likewise, neither gender nor number of children was related to balance. As predicted in hypothesis 1, greater job demands were significantly related to lower levels of balance. Also, as predicted in hypothesis 3, greater spousal support was significantly related to higher levels of balance. Consistent with the moderated mediation model, the relationship between job demands and work-family balance was not moderated by spousal support.

The second step in testing our model consisted of testing the model presented in Equation 2.1 after substituting the mediator WFC as a criterion for work-family balance. As shown in Table 2.2, we found that the prior day's WFC was unrelated to daily WFC. Neither gender nor number of children predicted daily WFC. Consistent with the mediation predicted in hypothesis 2, greater job demands were related to greater work-to-family conflict. As predicted by our model, we did not find that spousal support was related to WFC. Finally, there was not a significant interaction between job demands and spousal support on WFC.

The third step in testing the moderated mediation model involved examining FWE as the criterion. As shown in Table 2.2, we found that the previous day's FWE was significantly related to daily FWE, suggesting that observations were serially dependent. Neither gender nor number of children

Table 2.1. Descriptive Statistics, Correlations, and Scale Reliabilities

Variable	M	SD	1	2	3	4	5	6	7
1. Gender	0.50	0.50	—						
2. Number of children	2.33	1.04	.00	—					
3. Work-family balance	3.69	0.86	.05	-.06	—				
4. Work→family conflict	2.24	0.82	.00	.05	-.37	.74			
5. Family→work enrichment	3.21	0.81	.07	.00	.30	-.03	.84		
6. Job demands	2.46	1.02	-.10	.09	-.22	-.41	-.07	—	
7. Spousal support	3.70	0.89	.14	-.12	.31	-.04	.40	-.07	.88

Note. $r > .07$, $p < .05$. $r > .09$, $p < .01$. $r > .11$, $p < .001$. Cronbach's alpha reliability coefficients calculated on day 7 are reported on the diagonal; other statistics were calculated after pooling observations within-subjects.

Table 2.2. Hierarchical Linear Models of Work-Family Balance, Work-to-Family Conflict, and Family-to-Work Enrichment

	Work-Family Balance			Work→Family Conflict			Family→Work Enrich.		
	b	SE	t	b	SE	t	b	SE	t
W-F Balance day - 1	-.03	.04	-0.70	--	--	--	--	--	--
W→F Conflict day - 1	--	--	--	.04	.04	0.87	--	--	--
F→W Enrichment day - 1	--	--	--	--	--	--	.17	.04	4.26**
Gender	.00	.10	0.00	.06	.09	0.63	.08	.11	0.69
Number of children	-.03	.05	-0.53	-.03	.05	-0.72	.01	.05	0.09
Job demands (D)	-.17	.03	-5.12**	.26	.03	8.91**	-.08	.03	-2.93*
Spousal support (S)	.20	.05	3.64**	-.07	.05	-1.51	.26	.04	5.76**
D x S	-.03	.03	-1.16	-.01	.02	-0.52	-.02	.02	-1.05

Note. * $p < .01$. ** $p < .001$. The intercepts are: balance = 3.65, conflict = 2.58, enrichment = 3.30. Degrees of freedom range from 431–433.

was related to daily FWE. Contrary to the model shown in Figure 2.1, job demands were negatively related to FWE. Consistent with the mediation predicted in hypothesis 4, greater spousal support was associated with greater FWE. Finally, the interaction between demands and support on FWE was not significant.

As a final step in testing hypothesis 3 and in answering our first research question, we tested the model shown in Equation 2.2. As shown in 2.3, after removing the effect of WFC, job demands were still a significant predictor of work-family balance, although the effect was attenuated. Sobel tests indicated that the indirect effect from job demands to work-family balance was highly significant ($z = 4.44, p < .001$). This suggests that WFC is a partial mediator of the relationship between job demands and work-family balance. The interaction between WFC and spousal support was not significant. This result, coupled with the non-significant demands by support interaction on WFC, indicates that the indirect effect of job demands on balance is not moderated by spousal support.

As a final step in testing hypothesis 4 and in answering our second research question, we tested the model shown in Equation 2.3. As shown in Table 2.3, spousal support was still a significant predictor of work-family balance after removing the effect of FWE, although this effect was marginally attenuated. Sobel tests indicated that the indirect effect from spousal support to work-family balance was highly significant ($z = 3.08, p < .01$). The interaction between FWE and job demands was not significant. Thus, given that there was also no moderation of the relationship between spousal support and FWE, we find no evidence that the indirect effect of spousal support on work-family balance is moderated by job demands.

DISCUSSION

The primary purpose of this study was to develop a better understanding of the relationship between daily demands and resources and work-family balance. Despite popular use of the term *work-family balance,* there are few empirical studies on the subject and no longitudinal studies of which we are aware. Using a design where we solicited end-of-day responses from non-professional workers over two weeks, we found that job demands were related to decreased levels of daily work-family balance. We also found that a family resource, spousal support, was related to increased levels of daily balance. Moreover, we found that work-to-family conflict and family-to-work enrichment partially mediated the effect of demands and resources, respectively, on work-family balance.

Table 2.3. Hierarchical Linear Model Tests of Moderated Mediation Models of Work-Family Balance

	W-F Balance (WFC Mediator)			W-F Balance (FWE Mediator)		
	b	*SE*	*t*	*b*	*SE*	*t*
W-F balance previous day	-.03	.04	-0.75	-.03	.04	-0.79
Gender	.00	.11	0.02	.02	.10	0.15
Number of children	-.03	.05	-0.68	-.04	.05	-0.71
Job demands (D)	-.14	.03	-4.29**	-.13	.04	-3.10*
Spousal support (S)	.18	.05	3.22*	.15	.06	2.67*
D x S	-.04	.03	-1.48	-.04	.03	-1.46
Work→ family conflict (WFC)	-.18	.06	-3.06*	--	--	--
WFC x S	.04	.06	0.64	--	--	--
Family→ work enrich. (FWE)	--	--	--	.22	.07	3.31**
FWE x D	--	--	--	.05	.03	1.53

Note. $*p < .01$. $**p < .001$. WFC = work-to-family conflict. FWE = family-to-work enrichment. The value of the intercept for the WFC mediator model is 3.69 and for the FWE mediator model is 3.80. Degrees of freedom are 429.

Our results provide partial support for more elaborate models of work-family balance proposed by Greenhaus and Allen and Voydanoff (2005a). In both of those models, job demands are predicted to be negatively related to balance, and that assumption is supported by our results. In addition, family resources such as spousal support are predicted to be positively related to balance in those models, and that was also supported by our results. We examined basic demands and resources posited to affect work-family balance, but future research will need to examine the relationship between work-family balance and a broader array of demands and resources from both domains to provide further support for these developing conceptual models of balance. Such research will also be useful in determining the utility of distinguishing broadly between demands and resources (see Voydanoff, 2005a).

Despite recent conceptualizations of work-family balance as a state of low conflict and high enrichment between work and family roles (e.g., Frone, 2003; Barnett, 1998), our results suggest that balance is related to, yet distinct from these constructs. As suggested by Greenhaus and Allen, we found moderately strong relationships between work-to-family conflict and balance and family-to-work enrichment and balance. Further, although the indirect effects of demands and resources through conflict and enrichment respectively were strong, we observed only a modest decline in the relationship of demands and resources with balance after controlling for those mediators. This suggests that work-to-family conflict and family-to-work enrichment are only partial mediators, and that the existence of other mediating variables is likely. Given our results, obvious candidates are the complements to the mediators we studied, namely family-to-work conflict and work-to-family enrichment (Greenhaus & Allen). Future research should evaluate more elaborate models including both directions of work-family conflict and enrichment as mediators, as well as indicators of work-family fit (Voydanoff, 2005a).

We did not find that the indirect effect of job demands through work-to-family conflict was moderated by spousal support, nor was the indirect effect of spousal support through family-to-work enrichment moderated by job demands. The lack of a significant moderating influence of spousal support is consistent with prior research on work-family conflict and social support more generally (Carlson & Perrewe, 1999; Frone, Russell & Cooper, 1995). We maintain that the search for moderators of relationships with work-family balance is important, particularly for identifying practical solutions to persistent negative influences on balance. Other potential moderators not included in our study are organizational policies such as flextime (e.g., Hill et al., 2003; Voydanoff, 2005a) and stable dispositional variables such as personality or values.

One limitation of the study concerns the relatively homogenous sample. All of our participants were non-professionals from dual-earner families. Our results, therefore, may not be generalizable to other populations, such as professionals or single-earner parents. Future studies might include participants from a variety of backgrounds in order to compare the effects associated with different work and family contexts. A second limitation of the study is that all of the data were self-reported, leading to concerns about common method variance (Podsakoff, MacKenzie, Lee, & Podsakoff, 2003). These concerns could be addressed by collecting the same data from others, such as spouses or coworkers. Finally, we used a single-item measure of overall balance, and there is a clear need for research using more refined measures (Grzywacz & Carlson, in press).

Overall, this study provides much needed research on the often-discussed but poorly understood concept of work-family balance. We demonstrated that work demands and family resources are additively related to balance and that these effects can be partially understood in terms of the better-researched constructs work-family conflict and work-family enrichment. As future research explores mediators and moderators of work-family balance in more depth, we hope to see greater development of a theory of role balance (cf., Marks & MacDermid, 1996) as well as clearer prescriptions for policy makers and practitioners.

NOTE

Adam B. Butler, Department of Psychology, University of Northern Iowa; Brenda L. Bass, Department of Family Studies, University of Northern Iowa; Joseph G. Grzywacz, Department of Family and Community Medicine, Wake Forest University School of Medicine. This research was supported by a grant from the Alfred P. Sloan Foundation and the Graduate College and College of Social and Behavioral Sciences at the University of Northern Iowa. Direct all correspondence concerning this chapter to Adam Butler, Department of Psychology, University of Northern Iowa, Cedar Falls, IA 50614-0505. Email correspondence to adam.butler@uni.edu.

REFERENCES

Aiken, L. S., & West, S. G. (1991). *Multiple regression: Testing and interpreting interactions*. Thousand Oaks, CA: Sage.

Aryee, S., Srinivas, E. S., & Tan, H. H. (2005). Rhythms of life: Antecedents and outcomes of work-family balance in employed parents. *Journal of Applied Psychology, 90*, 132–146.

Barnett, R. C. (1998). Toward a review and reconceptualization of the work/family literature. *Genetic, Social & General Psychology Monographs, 124*, 125–182.

Baron, R. M., & Kenny, D. A. (1986). The moderator-mediator variable distinction in social psychological research: Conceptual, strategic and statistical considerations. *Journal of Personality and Social Psychology, 51*, 1173–1182.

Barrett, L. F., & Barrett, D. J. (n.d.). The Experience Sampling Program [PDA software and manual, Electronic version]. Boston, MA: Boston College. Retrieved from http://www2.bc.edu/~barretli/esp/index.html.

Bass, B. L., Linney, K. D., Butler, A. B. & Grzywacz, J. G. (2007). Evaluating PDAs in family research with non-professional couples. *Community, Work and Family, 10*, 57–74.

Bellavia, G., & Frone, M. R. (2005). Work-family conflict. In J. Barling, E. K. Kelloway, & M. R. Frone (Eds.), *Handbook of work stress* (pp. 113–147). Thousand Oaks, CA: Sage.

Butler, A. B., Grzywacz, J. G., Bass, B. L., & Linney, K. D. (2005a). Extending the demands-control model: A daily diary study of job characteristics, work-family conflict, and work-family facilitation. *Journal of Occupational and Organizational Psychology, 78*, 155–169.

———. (2005b, November). *Predicting work-family balance from work-family conflict and facilitation among couples*. Paper presented at the Annual Conference of the National Council on Family Relations, Phoenix, AZ.

Carlson, D. S., Kacmar, K. M., Wayne, J. H., & Grzywacz, J. G. (2006). Measuring the positive side of the work-family interface: Development and validation of a work-family enrichment scale. *Journal of Vocational Behavior, 68*, 131–164.

Carlson, D. S., Kacmar, K. M., & Williams, L. J. (2000). Construction and initial validation of a multi-dimensional measure of work-family conflict. *Journal of Vocational Behavior, 56*, 249–276.

Carlson, D. S., & Perrewe, P. L. (1999). The role of social support in the stressor-strain relationship: An examination of work-family conflict. *Journal of Management, 25*, 513–540.

Casper, W. J., Eby, L. T., Bordeaux, C., Lockwood, A., & Lambert, D. (2007). A review of research methods in IO/OB work-family research. *Journal of Applied Psychology, 92*, 28–43.

Eby, L. T., Casper, W. J., Lockwood, A., Bordeaux, C., & Brinley, A. (2005). Work and family research in IO/OB: Content analysis and review of the literature (1980–2002). *Journal of Vocational Behavior, 66*, 127–197.

Frone, M. R. (2003). Work-family balance. In J.C. Quick & L. E. Tetrick (Eds.), *Handbook of Occupational Health Psychology* (pp. 143–162). Washington, D.C.: American Psychological Association.

Frone, M. R., Russell, M., & Cooper, M. L. (1995). Relationship of work and family stressors to psychological distress: The independent moderating influence of social support, mastery, active coping, and self-focused attention. In R. Crandall, & P. L.

Perrewe (Eds.), *Occupational stress: A handbook* (pp. 129–150). Washingon, DC: Taylor and Francis.

Frone, M. R., Yardley, J. K., & Markel, K. S. (1997). Developing and testing an integrative model of the work-family interface. *Journal of Vocational Behavior, 50*, 145–167.

Greenhaus, J. H., & Allen, T. D. *Work-family balance: Exploration of a concept.* Manuscript submitted for publication.

Greenhaus, J. H., & Beutell, N. J. (1985). Sources of conflict between work and family roles. *Academy of Management Review, 10*, 76–88.

Greenhaus, J. H., Collins, K. M., & Shaw, J. D. (2003). The relation between work-family balance and quality of life. *Journal of Vocational Behavior, 63*, 510–531.

Greenhaus, J. H., & Powell, G. N. (2006). When work and family are allies: A theory of work-family enrichment. *Academy of Management Review, 31*, 72–92.

Grzywacz, J. G., & Butler, A. B. (2005). The impact of job characteristics on work-to-family facilitation: Testing a theory and distinguishing a construct. *Journal of Occupational Health Psychology, 10*, 97–109.

——. (2007). Work-family balance. In G. Fink (Ed.), *Encyclopedia of stress* (2nd ed., vol. 3, pp. 868–871). Oxford, UK: Academic Press.

——. (in press). Work-family conflict. In J. Barling (Ed.), *Handbook of organizational behavior.* Thousand Oaks, CA: Sage.

Grzywacz, J. G., Butler, A. B., & Almeida, D. (2008). Work, family, and health: Work-family balance as a protective factor against the stresses of daily life. In A. Newhall-Marcus, D. F. Halpern, & S. J. Tan (Eds.), *Changing realities of work and family.* Oxford, UK: Blackwell.

Grzywacz, J. G. & Carlson, D. S. (in press). Conceptualizing work-family balance: Implications for practice and future research. *Advances in Human Resource Development.*

Grzywacz, J. G., Carlson, D. S., Kacmar, K. M., & Wayne, J. H. (in press). Work-family facilitation: A multilevel perspective on the synergies between work and family. *Journal of Occupational and Organizational Psychology.*

Grzywacz, J. G., & Marks, N. F. (2000). Reconceptualizing the work-family interface: An ecological perspective on the correlates of positive and negative spillover between work and family. *Journal of Occupational Health Psychology, 5*, 111–126.

Gutek, B. A., Searle, S., & Klepa, L. (1991). Rational versus gender role explanations for work-family conflict. *Journal of Applied Psychology, 76*, 560–568.

Haddock, S. A., Zimmerman, T. S., Ziemba, S. J., & Lyness, K. P. (2006). Practices of dual earner couples successfully balancing work and family. *Journal of Family and Economic Issues, 27*, 207–234.

Hill, E. J., Hawkins, A. J., Ferris, M., & Weitzman, M. (2001). Finding an extra day a week: The positive influence of perceived job flexibility on work and family life balance. *Family Relations, 50*, 49–58.

Hill, E. J., Hawkins, A. J., Martinson, V., & Ferris, M. (2003). Studying "working fathers." *Fathering, 1*, 239–261.

Janssen, P. P. M., Peeters, M. C. W., de Jonge, J., Houkes, I., & Tummers, G. E. R. (2004). Specific relationships between job demands, job resources and psychological outcomes and the mediating role of negative work-home interference. *Journal of Vocational Behavior*, *65*, 411–429.

Kahn, R. L., Wolfe, D. M., Quinn, R. P., Snoek, J. D., & Rosenthal, R. A. (1964). *Organizational stress: Studies in role conflict and ambiguity*. New York: John Wiley & Sons.

Karasek, R. A., & Theorell, T. (1990). *Healthy work: Stress, productivity, and the reconstruction of working life*. New York: Basic Books.

Keene, J. R., & Quadagno, J. (2004). Predictors of perceived work-family balance: Gender difference or gender similarity. *Sociological Perspectives, 47*, 1-23.

Kenny, D. A., Bolger, N., & Kashy, D. A. (2002). Traditional methods for estimating multilevel models. In D. S. Moskowitz, & S. L. Hershberger (Eds.), *Modeling intraindividual variability with repeated measures data: Methods and applications* (pp. 1–24). Mahwah, NJ: Lawrence Erlbaum.

Kreft, I. G., De Leeuw, J., & Aiken, L. S. (1995). The effect of different forms of centering in hierarchical linear models. *Multivariate Behavioral Research, 30*, 1–21.

Lambert, C. H., Kass, S. J., Piotrowski, C., & Vodanovich, S. J. (2006). Impact factors on work-family balance: Initial support for border theory. *Organization Development Journal, 24*, 64–75.

Marks, S. R., & MacDermid, S. M. (1996). Multiple roles and the self: A theory of role balance. *Journal of Marriage and the Family, 58*, 417–432.

Martins, L. L., Eddleston, K. A., & Veiga, J. F. (2002). Moderators of the relationship between work-family conflict and career satisfaction. *Academy of Management Journal, 45*, 399–409.

Mesmer-Magnus, J. R., & Viswesvaran, C. (2005). Convergence between measures of work-to-family and family-to-work conflict: A meta-analytic examination. *Journal of Vocational Behavior, 67*, 215–232.

Morehead, A. (2001). Synchronizing time for work and family: Preliminary insights from qualitative research with mothers. *Journal of Sociology, 37*, 355–369.

Muller, D., Judd, C. M., & Yzerbyt, V. Y. (2005). When moderation is mediated and mediation is moderated. *Journal of Personality and Social Psychology, 89*, 852–863.

Podsakoff, P. M., MacKenzie, S. B., Lee, J. Y., & Podsakoff, N. P. (2003). Common method biases in behavioral research: A critical review of the literature and recommended remedies. *Journal of Applied Psychology, 88*, 879–903.

Quick, J. D., Henley, A. B., & Quick, J. C. (2004). The balancing act—At work and at home. *Organizational Dynamics, 33*, 426–438.

Singer, J. D. (1998). Using SAS PROC MIXED to fit multilevel models, hierarchical models, and individual growth models. *Journal of Educational and Behavioral Statistics, 23*, 323–355.

Voydanoff, P. (in press). The intersection of work and family demands and resources: Linking mechanisms and boundary-spanning strategies. In R. C. Crane & E. J. Hill (Eds.), *Handbook of families and work*. Lanham, MD: University Press of America.

———. (2004). The effects of work demands and resources on work-to-family conflict and facilitation. *Journal of Marriage and Family, 66*, 398–412.

———. (2005a). Toward a conceptualization of perceived work-family fit and balance: A demands and resources approach. *Journal of Marriage and Family, 67,* 822–836.

———. (2005b). The differential salience of family and community demands and resources for family-to-work conflict and facilitation. *Journal of Family and Economic Issues, 26,* 395–417.

Wayne, J. H., Randel, A. E., & Stevens, J. (2006). The role of identity and work-family support in work-family enrichment and its work related consequences. *Journal of Vocational Behavior, 69,* 445–461.

West, S. G., & Hepworth, J. T. (1991). Statistical issues in the study of temporal data: Daily experiences. *Journal of Personality, 59,* 609–662.

Chapter Three

Working Families Under Stress: Socially Toxic Time Cages and Convoys

by Phyllis Moen and Erin Kelly

ABSTRACT

America's working families are living under chronic stress as a result of a confluence of social forces—in the global economy, in the labor market, in technology, in families, and in gender values. In particular, there is a fundamental mismatch between working conditions and family needs and resources as a result of outdated time cages and convoys: the set of bureaucratic rules, regulations and expectations at any one time (cages) and over time (convoys) defining work-time durations, timing, pacing, and rhythms. These working conditions produce time pressures and insecurities while simultaneously limiting the flexibility and options of all family members, not only those in the workforce.

We develop a model theorizing that work demands, work-time rigidities, and uncertainties constitute toxic social ecologies, potentially harmful to the health and well-being of both workers and their families. A key mediator between toxic working conditions and family well-being is life-course fit: the cognitive assessments by family members of the congruence (or incongruence) between their needs and goals, on the one hand, and available resources on the other. The concept of life-course fit (or misfit) is a multidimensional indicator of family distress. Fundamental mismatches in the clockworks of paid work and family (or personal) needs and goals, along with the mismatches between time investments in paid work and job protections, mean that time and security have joined income as scarce resources in most American households. A second key mediator consists of family adaptive

*strategies, the (often gendered) adjustments family members make in the ab-
sence of a sense of life-course fit.*

*We argue that outdated work-time cages and convoys can be redesigned in
ways that enhance the quality and functioning of family life as well as the effectiveness of employees as citizens and on the job. Researchers and policy-
makers can help reduce the chronic stresses experienced by contemporary
families provided they recognize and investigate the possibility of redesigning
the constraining clockworks of paid work while recognizing that the unpaid
civic and family work accomplished by family members is key to health and
well-being, the glue binding society together.*

INTRODUCTION

When Reuben Hill studied families under stress in the 1960s, he described
stressors in terms of a crisis event or situation (such as having a husband/
parent away at war) that temporarily disrupts family functioning and is followed by a period of recovery. Today's families under stress also experience
stressful events such as job loss or a husband/wife/parent away at war, but it
is the proliferation of chronic stressors built into everyday life that is especially trying. Chronic stressors increasingly involve time deficits and uncertainties from which there is no recovery.

Most adults in contemporary American working families feel squeezed for
time. They also feel uncertain about the future. Research suggests this is a result of the inflexible timeclocks of paid work, the pace of new technologies,
rising job demands, the risks of a global economy, and the absence of synchrony between the timeclocks of family life and of jobs. Many American
women and men feel that time is speeding up, with the rhythms of working
days and work weeks, as well as the rhythms of occupational paths throughout adulthood, simultaneously inflexible and unpredictable. The clocks,
rhythms, and requirements of paid work are at odds with the clocks, rhythms,
and needs of family life, with insufficient time for rest, reflection, and renewal.

Families take the time to accomplish (unpaid) most of society's care work.
They also serve as a source of rest and restoration in the face of the pressures
experienced by the nation's workforce. The fact that all adults in the household are increasingly part of that workforce means additional time pressures
and stressors for families, as well as little time for either rest or restoration.
We focus in this chapter on the time binds and insecurity contemporary families confront, arguing that they are a result of the fundamental mismatch between a global risk economy, existing inflexible and outdated temporal

arrangements around paid work, and the resources for family well-being. Specifically, we theorize time rigidities in the layered clockworks embedded within organizational policies and practices as potential social toxins for the health and life quality of workers and their families. Existing bureaucratic work-time regimes contribute to the risk of toxicity. Also toxic are the uncertainties flowing from a changing social contract between employers and employees, producing rising risks of layoffs, cuts in benefits, and early retirement buyouts for members of working families at all socio-economic levels.

We coin or expand a number of life-course concepts to model these impacts. First, the terms *time cages* (at any one point) and *time convoy* (over the life course) capture the taken-for-granted organizational, bureaucratic, and cultural rules, routines, and regulations about time durations (such as the 40-hour or more work week), rhythms (such as the work day, the work week, and the school-work-retirement path), timing (such as norms about the age children "should" leave their parents' home), and biographical pacing (such as the timing and order of schooling, marriage, and job shifts and exits). What we call time cages and convoys are the structures and cultures of time embodied in organizational and government policies and practices. They are obsolete — at odds with the forces of change in the global economy, in the labor market, in technology, in families, and in gender values.

Second, we see time pressures and insecurities brought about in part by the speedup in work demands and activities as constituting *toxic social ecologies* (Garbarino, 1995) for workers and their families.

Third, we develop an understanding of *life-course fit* as the cognitive assessments by family members of the congruence between needs and goals, on the one hand, and available resources on the other. The fundamental mismatches in the clockworks of paid work and family (or personal) needs and goals, along with the mismatches between time investments in paid work and job protections, mean that time and security have joined income as scarce resources in most American households.

Fourth, we theorize that it is the absence of life-course fit that pushes working families to engage in *strategies of adaptation* that are often divided by gender (Acker, 1990). We model links between these concepts and processes in Figure 3.1.

In the following sections we consider each of these concepts in turn. We then ask whether the idea of balance is useful in theorizing and understanding possible means of loosening the time constraints surrounding paid work. We conclude with a call for researchers and policy-makers to cease conducting research and policy development premised on existing bureaucratic clockworks of jobs and occupational pathways as natural and hence, taken as given. Institutionalized patterns of working time and job attachment time

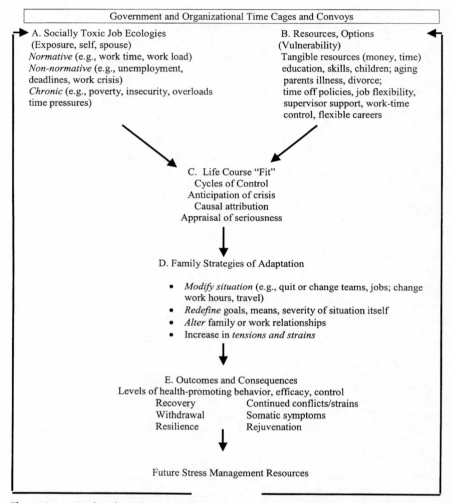

Figure 3.1.   **Toxic Job Ecologies, Work-Family Conflicts, Adaptations and Health: A Cycles of Control Model.**

over the life course are not immutable, but, rather, were socially constructed to fit the needs of employers and employees in the middle of the 20th century. (Far earlier, even the school year was constructed to meet the needs of agriculture at a time when children were needed to help with the planting and harvest.) Time-related policies and practices can be redesigned in ways that enhance the quality and functioning of family life as well as the effectiveness of employees on the job and as citizens. We argue that what is required is recognition of the possibility of redesigning the constraining clockworks of work—and of the need to do so.

TOXIC JOB ECOLOGIES

Toxicity typically refers to harmful health effects of materials (such as pesticides or waste) in the physical environment, an issue increasingly on the public agenda. But certain social environments can also be deleterious to health and well-being. Jim Garbarino (1995) defines a socially toxic environment in terms of the social world of children, concluding that the social context in which children are growing up has become harmful to their development. Similarly, Peter Frost recently published a book on *Toxic Emotions at Work* (2003).

We contribute to this theorizing about toxicity by defining *socially toxic job ecologies* (e.g., Bronfenbrenner, 2005) as particular constellations of job conditions that are harmful to employees' health and may also affect the health and well-being of other family members. These can be subdivided into normative job conditions, such as the institutionalized work day, work week, and work year, and job events that are non-normative, such as downsizing, plant closings, and cutbacks in salary, health insurance, or pensions. Both normative and non-normative conditions contribute to socially toxic chronicities, as when employees face a combination of chronically high workloads, chronic job insecurity, and little control of or ways to modify either. These conditions are recognized as unpleasant and impacting employees' families and personal lives. But they are so common as to be culturally accepted as normal—just the way things are (see A, Figure 3.1).

Stress at its most basic can be defined as the gap between resources and needs (or demands, such as between A and B on Figure 3.1) leading to role strains (C; see also Goode, 1960). Working environments characterized by high job demands and little job control have been found to increase stress, amplifying employees' physical as well as mental health risks (e.g., Karasek & Theorell, 1990), along with their assessments of work-family pressures and conflicts (Moen & Yu, 2000; Moen, Kelly, & Huang, 2008). Moreover, studies show the contagion of stressors on the job, touching the lives of other family members, including spouses and children (Almeida, Chandler, & Wethington, 1999; Almeida, McGonagle, Cate, Kessler, & Wethington, 2003; Crouter & Bumpus, 2001; Crouter, Bumpus, Head, & McHale, 2001; Crouter, Bumpus, Maguire, & McHale, 1999; Crouter & McHale, 2005; Larson & Almeida, 1999; McDonald & Almeida, 2004; Yorgason, Almeida, Neupert, Spiro, & Hoffman, 2006).

FAMILIES IN CAGES AND CONVOYS OF TIME

Individuals and families operate within the confines of *institutional (or bureaucratic) time*—what Sennett (1998) calls a *time cage*. We broaden the concept from time cages at one point in time to the more dynamic notion of *time convoys*—institutional (or bureaucratic) time constraints and expectations that shift over the life course.

Reuben Hill (1966) laid the groundwork for the study of families moving through time by theorizing the orderly flow of families through life cycles; that is, the patterned ways that families move through times of child-bearing, child-raising, and child-leaving (see also Aldous, 1996). But identifying the stages of a typical family cycle was seen by some as prescriptive; that is, a prototype of how families should be (O'Rand & Krecker, 1990). Moreover, as the nation moved through the 20th century, the typical family cycle represented an ever-smaller portion of the real-life distribution and experiences of families in the United States (Bianchi & Casper, 2005; Bianchi et al., 2006).

Hill's life cycle approach was foundational in that it emphasized the temporal nature of family life as it articulated with organizational time, such as the schooling of children and the retirement of the major breadwinner. Hill also located families in consumer time: he found that family members define themselves as "on" or "off" time in purchasing certain items—a home, or appliances, for example. Where families are in biographical and family time (that is, the ages of children and parents) and in social and institutional time (being, for example, ahead or behind the cultural and structural timetables as to when key transitions should take place (see Neugarten, 1996a, 1996b) is crucial to understanding family well-being.

Kahn and Antonucci (1980) first introduced the concept of *social convoys*: that lives are always lived in tandem with others, as networks of kin and friends move together through life. This builds on Elder's (1985) notion of linked lives. We propose that social convoys are also influenced by bureaucratic and normative time convoys: the legal as well as culturally expected ages of, for example, marriage, parenthood, children leaving the parental home, military service, and retirement.

Families have always confronted time-use norms, time budgets, and time needs that vary at different points in the life course. Reuben Hill (1970, 1971) described families as the great burden carriers of the nation. What is important is that over the last half-century families have changed, the workforce has changed, technologies have changed, and the economy has changed. What has not changed, except for speed ups and increasing demands, are the clockwork rules around the time and timing of jobs and career paths. These occupational and organizational time regimes are crucial, because they have become the framework behind the social organization of time in contemporary society, as well as the social organization of the life course for all family members, even children.

THE ABSENCE OF LIFE-COURSE FIT
AS FOSTERING TOXICITY

We develop the concept of *life-course fit* as an umbrella term for the congruence or incongruence between multiple obligations, needs, and goals, on the one hand, and the necessary resources with which to achieve them, on the other, as both play out over the life course. Consider, for example, work-family conflicts and strains. These are manifestations of poor fit at one point in time. But we could expect that the incidence, severity, and causes of work-family conflicts and strains would vary over the life course, in tandem with age-related, family and job changes, age-related shifts in both demands/needs and resources, and historical changes across generations. This means greater life-course fit (or misfit) at some ages and stages than others, and at different historical periods.

Standardizing Jobs and the Life Course

Families change through time, but so do jobs and occupational paths. A number of life-course scholars (e.g., Heinz & Marshall, 2003; Kohli, 1986; Mayer & Mueller, 1986; Moen, 2003, 2005; Moen & Roehling, 2005; Riley & Riley, 1989, 1994; Settersten & Mayer, 1997; Settersten & Owens, 2002) have pointed to the development of careers as providing the temporal and organizational blueprint for the life course, beginning with a period of preparation for the world of work (education), followed by years of continuous, full-time productive attachment to the workforce, and then retirement. By the middle of the 20th century this became the widely accepted *career mystique* (Moen & Roehling, 2005) even for those who could never achieve it. Continuous (full-time, full-year, unbroken) employment became the norm: the taken-for-granted, standardized, expected, and rewarded adult course, at least for professional white-collar and unionized blue-collar male employees. The career mystique promised success and fulfillment, a chance at the American Dream (or at least seniority and security) in return for a lifetime of unremitting hard work (Moen & Rowling, 2005; see also Osipow, 1973).

Although few employees may have believed they could reap the rewards from, or even follow this lock-step career mystique script, it nevertheless became the most consequential social clock in modern times, a time convoy standardizing not only adult lives but also family activities around workdays, workweeks, work years, and the life course. In the United States, an adulthood of uninterrupted full-time (or longer) employment in the primary labor market came to be seen as the path to security, status, and success, the only source of health care insurance, pensions, sick leave, and even paid vacations (Kalleberg, Reskin, & Hudson, 2000).

The whole edifice of labor market policies (such as unemployment insurance, the Fair Labor Standards Act, and Social Security) is still based on assumptions about lock-step paths from education to employment to retirement. Desirable jobs still require continuous employment, long hours, and heavy occupational commitments, as if employees have no other personal, family, or community goals, interests, or responsibilities. At the same time, even desirable jobs no longer provide job, economic, or retirement security.

Unstandardized Families

Employees are also family members, embedded within the temporal constraints and clockworks of human and family development at different ages and stages. These two distinctive convoys of time—shaping both family living and earning a living—are increasingly at cross purposes, contributing to an absence of life-course fit. Households where all adults—husbands and wives, single parents, singles—are in the workforce have no one full time on the home front to be emotionally present for children, to care for aging parents or other infirm relatives, or even to pick up the clothes on the floor, much less the pieces of frazzled workers' lives.

We theorize that the fundamental mismatch between families and labor markets—the absence of life-course fit—is emblematic of the social toxicity of jobs and the time convoys in which they are embedded. Government and corporate policies and practices have not kept pace with rising (individual and family) overloads, pressures, and uncertainties. And, since Americans must now compete for jobs on a global playing field, nothing is secure about their present or their future prospects, including their retirement.

The absence of life course fit between family-time goals, needs, and obligations and existing cages and convoys of time regulated by the market and by public policy is creating a tension between jobs and family life conducive to neither life quality nor health, much less optimal functioning on the job or at home. This tension is often experienced as work-family conflict, and is especially difficult for working families with children. Even middle-class professionals raising children are under chronic stress (Moen & Huang, 2008). Some families—those where adults have little education, few job skills, and minimal social or economic resources, such as single parents, immigrant families, and minority families—have always been vulnerable to toxic job events and chronic stress. But today, even families with educated and skilled adults who hold down desirable jobs are stretched thin in time, economic, and emotional resources.

In sum, existing bureaucratic time convoys perpetuate the social and temporal organization of paid work, occupational paths, and the life course, offering working families few options or flexibilities. Standardized jobs and trajectories, combined with unstandardized family needs and obligations, foster conditions of family risk and vulnerability—the absence of life-course fit. Through this prism of ill-fitting time convoys we view families' strategies of adaptation.

FAMILY ADAPTIVE STRATEGIES

In *Families Under Stress* (1971), Reuben Hill investigated how families adapt, along with the implications of various adaptive strategies. Hill's theorization of family stress adaptations presaged the contemporary life-course *cycles of control* model (Elder, 1974, 1985, 1994, 1998; Kelly & Moen, 2007; Moen & Chesley, 2008; Moen & Howery, 1988; Moen & Yu, 1999, 2000). Specifically, individuals and families seek a sense of control over their lives by making efforts to regain equilibrium (life-course fit) whenever needs, pressures, or goals outstrip the available resources with which to manage them (see C, Figure 3.1).

The concept of adaptive strategies (Elder, 1974; Conger & Elder, 1994; Hareven, 1982; Hill, Hawkins, Martinson, & Ferris, 2003; Hill, Martinson, & Ferris, 2004; Moen & Wethington, 1992) has encouraged life-course and family scholars to consider individuals and families as active decision-makers, the architects of their own biographies, even as they are enabled or constrained by existing (and often lagging) organizational and governmental policies and practices. Workers and their families respond to an absence of life-course fit by making strategic selections from the (often limited) pool of options available to them (see D, Figure 3.1). Some strategies are cobbled together by individual families; others are culturally endorsed as the "right" way to manage.

The Breadwinner-Homemaker Strategy

The adaptive strategy in the middle of the 20th century for white-collar and unionized blue-collar workers was the breadwinner-homemaker time divide. Men were seen (and saw themselves) as good family providers, devoting themselves fully to their jobs (Bernard, 1981; Townsend, 2002). During this time the occupational pathways became institutionalized as taken-for-granted time convoys consisting of built-in bureaucratic rules, regulations, and expectations for workers of various ages (related to seniority, benefits, job security, salary, work engagement) and built-in bureaucratic clockworks (related to what Merton [1957] called "socially expected durations" about the time and timing of the workday, the workweek, the work year, and working life). These legitimated expectations about paid work, occupational paths, family obligations, and the life course were gender—as well as age-graded—describing, constraining, and rewarding certain patterns of men's lives at work and women's lives at home. Men in middle-class white-collar and unionized blue-collar jobs could follow lock-step, orderly careers, investing a lifetime of energy and effort in their jobs, precisely because they had wives who took care of everything else.

Middle-class women's lives were governed by the social organization of time based on the feminine mystique (Friedan, 1963) that women's fulfillment comes from a lifetime of full-time care of their husbands, their children, and their suburban homes. In the middle of the 20th century, Betty Friedan (1963) captured the voices of suburban housewives, asking (as did Peggy Lee later on) "is that all there is?" She revealed the feminine mystique for what it was, a myth, a social invention creating imaginary divides between home and workplace, men and women, paid and unpaid work.

The Women-Doing-It-All Strategy

Betty Friedan's 1963 book and the growing women's movement questioned and eventually killed the feminine mystique. Middle-class women began instead to view the career mystique (offering guideposts to men's lives) as the path to their own self-development as well as gender equality. Middle-class married women moved into universities and employment in unprecedented numbers. (Poor women have always been in the workplace, only without advancement opportunities.) But many women neglected the fact that men's career mystique, the myth that hard work and long hours always pay off, emerged in tandem with and was bolstered by the feminine mystique, requiring a supportive wife in the home. Many feminists in the 1960s and 1970s failed to address the difficulty that continues to plague contemporary society: if all adults in a family are putting in long hours on paid jobs, who then will manage the family care side of everyday life?

Married women, including those raising children, moved into or remained in the workforce in remarkable numbers in the 1970s and 1980s, despite their second shift (Hochschild, 1989) of housework and family care. And yet working families—where all adults are in the workforce—were and are under considerable stress. How then are families managing in light of these disjunctures and dilemmas around time? Most American women have not simply traded one mystique for another—moving from strictures about the good mother or the good wife to the good worker. Rather, most are trying to have it all by being it all—the good wife, the good mother, and the good worker (Hochschild, 1997). The result? Women traded the feminine mystique for career mystique plus, the "plus" being the care they continue to provide their families. But the career mystique, the mental map underpinning labor market policies and organizational rules and regulations, requires a large and often inflexible time commitment. This makes doing both jobs well—at work and in family life— nearly impossible. Growing numbers of men who are trying to be egalitarian husbands and caring fathers while still climbing occupational ladders are discovering, as are women, the fundamental incompatibility between work and family goals and obligations, at least as they are currently configured.

The Neotraditional Strategy

Because of these incompatibilities, most American families make strategic choices as to how to allocate the family's paid and unpaid work. And, since men are typically in better jobs with better pay and better prospects, it makes sense, from a household economy perspective, to invest most of husbands'/fathers' time in paid work. Thus, men remain the principal occupants of desirable jobs. And men remain the principal breadwinners. Most dual-earner couples prioritize husbands' jobs (Pixley, 2008; Pixley & Moen 2003), following a neotraditional division of paid work and domestic work where husbands put in long hours on the job and their wives put in considerably fewer hours in paid work but do the bulk of the unpaid family work (Moen & Sweet, 2003; Moen and Yu, 1999, 2000; Townsend, 2002).

The next phase of feminism, emerging in the 1990s, saw women's double day as accounting for the enduring disparities in men's and women's occupations, status, mobility, and pay (e.g., Coltrane, 1996; Fenstermaker, 1997; Hertz, 1986; Hochschild, 1989; Moen,1992). The adaptive strategy sought but rarely achieved was for men to do their fair share of family work. But, since jobs come prepackaged as standardized time amounts and since wage rates have remained stagnant, it is impossible for most mothers and fathers to, for example, each work part time. To obtain health insurance and other benefits, some degree of security, and sufficient income, most couples in fact follow a neotraditional strategy (Moen & Sweet, 2003; see also Crompton, 2006) of having one spouse pursue the long hours of the career mystique and the other scale back on his or her job aspirations and time investments outside the home (Becker & Moen, 1999). In part as a result of discrimination, in part as a strategy to manage both their paid jobs and their unpaid family work, most women remain in the secondary labor market, working in part-time, temporary, or low-level jobs that come without the career mystique expectation of continuous, total commitment but also without the internal mobility ladders, skill development, security, financial, and other rewards associated with most desirable jobs.

This two-tier arrangement offered a gendered bifurcation of opportunities both within and across families, within and across the labor market. Desirable jobs in the primary labor market remained disproportionately occupied by middle-class men, along with men in unionized blue-collar occupations (Correll, 2007; Kalleberg, Reskin, & Hudson, 2000). Women, immigrants, minorities, and the poorly educated, by contrast, worked in the secondary labor market, with few protections or possibilities. Especially vulnerable to chronic stress have been families whose primary earners are in the secondary labor market, creating a toxic environment for families without health insurance, pensions, unemployment insurance, and disability insurance (since all rest on the edifice of the lock-step career mystique). Those excluded from the primary labor market are outsiders.

The Balance and Opting-Out Strategies

One popular media response has been to define the issue as one of balance and, almost exclusively, as a women's problem (Kelly, 1999, 2005a; Moen, 1992; Moen & Yu, 1999, 2000). Workers, especially those who are also wives, mothers, and/or caregivers of aging parents, are exhorted in magazines and on television to balance the work and home aspects of their lives. This perpetuates the view of stressed out families as private troubles rather than a public issue (cf. Becker & Moen, 1999; Mills, 1959).

The culture and organization of working time remains unmodified, as, for the most part, do men's life paths; it is women who are expected to adapt (balance) to these established patterns. Accordingly, it is women who accommodate to the structural lag (e.g., Riley, Kahn, & Foner, 1994) resulting from the changing realities of the work/family time interface. They frequently do so by (1) choosing routine jobs with contained demands (frequently without career ladders or benefits), (2) moving in and out of the labor force and in and out of part-time jobs, (3) being less willing to relocate or travel for their own advancement and typically working fewer hours than men (Roehling, Roehling, & Moen, 2001). These strategies produce intermittent job histories for women, as they move to facilitate their husbands' (but not their own) jobs, leave the workforce for a time to care for children or aging parents, or opt out when health difficulties or other events make it impossible to continue as a two-job family (Stone, 2007).

Thus, despite a half-century of social movement actions, lobbying, and legislation aimed at gender equality, a half-century of research on families and work documenting the persistence of time pressures, overloads, and strains, a half-century studying gender inequality, the bureaucratic and cultural time convoys shaping the rhythms of families, jobs, and the life course remain gender-graded as well as age-graded, typically producing diverging paths for men and women.

Today, both wives and husbands are seeking ways not just to achieve balance but also to resolve the time conflicts between their home lives and their work lives. Both men and women increasing want to be actively engaged in their families and personal lives as well as in their jobs.

The Living with Stress Strategy

Contemporary Americans now share many experiences regardless of gender, not all of them favorable. Higher education is less affordable, often made possible only through costly school loans. Still, unprecedented numbers of Americans are college-educated, hoping for interesting, challenging, and secure jobs, but confronting the ambiguities, uncertainties, and workloads of jobs in a global risk economy (Moen & Orrange, 2002; Orrange, 2007). Both men and women are now vulnerable to forced early retirements, layoffs, benefit loss, and the demise of pensions.

Women—and growing numbers of men—are moving in and out of roles in families, in the workplace, and in educational institutions at unprecedented rates. In part this reflects the dislocations of a global economy; today even middle-class white and unionized blue-collar workers find that neither job nor economic security come with seniority. Corporations now regularly merge, downsize, and become bankrupt, in good times as well as bad. What life-course scholars increasingly find in both men's and women's biographies are more discontinuities than continuities—in families, in paid work, across the generations, and in personal experience and development (Elder & O'Rand, 1995; Han & Moen, 1999a, 1999b; Moen & Han, 2001a, 2001b; Pavalko & Smith, 1999; Rindfuss, Swicegood, & Rosenfeld, 1987; Settersten & Mayer, 1997; Williams & Han, 2003).

Men still earn more than women, but neither men's nor women's salaries are now sufficient to support families on one income (Jacobs & Gerson, 2004). Suburbs still have appeal for those who can afford them, but there are now escalating costs for good housing in good school districts in safe neighborhoods, and defaults on mortgages are common. What were amenities in the 1950s—air conditioning, color televisions, fancy appliances—most Americans now define as necessities (Schor, 1992).

Today there is no normal life path. Chronologies once taken for granted have disappeared. Marriage and children have come to be more optional than inevitable. Americans marry later or not at all, postpone parenthood, have fewer children or none at all, move in and out of jobs, in and out of schooling, in and out of marriage or partnerships, and in and out of retirement. In part, many of these shifts reflect men's and women's efforts to reduce conflicting work and family demands, as well as the complexities of putting the pieces of life (such as two jobs plus family) together. In part, it reflects the deinstitutionalization of the primary labor market, with its ordered career tracks, security with seniority, and generous benefits, including health care and pensions (Carre, Ferber, Golden, & Herzenberg, 2000; Cornfield, Campbell, & McCammon, 2001). In part, it reflects the cultural norm of gender equality confronting institutional arrangements (time cages and convoys) built decades ago around jobs and careers requiring full-time, full-life commitments.

Family life has changed considerably over the past 50 years (Bianchi & Casper, 2005; Bianchi, Milkie, Sayer, & Robinson, 2000; Bianchi, Robinson, & Milkie, 2006). Most children are now raised in households in which all adults work for pay, reconfiguring the shape and culture of childhood in ways dictated by the time and energy demands of parents' jobs. In the vast majority of families, neither men nor women nor their children have the luxury of a supportive full-time homemaker, or grandparents living down the road. Family time has become scheduled and frantic, leaving less free time for everyone. Work time spills over well beyond the official work day or work week, and still many feel there is too much to do and too little time to do it (Galinsky, Bond, Kim, Backon, Brownfield, & Sakai, 2005). New communication technologies mean that workers and family members are constantly accessible, with the lines between paid work and home increasingly blurred (Chesley, 2006).

Blaming women, working parents, or working families for not balancing their lives seems an egregious case of blaming the victims for what is clearly and increasingly a public issue: the toxicity of paid work and career pathways as currently structured.

WHAT IS TOXIC ABOUT PAID WORK?

The United States is experiencing radical transformations in the nature of the workforce and the nature of the retired force, as well as in families, communities, and virtually all aspects of the contemporary life course. On this moving platform of change, contemporary working families are hard pressed to find effective strategies that enable them to adapt to the changing realities of paid work. We identify five potentially toxic forces and conditions.

Job and Economic Insecurity

Contributing to the toxicity of working families is a global, highly competitive, information economy that has made career ladders and prospects now less predictable, secure, or stable. The old contract between employers and employees (the often informal tradeoff awarding security to workers in return for their commitment) is quickly disappearing (Kelly & Kalev, 2006; Stone, 2004; Sweet, Moen, & Meiksins, 2007), along with the dismantling of social safety nets and the economic risks accompanying digitalization and off-shore outsourcing (Cappelli, 1999; Cappelli, Bassi, Knoke, Katz, Osterman, & Useem, 1997; Kalleberg, 2000; Osterman, 1996; 1999; Rubin, 1996).

There is a large body of evidence demonstrating unemployment is toxic for families, and yet layoffs and downsizing are now commonplace. We theorize that job insecurity and insufficient wages are also toxic, fostering uncertainty and risk and contributing to escalating debt. Living with these toxicities creates conditions of chronic stress; they also reduce the ability of families to anticipate, plan, and budget for the future. Today's economic climate is producing new insecurities and ambiguities about the availability of optimal or even sustainable life pathways.

Escalating Job Demands

In light of a competitive global risk economy the *time and psychological demands of jobs* have escalated, producing a chronic time deficit in most households. Studies show that sufficient sleep is essential to health, and yet few working Americans report getting the required 7 or 8 hours (Bianchi, Robinson, & Milkie, 2006).

Unexpected Retirements

Also as a consequence of the competitive globalization of work with its outsourcing, offshoring, and automating of jobs, workers in their 50s and 60s find themselves forced to retire (encouraged by the carrot of a retirement package and the stick of possibly being laid off) years before they intended to do so (Han & Moen, 1999a; Moen, Sweet, & Swisher, 2005). Even though the American workforce is aging, growing numbers of workers in their 50s and early 60s are retiring unexpectedly from their primary career jobs, frequently as a result of corporate restructuring, mergers, and bankruptcies. Most of those in their 60s and 70s are retired, but ambivalent about full-time, unending leisure, with many wanting opportunities to remain engaged in meaningful activities, paid or unpaid (Moen et al., 2000).

The Absence of Control

Research and theory point to the absence of a sense of control as contributing to psychological distress stress and poor health (Karasek & Theorell, 1990). We extend this body of work to theorize that the absence of *control over working time* is important for life quality, but few members of working families have the freedom to modify their jobs or the flexibility to decide when, where, and how much they work (Kelly & Moen, 2007; Clarkberg & Moen, 2001). Today most working husbands have working wives; most children have both parents in the workforce. This reconfiguration of the workforce and of family circumstances is producing a dearth of time for families, communities, and the quality of American lives. The workforce is older than ever before, with older workers often desiring fewer time demands, more control, and greater flexibility. The leading edge of the baby boom generation began turning 60 in 2006.

Gender Disparities

Feminist scholars in the United States are beginning to frame gender disparities as well as family and individual pressures and strains as originating in and sustained by the social organization of time in paid work and occupational career paths, along with gender stereotypes that ignore or discount the time spent in the unpaid work of family and community (See Table 3.1, as well as Bailyn, 1993; Bem, 1993; Correll, 2007; Folbre, 2001; Moen, 1992, 2003, 2005; Moen & Roehling, 2005; Williams, 2000). When existing temporal arrangements are at odds with gender equality or with the needs and goals of families and family members, the family resources for adaptation are constrained.

CONCLUSIONS

Jobs are the lynchpins anchoring individuals and families to the larger society. They are essential to the family economy, determining social status and life chances, and shaping family members' identities, lifestyles, and life quality. This means that families cannot be understood except in transaction with and embedded within the bureaucratic time cages and time convoys institutionalized around paid work and occupational pathways. In this chapter we have shown the difficulties contemporary working families face in the light of outdated work-time and career convoys created mid-20th century, when wages were growing and most married middle-class mothers were full-time homemakers. Historically, America and other advanced societies have operated on the premise that wives and mothers would (and should) do the domestic carework of society in order to free husbands and fathers to work in the paid economy. The fact that women now constitute almost half the workforce challenges well-entrenched employment and work-hour policies and practices designed for a predominantly male workforce, a workforce without childcare, eldercare, or other domestic responsibilities.

Our thesis is that the outdated time cages and convoys of paid work, together with the uncertainties and frantic pace of a global information economy, foster toxic ecologies for workers and families. Contributing to these toxicities are various combinations of time pressures, financial pressures, and insecurities about the future. Individuals and families seek to resolve the misfit producing these pressures through strategies of adaptation. Unfortunately, most of these strategies tend to reproduce gender distinctions and inequalities at work and home.

Implications for Theory and Research

Scholars from a range of disciplines have until recently based their theoretical arguments and empirical investigations of paid work, family work, work-family issues, mobility, and inequality on conventional taken-for-granted mental maps and framings of time. For example,. Americans, including social scientists, typically think of *work* as paid work. (For many years, economists and others defined *leisure* as everything that was not paid work, thereby making homemakers into ladies of leisure). This leads to a convenient dichotomy—work versus nonwork (often depicted as *family* or *life* as in work-family or work-life). Such conventional divides are typical in scholarly journals, government reports, and the popular media. These mental maps may be a useful heuristic, but direct attention to some things and away from others. For example, the layered complexities and the dynamics of families in transaction with labor markets get lost in the focus on work-family conflict, which is invariably studied at the micro-level. One can think of three worlds of work: market work, civic work, and family work (see Table 3.1). Moreover, each of these three types of work can be paid or unpaid. The layered complexities and the dynamics of families in transaction with labor markets

Table 3.1   Rethinking Work: Three Worlds of Paid and Unpaid Work

	Market Work	*Civic Work*	*Family/Care Work*
Paid Workforce	Entrepreneurs Employees Contract Employees	Philanthropists Social Entrepreneurs Elected Officials Employees in NGOs and govt. agencies	Family entrepreneurs and employees in family businesses Paid domestic, childcare, and home health care workers
Unpaid Workforce	Unpaid overtime work Interns Corporate spouses Corporate employee volunteers Corporate retiree volunteers	Formal volunteer Workers Community organizers Participant neighborhood groups Member civic organizations, Informal ad hoc volunteers Public service (e.g., board, panels)	Relative in family business Regular care provider of children, aging parents, other relatives Informal ad hoc volunteering for children, relatives, neighbors ("Helping out"— Wilson & Musick) Housework Self-care, Development

get lost when paid (market) work is contrasted only with unpaid (family) work.

What matters, in scholarship as much as policy, is what is named and counted. Think about the things we as a nation, and as occupational, family, and life course scholars, define, study, and count. Think about the things that remain undefined, uncounted. The toxicity of working conditions, and especially of invisible time cages and convoys creating or contributing to these conditions, are only beginning to be investigated.

Even more troubling is the matter of selection bias: much of the scholarship on inequality and work-family issues states (in the description of the sample) that the researchers are restricting their sample to those employed in full-time jobs. And yet a common dual-earner family strategy is to allocate one partner to the full-time workforce and the other partner into part-time or contingent jobs, or even out of the workforce for the time, something that is lost when the sample is restricted to full-time employees (see Stone, 2007;

Moen, 2008). The example of dual-earner couples also underscores the importance of studying *linked lives*. Couples make decisions as couples; and yet scholars tend to model the behavior and experiences of individuals, not dyads.

Families as concrete repositories and constellations of roles, risks, and relationships are where abstract national and global economic, technological, and demographic forces play out in real time. Studying family and individual adaptive strategies and life-course "fit" provides useful points of entry for rendering visible what are often outdated shared understandings and taken-for-granted rules, the time convoys operating within and across the institutions of family, labor markets, business, and social policy development and regulation (Bianchi et al., 2000; Bianchi, Robinson, & Milkie, 2006; Schneider & Waite, 2005). We argue that scholarship should move away from dichotomies (paid work–unpaid family work; primary–secondary workforces; employed–retired; careers–jobs) to a vision of lives as layered constellations of paths, perspectives, and constrained prospects (see also MacDermid, Roy, & Zvonkovic, 2005) embedded within relationships, as well as bureaucratic time cages and convoys of expectations, practices, and policies.

Our life-course framing of families under chronic stress implies that: (1) simple assumptions about work-family balance portray a limited snapshot of a much more complicated, variegated, and dynamic phenomenon; (2) family members' adaptive strategies can only be captured by considering the linked lives of couples and families, since they often involve within-family (and gendered) trade-offs (Moen & Hernandez, 2008); (3) work, family, community, and personal ties, demands, and resources shift over the life course, as do their meanings, producing shifts in perceptions of life-course fit; and (4) historical, cultural, and institutional forces, and especially work-time and lay-off policies and norms, provide a backdrop of constraint, uncertainty, and risk against which individuals and families make strategic occupational and family choices. It is in the contexts of outdated (and, as we argue, potentially toxic) time convoys that family members experience and define the consequences of their pragmatic adaptations, often seeking to once again make strategic course corrections to improve or at least sustain some measure of life-course fit. Our point is that these are not the private troubles of individual families. Time cages and convoys are socially constructed, socially sustained, and can be socially reconstructed. Can scholars help to reframe the terms of discourse and the policies shaping the family and work interface? Berger and Luckmann (1966; p. 81) remind us that "the relationship between knowledge and its social base is a dialectic one, that is, knowledge is a social product and knowledge is a factor in social change."

Policy Implications

Few public policy makers or business leaders challenge the chronicities built into the career mystique, seemingly taking for granted the mental maps and bureaucratic clocks and calendars creating and sustaining work days, work weeks, work years, work lives. In particular, business and government officials do not question the existing social, temporal, and spatial organization of paid work on the job and unpaid family work on the home front. The first author remembers talking to a public official in Washington, DC, several decades ago, a person influential in shaping civil service labor force policies, who said "Women are simply going to have to decide, do they want good jobs or families. They can't have both." Much has changed. Today, the rhetoric in such policy circles is more about balance than choice of one role over another. But, except for the provision of unpaid leaves for a portion of the workforce (FMLA), public policies still assume—and tacitly reinforce—that employment and family caregiving are separate enterprises and that people who try to have it all must figure out on their own how to do so.

In Europe, career and life-course regimes have been a function of the state, with educational, welfare, and labor policies providing exit and entry portals into and out of various roles at particular ages and in particular circumstances. European social security policies concerning risks (of poor health, lay offs, unemployment, childcare, aging) have long been in place, providing support but also structuring the life course (Blossfeld & Hofmeister, 2006; Heinz, 1999; Kelly, 2005b; Marshall, Heinz, Krüger, & Verma, 2001).

In the United States, the life course regime became institutionalized more as a function of the market, not explicit state action. Myriad private policies developed around hiring, firing, promotions, geographical mobility, occupational mobility, career paths, retirement, security, compensation, benefits, and opportunities that, in combination with related public sector regulations, created and now perpetuate the multiple timeclocks of paid work.

Despite these different origins, what we see in both Europe and North America are deeply rooted organizational and cultural practices that reify the lock-step life course: first full-time, uninterrupted education, then full-time, uninterrupted employment, then full-time, uninterrupted retirement. The difference is that in Europe, family and personal transitions are also incorporated into the life course regime, while in the United States the focus is almost exclusively on the time convoys of paid work.

The United States has yet to achieve consensus as to what the nature of gender equality, well-functioning working families, or the ideal work-family interface should look like (see Moen & Coltrane, 2005). This is a matter of pivotal importance in seeking to understand the absence of coherent public and private sector response to the fundamental incompatibility between occupational and family career paths and the strains and insecurities of a global risk economy. Especially in the absence of consensus about the care of young children and of government mandates, the United States is seriously constrained from adopting social policies and institutional arrangements that can lessen toxic job ecologies, enabling families and family members to lead more enriched, healthy, secure, and sane lives.

The Way Forward?

We are in the midst of transformations in both the labor market and the family as social institutions. Working families are experiencing converging divergences (Moen & Spencer, 2006) in that even middle-class; privileged households now confront risk and uncertainty on the job and off, as well as some of the stresses and overloads common to life in working-class households. Working families and individual members of particular families also converge in that they share some common visions and myths about being good providers, good mothers and fathers, and good workers (Coltrane, 2004). But there is also unprecedented divergence in the sheer range of actual family and employment arrangements, as opposed to the outdated temporal blueprints about the time, order, and timing of life course transitions (Daly & Beaton, 2005; Moen, 2003; Moen & Roehling, 2005; Sweet & Moen, 2006). All kinds of families and all kinds of family members are caught up in multilayered dislocations and ambiguities of 21st century life: a global economy and the corresponding restructuring of work and risk, a legal and organizational framework endorsing gender equality in an institutional environment reinforcing gender strategies in households, markets, and businesses. But families and family members experience these dislocations and ambiguities differently given their distinctive age, gender, occupational, resource, and life stage circumstances—the shared and distinctive institutional ecologies in which each is embedded (Bronfenbrenner, 1986, 2005; Gerstel & Sarkisian, 2006; Heymann, 2001; Marshall, et al, 2001; Moen, Elder, & Lüscher, 1995; Savin-Williams, 2001; Settersten, 1999).). Scholars can help to reframe the challenges confronting working families as necessitating both strong safety nets and the transformation of existing timeclocks of paid work.

The difficulty is, both individuals and organizations are inherently resistant to change. Moreover, most employees and employers in the U.S. see work-family conflicts and dislocations as private troubles, not pubic issues. Policies and practices have yet to be developed in response to the ambiguities, chronic stresses, and uncertainties of toxic working environments. Why is that the case? Powell and DiMaggio (1991, p. 194) point out that existing social arrangements provide a guide to action and produce shared expectations that, in turn, foster psychological security. Attempts to change existing arrangements are often resisted because they disrupt the taken-for-granted routines of daily living, even when these routines are potentially toxic. The U.S. government is particularly reluctant to mandate changes in the social and temporal organization of paid work. Moreover, the existing safety net of state-provided welfare applies mostly to those older than age 65.

There are, however, important "pockets of innovation" leading change in the private-sector that suggest potential ways forward. For example, our current research examines an innovation undertaken in a large retail organization headquarters (Best Buy). This "Results Only Work Environment" (ROWE) (see www.culturerx.com) is an innovative program encouraging teams and supervisors to focus on results, not time at work, as the metric of productivity. ROWE challenges the current organizational culture of time, redesigning work by permitting employees in teams to control where and when their work is done. This program is unusual, compared to other flexible work initiatives in companies, because it explicitly encourages insiders to question the taken-for-granted and often unnoticed expectations and assumptions about time that permeate the corporate culture (Kelly & Moen, 2007; Moen, Kelly, & Chermack, in press; see also www.flexiblework.umn.edu).

New and more appropriate policies and practices will come about only when the economic and social costs of doing nothing outweigh the costs of change. One important step is to document job toxicities as well as the costs to families and to corporations of adults under stress. Research can offer new metrics, beyond GNP and the bottom line, for capturing and weighing the costs of doing nothing and the costs of change. Scholars can also challenge existing taken-for-granted categories and concepts, offering alternative ways to frame both work and family. For example, Moen (2007) suggests the idea of "Not so Big" jobs, and Kelly and Moen (2007) underscore the importance of greater employee control over their work-time and schedules.

Outmoded conventions and stereotypes, false myths like the career mystique, and conventional mental maps of families and work—all are contributing to toxic work ecologies placing working families under stress, especially the challenges of converging forces of change in the workforce, in technologies, in a global economy. Conventional mental maps also operate as real impediments to imagining new work-time calendars and chronologies. We believe that having employees customize where and when their work is done (so long as quality results are achieved) is one possible avenue, as is offering employees' more options in and greater customization of career paths in order to facilitate better life-course fit. Existing time cages and convoys are not immutable. They were socially constructed in past times for a labor market, a family structure, and an economy that no longer exist. As such, they can be reconfigured. Doing so, we believe, would be a key investment in the health of the nation's workforce and the nation's families.

NOTE

Phyllis Moen, Ph.D., is McKnight Presidential Endowed Chair in Sociology at the University of Minnesota. Erin L. Kelly, Ph.D., is an associate professor of sociology at the University of Minnesota. Direct correspondence to Phyllis Moen, Ph.D., 909 Social Science Building, 267 19th Avenue South, Minneapolis, MN 55455. Phone: 612-625-5843; FAX: 612-624-7020; Email: phylmoen@umn.edu. This research was supported by a grant from the Alfred P. Sloan Foundation (#2002-6-8; http://www .sloan.org). We especially appreciate Kathleen E. Christensen, who has led the foundation's work-family initiative. This research was conducted as part of the Workplace, Family, Health and Well-being Network, which is funded by a cooperative agreement through the National Institutes of Health and the Centers for Disease Control and Prevention and National Institute of Child Health and Human Development (Grant # U01HD051217, U01HD051218, U01HD051256, U01HD051276), National Institute on Aging (Grant # U01AG027669), Office of Behavioral and Science Sciences Research, and National Institute of Occupational Safety and Health (Grant # U010H008788). The contents of this publication are solely the responsibility of the authors and do not necessarily represent the official views of these institutes and offices. Special acknowledgement goes to Extramural Staff Science Collaborator, Rosalind Berkowitz King, Ph.D. (NICHD), and Lynne Casper, Ph.D. (now of the University of Southern California), for design of the original Workplace, Family, Health and Well-Being Network Initiative. Persons interested in learning more about the Network should go to https://www.kpchr.org/workplacehealth. We especially appreciate Jane Peterson's extensive bibliographic work.

REFERENCES

Acker, J. (1990). Hierarchies, jobs, bodies: A theory of gendered organizations. *Gender and Society, 4,* 139–158.

Aldous, J. (1996). Family time and its divisions. In J. Aldous (Ed.), *Family careers: Rethinking the developmental perspective* (pp. 29–45). Thousand Oaks, CA: Sage.

Almeida, D. M., Chandler, A., & Wethington, E. (1999). Daily spillover between marital and parent child conflict. *Journal of Marriage and the Family, 61,* 49–61.

Almeida, D. M., McGonagle, K. A., Cate, R., Kessler, R. C., & Wethington, E. (2003). Psychological modifiers of emotional reactivity to marital arguments: Results from a daily diary study. *Marriage and Family Review, 34,* 89–113.

Bailyn, L. (1993). *Breaking the mold: Women, men, and time in the new corporate world.* New York: Free Press.

Becker, P. E., & Moen, P. (1999). Scaling back: Dual-career couples' work-family strategies. *Journal of Marriage and the Family, 61,* 995–1007.

Bem, S. L. (1993). *The lenses of gender: Transforming the debate on sexual inequality.* New Haven, CT: Yale University Press.

Berger, P. L., & Luckmann, T. (1966). *The social construction of reality: A treatise in the sociology of knowledge.* New York, NY: Anchor/Doubleday.

Bernard, J. (1981). The good provider role. *American Psychologist, 36,* 1–12.

Bianchi, S. M., & Casper, L. M. (2005). Explanations of family change: A family demographic perspective. In V. L. Bengtson, A. C. Acock, K. R. Allen, P. Dilworth-Anderson, and D.M. Klein (Eds.), *Sourcebook of family theory and research: An interactive approach* (pp. 93–117). Thousand Oaks, CA: Sage.

Bianchi, S. M., Milkie, M. A., Sayer, L. C., & Robinson, J. P. (2000). Is anyone doing the housework? Trends in the gender division of household labor. *Social Forces, 79,* 2–39.

Bianchi, S. M., Robinson, J. P, & Milkie, M. A. (2006). *Changing rhythms of American family life.* New York: Russell Sage.

Blossfeld, H.-P., & Hofmeister, H. (2006). *Globalization, uncertainty and women's careers: An international comparison.* Northampton, MA: Edward Elgar.

Bronfenbrenner, U. (1986). Ecology of the family as a context for human development: Research perspectives. *Developmental Psychology, 22,* 723–742.

Bronfenbrenner, U. (Ed.). (2005). *Making human beings human: Bioecological perspectives on human development.* Thousand Oaks, CA: Sage.

Cappelli, P. (1999). Career jobs are dead. *California Management Review, 42,* 147–167.

Cappelli, P., Bassi, L., Knoke, D., Katz, H., Osterman, P., & Useem, M. (1997). *Change at work.* New York: Oxford University Press.

Carre, F., Ferber, M. A., Golden, L., & Herzenberg, S. A. (2000). *Nonstandard work: The nature of challenges of changing employment arrangements.* Champaign, IL: Industrial Relations Research Association.

Chesley, N. (2006). Families in a high tech age: Technology usage patterns, work and family correlates, and gender. *Journal of Family Issues, 27,* 587–608.

Clarkberg, M., & Moen, P. (2001). Understanding the time-squeeze: Married couples preferred and actual work-hour strategies. *American Behavioral Scientist, 44,* 1115–1136.

Coltrane, S. (1996). *Family man: Fatherhood, housework, and gender equity.* New York: Oxford University Press.

———. (2004). *Families and society.* Belmont, CA: Wadsworth/ITP.

Conger, R. D., & Elder, G. H., Jr. (1994). *Families in troubled times: Adapting to change in rural America.* Hawthorne, NY: Aldine.

Cornfield, D. B., Campbell, K. E., & McCammon, H. J. (2001). *Working in restructured workplaces: Challenges and new direction for the sociology of work.* Thousand Oaks, CA: Sage.

Correll, S. J. (2007). *Social psychology of gender: Advances in group processes,* vol. 24. New York: Elsevier Science.

Crompton, R. (2006). *Employment and the family: The reconfiguration of work and family life in contemporary societies.* New York: Cambridge University Press.

Crouter, A. C., & Bumpus, M. F. (2001). Linking parents' work stress to children's and adolescents' psychological adjustment. *Current Directions in Psychological Science, 10,* 156–159.

Crouter, A. C., Bumpus, M. F., Head, M. R., & McHale, S. M. (2001). Implications of overwork and overload for the quality of men's family relationships. *Journal of Marriage and Family, 63,* 404–416.

Crouter, A. C., Bumpus, M. F., Maguire, M. C., & McHale, S. M. (1999). Linking parents' work pressure to adolescents' well-being: Insights into dynamics in dual-earner families. *Developmental Psychology, 35,* 1453–1461.

Crouter, A. C., & McHale, S. M. (2005). Work, family, and children's time: Implications for youth. In S. Bianchi, L. Casper, & R. B. King (Eds.), *Work, family, health, and well-being.* Mahwah, NJ: Lawrence Erlbaum.

Daly, K. J., & Beaton J. (2005). Through the lens of time: How families live in and through time. In V. Bengtson, D. Klein, A. Acock, K. Allen, & P. Dilworth-Anderson, (Eds.), *Sourcebook of family theory and methods* (pp. 241–254). Thousand Oaks, CA: Sage.

Elder, G. H., Jr. (1998). The life course as developmental theory. *Child Development, 69,* 1–12.

―――. (1994). Time, human agency, and social change: Perspectives on the life course. *Social Psychology Quarterly, 47,* 4–15.

―――. (1985). *Life course dynamics: Trajectories and transitions, 1968–1980.* Ithaca, NY: Cornell University Press.

―――. (1974). *Children of the great depression.* Chicago, IL: University of Chicago Press.

Elder, G. H., Jr., & O'Rand, A. M. (1995). Adult lives in a changing society. In J. S. House, K. Cook, & G. Fine (Eds.), *Sociological perspectives on social psychology* (pp. 452–475). Needham Heights, MA: Allyn & Bacon.

Fenstermaker, S. (1997). Telling tales out of school: Three short stories of a feminist sociologist. In B. Laslett & B. Thorne (Eds.), *Feminist sociology: Life histories of a movement.* (pp. 209–228). New Brunswick, NJ: Rutgers University Press.

Folbre, N. (2001). *The invisible heart: Economics and family values.* New York: The New Press.

Friedan, B. (1963). *The feminine mystique.* New York: Bantam Doubleday Dell.

Frost, P. (2003). *Toxic emotions at work: How compassionate managers handle pain and conflict.* Boston, MA: Harvard Business School Press.

Galinsky, E., Bond, J. T., Kim, S. S., Backon, L., Brownfield, E., & Sakai, K. (2005). *Overwork in America: When the way we work becomes too much.* New York: Families and Work Institute.

Garbarino, J. (1995). *Raising children in a socially toxic environment.* San Francisco: Jossey-Bass Publishers.

Gerstel, N., & Sarkisian, N. (2006). A sociological perspective on families and work: The import of gender, class, and race. In M. Pitt-Catsouphes, E. Kossek, & S.

Sweet (Eds.), *The work and family handbook: Multi-disciplinary perspectives, methods, and approaches* (pp. 237–266). Mahwah, NJ: Lawrence Erlbaum.

Goode, W. J. (1960). A theory of role strain. *American Sociological Review, 25,* 483–496.

Han, S.-K., & Moen, P. (1999a). Clocking out: Temporal patterning of retirement. *American Journal of Sociology, 105,* 191–236.

———. (1999b). Work and family over time: A life course approach. *The Annals of the American Academy of Political and Social Sciences, 562,* 98–110.

Hareven, T. K. (1982). *Family time and industrial time.* New York: Cambridge University Press.

Heinz, W. R. (1999). *From education to work: Cross-national perspectives.* New York: Cambridge University Press.

Heinz, W. R., & Marshall, V. W. (2003). *The social dynamics of the life course. Transitions, institutions, and interrelations.* Hawthorne, NY: Aldine de Gruyter.

Hertz, R. (1986). *More equal than others: Women and men in dual-career marriages.* Berkeley, CA: University of California Press.

Heymann, J. (2001). *The widening gap: Why America's working families are in jeopardy and what can be done about it.* New York: Basic Books.

Hill, E. J., Hawkins, A. J., Martinson, V., & Ferris, M. (2003). Studying "working fathers": Comparing fathers' and mothers' work-family conflict, fit, and adaptive strategies in a global high-tech company. *Fathering, 1,* 239–261.

Hill, E. J., Martinson, V., & Ferris, M. (2004). New-concept part-time employment: A work-family adaptive strategy for women professionals with small children. *Family Relations, 53,* 282–292.

Hill, R. (1966). Contemporary developments in family theory. *Journal of Marriage and the Family, 28,* 10–26.

———. (1970). *Family development in three generations.* Cambridge, MA: Schenkman Publishing.

———. (1971). *Families under stress: Adjustment to the crises of war separation and reunion.* New York: Harper and Brothers.

Hochschild, A. (1989). *The second shift.* New York: Avon Books.

———. (1997). *The time bind: When work becomes home and home becomes work.* New York: Metropolitan Books.

Jacobs, J. A., & Gerson, K. (2004). *The time divide: Balancing work and family in contemporary society.* Cambridge, MA: Harvard University Press.

Kalleberg, A. L. (2000). Nonstandard employment relations: Part-time, temporary, and contract work. *Annual Review of Sociology, 26,* 341–365.

Kalleberg, A. L., Reskin, B. F., & Hudson, K. (2000). Bad jobs in America: Standard and nonstandard employment relations and job quality in the United States. *American Sociological Review, 65,* 256–278.

Kahn, R. L., & Antonucci, T. C. (1980). Convoys over the life course: Attachment, roles, and social support. In P. B. Baltes & O. Brim (Eds.), *Life-span development and behavior* (pp. 253–286). New York: Academic Press.

Karasek, R. A., & Theorell, T. (1990). *Healthy work: Stress, productivity, and the reconstruction of working life.* New York: Basic Books.

Kelly, E. (2005a). Discrimination against caregivers? Gendered family responsibilities, employer practices, and work rewards. In L. B. Nielsen & R. L. Nelson (Eds.), *The handbook of employment discrimination research* (pp. 341–362). New York: Kluwer Academic Publishers.

———. (2005b). Work-family policies: The United States in international perspective. In M. Pitt-Catsouphes, E. Kossek, & S. Sweet. (Eds.), *Work-family handbook: Multi-disciplinary perspectives and approaches*. (pp. 99–123). New York: Lawrence Erlbaum Associates.

———. (1999). Theorizing corporate family policies: How advocates built "the business case" for "family-friendly" programs. *Research in the Sociology of Work, 7,* 169–202.

Kelly, E. L., & Kalev, A. (2006). Managing flexible work arrangements in US organizations: Formalized discretion or "a right to ask." *Socio-Economic Review, 4,* 379–416.

Kelly, E., & Moen, P. (2007). Rethinking the clockwork of work: Why schedule control may pay off at home and at work. *Advances in Developing Human Resources, 9,* 487–506.

Kohli, M. (1986). The world we forget: A historical review of the life course. In V. W. Marshall (Ed.), *Later life: The social psychology of aging* (pp. 271–303). Beverly Hills, CA: Sage.

Larson, R. W., & Almeida, D. M. (1999). Emotional transmission in the daily lives of families: A new paradigm for studying family process. *Journal of Marriage and the Family, 61,* 5–20.

MacDermid, S. M., Roy, K., & Zvonkovic, A. M. (2005). Don't stop at the borders: Theorizing beyond dichotomies of work and family. In V. Bengtson, D. Klein, A. Acock, K. Allen, & P. Dilworth-Anderson (Eds.), *Sourcebook of family theory and research* (pp. 493–507). Thousand Oaks, CA: Sage Publications.

Marshall, V. W., Heinz, W. R., Krüger, H., and Verma, A. (2001). *Restructuring work and the life course.* Toronto: University of Toronto Press.

Mayer, K. U., & Mueller, W. (1986). The state and the structure of the life course. In A. B. Sorenson & L. R. Sherrod (Eds.), *Human development and the life course: Multidisciplinary perspectives F.E.W.* (pp. 217–245). Hillsdale, NJ.: Laurence Erlbaum.

McDonald, D. A., & Almeida, D. M. (2004). The interweave of fathers' daily work experiences and fathering behaviors. *Fathering, 2,* 235–251.

Merton, R. K. (1957). *Social theory and social structure.* New York: The Free Press.

Mills, C. W. (1959). *The sociological imagination.* New York: Oxford University Press.

Moen, P. (2008). It's constraints, not choices. *Science, 319*(5865), 903–904.

———. (2007). Not so big jobs and retirements: What workers (and retirees) really want. *Generations, 31,* 31–36.

———. (2005). Beyond the career mystique: "Time in," "time out," and second acts. *Sociological Forum, 20,* 189–208.

———. (2003). *It's about time: Couples and careers.* Ithaca, NY: Cornell University Press.

———. (1992). *Women's two roles: A contemporary dilemma.* Westport, CT: Greenwood Publishing.

Moen, P., & Coltrane, S. (2005). Families, theories, and social policy. In V. Bengtson, D. Klein, A. Acock, K. Allen, & P. Dilworth-Anderson, (Eds.) *Sourcebook of family theory and methods* (pp. 543–565). Thousand Oaks, CA: Sage Publications.

Moen, P., & Chesley, N. (2008). Toxic job ecologies, time convoys, and work-family conflict: Can families (re)gain control and life-course "fit"? In K. Korabik, D. S. Lero, & D. L. Whitehead (Eds.), *Handbook of work-family integration: Research, theory, and best practices* (pp. 95–122). New York: Elsevier.

Moen, P., Elder, G. H., Jr., & Lüscher, K. (1995). *Examining lives in context: Perspectives on the ecology of human development.* Washington, DC: American Psychological Association.

Moen, P., & Han, S.-K. (2001a). Reframing careers: Work, family, and gender. In V. Marshall, W. Heinz, H. Krüger, and A. Verma (Eds.), *Restructuring work and the life course* (pp. 424–445). Toronto, Canada: University of Toronto Press.

———. (2001b). Gendered careers: A life course perspective. In R. Hertz and N. Marshall (Eds.), *Working families: The transformation of the American home* (pp. 42–57). Berkeley, CA: University of California Press.

Moen, P., & Hernandez, E. (in press). Linked lives: Social and temporal convoys over the life course. In G. Elder & J. Giele, (Eds.), *The craft of life course studies.* New York: Guilford Press.

Moen, P., & Howery, C. B. (1988). The significance of time in the study of families under stress. In D. Klein & J. Aldous (Eds.), *Social stress and family development* (pp. 131–156). New York: Guilford Press.

Moen, P., & Huang, Q. (in press). Customizing careers by opting out or shifting jobs: Dual-earners seeking life-course "fit." In K. Christensen & B. Schneider (Eds.), *Achieving Workplace Flexibility in the U.S.: Insights from Abroad.*

Moen, P., Kelly, E. L., & Huang, R. (in press). Fit inside the work-family black box: An ecology of the life course cycles of control reframing. *Journal of Occupational and Organizational Psychology.*

Moen, P., Kelly, E., & Magennis, R. (in press). Gender strategies: Socialization, allocation, and strategic selection processes shaping the gendered adult course. In M. C. Smith (Ed.), *The handbook of research on adulthood: Adult development and learning.* London: Routledge/Taylor & Francis Publishers.

Moen, P., & Orrange, R. (2002). Careers and lives: Socialization, structural lag, and gendered ambivalence. In R. Settersten and T. Owens (Eds.), *Advances in life course research: New frontiers in socialization* (pp. 231–260). London: Elsevier Science.

Moen, P., & Roehling, P. V. (2005). *The career mystique: Cracks in the American dream.* Boulder, CO: Rowman & Littlefield.

Moen, P., & Spencer, D. (2006). Converging divergences in age, gender, health, and well-being: Strategic selection in the third age. In R. Binstock & L. George (Eds.), *Handbook of aging and the social sciences* (pp. 127–144). Burlington, MA: Elsevier Academic Press.

Moen, P., & Sweet, S. (2003). Time clocks: Work-hour strategies. In P. Moen (Ed.), *It's about time: Couples and careers* (pp. 17–34). Ithaca, NY: Cornell University Press.

Moen, P., Sweet, S., & Swisher, R. (2005). Embedded career clocks: The case of retirement planning. In R. Macmillan (Ed.), *Advances in life course research: The structure of the life course: Individualized? standardized? differentiated?* (pp. 237–265). New York: Elsevier.

Moen, P., & Wethington, E. (1992). The concept of family adaptive strategies. *Annual Review of Sociology, 18,* 233–251.

Moen, P, & Yu, Y. (2000). Effective work/life strategies: Working couples, work conditions, gender and life quality. *Social Problems, 47,* 291–326.

——. (1999). Having it all: Overall work/life success in two-earner families. *Research in the Sociology of Work, 7,* 109–139.

Neugarten, B. L. (1996a). New perspectives on aging and social policy. In D. A. Neugarten (Ed.), *The meanings of age: Selected papers of Bernice L. Neugarten* (pp. 366–376). Chicago: University of Chicago Press.

—— (1996b). Social implications of life extension. In D. A. Neugarten (Ed.), *The meanings of age: Selected papers of Bernice L. Neugarten* (pp. 339–345). Chicago: University of Chicago Press.

O'Rand, A. M., & Krecker, M. L. (1990). Concepts of the life cycle: Their history, meanings and uses in the social sciences. *Annual Review of Sociology, 16,* 241–62.

Orrange, Robert M. (2007). *Work, family, and leisure: Uncertainty in a risk society.* Lanham, MD: Rowman & Littlefield Publishers, Inc.

Osipow, S. H. (1973). *Theories of career development* (2nd Edition). New York: Meredith Corporation.

Osterman, P. (1996). *Broken ladders: Managerial careers in the new economy.* UK: Oxford University Press.

Osterman, P. (1999). *Securing prosperity: The American labor market: How it has changed and what to do about it.* NJ: Princeton University Press.

Pavalko, E. K., & Smith, B. (1999). The rhythm of work: Health effects of women's work dynamics. *Social Forces, 7,* 1141–62.

Pillemer, K., Moen, P., Wethington, E., and Glasgow, N. (Eds.). 2000. *Social Integration in the Second Half of Life.* Baltimore: The Johns Hopkins Press.

Pixley, J. E. (2008). Life course patterns of career-prioritizing decisions and occupational attainment in dual-earner couples. *Work and Occupations, 35,* 127-163.

Pixley, J. E., & Moen, P. (2003). Prioritizing careers. In P. Moen (Ed.), *It's about time: Couples and careers* (pp. 183–200). Ithaca, NY: Cornell University Press.

Powell, W., & DiMaggio, P. (1991). *The new institutionalism in organizational analysis.* Chicago: University of Chicago Press.

Riley, M., Kahn, R., & Foner, A. (1994). *Age and structural lag: The mismatch between people's lives and opportunities in work, family and leisure.* New York: Wiley.

Riley, M. W., & Riley, J. W., Jr. (1989). The lives of old people and changing social roles. *The Annals of the American Academy of Political and Social Science, 503,* 14–28.

———. (1994). Structural lag: Past and future. In M. W. Riley, R. L. Kahn, and A. Foner (Eds.), *Age and structural lag: Society's failure to provide meaningful opportunities in work, family and leisure* (pp. 15–36). New York: Wiley and Sons.

Rindfuss, R. R., Swicegood, C. G., & Rosenfeld, R. A. (1987). Disorder in the life course: How common and does it matter? *American Sociological Review, 52,* 785–801.

Roehling, P. V., Roehling, M. V., & Moen, P. (2001). The relationship between work-life policies and practices and employee loyalty: A life course perspective. *Journal of Family and Economic Issues, 22,*141–170.

Rubin, B. A. (1996). *Shifts in the social contract: Understanding change in American society*. Thousand Oaks, CA: Pine Forge Press.

Savin-Williams, R. (2001). *Mom, Dad, I'm gay: How families negotiate coming out.* Washington, DC: American Psychological Association Press.

Schneider, B. & Waite, L. J. (2005). *Being together, working apart: Dual-career families and the work-life balance*. New York: Cambridge University Press.

Schor, J. (1992). *The overworked American: The unexpected decline of leisure*. New York: Basic Books.

Sennett, R. (1998). *The corrosion of character: The personal consequences of work in the new capitalism.* New York: W.W. Norton.

Settersten, R. (1999). *Lives in time and place: The problems and promises of developmental science*. Amityville, NY: Baywood Publishing Company.

Settersten, R. A., Jr., & Mayer, K. U. (1997). The measurement of age, age structuring, and the life course. *Annual Review of Sociology, 23,* 233–61.

Settersten, R. A., Jr., & Owens, T. (2002). *Advances in life course research: New frontiers in socialization*. London: Elsevier Science.

Stone, K. V. W. (2004). *From widgets to digits: Employment regulation for the changing workplace*. New York: Cambridge University Press.

Stone, P. (2007). *Opting out? Why women really quit careers and head home.* Los Angeles: University of California Press.

Sweet, S., & Moen, P. (2006). Advancing a career focus on work and family: Insights from the life course perspective. In M. Pitt-Catsouphes, E. E. Kossek, and S. Sweet (Eds.), *The work and family handbook: Multi-disciplinary perspectives and methods* (pp. 189–208). Mahwah, NJ: Lawrence Erlbaum Associates.

Sweet, S., Moen, P., & Meiksins, P. (2007). Dual earners in double jeopardy: Preparing for job loss in the new risk economy. In B. A. Rubin (Ed.), *Research in the sociology of work, Volume 17: Work place temporalities* (pp. 445–469). New York: Elsevier.

Townsend, N. (2002). *The package deal: Marriage, work, and fatherhood in men's lives*. Philadelphia: Temple University Press.

Weymann, A. (2003). Future of the life course. In J. T. Mortimer and M. J. Shanahan (Eds.), *Handbook of the life course* (pp. 703–714). New York, NY: Kluwer & Plenum.

Williams, J. (2000). *Unbending gender: Why family and work conflict and what to do about it*. New York: Oxford University Press.

Williams, S., & Han, S.-K. (2003). Career clocks: Forked roads. In P. Moen (Ed.), *It's about time: Couples and careers* (pp. 80–97). Ithaca, NY: Cornell University Press.

Yorgason, J. B., Almeida, D. M., Neupert, S. D., Spiro, A., & Hoffman, L. (2006). A dyadic examination of daily health symptoms and emotional well-being in later life couples. *Family Relations, 55,* 613–624.

Chapter Four

The Effects of Job Stress on the Family: One Size Does Not Fit All

by Rena L. Repetti and Darby Saxbe

ABSTRACT

This chapter focuses on how families and individuals adapt and respond to demands and constraints placed by the workplace, arguing that it is time to move beyond "one size fits all" models in our understanding of work-family spillover. We begin with a review of research indicating that the effects of job stressors on family life vary according to the gender and the psychological well-being of the individual worker, characteristics of the family, and characteristics of other family members. Explanations for why and how the individual and family difference variables may exert their influence are discussed. Physiological responses to stress may mediate some of the observed moderator effects, and the social, emotional, and physical milieu to which employees return after work may explain other differences.

MODERATORS OF WORK-FAMILY LINKAGES

Work-family researchers find that families differ in how they are influenced by parents' experiences at work (Crouter & Helms-Erikson, 1997; Crouter & Bumpus, 2001; Perry-Jenkins & Gillman, 2000; Perry-Jenkins, Repetti, & Crouter, 2000; Repetti, 2005). Our review focuses on non-uniformities in the effects that job stressors have on families; summarizing evidence for a number of variables that appear to act as moderators.

Sex Differences

Although gender is probably the most frequently examined group difference variable in the work-family literature, few studies of the effects of job stressors have considered variability in the impact of women's versus men's experiences. However when gender is examined, differences are often found. For example, in one study of dual-earner families, mothers' descriptions of the interpersonal atmosphere at work predicted changes in both maternal and paternal parenting three months later. Both mothers' and fathers' interactions with their year-old infants were more negative (e.g., more intrusive) and less positive (e.g., less sensitive and responsive) when the mother reported a negative social climate at work. Fathers' work experiences were unrelated to either parents' play behavior (Costigan, Cox, & Cauce, 2003).

An unusual feature of the study by Costigan and colleagues is the fact that all of the mothers in the sample were employed full-time. In most studies of dual-earner families, a substantial proportion of the women are employed part-time but almost all of the men are employed full-time. Moen and Yu (2000) consider these full-time/part-time dual-earner arrangements to be a modified form of the traditional husband breadwinner/wife homemaker model. Although these couples represent many dual-earner U.S. families, particularly those with young children at home, they do not present equivalent male and female samples for comparing the effects of stressful work experiences. In the Costigan et al. (2003) study, mothers and fathers devoted a similar amount of time to work each week, and the effects of their experiences could be reasonably compared.

Gender differences have also been observed in the short-term effects of job stressors on marital interaction. The studies described below used daily-report methodologies with samples of dual-earner couples; in all cases, the average work week of the wives was shorter than that of the husbands. Bolger, DeLongis, Kessler, and Wethington (1989) found that husbands' reports of "tensions or arguments" at work predicted an increase in the same type of interpersonal stress at home later that evening. On the other hand, wives' reports of problems at work did not have a short-term impact on their marital interactions. It is possible that the difference was due to the gender difference in job hours; wives were employed an average of 22 hours per week compared to the husbands' average of 43 hours.

A recent study found that wives were more socially withdrawn following a higher-paced workday (Schulz, Cowan, Cowan, and Brennan, 2004). However their husbands showed no association between the workday's pace and their marital behavior later at home. Story and Repetti (2006) replicated this pattern in another daily diary study using the same measure of marital with-drawal. Among wives, higher workload days were followed by withdrawal but there was no evidence for increased withdrawal among the husbands. The Story and Repetti study did not, however, replicate the gender pattern re-ported by Bolger et al. (1989), in which only husbands' job experiences pre-dicted marital arguments. Story and Repetti (2006) found that both husbands and wives described more marital anger (and more marital withdrawal) after days when they had more distressing interactions with coworkers and super-visors.

Thus, it may be that daily job stressors, such as work overload and inter-personal problems at work, have a greater impact on women's parenting and marital behavior than on men's behavior. A greater impact of workload on wives' involvement and responsiveness during marital interaction was ob-served in two daily diary studies despite the fact that in both samples the av-erage husband worked 15–18 more hours each week.[1] The gender difference may be consistent with Moen and Yu's (2000) finding that wives in two-earner couples report higher levels of distress and less confidence in their own ability to cope with difficulties than do husbands. There is a clear need for the continued investigation of possible gender differences in the effects of job stressors on behavior in the family. In particular there is a shortage of re-search comparing women and men who devote the same number of hours to their jobs each week.

Psychological Well-Being

Virtually all models of job stress influences on family interaction cast indi-vidual emotional and psychological functioning in key mediating roles (Perry-Jenkins et al., 2000). The assumption is that stressors affect a worker's energy, mood, and cognitions which, in turn, influence his or her social be-havior at home. The logical next step, therefore, is to consider how stable dif-ferences in personality or other psychological factors help to fashion the im-pact that job stressors do (or do not) have on an individual's behavior at home. Two studies of employed women found that a mother's psychological well-being moderated the association between her work experiences and her parenting behavior. In a daily-report study of employed mothers and their pre-school-age children, a higher-workload day was followed by more withdrawn and aversive behavior during the parent-child reunion, but this effect was ob-served only in the more distressed group of mothers (Repetti & Wood, 1997a). Among mothers who reported few symptoms of depression or anxi-ety, daily workload had no impact on subsequent interactions with their children. A different job stressor, negative social interactions at work, had the same short-term impact on parenting, but only among the mothers who reported more Type A behaviors, such as generally feeling pressed for time or getting upset at having to wait. In each case, once individual differences in personality or emotional well-being were considered, it was only the more distressed mothers who reacted to daily variations in job stressors.

A study that investigated how the length of a maternity leave might affect the quality of mother-infant interactions found a negative impact of a short maternity leave (six weeks or less) among the mothers who experienced postpartum depressive symptoms (Clark, Hyde, Essex, & Klien, 1997). For those mothers, a shorter leave was associated with fewer positive behaviors with the baby, like a warm tone of voice, a cheerful mood, and expressions of pleasure and enjoyment. For other mothers, however, a quick return to work was not associated with less positive maternal affect or behavior.

A pattern emerges in these two studies. For some women, stressful occupational conditions—a short maternity leave, an especially busy day or tense social interactions at work—had no detectable impact on parenting. But the same experiences were associated with variations in parenting among women who showed some signs of psychological distress. This suggests that emotional and psychological functioning are important sources of individual differences in responses to stressful employment experiences.

Characteristics of the Family

Just as individual differences play a role in determining how job stressors are carried into the home, characteristics of the household to which that individual returns are also a factor. The family's stage in its life cycle, the quality of relationships, and the division of labor within the home are all examples of family-level variables that have been found act as moderators.

An analysis of survey data from the 1992 National Study of the Changing Workforce found that men and women who were part of dual-earner couples faced more conflict in balancing work, personal, and family life if they had children living at home. They also described higher levels of stress and overload, and less mastery and control over their lives compared to dual-earner couples without children (Moen & Yu, 2000). Grzywacz, Almeida, and McDonald (2002) reported similar findings in a representative sample of employed individuals in the United States. The survey included questions about negative spillover from work to home, such as whether respondents thought their jobs reduced the effort they put into activities at home. Results indicated that negative spillover varied across the life cycle, with a decline beginning when employees were in their mid-50s. Similarly, the odds that work and family stressors would both occur on the same day gradually increased across young adulthood and midlife, but then declined during the later years. Thus, reports of negative spillover from work to home were strongest during the years when children are present, which is when labor and responsibilities in the family peak; this is the life stage that is most often studied by work-family researchers.

A good example of that tradition is research conducted by the Alfred P. Sloan Foundation's Center on Everyday Lives of Families (CELF) at UCLA. Our group studied a sample of dual-earner families with school-aged children through videotaping and other intensive data collection methods to obtain a rich and detailed picture of a week in their lives. One analysis found that, among fathers who were less happily married, more stressors at work were associated with observations of more intense and more negative social behavior with wives and school-aged children on weekday afternoons and evenings (e.g., more talking and more expressions of negative emotion). For the fathers in happier marriages, job stressors were linked with observations of less intense and less negative family interactions. Fathers' psychological distress also acted as a moderator, strengthening the connection between stressors at work and negative social behavior at home (Wang, Repetti, & Campos, 2008). Interestingly, there was no reliable evidence of a connection between the mothers' stressors at work and mothers' social behavior, whether or not individual or relationship distress was tested as a moderator. Another investigation, comparing parental monitoring in different groups of dual-earner families, uncovered a similar pattern. When fathers were employed in high-stress jobs, families were less adept at monitoring young sons, but only if the parents also described an unhappy marriage (Bumpus, Crouter, & McHale, 1999). That is, on average, there were no differences in how knowledgeable parents were about their children's daily lives, but parental monitoring differences were found when marital quality was considered. In families with young sons and less happy marriages, more employment demands on the father (but not more demands on the mother) were associated with the parents being less aware of their children's daily experiences, activities, and whereabouts. The findings from these two studies suggest that the well-being of a marriage, perhaps in combination with parent gender, helps to determine whether a stressful job has a negative impact on family behavior.

The quality of family relationships has also been found to moderate short-term associations between job stressors and family life. In the Schulz et al. (2004) daily-diary study mentioned above, couples with varying levels of marital satisfaction differed in the extent to which daily experiences at work were linked to marital interactions after work. For example, overall, when husbands left work in a more negative mood they were less likely to engage in angry marital behaviors (e.g., being argumentative, acting unkind and impatient with their wives). However, this effect was particularly strong among the men who were more satisfied with their marriages. Husbands in less satisfying marriages were not as likely to reduce their expressions of anger following a stressful day at work. Story and Repetti (2006) found that the short-term effects of work stressors on marital interaction differed for high-conflict and low-conflict families. Those with more conflictual social climates were more reactive to daily job stressors; both the husbands and the wives in those households were more likely to express anger and to withdraw from marital interaction on evenings following busy and interpersonally stressful days. Thus, feelings of irritability and frustration were more likely to be brought home when expressions of anger were generally more accepted or commonplace, and the spouses were also more likely to withdraw from their partners on stressful days, perhaps in an attempt to limit such unpleasant interactions.

The findings from these four studies point to the importance of the general quality of family relationships in guiding whether and how job stressors have an impact. In particular, a poor marriage or a high level of conflict and anger in the home may increase that family's vulnerability to negative spillover effects. Put another way, more satisfying and harmonious relationships may protect families from a potentially harmful carryover of job stress into the home.

The way that housework and childcare are divided between spouses also sets the stage for the influence of job stressors. An interview and questionnaire study of employed women who were pregnant at the start of the study examined how employment experiences at 4 months post-partum affected the mothers' feelings of role overload (feeling "pulled apart from having to juggle conflicting obligations" and doing "just too much"). On average, work hours were not associated with experiences of role overload; the link depended on how satisfied women were with the extent of their partners' contributions to household and family chores. Among women who were satisfied with the division of labor, there was little difference in feelings of role overload between those who worked long hours and those who worked fewer hours each week. However, among women who were dissatisfied with the division of labor in their homes, more work hours predicted greater role overload (Hyde, Essex, Clark, & Klein, 2001). As others have noted, at this point in society's adjustment to the influx of women into the paid labor force, an individual's employment hours, share of household labor, and gender are all inextricably intertwined. Therefore, any attempt to analyze how families differ in their responses to job stressors, must take all three variables into account.

Characteristics of Other Family Members

Besides characteristics of the employed individual and of the family, the characteristics of spouse and children also help to shape how jobs affect home life. A good example is the spouse's job characteristics, as illustrated by a study of how authority at work related to division of household labor (Brayfield, 1992). The wife's share of traditionally female tasks—cooking, laundry, housecleaning—was predicted by an interaction between her own authority at work and a measure that compared her authority to her husband's authority at work. For example, among women in supervisory roles, more authority at work (relative to husband's) was associated with a reduced share of household labor; an effect that was even stronger among women in top management. Thus, husbands' job characteristics helped to shape the link between wives' positions at work and their labor at home.

Characteristics of children may also act as moderators of work-family linkages (Greenberger, O'Neil, & Nagel, 1994). A study of parental monitoring found that, on average, there were no differences between the single-earner families and the dual-earner families with respect to parents' day-to-day knowledge about their school-aged children's lives, nor with respect to children's behavior problems (Crouter, MacDermid, McHale, & Perry-Jenkins, 1990).[2] But there were sub-group differences. Sons, but not daughters, in dual-earner families were more likely than other children to get into trouble, quarrel, and fight, but only if their parents were not keeping track of their daily activities and experiences. The conduct of sons in dual-earner families who were well monitored did not differ from the conduct of other children. The moderating role of child characteristics is probably most evident when parenting behavior is the outcome of interest. For example, in the maternity leave study mentioned earlier, infant temperament was a significant moderator. If the infant had a difficult or fussy temperament, a relatively quick return to work was associated with less positive maternal affect and behavior with the baby (Clark, Hyde, Essex, & Klein, 1997).

To summarize, researchers are interested in understanding variability in how families are affected by experiences in the workplace. When those questions are posed in studies with adequate sample sizes, differences are often found. Our review of the research literature suggests that the gender, personality, and psychological well-being of the employed individual and of other family members all help to determine how job stress influences family life. The stage of life and quality of relationships in the family, the manner in which labor is divided in the household, and the spouse's job characteristics are other factors that appear to shape work-family linkages. The next two sections of this chapter discuss some possible explanations for why and how those individual and family difference variables exert their influence.

STRESS PHYSIOLOGY

Recently, researchers have begun to focus attention on the biological under-pinnings of personality and health differences, exploring how inherited or ac-quired biological characteristics might shape both individual reactivity and coping strategies in the face of stress. While the stress physiology literature has not yet been extensively applied to work-family research, this work has direct bearing on some of the variables already described in this chapter, such as gender, marital quality, and psychological well-being.

Stress physiology, defined in terms of reactivity to threatening or demand-ing situations, and the ability to modulate or recover from one's response to stressors, has attracted a great deal of research interest in recent years. Given the increasing accessibility of biological measures of cortisol, heart rate, blood pressure, skin conductance, and proinflammatory cytokines, re-searchers have begun to link these markers of physiological functioning to daily experiences, ranging from marital conflict to high workload (Robles & Kiecolt-Glaser, 2003; Steptoe et al, 1998). Both experimental and naturalistic research on stress responses have found individual variability in stress-re-sponding systems like the hypothalamic pituitary adrenocortical (HPA) axis, which releases the hormone cortisol, and the sympathetic and parasympa-thetic systems (Dickerson & Kemeny, 2004; Gevirtz, 2000). Additionally, the notion of allostatic load, introduced to explain the long-term effects of chronic wear and tear on biological self-regulatory systems (McEwan, 1998), has helped researchers build a conceptual framework for understanding asso-ciations between individual differences, everyday stress, and health.

Given evidence that stress responses can be shaped by genes and early ex-periences, apparently leading to pervasive individual differences in reactivity (Yehuda & McEwan, 2004), it is no wonder that couples and families cope differently with the daily hassles of work, marriage, and parenting. For in-stance, we have discussed gender as one factor that may be implicated in dif-ferent responses to work stress. There is a burgeoning research literature sug-gesting that women and men may show different levels of reactivity to both work and family stressors. For example, some researchers have suggested that the HPA axis (cortisol) response to acute laboratory stressors is larger in men than in women (Lovallo & Thomas, 2000). One study (Ennis, Kelly, & Lambert, 2001) found that cortisol levels increased in men and decreased in women in anticipation of a stressful exam.

Interestingly, several studies have found that women are more physiologi-cally reactive to interpersonal conflict than are men, despite men's typically stronger response to laboratory stressors (cf., Kiecolt-Glaser & Newton, 2001). For example, among patients with hypertension, wives showed blood pressure changes during marital conflict that were related to hostility and overall marital quality, while husbands did not (Ewart, Taylor, Kraemer, & Agras, 1991). Wives also appear to show a greater epinephrine response to marital conflict (Malarkey, Kiecolt-Glaser, Pearl, & Glaser, 1994). One study combined an achievement challenge—a public speaking task that was either rated or not rated for verbal competence—with a disagreement/communion challenge—husbands and wives were either assigned to the same or opposing sides in a discussion. The disagreement condition was associated with elevated blood pressure and heart rates among wives, but not husbands (Smith et al., 1998), while the achievement challenge affected men's, but not women's, heart rate and blood pressure (Brown & Smith, 1992). This finding might help to explain why interpersonal problems at work were salient for the mothers' behavior but not for the fathers' behavior in a study described in the first part of this chapter (Costigan et al., 2003). That is, if women show greater physiological responses to interpersonal stressors, which could include interactions taking place both at work and at home, they might also show more enduring carryover effects after exposure to these types of stressors. In contrast, men might be more responsive to work stressors relevant to achievement. Although this hypothesis has not been explicitly tested, and is not fully supported by the findings of sex differences summarized in this chapter, it offers an example of the type of research question that stress physiology research can inform.

Another relevant gender difference has emerged in research on physiological unwinding, or the process of shedding tensions generated at work. Several studies suggest that, while both sexes appear physiologically aroused at work, working fathers may recover more rapidly after the workday ends. A study that measured the physiological stress levels of male and female managers found rapid after-work unwinding among the male managers, with decreased levels of blood pressure, norepinephrine excretion, and cortisol excretion during the evening hours. In contrast, female managers' physiological stress levels stayed closer to their daytime levels (Frankenhaeuser et al., 1989; Lundberg & Frankenhaeuser, 1999). Other researchers have reported that working women exhibit higher levels of physiological arousal on rest days than men do, signaling a lack of recovery, and that women with children tend to excrete more evening cortisol than women without children (Pollard, Ungpakorn, Harrison, & Parkes, 1996; Luecken et al., 1997). Marital satisfaction may play a role in the unwinding process, at least for women. Our study of cortisol patterns in dual-earner parents found that men and happily married women seemed to show a larger-than-usual drop in cortisol after a busier-than-usual workday, an apparent sign of exaggerated recovery from work, but that maritally dissatisfied women did not show the same drop-off (Saxbe, Repetti, & Nishina, 2008). These physiological differences may extend from women's greater share of domestic responsibilities, although much more research in this area is warranted.

As discussed earlier, individual differences in psychological well-being may also affect coping responses to work-family challenges. Physiological researchers have found some links between mental health and stress physiology. For example, in cortisol research, clinical depression has been associated with both blunted reactivity to, and poor recovery from, laboratory stressors (Burke, Davis, Otte, & Mohr, 2005). In other words, patients with depression seem to have an unresponsive and sluggish pattern of cortisol activity. An analogous result appears in naturalistic research, which has linked depression with a flattened diurnal cortisol slope (Miller, Chen, & Zhou, 2007). Cortisol levels typically peak in the morning and drop during the day, but a person with depression might exhibit both a lower morning cortisol level and then a plateau. In other mental disorders, such as PTSD, cortisol patterns also appear dysregulated—in PTSD and in Chronic Fatigue Syndrome, for example, cortisol levels are often lower than normal (Fries, Hesse, Hellhammer, & Hellhammer, 2005). These kinds of differences in physiology may help to explain how psychological health affects coping with work-family stress. If psychological problems lead to disruptions in stress responses and self-regulatory systems, they might deplete energy reserves, increase feelings of fatigue, and impair the ability to react quickly and effectively to the small, chronic stressors that are part of the life both at work and at home. While this remains speculative, it is possible that subjective states characterized by low energy, tiredness, or slow recovery from a stressor (feeling worked up even after a threat has passed, for example) might inform family members' behavior at home. For example, social withdrawal, a common response to difficult workdays, has been described as a short-term coping response to daily stress because it might help to restore a family member's mood or arousal level (Repetti, 1992). We can speculate that a family member whose stress-responding capabilities are already compromised by allostatic load or depression might exhibit this behavior more frequently, or might require a more prolonged period of social withdrawal in order to recover adequately.

In summary, physiological paradigms can help work-family researchers understand the interrelationships between daily stress, individual differences, and even long-term health. Stress responses can influence mood and coping resources, just as our daily lives and demands help to shape their functioning.

THE AFTER-WORK CONTEXT

When they leave work at the end of the day, employees face a new set of challenges and rewards, stressors and supports, and constraints on their energy and time. The nature and length of their commute home, whether or not there is an opportunity to relax and unwind before jumping into family life, and the child care and household responsibilities waiting for them at home are just a few features of the after-work environment that shape how employed members feel, think, and behave. For example, in a study of emotion transmission, Larson and Gillman (1999) found that time alone reduced the transmission of anger and anxiety from mothers to their adolescent children. The buffering effect of time alone was not due to a decrease in the total amount of time spent with the child. Solitary time appeared to have an independent beneficial effect by limiting the transmission of negative emotion when the mother and adolescent were together, suggesting that work-family negative emotion spillover may be less likely to occur if the employed parent has some time alone after work. It also offers one explanation for why social withdrawal may be a common coping strategy for employed parents after a stressful day at work. The possibility of some private time after work may contribute to the variability in work-family linkages observed among families that differ in division of household labor and ages of children. The physical environment also plays a role; residential attributes can enhance or limit possibilities for restorative processes after work by influencing exposure to daily hassles (e.g., troublesome neighbors) and ambient stressors (e.g., noise) (Hartig & Lawrence, 2003).

The needs, demands, emotions, and social behavior of family members are all part of the social world an employee enters as or she crosses the threshold from job to home at the end of the workday; these features of the social environment may be crucial to determiining how an individual's response to job stressors is expressed in the home and the extent to which restoration can occur. The behaviors of spouse and children may be the proximal variables that explain why some of the characteristics of families and their members act as moderator variables in the research literature discussed earlier. Support from a spouse is an important aspect of the after-work social environment. Family researchers have noted that emotional support from a spouse can help shield the marital relationship from the negative consequences of all kinds of stressors (Conger, Rueter, & Elder, 1999). Marital support may also take the form of helping with household chores and other demands on stressful days (Bolger et al., 1989), which may also facilitate the distressed partners' withdrawal-based coping. One study found that air traffic controllers were less likely to exhibit anger, and were more likely to withdraw from marital interaction, after high workload days at the airport if they received more support from their wives that evening (Repetti, 1989). Perhaps the support that the air traffic controllers got from their wives allowed a period of emotional recuperation, something that may be critical to avoiding negative emotional spillover after a stressful day at work.

Although it has not been the focus of much research in this area, the behavior of children when families are together at the end of the workday is also important in shaping work-family linkages. For instance, developmental psychologists have found that disruptive and difficult child and adolescent behaviors predict increases in parental criticism (Frye & Garber, 2005) and arguments between parents (Jenkins, Simpson, Dunn, Rasbash, & O'Connor, 2005), as well as declines in nurturant parenting and increases in harsh and inconsistent parenting (Rueter & Conger, 1998). This line of research indicates that what children do influences not only how parents behave with their children, but also how they behave with their spouses. It therefore makes sense for work-family researchers to consider how children contribute to the social situations that employed parents face at the end of the workday. For instance, Repetti and Wood (1997b) analyzed videotapes of the daily parent-child reunions of employed mothers as they retrieved their preschoolers from worksite daycare centers. When mothers showed signs of withdrawing—by speaking less and expressing less affection than on other days—their children responded by increasing attempts to engage the parent in the interaction, for instance by displaying more positive behaviors and asking more questions. Combined with the finding that these mothers were more socially withdrawn after high-stress days at work (Repetti & Wood, 1997a), we see that even young children can engage in behaviors that redirect their parents' responses to job stress.

In the CELF study mentioned earlier, intensive videotaping to examine a week in the life of a sample of dual-earner families. One set of analyses examined how returning parents were welcomed home by the rest of the family at the end of the workday. When parents arrived home, family members were about as likely to be distracted and to treat the reunion as a side event as they were to be fully engaged in greeting and welcoming the parent (Ochs, Graesch, Mittmann, Bradbury, & Repetti, 2006). Children were particularly likely to be distracted when fathers returned home, perhaps reflecting the fact that fathers were often the final family member to arrive home at the end of the day and, by then, children often had been in the home for some time and were entrenched in an activity. The greeting behavior (or lack thereof) reported by the CELF researchers raises a question about the extent to which family members' behavior may promote a particular type of response to a stressful day at work. Perhaps ignoring a parent or spouse when he or she returns home promotes social withdrawal as a way of coping with a stressful day. Alternatively, displays of appreciation and affection from family members might promote a different type of response after a hard day at work, perhaps more discussion of what went on that day. The findings from these two naturalistic observational studies illustrate that, when an individual's behavior is studied, not as an isolated specimen, but embedded within the social context of the family, a new picture of work-family processes emerges. A spouse or parent can no longer be cast as an actor in full control of his or her actions; the contributions of the behavior, attitudes, motivations, and interests of other family members must be acknowledged.

In sum, a careful consideration of the social and physical world that employees enter as they leave work each day may help researchers uncover processes that explain the why and how occupational experiences have different effects on families.

FUTURE DIRECTIONS FOR RESEARCH

Individuals and families respond in variety of ways to job stressors; researchers have begun to identify the sources of those differences and to describe how they influence work-family linkages. Our review points to variables that seem to play a role, but the findings are not always consistent. A more strategic use of sampling methods would improve our ability to identify reliable patterns of group differences and moderator effects. Large random samples may provide enough variance to detect interaction effects. However, the sampling methods and sizes required to adequately represent the full range of individual and family characteristics are often not practical or feasible, particularly with more intensive data collection methods. Another strategy is to focus on selected samples in which the effects of moderators might be easier to observe. To the extent that some sources of variance are, in a sense, controlled by the sample's homogeneity (e.g., families with children in a particular age range), there is greater opportunity for the effects of other characteristics of interest (e.g., marital quality) to be detected (Repetti, 2005; Repetti & Wang, in press).

At the same time that researchers strive to identify moderator variables, we also need hey must also begin to describe the processes that underlie those interactions. Our chapter points to some promising directions for future work, for example, physiological mechanisms might explain sex differences or the moderating effects of psychological distress. Details about the social situations that confront employees when they leave the workplace at the end of the day will help us to understand how certain characteristics of families (e.g., relationship quality) and of their members (e.g., child age) shape the impact of job stressors. Work-family researchers will need to use a broader range of methods, like naturalistic observations and physiological measures, to investigate those processes and to move beyond "one size fits all" models.

NOTES

Rena Repetti, Ph.D., is a professor and Darby Saxe, M.A., is a graduate student in the Department of Psychology at the University of California, Los Angeles. Both authors thank the Alfred P. Sloan Foundation and the Center on Everyday Lives of Families at UCLA for supporting their research. A Graduate Research Fellowship from the National Science Foundation also supported Darbe Saxbe's work on this paper.

1. On average, husbands worked 43 and 47 hours per week and wives worked 25 and 32 hours per week in the Schulz et al (2004) and the Story and Repetti (2006) studies, respectively.

2. In dual-earner families the mothers were employed at least 15 hours per week, and in single-earner families mothers either were employed less than 15 hours or did not work outside the home at all.

REFERENCES

Bolger, N., DeLongis, A., Kessler, R. C., & Wethington, E. (1989). The contagion of stress across multiple roles. *Journal of Marriage and the Family, 51*, 175–183.

Brayfield, A. A. (1992). Employment resources and housework in Canada. *Journal of Marriage and the Family, 54*, 19–30.

Brown, P. C., & Smith, T. W. (1992). Social influence, marriage, and the heart: Cardiovascular consequences of interpersonal control in husbands and wives. *Health Psychology, 11*, 88–96.

Bumpus, M. F., Crouter, A. C., & McHale, S. M. (1999). Work demands of dual-earner couples: Implications for parents' knowledge about children's daily lives in middle childhood. *Journal of Marriage and the Family, 61*, 465–475.

Burke, H. M., Davis, M. C., Otte, C., & Mohr, D. C. (2005). Depression and cortisol responses to psychological stress: A meta-analysis. *Psychoneuroendocrinology, 30*, 846–856.

Clark, R., Hyde, J. S., Essex, M. J., & Klein, M. H. (1997). Length of maternity leave and quality of mother-infant interactions. *Child Development, 68*, 364–383.

Conger, R. D., Rueter, M. A., & Elder, G. H., Jr. (1999). Couple resilience to economic pressure. *Journal of Personality and Social Psychology, 76*, 54–71.

Costigan, C. L., Cox, M. J., & Cauce, A. M. (2003). Work-parenting linkages among dual-earner couples at the transition to parenthood. *Journal of Family Psychology, 17*, 397–408.

Crouter, A. C., & Bumpus, M. F. (2001). Linking parents' work stress to children's and adolescents' psychological adjustment. *Current Directions in Psychological Science, 10*, 156–159.

Crouter, A. C., & Helms-Erikson, H. (1997). Work and family from a dyadic perspective: Variations in inequality. In S. Duck (Ed.), *Handbook of personal relationships,* 2nd ed. (pp. 487–503). Hoboken, NJ: John Wiley & Sons.

Crouter, A. C., MacDermid, S. M., McHale, S. M., & Perry-Jenkins, M. (1990). Parental monitoring and perceptions of children's school performance and conduct in dual- and single-earner families. *Developmental Psychology, 26*, 649–657.

Dickerson, S. S., & Kemeny, M. E. (2004). Acute stressors and cortisol responses: A theoretical integration and synthesis of laboratory research. *Psychological Bulletin, 130*, 355–391.

Ennis, M., Kelly, K. S., & Lambert, P. L. (2001). Sex differences in cortisol excretion during anticipation of a psychological stressor: Possible support for the tend-and-befriend hypothesis. *Stress and Health, 17*, 253–261.

Ewart, C. K., Taylor, C. B., Kraemer, H. C., & Agras, W. S. (1991). High blood pressure and marital discord: Not being nasty matters more than being nice. *Health Psychology, 10*, 155–163.

Frankenhaeuser, M., Lundberg, U., Fredriksson, M., Melin, B., Tuomisto, M., & Myrsten, A. (1989). Stress on and off the job as related to sex and occupational status in white collar workers. *Journal of Organizational Behavior, 10*, 321–46.

Fries, E., Hesse, J., Hellhammer, J., & Hellhammer, D. H. (2005). A new view on hypocortisolism. *Psychoneuroendocrinology, 30*, 1010–1016.

Frye, A. A., & Garber, J. (2005). The relations among maternal depression, maternal criticism, and adolescents' externalizing and internalizing symptoms. *Journal of Abnormal Child Psychology, 33*, 1–11.

Gevirtz, R. (2000). The physiology of stress. In D. T. Kenny, J. G. Carlson, F. J. McGuigan, & J. L. Sheppard (Eds.), *Stress and health: Research and clinical applications* (pp. 53–71). Amsterdam: Harwood Academic Publishers.

Greenberger, E., O'Neil, R., & Nagel, S. K. (1994). Linking workplace and homeplace: Relations between the nature of adults' work and their parenting behaviors. *Developmental Psychology, 30*, 990–1002.

Grzywacz, J. G., Almeida, D. M., & McDonald, D. A. (2002). Work-family spillover and daily reports of work and family stress in the adult labor force. *Family Relations: Interdisciplinary Journal of Applied Family Studies, 51*, 28–36.

Hartig, T., & Lawrence, R. J. (2003). Introduction: The residential context of health. *Journal of Social Issues, 59*, 455–472.

Hyde, J. S., Essex, M. J., Clark, R., & Klein, M. H. (2001). Maternity leave, women's employment, and marital incompatibility. *Journal of Family Psychology, 15*, 476–491.

Jenkins, J., Simpson, A., Dunn, J., Rasbash, J., & O'Connor, T. G. (2005). Mutual influence of marital conflict and children's behavior problems: Shared and nonshared family risks. *Child Development, 76*, 24–39.

Kiecolt-Glaser, J., & Newton, T. (2001). Marriage and health: His and hers. *Psychological Bulletin, 127*, 472–503.

Larson, R. W., & Gillman, S. (1999). Transmission of emotions in the daily interactions of single-mother families. *Journal of Marriage and the Family, 61*, 21–37.

Lovallo, W. R., & Thomas, T. L. 2000. Stress hormones in psycho-physiological research. In: Cacciopo, J., Tassinary, L., Bernston, G. (Eds.), *Handbook of Psychophysiology*, 2nd ed. (pp. 342–367). Cambridge, UK: Cambridge University Press.

Luecken, L., Suarez, E., Kuhn, C., Barefoot, J., Blumenthal, J., Siegler, I., & Williams, R. (1997). Stress in employed women: impact of marital status and children at home on neurohormone output and home strain. *Psychosomatic Medicine, 59*, 352–359.

Lundberg, U., & Frankenhaeuser, M. (1999). Stress and workload of men and women in high ranking positions. *Journal of Occupational Health Psychology, 4*, 142–151.

Malarkey, W., Kiecolt-Glaser, J. K., Pearl, D., & Glaser, R. (1994). Hostile behavior during marital conflict alters pituitary and adrenal hormones. *Psychosomatic Medicine, 56*, 41–51.

McEwan, B. S. (1998). Protective and damaging effects of stress mediators. *New England Journal of Medicine, 338*, 171–179.

Miller, G. E., Chen, E., & Zhou, E. S. (2007). If it goes up, must it come down? Chronic stress and the hypothalamic-pituitary-adrenocortical axis in humans. *Psychological Bulletin 133*, 25–45

Moen, P., & Yu, Y. (2000). Effective work/life strategies: Working couples, work conditions, gender, and life quality. *Social Problems, 47*, 291–326.

Ochs, E., Graesch, A. P., Mittmann, A., Bradbury, T., & Repetti, R. (2006). Video ethnography and ethnoarchaeological tracking. In M. Pitt-Catsouphes, K. Kossek & S. Sweet (Eds.), *The work and family handbook: Multi-disciplinary perspective, methods, and approaches* (pp.387–409). Mahwah, NJ: Lawrence Erlbaum.

Perry-Jenkins, M., & Gillman, S. (2000). Parental job experiences and children's well-being: The case of two-parent and single-mother working-class families. *Journal of Family and Economic Issues, 21*, 123–147.

Perry-Jenkins, M., Repetti, R. L., & Crouter, A. C. (2000). Work and family in the 1990's. *Journal of Marriage and the Family, 62*, 981–998.

Pollard, T., Ungpakorn, G., Harrison, G., & Parkes, K. (1996). Epinephrine and cortisol responses to work. *Annals of Behavioral Medicine, 18*, 229–237.

Repetti, R. L. (1989). Effects of daily workload on subsequent behavior during marital interaction: The roles of social withdrawal and spouse support. *Journal of Personality and Social Psychology, 57*, 651–659.

———. (1992). Social withdrawal as a short-term coping response to daily stressors. In H. S. Friedman (Ed.), *Hostility, coping, & health* (pp.151–165). Washington, DC: American Psychological Association.

———. (2005). A psychological perspective on the health and well-being consequences of parental employment. In S. M. Bianchi, L. M. Casper, & R. B. King (Eds.), *Work, family, health, and well-being* (pp. 245–258). Mahwah, NJ: Lawrence Erlbaum.

Repetti, R. L., & Wang, S. (in press). Parent employment and chaos in the family. In G. Evans & T. Wachs (Eds.), *Chaos and children's development: Levels of analysis and mechanisms*. Washington, DC: APA Books.

Repetti, R. L., & Wood, J. (1997a). Effects of daily stress at work on mothers' interactions with preschoolers. *Journal of Family Psychology, 11*, 90–108.

———. (1997b). Families accommodating to chronic stress: Unintended and unnoticed processes. In B. H. Gottlieb (Ed.), *Coping with chronic stress* (pp. 191–220). New York: Plenum Publishing.

Robles, T. F., & Kiecolt-Glaser, J. K. (2003). The physiology of marriage: pathways to health. *Physiology and Behavior, 79*, 409–16.

Rueter. M. A., & Conger, R. D. (1998). Reciprocal influences between parenting and adolescent problem-solving behavior. *Developmental Psychology, 34*, 1470–1482.

Saxbe, D., Repetti, R. L., & Nishina, A. (2008). Marital satisfaction, recovery from work, and diurnal cortisol among men and women. *Health Psychology, 27*, 15–25.

Schulz, M. S., Cowan, P. A., Cowan, C. P., & Brennan, R. T. (2004). Coming home upset: Gender, marital satisfaction, and the daily spillover of workday experience into couple interactions. *Journal of Family Psychology, 18*, 250–263.

Smith, T. W., Gallo, L. C., Goble, L., Ngu, L. Q., & Stark, K. A. (1998). Agency, communion, and cardiovascular reactivity during marital interaction. *Health Psychology, 17*, 537–545.

Steptoe, A., Wardle, J., Lipsey, Z., Mills, R., Oliver, G., & Jarvis, M. (1998). A longitudinal study of work load and variations in psychological well-being, cortisol, smoking, and alcohol consumption. *Annals of Behavioral Medicine, 20*, 84–91.

Story, L. B., & Repetti, R. L. (2006). Daily occupational stressors and marital behavior. *Journal of Family Psychology, 20*, 690–700.

Wang, S., & Repetti, R. L. (2008). *Work and family relationships: Links between job stress, distress, and social behavior at home*. Unpublished manuscript.

Yehuda, R., & McEwen, B. (2004). Biobehavioral stress response: Protective and damaging effects. *Annals of the New York Academy of Sciences, 1032*, 1–7.

Young, A. H. (2004). Cortisol in mood disorders. *Stress: The International Journal on the Biology of Stress, 7*, 205–208.

Chapter Five

How Family-Supportive Work Environments and Work-Supportive Home Environments Can Reduce Work-Family Conflict and Enhance Facilitation

Elianne F. van Steenbergen, Naomi Ellemers, and Ab Mooijaart

ABSTRACT

In an attempt to help employees manage their work and family responsibilities, many organizations offer work-family benefits or programs to their employees, such as formal arrangements for flextime or childcare facilities. However, a substantial body of research suggests that, more than having work-family benefits or arrangements available to them, it is important for employees to receive informal support in their work environments. That is, employees in family-supportive work environments (e.g., managerial and co-worker support for family issues) experience fewer problems in combining their work and family roles (lower work-family conflict). In this chapter, we extend this line of research by also examining informal support in the home environment, thus assessing the family supportiveness of the work environment as well as the work supportiveness of the home environment. Moreover, we not only examine whether employees in supportive work and home environments experience fewer problems in combining work and family, but also whether support at work and at home might have the capacity to induce a positive exchange between people's work and family roles (work-family facilitation). We present data from a survey study among 301 Dutch employees in a multinational financial services organization. Our findings indicate that supportive work and home environments have the capacity to reduce the extent to which employees experience conflict between their work and family roles, and also seem to stimulate experiences of work-family facilitation. Moreover, we found intriguing gender differences, indicating that the work

and home environments have a different impact upon men's and women's
ability to combine their work and family lives.

With the dual-earner family as predominant model in current society, most employees—male and female—combine their work with some sort of family responsibility (Bond, Thompson, Galinsky, & Pottras, 2002; United Nations Statistics Division, 2006). In response to this new reality, many contemporary organizations offer their employees work-family benefits to support them in their efforts to balance their work and family lives (Thompson & Pottras, 2005). These benefits include, for instance, formal arrangements for flextime, parental leave, child-care facilities, or facilities for telecommuting.

However, a growing body of research suggests that the informal work environment, such as the organizational culture or the degree to which a supervisor accommodates and understands family issues, has more impact on employees' ability to manage work and family roles than the formal benefits organizations offer. That is, increasing studies show that experiences of work-family conflict are related more to family support within the organizational culture, as well as supervisor and co-worker support for the family domain, than to the availability or use of concrete work-family benefits (Allen, 2001; Hammer, Neal, Newsom, Brockwood, & Colton, 2005; Kluwer, Boers, Heesink, & Van de Vliert, 1997; Thompson, Beauvais, & Lyness, 1999; Thomas & Ganster, 1995). *Work-family conflict* here refers to the feeling that work and family roles are incompatible in some respect, as a result of which participation in one role makes it more difficult to fulfill the requirements of the other role (Greenhaus & Beutell, 1985). For instance, in a sample of more than 3,000 American employees from the 2002 Study of the Changing Workforce, Thompson and Pottras (2005) examined whether employees' conflict experiences depend on two types of conditions available to them: family-friendly benefits (family benefits and alternative work schedules) or the extent to which they received informal family support in their work environment (supportive organizational culture, supervisor support, and co-worker support). Family-friendly benefits were not associated with the level of conflict employees experienced, whereas higher levels of informal family support related to significantly lower levels of conflict reported by these employees. In addition, Behson (2005) used the statistical technique of dominance analysis to test the relative contribution of formal benefits versus informal support to conflict experiences of employees who participated in the 1997 National Study of the Changing Workforce. Again, strong support was found for the dominance of informal support over formal benefits in explaining variance in conflict experiences, as 95% of the total variance that was explained in the conflict experiences of employees was explained by informal support, whereas less than 5% was attributable to the formal benefits organizations offered.

Thus, more than having work-family benefits formally available to them, it seems important for employees to have supervisors and co-workers who are understanding and accommodating of family issues and empathize with employees' desire to seek a balance between work and family responsibilities (Thomas & Ganster, 1995). Examples might include a supervisor who allows personal calls home and is open to discuss family issues or problems, or colleagues who understand when one has to leave early to pick up a child from day care or school, or a dependent parent from a caregiver (Thomas & Ganster, 1995; Thompson & Pottras, 2005). Moreover, the degree to which cultural norms within the organization prescribe working long hours, prioritizing work over family, and collective beliefs about whether using work-family benefits will jeopardize one's career have an important influence on the level of conflict that employees experience (e.g., Allen, 2001; Poelmans et al., 2003; Thompson et al., 1999). These day-to-day interactions employees have with their supervisors and co-workers and the prevalent organizational norms most strongly affect the work-family interface.

This important body of research has, in our opinion, three central shortcomings as a result of which the picture still remains incomplete. First, prior studies remained almost exclusively focused on formal and informal characteristics of the work environment, thus only addressing the organizational contribution to conflict experiences (Allen, 2001; Behson, 2005; Thompson et al., 1999; Thompson & Pottras, 2005; Voydanoff, 2004a). They neglect the contribution of the home environment, such as receiving support from one's spouse or other family members for work requirements or the norms that characterize one's home environment. In the present study we will examine both work and home environments.

A second shortcoming is the one-sided focus of the literature on the negative side of combining work and family roles. Prior studies almost exclusively examined whether the nature of the work environment is associated with higher or lower levels of conflict. This approach suggests that the best possible outcome is to have no conflict, and neglects the possibility that work and family roles can also benefit each other. As a result, it remains unknown whether supportive environments might also have the capacity to induce work-family facilitation, which occurs when participation in the work role is made easier by virtue of the family role or vice versa (van Steenbergen, Ellemers, & Mooijaart, 2007; Wayne, Musisca, & Fleeson, 2004). To address this, we will assess how work and home environments affect facilitation as well as conflict.

Third, prior studies address conflict in a general sense, thus neglecting different types of conflict (and facilitation). In the present research, we comply with the call to provide a finer-grained examination of the work-family interface (Adams, et al., 1996; Poelmans et al., 2003) by analyzing whether types of conflict and facilitation are affected differently by the supportiveness of the work and home environments.

FAMILY-SUPPORTIVE WORK ENVIRONMENTS AND WORK-SUPPORTIVE HOME ENVIRONMENTS

Despite calls in the work-family literature to assess employees' home situations with the same precision as their work situations (e.g., Geurts & Demerouti, 2003), previous research has focused on the organizational contribution to employees' conflict experiences in role combination (Allen, 2001; Behson, 2005); Thompson et al., 1999; Thompson & Pottras, 2005; Voydanoff, 2004a). Because work characteristics are believed to be the primary antecedents of work-to-family (WF) conflict (Frone et al., 1992), most studies address this WF direction of conflict, thus only capturing the extent to which work negatively interferes with family life (e.g., Behson, 2005; Dikkers, Geurts, den Dulk, Peper, & Kompier, 2004; Thompson et al., 1999; Voydanoff, 2004a). From this literature it is apparent that cross-domain support—support provided by one domain (work) for the other domain (family) related to lower WF conflict among employees. That is, as described, a family-supportive work environment relates to lower WF conflict. In the present study, we also examine the reverse: whether perceived support within the home domain for work issues can help lower levels of family-to-work (FW) conflict.

With regard to the work environment, we assess supervisor and co-worker support for the family domain (Thomas & Ganster, 1995; Lapierre & Allen, 2006; Kluwer et al., 1997), as well as the supportiveness of two components of the organizational culture. First, we assess the extent to which cultural norms prescribe long work hours, hereafter referred to as *organizational time demands* (Thompson et al., 1999; Thompson & Pottras, 2005; Poelmans, 2003; Kluwer et al., 1997). The second component consists of the perceived *negative career consequences* when using work-family benefits or devoting time to family responsibilities. This refers to employees' reluctance to use work-family benefits or devote more time to their family responsibilities out of fear that having less face time at work is interpreted as a lack of commitment, which will jeopardize their careers (Poelmans, 2003; Thompson et al., 1999; Voydanoff, 2004a). Obviously, a supportive work environment is characterized by high levels of supervisor and co-worker support and the perception of limited organizational time demands and few negative career consequences when using work-family benefits.

The supportiveness of the home environment has received surprisingly little scientific attention. To our knowledge, there are only two studies in the literature that relate conflict experiences of employees to the support they receive for work issues within the family domain (cross-domain support). In the study by Kossek, Colquitt, and Noe (2001), employees of an American university rated their family climates on the extent to which they could (a) share concerns about their work and (b) were expected to sacrifice work performance for the sake of family duties. In the same vein, they rated their work climate on the extent to which they could (a) share concerns about their families and (b) were expected to sacrifice family performance for the sake of work performance. In this study, a work climate that expected employees to make family sacrifices was especially related to higher levels of WF conflict, whereas a family climate that emphasized making work sacrifices was related to higher levels of both WF and FW conflict (Kossek et al., 2001). In addition, Lapierre and Allen (2006) found that employees who felt that their family members supported work saw the family as less interfering with work (FW conflict), whereas the extent to which their supervisors were supportive of family responsibilities was related to lower experiences of work interfering with family (WF conflict). Moreover, studies that did not assess cross-domain support, but focused on the general support received at home in terms of emotional support, recognition, feedback, or appreciation (example item: "How much does your spouse or partner really care about you?") show that family resources such as spousal support and support from other family members relate to lower reported FW conflict (Adams et al., 1996; Aryee, Srinivas, Tan, 2005; Carlson & Perrewé, 1999; Grzywacz & Marks, 2000).

In the present research, we examine the work supportiveness of the home environment as follows: In parallel to the indicators of support in the work environment, we first examine support of partner. Just as conflict experiences are likely to depend on the family supportiveness of one's supervisor at work (e.g., Thomas & Ganster, 1995; Thompson & Pottras, 2005), we posit that the level of conflict one experiences should also depend on having a partner at home who is supportive and sensitive to work responsibilities and will help accommodate a balance between work and family. In the same vein, we argue that receiving support from other family members and friends for work issues and for finding a balance between work and family could be an important resource, comparable to co-worker support at work, when juggling work and family responsibilities. Furthermore, comparable to the components that can make an organization a greedy institution (organizational time demands and negative career consequences when using work-family benefits;

e.g., Thompson et al., 1999), we examine two components that can make the home environment greedy. Mirroring organizational time demands, we examine demands in the home environment that require a person to be present to do certain activities at specified times (Poelmans et al., 2003). In the case of the home environment, this might include being responsible for caring tasks at specified times (e.g., taking the children to school, cooking dinner), or being expected to be home for dinner or family activities at set times. Just as organizational time demands influence conflict experiences, one would expect that time demands from one's home environment affect conflict, thus creating the well-known time-bind between work and family life (Hochschild, 1997). Finally, as employees can be reluctant to use work-family benefits out of fear that having less face time in the office will jeopardize their careers (Thompson et al., 1999), individuals could be reluctant to take on a promotion or a more demanding job when they perceive this will negatively affect their lives at home. Especially when a more demanding job or more demanding work tasks would require being away from home more (e.g., traveling for work, dinners with clients), one could fear that having less face time at home communicates a lack of commitment that will hurt one's relationships. We refer to the perception that work-related absence from home would jeopardize one's relationships as *negative relationship consequences*.

CONFLICT AND FACILITATION

The second shortcoming of the research was the predominant focus on the negative side of combining work and family roles. Most studies in the work-family literature implicitly or explicitly adopted a scarcity perspective on human energy. They assume that personal resources of time, energy, and attention are finite, as a result of which devotion of attention to one role necessarily implies that fewer resources can be spent on another role (Voydanoff, 2004a). Research within this tradition searched for possibilities to reduce or prevent work-family conflict. Theoretically, this scarcity perspective was opposed by role expansion theory (Marks, 1977), which posits that human energy is abundant and expandable and that roles can also positively affect one another. However, scholars only recently started to pay empirical attention to the concept of work-family facilitation, which refers to the idea that participation in the work role is made easier by virtue of the family role or vice versa (van Steenbergen et al., 2007; Wayne, Musisca, & Fleeson, 2004). As a result, research on facilitation and ways to enhance facilitation (as opposed to reducing conflict) is still relatively scarce.

Two recent studies, however, suggest that supportive environments might also enhance facilitation among employees. That is, Voydanoff (2004b) found that having a family-supportive supervisor was related to lower WF conflict, but also to higher levels of WF facilitation. In addition, Thompson and Pottras (2005) found that perceiving one's supervisor and co-workers as family supportive related to lower WF conflict as well as higher levels of general facilitation (they did not distinguish between WF and FW facilitation). Moreover, studies assessing general support instead of cross-domain support indicate that receiving support at home from spouse, family, and friends predicted the level of FW facilitation employees experienced (Aryee et al., 2005; Grzywacz & Marks, 2000).

In the present research, we examine family support for the work environment as well as work support for the home environment, and relate them to employees' WF and FW conflict and facilitation experiences. In previous work, scholars have argued that characteristics of the work environment predict the WF direction of conflict and facilitation experiences, whereas characteristics of the home environment are the primary antecedents of the FW direction (e.g., Frone et al., 1992). However, in the empirical literature, exceptions to this pattern have been found, in that characteristics of the work environment related to the FW direction and characteristics of the home environment related to the WF direction of conflict and facilitation experiences (e.g., Aryee et al., 2005; Geurts et al., 2005; Grzywacz & Marks, 2000; Kossek et al., 2001). This seems to suggest that supportive work and home environments benefit employees' general ability to balance work and family roles (Allen, 2001). In the present research, we therefore predict that supportive work and home environments relate to lower conflict and higher levels of facilitation among employees. Thus, we hypothesize that the support components of the work environment (supportive supervisor, supportive co-workers) relate to lower conflict and higher levels of facilitation, whereas organizational time demands and negative career consequences relate to higher conflict and lower levels of facilitation. In the same vein, we expect that the support components of the home environment (supportive partner, supportive family and friends) relate to lower conflict and higher levels of facilitation, whereas home time demands and negative relationship consequences relate to higher conflict and lower levels of facilitation.

DIFFERENT TYPES OF CONFLICT AND FACILITATION

There are different ways in which work and family roles can hinder and benefit one another. However, little is known about how the different components that make a work or home environment supportive relate to the different types of conflict or facilitation experiences that people can have. This is unfortunate because different types of conflict and facilitation are known to have specific relationships with outcome variables (Bruck, Allen, & Spector, 2002; van Steenbergen et al., 2007). Moreover, knowing exactly which types of conflict or facilitation are affected would further our understanding of the subtleties of work-family dynamics (Adams et al., 1996; Poelmans et al., 2003) and could assist practitioners in designing interventions tailored to specific needs of individuals or organizations.

From prior studies that adopted a scarcity perspective on human energy, we know that individuals can experience energy-based, time-based, behavioral, and psychological conflict (Carlson, Kacmar, & Williams, 2000; Carlson & Frone, 2003). Energy-based conflict exists when energy depleted by one role makes it difficult to fulfill the requirements of another role (e.g., too tired from family responsibilities to concentrate on work). Time-based conflict occurs "when time devoted to one role makes it difficult to fulfill the requirements of another role" (e.g., a project at work precludes a family activity). Behavioral conflict exists "when behavior required in one role makes it difficult to fulfill the requirements of another role" (e.g. difficulties in switching from a tough managerial role to a caring family role, Greenhaus & Beutell, 1985, p. 76). Finally, psychological conflict refers to "the psychological preoccupation with one role, while performing another role that interferes with one's ability to become engaged in that last role." For instance, someone keeps thinking about home-life matters while at work, which may render him or her unable to concentrate on work (Carlson & Frone, 2003, p. 518; Greenhaus, 1988).

We will also examine the effects of different types of facilitation. Based on premises of the role expansion theory (Marks, 1977; Barnett & Hyde, 2001) and prior empirical studies on facilitation (e.g., Ruderman, Ohlott, Panzer, & King,, 2002; Wayne et al., 2004), we argued earlier (van Steenbergen et al., 2007) that individuals can also experience different types of facilitation, in parallel to the different types of conflict. In both qualitative and quantitative data, we found support for the distinction between energy-based, time-based, behavioral, and psychological facilitation. These types of facilitation were statistically distinguishable from the different types of conflict and demonstrated specific relationships with outcome variables we measured in the work, home, and health domains. Individuals experience energy-based facilitation when the energy obtained in one role makes it easier to fulfill the requirements of another role (van Steenbergen et al., 2007). As an interviewee in that previous research indicated: "It is fun being a dad. It gives you a lot of pleasure and positive energy, which makes itself felt at work" (p. 285). Moreover, people can experience time-based facilitation, occurring when the time devoted to one role stimulates or makes it easier to effectively manage and use the time in another role. For instance, the time people spend on parenting tasks (picking up the children on time, etc.) can make it easier for them to prioritize the tasks they take on at work and can stimulate them to use their time at work more effectively. Behavioral facilitation occurs when behavior required or learned in one role makes it easier to fulfill the requirements of another role, as expressed by an interviewee (van Steenbergen et al., 2007, p. 285), "At work I function in a dynamic field where a lot of power and strategic games go on. So, I do not lose my head quickly when some problem arises at home. I have learned to deal with problems; I have those skills." Finally, psychological facilitation refers to the ability to put matters associated with one role into perspective by virtue of another role, which makes it easier to fulfill the requirements of the first role. For instance, participating in family activities can help one to put work matters into perspective, which benefits that person's functioning at work. To our knowledge, no prior study examined how supportive work and home environments affect different facilitation experiences of individuals. In the present research, we will explore how the components of supportive work and home environments relate to energy-based, time-based, behavioral, and psychological WF and FW conflict and facilitation experiences.

In doing this, we will explicitly examine whether there are any gender differences, as there are indications that supportive environments can affect men and women differently (Grzywacz & Marks, 2000). For instance, a previous study revealed that organizational time demands only predicted the level of conflict men reported, whereas perceptions that one could make use of work-family benefits and having a family-supportive supervisor significantly predicted women's conflict experiences (Kluwer et al., 1997).

METHOD

Sample and Participants

A multinational financial service organization gave us permission to conduct a survey study and provided us with the work addresses of a random sample of 750 of their Dutch employees. In line with prior studies (e.g., Grzywacz & Marks, 2000), we did not limit our sample to employees with children because this would reflect a too-narrow conceptualization of family, as childless adults can also carry family responsibilities to parents, siblings, and others. The response rate was 48.4%, with 363 surveys returned. A detailed description of the statistical characteristics of the scales that measure the different types of facilitation and examine their relationships with different categories of outcome variables is available in van Steenbergen et al. (2007).

Consistent with previous studies (e.g., Frone et al., 1992), we excluded employees ($N = 11$) who worked less than 20 hours per week. In accordance with our objective to study support of partners we limited the sample to employees who were married or cohabiting ($N = 301$).

The 301 participants consisted of 185 males and 116 females. Males were contracted to work for an average of 36.64 hours a week, whereas females contracted to work 31.23 hours). Average organizational tenure was 17.56 years for males and 10.15 years for females. Of males, 5.4% indicated being in the age category "29 years or less," 30.3% were "between 30 and 39," 34.6% were "between 40 and 49," and 29.7% were "50 years or older." For females these percentages were, respectively, 14.7%, 47.4%, 29.3%, and 8.3%. About half of the males (50.3%) had received higher education (university or higher vocational education), 49.7% had completed lower education (lower vocational education or high school). Of females, 56% had received higher education. A large number of males and females had at least one child (77.3% and 60.5%). For males with children, 24.1% had a youngest child who was not yet attending school (0–3 years old), 31.0% had a child in the Dutch elementary school age (4–12 years old), 20.0% had a youngest child in the Dutch high school age (13–21 years old), and 24.8% had a youngest child aged 22 years or older For females these percentages were, respectively, 46.6%, 30.1%, 15.1%, and 8.2%. The organization's salary system consists of 15 ascending salary categories, ranging from $1 = lowest$ to $15 = highest$ in pay. The average salary category for men was 9.40 and for women 7.89.

Measures

We measured supervisor support with three items adapted from Thompson et al. (1999): "My direct manager is sympathetic toward my family related responsibilities," "My direct manager is accommodating of family-related needs," and "My direct manager gives me enough scope to balance my work and family life" ($\alpha = .91$). Co-worker support was measured with the same items only this time these referred to co-workers ($\alpha = .91$). Both organizational time demands ($\alpha = .73$) and negative career consequences ($\alpha = .73$) were measured with two items developed by Thompson et al. (1999). Sample items are, respectively, "Employees are often expected to take work home at night and/or on weekends" and "To turn down a promotion or transfer for family-related reasons will seriously hurt one's career progress in my organization." Support of partner and support of family and friends were both measured with three items (e.g., "My partner is accommodating of my work-related obligations" and "My family (other than spouse) and friends are accommodating of my work-related obligations" ($\alpha = .86$ and $\alpha = .90$, van Steenbergen & Ellemers, 2003). Negative relationship consequences and home time demands were both measured with two items, e.g., "Accepting a promotion or a more demanding job would have negative consequences for the relationship with my partner" and "At home it is expected of me that I spend a lot of hours on caring tasks" (van Steenbergen & Ellemers, 2003).

The reliability coefficients for these last two measures were somewhat low ($\alpha = .65$ and $\alpha = .67$. However, we corrected for measurement error in our analyses. To ascertain that the four components of the work environment and the four components of the home environment were statistically distinct, we conducted confirmatory factor analyses. Results supported the proposed 8-factor solution, which demonstrated close fit to the data ($\chi^2 (142) = 288.35$, $p < .001$, CFI $= .93$, GFI $= .86$, IFI $= .93$, RMSEA $= .08$), and fit the data better than alternative models.

We used the three-item scales by Carlson et al. (2000) to examine energy-based, time-based, and behavioral conflict. Sample items are, respectively: "Due to all the pressures at work, sometimes when I get home I am too stressed to do the things I enjoy"; "I have to miss activities at home due to the amount of time I must spend on work"; "The problem-solving behaviors I use in my job are not effective in resolving problems at home." All scales demonstrated good reliability, ranging from $\alpha = .71$ to $\alpha = .92$, except for behavioral WF ($\alpha = .57$). However, we did correct for measurement error in our analyses. The three-item scales by Carlson and Frone (2003) measured psychological WF and FW conflict ($\alpha = .88$, $\alpha = .81$, e.g., "When I am at home, I often think about work-related problems."

We used our own three-item scales to measure energy-based, time-based, behavioral, and psychological WF and FW facilitation (van Steenbergen et al., 2007). Sample items are: "Because I relax and regain my energy at home, I can better focus on performing my work" (energy-based FW facilitation); "The amount of time I spend on my home life stimulates me to use my time at work effectively" (time-based FW facilitation); "The skills I use at work help me to better handle matters at home" (behavioral WF facilitation); "Because of my work, I am better able to put home-related matters into perspective" (psychological WF facilitation). Reliability for all scales was high (range $\alpha = .71$ to $\alpha = .86$). Results from confirmatory factor analyses supported that the eight conflict and eight facilitation types were statistically distinct, as the proposed 16-factor solution demonstrated good fit to the data ($\chi^2 (869) = 1428.99$, $p < .001$, CFI $= .91$, GFI $= .83$, IFI 5 .92, RMSEA $= .05$), and fit the data better than alternative models (see also van Steenbergen et al., 2007).

RESULTS

First, we examined whether men and women differed in the extent to which they experienced their work and home environments as supportive or whether there were any gender differences in the level of conflict or facilitation. MANCOVA analyses (in which we corrected for differences in working hours, organizational tenure, age, education, age of youngest child, and salary) revealed no gender differences in perceived level of support received at work ($F(4) = 0.95$, ns) or at home ($F(4) = 1.14$, ns), nor in the level of conflict experienced ($F(8) = 1.65$, ns). However, women did experience higher levels of facilitation than men ($F(8) = 2.51$, $p < .01$). Specifically, women experienced significantly higher levels of time-based WF facilitation, psychological WF facilitation, behavioral WF and FW facilitation, and marginally higher levels of time-based FW facilitation.

We used path analysis (EQS 6.0) to further analyze the data for men and women separately. Using separate data sets, we built path models in which the components of the work and home environments predicted conflict and facilitation. Because the current sample sizes were not sufficiently large to use latent variables, the items for each scale were averaged to create single indicators for each construct. To correct for random measurement error we fixed the loadings from indicator to construct to the square root of the coefficient alpha internal consistency estimate for each construct, and fixed their respective error terms to 1 minus alpha. This approach is consistent with previous work (Carlson & Perrewé, 1999; Frone et al., 1992; Williams & Hazer, 1986). The home and work indicators were allowed to correlate, as were the conflict and facilitation indicators. Furthermore, we used the Wald test to determine which of these paths could be set to zero without significant loss of model fit (reference to Wald test). Model fit was evaluated with the chi-square statistic and the fit indices GFI, CFI, IFI, and the RMSEA. In general, models with fit indices greater than .90, and a RMSEA smaller than or equal to .08, indicate a good fit between the model and the data (Browne & Cudeck, 1989). The model for men demonstrated good fit with the data ($\chi^2 (93) = 85.95$, $p = .69$, CFI $= 1.00$, GFI $= .96$, IFI $= 1.00$, RMSEA $= .01$), as did the model for women ($\chi^2 (96) = 71.61$, $p = .97$, CFI $= 1.00$, GFI $= .95$, IFI $= 1.00$, RMSEA $= .01$). To facilitate interpretation, we present the results for both men and women in two separate figures. Figures 5.1A and 5.1B depict the prediction of conflict and facilitation for men. Figures 5.2A and 5.2B

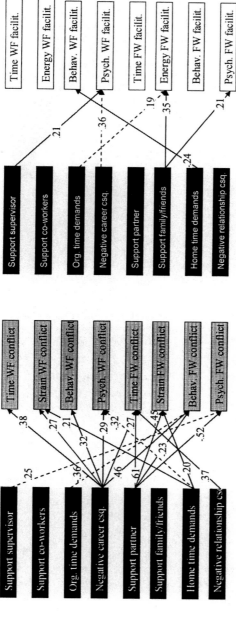

Figure 5.1A. Prediction of Men's Conflict Experiences.

Figure 5.1B. Prediction of Men's Facilitation Experiences.

Note: We expected that the support components would relate to lower conflict and higher facilitation, and that organizational (home) time demands and negative career (relationship) consequences would relate to higher conflict and lower facilitation. Findings that contradict this expectation are represented by dotted paths.

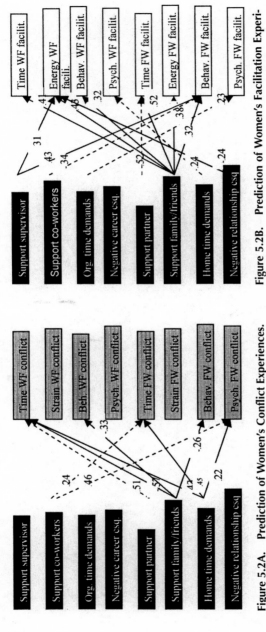

Figure 5.2A. Prediction of Women's Conflict Experiences.

Figure 5.2B. Prediction of Women's Facilitation Experiences.

Note: We expected that the support components would relate to lower conflict and higher facilitation, and that organizational (home) time demands and negative career (relationship) consequences would relate to higher conflict and lower facilitation. Findings that contradict this expectation are represented by dotted paths.

depict these relationships for women. The figures depict the standardized solution and only reflect the significant (p < .01) relationships. The paths in the figures are depicted as either solid or dotted lines. We hypothesized that the support components would relate to lower conflict and higher facilitation, and that organizational (home) time demands and negative career (relationship) consequences would relate to higher conflict and lower facilitation. Solid lines represent findings that were consistent with this hypothesis; observations that did not fit this prediction are represented by dotted lines. For men, 17 paths were consistent with this prediction and five were not. For women, 16 paths were consistent with this prediction and six were not. We describe these results in 5.1A, 5.1B, 5.2A, and 5.2B.

The Impact of a Supportive Work Environment

Regarding the impact of the work environment on men's ability to combine work and family, 5.1A and 5.1B show that for men the perception of negative career consequences was an influential component. The perception that devoting more time to family responsibilities—thus having less face time in the office—would have negative consequences for their career progress related to higher levels of almost every type of conflict we examined. Supervisor support was related to the perception that their work helped them to put their home-life matters into perspective, benefiting their functioning at home (higher psychological WF facilitation). Co-worker support was unrelated to men's conflict or facilitation experiences. In addition, we observed some relationships that were inconsistent with our expectation. That is, supervisor support was related to higher psychological FW conflict. Thus, receiving supervisor support related to more preoccupation with home-life matters while at work. In addition, the perception of negative career consequences had a beneficial effect in that it related to higher psychological WF facilitation. Finally, organizational time demands did not seem to have detrimental effects because they related to lower conflict and higher facilitation. We will discuss these findings later.

For women (Figure 5.2A and 5.2B), a totally different picture emerged. Negative career consequences, an influential component for men, was unrelated to conflict and facilitation for women. For women, supervisor support was related to higher levels of facilitation. That is, women who reported higher levels of support from their supervisors indicated to a higher degree that work provided them with extra energy that benefited their lives at home (energy-based WF facilitation). Moreover, women who reported more support from their supervisors also used in their work the skills and behaviors they acquired at home (behavioral FW facilitation). We also observed some unexpected relationships. While this was not the case for men, co-worker support was related to women's conflict and facilitation experiences. However, it seemed to have detrimental effects because higher levels of support from co-workers in fact related to higher levels of time-based FW and psychological FW conflict and lower levels of behavioral FW facilitation. Thus, for women, having co-workers who understand of family issues and accommodate a balance between work and family seems to go hand-in-hand with higher perceptions that their family life negatively interferes with their work. As was the case for men, organizational time demands did not seem to have detrimental effects. Women who experienced higher time demands experienced higher psychological FW facilitation, thus perceiving that their home life enabled them to put work matters into perspective, which benefited their work.

The Impact of a Supportive Home Environment

The relationships between the home environment and conflict and facilitation were again fundamentally different for men and women. For men, receiving support from their partners was highly beneficial in the sense that it related to lower levels of all types of conflict in which family negatively interferes with work. Partner support was unrelated to men's facilitation experiences. However, men who received higher levels of support from family and friends experienced to a higher degree that their home lives provided them with extra energy and psychological benefits that positively affected their work (higher energy-based FW and psychological FW facilitation). Furthermore, men who reported high levels of home time demands (e.g., being expected to take on caring tasks at specified times) reported higher levels of both energy-based WF and FW conflict. Finally, for men, the perception that work-related absence from home would jeopardize their relationship (negative relationship consequences) was for men related to the experience that the time they spent on their home lives negatively interfered with their work (time-based FW conflict). This is all in line with our predictions. Inconsistent, however, is the finding that higher levels of home time demands also went hand-in-hand with lower preoccupation with work matters while at home (lower psychological WF conflict).

For women, support from family and friends seems to be an important resource in combining work and family roles. Women who indicated higher levels of support experienced lower levels of time-based and behavioral WF and FW conflict. Moreover, the more support women received from family and friends, the more they experienced that the time they spent on one role allowed them to use the time in the other role more efficiently (time-based WF and FW facilitation). The more women experienced that one role provided them with extra energy that could be used in the other role (energy-based WF and FW facilitation), and the more they experienced that one role taught them new skills and behaviors that were also useful in the other role (behavioral WF and FW facilitation). Perceptions of high home time demands were detrimental in the sense that they related to higher time-based WF and FW conflict and higher psychological FW conflict. Thus, being expected to perform a lot of caring tasks related to feelings of a time bind between work and family and higher levels of preoccupation with home-life matters while at work. When women perceived to a higher degree that work-related absence from home would jeopardize their relationship (negative relationship consequences), they experienced to a lower degree that their work gave them extra energy that benefited their home life (lower energy-based WF facilitation). We also observed some unexpected relationships. Although partner support consistently related to lower levels of conflict experiences for men, receiving partner support had adverse effects for women. For women, higher levels of partner support related to higher conflict experiences and lower facilitation experiences. In addition, home time demands for women related to the perception that their work helped them to put their home-life matters into perspective, benefiting their functioning at home (higher psychological WF facilitation).

When comparing these results for men and women, the differences are striking. The supportiveness of the work and home environment primarily seem to affect men's conflict experiences (more paths), whereas for women they relate more to their facilitation experiences. Moreover, only one specific path was the same across gender (support of family and friends relating to higher energy-based FW facilitation). This indicates that receiving support at work and at home has a fundamentally different influence on men's and women's ability to manage work and family roles.

DISCUSSION

The objective of this research was to gain more insight into the effects of support in the work and home environments on employees' ability to balance their work and family lives. This research contributes to the work-family literature in several ways. First, whereas prior studies predominantly focused on the organizational contribution to conflict experiences, the present research also provides insight into how the home environment relates to these experiences. Second, rather than merely examining conflict experiences, we also examined the positive side of role-combining by also investigating facilitation. In this way, we were able to shed more light on possible ways to enhance the experience of facilitation by creating supportive work and home environments. Third, by examining different types of conflict and facilitation that individuals can experience and explicitly focusing on possible gender differences, we provided a fine-grained analysis of how supportive work and home environments differentially related to conflict and facilitation across gender.

Supportive Work and Home Environments and the Experience of Conflict

The present findings provide strong support for the need to examine both the work and home environments when investigating experiences of conflict between work and family roles. Furthermore, these findings suggest that support for family issues at work and support for work issues at home affect employees' general ability to balance work and family roles (Allen, 2001), as the work and home environments related to conflict and facilitation experiences in both the WF and FW directions. Our findings replicated recent studies showing that support of family members for the work domain relates to lower reported conflict (Kossek et al., 2001; Lapierre & Allen, 2001). Our study extended these findings by showing that specific components of a work-supportive home environment were differentially related to different types of conflict experiences reported by men and women. For instance, receiving support of one's partner strongly related to lower levels of conflict for men, whereas for women support from family and friends was far more important than partner support in this regard.

Supportive Work and Home Environments and the Experience of Facilitation

Because of the dominant focus on conflict in the work-family literature, research on the experiences of facilitation between work and family roles and possibilities to enhance these experiences is scarce. Two recent studies, however, found that employees who received support from their supervisors and co-workers for family issues experienced higher levels of facilitation between their work and family lives (Thompson & Pottras, 2005; Voydanoff, 2004b). The present study adds to this literature by showing that both family-supportiveness of the work environment and work-supportiveness of the home environment relate to facilitation experiences of employees. In our study, supervisor support and support from family and friends were consistently related to increased levels of facilitation for both men and women. Thus, the present study indicates that supportive environments—besides reducing conflict—

have the capacity to stimulate facilitation. Supervisors seem to be in a key position to stimulate experiences of facilitation among employees, whereas support of family and friends is vital at home. However, it is important to note that we also found instances where receiving support did not have the expected beneficial effects, or where demands at work or at home did not seem to have detrimental effects. We discuss these results below in more detail.

Different Effects for Men and Women

In this study, men and women did not differ in the extent to which they rated their work and home environments as supportive. However, there were strikingly few similarities between men and women in terms of how the different components of the work and home environments related to their experiences in balancing work and family. This suggests that the impact of the work and home environments on conflict and facilitation is fundamentally different for men and women.

For men, the perception that devoting more time to family responsibilities (and thus having less face time at work) would jeopardize their careers was a strong predictor of conflict between work and family. Interestingly, in several studies within the Dutch context, where the present study was also carried out, men indicated the wish to work fewer hours per week while women indicated the wish to participate more hours in the work force (Schippers, 2001). Moreover, a recent study indicates that the wage penalty associated with working part-time is more severe for men than women (Hirsch, 2005). The present study suggests that the perceived (and real) negative career consequences for men play a role here, causing men to experience conflict, and possibly hindering couples to divide paid and unpaid work in a different, less traditional manner. With regard to the work supportiveness of the home environment, men especially benefited from receiving support from their partners related to reduced negative family interference with work.

Consistent with previous findings, women especially benefited from receiving support from their supervisors at work (Thomas & Ganster, 1995; Kluwer et al., 1997), and from receiving support from family and friends at home. For women, having a family-supportive supervisor related to enhanced experiences of facilitation, and having family and friends who were supportive of work issues related to lower conflict as well as higher facilitation between work and family. These different patterns for men and women underscore the importance of explicitly examining the role of gender in future work-family interface (instead of merely controlling for gender in statistical analyses), and, possibly, to develop different organizational policies to help avoid conflict and enhance facilitation for men and women.

Demands Not Always Detrimental and Support Not Always Beneficial

Intriguingly, the present findings suggest that demands at work and at home do not always have detrimental effects and that the effects of support are not always beneficial. This indicates that striving for higher levels of support and lower demands is neither a panacea to reduce conflict nor a magic way to enhance facilitation, but rather that the picture is more complicated. In our study, demands in terms of organizational and home time demands or negative career consequences had unpredicted effects in that they were also related to higher levels of psychological and energy-based facilitation and lower psychological conflict. Previous studies also found instances where job demands in terms of time pressure and workload and demands from friends related to higher, not lower levels of facilitation (Grzywacz & Marks, 2000; Voydanoff, 2004a). The authors of this previous work explained that their measures of demands might also have picked up unmeasured aspects of job quality or work engagement, which could explain this positive relationship between demands and facilitation. Another explanation, in our view, is that low levels of demands are not by definition preferable. A certain level of demands can also be stimulating or motivating; only high levels of demands become detrimental.

Moreover, we found that for women, higher levels of co-worker and partner support for family issues were associated with higher levels of conflict. Because data for this study were collected at a single point in time, issues of reverse causality could play a role. In addition, for example, partners and coworkers who give support may relate to higher conflict because individuals ask for and receive more support at times of higher conflict. Although supportive work and home environments are widely regarded as antecedents of conflict and facilitation (Allen, 2001; Carlson & Perrewé, 1995; Voydanoff, 2004a), future longitudinal research is needed to fully rule out the possibility of reverse causation. However, this finding also relates to prior inconsistent findings in the literature on the role of social support. For instance, Fernandez (1995) found that social support of co-workers can exacerbate self-reported conflict. She referred to this effect as the "reverse buffering effect" and argued that talking with co-workers can also legitimize and highlight negative feelings, thus increasing conflict or dissatisfaction. Although this interpretation is post hoc and hence remains speculative, it could explain the present findings. Combining work and family responsibilities is traditionally seen as a women's issue and it is often assumed that women experience most difficulties in combining these different responsibilities. Possibly, in talking with co-workers and one's partner, this negative side is most often highlighted and discussed, thus exacerbating experiences of conflict. Clearly, these interesting findings merit future research on the role of constructive or destructive support.

A Fine-Grained Analysis

We complied with the call to examine different types of conflict and facilitation (Adams, et al., 1996; Poelmans, et al., 2003). Energy-based, time-based, behavioral, and psychological WF and FW conflict and facilitation experiences had different antecedents in the work and home environments, thus supporting the need to distinguish between these experiences instead of examining generalized conflict and facilitation. Considering that different types of conflict and facilitation are also differentially related to outcomes in the work, home, and health domains, such as job performance, home life satisfaction, and depression (Allen & Spector, 2002; van Steenbergen et al., 2007), the present approach is a first step towards designing tailored interventions that address specific aspects of conflict and facilitation among men and women.

What about Work-Family Benefits?

As described in the beginning of this chapter, previous research consistently showed that informal support in the work environment is more strongly related to success in role combination than the formal work-family benefits offered by organizations (e.g., Behson, 2006 2005?; Thompson & Pottras, 2005). Therefore, in our research we focused on the extent to which individuals receive this informal support within their work and home environments. However, by no means do we wish to imply that work-family benefits are unimportant or that organizations could stop offering them. Although the relationship between informal support and conflict is generally stronger, previous studies showed that work-family benefits are related to lower conflict experiences of employees (Thomas & Ganster, 1995). Moreover, offering work-family benefits does seem to signal to employees that the organization cares about their well-being, which can positively affect their attitudes (cf. social exchange theory), thus relating to higher levels of employees' affective commitment to their organization as well as higher levels of job satisfaction (Hammer et al., 2005; Thompson et al., 1999). This indicates that from the perspective of fostering organizational commitment and job satisfaction, offering benefits is clearly beneficial.

Future Research Directions

Our research showed that the supportiveness of the work and home environments were differentially related to different types of conflict and facilitation experiences of male and female employees. Therefore, we stress the importance of examining the effects of both the work and the home environments on individuals' experiences in combining their work and family roles in future research. In doing so, it is important to distinguish between different types as well as different directions (WF and FW) of conflict and facilitation. In view of the substantial gender differences we observed, we underscore the need to carefully examine, both theoretically and empirically, the role of gender in future work-family research.

Because this research represents a single study that was carried out in the Netherlands, additional research should assess the robustness of our findings in other contexts. Although most work-family research has been conducted in the United States, empirical research within Europe also demonstrated that conflict experiences of employees were much more related to the informal context than the use or availability of formal work-family benefits (Dikkers et al., 2004; Kluwer et al., 1997). We are unaware of studies that systematically compare the informal family support of work environments in different national contexts; such comparative studies between countries are interesting and necessary (Poelmans et al., 2003).

A limitation of the present study is that our sample size was relatively small. Although we took precautions to address this in our analyses (e.g., by creating single indicators for each construct, cf. Frone et al., 1992), future research should aim for larger samples.

Furthermore, research that further extends our insight into antecedents of facilitation would make a strong contribution to the literature and would be of great practical use. Further, focusing on the applied perspective, we call for researchers and practitioners in this area to collaborate in designing ways to teach managers how to deal with work-family issues, to be supportive, and how to open up for discussion cultural norms that are perceived by employees as hindering facilitation. Of course, such interventions should be supported by top management. Managers can be taught to create a "win-win" between important organizational and employee interests. In the same vein, we call for designing (and measuring the effects of) interventions that aim to enable couples to better balance their work and family lives. Finally, we call for work-family researchers to include objective outcome measures in their studies (e.g., sales rates, objective health indicators) to demonstrate in financial terms, if possible, the benefits to employers of supporting employees in balancing their work and family lives.

CONCLUSION

In conclusion, this research indicates that employees' ability to combine work and family depends upon the extent to which their work environment is family supportive as well as the extent to which their home environment is supportive of work issues. A family-supportive work environment and a work-supportive home environment do not only seem to reduce the extent to which employees experience conflict between their work and family roles, but also seem to stimulate employees' positive exchange between their work and family lives (facilitation). Finally, this study revealed important gender differences, thus providing a more complete picture of the different effects the work and home environments can have on men's and women's ability to combine work and family.

NOTE

Elianne van Steenbergen, Naomi Ellemers, Department of Social and Organizational Psychology, and Ab Mooijaart, Department of Methods and Statistics, Leiden University, The Netherlands. This work was conducted at Leiden University. Elianne van Steenbergen is now at Utrecht University, the Netherlands. Correspondence concerning this article should be addressed to her at Utrecht University, Department of Social and Organizational Psychology, PO Box 80.140, 3508 TC Utrecht, The Netherlands. Phone, +31 (0)30 2536711, Fax: (0)30 2534718, E-mail: E.F.vanSteenbergen@uu.nl

REFERENCES

Allen, T. D. (2001). Family-supportive work environments: The role of organizational perceptions. *Journal of Vocational Behavior, 58,* 414–435.

Adams, G. A., King, L. A., & King, D. (1996). Relationships of job and family involvement, family social support, and work-family conflict with job and life satisfaction. *Journal of Applied Psychology, 81,* 411–420.

Aryee, S., Srinivas, E. S., & Tan, H. H. (2005). Rhythms of Life: Antecedents and outcomes of work-family balance in employed parents. *Journal of Applied Psychology, 90,* 132–146.

Barnett, R. C., & Hyde, J. S. (2001). Women, men, work, and family: An expansionist theory. *American Psychologist, 56,* 781–796.

Behson, S. J. (2005). The relative contribution of formal and informal work-family support. *Journal of Vocational Behavior, 66,* 487–500.

Bond, J. T., Thompson, C., Galinsky, E., & Pottras, D. (2002). *Highlights of the national study of the changing workforce.* New York: Families and Work Institute.

Browne, M. W., & Cudeck, R. (1989). Single sample cross-validation indices for covariance structures. *Multivariate Behavioral Research, 24,* 445–455.

Bruck, C. S., Allen, T. D., & Spector, P. E. (2002). The relation between work-family conflict and job satisfaction: A finer grained analysis. *Journal of Vocational Behavior, 60,* 336–353.

Carlson, D. S., & Frone, M. R. (2003). Relation of behavioral and psychological involvement to a new four-factor conceptualization of work-family interference. *Journal of Business and Psychology, 17,* 515–535.

Carlson, D. S., Kacmar, K. M., & Williams, L. J. (2000). Construction and initial validation of a multidimensional measure of work-family conflict. *Journal of Vocational Behavior, 56,* 249–276.

Carlson, D. S., & Perrewé, P. L. (1999). The role of social support in the stressor-strain relationship: An examination of work-family conflict. *Journal of Management, 25,* 513–540.

Dikkers, J., Geurts, S., Dulk, L. den, Peper, B., & Kompier, M. (2004). Relations among work-home culture, the utilization of work-home arrangements, and work-home interference. *International Journal of Stress Management, 11,* 323–245.

Fernandez, D. R. (1995). Career plateau response as a function of personal and coping strategies. Unpublished doctoral dissertation, Florida State University, Gainesville.

Frone, M. R., Russell, M., & Cooper, M. L. (1992). Antecedents and outcomes of work-family conflict: Testing a model of the work-family interface. *Journal of Applied Psychology, 77,* 65–78.

Geurts, S. A. E., & Demerouti, E. (2003). Work/non-work interfaces: A review of theories and findings. In M. J. Schabracq, J. A. M. Winnubst, & C. L. Cooper (Eds.), *Handbook of work & health psychology.* West Sussex, UK: John Wiley & Sons.

Geurts, S. A. E., Taris, T. W., Kompier, M. A. J., Dikkers, J. S. E., van Hooff, M. L. M., & Kinnunen, U. M. (2005). Work-home interaction from a work psychological perspective: Development and validation of a new questionnaire, the SWING. *Work & Stress, 19,* 319–339.

Greenhaus, J. H. (1988). The intersection of work and family roles: Individual, interpersonal, and organizational issues. *Journal of Social Behavior and Personality, 3,* 23–44.

Greenhaus, J. H., & Beutell, N. (1985). Sources of conflict between work and family roles. *Academy of Management Review, 10,* 76–88.

Grzywacz, J. G., & Marks, N. F. (2000). Reconceptualizing the work-family interface: An ecological perspective on the correlates of positive and negative spillover between work and family. *Journal of Occupational Health Psychology, 5,* 111–126.

Hammer, B., Neal, M. B., Newsom, J. T., Brockwood, K. J., Colton, C. L. (2005). A longitudinal study of the effects of dual-earner couples' utilization of family-friendly workplace supports on work and family outcomes. *Journal of Applied Psychology, 90,* 799–810.

Hirsch, B. T. (2005). Why do part-time workers earn less? The role of worker and job skills. *Industrial and Labor Relations Review, 58,* 525–551.

Hochschild, A. R. (1997). *The time bind: When work becomes home and home becomes work.* New York: Holt.

Kluwer, E. S., Boers, S., Heesink, J. A. M., & Vliert, E. van der (1997). Rolconflict bij tweeverdieners: De invloed van een "zorgvriendelijke" werkomgeving. *Gedrag en Organisatie, 10(4)* 223–241.

Kossek, E. E., Colquitt, J. A., & Noe, R. A. (2001). Caregiving decisions, well-being, and performance: The effects of place and provider as a function of dependent type and work-family climates. *Academy of Management Journal, 44,* 29–44.

Lapierre, L., & Allen, T. D. (2006). Work-supportive family, family-supportive supervision, use of organizational benefits, and problem focused coping: Implications for work-family conflict and employee well-being. *Journal of Occupational Health Psychology, 11,* 169–181.

Marks, S. P. (1977). Multiple roles and role strain: Some notes on human energy, time and commitment. *American Sociological Review, 42,* 921–936.

Poelmans, S., Allen, T. D., Spector, P. E., O'Driscoll, M., Cooper, C. L., & Sanchez, J. I. (2003). A cross-national comparative study of work/family demands and resources. *International Journal of Cross Cultural Management, 3,* 275–288.

Ruderman, M. N., Ohlott, P. J., Panzer, K., & King, S. (2002). Benefits of multiple roles for managerial women. *Academy of Management Journal, 45,* 369–386.

Schippers, J. J. (2001). *Arbeidsmarkt- en emancipatiebeleid: De vraag naar diversiteit.* Oratie rede, Universiteit Utrecht.

Thomas, L. T., & Ganster, D. C. (1995). Impact of family supportive work variables on work-family conflict and strain: A control perspective. *Journal of Applied Psychology, 80,* 6–15.

Thompson, C. A., Beauvais, L. L., & Lyness, K. S. (1999). When work-family benefits are not enough: The influence of work-family culture on benefit utilization, organizational commitment, and work-family conflict. *Journal of Vocational Behavior, 54,* 392–415.

Thompson, C. A., & Pottras, D. J. (2005). Relationships among organizational family support, job autonomy, perceived control, and employee well-being. *Journal of Occupational Health Psychology, 10,* 100–118.

United Nations Statistics Division (2006). Statistics and indicators on women and men. Demographic and social. Retrieved: 4 May 2007 from http://unstats .un.org.

Van Steenbergen, E. F., & Ellemers, N. (2003). De wederzijdse win-win van zorgvriendelijk werken en werkvriendelijk zorgen. *Jaarboek Sociale Psychologie 2003.* Delft: Eburon.

Van Steenbergen, E. F., Ellemers, N., & Mooijaart, A. (2007). How work and family can facilitate each other: Distinct types of work-family facilitation and outcomes for women and men. *Journal of Occupational Health Psychology, 12,* 279–300.

Voydanoff, P. (2004a). The effects of work demands and resources on work-to-family conflict and facilitation. *Journal of Marriage and the Family, 66,* 398–412.

—— (2004b). Implications of work and community demands and resources for work-to-family conflict and facilitation. *Journal of Occupational Health Psychology, 9,* 275–285.

Wayne, J. H., Musisca, N., & Fleeson, W. (2004). Considering the role of personality in the work-family experience: Relationships of the big five to work-family conflict and enrichment. *Journal of Vocational Behavior, 64,* 108–130.

Williams, L. J., & Hazer, J. T. (1986). Antecedents and consequences of satisfaction and commitment in turnover models: A reanalysis using latent variable structural equation methods. *Journal of Applied Psychology, 71,* 219–231.

Chapter Six

Reducing Conceptual Confusion: Clarifying the Positive Side of Work and Family

Julie Holliday Wayne

ABSTRACT

Scholars have theorized (e.g., Sieber, 1974; Marks, 1977), and empirical evidence supports (e.g., Grzywacz & Marks, 2000; Wayne, Musisca, & Fleeson, 2004), that work and family can have beneficial effects on one another. Numerous constructs reflecting the positive side of the work-family interface have been proposed, including enhancement, positive spillover, enrichment, integration, and facilitation. Most often, these terms are used interchangeably without specific definitions and well-understood distinctions, leading to conceptual ambiguity and confusion. The present chapter provides a framework that clarifies each of these constructs and explains their interrelationships and distinctions. Then, each construct is explained in terms of its definition, measurement, and research findings. Further, the chapter highlights how researchers might test a process and episodic view of the positive work-family interface. The chapter concludes with implications of this framework for future research and theory.

Historically, the idea that work and family can benefit each other was introduced thirty years ago. Sieber (1974) and Marks (1977) first challenged the "scarcity of resources" hypothesis and argued that involvement in multiple roles provides benefits that may outweigh its costs. This sociological theory, referred to as Role Enhancement Theory, provided the theoretical basis for the positive influence of multiple roles and broadened the lens on the work-family interface beyond the conflict perspective. Subsequent empirical research spanning several disciplines demonstrated that work and family can have beneficial effects on one another (e.g., Barnett & Hyde, 2000; Grzywacz & Marks, 2000a; Kirchmeyer, 1992; Wayne, Musisca, & Fleeson, 2004). In recent years, interest in the positive connections between work and family has grown. Theoretical and empirical advancement is hindered, however, by conceptual ambiguity and confusion in the literature.

As often happens in a developing area of research, researchers have either neglected to define or have used different definitions of and labels for similar constructs across studies. Also, some terms that represent distinct constructs have been used interchangeably. For example, *positive spillover* has been defined as how one role supports, facilitates, or enhances the other (Crouter, 1984; Kirchmeyer, 1992); as when "experiences, thoughts, and feelings of one role spillover to positively influence the experiences, thoughts, and feelings in another role" (Stephens, Franks, & Atienza, 1997); and as effects of work and family on one another that make the two domains similar (Edwards & Rothbard, 2000). *Work-family integration* is another construct label that has been used and defined as when positive attitudes spill over or when resources in one role enrich the other (Greenhaus & Parasuraman, 1999) and as when participation in one role enhances the quality of life in the other (Friedman & Greenhaus, 2000). Other scholars have used the term *work-family facilitation,* which Frone (2003) defined as the "extent to which participation in one role is made easier by virtue of the experiences, skills, or opportunities gained in the other." Most recently, Greenhaus and Powell (2006) used the term *work-family enrichment,* which they define as "the extent to which experiences in one role improve the quality of life in the other role," and they state that enrichment is synonymous with enhancement, positive spillover, and facilitation.

As noted by Hanson and colleagues (2006), distinctions among these constructs are not well understood and more often than not, they are considered synonymous. The use of varied definitions for the same construct is a problem, but even more problematic is the use of varied labels for similar definitions. Given this conceptual ambiguity in the literature, it is reasonable to expect that researchers interested in the positive side of the work-family interface might be asking: "What should I call what I am studying?" "How should I measure it?" "Are all these constructs the same?" and "If they are different, how do they all fit together?" Given the growing interest in this topic, the time has come to resolve some of these unanswered questions.

The primary purpose of this chapter is to provide a framework that clarifies each of these constructs and explains their interrelationships and distinctions. Despite the fact that some of these constructs have been considered synonymous and used interchangeably in the past, as elaborated below, each of these constructs is distinct. The chapter begins with an organizing framework of the constructs. Then, each construct is discussed in more detail in terms of its definition, measurement, and research findings. Further, the implications of this framework for future research and theory are discussed. Although it is not a purpose of the present paper to identify and test an empirical model, both a process and episodic model of the positive connections between work and family are offered in order to stimulate future research. The models offered, though they build upon existing conceptual models (Greenhaus & Powell, 2006; Voydanoff, 2004), are distinctive in that they include various core constructs of the positive side of the work-family interface rather than a single construct.

To facilitate discussion of each construct, a summary of the primary literature is provided in Table 6.1. Several important aspects of this growing literature are evident from this table. First, literature on the positive side of the work-family interface has expanded rapidly, especially since 2004. Further, one can note the degree to which various terms have been used (e.g., spillover, enhancement, enrichment, facilitation) to represent the positive interplay between work and family and the fact that researchers themselves note the assumption of similarity across conceptual labels. Both Carlson, Kacmar, Wayne, & Grzywacz,. (2006) and Hanson et al. (2006) in their scale development efforts recognized the need to more carefully define and distinguish among these constructs. Greater elaboration of these constructs and their similarities and distinctions is needed. This chapter provides a way of thinking about the positive side of the work-family interface that should serve to reduce conceptual confusion, foster theoretical, measurement, and empirical development, and guide researchers in the choice of constructs most relevant to their research interests.

A FRAMEWORK OF THE CONSTRUCTS THROUGH WHICH WORK AND FAMILY BENEFIT ONE ANOTHER

Figure 6.1 provides a framework of the constructs through which work and family benefit one another. The framework is broadly introduced here and each construct is elaborated later. The basic construct through which work and family benefit each other is *individual enhancement*. More specifically, through an individual's engagement in a domain (A), he or she acquires gains, benefits, or privileges within that particular domain. For example, an individual may experience positive mood or enhanced self-esteem through his or her involvement in the family, and enhanced mood and esteem represent gains to the individual in the family. Likewise, an individual may develop new skills and behaviors in the

Table 6.1. Chronological Summary of the Primary Literature on the Positive Side of the Work-Family Interface

Scholar and Journal	Conceptual Label	Conceptual Definition	Primary Contribution	Underlying Processes	Measurement
Sieber (1974) *American Sociological Review*	Role Expansion	N/A	Role accumulation can lead to notable gains for individuals and systems because specific privileges and psychological benefits frequently accompany role occupancy.	Privileges / Status security / Status enhancement / Personality enrichment	N/A
Marks (1977) *American Sociological Review*	Role Expansion	N/A	Role strain is not inevitable because different roles require and are given different levels of time, energy, and commitment. Individuals' active engagement in roles expands rather than drains psychological energy.	N/A	N/A
Crouter (1984) *Human Relations*	Positive Family-Work Spillover	How family life supports, facilitates, or enhances work life	Qualitative interviews focusing on nonwork-to-work "positive spillover." Two types of spillover emerged from interviews: Educational and psychological spillover.	*Educational* Skills, attitudes, perspectives / *Psychological* Energy, attention span, mood	N/A
Barnett & Baruch (1985)	Quality of Role Experience	The extent to which the	Role occupancy involves both rewards and		

Source	Term	Definition	Description	Dimensions	Items
Journal of Personality and Social Psychology		challenges, and it is the relative level of rewards to challenges or "balance" that affects individuals.	benefits of being in a role outweigh the burdens of that role		9 Work → Family Items developed by authors Overall career-family Career-marriage Career-parenting
Tiedje and colleagues (1990) *Journal of Marriage and the Family*	Compatibility	The extent to which work-family rewards are high and work-family challenges are low	Rewards and challenges of multiple role occupancy are independent, and certain typologies (e.g., high reward low challenge) yield more salutary outcomes than other typologies (e.g., high reward, high challenge).		
Kirchmeyer (1992) *Basic and Applied Social Psychology*	Positive Nonwork-work Spillover	Referred to Crouter's (1984) definition	Measured the four types of gains from role occupancy outlined by Sieber, and found that role gains outside of work were correlated with favorable work-related outcomes and that positive spillover was modestly correlated with negative spillover.	Privileges Status security Status enhancement Personality enrichment	15 Nonwork→Work Items developed by author Averaged for general, unidimensional measure of the nonwork→work direction

(continued)

Table 6.1. (*continued*)

Scholar and Journal	Conceptual Label	Conceptual Definition	Primary Contribution	Underlying Processes	Measurement
Marshall & Barnett (1993) *Journal of Community and Applied Social Psychology*	Gains	Personal rewards of being involved in work and family roles	Women and men in dual-earner couples generally report more gains from combining work and family than strains, and gains are associated with contextual resources (e.g., support) and individual characteristics (e.g., sex-role attitudes).		
Stephens and colleagues (1997) *Psychology and Aging*	Positive Spillover	When experiences, thoughts, & feelings of one role spill over to positively influence the experiences, thoughts, & feelings in another role.	Found that the employment role and the role of caregiver for a dependent parent yielded gains for each other, and these gains occurred through greater confidence and mood. Also noted small, non-significant associations between negative and positive spillover.	Confidence Moods	3 Caregiver→ employment 3 Employment→ Caregiver items developed by authors Summed for general, unidimensional measure for each direction

Greenhaus & Parasuraman (1999) *Handbook of Gender and Work*	Integration	Positive attitudes spill over or when resources in one role enrich the other.	Summarized the literature and suggested that enhancement was distinct from conflict, and that enhancement occurred through spill over of psychological states such as attitude and mood.	Attitudes Mood Resources	N/A
Edwards & Rothbard (2000) *Academy of Management Review*	Spillover	Effects of work and family on one another that make the two domains similar.	Translate linking mechanisms into causal relationships between work and family constructs.	Mood Values Skills Behaviors	N/A
Grzywacz & Marks (2000) *Journal of Occupational Health Psychology*	Positive Spillover	Participation in one role leads to better functioning in the other domain.	Measured positive and negative spillover from work-to-family and family-to-work; demonstrated distinction between positive and negative spillover.	Work→Family Behavior & Skills Family→Work Support, Renewed Energy & Love	Work→Family and 3 Family→Work Items Averaged for general, unidimensional measure of each direction
Friedman & Greenhaus (2000) *Work and Family: Allies or Enemies?*	Integration	Participation in one role enhances the quality of life in the other.	Proposed that Resources, Involvement, and Emotional Gratification determine whether work-family integration or conflict occurs.	Resources Involvement Emotional Gratification	N/A

(continued)

Table 6.1. *(continued)*

Scholar and Journal	Conceptual Label	Conceptual Definition	Primary Contribution	Underlying Processes	Measurement
Sumer & Knight (2001) *Journal of Applied Psychology*	Positive Spillover	Satisfaction in one life domain causes satisfaction in the other. Positive spillover is when one role facilitates or enhances the other.	Considered the influence of individual differences in terms of attachment style to positive and negative spillover. Securely attached individuals experienced more positive spillover. Found no to small negative correlations between positive and negative spillover.	Work→Family Knowledge, Skills, and Perspectives / Family→Work Skills, Support, Energy, Ideas, Satisfaction Spillover	4 Work→Family and 5 Family→Work items developed by authors / General, unidimensional measure of each direction
Ruderman et al. (2002) *Academy of Management Journal*	Synergies Across Multiple Roles		Used qualitative data to examine how women's' personal lives benefit their managerial roles.	Interpersonal skills Psychological Emotional support Multi-tasking Personal interests Leadership	N/A
Grzywacz, Almeida, & McDonald (2002) *Family Relations*	Spillover	Extent to which participation in one domain impacts participation	Used two national data sets including a survey and 8-day daily diary study to examine the distribution of positive and negative spillover in the adult	Dimensions not explicitly given though sample items are	MIDUS 3 items W–F 3 items F–W

Citation	Term	Definition	Description		
Frone (2003) *Handbook of Occupational Health Psychology*	Facilitation	Extent to which participation in one role is made easier by virtue of the experiences, skills, or opportunities gained in the other.	labor force—e.g., age was related to reports of spillover. Reviewed the literature on conflict and facilitation. Argued that facilitation is a more appropriate label for the concept than "positive spillover" because it implies both valence (i.e., positive) and causation. Called for more theory and research around the facilitation concept.	N/A	N/A
Voydanoff (2004) *Journal of Marriage & Family*	Facilitation	Cognitive appraisal of the benefits of one domain for the other; a form of synergy in which resources in one role enhance or make easier participation in the other role.	Used data from National Study of Changing Workforce and demonstrated the relation of work demands to conflict and resources to facilitation.	W–F Energy, mood	NSCW 2 items W–F

(continued)

Table 6.1. *(continued)*

Scholar and Journal	Conceptual Label	Conceptual Definition	Primary Contribution	Underlying Processes	Measurement
Wayne, Musisca, & Fleeson (2004) *Journal of Vocational Behavior*	Facilitation	By virtue of participation in one role, one's performance or functioning in the other role is enhanced.	Examined relation of Big Five to conflict & facilitation and their relation to domain satisfaction and effort. Extraversion predicted facilitation; facilitation predicted domain satisfaction and effort.	WFF: skills, behaviors, and positive mood FWF: positive mood, support, or a sense of accomplishment	Items from MIDUS 4 items W–F 4 items F–W
Grzywacz & Butler (2005) *Journal of Occupational Health Psychology*	Facilitation (notes same as various conceptual labels including enhancement, integration & positive spillover	Extent to which participation in one role is made easier by skills, experiences, & opportunities gained in another domain (Frone, 2003).	Resource rich jobs (autonomy, variety, complexity, and social skills) enable WFF.	Behavior "things" one does and skills used	Items from MIDUS 3 items W–F

Source	Construct	Definition	Findings/Description	Items	Measure
Hill (2005) *Journal of Family Issues*	Facilitation (also "called positive spillover or work-family enrichment")	Uses Frone (2003)	Facilitation positively predicts domain satisfaction (e.g., life, job, family, marital) and negatively predicts stress.	N/A (Items not described)	National Study of Changing Workforce (NCSW) items Work->Family: 2 items Family-> Work: 1 item
Hammer et al. (2005) *Journal of Occupational Health Psychology*	Positive spillover ("work/family enrichment/ positive spillover")	Refers to Edwards & Rothbard (2000) and the way occupation of one role results in perceived gains in another (Stephens, 1997).	Longitudinal study of 234 dual-earner couples in which positive spillover was negatively related to depression and longitudinal crossover of positive spillover on spouse's depression.	N/A	6 items adapted from Stephens et al. (1997) 3 Work–Family 3 Family–Work
Greenhaus & Powell (2006) *Academy of Management Review*	Enrichment	Extent to which experiences in one role improve the quality of life in the other role.	Proposed a theoretical model of enrichment including research propositions that reflect two paths: an instrumental and an affective path. Reviews conceptual and empirical studies of enrichment.	N/A	N/A

(continued)

Table 6.1. *(continued)*

Scholar and Journal	Conceptual Label	Conceptual Definition	Primary Contribution	Underlying Processes	Measurement
Wayne, Randel, & Stevens (2006) *Journal of Vocational Behavior*	Enrichment	Used Greenhaus & Powell (2006): "experiences in one role improve quality of life for individual in the other role."	Considered identity and formal and informal domain support as predictors of enrichment and its relation to organizational commitment and turnover intentions. Found informal & emotional support associate with greater enrichment. Enrichment predicted commitment and turnover.	Affective	3 Work–Family 3 Family–Work
Witt & Carlson (2006) *Journal of Occupational Health Psychology*	Enrichment (notes alternative labels are "enhancement facilitation, & positive spillover"	Greenhaus & Powell (2006): domain yields resources that can be applied to enhance other domain.	FWC, but not FWE, relate to supervisor-rated job performance.	FW Personal and status enhancement WF Skills, values, affect	8 Family–Work from Kirchmeyer (1992) 11 Work–Family developed by authors

Citation	Term	Definition	Key findings	Subdimensions	Items
Williams et al., (2006) *Journal of Occupational Health Psychology*	Spillover (notes facilitation and spillover used "interchange-ably")	Compatibility in which resources in one role assist participation in another (Voydanoff, 2004).	Examined the relationship between positive and negative spillover and sleep quality. Only positive FW spillover was related to better quality sleep after controlling for important situational factors.	N/A	#/type of items by direction not described — Same items from MIDUS used by Grzywacz & Marks (2000)
Thompson & Prottas (2006) *Journal of Occupational Health Psychology*	Spillover	N/A	Job autonomy and informal organizational support positively predict positive spillover.	N/A	4 items including both directions (W–F and F–W) from the NSCW
Carlson et al. (2006) *Journal of Vocational Behavior*	Enrichment	Extent to which experiences in one role improve the quality of life, namely performance or affect, in the other role.	Five-study development and validation of a multidimensional scale to measure enrichment; explicitly incorporated enhanced functioning for the individual in the receiving domain to differentiate from positive spillover and facilitation.	W–F Developmental Affective Capital F–W Developmental Affective Efficiency	18 items 9 W–F 9 F–W

(continued)

Table 6.1. *(continued)*

Scholar and Journal	*Conceptual Label*	*Conceptual Definition*	*Primary Contribution*	*Underlying Processes*	*Measurement*
Hanson, Hammer, & Colton (2006) *Journal of Occupational Health Psychology*	Positive Spillover	Edwards & Rothbard (2000): affect, skills, values, & behaviors from originating to receiving domain, thus having beneficial effects.	Developed and validated a multidimensional scale of positive spillover.	Behaviors Values Affect	Work–Family Family–Work
Wayne et al. (2007) *Human Resource Management Review*	Facilitation	Engagement in domain yields development al, affective, capital, or	Introduces the Resource-Gain-Development perspective to explain why facilitation occurs and to propose its primary correlates.	N/A	N/A

		efficiency gains which enhance functioning of another domain.	Provides an exemplar model of correlates of WFF.		N/A
Grzywacz et al. (2007) *Journal of Occupational & Organizational Psychology*	Facilitation	Engagement in one social system contributes to growth in another social system.	Notes the need for a construct that captures the influence of work and family on system-level outcomes. Defines facilitation as such a construct and elaborates its theoretical basis.	N/A	

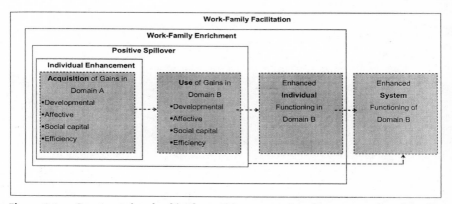

Figure 6.1.   Constructs involved in the positive connections between work and family.

work domain. When an individual acquires gains from his or her engagement in a domain, it represents individual enhancement.

The other domain (B) cannot benefit from the individual's enhancement, however, without the individual transferring the gains to the other domain. For example, for family to benefit work, the positive mood acquired at home must carryover and be used in the work domain. Similarly, new skills learned at work must be applied at home. When the gains acquired in one domain are used in the other domain, this is *positive spillover*. Whereas spillover does imply that gains are transferred across domains, it does not imply that the use of the gains improves the individual's performance or quality of life in the other domain. For that to occur, the individual must successfully apply the gains in the other domain. If the gains are applied successfully and enable the individual to function more effectively in the latter role, then *work-family enrichment* occurs.

Most organizational scholarship focuses on the individual as the primary unit of analysis, and therefore, consideration of the positive connections between work and family typically stops here. In order to truly recognize the positive impact that work and family can have on one another, researchers must consider not only the individual as the unit of analysis but also the system itself. Thus, as other scholars have recommended (e.g., Eby, Casper, Lockwood, Bordeaux, & Brinley, 2005), this chapter expands our consideration of the positive connections between work and family to include the level of analysis of the system (e.g., Grzywacz, Carlson, Kacmar, & Wayne, 2007; Wayne, Grzywacz, Carlson, & Kacmar, 2007). When gains are transferred in a way that ultimately yields enhanced functioning of the system (e.g., family or work), this represents *work-family facilitation* (Grzywacz et al., 2007; Wayne, Grzywacz et al., 2007).

Following this general overview that highlights the distinctions among these constructs, the chapter discusses each construct more thoroughly by defining each, describing its past measurement and research findings, and discussing future directions.

AN ELABORATION OF THE "INDIVIDUAL ENHANCEMENT" CONSTRUCT

Conceptual definition. Individual enhancement occurs when, through an individual's engagement in a life domain, she or he experiences gains within that domain. Gains are the inherent privileges and benefits that Sieber (1974) and Marks (1977) argued result from engagement in a life domain or system, and they are the initial means by which work and family can benefit each other. Individual gains occur at the level of the individual worker and family member, such as when an individual's thoughts, feelings, or behaviors are altered or capital is acquired by engaging in a given domain (Wayne, Grzywacz et al., 2004). Theory supports the suggestion that individuals derive gains from involvement in life domains. For example, Sieber proposed that individuals occupying multiple roles accrue benefits such as role privileges, status security, resources, and personality enrichment, which lead to greater role gratification. Moreover, empirical evidence suggests that individuals in multiple roles enjoy better health and financial security (e.g., Waldron, Weiss, & Hughes, 1998), a stronger sense of identity (e.g., Thoits, 1983), and greater social support (e.g., Greenberger & O'Neil, 1993) (see Barnett & Hyde, 2001; Grzywacz & Butler, 2005; Grzywacz et al., 2007). The focus in role accumulation and expansion theory has been on demonstrating that individuals benefit from involvement in and satisfaction with both work and family domains (Greenhaus & Powell, 2006). The emphasis here is on explaining and differentiating the constructs linking involvement in one domain with individual or system benefits in another, as depicted in Figure 6.1. The root construct is individual enhancement, which occurs when an individual derives gains in an originating domain and these can ultimately benefit the other domain. Importantly, enhancement is an intra-role phenomenon. That is, these benefits are derived by the individual from within a particular role. Enhancement, however, does not inherently involve the display or use of these benefits within any other role.

Empirical and theoretical support. Carlson, et al. (2006) conducted a review of the literature to identify the different types of gains generated by an individual's engagement in a domain that can positively influence another. Their review revealed 15 different gains ranging from additional economic resources (e.g., salary, health insurance; Sieber, 1974), to the acquisition of new skills and perspectives (Crouter, 1984) to improvements in self-confidence and mood (Marks, 1977; Stephens et al., 1997). They organized these into four broad categories capturing the major individual gains acquired in a life domain. *Developmental gains* occur when the individual acquires new skills, knowledge, behaviors, values, or perspectives within a domain. For example, parents might develop greater patience because of interacting with their children or individuals may learn better negotiating skills through activities at work. Individuals engaged in a domain might also generate *affective gains* or experience positive alteration in moods, attitudes, or other aspects of emotion, such as confidence or positive mood that might result when an individual experiences success or receives emotional support within a domain. An individual might also acquire *capital gains*, such as economic, social, or health assets, within a domain. For example, an individual might generate income, networking relationships, or better physical fitness through engagement in the work domain. A final individual gain is *efficiency,* which occurs when an individual's focus or attentiveness is induced by his or her involvement in a life domain. For example, an individual's numerous responsibilities within his family may increase his focus and attention. In summary, individual enhancement occurs when through engagement in a domain an individual acquires developmental, affective, capital, or efficiency gains.

Measurement issues. Given that this construct is the starting point through which work and family domains can benefit one another, it is important to consider how enhancement might be studied empirically. When measuring each construct, it is essential that items are written to reflect conceptual definitions. Thus, an item written to correspond to individual enhancement should reflect that it is an intra-role phenomenon in which an individual acquires gains. An example item to measure enhancement due to affective gains would be: "My job puts me in a good mood." Such self-report measures of enhancement would allow researchers to examine the degree to which involvement in a domain generates particular gains for the individual. Although work-family scholars may not be interested in measuring enhancement for its own sake, this initial construct helps us understand the process by which work and family can ultimately benefit one another.

The acquisition of developmental, affective, capital, or efficiency gains is of personal benefit to the individual within the originating domain, but is not sufficient for work-family enrichment or facilitation to occur. Although individuals may personally benefit from role participation by the gains they acquire, this enhancement may not yield change in the individual's activities in the other domain or changes in the other system's dynamics (Grzywacz & Butler, 2005). For example, consider a mother of three children who is deeply engaged in her family and who acquires great skill (e.g., multitasking) and positive emotion from it (i.e., affective and developmental enhancement). For the woman who lacks interest in her job or lacks opportunity to apply her multitasking skills, improved functioning for that individual at work (i.e., enrichment) or for the larger work system (i.e., facilitation) is unlikely (Grzywacz & Butler, 2005; Marks & MacDermid, 1996). Thus, enrichment and facilitation occur only when the positive individual gains created in one role are (1) transferred to another domain (i.e., spillover) and (2) result in enhanced functioning for the individual (i.e., enrichment) or system (i.e., facilitation).

AN ELABORATION OF THE
"POSITIVE SPILLOVER" CONSTRUCT

Conceptual definition. Positive spillover is a mechanism by which gains in the originating domain can be linked to enhanced functioning in the other domain, for either the individual or the system. As already noted and as can be seen in Table 6.1, multiple definitions of positive spillover have been used. In their review of the literature, Edwards and Rothbard (2000) defined spillover as the effects of work and family on one another that make the two domains similar. They proposed that spillover occurs when mood, values, skills, or behavior in one domain affects mood, values, skills, or behavior in the other domain in a similar fashion (either directly or indirectly).

From these multiple definitions in the literature, the common notion is that spillover involves experiences in one domain being applied to another. As such, positive spillover is defined here as an inter-role phenomenon involving the transference of developmental, affective, capital, or efficiency gains acquired in one domain to another domain. For example, skills learned at work are used in the family; or a positive mood experienced in the family is carried to and displayed at work. Positive spillover—like enrichment and facilitation to come—is considered bidirectional, meaning, importantly, that the same core process occurs for both work benefiting family and family benefiting work. Thus, in describing these inter-role constructs, the direction of the relationship should be noted (i.e.,. work-family spillover or family-work spillover).

Empirical and theoretical support. Research supports the notion that developmental, affective, capital, and efficiency gains acquired in one domain are applied in the other domain. In terms of developmental gains, Crouter (1984) found that employees applied participative management skills from work with their families, and parents reported learning skills or acquiring new perspectives that could be applied on their jobs, indicating a direct transfer of skills from one domain to another. For example, one father reported using the listening skills he learned at work with his teenage son. Another father (De-Long & DeLong, 1992) reported using a technique with his children that he had developed for his employees to give feedback on what he was doing well or needed improving. He said, "One day, I thought, why don't I try this with my four children?" (p. 176). Capital gains are transferred, for example, when coworkers provide referrals for childcare or healthcare providers that can provide workers with new or better alternatives for accomplishing family responsibilities (Grzywacz & Butler, 2005). Efficiency gains acquired in the family might also be transferred to work. Female managers reported that one of six primary ways that their personal lives enhanced their work lives was by their handling of multiple tasks (Ruderman, Ohlott, Panzer, & King, 2002). Finally, confidence, esteem, and positive mood, or affective gains, from one domain are transferred to the other, as evidenced by the positive relationship between work and family satisfaction (Friedman & Greenhaus, 2000) and research indicating that positive affect at work is related to greater engagement in family life for men (Rothbard, 2001).

The transference of gains across domains is generally an intentional process with the exception of affective gains, as noted by Greenhaus and Powell (2006). For example, the choice to use decision making skills learned at work in the family or to use income from work to hire quality childcare are intentional decisions, whereas people likely do not make a conscious decision to transfer positive mood or self-esteem.

Distinction from other constructs. As noted in Table 6.1, much of the empirical literature to date has used the label *positive spillover,* and other recent labels have been equated with positive spillover, including work-family integration (Greenhaus & Parasuraman, 1999), work-family facilitation (Frone, 2003), and work-family enrichment (Greenhaus & Powell, 2006). Just as it is important to distinguish negative spillover from work-family conflict, it is important to distinguish positive spillover from work-family enrichment. In conceptualizing the positive spillover construct, it is critical to separate the process of positive spillover (the transference of gains across domains) from its potential results in the receiving domain (enhanced functioning for the individual or system) (refer to Figure 6.1).

The transference of these gains, that is, positive spillover, is a necessary but insufficient condition for enhanced individual or system functioning. For example, one might use a directive decision style learned at work with one's family (i.e., positive spillover) but with little success, because this style does not fit the demands of a family that values nurturance and self-direction (Greenhaus & Powell, 2006). Although positive spillover often results in enhanced functioning, it is not a given, and therefore, should not be considered part of the spillover construct. Additionally, when gains are successfully applied, positive spillover may contribute to enhanced individual or system functioning but not necessarily both. The use of the focal worker's income to hire quality childcare (i.e., positive spillover), for example, may not enhance his or her functioning in the family (i.e., work-family enrichment) but instead may enhance functioning of the system, such as improving parent-child interactions (i.e., work-family facilitation). Likewise, an individual's use at work of multitasking developed in the family may translate into enhanced individual job performance (i.e., family-work enrichment) but not to the performance of his or her workgroup or organization (i.e., family-work facilitation). For these reasons, the process of spillover should be distinguished from its potential results for individual or system functioning.

Measurement issues. As defined here, a second key construct in the positive side of the work-family interface is positive spillover that occurs when the developmental, affective, capital, and efficiency gains acquired in one domain are intentionally or unintentionally transferred to the other domain. In terms of measurement of positive spillover, therefore, responding affirmatively to the statement "Being in a good mood at work puts me in a good mood at home" would exemplify positive work-family spillover of affective gains, and "I use skills I learn in the family at work" would exemplify positive family-work spillover of developmental gains.

Until recently, most research on the positive side of the work-family interface has been conducted with ad hoc measures of the central construct that have not been subjected to rigorous development and validation procedures. As often happens, once these measures are published, other researchers use or adapt them in their studies. At times, the same scale (e.g., MIDUS) has been used to measure both positive spillover (e.g., Grzywacz & Marks, 2000) and facilitation (Wayne et al., 2004) and use of varying labels may confuse and deter from theory building related to these constructs (Hanson et al., 2006). Further, most of these measures do not reflect the multidimensional nature of the construct. Aside from the problem of conceptual ambiguity of construct labels and definitions, measures have not been considered as carefully as needed for this research to advance.

Some efforts that claim to measure positive spillover actually capture enrichment or a combination of the two constructs as defined here. For example, Grzywacz and Marks (2000a) purported to measure positive spillover with items such as "The things you do at work help you deal with personal and practical issues at home"; and Hammer et al. (2002) used similar items to measure positive spillover: "Having a successful day at work puts me in a good mood to handle my family responsibilities." Based upon the conceptual framework applied here, these items go beyond spillover to assess enhanced functioning for the individual. That is, they capture developmental and affective work-family enrichment, respectively, because they go beyond spillover (i.e., use of gain) to effective accomplishment of role responsibilities in the receiving domain. Others (e.g., Kirchmeyer, 1992; Sumer & Knight, 2001) include items measuring positive spillover ("Being a parent gives me access to certain facts and information which can be used at work") and enrichment ("Being a parent helps me understand the people at work better") within the same measure. Researchers should consider the conceptual distinctions among constructs provided here to create distinct and appropriate measurements of each construct.

A dire need in this research domain has been the need for a well-developed and validated measure. Hanson and colleagues (2006) created a multidimensional scale to measure positive spillover. They defined positive spillover (based on Edwards and Rothbard, 2000) as "the transfer of positively valenced affect, skills, behaviors, and values from the originating domain to the receiving domain, thus having beneficial effects on the receiving domain" (p. 251). From this definition, they created new items and adapted items from existing measures. Their final scale includes 22 items that capture both directions of positive spillover (work-to-family and family-to-work) as well as three types (affective, behavior-based, and value-based). A sample item measuring affective spillover is "Being in a positive mood at work helps me to be in a positive mood at home," which clearly reflects the conceptual definition of positive spillover provided here. Some items assess the degree to which gains in one domain create a beneficial result for the individual in the receiving domain (e.g., "Values developed at work make me a better family member"). Such items are consistent with Hanson et al.'s definition of positive spillover but not with the definition provided here. For purposes of conceptual elaboration and distinction, separating the process (transfer of gains) from the result (being a better family member) is important. Whether this conceptual distinction is important empirically, however, is a question that remains to be answered.

Often, rather than being interested in the objective occurrence of spillover and its correlates, of primary interest to work-family scholars is the individual's cognitive appraisal of the degree to which involvement in one domain ultimately interferes with (in the case of work-family conflict) or enhances (in the case of work-family enrichment) performance in another domain. In previous research, work-family conflict and to a lesser extent, work-family enrichment, have been examined as cognitive linking mechanisms between work and family characteristics, such as demands, resources, and outcomes

(Voydanoff, 2004). Given the importance of this focal construct to the work-family interface, let us turn our attention to it now.

AN ELABORATION OF THE "WORK-FAMILY ENRICHMENT" CONSTRUCT

Conceptual definition. Work-family enrichment is defined by Greenhaus and Powell (2006) as the extent to which experiences in one role improve the quality of life, namely performance or affect, in the other role. They proposed that enrichment occurs when resource gains generated in Role A promote performance in Role B. Implicitly, they refer to enhanced role performance for the individual within the receiving domain. Further, they suggested that enrichment occurs when resources gained from one role either directly improve individual performance in the other role, referred to as the instrumental path, or indirectly through their influence on positive affect, the affective path. Using terminology from the framework given here, then, work-family enrichment occurs when the developmental, affective, capital, or efficiency gains acquired in one domain are transferred to and improve individual functioning such as performance or affect in another domain (see Figure 6.1). Thus, enrichment builds on the more basic notion of positive spillover. The subtle, yet important, distinction between the two constructs is that with spillover, gains from one domain can be transferred yet not improve functioning of the individual in the other role. For enrichment to occur, gains must not only be transferred to another role but successfully applied in ways that result in improved functioning for the individual. Spillover and enrichment are overlapping but distinct constructs. Such a conceptual distinction has not been made previously in the work-family literature; yet, as with the conflict literature, spillover and enrichment should not be considered conceptually synonymous.

Recently, Greenhaus, Allen, and Spector (2006) offered a definition of work-family conflict that explicitly recognizes that a negative impact on performance is a necessary condition for work-family conflict to have occurred. Whereas work-family conflict is commonly defined as when roles are mutually incompatible such that participation in one role is more difficult because of participation in another (Greenhaus & Beutell, 1985), their recent definition of conflict is "the extent to which experiences in one role result in diminished performance in the other role." Their definition of work-family conflict, like that of work-family enrichment given here, purposefully captures the fundamental feature of the construct: the resulting improvement (or decrement) of performance in the receiving domain.

Empirical and theoretical support. Theoretical and empirical research supports the contention that positive spillover of developmental, affective, capital, and efficiency gains should lead to enhanced individual functioning in the receiving domain. The example from Crouter's (1984) research of the father applying communications skills learned at work with his teenage son implies enhanced performance in his role as a parent. Skills and behaviors learned in one domain that are applied successfully to another should yield enhanced individual performance in the receiving domain. Rothbard (2001) proposed that the positive spillover of affect increases psychological availability, an outward rather than inward focus, and greater energy in the receiving domain, all of which should generally result in enhanced individual functioning. Capital gains such as social, income, or health assets that are transferred to a receiving domain should improve individual functioning, or performance or affect, within that domain. Networking at work, for example, has been shown to relate to family satisfaction (Friedman & Greenhaus, 2000). Finally, positive spillover of efficiency from one's family should yield enhanced work role performance such as more efficient completion of job-related tasks. Enrichment is defined as when the gains acquired in one domain are transferred and yield improved individual functioning in the receiving domain.

Measurement issues. Like work-family conflict, enrichment consists of cognitive appraisals of the effects of the individual's involvement in one domain on his or her performance or affect in the other domain (Voydanoff, 2004). Whereas conflict is perceived when the relationship between the person and environment is appraised by the individual as endangering his or her well-being, enrichment is likely perceived when the person-environment relationship is appraised as enhancing his or her well-being (Voydanoff, 2004). In other words, to the degree that an individual perceives that gains acquired in one domain enhance his or her functioning in the other, he or she will report work-family enrichment. Thus, in terms of measurement and in comparison to enhancement and positive spillover, an example item reflecting enrichment would be: "Involvement in my job puts me in a positive mood, which helps me be a better family member." Consistent with its conceptual definition, this measurement of enrichment captures the individual's cognitive appraisal of both the transfer of gains *and* the resulting improvement for him or her in the receiving domain.

Carlson et al. (2006) recently developed and validated a scale to measure work-family enrichment. In their scale, they were careful to develop items that captured enhanced individual role performance or affect, not just positive spillover. Sample items from their scale include: "My involvement in my work helps me to acquire skills/puts me in a good mood/provides a sense of accomplishment and this helps me be a better family member," measuring developmental, affective, and capital work-family enrichment, respectively. They found empirical support for their proposed multiple dimensions of enrichment, albeit different dimensions for work-family than family-work enrichment. Specifically, they found support for developmental, affective, and capital-based work-family enrichment and developmental, affective, and efficiency-based family-work enrichment.

One would clearly expect an association between an individual's report of positive spillover and of enrichment; again, whether this conceptual distinction is an important practical distinction should be addressed empirically. However, as explained elsewhere in this chapter, one can reasonably argue that positive spillover (use of gains in another domain) does not necessarily and always lead to enrichment (enhanced performance or satisfaction for the individual). Therefore, at this stage of theory building and empirical research, it is safest to assume that they are empirically as well as conceptually distinct concepts.

Enhancement, spillover, and enrichment place primary emphasis on individuals, either in terms of benefits they receive from or their activities within a role (Grzywacz & Butler, 2005; Grzywacz et al., 2007). Although better functioning individuals likely contribute to better functioning families and organizations, there is a large inferential gap between individual and system-level functioning (Grzywacz & Butler, 2005; Grzywacz et al., 2007). In their comprehensive review, Eby et al. (2005) suggested the importance of understanding whether work and family benefit each other and what factors contribute to these beneficial effects. Thus, a construct is needed that captures the consequences for work and family of individuals' participation in both domains (Grzywacz & Butler, 2005; Grzywacz, et al., 2007; Wayne et al., 2007).

AN ELABORATION OF THE WORK-FAMILY FACILITATION CONSTRUCT

Conceptual definition. Work-family facilitation is a construct that captures the influence of engagement in one domain on functioning of the other system (Grzywacz et al., 2007; Wayne et al., 2007). Recently, researchers have elaborated upon the conceptual underpinnings of this construct (Grzywacz et al., 2007), as well as its likely correlates (Wayne et al., 2007).

Facilitation occurs when an individual's engagement in one domain of life (e.g., work or family) creates gains (i.e., developmental, affective, capital, or efficiency) that result in enhanced functioning of another life domain (e.g., family or work) (Wayne, et al., 2004; 2007). That is, individual engagement ultimately creates enhanced functioning for the *receiving system*. Enhanced functioning refers to a relatively enduring improvement in the operation, processes, or quality of life of the system (Wayne, Grzywacz, et al., 2004; 2007). Each life domain is a social system comprising elements that interact to create distinguishable subsystems (Bronfenbrenner, 1989). In families, for example, the marital dyad and parent-child dyads are subsystems of the larger family system. Likewise, there are definable subsystems in organizations such as departments, work teams, and supervisor-subordinate dyads. System improvement indicative of facilitation would be relatively enduring changes in such things as leader-member exchange or work-unit productivity in the workplace, and marital equity or cohesion in the family (Grzywacz & Butler, 2005). Thus, facilitation is a system-level construct that indicates that through an individual's involvement in one domain, there is enhanced functioning of another system or within its subsystems. For further elaboration of the conceptual foundation for facilitation, including a thorough definition and illustrations of how it occurs, consult Grzywacz et al. (2007).

Although Grzywacz et al. (2007) and Wayne et al. (2007) provide a needed and thorough discussion of facilitation as a focal construct, they do not fully consider facilitation's relationship to other core "positive" constructs. It is important to consider how facilitation occurs through enhancement, spillover, and/or enrichment. Enhanced system functioning indicative of facilitation can occur directly from positive spillover or indirectly through enrichment as depicted in Figure 6.1. In other words, enhanced functioning for the individual within the receiving domain is not necessary for enhanced functioning of the system to occur. Assume, for example, that through networking and income gained at work, an individual is able to transfer those gains to the family and hire quality in-home childcare. The transfer of these gains (i.e., positive spillover) may lead to better parent-child interactions (i.e., facilitation) without any change to the individual worker's functioning in the family (i.e., enrichment). Thus, positive spillover can lead directly to work-family facilitation. Alternatively, facilitation may also follow from work-family enrichment. For example, one father reported that after numerous disastrous family vacations, he applied his participative management skills learned at work and allowed his children a voice in planning the vacation (DeLong & DeLong, 1992). Applying this skill in the family (i.e., spillover) enabled him to perform more effectively as a parent (i.e., enrichment), which resulted in more enjoyable vacations with less conflict and presumably, better parent-child interactions (i.e., facilitation). Thus, positive spillover can lead to work-family facilitation indirectly through work-family enrichment.

Measurement issues. Given that work-family facilitation is a new construct, it is important to address how it might be measured in research. Facilitation might be measured via self-report in that respondents report the degree to which they perceive that their involvement in a domain positively benefits the functioning of the other system. Consider, for example, a situation in which through wellness resources at work such as exercise or cooking classes, an individual develops health assets which she or he transfers to the family. To assess work-family facilitation, one could use items such as: "My work provides me with information and advice that helps my family function better," where the item captures the respondent's perception of the transfer of gains and improved functioning of the family system. A potential problem with self-report at this level of analysis, however, is that we may be asking respondents to report more than they are capable of knowing (Nisbett & Wilson, 1977). In other words, respondents may find it difficult to accurately assess the degree to which their involvement in one domain directly caused improvements to the other system. Moreover, individuals may perceive that the system is benefiting and functioning better when objectively it is not. Researchers should consider what phenomenon they are truly interested in studying. If they are interested in respondents' perceptions of work-family facilitation, then such a self-report measure would be appropriate. If, however, researchers want objective and quantifiable evidence of facilitation, then they should relate positive spillover or enrichment or both to system-level outcomes. For example, to determine whether the transfer of health assets (such as cooking classes) improved family functioning, one could investigate the relation of this positive spillover to the number of family illnesses. Finding significant positive relationships would indicate that involvement in one domain influenced the functioning of the system and would illuminate some of the mechanisms by which this occurred.

GUIDING FUTURE RESEARCH: EMPIRICAL TESTS OF MODELS OF POSITIVE WORK-FAMILY CONNECTIONS

The process view. Thus far, this chapter has outlined the constructs involved in the positive connections between work and family and has defined and distinguished among them (refer to Figure 6.1). Importantly, although intended for the primary purpose of providing a conceptual schema of these constructs, this framework suggests the potential process by which involvement in one domain ultimately influences individual and system

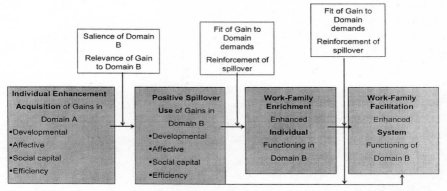

Figure 6.2.   The process involved in the positive connections between work and family.

functioning in another. Building from the conceptual foundation already provided, I now elaborate on this process, including relevant moderating conditions (refer to Figure 6.2).

The process of the positive connections between work and family begins when, through an individual's engagement in a domain, he or she acquires developmental, affective, capital, or efficiency gains (*individual enhancement*). For the process to continue, these gains must be transferred to the other domain (*spillover*). Based on expectancy theory (Vroom, 1964), Greenhaus and Powell (2006) proposed moderating factors that influence whether gains acquired in one domain are transferred to another. According to expectancy theory, an individual is most likely to engage in a behavior (e.g., the transfer of a gain) when the potential outcome of that behavior is highly valued and likely to lead to a desired outcome. Thus, individuals more readily transfer gains to a role when it is highly salient to the individual because he or she places high value on performing well in a role that is central to their self-concept (Thoits, 1991). Likewise, individuals transfer gains when they believe that the gain is highly relevant to performance in role B because it enables them to achieve the desired outcome of improved role performance (Greenhaus & Powell, 2006). Thus, individual enhancement (or gains acquired in domain A) likely leads to positive spillover to domain B when (1) domain B is highly salient for the individual and (2) when he or she perceives relevance of the gain to that domain (Greenhaus & Powell, 2006).

Generally speaking, when positive spillover occurs, it should lead to enhanced functioning in the receiving domain for either the individual, the system, or both. As already noted, however, positive spillover does not always translate into enhanced functioning. The degree to which enrichment or facilitation follows from positive spillover likely depends upon at least two primary factors. First, enhanced functioning for the individual or system is more likely when the receiving domain is receptive to and reinforcing of the use of gains acquired in the generating domain (Grzywacz & Butler, 2005). For example, an individual may learn new negotiation or conflict management skills at work that he or she uses at home (i.e., spillover). If the display of this gain in the family is not reinforced in some way by family members or through the experience of more effective conflict resolution, then enhanced functioning for the individual or the family is not likely to occur. Similarly, if an individual derives health assets from work that s/he uses at home (spillover) but family members refuse to eat healthy food or participate in exercise, then system-level change (facilitation) will not occur. Moreover, following the tenets of reinforcement theory, without reinforcement the transfer of these gains across domains is less likely to recur. An individual gain that is transferred to the receiving domain (spillover) needs to be met with reinforcing circumstances to realize enhanced individual or system functioning (Grzywacz & Butler, 2005).

Second, enhanced individual and system functioning are more likely to occur when there is actual or perceived fit between the gains acquired from one domain and the role demands and experiences of the other (Greenhaus & Powell, 2006). In other words, positive spillover is more likely to lead to enrichment or facilitation when the experiences or activities in the receiving domain require the developmental, affective, capital, or efficiency gains obtained in the generating domain. For example, developmental gains in the form of conflict management skills will be more helpful to functioning in the family for someone who has more conflict situations in which to use those skills, such as a father with a teenage son (Crouter, 1984) rather than someone with no caregiving demands. The use of capital gains from work transferred to home to hire live-in childcare may not enhance functioning in the family if it creates less intimate parent-child interactions (Greenhaus & Powell, 2006). Thus, positive spillover more readily leads to enhanced functioning for the individual (i.e., work-family enrichment) or system (i.e., work-family facilitation) when gains acquired in one role are reinforced and when they are consistent with demands of the other role.

Future research can empirically examine the entire theoretical process provided in Figure 6.2. This framework generates numerous research questions such as: To what degree does acquiring gains (enhancement) in a domain result in positive spillover across domains? And does this depend upon salience and relevance of the gain as suggested here? Further, how strong is the relationship between the use of gains across domains (spillover) and perceived improvement for the individual in the domain (enrichment)? Is the strength of this relationship affected by reinforcement of and fit of gains? Is the conceptual distinction between spillover and enrichment important empirically, or are these constructs so overlapping that they can be treated synonymously? Finally, does positive spillover or enrichment ultimately result in enhanced system functioning (facilitation)? If this occurs, does it do so through spillover, enrichment, or both? Addressing such questions provides a deeper, richer perspective on the work-family interface beyond the more typical cross-sectional antecedent-consequence approach. Testing of this process model would suggest that mediators and moderators be included. In terms of methodology, experience sampling (e.g., Butler, Grzywacz, Bass, & Linney, 2005; Williams & Alliger, 1994) and other repeated measures techniques would be necessary and fruitful, as would collecting data from others within the system.

The episodic view. Typically, researchers practically or theoretically desire to capture a snapshot view of the work-family interface. In this case, the greatest interest for work-family scholars will be examining primary correlates of the construct of work-family enrichment in the form of an empirical model. Rather than objectively assessing individual elements of this process (e.g., enhancement, spillover, and enrichment), it is important to note that this approach typically considers work-family enrichment as a perceptual variable that subsumes some of the other constructs. That is, work-family enrichment includes the individual's cognitive appraisal of the degree to which gains acquired in one domain (enhancement) are transferred to another (spillover) and enhance his or her functioning. This is much the same as measures of work-family conflict in which the time, strain, or behavior from one role are transferred to another and ultimately interfere with functioning of that role. An item used to measure work-family conflict such as, "Tension and anxiety from my family life often weaken my ability to do my job" (Carlson, Kacmar, & Williams, 2000) measures the individual's perception of the extent to which involvement in domain A (family) creates tension and anxiety that ultimately interfere with performance in domain B (work) (Carlson et al., 2006). Such perceptual measures of work-family enrichment or conflict are then considered a cognitive linking mechanism between work-family antecedents and outcomes (Voydanoff, 2004).

Although it is beyond the purposes of this paper to delineate specific predictors and hypotheses, building from the basic conceptual framework provided in this chapter, Figure 6.3 suggests a general model of antecedents, moderators, and outcomes of enrichment. Scholars have tended to agree that environmental resources are primary contributors to the positive connections between work and family (e.g., Grzywacz & Butler, 2005; Wayne, Grzywacz, Carlson, & Kacmar, 2005; Voydanoff, 2004; Witt & Carlson, 2006). Resources in the family domain predict family-work enrichment, and resources

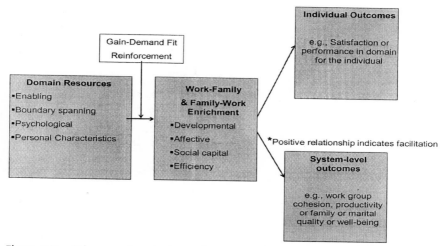

Figure 6.3. Primary antecedents, moderators, and consequences of work-family enrichment.

in the work domain predict work-family enrichment. As suggested by Voydanoff (2004), the richness of enabling, boundary spanning, psychological and personal resources in a domain likely influences the individual's appraisal of the degree to which that domain provides gains that enhance his or her functioning in the other domain.

Following Greenhaus and Powell (2006) and others (e.g., Wayne et al., 2007), the degree to which resources predict work-family enrichment likely depends upon the degree of reinforcement received and the degree to which the gains from one domain fit the demands of another (Greenhaus & Powell, 2006; Grzywacz et al., 2005). For example, the availability of family supportive programs is likely more strongly predictive of work-family enrichment for those with caregiving needs (that is, a fit between the available domain resource and the need in the receiving environment). Thus, the moderating conditions of reinforcement and fit should be considered in future empirical tests. Finally, researchers would likely also be interested in testing the objective outcomes of individuals' cognitive appraisal of work-family enrichment. A large body of research has investigated and found negative individual outcomes of work-family conflict. Likewise, researchers should examine affective and behavioral outcomes with the expectation that enrichment would favorably relate to these outcomes.

Whereas the ultimate desire is that work-family enrichment serves to improve family and organizational functioning, empirical evidence is needed to support this assumption. Researchers should examine system-level outcomes of enrichment to investigate the occurrence of facilitation. Wayne and colleagues (2007) elaborate on the likely outcomes of facilitation such as family well-being or work unit productivity (Grzywacz & Butler, 2005; Wayne et al., 2007). The occurrence of work-family facilitation would be supported by a positive relationship between work-family enrichment and these system-level outcomes.

SUMMARY AND CONTRIBUTIONS

In summary, the present framework was designed to answer questions researchers interested in the positive side of the work-family interface are likely facing due to construct confusion: "What should I call what I am studying?" "How should I measure it?" "Are all these constructs the same?" and "If they are different, how do they all fit together?" This chapter provided conceptual definitions of each construct previously proposed in the literature, including enhancement, positive spillover, enrichment, and facilitation. The chapter also highlighted their similarities and distinctions, provide a pictorial representation of how they fit together, and discussed potential measurement issues surrounding each.

These conceptual distinctions among constructs are important not only in terms of clarity, organization, and communication in the literature but are also essential in terms of furthering research and theory. Without a thorough understanding of the various constructs involved in the positive connections between work and family, theory cannot advance. From the process model of the mechanisms that enable work and family to benefit one another, theory can further elaborate the why, when, and how of the positive connections between work and family.

Researchers should also be better able to identify the appropriate theoretical construct of interest. Researchers interested in the degree and type of gains acquired by an individual within a domain would focus on individual enhancement, and those interested in the transfer of those gains across domains would be interested in studying positive spillover. For those whose interest is in the degree to which involvement in one domain provides gains that improve individuals' functioning in the other, their construct of interest would be work-family enrichment. This chapter also discusses an emerging, system-level construct, facilitation (Grzywacz & Butler, 2005; Wayne, Grzywacz et al., 2004), for researchers interested in capturing the impact of work on family and vice versa.

This framework should provide a common language upon which scholars can rely to reduce confusion and make appropriate comparisons and conclusions across studies. After having first identified the appropriate construct, researchers must determine ways to appropriately measure it. Thus, this chapter links these conceptual definitions to potential measures in order to move research forward. Researchers should carefully consider their construct of interest and ensure it is measured validly without contamination across constructs.

Finally, given the likely interest in the construct of work-family enrichment, the chapter provides a general model of potential correlates of this construct, highlighting (1) four domain resources that can create work-family enrichment; (2) moderating factors of this relationship, and (3) possible individual-level outcomes of enrichment as well as system-level outcomes that would provide evidence of work-family facilitation.

Lambert and Kossek (2005) noted that there is little consensus on the language and core concepts used in the work-family literature and that often, the reason for selection of particular terminology is not explained. They added that "one wonders how much thought was given to choosing among different conceptualizations." As they stated, scholars can advance the work-life field by carefully considering and explaining the theoretical origins of the terminology they use. From the conceptual foundation provided here, it is hoped that scholars can better understand and justify their choice of conceptualization so that research and theory on the positive side of the work-family interface can flourish.

NOTE

Julie Holliday Wayne, Ph.D., is visiting assistant professor at the Calloway School of Business & Accountancy, Wake Forest University. The author gratefully acknowledges the suggestions of Dawn Carlson, Joe Grzywacz, and Micki Kacmar on an earlier version of this manuscript and their contributions to Table 6.1.

REFERENCES

Barnett, R. C., & Hyde, J. S. (2001). Women, men, work, and family: An expansionist theory. *American Psychologist, 56*, 781–796.

Bronfenbrenner, U. (1989). Ecological systems theory. In R. Vasta (Ed.), *Six theories of child development. Annals of child development: A research annual (6,* pp. 187–249). Greenwich, CT: JAI Press.

Butler, A. B., Grzywacz, J. G., Bass, B. L., & Linney, K. D. (2005). Extending the demands control model: A daily diary study of job characteristics, work-family conflict and work-family facilitation. *Journal of Occupational and Organizational Psychology, 78,* 155–169.

Carlson, D. S., Kacmar, K. M., Wayne, J. H., & Grzywacz, J. G. (2006). Measuring the positive side of the work-family interface: Development and validation of a work-family enrichment scale. *Journal of Vocational Behavior, 68,* 131–164.

Carlson, D. S., Kacmar, M. K., & Williams, L. J. (2000). Construction and validation of a multidimensional measure of work-family conflict. *Journal of Vocational Behavior, 56,* 249–276.

Crouter, A. C. (1984). Spillover from family to work: The neglected side of the work family interface. *Human Relations, 37,* 425–442.

DeLong, T. J., & DeLong, C. C. (1992). Managers as fathers: Hope on the homefront. *Human Resource Management, 31,* 171–181.

Eby, L. T., Casper, W. J., Lockwood, A., Bordeaux, C., & Brinley, A. (2005). Work and family research in IO/OB: Content analysis and review of the literature (1980–2002). *Journal of Vocational Behavior, 66,* 124–197.

Edwards, J. R., & Rothbard, N. P. (2000). Mechanisms linking work and family: Clarifying the relationship between work and family constructs. *Academy of Management Review, 25,* 178–199.

Friedman, S. D., & Greenhaus, J. H. (2000). *Work and–family—allies or enemies? What happens when business professionals confront life choices.* New York: Oxford University Press.

Frone, M. R. (2003). Work-family balance. In J. C. Quick, & L. E. Tetrick (Eds.), *Handbook of occupational health psychology* (pp. 143–162). Washington, DC: American Psychological Association.

Greenberger, E., & O'Neil, R. (1993). Spouse, parent, worker: Role commitments and role-related experiences in the construction of adults' wellbeing. *Developmental Psychology, 29,* 181–197.

Greenhaus, J. H., Allen, T. A., & Spector, P. E. (2006). Health consequences of work-family conflict: The dark side of the work-family interface. In P. L. Perrewe & D. C. Ganster (Eds.), *Research in occupational stress and well-being* (pp., 61–98). Amsterdam: JAI Press.

Greenhaus, J. H., & Beutell, N. J. (1985). Sources of conflict between work and family roles. *Academy of Management Review, 10,* 76–88.

Greenhaus, J. H., & Parasuraman, S. (1999). Research on work, family, and gender: Current status and future directions. In G. N. Powell (Ed.), *Handbook of gender and work* (pp. 391–412). Thousand Oaks, CA: Sage.

Greenhaus, J. H., & Powell, G. N. (2006). When work and family are allies: A theory of work family enrichment. *Academy of Management Review, 31*(1), 72–92.

Grzywacz, J. G., Almeida, D. M., & McDonald, D. A. (2002). Work–family spillover and daily reports of work and family stress in the adult labor force. *Family Relations, 51,* 28–36.

Grzywacz, J. G., & Butler, A. B. (2005). The impact of job characteristics on work-to-family facilitation: Testing a theory and distinguishing a construct. *Journal of Occupational Health Psychology, 10,* 97–109.

Grzywacz, J. G., Carlson, D. S., Kacmar, K. M., & Wayne, J. H. (2007). Work-family facilitation: A multilevel perspective on the synergies between work and family. *Journal of Occupational and Organizational Psychology, 80,* 559–574.

Grzywacz, J. G. & Marks, N. F. (2000a). Reconceptualizing the work-family interface: An ecological perspective on the correlates of positive and negative spillover between work and family. *Journal of Occupational Health Psychology, 5,* 111–126.

————. (2000b). Family, work, work-family spillover and problem drinking during midlife. *Journal of Marriage and the Family, 62,* 336–348.

Grzywacz, J. G., Wayne, J. H., Carlson, D. S., & Kacmar, K. M. (under review.). *Work-family facilitation: A multilevel perspective on the synergies between work and family.*

Hammer, L. B., Cullen, J. C., Caubet, S., Johnson, J., Neal, M. B., & Sinclair, R. R. (2002, April) *The effects of work-family fit on depression: A longitudinal study.* Paper presented at the Annual Conference of the Society for Industrial and Organizational Psychology, Toronto, Canada.

Hammer, L. B., Cullen, J. C., Neal, M. B., Sinclair, R. R., & Shafiro, M. V. (2005). The longitudinal effects of work-family conflict and positive spillover on depressive symptoms among dual-earner couples. *Journal of Occupational Health Psychology, 10,* 138–154.

Hanson, G. C., Hammer, L. B., & Colton, C. L. (2006). Development and validation of a multidimensional scale of perceived work-family positive spillover. *Journal of Occupational Health Psychology, 11,* 249–265.

Hill, E. J. (2005). Work-family facilitation and conflict, working fathers and mothers, work-family stressors and support. *Journal of Family Issues, 26,* 793–819.

Kirchmeyer, C. (1992). Perceptions of nonwork-to-work spillover: Challenging the common view of conflict-ridden domain relationships. *Basic and Applied Social Psychology, 13,* 231–249.

Lambert, S. J., & Kossek, E. K. (2005). Future frontiers: Enduring challenges and established assumptions in the work-life field. In Kossek, E. K., & Lambert, S. J. (Eds.), *Work and life integration: Organizational, cultural, and individual perspectives.* Mahwah, NJ: Lawrence Erlbaum Press.

Marks, S. R. (1977). Multiple roles and role strain: Some notes on human energy, time and commitment. *American Sociological Review, 42,* 921–936.

Marks, S. R., & MacDermid, S. M. (1996). Multiple roles and the self: A theory of role balance. *Journal of Marriage and the Family, 58,* 417–432.

Nisbett, R. E., & Wilson, T. D. (1977). Telling more than we can know: Verbal reports on mental processes. *Psychological Review, 84,* 231–259.

Rothbard, N. (2001). Enriching or depleting? The dynamics of engagement in work and family roles. *Administrative Science Quarterly, 46,* 655–684.

Ruderman, M. N., Ohlott, P. N., Panzer, K., & King, S. N. (2002). Benefits of multiple roles for managerial women. *Academy of Management Journal, 45,* 369–386.

Sieber, S. D. (1974). Toward a theory of role accumulation. *American Sociological Review 39,* 567–578.

Stephens, M. A., Franks, M. M., & Atienza, A. A. (1997). Where two roles intersect: Spillover between parent care and employment. *Psychology and Aging, 12,* 30–37.

Sumer, H. C., & Knight, P. A. (2001). How do people with different attachment styles balance work and family? A personality perspective on work-family linkage. *Journal of Applied Psychology, 86,* 653–663.

Thoits, P. A. (1983). Multiple identities and psychological well-being: A reformulation and test of the social isolation hypothesis. *American Sociological Review, 48*, 174–187.

———. (1991). On merging identity theory and stress research. *Social Psychology Quarterly, 54*, 101–112.

Thompson, C. A., & Prottas, D. J. (2005). Relationships among organizational family support, job autonomy, perceived control, and employee well-being. *Journal of Occupational Health Psychology, 10*, 100–118.

Tiedje, L. B., Wortman, C. B., Downey, G., Emmons, C., Biernat, M., & Lang, E. (1990). Women with multiple roles: Role-compatibility perceptions, satisfaction, and mental health. *Journal of Marriage and the Family, 52*, 63–72.

Voydanoff, P. (2004). The effects of work demands and resources on work-to-family conflict and facilitation. *Journal of Marriage and Family, 66*, 398–412.

Vroom, V. H. (1964). *Work and motivation*. New York: Wiley.

Waldron, I., Weiss, C. C., & Hughes, M. E. (1998). Interacting effects of multiple roles on women's health. *Journal of Health and Social Behavior, 39*, 216–236.

Wayne, J. H., Musisca, N., & Fleeson, W. (2004). Considering the role of personality in the work-family experience: Relationships of the Big Five to work-family conflict and facilitation. *Journal of Vocational Behavior, 64*, 108–130.

Wayne, J. H., Grzywacz, J. G., Carlson, D. S., & Kacmar, K. M. (2004, April). *Work-family facilitation: A theoretical review of the construct*. Paper presented at the Annual Conference of the Society for Industrial and Organizational Psychology, Chicago, IL.

———. (2007). Work-family facilitation: A theoretical explanation and model of primary antecedents and consequences. *Human Resource Management Review, 17*, 63–76.

Wayne, J. H., Randel, A. E., & Stevens, J. (2006). The role of identity and work-family support in work-family enrichment and its work-related consequences. *Journal of Vocational Behavior, 69*, 445–461.

Williams, A., Franche, R. L., Ibrahim, S., Mustard, C. A., & Layton, F. R. (2006). Examining the relationship between work-family spillover and sleep quality. *Journal of Occupational Health Psychology, 11*, 27–37.

Williams, K. J., & Alliger, G. M. (1994). Role stressors, mood spillover, and perceptions of work-family conflict in employed parents. *Academy of Management Journal, 37*, 837–868.

Williams, S., Zainuba, M., & Jackson, R. (2003). Affective influences on risk perceptions and risk intention. *Journal of Managerial Psychology, 18*, 126–137.

Witt, L. A., & Carlson, D. S. (2006). The work-family interface and job performance: Moderating effects of conscientiousness and perceived organizational support. *Journal of Occupational Health Psychology, 11*, 343–357.

Chapter Seven

The Intersection of Work and Family Demands and Resources: Linking Mechanisms and Boundary-Spanning Strategies

by Patricia Voydanoff

The work-family interface can be understood as multiple intersections between work and family demands and resources. Various combinations of work and family demands and resources can have additive and interactive effects on work and family role performance and quality and individual well-being. In addition, work and family demands and resources influence outcomes through linking mechanisms in which individuals assess the extent to which resources are adequate to meet demands and through boundary-spanning strategies in which they take actions to reduce demands and increase resources. This chapter elaborates a conceptual model that focuses on how work and family demands and resources intersect to affect work and family role performance and quality and individual well-being through linking mechanisms and boundary-spanning strategies.

Extensive research has documented relationships between diverse work and family characteristics and work and family role performance and quality and individual well-being. Work and family characteristics can be subsumed under two categories: demands and resources. Demands are structural or psychological claims associated with role requirements, expectations, and norms to which individuals must respond or adapt by exerting physical or mental effort. Resources are structural or psychological assets that may be used to facilitate performance, reduce demands, or generate additional resources. Work and family demands and resources are of two types: within-domain and boundary-spanning. Within-domain demands and resources are associated with characteristics such as the structure and content of activities in one domain (e.g., job pressure and autonomy or time spent caring for family members), whereas boundary-spanning demands and resources are inherently part of two domains (e.g., bringing work home and a supportive work-family culture). Although boundary-spanning demands and resources originate in one domain, they serve as demands and resources in other domains. For example, when individuals work at home or perform family activities at work, they are operating in both domains at the same time. When employers acknowledge and address employee family needs through a supportive work-family culture and policies, the two domains are partially integrated.

Role performance encompasses behaviors performed at work and in the home, whereas role quality refers to positive and negative affect, such as positive and negative moods and emotions derived from work and family activities. Work outcomes include job performance and productivity, attendance-related issues, and job satisfaction and stress. Family outcomes encompass family role performance, family role quality, and child development outcomes. Individual outcomes incorporate several aspects of psychological and physical well-being, for example, depression, psychological distress, and physical health and illness. These outcomes have implications for the system-level functioning of workplaces and families.

DIRECT EFFECTS OF WORK AND FAMILY DEMANDS AND RESOURCES ON OUTCOMES

Extensive research has documented that within-domain and boundary-spanning demands and resources are directly related to work and family role performance and quality and individual well-being. (See Voydanoff, 2007, for a recent review.) However, the rationale for these relationships differs for within-domain demands, within-domain resources, boundary-spanning demands, and boundary-spanning resources. In addition, demands and resources may affect outcomes in two ways: in an additive fashion in which each demand or resource contributes independently to outcomes or in an interactive way in which the effect of one demand or resource on outcomes is contingent on the level of another demand or resource. The most commonly studied and theoretically most interesting interaction occurs when resources in one domain buffer the effects of a demand in another domain.

Within-Domain Demands

Within-domain demands, which are characteristics associated with the structure and content of a domain, are of two types: time-based and strain-based. Time-based demands reflect the idea that time is a fixed resource, that is, time spent in activities in one domain is not available for activities in another domain. Time-based demands are related to outcomes through a process of resource drain in which the time or involvement required for participation in one domain limits the time or involvement available for participation in another domain. Resource drain from one domain limits role performance and quality in other domains and reduces individual well-being. Time-based demands include the amount of time in paid work (the number and scheduling of work hours) and family work (time caring for children and elderly parents and time in household work). (See Table 7.1 for a listing of frequently studied work and family demands and resources).

Strain-based demands influence work and family role performance and quality and individual well-being through a process of negative psychological spillover in which the strain associated with participating in one domain is carried over to another domain such that it creates strain in the second domain. This strain hinders role performance and quality, thereby reducing individual well-being. Psychological spillover operates through transmission processes in which conditions in one domain are associated with psychological responses, which are then transferred into attitudes and behavior in another domain. Negative transmission processes include negative emotional arousal, interpersonal withdrawal, energy depletion, and stress (Piotrkowski, 1979; Rothbard, 2001). Strain-based demands include characteristics associated with the social organization of work (job demands and job insecurity) and family social organization (marital conflict, children's problems, caregiver strain, and unfairness in household work).

Within-Domain Resources

Within-domain work and family resources engender processes that improve role performance and quality and individual well-being when they are applied across domains. They include enabling resources and psychological rewards. Enabling resources from one domain may generate resources in another domain that provide the means for enhancing participation in the second domain. Enabling resources generally are associated with the structure or content of domain activities, for example, skills and abilities developed through domain activity, behaviors associated with role activities, and the availability of social support from others involved in the domain. Enabling resources in one domain increase the competence and capacities of individuals to perform in other domains. For example, interpersonal communication skills developed at work or at home, may facilitate constructive communication with members of other domains. In addition, positive participation in domain activities may be associated with energy creation that enhances participation in

Table 7.1. Work and Family Demands and Resources

	Work	Family
Within-domain demands		
Time-based demands	Time in paid work	Time caring for children
Resource drain	Nonstandard work schedules	Time caring for elderly relatives
		Time in household work
Strain-based demands	Job demands	Marital conflict
Psychological spillover	Job insecurity	Children's problems
		Caregiver strain
		Unfairness in household work
Within-domain resources		
Enabling resources	Autonomy	Family adaptability and cohesion
Resource generation	Skill utilization	Spouse support
	Supervisor and coworker support	Kin support
Psychological rewards	Meaning	Meaning
Psychological spillover	Pride	Pride
	Respect	Respect

Boundary-spanning demands		
Transitions		
Low permeability	Overnight travel Commuting time	Commuting time
Role blurring		
High permeability	Work activities at home Work-to-family boundary permeability	Family activities at work Family-to-work boundary permeability
Boundary-spanning resources		
Work supports		
Boundary flexibility	Flexible work schedules Dependent care	Spouse and kin child and elder care Spouse and kin household work
Family supports		
Boundary flexibility	Time off for family Part-time work	Spouse employment
Normative support		
Boundary flexibility	Supervisor work-family support Supportive work-family culture	Spouse and kin work-family support

Source: Voydanoff (2007).

other domains (Marks, 1977). This improved performance is accompanied by role quality and individual well-being. Enabling resources include job autonomy, skill utilization, and workplace support in the work domain and family adaptation and cohesion and spouse and kin support in the family domain.

In early work on psychological rewards, Sieber (1974) proposed that rewards from one domain may facilitate participation in another domain. These rewards included privileges, status security and enhancement, and personality enrichment. Rewards also include psychological resources that are associated with feeling esteemed and valued and intrinsic rewards such as meaningful activities. These rewards may be accompanied by psychological benefits, such as motivation, a sense of accomplishment, self-esteem, and ego gratification. They may affect other domains through processes of positive psychological spillover. Positive transmission processes include positive emotional arousal, interpersonal availability, energy creation, and gratification (Piotrkowski, 1979; Rothbard, 2001). Psychological rewards include meaning, pride, and respect associated with performing work and family activities.

Boundary-Spanning Demands

Boundary-spanning demands and resources are expected to influence outcomes through different processes than do within-domain demands and resources. Work-family border theory (Clark 2000) provides a useful framework for understanding the processes through which boundary-spanning demands and resources influence outcomes. It views relationships between domains as a continuum ranging from segmentation to integration. At the segmentation end of the continuum, the work and family domains are mutually exclusive with distinctive mentalities and no physical or temporal overlap. At the integration end of the continuum, work and family are indistinguishable in terms of the people, tasks, and thoughts involved (Clark, 2000; Nippert-Eng, 1996). Work-family border theory further posits that the extent of segmentation or integration is associated with the degree of permeability and flexibility of the boundaries between domains. Permeability refers to the degree to which elements from one domain enter into another domain, for example, an individual making family-related appointments while at work. Flexibility is the extent to which temporal and spatial boundaries allow roles to be enacted in various settings and at various times, for example, flexible work schedules in which an individual can vary starting and ending work times to meet family needs. Segmentation is characterized by low permeability and inflexible boundaries, whereas integration is associated with high permeability and flexible boundaries (Clark, 2000).

Boundary-spanning work and family demands and resources derive from the boundary permeability and flexibility associated with varying degrees of segmentation or integration. Boundary-spanning demands encompass boundary permeability across domains, whereas boundary-spanning resources incorporate boundary flexibility. Low boundary permeability is accompanied by more difficult transitions across domains, which may result in decreased role performance and quality and individual well-being. Demands associated with difficult role transitions include overnight travel for work and commuting time. High permeability also is associated with role blurring or blending, in which distinctions between roles become unclear. Demands associated with role blurring include the performance of work responsibilities at home or family duties at work and permeable work-family boundaries.

Boundary-Spanning Resources

Boundary-spanning resources address how work, family, and community domains connect with each other in terms of boundary flexibility. Boundary flexibility refers to the degree to which temporal and spatial boundaries permit role activities to be performed in various settings and at various times, that is, flexibility regarding when and where activities are performed. Work-based boundary-spanning resources include the availability or use of workplace policies and programs that enhance the flexibility of the temporal boundary between work and family. These policies and programs may improve flexibility in two ways: work supports and family supports. Work supports (e.g., flexible work schedules and dependent care benefits) help employees accommodate their family responsibilities without reducing work hours or the amount of work that is performed. Family supports (e.g., the ability to take time off from work for family responsibilities, and part-time work) enhance flexibility by reducing an individual's time at work. In addition, normative support can increase boundary flexibility by providing organizational support for workers to use these policies and programs to coordinate work and family obligations and activities.

Family-based boundary-spanning resources also include work supports, family supports, and normative support. Spouses and kin can increase the ability of individuals to meet the temporal demands of their work roles by performing additional dependent care and household work activities, which frees up time for work activities. In addition, one spouse may be the major provider so that the other spouse can devote more time to family activities. Family members also may provide normative support to individuals who are attempting to combine work and family activities by acknowledging the value of such attempts and giving instrumental and emotional social support.

Boundary-spanning resources may enhance cross-domain role performance and quality and individual well-being through increased flexibility of the temporal boundary between work and home, legitimacy for the use of work-family policies, spouse and kin assistance, community-based programs, and normative work-family support from family, community, and friends.

Cross-Domain Buffering Effects of Resources on Relationships between Demands and Outcomes

In addition to having direct additive effects on role performance and quality and individual well-being, demands and resources may combine in more complex ways to influence outcomes. For example, theories of occupational stress and family resilience propose that resources may buffer the effects of demands on outcomes. These within-domain approaches provide a framework for examining similar relationships that may occur across domains. Occupational stress theory includes two approaches that are relevant to understanding the combined effects of demands and resources on outcomes within the work domain. The most prominent is the job demand-control model in which job resources are expected to buffer the effects of job demands on job strain and individual well-being. This model is based on the assumption that the level of psychological demands combines with the level of decision latitude to influence psychological strain or physical illness and psychological growth. Job demands focus on time demands, monitoring demands, and problem-solving demands, whereas decision latitude includes decision or task authority and skill discretion. Recently, social support has been added to the model as a resource that operates similarly to control in relation to job demands and health outcomes (de Lange et al., 2003; van der Doef & Maes, 1999). The second approach focuses on rewards rather than enabling resources as a potential buffer. The effort-reward approach proposes that an imbalance between work effort and rewards (i.e., situations of high effort and low reward) leads to adverse physical and psychological health consequences. High effort results from the demands of the job or the motivations of workers in demanding situations such as need for control. Rewards include money, esteem, and status control (Siegrist, 1998).

The family resilience literature views resilience as a process in which risks and protective factors interact in relation to a family's ability to fulfill important family functions such as family solidarity, economic support, nurturance and socialization, and protection. Risks that endanger these family outcomes include non-normative family demands and the family's shared meanings of these demands. Family protective factors, such as family cohesiveness, flexibility, and communication patterns, may buffer the relationships between risks and outcomes (Patterson, 2002).

These approaches suggest that, in addition to additive effects of work and family demands and resources on outcomes, resources from one domain may buffer the negative effects of demands from another domain on work and family role performance and quality and individual well-being. Few studies have examined such effects and only a few of the possible combinations of demands, resources, and outcomes have been considered. Some of these studies reveal buffering effects, whereas others do not. (See Voydanoff, 2007, for a review.) These mixed findings suggest that cross-domain resources may buffer the effects of work and family demands on outcomes under some conditions. More rigorous research is needed to assess these conditions. Existing studies have used small and specific samples and measures with undetermined psychometric properties.

The implications for work-family policy differ for additive and buffering effects. When demands and resources have additive effects on role performance and quality and individual well-being, resources reduce negative outcomes but do not address the negative effects of demands on outcomes. Thus, the negative consequences associated with demands remain unchanged, whereas resources have independent compensating effects on outcomes. However, if resources buffer the effects of demands on outcomes, the negative effects of demands are reduced or eliminated. Thus, demands no longer contribute to outcomes and increasing resources is sufficient to protect against the negative effects of demands. When additive effects occur, policies that only increase resources are insufficient to reduce the negative effects of demands on well-being. Thus, it is important to investigate such relationships further.

MECHANISMS LINKING WORK AND FAMILY DEMANDS AND RESOURCES TO OUTCOMES

In addition to having direct effects on role performance and quality and individual well-being, work and family demands and resources may influence outcomes indirectly through work-family linking mechanisms such as perceived work-family conflict, facilitation, fit, and balance. Linking mechanisms are cognitive appraisals of the effects of the work and family domains on each other. According to Lazarus and Folkman (1984), cognitive appraisal is the process of deciding whether an experience is positive, stressful, or irrelevant with regard to well-being. A stressful appraisal occurs when individuals perceive that the demands of the environment exceed their resources, thereby endangering their well-being. Thus, perceptions of work-family conflict, facilitation, fit, and balance derive from assessing the relative demands and resources associated with work and family roles and their impact on role performance and quality and individual well-being.

Work-Family Conflict and Work-Family Facilitation

A conceptualization of work-family conflict and facilitation. Perceived work-family conflict and work-family facilitation are the two most commonly studied mechanisms linking work and family demands and resources in one domain to role performance and quality and individual well-being in the other domain. Work-family conflict is a form of inter-role conflict in which the demands of work and family roles are seen as incompatible in some respect so that participation in one role is more difficult because of participation in the other role (Greenhaus & Beutell, 1985). It is a form of demands-abilities misfit in which time demands, strain, or skills in one domain create work-family conflict by reducing abilities in the other domain such that demands in the other domain are not met (Edwards and Rothbard, 2005). In this context, abilities are comparable to resources. Work-family conflict can take two forms: work-to-family conflict in which the demands of work make it difficult to perform family responsibilities and family-to-work conflict in which family demands limit the performance of work duties. Work demands generally are associated with work-to-family conflict, whereas family demands are the proximal sources of family-to-work conflict.

Work-family facilitation is a form of synergy in which resources associated with one role enhance or make easier participation in the other role (Voydanoff, 2004). Thus, resources in one domain increase resources in the other domain, thereby facilitating performance in the other domain. It can operate from work to family or from family to work. Work resources are expected to influence work-to-family facilitation, whereas family resources affect family-to-work facilitation. Work-family conflict and facilitation are only slightly correlated with each other and the four components of conflict and facilitation form separate factors in a factor analysis (Grzywacz & Marks, 2000).

Figure 7.1 presents a conceptual model in which work-family conflict and facilitation serve as linking mechanisms. Within-domain and boundary-spanning demands and resources are associated with work-family conflict and facilitation. Conflict and facilitation influence outcomes via their relationships with boundary-spanning strategies and work-family balance. The model suggests that within-domain demands, within-domain resources, and boundary-spanning demands and resources operate differently in relation to work-family conflict and facilitation. Within-domain demands are expected to be positively associated with work-family conflict, whereas within-domain resources are expected to be positively related to work-family facilitation. This

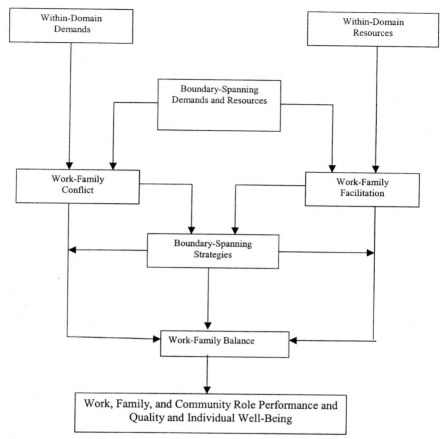

Figure 7.1.   The Conceptual Model with Work-Family Conflict and Facilitation as Linking Mechanisms. Source: Voydanoff (2008).

differential salience approach proposes that within-domain demands are relatively salient for work-family conflict because they are associated with processes that limit the ability of individuals to meet obligations in another domain (i.e., resource drain and negative psychological spillover). Within-domain resources are relatively salient for work-family facilitation because they engender processes that improve one's ability to participate in other domains (i.e., enabling resources and positive psychological spillover) (Voydanoff, 2004).

In contrast to the prediction of differential salience of within-domain demands and resources for work-family conflict and facilitation, boundary-spanning demands and resources are expected to have comparable salience for work-family conflict and facilitation. Boundary-spanning demands and resources also are expected to be related to both directions of conflict and facilitation, for example, work-based demands are expected to be associated with both work-to-family and family-to-work conflict and facilitation. Because boundary-spanning demands and resources focus on aspects of role domains that directly address how they connect with each other (i.e., boundary permeability and flexibility), the processes relating them to conflict and facilitation are expected to operate similarly in both directions and for both demands and resources.

In addition to these direct effects of work and family demands and resources on work-family conflict and facilitation, demands and resources may interact in relation to conflict such that the effects of a given work (family) demand on conflict may depend on the level of a given family (work) resource. In this situation, a work (family) resource would buffer the negative effects of a family (work) demand on conflict. For example, a buffering effect would exist if a positive relationship between time caring for children and family-to-work conflict were reduced for those with high workplace support. Empirical research is needed to determine the extent to which and the circumstances under which these buffering effects may occur.

Assessing work-family conflict and facilitation. Over the past twenty-five years, several measures of work-family conflict have been developed that have acceptable levels of internal consistency and discriminant validity. (See Tetrick and Buffardi, 2006, for a review.) Measures of work-family conflict assess the extent to which demands in one domain have negative effects on role performance and quality in the second domain. They vary in the extent to which they focus on the specific demand in one domain (time, strain, or behavior) or on specific aspects of role performance and quality in other domain (participation in activities, psychological availability, or psychological stress). However, they do consistently address the connection between the two by using linking phrases such as "interferes with", "makes it difficult", and "keeps me from". Examples of various types of items include: "Tension and anxiety from my family life often weakens my ability to do my job", "I am often so emotionally drained when I get home from work that it prevents me from contributing to my family", "My work keeps me from my family activities more than I would like", and "I have to miss work activities due to the amount of time I must spend on family responsibilities" (Carlson, Kacmar, & Williams, 2000).

Because work-family facilitation has only recently been incorporated in studies of the work-family interface, only a few well-developed measures exist. These measures assess the extent to which enabling resources and positive psychological spillover in one domain enhance role performance or quality in the other domain. As with work-family conflict, the items vary in the extent to which they focus on the nature of the resource or the type of outcome, for example, "Skills developed in my family life help me in my job" or "Values that I learn through my work experiences assist me in fulfilling my family responsibilities" (Hanson, Hammer, & Colton, 2006). Another recently developed measure focuses explicitly on enhanced role performance by incorporating becoming a better family member/worker into each item, for example, "My involvement in my work puts me in a good mood and this helps me be a better family member" (Carlson, Kacmar, Wayne, & Grzywacz, 2006). The need to consider both the demand or resource and the outcome in measures of conflict and facilitation is emphasized by a recent study by Hill et al. (this volume). This study asked open-ended questions about the ways in work (home life) positively influence home life (work). Respondents identified aspects of one domain that facilitated the other domain (i.e., enabling resources, positive psychological spillover, and boundary flexibility) as well as aspects of one domain that were facilitated by the other domain (role performance and quality and individual well-being). This suggests that respondents perceive the linkages between resources in one domain and role performance and quality in another domain.

However, other scholars suggest that incorporating relatively specific demands, resources, or outcomes into the questions confounds sources and outcomes with conflict (and by extension, facilitation). Bellavia and Frone (2005) are concerned that time, strain, and behavior demands are sources of work-family conflict and therefore should not be considered as "forms" of conflict or specified in measures of conflict. Conflict should be assessed with items that are as general as possible. For example, an item in the Netemeyer, Boles, and McMurrian scale (1996) reads as follows: "The demands of my work interfere with my home and family life". MacDermid (2005) expresses similar concerns about confounding work-family conflict with work, family, and stress-related outcomes (i.e., job and family role performance and satisfaction and individual well-being). However, these issues may be embedded in the effort to assess individuals' cognitive appraisals of the effects of work and family demands and resources on cross-domain role performance and quality and individual well-being.

Work-Family Fit

A conceptualization of work-family fit. A third important linking mechanism is work-family fit. This chapter conceptualizes work-family fit from the perspective of the person-environment fit approach to occupational stress. The basic tenet of person-environment fit theory is that stress arises from the lack of fit or congruence between the person and the environment rather than from either one separately (Edwards & Rothbard, 2005). Fit is of two types: demands-abilities and needs-supplies. Demands include quantitative and qualitative job requirements, role expectations, and group and organizational norms, whereas abilities include aptitudes, skills, training, time, and energy that may be used to meet demands. Fit occurs when the individual has the abilities needed to meet the demands of the environment. Strains are expected to increase as demands exceed abilities. Needs encompass biological and psychological requirements, values, and motives, whereas supplies consist of intrinsic and extrinsic resources and rewards that may fulfill the person's needs, such as food, shelter, money, social involvement, and the opportunity to achieve. Fit exists when the environment provides the resources required to satisfy the person's needs, whereas strains occur when needs exceed supplies. Misfit, which occurs when demands and needs exceed abilities and supplies, results in strains and illness as well as coping behavior and cognitive defense to improve fit, whereas fit can create positive mental and physical health outcomes.

Building on this previous work, work-family fit is defined as a form of inter-role congruence in which the resources associated with one role are sufficient to meet the demands of another role such that participation in the second role can be effective. Work-family fit has two dimensions: work demands-family resources fit in which family-related resources are adequate to meet demands of the work role and family demands-work resources fit in which work-related resources are sufficient to satisfy family demands. Figure 7.2 presents a conceptual model that incorporates work-family fit as a linking mechanism. Within-domain demands and resources are expected to be differentially salient for the two dimensions of work-family fit. Within-domain work demands and within-domain family resources combine to influence work demands-family resources fit, whereas family demands and work resources are relevant for family demands-work resources fit. The extent to which enabling resources and psychological rewards in one domain meet or counteract the time-based and strain-based demands in the other domain determines the level of fit. For example, spouse and kin support may contribute to work demands-family resources fit by helping employees deal with work demands such as job pressure and insecurity. Job autonomy and meaningful work may increase family demands-work resources fit by making it easier for individuals to address strain-based family demands emanating from spouse, children, or kin.

In contrast to within-domain demands and resources, work-based and family-based boundary-spanning demands and resources are expected to be associated with both dimensions of fit. Boundary-spanning demands (e.g., com-

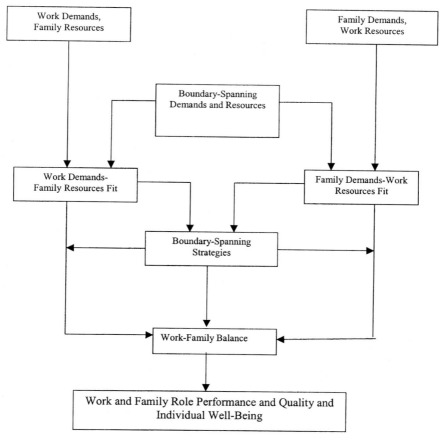

Figure 7.2.   The Conceptual Model with Work-Family Fit as a Linking Mechanism.
Source: Voydanoff (2005b).

muting time and overnight travel for work) limit the ability of individuals to make transitions between the work and family domains. This increases the level of demands both at work and at home, which decreases both types of fit. Boundary-spanning demands that create role blurring across domains (e.g., bringing work home and family interruptions and distractions at work) also decrease both types of fit by increasing both work and family demands. Boundary-spanning resources may have positive effects on both dimensions of work-family fit. Workplace policies that facilitate the coordination of work and family responsibilities and normative support for such policies provide additional resources to meet the demands of work and family life. For example, flexible work schedules may improve work demands-family resources fit by adjusting the timing of work, thereby improving the match between a work demand and a family's ability to meet the demand. Flexible schedules also may facilitate a family's ability to care for children or other relatives, thereby increasing family demands-work resources fit.

The ways in which work and family demands and resources combine to influence the two types of work-family fit have not been explored. As with the direct effects of work and family demands on role performance and quality and individual well-being, it is possible that demands and resources combine additively to influence work-family fit. In this case, low work (family) demands and high family (work) resources would be associated with work demands-family resources fit (family demands-work resources fit). For example, such an independent compensating effect would occur if relatively short work hours and high spouse support were associated with high work demands-family resources fit. In addition, demands and resources may have interactive effects on fit such that a work (family) resource would buffer the negative effects of a family (work) demand on fit. For example, a buffering effect would occur if the negative relationship between long hours and work demands-family resources fit were reduced for those with high spouse support.

Assessing work-family fit. Studies of person-environment fit in the workplace have used three methods of measuring perceived fit—the atomistic, molecular, and molar approaches (Edwards, Cable, Williamson, Lambert, & Shipp, 2006). In the atomistic approach, aspects of the perceived environment and perceived person are measured separately and combined in some way, for example, difference scores. The molecular approach directly assesses the perceived discrepancy between dimensions of the perceived environment and the perceived person, for example, by asking whether a job requires more (or less) training than the individual has. The molar approach is a direct assessment of perceived fit, for example, a rating of the extent to which an individual's training is a good fit with the requirements of the job. In addition, one may assess overall atomistic, molecular, or perceived fit by using summary judgments, for example, by asking about the overall fit between the demands of the job and the abilities of the person.

Although the measurement of work-family fit is quite undeveloped, a few researchers have taken initial steps. Drawing on person-environment fit theory, Pittman (1994) suggested that family members weigh the demands on them with the benefits that the job and work organization provide. His measure, which focused on family demands-work resources fit, asked questions about the extent to which the military provides a good environment for child-drearing, satisfaction with living conditions, and organizational sensitivity to the needs of family members. Expanding on this approach, DeBord, Canu, and Kerpelman (2000) and Teng (1999) proposed a two-dimensional model of work-family fit. The first dimension conceives of fit as the congruence of work demands with family abilities or expectations regarding meeting work demands, whereas the second dimension is the match of work supplies or rewards with family needs or goals. Teng's measure of work demands-family abilities fit assessed concern about several work demands, whether family members feel these demands are more difficult than expected, and how well family members are dealing with the demands. The work rewards-family needs items asked how well the rewards and benefits of the job meet individual and family needs.

In addition, two other studies have presented measures of family demands-work resources fit. Barnett, Gareis, and Brennan (1999) considered fit in terms of the ability of employees to develop and optimize strategies to meet family needs in the workplace. They measured fit by asking how well the number and distribution of physicians' and their partners' work hours and work-schedule flexibility meet their own, their partners', and their children's needs. More recently, Barnett and Gareis (2006) conceptualized community resource fit as the extent to which community resources are available and well-matched to the needs of families. They developed six subscales to measure community resource fit. These subscales address work resources, school resources, after-school programs, and public, school, and after-school transportation.

Teng's (1999) measure is the most comprehensive; however, the measures of the two types of fit are not comparable. The measure of work demands-family abilities fit consists of the additive combination of work demands and family abilities, whereas the work rewards-family needs measure is a direct appraisal of how well job rewards and benefits meet individual and family needs. Other measures assess specific aspects of family demands-work resources fit such as the extent to which work hours, work schedule, and job flexibility meet individual and family needs (Barnett et al., 1999; Barnett & Gareis, 2006) or whether the military is responsive to family needs (Pittman, 1994).

Despite the limited availability of measures of work-family fit, previous measures provide a place to start in the development of more precise and comprehensive measures. Measurement approaches used in the study of person-environment fit in the work domain also are useful. It is essential that measures directly address the extent to which resources in one domain address demands in the other domain. This can be done by using either the molecular or the molar approaches to person-environment fit. In the molecular approach, questions would ask individuals to compare their level of resources in one domain to the level needed to meet demands in the other domain. For example, a question could ask "How much help is available (do you receive) from your supervisor to meet your family's needs? ($+2$ = much more than I need, $+1$ = somewhat more than I need, 0 = about what I need, -1 = somewhat less than I need, -2 = much less than I need)." Questions using the molar approach would address the level of fit by asking about the extent to which resources in one domain meet demands in the other domain. For example, "How much does support from your spouse help you handle the demands from your job? (1 = not at all, 2 = not too much, 3 = somewhat, 4 = a lot)." The Teng (1999) measure of work rewards-family measure follows this approach by asking how well the following rewards and benefits of the job meet family needs: income, other financial benefits, support from workers and supervisors, and amount of control over working conditions. Items assessing a range of enabling resources, psychological rewards, and boundary-spanning resources could be combined into scales using the molecular and molar approaches. Molecular and molar global assessments also could be made, for example, "How much help is available (do you receive) from members of your family to meet the demands of your job?" or "How much do the rewards and benefits of your job help you meet your family's needs?"

Such measures of work-family fit would differ from assessments of work-family conflict and facilitation in important respects. Although demands are expected to be relatively strongly associated with work-family conflict and resources with work-family facilitation, work-family fit is derived from a combination of demands and resources. Work-family conflict and facilitation are components of work-family fit in that the decrease of resources associated with conflict and the increase of resources associated with facilitation may affect the extent to which work (family) resources are adequate to meet family (work) demands. Thus, work-family fit is a more comprehensive linking mechanism than work-family conflict and facilitation that requires more complex measurement instruments.

Work-Family Balance

A conceptualization of work-family balance. The fourth and final linking mechanism is work-family balance. Some scholars have viewed work-family balance in terms of work-family conflict and facilitation. They have defined work-family balance as the absence of work-family conflict or as low levels of work-family conflict and high levels of work-family facilitation (Voydanoff, 2007). Tetrick and Buffardi (2006) refer to work-to-family conflict, family-to-work conflict, work-to-family facilitation and family-to-work facilitation as the four components of work-family balance. Either reducing work-family conflict or increasing work-family facilitation increases balance. Conceptually, however, it makes more sense to view work-family conflict and facilitation as precursors of work-family balance. Figure 7.1 proposes that demands and resources influence work-family conflict and facilitation, which in turn are related to work-family balance, either directly or through the effects of boundary-spanning strategies. Similarly, Greenhaus and Allen (in press) present a model in which work and family experiences and dispositional characteristics are associated with work-family conflict and work-family facilitation, which in turn are related to the elements of work-family balance, that is, effectiveness and fulfillment in work and family roles and feelings of work-family balance. A recent study has supported parts of these models (Butler, Bass, & Grzywacz, this volume).

Extending this approach, this chapter defines work-family balance as a form of inter-role congruence in which work and family resources are sufficient to meet work and family demands such that participation is effective in both domains. Figure 7.2 proposes that work and family demands and resources influence the two dimensions of work-family fit, which result in work-family balance, either directly or through the use of boundary-spanning strategies. Thus, work-family balance combines the extent to which family resources are adequate to meet work demands and the extent to which work resources meet family demands with the effects of boundary-spanning strategies to yield an overall appraisal of the level of harmony, equilibrium, and integration of work and family life. Although the model proposes that the two dimensions of work-family fit have additive effects on work-family balance, the relative importance of the two dimensions may vary among individuals. The extent to which the work or family role is relatively salient may influence these relationships. (See Greenhaus & Allen, in press, for a conceptualization of work-family balance that incorporates domain salience as part of the definition of balance.)

The premise of a direct relationship between fit and balance is consistent with the model of Edwards and Rothbard (2005), who propose that work and family person-environment fit have additive effects on strain. Work-family fit provides a more inclusive precursor of work-family balance than conflict and facilitation do. Work-family fit is a direct assessment of the extent to which resources are adequate to meet demands, whereas conflict and facilitation reference only the effects of demands and resources respectively on cross-domain role performance and quality.

Assessing work-family balance. Most studies of work-family balance use a single-item measure that assesses individual appraisals regarding the level of satisfaction or success with the balance between work and family life or the balance of work and family demands or responsibilities. Such measures provide useful global assessments of work-family balance. When the question references balancing work and family demands or responsibilities rather than overall work and family life, however, the consideration of resources as part of the process is implied but not directly considered. Single-item global measures of work-family balance as conceptualized here might read: "How much do the rewards and support from your job and family help you meet demands at work and at home—not at all, not too much, somewhat, a lot?" or "How often do you have enough help and support from your job and family so that you can adequately perform your duties at home and work—never, sometimes, often, all the time?"

It is encouraging to note that multi-item scales of work-family balance are under development. Some are more relevant to the demands and resources approach presented in this chapter than others are, however. Perhaps the most compatible are those that assess individual abilities to perform activities in both the work and family domains effectively. For example, the Valcour (2007) scale assesses the level of satisfaction with the way respondents divide their time and attention between work and personal or family life, how well their work and personal or family life fit together, their ability to balance the needs of their job with their personal or family life, and their opportunity to perform their job well and yet be able to perform home-related duties adequately. A scale being developed by Joplin, Shaffer, Lau, and Francesco (2003) includes subscales measuring equilibrium (I feel fulfilled in all aspects of my life), control (e.g., I manage all aspects of my life effectively), and synchrony (My personal life and my work life are complementary). In addition, the Hill, Martinson, Ferris, and Baker (2004) scale contains items on the extent to which work resources such as flexibility and time away from work are sufficient to maintain balance as well as questions regarding overall balance. These measures provide an overall assessment or appraisal of the extent to which the balance of work and family demands and resources permits adequate role performance in work and family life.

Some scholars who conceive of work-family fit and balance as consisting of work-family conflict and facilitation use measures of work-to-family conflict, family-to-work conflict, work-to-family facilitation, and family-to-work facilitation as indicators of fit and balance (Tetrick & Buffardi, 2006). No independent measures of work-family fit and balance are used, thus confounding fit and balance with conflict and facilitation. This chapter argues that the sources and consequences of work-family fit and balance are better understood when specific demands and resources are examined rather than relying on appraisals of conflict and facilitation as representations of fit and balance. When measures of conflict and facilitation are used as indicators of fit, the analysis is one step removed from the demands and resources associated with work and family roles (e.g., it is not clear which demands are creating the conflict or which resources are associated with facilitation).

Work-Family Balance and Outcomes

The final stage of the conceptual models proposes that work-family balance is positively associated with work, family, and community role performance and quality and individual well-being. A global assessment of balance between the work and family domains is posited to improve performance and quality in both domains as well as to have positive effects on community role performance and quality and individual well-being. It also is possible that role performance is a precursor of role quality. Greenhaus and Powell (2006) propose that performing well in a role is likely to be reflected in increased positive affect.

CHANGING DEMANDS AND RESOURCES THROUGH BOUNDARY-SPANNING STRATEGIES

A Conceptualization of Work-Family Boundary-Spanning Strategies

In the previous section, linking mechanisms were viewed as primary cognitive appraisals, that is, the process of deciding whether situations are positive, stressful, or irrelevant with regard to well-being. Primary appraisal is the initial step in a process that links demands and resources to individual outcomes. A primary appraisal asks the question, "Am I in trouble or being benefited, now or in the future, and in what way?" An accompanying question is "What if anything can be done about it?" (Folkman & Lazarus, 1984: 31). This second question is referred to as secondary appraisal. Secondary appraisal encompasses ways in which to address stressful primary appraisals by considering the relative availability and potential effectiveness of various coping options. These appraisal processes operate hand in hand with coping, which is defined as "constantly changing cognitive and behavioral efforts to manage specific external and/or internal demands that are appraised as taxing or exceeding the resources of the person" (p. 203). Coping can be of two interrelated forms. Problem-focused coping is the mobilization of actions to reduce or eliminate the problem, whereas emotion-focused coping is aimed at regulating the emotions associated with the stressful situation.

The analysis of work-family boundary-spanning strategies extends this conceptualization by applying it to processes that mediate and moderate the effects of work and family demands and resources on work and family role performance and quality and individual well-being. Work-family boundary-spanning strategies are a subset of problem-focused coping behaviors that specifically address work and family demands and resources. They are actions taken by individuals and families to reduce or eliminate a perceived lack of congruence between work and family demands and resources. Individuals also may use boundary-spanning strategies to further improve a relatively high level of congruence between demands and resources.

The model presented in Figure 7.2 indicates that boundary-spanning strategies may mediate and moderate relationships between work-family fit and work-family balance. Similar processes are expected for work-family conflict and facilitation. (See Figure 7.1.) Thus, linking mechanisms associated with primary appraisal and boundary-spanning strategies derived from secondary appraisal and coping form an integrated process that links demands and resources with outcomes. The model relates to routines that individuals and families adopt to meet challenges that occur over time rather than specific daily incidents that are not covered by previously established routines. (See Powell & Greenhaus, 2006, for an analysis of the management of specific incidents of work-family conflict.)

Boundary-spanning strategies can address an incongruence between demands and resources in two ways—by reducing demands or increasing resources. Table 7.2 presents a relatively comprehensive list of possible strategies. Some strategies change work and family roles so that within-domain and boundary-spanning demands are reduced. When demands are reduced in one domain, resources in the other domain are better able to meet these lowered demands. Strategies that may reduce within-domain work demands include cutting work hours and refusing overtime, changing work schedules, and reducing work responsibilities, whereas within-domain family demands may be addressed by spending less time with family members, limiting child and elder care and household work, and improving relationships with family members. Work- and family-based boundary-spanning demands may be reduced by limiting overnight travel for work, reducing commuting time, and establishing firmer work-family boundaries.

Extant research on boundary-spanning strategies has focused almost exclusively on the boundary-spanning strategies just described. However, other strategies may increase within-domain and boundary-spanning resources. Additional resources in one domain make it easier for individuals and families to meet demands in another domain. Strategies that may increase within-domain resources include taking a more enriching or rewarding job, gaining job

Table 7.2.   Work and Family Boundary-Spanning Strategies

	Work	Family
Reduce within-domain demands		
Time-based demands	Cut work hours Refuse overtime Change work schedule	Spend less time with spouse and family Limit childbearing Spend less time caring for children and elderly relatives Do less household work
Strain-based demands	Take less demanding job Refuse promotions Refuse work assignments	Improve relationships with spouse, children, and elderly relatives Reduce commuting time
Reduce boundary-spanning demands		
Transitions	Refuse or limit overnight travel Reduce commuting time	Establish work-family boundaries
Role Blurring	Establish work-family boundaries	
Increase within-domain resources		
Enabling resources	Take more enriching job Become self-employed	Improve family adaptability and cohesion Use or improve family and kin support Improve meaning, pride, and respect within the family

(contiued)

Table 7.2. (*continued*)

	Work	Family
Psychological rewards	Take more rewarding job Become self-employed	
Increase boundary-spanning resources		
Work supports	Use available work support policies Take job with work support policies	Hire child and elder care services Hire household services Spouse and kin do more child and elder care and household work Increase employment of family members Use or improve work-family support
Family supports	Use available family support policies Take job with family support policies	
Normative support	Use available supervisor work-family support and supportive work-family culture Take job with supervisor work-family support and supportive work-family culture	

flexibility and rewards by becoming self-employed, using family and kin support, and improving family adaptation and cohesion. Although they generally have not been considered as such in the literature (but see Voydanoff, 2002), the use of available work supports, family supports, and normative support are work-based boundary-spanning strategies because they increase work-based boundary-spanning resources. Family-based boundary-spanning resources can be expanded by hiring child and elder care and household services, having family members do more paid work or dependent care and household work, and using or improving work-family support from family members.

Assessing the Effectiveness of Boundary-Spanning Strategies

There is limited empirical support for the proposition that boundary-spanning strategies mediate or moderate the effects of work-family conflict, facilitation, or fit on work-family balance. This is due partly to a dearth of studies; however, other issues are involved. First, cross-sectional studies may confound preventing with reducing work-family conflict and misfit and, second, some strategies may not be effective in reducing conflict and misfit.

The use of boundary-spanning strategies is inherently part of a temporal process, which has important implications for causal order in the model. Depending on the timing, these actions may prevent work-family misfit (or conflict) in the first place. Thus, a given strategy can have a negative relationship to work-family misfit (a preventive effect), can be positively related to work-family balance (a therapeutic effect), or can have a buffering effect on the relationship between work-family fit and work-family balance (Bowen, 1998). Bowen's study of leader support documented that all three types of relationships can exist simultaneously. (See Greenhaus & Parasuraman, 1994, for a comparable approach that viewed social support as stress-preventing, health-sustaining, and buffering in relation to stress and well-being.)

Individuals and families may prevent work-family conflict and misfit and enhance work-family facilitation by limiting work and family demands and/or enhancing resources such that a satisfactory congruence between demands and resources exists. In addition, individuals and families can take preventive action by using boundary-spanning strategies when they anticipate increased demands such as the birth of a child or additional responsibilities in a new or existing job. These strategies could either reduce demands or increase resources. For example, when a birth is expected, an individual may decide to work part-time job for a period of time. Or an individual may obtain additional assistance with child or elder care from family members or hired services in preparation for increased responsibilities at work.

A therapeutic effect occurs when individuals and families use boundary-spanning strategies to reduce the negative effects of work-family misfit (or conflict) on work-family balance. Thus, when individuals experience work-family misfit, they respond by using strategies that either reduce demands or increase resources. Thus, at the beginning of this process, misfit is positively related to the use of boundary-spanning strategies. If the strategies are effective, they then become negatively associated with misfit. Thus, cross-sectional research may confound the preventive use of strategies and the effective use of strategies over time with the initial association between experiencing misfit and the use of strategies. Longitudinal or experimental study designs are required to assess the temporal processes involved with the use of boundary-spanning strategies. (See Allen & Shockley, in press, and van Steenbergen, Ellemers, & Mooijaart, in press, for similar arguments.)

Boundary-spanning strategies also may moderate the effects of work-family misfit (or conflict) on balance by buffering the negative effects of misfit on balance. In this situation, the negative relationship between misfit and balance decreases when boundary-spanning strategies are used. For example, the negative relationship between work-family misfit and balance may be weaker for those who cut work hours, increase work-family support, or use community services such as after-school programs. Thus, the negative relationship between misfit and balance exists only for those who do not use boundary-spanning strategies.

In addition, boundary-spanning strategies may have feedback effects on the work-family interface. The successful use of these strategies can change work and family demands and resources such that they can promote work-family fit. For example, reducing work hours or working at home may facilitate the performance of family roles, thereby leading to work-family fit.

Second, boundary-spanning strategies may not always be effective in reducing work and family demands or increasing work and family resources. In some situations, the demands are too high for the available strategies to reduce effectively. For example, a qualitative study (Roy, Tubbs, & Burton, 2004) describes the proactive use of strategies that stagger and decrease obligations and expand resources among low-income families. However, when demands are extremely high, the use of these strategies is accompanied by psychological and physical health costs.

In addition, some strategies are generally more effective than others. Voydanoff's (2005a) review revealed that family support policies generally are negatively associated with work-family conflict, whereas work support policies are not. Family support policies reduce the overall amount of time spent in paid work through time off from work or part-time work; work support policies provide schedule flexibility or dependent care without reducing the overall work load. Others have suggested that normative support though work-family support from supervisors and a supportive work-family culture are more effective than formal work or family support policies (van Steenbergen et. al., this volume).

Some have suggested that strategies are effective only when certain conditions are met, for example, limiting work hours or job-related travel may reduce work-family misfit if a person's or family's career goals also are modified but may not if the changes are seen as a necessary but not desired adjustment to work-family role misfit. Grzywacz, Jones, and Casey (this volume) concluded that control over timing is critical for policies such as flextime to be effective.

Some strategies may be effective in relation to one linking mechanism but not another. Powell and Greenhaus (2007) suggest that individuals may prefer to segment work and family roles in order to prevent work-family conflict. However, their study indicates that a preference for segmentation also limits work-family facilitation because it may prevent the transfer of resources from one domain to another. To further our understanding of the role of boundary-spanning strategies in reducing the effects of work-family conflict and misfit on balance and individual, work, and family outcomes, it is necessary to conduct studies that examine the ways in which specific boundary-spanning resources operate over time.

CONCLUSION

Drawing on a demands and resources approach, this chapter presents and elaborates two conceptual models that propose linkages between work and family demands and resources and work and family role performance and quality and individual well-being. The first suggests that within-domain demands and boundary-spanning demands and resources influence work-family conflict, whereas within-domain resources and boundary-spanning demands and resources affect work-family facilitation. The second posits that work, family, and boundary-spanning demands and resources combine to create two dimensions of work-family fit. Work demands-family resources fit derives from work demands, family resources, and boundary-spanning demands and resources, whereas family demands-work resources fit results from family demands, work resources, and boundary-spanning demands and resources. Work-family conflict and facilitation and the two dimensions of work-family fit combine with boundary-spanning strategies to influence work-family balance. Work-family balance then affects work and family role performance and quality and individual well-being.

These relatively comprehensive models reveal the importance of examining not only the demands that may reduce work-family conflict, fit, and balance but also the resources that may enhance work-family facilitation, fit, and balance. Thus, work-family policies and programs should include the enhancement of work, family, and boundary-spanning resources as well as the reduction of work, family, and boundary-spanning demands. Both can occur either by developing policies and programs that reduce demands and increasing resources independently (e.g., by reducing work hours or increasing job autonomy) or by designing policies that address demands and resources jointly (e.g., by creating a supportive work-family culture that focuses on flexibility in meeting family demands such as caregiving for children or parents). In addition, boundary-spanning strategies can be effective in reducing work-family conflict and misfit by decreasing work and family demands and increasing work and family resources.

Obviously, the model is an oversimplification of the components and the mechanisms linking them to each other. Both need further elaboration in empirical tests of the model. The most critical need is to further specify the model as a temporal process. This requires a methodology that is qualitative, at least initially, and longitudinal. Particular aspects of the work-family interface, that is specific combinations of work and family demands and resources, need to be studied over time. Tracking the effects of a change in either work or family demands and resources on responses to the work-family interface would be useful, for example, a major promotion, changes in work hours or scheduling, or the birth of a child. (See, for example, the Holtzman and Glass, 1999, longitudinal study of the factors associated with changes in job satisfaction following the birth of a child). Longitudinal data also are needed to address the thorny problems mentioned above, namely, the role of preventive versus therapeutic boundary-spanning strategies. A longitudinal approach can be extended further by considering responses to the work-family interface over the life course. For example, Kofodimos (1990) discussed a "spiraling imbalance" between work and family over the careers of executives as they increasingly make decisions favoring work over family responsibilities.

The models presented here are based on our current state of knowledge. This knowledge base is inadequate for the construction and presentation of a completely developed model. Additional research undoubtedly will result in revisions of the conceptual model. Furthermore, improved model development requires better measures of work-family linking mechanisms and boundary-spanning strategies and more methodologically sophisticated studies that examine the relationships proposed in the model.

NOTE

Patricia Voydanoff, Ph.D., is a senior research associate at the Fitz Center for Leadership in Community, University of Dayton. Address correspondence to Patricia Voydanoff, Fitz Center for Leadership in Community, Dayton, OH 45469-1445; Phone: 937-229-4614; Email: Patricia.Voydanoff@notes.udayton.edu.

REFERENCES

Allen, T. D., & Shockley, K. (in press). Flexible work arrangements: Help or hype? In D. R. Crane & E. J. Hill (Eds.), *Handbook of families and work*. Lanham, MD: University Press of America.

Barnett, R. C., & Gareis, K. C. (2006). Antecedents and correlates of parental after-school stress. *American Behavioral Scientist, 49,* 1382–1399.

Barnett, R. C., Gareis, K. C., & Brennan, R. T. (1999). Fit as a mediator of the relationship between work hours and burnout. *Journal of Occupational Health Psychology, 4,* 307–317.

Bellavia, G. M., & Frone, M. R. (2005). Work-family conflict. In J. Barling, E. K. Kelloway, & M. R. Frone (Eds.), *Handbook of work stress* (pp. 113–147). Thousand Oaks: Sage.

Bowen, G. L. (1998). Effects of leader support in the work unit on the relationship between work spillover and family adaptation. *Journal of Family and Economic Issues, 19,* 25–52.

Butler, A. B., Bass, B. L., & Grzywacz, J. G. (in press). Job demands, spouse support, and work-family balance. In D. R. Crane & E. J. Hill (Eds.), *Handbook of families and work*. Lanham, MD: University Press of America.

Carlson, D. S., Kacmar, K. M., Wayne, J. H., & Grzywacz, J. G. (2006). Measuring the positive side of the work-family interface. *Journal of Vocational Behavior, 68,* 131–164.

Carlson, D. S., Kacmar, K. M., & Williams, L. J. (2000). Construction and initial validation of a multidimensional measure of work-family conflict. *Journal of Vocational Behavior, 56,* 249–276.

Clark, S. C. (2000). Work/family border theory. *Human Relations, 53,* 747–770.

DeBord, K., Canu, R. G., & Kerpelman, J. (2000). Understanding work-family fit for single parents moving from welfare to work. *Social Work, 45,* 313–324.

de Lange, A. H., Taris, T. W., Kompier, M. A. J., & Houtman, I. L. D. (2003). "The *very* best of the millennium": Longitudinal research and the demand-control-(support) model. *Journal of Occupational Health Psychology, 8,* 283–305.

Edwards, J. R., Cable, D. M., Williamson, I. O., Lambert, L. S., & Shipp, A. J. (2006). The phenomenology of fit. *Journal of Applied Psychology, 91,* 802–827.

Edwards, J. R., & Rothbard, N. P. (2005). Work and family stress and well-being. In E. E. Kossek & S. J. Lambert (Eds.), *Work and life integration* (pp. 211–242). Mahwah, NJ: Erlbaum.

Greenhaus, J. H., & Allen, T. D. (2008). Work-family balance: Exploration of a concept. Manuscript submitted for publication.

Greenhaus J. H., & Beutell, N. J. (1985). Sources of conflict between work and family roles. *Academy of Management Journal, 10,* 76–88.

Greenhaus, J. H., & Parasuraman, S. (1994). Work-family conflict, social support and well-being. In M. J. Davidson and R. J. Burke (Eds.), *Women in Management: Current Research Issues* (pp. 213–229). London: Paul Chapman Publishing.

Greenhaus, J. H., & Powell, G. N. (2006). When work and family are allies. *Academy of Management Review.31,* 72–92.

Grzywacz, J. G., Jones, F. A., & Casey, P. R. (in press). Workplace flexibility. In D. R. Crane & E. J. Hill (Eds.), *Handbook of families and work.* Lanham, MD: University Press of America.

Grzywacz, J. G., & Marks, N. F. (2000). Reconceptualizing the work-family interface. *Journal of Occupational Health Psychology, 5,* 111–126.

Hanson, G. C., Hammer, L. B., & Colton, C. L. (2006). Development and validation of a multidimensional scale of perceived work-family positive spillover, *Journal of Occupational Health Psychology, 11,* 249–265.

Hill, E. J., Allen, S., Jacob, J., Bair, A. F., Bikhazi, S. L., Cox, A., Martinengo, G., Trost, T., Walker, E. (in press). Work-family facilitation. In D. R. Crane & E. J. Hill (Eds.), *Handbook of families and work.* Lanham, MD: University Press of America.

Hill, E. J., Martinson, V. K., Ferris, M., & Baker, R. Z. (2004). Beyond the mommy track. *Journal of Family and Economic Issues, 25,* 121–136.

Holtzman, M., & Glass, J. (1999). Explaining changes in mothers' job satisfaction following childbirth. *Work and Occupations, 26,* 365–404.

Joplin, J. R. W., Shaffer, M. A., Lau, T., & Francesco, A. M. (2003, August). Life balance: Developing and validating a cross-cultural model. Paper presented at the Annual Meeting of the Academy of Management, Seattle, WA.

Kofodimos, J. R. (1990). Why executives lose their balance. *Organizational Dynamics, 19,* 58–73.

Lazarus, R. S., & Folkman, S. (1984). *Stress, appraisal, and coping.* New York: Springer.

MacDermid, S. M. (2005). (Re)considering conflict between work and family. In E. E. Kossek & S. J. Lambert (Eds.). *Work and life integration* (p. 40). Mahwah, NJ: Erlbaum.

Marks, S. R. (1977). Multiples roles and role strain. *American Sociological Review, 42,* 921–936.

Netemeyer, R. G., Boles, J. S., & McMurrian, R. (1996). Development and validation of work-family conflict and family-work conflict scales. *Journal of Applied Psychology, 81,* 400–410.

Nippert-Eng, C. E. (1996). *Home and work.* Chicago: University of Chicago Press.

Patterson, J. M. (2002). Integrating family resilience and family stress theory. *Journal of Marriage and Family, 64,* 349–360.

Piotrkowski, C. (1979). *Work and the family system.* New York: Free Press.

Pittman, J. F. (1994). Work/family fit as a mediator of work factors on marital tension. *Human Relations, 47,* 183–209.

Powell, G. N., & Greenhaus, J. H. (2006). Managing incidents of work-family conflict. *Human Relations, 59,* 1179–1212.

Powell, G. N., & Greenhaus, J. H. (2007, August). Influence of sex, gender self-scheme, and segmentation preferences on work-to-family enrichment. Paper presented at the annual meeting of the Academy of Management, Philadelphia.

Rothbard, N. P. (2001). Enriching or depleting? The dynamics of engagement in work and family roles. *Administrative Science Quarterly, 46,* 655–684.

Roy, K. M., Tubbs, C. Y., & Burton, L. M. (2004). Don't have no time: Rhythms and the organization of time for low-income families. *Family Relations, 53,* 168–178.

Sieber, S. D. (1974). Toward a theory of role accumulation. *American Sociological Review, 39,* 567–578.

Siegrist, J. (1998). Adverse health effects of effort-reward imbalance at work. In C. L. Cooper (Ed.), *Theories of organizational stress* (pp. 190–204). New York: Oxford University Press.

Teng, W. (1999). *Assessing the work-family interface.* Unpublished doctoral dissertation, Auburn University, Auburn, AL.

Tetrick, L. E., & Buffardi, L. C. (2006). Measurement issues in research on the work-home interface. In F. Jones, R. J. Burke, & M. Westman (Eds.), *Work-life balance: A psychological perspective* (pp. 90–114). Hove, UK: Psychology Press.

Valcour, M. (2007). Work-based resources and work-family balance. *Journal of Applied Psychology, 92,* 1512–1523.

van der Doef, M., & Maes, S. (1999). The job demand-control (-support) model and psychological well-being: A review of 20 years of empirical research. *Work & Stress, 13,* 87–114.

van Steenbergen, E. F., Ellemers, N., & Mooijaart, A. (in press). Combining work and family. In D. R. Crane & E. J. Hill (Eds.), *Handbook of families and work.* Lanham, MD: University Press of America.

Voydanoff, P. (2002). Linkages between the work-family interface and work, family, and individual outcomes. *Journal of Family Issues, 23,* 138–164.

––––– (2004). The effects of work demands and resources on work-to-family conflict and facilitation. *Journal of Marriage and Family, 66,* 398–412.

––––– (2005a). Consequences of boundary-spanning demands and resources for work-family conflict and perceived stress. *Journal of Occupational Health Psychology, 10,* 491-503.

––––– (2005b). Toward a conceptualization of work-family fit and balance: A demands and resources approach. *Journal of Marriage and Family, 67,* 822–836.

–––––. (2007). *Work, family, and community: Exploring interconnections.* Mahwah, NJ: Erlbaum.

––––– (2008). A conceptual model of the work-family interface. In K. Korabik, D. S. Lero, & D. L. Whitehead (Eds.), *Handbook of work-family integration* (pp. 37–55). New York: Elsevier.

Chapter Eight

Work and Family Health in a Global Context

by S. Jody Heymann

This chapter will discuss findings from the Project on Global Working Families in the context of changing global demographics. Qualitative interviews of more than one thousand caregivers have been conducted in six countries and quantitative analyses have been conducted of national surveys covering 55,000 households in seven countries. Striking commonalities are evident across countries and levels of development. This chapter will also discuss some of the public policies that can help protect working families from a range of problems—from exploitative working conditions to caregiving crises to more common challenges such as time conflicts.

DRAMATIC TRANSFORMATIONS

Gabriela Saavedra's home in Tegucigalpa, Honduras, initially crudely built with scrap wood, was visibly crumbling when we met her.[1] When Gabriela was in elementary school, she and her three siblings inherited the house after their mother died of uterine cancer that had gone undiagnosed and untreated for too long. At nineteen years old, Gabriela was renting out the eight-foot-wide downstairs of the shack, although "renting out" was a euphemism: the woman downstairs was dying of uterine cancer herself and had not been able to pay rent for months. Kicking her out or demanding rent was an impossible prospect for Gabriela, who had witnessed her own mother's painful death. To get to Gabriela's room in the shack, you had to climb a broken wooden ladder propped against an outside wall—a feat she had to undertake while carrying her 19-month-old toddler, Ana Daniel.

Lately, Ana Daniel had been battling repeated respiratory infections, a health problem for which she faced a heightened risk due to the early termination of breast-feeding; Gabriela had to return to work less than two months after her birth. Worried about her daughter's condition, Gabriela attempted to seal up any drafts by using cardboard to cover the bent wooden boards that served as her walls. Ana Daniel had not seen a doctor since Gabriela could not bring her to the clinic during the day due to her long work days in the factory and lack of leave, "Sometimes I would come back late from work, very tired, and she would be very sick, barely being able to breathe," Gabriela explained.

Sitting in a chair in a weathered Nike sweatshirt, Gabriela described her job at the sweatshop making clothes for exportation. She worked from 7:00 a.m. until at least 6:00 p.m., seven days a week. Many nights, with no prior notice, the Korean owners would mandate everyone stay until 9:00 or 11:00 p.m. On several occasions, employees had been required to work shifts until 5:00 the next morning, leaving no time for sleep before the morning commute back to the factory. It was made clear to Gabriela and the other workers that if they declined the overtime hours, they would lose their jobs.

Sleep deprivation created dangerous conditions for Gabriela at work. "I was sewing at 3:00 a.m., and I couldn't do it any more because I was so tired. I almost cut off a finger." She told us of others who had worked at the factory and suffered serious injuries due to extreme fatigue. Wages earned for this hazardous work during overtime hours were even lower than her usual pay. Gabriela noted, "I've heard that overtime at night should be paid at 200% of normal wages, but they pay only 75% [of normal wages]."

Despite working seven days a week (making 100 shirts an hour for 11 to 22 hour shifts), Gabriela earned only 400 lempiras, or 26 U.S. dollars a week. Food was expensive at the factory—$1.00 to $1.50 a meal—but the fifteen minutes allotted for a lunch break left no time for alternatives. Even if she ate the factory food only once during an excruciatingly long workday, Gabriela spent $7–$10 of her weekly salary on her own meals. Another $10 was used to pay for formula and diapers for her daughter. That left $6–$9 a week for any other necessities. Gabriela could not afford to lose any of the limited wages she earned, therefore she worked even when she was sick. She also worked when Ana Daniel was sick.

While her mother-in-law had initially helped to care for Ana Daniel, she stopped offering this help freely after the death of Gabriela's husband, Daniel. On his way home with a full two weeks' wages and a present for their daughter to celebrate a holiday for children, Daniel was attacked and murdered. Afterwards, Gabriela's mother-in-law would only care for Ana Daniel if Gabriela agreed to give the child up. Gabriela's stepmother had helped out for a time, but she too had to return to work. Not long before our interview,

Gabriela's ten-year-old stepsister had started caring for the toddler, but she was to return to school within weeks of our departure. Gabriela had no idea what she would do then.

When Gabriela was asked what one thing she would change in her life if she could, she answered without hesitation. She spoke at once—not of the condition of her home or of her poverty—but of caring for Ana Daniel: "I would like to work fewer hours. I would like to have someone who could take care of my daughter over here. And I would like to leave work earlier to be able to spend more time with her."

Despite her mother's devotion to her well-being, Ana Daniel did not have a chance at a healthy childhood if her mother continued to work in the sweatshop. Gabriela's pay was too low for them both to eat adequately. There was no money to repair the burned-out holes in the side of their shack or to fix the missing rungs on the ladder that could one day trip Ana Daniel and cause her to fall more than a dozen feet to the ground. There was not enough money to pay for water cleaned of the diarrhea-inducing pathogens that constitute one of the leading causes of malnutrition and death of children younger than five. Moreover, Gabriela's punishing work schedule left her no time to be a parent, and Ana Daniel was at risk of being locked alone at home with no one to care for her.

Gabriela and Ana Daniel are far from alone. Millions of parents labor under conditions that damage their children's lives, as well as their own. The anti-sweatshop movement has brought much-needed attention to the draconian conditions under which many adults must labor around the world, but globally we have turned a blind eye to the ways in which the devastating circumstances confronted by many adults are also ravaging their families.

INDELIBLE TRANSFORMATIONS

During the past fifty years, three distinct factors have led to major transformations of family life. These forces paradoxically have the potential to either lift families out of poverty or to compromise children's well-being. First, fathers and mothers worldwide have been increasingly drawn into the formal labor force—simultaneously providing more opportunities while creating new obstacles to caregiving. Globally, there are at least 900 million children being raised in households in which all adults work.[2] Second, urbanization has pulled nuclear families toward new job opportunities and away from extended-family support. Finally, these transformations have occurred in an era of increased economic globalization, which has increased access to lower-cost goods and services but also decreased workers' ability to bargain for decent wages and benefits.

The confluence of changes in labor force participation, urbanization, and the current form of globalization have raised critical new questions and concerns for families on a global scale: Have these transformations helped to ameliorate the poverty endured by parents and children around the world? If not, why not? With more adults working and struggling to earn enough to support their families, who will care for infants and toddlers? How will adults keep their jobs while caring for children sick with fever, diarrhea, or pneumonia? How can parents ensure that their young children receive essential preventive care such as immunizations, or receive breast milk, the best protection against infant malnutrition and illnesses frequent in poor nations around the world? Changes in the nature of work and family life are felt from Detroit to Delhi. Moreover, the lives of families across the planet are becoming more interdependent and the likelihood is increasing that parents and children in Great Britain and Gabon, the United States and the Ukraine, will either sink or swim together.

THE PROJECT ON GLOBAL WORKING FAMILIES

In order to capture the many ways in which these dramatic demographic changes are reshaping families and work around the world, my research team examined conditions in a wide variety of global settings. Our goal was to gain a better understanding of the differences and commonalities among the experiences of working adults and their families across national borders, social classes, occupations, genders, and ethnicities. While the selected countries share the marked demographic and labour transformations described above, they represent very different contexts geographically, politically, economically, and socially. Beyond representing different regions around the world, these countries also represent high-, medium-, and low-income nations; have economies driven variously by natural resource extraction, manufacturing, and services; and include democratic as well as socialist governments.

We analyzed large, nationally representative, closed-ended, publicly available household-level surveys of more than 55 thousand households in Botswana, Brazil, Mexico, Russia, South Africa, the United States, and Vietnam. In conjunction with this quantitative data analysis, we undertook more than one thousand qualitative, in-depth, open-ended interviews in Mexico, Botswana, Vietnam, the United States, Honduras, and Russia. We spoke with working families, employers, teachers, childcare providers, and healthcare providers. In order to understand how these experiences map onto the actual work protections in place in different countries, we went on to investigate how national-level public policies worldwide compare in meeting the needs of working families. In 180 nations, we compared available policies relevant to infant and toddler care, early education, care for school-age children, elder care, parental leave, and leave to care for other family needs.

It is clear from our research that around the world, in industrialized and developing countries alike, changes in working conditions are threatening children's health and development and the well-being of families. Equally clear is the fact that this does not have to be the case: solutions exist across countries and across the socioeconomic spectrum.

PROMOTING CHILDREN'S HEALTH: HOW DO WORKING CONDITIONS AFFECT PREVENTION?

The major global killers of children are preventable. Statistics on the millions of children worldwide who die needlessly of avoidable diseases, as well as the far greater number who live with preventable illnesses, injuries, and disabilities, are well known. Initiatives to increase rates of vaccination, breast-feeding, and preventive prenatal care, among other approaches, have been developed and launched. Many of these efforts could not be more crucial to the health of our world's children.

Although efforts are made to improve child health, a crucial hole in the safety net has been ignored. Prevention requires the time and active involvement of children's parents and caregivers to ensure, for example, that children receive immunizations on time, have access to clean water to prevent diarrhea, and receive life-saving treatment if they develop diarrhea or respiratory infections. Yet little or no attention has been paid to identifying who actually has the opportunity to care for children's health and safety and to the role parental working conditions play in the ability to provide this care.

Parents we interviewed around the world told us that their experiences at work eroded their children's health in ways ranging from children being unable to make needed doctors' appointments to children receiving inadequate preventative care or any care at all while sick. Thirty-five percent of the families we met in Botswana, 21% in Mexico, 41% in the United States, and 25% in Vietnam felt this way.

Breast-feeding. Breast-feeding provides a vital example of the importance of understanding parental working conditions. The four leading causes of death in children worldwide include problems related to delivery in the first month of life (20%), respiratory infections (18%), diarrhea (17%), and vaccine-preventable diseases (15%) (UNICEF, 2001). Breast-feeding is a major factor in the prevention of two of these four: diarrheal diseases and respiratory infections. Breast-feeding can dramatically reduce the risk of death from diarrheal diseases, a crucial consideration because in developing countries alone, two million children die from diarrheal diseases every year (WHO, 1998). In fact, breast-fed infants have significantly lower rates of gastrointestinal infections (Dewey, Heinig, & Nommsen-Rivers, 1995; Feachem & Koblinsky, 1984; Howie, Forsyth, Ogston, Clark, & Florey, 1990; Lepage, Munyakazi, & Hennart, 1982), respiratory tract infections (Cerqueiro, Murtagh, Halac, Avila, & Weissenbacher, 1990; Howie et al., 1990; Watkins, Leeder, & Corkhill, 1979; Wright, Holberg, Martinez, Morgan, & Taussig, 1989), otitis media (Aniansson et al., 1994; Duncan et al., 1993), meningitis (Arnold, Makintube, & Istre, 1993), and other infections (Cunningham, D.B. Jelliffee, & E.F. Jelliffee, 1991; Feachem & Koblinsky, 1984). Overall, the chances of early death are one and a half to five times less for children who are breast-fed (Feachem & Koblinsky, 1984; Habicht, DaVanzo, & Butz, 1986; Hobcraft, McDonald, & Rutstein, 1985; Jason, Nieburg, & Marks, 1984).

While the many benefits of breast-feeding are well established and while there is no inherent conflict between employment and breast-feeding, the working conditions of many employed mothers preclude adequate breast-feeding opportunities. New mothers often have to end breast-feeding dangerously early, at times without even being able to afford or obtain adequate nutritional substitutes for breast milk. When jobs do not guarantee maternity leave or breaks for breast-feeding during the workday, or if children are being cared for far from the workplace, breast-feeding is often impossible.

The family of Maria Gonzalez, who lived in Buenas Nuevas, Honduras, described an all-too-frequent experience. Their oldest daughter, twenty-three-year-old Leti Marta, had a job as a secretary. Leti earned the sole income to support her seven-month-old baby, Marcela, since the child's father had abandoned her during the pregnancy. Leti's job only allowed her forty-two days off after the birth, and Maria therefore helped to raise the infant. When the maternity leave ended, so did the breast-feeding. Leti tried to express milk, but she was unable to sustain this while working. Maria fed her granddaughter milk "from a can," but by the age of seven months, the little girl was anemic and pale as a ghost. Having been weaned too young, she suffered from acute malnutrition and was falling off the growth chart, weighing at seven months what she should have weighed at four.

An inherent incompatibility between breast-feeding and work is not the cause of children suffering from illnesses and dying prematurely when they are deprived of the protective benefits of breast milk. Employers and working mothers have demonstrated that when childcare is available near the workplace and when breaks are available for breast-feeding, mothers are able to successfully continue their jobs while breast-feeding their infants throughout the first year of life.

When employers make it feasible for parents to work while caring for their children, the ability to hold a job and breast-feed becomes a realistic practice in a diversity of settings. Mandipa Kazapula described her experience breast-feeding while working in Botswana. At 29 years old, Mandipa was the mother of three children between the ages of one and ten. She worked as a local police officer, but Mandipa's employer understood the importance of making it possible for her to care for her infant while working. Because of this, Mandipa explained, "I had a feeding hour at 11 o'clock [in the morning] so I could come home. In the evening I could come home and feed."

Halfway around the world from Mandipa's job as a police officer, Truong Thi Nhu Quynh was employed as a public-school teacher in Vietnam. She recounted how she breast-fed her son for eighteen months while at work:

> While my son was little. . . . while I was working, I often came home to nurse him every two classroom periods. Having done so, I felt near my son, although I went to work. The headmaster used to care for teachers in the school. By doing that, the teachers could work well. The assigned workload would never be four or five hours continuously, which would have made it impossible for me to go home to nurse my child. . . . I would teach two periods straight and then could go home. I would have to come back for more teaching, but that type of arrangement helped me nurse my child.

Immunizations, safe drinking water, and infectious diseases. Vaccinations provide another important example of a crucial and readily practicable method of preventing childhood illness and death. Yet immunization programs in many parts of the world are currently structured so that parents or other adult care providers must take time off from work to bring their children to clinics or physicians' offices for shots or be home during the day when immunization campaigns occur.

Dr. Marcelo Javaloyas was the director of a health clinic serving many of the neighborhoods we visited in Tegucigalpa. Dr. Javaloyas described how difficult it was to effectively immunize children in many of the working-poor households where parents lacked childcare. These parents had no way to take leave from work during the day to bring the children to the clinic. Moreover, when making home visits, doctors and nurses found countless children at home alone. There were no adults available to confirm which shots the children needed and the children were unable to locate their *carnets*, or immunization cards, making it impossible to administer the vaccinations.

Due to the difficult working conditions faced by parents in lower-income families, poor children are more likely to lack immunizations than those who are better-off economically—even when the vaccines are freely available.

Studies in Haiti, Indonesia, and the United States have all found that parents cite conflicts with work schedules as a significant barrier to getting their children immunized (Coreil, Augustin, Halsey, & Holt, 1994; Fielding, Cumberland, & Pettitt, 1994; Lannon et al., 1995; McCormick, Bartholomew, Lewis, Brown, & Hanson, 1997).

Work does not need to be an obstacle to child health. Even the provision of very basic benefits, such as paid leave and flexibility, would allow parents the opportunity to bring their children for immunizations and other essential preventive care. Immunization campaigns could extend to cover the children of parents working weekday shifts if they occurred on weekdays in childcare centers and preschools or in clinics on weekends or evenings.

Beyond immunizations, Dr. Javaloyas told us how the lack of available adults increases the chances that children will suffer repeated infections:

> A boy of one year of age comes to the health center. The doctor who sees him finds out that the medical record at age one is extensive, and that attracts his attention. He starts going through it, and he realizes that the kid has had diarrhea problems. He then checks that the diarrhea problems started at six months of age. The doctor then asks the mom if she breast-fed the kid. She says that she did, but only for the first six months. That means that for that time the kid was better protected. . . . Then the doctor asks: "After six months, who was taking care of the child?" "My ten year old daughter." "How many children live at home?" "Six."

What it takes to prevent diarrhea is well understood. Beyond breastmilk, children need access to safe drinking water. The most straightforward way to ensure this is either through indoor plumbing or outdoor standpipes that deliver water free of microbes. In areas of the world where water is drawn directly from rivers or streams and where water from pipes still carries bacteria, solutions such as boiling water and peeling or cooking fruits and vegetables can eliminate most sources of diarrhea. In order to do these basic things, however, adults need to have adequate time; safe water and food preparation takes a great deal longer when, for example, fuel must be gathered in order to boil water. As a global community, we have been well aware of these facts for a long time but have failed to look at the feasibility of creating circumstances that would allow adults in poor countries to take these primary precautions for the health of their children.

Injuries. Preventing injury as well as illness requires that adults are available to care for children. For the families we interviewed, the rates of accidents occurring while parents were at work were high in all countries due to the inadequate availability of care. Children experienced accidents or emergencies while parents were at work in 53% of the families we spoke with in

Botswana, in 47% of the families we interviewed in Mexico, and in 38% of those we interviewed in Vietnam.

Injury rates skyrocket when children are left home alone or in the care of other children. In Villa Franca, one of the poorer neighborhoods high on the hills surrounding Tegucigalpa, Eva Martinez raised five children alone on the small earnings she made washing and ironing the clothes of other families. Every day, she went from house to house in another poor neighborhood asking how she could help families for the minimal amount of money they could afford to pay her. Her earnings barely fed and clothed her children and left no income to pay for childcare. Eva had no choice but to leave her children alone when she went out in search of work.

She spoke to us about the crises that occurred when her children went without any adult supervision. Eva's son was only seven and was left watching her then 3- year-old daughter. One afternoon, the two went off alone to buy some food. Her daughter fell down one of the hillside escarpments surrounding the city and broke her leg. On another occasion, a different daughter cut off the tip off her finger trying to prepare food. She sliced all the way through the nerves, damaging them irreparably. Yet another time, when all four daughters had been left alone with her oldest son, one of the preschool girls climbed the wooden ladder that ran from the base of their one-room home to the roof. The girl fell the entire distance from the roof to the ground. Eva returned from work to find her daughter unconscious and still bleeding. She was taken to the hospital, where she stayed for weeks with a fractured skull. The hospital bill, totaling more than 2,000 lempira ($115)—far more than Eva's meager monthly earnings—sent the family further into debt. While Eva was painfully aware of the risks of leaving her children unattended, she also knew they would starve if she did not work.

Injuries resulting from children being left home alone take place in both high- and low-income countries, differing only by the nature of the injury. In the United States, Caroline Hardin described how her son had cut his arm while waiting for her to come home from work:

> There's some glass doors that go between here and the living room. [My children] were fooling around together. Cassie tried to lock Troy out, and he pushed against the glass door. There must have been a fissure in the glass or something, but it broke and his arm went right through. He really cut himself [and had to go to the hospital emergency room].

At times, parents left their children home alone because they could not afford any childcare. At other times parents left their children in the only care they could afford: informal care by poor-quality providers. Thatayaone Marumoagae lived in Gaborone, Botswana, and sold clothing at the main bus terminal. Poorly paid, he could afford only low-quality informal care for his young son. When the caregiver left the child alone, Thatayaone's son was hit by a car. "He was trying to go to the other side of the road, just to get out of our house to the neighbor's house. A transport car, taxi, ran over him, and we were informed that he had gotten in a car accident. By the time they informed us, he was already in so much pain he couldn't stand it."

Healthcare professionals we interviewed in each country witnessed illnesses and injuries resulting from children being left at home alone, in the care of other siblings, or in inadequate care.

CARING FOR SICK FAMILY MEMBERS

The timing and types of preventive healthcare that children need are generally predictable. One can tell in advance when children will require immunizations and until what age they need to be breast-fed. Preventing exposure to injury involves the expected: ensuring that children have decent routine supervision and care. Addressing the needs of sick children, however, is different because the onset of illness cannot commonly be anticipated. When it comes to caring for sick children, the question is whether work environments in the global economy have the flexibility to bend when a problem arises, allowing parents to provide adequate care, or whether the system fails. When children become acutely ill or suffer from chronic health conditions, is there anyone available to take care of them?

Parents play a critical a role in caring for children recovering from illnesses, taking them to the physician, obtaining and administering medicine, and providing daily care when children cannot attend routine childcare or school. A long-standing body of research has demonstrated that children recover more rapidly from illnesses and injuries when cared for by parents (Mahaffy, 1965; Palmer, 1993; van der Schyff, 1979). Parents' involvement has been shown to speed children's recovery, whether they are having an outpatient procedure or require hospitalization (Kristensson-Hallstron, Elander & Malmfors, 1997; Taylor & O'Connor, 1989). Benefits to children's health have been reported for health problems ranging from epilepsy (Carlton-Ford, Miller, Brown, Nealeigh, & Jennings, 1995) to asthma and diabetes (Anderson, Miller, Auslander, & Santiago, 1981; Hamlett, Pellegrini, & Katz, 1992; LaGreca et al., 1995), among other conditions.

My research team's work has demonstrated that the working conditions of parents play a critical role in determining whether parents can care for their children when they become sick (Heymann, 2006; Heymann, Fischer, &

Engelman, 2003; Heymann, 2000; Heymann, Toomey, & Furstenberg, 1999; Heymann & Earle, 1996; Miller, Gruskin, Rajaraman, Subramanian, & Heymann, 2006; Vo, Penrose, & Heymann, 2007). The risky circumstances faced by children when they were sick paralleled many of the situations they dealt with when they were well. Sick children were at times left home alone, left in the care of young children, taken to their parents' workplaces, or left in the hands of inadequate caregivers. But severe consequences of such inadequate care were more immediate because the children were already ill. Overall, in the countries that we studied, 17% of children had been left home alone when they were sick: specifically, 28% in Botswana; 16% in Mexico; and 7% in Vietnam.

Causes of children left home alone sick. Sick children are not left alone because their parents care less, understand less well what their children need, or have different values or feelings than other parents. Children are placed at risk because parents have little or no choice: in every country we studied, parents faced untenable choices when it came to caring for sick children. More than a quarter of families in Botswana, where the health impacts of the HIV epidemic are devastating, had to leave children home alone when they were sick. While the numbers of parents leaving ill children home alone were lower in Mexico and Vietnam, a significant number of the parents who stayed home to care for their sick children lost pay and jobs. Twenty-eight percent of the parents we interviewed in Botswana had lost pay, had difficulty retaining their jobs, or lost job promotions because of the need to care for sick children, as did 48% of working parents in Mexico and 62% in Vietnam. Parents living in poverty were the most likely to confront no-win situations when their children were sick. Two-thirds of poor families had left children home alone sick or lost needed income in order to care for their children, compared to less than half of working families living above the poverty line.

This costly dilemma was clearly depicted by the experience of Tshegofatso Walone in Botswana. Tshegofatso had five children of her own, aged 13 to 22, and was also the primary caregiver for her 3-year-old grandson. She made a living cleaning a public building, and the few dollars she earned per day left little for her family. She found herself having to choose between the most basic necessities: one month, buying uniforms so her children could attend school and consequently not being able to pay for electricity and, the next month, paying for the electricity but not buying school essentials.

Although Tshegofatso knew that leaving her children home alone when they fell ill was a terrible option, "When you are away and there is a sick child at home, there is no one to care for that child by giving medication and bathing the child." When asked what she did when a child became sick, she explained: "Sometimes I ask permission to go and take care of this child or even take leave." However, she often could not afford to miss work because the leave was not paid. Tshegofatso described an incident that occurred when she had had to leave a sick child at home alone:

> At half-past seven, when I was going to work, my last born was sick. He was vomiting, had diarrhea and stomach complaints. I left him with my neighbor, but the neighbor didn't care for my child. She just left him there vomiting. Immediately when I came home I thought my child looked worse. I took him to the hospital around half-past six, and he was tired and pale. I had wanted to leave the job, but then I had thought, what would I give this child?

While there are many capacity-building programs designed to increase parental knowledge about recognizing different illnesses and about which actions to take, there are not enough programs or policies aimed at ensuring that parents have the chance to provide the kind of care they already know is important. Tshegofatso Walone and the other parents we interviewed were well aware that their children needed them when they were sick. The trouble was that they could not afford to take unpaid leave and even fewer could afford to lose their jobs. Knowledge and parenting skills were not an issue; rather the problem was a lack of opportunity.

Children sent to school or brought to work sick. Unable to adjust their hours or take paid leave from work, many caregivers' only alternative to leaving sick children home alone was to send sick children to school or daycare or bring them along to work.

In the United States, Donna Saffioti, a childcare provider at a preschool center, described a common situation:

> The children who are older and are able to speak say, "Oh, I had medicine this morning" and most of the time, we attributed that to Tylenol. A couple of hours later we check the temperature, and it shoots right up because they had Tylenol at the house to keep the temperature down. . . . That goes back to the demands on [the parents'] jobs. It's just hard for them to take time off. . . . And so they think maybe we won't catch that, and then the child could be here all day and they wouldn't have to miss work.

When parents sent their children to school or daycare sick, other children rapidly became infected. Bringing children to work was not a much better option since parents were often unable to provide adequate care while working. In Vietnam, Thi Nhung described one episode when her preschool-aged daughter became sick:

> Her father was at work; he couldn't come home. It was time for me to go teach; I couldn't stay home. I had to take her with me to school. I let her sit and play

[outside] by herself, although she was sick. That day she had a fever and a cold. The other people saw her playing out there. . . . She was very cold. She didn't dare to say anything nor leave. . . . I was teaching in the classroom. I couldn't bring her in. . . . Naturally, I was worried because she was little. . . . I was worried that she would go somewhere and be missing and I can't find her. Whenever a student asked to go out [of my classroom], I would ask that student to see where my child was, to see whether she was still there.

When parents could rely on extended family members for help, children were about half as likely to be sent to school or daycare sick. More importantly, irrespective of the availability of extended family members, when parents had decent conditions at work—such as access to any amount of leave at all—the impact was enormous: the likelihood that children were sent to school or daycare sick was effectively reduced by half.

CARING FOR CHILDREN WITH SPECIAL NEEDS

The untenable choices that parents are all too often forced to make between effectively caring for a sick child and earning an income sufficient to meet their family's most basic needs are magnified many times over when a child in the family has a disability or a chronic medical condition. Worldwide, 150 million children were living with disabilities or chronic conditions at the end of the 20th century, and this number has been rising (UNICEF, 1999).

Kereng Seetasewa of Botswana had four children, the youngest of whom, 5-year-old Kesego, had been severely disabled by cerebral palsy. Over time, nerve damage, along with disuse and misuse, had caused the muscles in Kesego's legs to contract, rendering them barely functional. No early intervention, physical therapy, or childcare was available to Kereng for her daughter, nor would any employer who paid a decent wage allow Kereng to bring the child to work. For a long period, Kereng could not find a job. She ended up doing piecework for women who wanted their laundry done. They paid little but at least allowed her to bring Kesego. Although this was better than leaving her child alone, it was still difficult for both mother and child:

It's not easy, because when I get to work, I have to set Kesego aside and do my duties. When she cries, I give her whatever she wants and I continue. There are times when she doesn't feel well and I have to work with her on my back. When she's really sick, I tell my employer that I have to take Kesego to the hospital. With my current employer, Kesego has never been hospitalized. But with my first two employers, there was a time when she was hospitalized.

While the lack of childcare affected Kereng and her employers, the most devastating effect was on Kesego. Although she needed an operation to get her legs straightened so that they would be more functional, Kereng faced an impossible bind: "They wanted to straighten her legs, but I adamantly refused. . . . If they were to straighten her legs, it could mean that she would only be able to sit [for a long period]. . . . If she's just in a sitting position, she cannot crawl. And if she can't crawl, I can't go to work." Kereng needed Kesego to be able to crawl because she could not carry Kesego all day on her back during the recovery period from the operation. Getting the operation for Kesego would have meant the loss of the income that the family depended on for survival.

In Vietnam, Bui Thi Phuong Khanh had a clerical job in a factory and was raising her son, Toan, on her own. From birth, it was clear that Toan had problems: his intestines were herniating through the abdominal wall but the surgeons recommended that he wait for surgery until he was older. With this condition, Toan required a great deal of care as a toddler. Phuong Khanh explained:

> I was only told by the daycare teacher, "Because of your child's condition, the district yelled at us and wouldn't let me keep your child here. It would be very dangerous. [They said that] I have to return [him] to the mother of the child because this is a very special situation." That was what happened. However, I didn't hear directly from the Department of Health. I was very sad. I cried in front of my manager's office and asked if I could bring my child to work with me. I would not be able to bring the food home if I was home taking care of my child. . . . I shed tears. A few noticed and asked me why I was sad. I told them about my child's condition and wasn't sure who to send him to. We would both die of starvation if I was home taking care of my child. They told me to bring my child in to work after they heard my story.

While she was fortunate in the end to be able to take her child to work—many employers would not have allowed her to do so—this arrangement was still far worse for her son than being able to attend a childcare center. Like other children, Toan needed a chance to be with his peers and opportunities to learn and grow. In reality, it was not too hazardous for Toan to attend childcare; the staff there would have been able to look after his needs more closely than Phuong Khanh (or any other parent) could while working. Instead, during the day, Toan's early education and development consisted of lying next to Phuong Khanh's table while she worked.

The barriers that Phuong Khanh and Toan faced were unnecessary. In contrast, a childcare center had accepted Pham Dieu Hien's son, Liep, despite his health problems involving both refractory seizures and developmental delays. Hien, her husband and in-laws could readily see the difference it was making in the child's basic life skills. Hien explained:

> My son is learning to be independent. The teachers teach the children to be independent. My son, when he was at home, I had to spoon feed him. It was very difficult. He was very lazy at eating. Each time when he ate, his grandfather and then his grandmother had to entice him every way. But since he has entered childcare, he has learned to sit at the table and feed himself.

Hien was grateful to have found a childcare center that would take her son. Even though it cost half of all the money she earned, she was still able to save some of her wages to pay for his medicine.

While far better than having no early development program, the childcare center was not totally equipped to meet Liep's needs. They accepted and cared for him, but the childcare providers were sometimes overwhelmed by his behavioral problems. Moreover, they had received no training in what to do and were frightened by the seizures. As a result, their response, no matter how many times a seizure occurred, was always to call Hien. Describing a recent incident, Hien recounted: "All of a sudden, he had a seizure. His eyes rolled up. His teacher was scared. She had to call home. I was working at the company; my family had to call me to go pick up my son." A bit of education in the straightforward measures needed to deal with the seizures would have gone a long way in this case. In addition, the teachers could be trained that Liep—like most children being treated for epilepsy—only needed to see a doctor if he had concurrent illnesses and that it was unnecessary for him to be examined or to go home with every seizure.

In Mexico City and Milan, in Houston and Ho Chi Minh City, most childcare centers and schools remain poorly prepared to deal with even the most common chronic children's health conditions, be they asthma or epilepsy. The great early childhood care and education benefits that Liep gained when he was able to attend the childcare center were clear. All children—regardless of conditions they are born with—should have similar opportunities. To achieve this, childcare providers will need training and support.

IMPACT ON PARENTS: PERPETUATING THE POVERTY CYCLE

Around the world, parents spoke of the difficulties of being able to care for sick children and earn a living simultaneously. In these circumstances, something had to be given up, and parents often not only lost wages, but also missed opportunities for advancement in their jobs. Of the parents we interviewed about this, 12% in the United States, 21% in Botswana, 45% in Mexico, and 58% in Vietnam had lost pay when having to be absent from work to care for a sick child. Losing out on job promotions or having trouble keeping a job when caring for sick children was also common: 14% of the parents in Botswana, 13% in the United States, 11% in Mexico, and 8% in Vietnam. For families with a child suffering from a chronic condition, damaging economic consequences were especially frequent: three out of four either lost pay, promotions, or the job itself when caring for their child's health problems.

This negative trade-off between the caring for the health of children and making ends meet creates a vicious cycle of poverty for poor families with sick children. When parents take time off without paid leave or flexibility in order to provide much needed care for ill children, the cost is much greater than simply lost wages. Parents pay up to triple damages in wages for each day missed or they risk job loss. Already living in poverty, this income loss means that the parents can not afford food, fuel, or other essentials, further compromising the well-being of family members. If a parent chooses to go to work in an effort to avoid such penalties, the sick child is often left alone or in lesser care and their health deteriorates.

Like so many other aspects of the experiences of working parents and their children, income and job loss transcended borders. Refilwe Keetetswe of Botswana risked losing both her pay and her work to care for her child. In the end, she lost any chance at promotion. A mother of two, Refilwe worked at a bank. She explained:

> At times, my child would get sick and I couldn't afford a caretaker, so I had to stay home. If you stay home for three days, it appears on your record. At the end of the year, you don't get an increment for that. At times I had to stay for three to four days, or I'd take my son to Molepolole until I'd find someone to look after my child in Gaborone. At times he was sick, the caretaker had left, and there was no one to look after him. They'd ask me if I still needed a job or did I need to go and look after my child. That's what they'd say. . . . It was so difficult."

Even when parents were not fired from their jobs, the risk of being laid off weighed heavily on the choices they made. In Moscow, we spoke with 52-year-old Viktoriya Daniilovna Kozlova, who was working as a transportation dispatcher and raising two sons. Fearing losing her job in a setting where there was no support for working parents and in an economy where jobs were scarce, Viktoriya felt unable to take any time off to provide care when her children were sick. "We need money. My child is sick and I would be happy to stay home, but I need money," she explained. "I cannot even take one day a week because I'm afraid I will be fired." The experiences of the families we interviewed around the world made clear that it was, in fact, the poor who were most likely to lose pay, promotions, and jobs while meeting their care-giving responsibilities.

Irene Echeverria Perez knew a lot about how hard it was to be absent from her work washing dishes in a hotel in Mexico to care for her son, who had been born with a serious heart condition. Irene was constantly torn between taking leave to care for him directly and earning the money necessary to pay for his medical care. She explained: "They don't pay. No, they don't pay. If you don't work, they don't pay you. . . . [It is] 1,000 pesos every two weeks that I receive. If I work a day less, it's less money." She went on to describe how missing a day of work without permission meant a three-day pay cut. At only 9 months old, Irene's son died while she was at work. She was tormented by the possibility that he might have survived longer if she had been at home, but there was no way she could feed her son and daughter if she missed more days at a cost of three days worth of wages for every one day missed without permission. The doctors had to give her tranquilizers when she learned of her son's death. Six years later, her mental health was still fragile.

Such unbearable choices do not have to be the norm. If we recognize that caring for sick family members is one of the most common dilemmas faced by those working the world over, we can create the kinds of decent working conditions that take this into account. Ninety percent of the problem could be addressed if parents were granted a basic amount of paid leave and flexibility to care for sick children. The dangers to child health posed by being left home alone sick or sent to school sick and spreading infections to others, and the threats to the welfare of parents facing unconscionable conflicts, would easily by avoided.

BRIDGING THE GAP

Meeting preventive and curative health needs. As detailed in this chapter, far too many parents are currently forced to make devastating choices between working to earn enough to subsist and being able to meet their children's most basic needs. What makes these risks to children's health and their resultant tragedies so intolerable is how utterly preventable they are.

There is no inevitable conflict between the ability of parents to support their family economically and their ability to care for their children when they are sick. Working conditions that allowed parents to take leave from work—through either paid leave or flexibility—halved the risk of parents having to leave children home alone sick. Similarly, the risk that parents would have to send a child to school or daycare sick was significantly ameliorated—by one-half—when parents had paid leave from work or flexibility on the job. Instances of leaving children home alone sick were rare where working parents could both take some paid leave and had flexibility in their jobs. In fact, children from these families were less than one-quarter as likely to be left home alone sick as those from families that did not have both of these workplace benefits.

Caring for children's health was a top priority for the overwhelming majority of parents in every city, town, and village we visited. Worldwide, when parents' right to adequately address their children's health needs was protected at work, parents were empowered and did provide the care their children required. The question was whether or not their working conditions allowed them to do so. In rural and urban areas, in informal and formal sector work, parents were willing to help employers "get the job done" while caring for their children's health.

In addition to the role of parental working conditions in determining child health, the availability of high-quality childcare is equally important. Parents who had access to formal childcare were the least likely to have left a child home alone sick. Six percent of those who used formal childcare had left their child home alone sick compared to 22% of those who only used informal care.

Such simple protections significantly enable parents to provide the fundamental aspects of preventive care and health promotion as well as address the unpredictable and urgent health needs of their children.

Coordinated policies. One critical question regarding sick children is whether the policies of workplaces and childcare centers are coordinated — that is, if a child is prevented from attending a childcare center because of illness, can working parents stay home to provide care? As it turns out, all too often, the policies are out of sync: rules require that parents keep children home, but do not allow parents to stay home from work. This begs the obvious question: who is supposed to care for the sick child?

The cases where work and child care policies are consistent illustrate that solutions are feasible. For example, Paulina Vasquez described what happened when her son got sick at daycare while she was working for an employer mandated to provide coverage through Mexican social security:

> When he's been sick, [the daycare staff have] called me right away at my work. They would tell me that the baby was sick. I would ask for permission at my work — we can ask for permission in these cases — and go to the daycare center. The doctor would tell me what was wrong and give me a referral sheet for medical consultation. With that sheet I would go to the clinic the same day, since there they would get his fever under control or stop his diarrhea. They would suspend the baby from the daycare center for several days, but they would do the same thing to me. Thus, both of us were protected. They would give me a

three-day permission not to go to work, which is usually the time it takes for the child to get better. When he was stable again, he would go back to his school and I would go to work.

The same social security that provided her childcare also provided her health-care and regulated when she could receive paid leave. Sensibly, the rules corresponded. Having benefits for both mother and child come from one source does not necessarily guarantee coordination; frequently, employers who provide childcare will simultaneously set incongruent leave policies for employees. Public policies that are well-constructed and effective, however, can ensure coordination even when childcare is provided by someone other than the employer.

CHILDREN AND FAMILIES IN A GLOBALIZED ECONOMY

While there remains a great deal more to learn about the conditions in which young children are being raised and the struggles that their working parents are facing worldwide, the evidence could not be clearer on several essential points:

- Too often, young children are being left home alone, in the care of other young children or in other grossly inadequate care.
- The health and development of all of these children are jeopardized, as is the education of the only slightly older children when they are pulled out of school to provide care.
- The lack of decent working conditions and social supports makes it nearly impossible for millions of parents to balance caring well for their children with earning an income to support them, and this prevents millions of families from exiting poverty.

We know how access to paid leave affects families, and the importance of enabling parents to care for their sick and hospitalized children. We also understand the critical impacts of the availability of childcare and extended educational opportunities on the chances of young children in poverty surviving and thriving. The global response will turn on political will more than knowledge. How the global community decides to address the barriers families are up against in meeting children's needs will reflect our fundamental values. Do we really believe that all children should be given the best chance at a healthy life? Do adults have not only an obligation to support themselves and those who depend upon them economically, but also a right and responsibility to care for others? Are we willing to create a world that embodies this? To do so, we will need societal rules that respect the ability to care for children and other vulnerable family members.

The tragedies of our global inertia when it comes to establishing these human priorities are evident in too many of the deaths of children from preventable malnutrition, diarrhea, disease, and injuries. For the preschool and school-age children worldwide who have no chance to learn before entering school, who are left alone with no adults available, who are pulled out of school to care for their younger siblings, who are without any care when they are sick, these tragedies are enacted recurrently in their lives. The same is true for the adults who lose bad jobs and end up in worse ones when they seek to care for their children and for those families who have no chance at exiting poverty.

To date, the global economy has freed the flow of capital far more than it has freed the movement of labor. Likewise, systems have been put in place to protect the rights of capital in ways that have far outpaced the protections for working parents and their children. World Trade Organization agreements that provide for substantial sanctions when countries violate agreements regarding the free flow of goods provide one example. In contrast, the accords ensuring decent working conditions for laborers are ratified on a voluntary basis, and their enforcement mechanisms are weak.

A race to the bottom is not an inherent feature of globalization. Increased social and economic relations across countries can just as readily lead to widely shared economic advancements as they can result in a deterioration of working conditions. Establishing a universal set of basic labor standards is one way to ensure that we avoid a race to the bottom in working conditions. These standards need to comprise the kind of conditions essential to humane survival both for adults and the children they care for, including a living wage, parental leave, flexibility, and reasonable hours. At the same time, we need to widen the educational opportunities that make it possible for all to gain from a global economy by ensuring that children in poor countries and poor children in affluent countries have access to early education and quality primary and secondary schools. This can only be done if children are not compelled to leave school at young ages because their parents' earnings are too low to ensure survival. Just as a world where all children can eat is not too lofty a dream, neither is a world where children are not left alone or pulled out of school to act as childcare providers, and where all children have adults who can care for them when they are healthy and when they are sick.

NOTES

Jody Heymann, Ph.D., MD, is a Canada Research Chair in Global Health and Social Policy and Professor (joint appointment with Political Science, Epidemiology, Biostatistics and Occupational Health) at McGill University, Montreal, Quebec, Canada. This chapter is based on research presented in *Forgotten Families: Ending the Growing Crisis Confronting Children and Working Parents in the Global Economy* (Oxford University Press, 2006).

1. All names have been changed to protect respondents' confidentiality. While recognizing cultural differences in the practice of referring to individuals by name, for consistency each person is introduced by full name and then the first name only is used in subsequent references to that person.

2. To calculate this figure, detailed household survey information was used from a sample of widely divergent countries.

REFERENCES

Anderson, B .J., Miller, J. P, Auslander, W. F., & Santiago, J. V. (1981). Family characteristics of diabetic adolescents: Relationship to metabolic control. *Diabetes Care, 4*(6), 585–94.

Aniansson, G., Alm, B., Andersson, B., Hakansson, A., Larsson, P., Nylen, O., Peterson, H., Rigner, P., Svanborg, M., Sabharwal, H., & Svanborg, C. (1994). A prospective cohort study on breast-feeding and *otitis media* in Swedish infants. *Pediatric Infectious Disease Journal, 13*(3), 183–88.

Arnold, C., Makintube, S., & Istre, G. R. (1993). Day care attendance and other risk factors for invasive *Haemophilus influenzae* type B disease. *American Journal of Epidemiology, 138*(5), 333–40.

Carlton-Ford, S., Miller, R., Brown, M., Nealeigh, N., & Jennings, P. (1995). Epilepsy and children's social and psychological adjustment. *Journal of Health and Social Behavior, 36*(3), 285–301.

Cerqueiro, M., Murtagh, P., Halac., A., Avila, M., & Weissenbacher, M. (1990). Epidemiologic risk factors for children with acute lower respiratory tract infection in Buenos Aires, Argentina: A matched case-control study. *Reviews of Infectious Diseases, Suppl. 8*(12), S1021–28.

Coreil, J., Augustin, A., Halsey, N. A., & Holt, E. (1994). Social and psychological costs of preventive child health services in Haiti. *Social Science and Medicine, 38*(2), 231–38.

Cunningham, A. S., Jelliffee, D. B., & Jelliffee, E. F. (1991). Breast-feeding and health in the 1980s: A global epidemiologic review. *Journal of Pediatrics, 118*(5), 659–66.

Dewey, K., Heinig, M. J., & Nommsen-Rivers, L. (1995). Differences in morbidity between breast-fed and formula-fed infants. Part I. *Journal of Pediatrics, 126*(5), 696–702.

Duncan, B., Ey, J., Holberg, C. J., Wright, A. L., Martinez, F. D., & Taussig, L. M. (1993). Exclusive breast-feeding for at least 4 months protects against *otitis media*. *Pediatrics, 91*(5), 867–72.

Feachem, R. G., & Koblinsky, M. A. (1984) Interventions for the control of diarrhoeal diseases among young children: Promotion of breast-feeding. *Bulletin of the World Health Organization, 62*(2), 271–91.

Fielding, J. E., Cumberland, W. G., & Pettitt, L. (1994). Immunization status of children of employees in a large corporation. *Journal of the American Medical Association, 271*(7), 525–30.

Hamlett, K. W., Pellegrini, D. S., & Katz, K. S. (1992) Childhood chronic illness as a family stressor. *Journal of Pediatric Psychology, 17*(1), 33–47.

Heymann, J., and Barrerra, M. (2008). *Addressing poverty in a globalised economy.* London: Policy Network

Heymann, S. J. (2000). *The widening gap: Why America's working families are in jeopardy—and what can be done about it.* New York: Basic Books.

———. (2006). *Forgotten families: Ending the growing crisis confronting children and working parents in the global economy.* New York: Oxford University Press.

Heymann, S. J., Earle, A., & Hayes, J. (2007). *The Work, Family, and Equity Index: How does the United States measure up?* Boston and Montreal: Project on Global Working Families and the Institute for Health and Social Policy.

Heymann, S .J. & Earle, A. (1996). Parental availability for the care of sick children. *Pediatrics, 98*(2), 226–30.

Heymann, S. J., Fischer, A., & Engelman, M. (2003). Labor conditions and the health of children, elderly and disabled family members. In S .J. Heymann (Ed.), *Global inequalities at work: Work's impact on the health of individuals, families, and societies* (pp. 75–104). New York: Oxford University Press.

Heymann, S .J., Toomey, S., & Furstenberg, F. (1999). Working parents: What factors are involved in their ability to take time off from work when their children are sick? *Archives of Pediatrics and Adolescent Medicine, 153*(8), 870–74.

Habicht, J., DaVanzo, J., & Butz, W. P. (1986). Does breastfeeding really save lives, or are apparent benefits due to biases? *American Journal of Epidemiology, 123*(2), 279–90.

Hobcraft, J. N., McDonald, J., & Rutstein, S. O. (1985) Demographic determinants of infant and early child mortality: A comparative analysis. *Population Studies, 39*(21), 363–85.

Howie, P., Forsyth, J. S., Ogston, S. A., Clark, A., & Florey, C. D. (1990). Protective effect of breast-feeding against infection. *British Medical Journal, 300*(6716), 11–16.

Jason, J., Nieburg, P., & Marks, J. S. (1984). Mortality and infectious disease associated with infant-feeding practice in developing countries, Part 2. *Pediatrics, 74*(4), 702–27.

Kristensson-Hallstron, I., Elander, G., & Malmfors, G. (1997). Increased parental participation in a pediatric surgical day-care unit. *Journal of Clinical Nursing, 6*(4), 297–302.

LaGreca, A., Auslander, W. F., Greco, P., Spetter, D., Fisher, E. B., & Santiago, J. V. (1995). I get by with a little help from my family and friends: Adolescents' support for diabetes care. *Journal of Pediatric Psychology, 20*(4), 449–76.

Lannon, C., Brack, V., Stuart, J., Caplow, M., McNeill, A., Bordley, W. C., et al. (1995). What mothers say about why poor children fall behind on immunizations: A summary of focus groups in North Carolina. *Archives of Pediatrics and Adolescent Medicine, 149*(10), 1070–75.

Lepage, P., Munyakazi, C., & Hennart, P. (1982). Breastfeeding and hospital mortality in children in Rwanda. *Lancet I, 8268,* 403.

Mahaffy, P. R. (1965). The effects of hospitalization on children admitted for tonsillectomy and adenoidectomy. *Nursing Research, 14*(1), 12–19.

McCormick, L. K., Bartholomew, L. K., Lewis, M. J., Brown, M. W., & Hanson, I. C. (1997). Parental perceptions of barriers to childhood immunization: Results of focus groups conducted in an urban population. *Health Education Research, 12*(3), 355–62.

Miller, C., Gruskin, S., Rajaraman, D., Subramanian, S. V., Heymann, J. (2006). Orphan care in Botswana's working households: Growing responsibilities in the absence of adequate support. *American Journal of Public Health, 96,* 1429–35.

Palmer, S .J. (1993). Care of sick children by parents: A meaningful role. *Journal of Advanced Nursing, 18*(2), 185–91.

Taylor, M. R. & O'Connor, P. (1989). Resident parents and shorter hospital stay. *Archives of Disease in Childhood, 64*(2), 274–76.

UNICEF. (2001). *The state of the world's children 2001.* New York: Oxford University Press.

UNICEF. (1999). Children with disabilities. *Education update, 2*(4). Retrieved July 30, 2004, from http://www.unicef.org/girlseducation/vol2disabileng.pdf

van der Schyff, G. (1979). The role of parents during their child's hospitalization. *Australian Nurses Journal, 8*(11), 57–61.

Vo, P. H., Penrose, K., & Heymann, S. J. (2007). Working to exit poverty while caring for children's health and development in Vietnam. *Community, Work and Family, 10*(2), 179–199.

WHO. (1998). *Reducing mortality from major killers of children* (Fact Sheet No. 178). Geneva: WHO Division of Child Health and Development.

Watkins, C. J., Leeder, S. R., & Corkhill, R. T. (1979). The relationship between breast and bottle feeding and respiratory illness in the first year of life. *Journal of Epidemiology and Community Health, 33*(3), 180–82.

Wright, A., Holberg, C. J., Martinez, F. D., Morgan, W. J., & Taussig, L. M. (1989). Breast feeding and lower respiratory tract illness in the first year of life. *British Medical Journal, 299*(6705), 946–49.

Chapter Nine

When Employees Must Choose between Work and Family: Application of Conservation of Resources Theory

by Dawn S. Carlson, Julie Holliday Wayne, and Kenneth J. Harris

ABSTRACT

Based on Conservation of Resources theory, this study examined factors that threaten resources when individuals are faced with competing work and family demands and the subsequent conflict they experience. Using scenario-based research and a sample of 174 working individuals, this study examined three factors from both the work and family domains that may influence the decision to participate in a work event versus a family event: pressure, salience, and importance. Both work and family salience and family importance were significant predictors of the choice of activity. Participants were then asked about the inter-role conflict they expected to experience when attending the activity they had chosen. Also, we examined the degree of engagement in the chosen role and perceived jeopardy to other-role relationships and how they affected perceived conflict. We found that if they chose work, perceptions of jeopardizing family relationships predicted greater family-to-work conflict. However, if they chose the family event, the more engaged they were in the family activity the less work-to-family conflict they expected to experience. Practical implications of the findings are discussed.

At one time or another, all employees have experienced a situation in which there has been a direct conflict between their work and family demands. For example, some have had to decide whether to leave work to care for a sick family member. Others have had to decide whether they should leave, postpone, or not attend a family event because an unexpected meeting or crisis has arisen at work. Although scholars have extensively considered factors that promote ongoing conflict between work and family and the negative consequences of it, very little attention has focused on how people make decisions when faced with such competing work and family demands.

Consider the following scenario that illustrates the competing work and family demands that an employee might face:

> You have spent the past few weeks planning your child's birthday party, which is scheduled to occur in two days, on Saturday. The invitations have been sent, the cake is ordered, out-of-town family members are scheduled to arrive, and the presents are bought. There are still many things you need to prepare in advance of and on the day of the party. Also, you have been very busy working on an important project at work on which you are the project manager. Because of deadlines and unexpected issues with the project, your boss has arranged an urgent meeting for your team to meet with the client for Saturday, and both your boss and the client insist that you are there.

If you were in this situation and faced with a decision regarding which event to attend, what would you choose? What factors would influence your decision? Would it matter, for example, that the birthday party was for your child rather than a friend? Similarly, would it matter that you were the team leader rather than just a team member? Would your personal values and priorities regarding work and family influence your choice? Despite the importance of understanding what factors influence people's decisions when faced with simultaneous demands, research has examined very few such factors.

Beyond understanding the factors influencing the decision-making process, it is important to understand the potential consequences of individuals' decisions. That is, once the individual has decided to attend an event (either the party or the team meeting), what are his or her attitudes and behaviors during the event? Is the individual likely to be focused and engaged while at the event, or distracted? Does she believe that her decision will jeopardize her relationships at work or in the family? And, to what degree does he anticipate that attending the event will generate conflict between his work and family roles? Answers to questions like these are important for researchers to address because individuals' attitudes and behaviors at the event likely influence processes and performance within work and family systems.

Whereas there is vast knowledge regarding factors generating ongoing work-family conflict and its consequences, it, few studies have investigated forces that influence decisions to participate in competing activities at one point in time (for exceptions, see Greenhaus & Powell, 2003; Powell & Greenhaus, 2006). Based on role theory (Kahn, Wolfe, Quinn, Snoek, & Rosenthal et al., 1964) and scarcity theory (Edwards & Rothbard, 2000;

Marks, 1977; Sieber, 1974). Greenhaus and Powell (2003) examined three predictor variables of the decision to participate in a work or family activity. Specifically, they examined whether pressure and support from role senders and an individual's work and family role salience influenced event choice. Building on these theories, they argued that the devotion of resources to one role necessitates the devotion of lesser resources to the other role. Using scenario research, they found that strong pressure from work and family role senders as well as an individual's work and family salience predicted the decision individuals made to participate in a work vs. a family activity. Their work provides a solid foundation on which to build, and future research needs to examine other factors that influence decision choice.

The current research is designed to build on the previous work of Greenhaus and Powell (2003) in two primary ways. Like Greenhaus and Powell, we use a scenario-based conflict episode to examine the influence of role sender pressure as well as an individual's role salience as predictors of the decision to participate in an activity. We extend their work by also considering the importance of the event as a factor that would influence the decision to participate in an activity. In the opening scenario, we asked the reader to consider whether he or she would be more willing to attend a family over work event if the birthday party was for one's child rather than a friend because the importance or significance of the event likely influences one's choice. We examine the causal effect of the event's importance on people's choice in a work-family conflict episode in an experimental setting.

The second way in which we build upon the work of Greenhaus and Powell (2003) is that we consider the consequences of the individual's choice. That is, we examine people's beliefs following their event choice and examine how these beliefs influence their expected conflict between work and family. More specifically, following the choice of event, we examine people's reported engagement in the event and the degree to which people believe that their choice would jeopardize their work and family relationships. Finally, we examine whether engagement and beliefs about jeopardized relationships ultimately influence the degree to which people expect the event will generate conflict between their work and family roles.

THEORETICAL FOUNDATION: CONSERVATION OF RESOURCES THEORY

To understand what factors influence event choice and why they might do so, we apply Conservation of Resources (COR) theory (Hobfoll, 1989; 2001). Conservation of Resources theory is a "broad-based motivational theory"

(Hobfoll, 2001) with a central tenet stating that individuals strive to obtain and maintain resources that serve as means to attain goals. Loss of resources leads to defensive behaviors to avoid losing more resources. Furthermore, when not confronted with stressors, people strive to develop resource surpluses in order to offset the possibility of future loss.

COR theory can be applied when employees experience role conflict and are forced to make decisions as to how to allocate their resources. According to COR theory, they do this in a way that will protect their resources or avoid losing additional resources. Thus, people develop a strategy based on anticipated outcomes of a situation. Then, based on that expectation, individuals determine the investment of resources given their resource pool. Those actions result in resource gains or losses, and subsequently, the outcome is the level of stress that follows (Hobfoll, 2001). This theory goes beyond previous models in that it states what behaviors people will engage in when confronted with stress. Specifically, when confronted with stress, individual strive to minimize net loss of resources (Hobfoll, 1989).

The foundation for understanding this theory is through resources, in that people must decide how to allocate resources to obtain the best outcome for themselves. Hobfoll defined resources as "objects, personal characteristics, conditions or energies that are valued by the individual or that serve as a means for attainment of these objects, personal characteristics, conditions, or energies." (Hobfoll, 1989, p. 516) Examples of resources are relationships in family, such as marriage, and at work, such as with coworkers, which when valued by the individual may be stress reducing (Hobfoll, 1989) or when threatened, may be stress inducing. We measure and manipulate the value of work-family resources in the form of an individual's self-defined role salience and externally generated role activity importance and role sender pressure. We do so because according to COR theory, the more valuable the resource, the more one should act in ways to protect that resource. Presumably, then, the greater the salience, pressure, and importance, the more valued the resource should be, and hence, the more one should behave in a way to protect that resource and choose that role-related activity.

PART 1: EVENT DECISION

As individuals are faced with competing role demands, they must make resource allocation decisions and thus decide which role to invest in or protect. In the first part of the current study we were interested in gaining greater understanding of how different factors influence the allocation decision people make when forced to choose between a work and a family event.

Work and Family Pressure

COR theory would suggest that when individuals are confronted with a stressor they react in a way to "minimize net loss of resources" (Hobfoll, 1989, p. 517). This idea has been applied to the competing demands of work and family, and researchers found that work and family role stressors lead to greater experiences of conflict (Grandey & Cropanzano, 1999). One such potential stressor that an individual may experience when work and family demands collide is the amount of pressure they feel from multiple role senders. That is, when a role sender (such as a spouse or boss) places strong pressure to attend an event, more stress is generated than when the role sender exhibits weak pressure. In fact, pressure from role senders has been found to significantly influence choice between conflicting work-family events (Greenhaus & Powell, 2003; Powell & Greenhaus, 2006).

COR theory would suggest that when an individual feels pressure to participate in a particular activity, he or she would be more likely to do that in order to avoid the loss of that resource. Loss may come in the form of not being able to successfully accomplish a goal or not having a good relationship with family (Hobfoll, 2001). In either case, the more pressure role senders exert, the more likely an individual is to feel that resource is threatened and therefore, act in ways to conserve that resource. While our theoretical foundation is different, this relationship is consistent with previous research that has demonstrated that demands in the form of role pressure determined role-related behavior (Greenhaus & Powell, 2003; Powell & Greenhaus, 2006). Therefore, we predict,

Hypothesis 1a: When faced with simultaneous demands, individuals are more likely to choose work when pressure to choose the work activity is strong rather than weak.

Hypothesis 1b: When faced with simultaneous demands, individuals are more likely to choose family when pressure to choose the family activity is strong rather than weak.

Work and Family Salience

The second predictor we included, work and family role salience, was also found by Greenhaus and Powell (2003) to be a significant predictor of role-related behavior. What is different between this predictor and the others of pressure and importance is that it is internally rather than externally generated. The idea of salience is rooted in social identity theory, which suggests that individuals have demanding role expectations in roles that are critical to one's self identity (Tajfel & Turner, 1985; Thoits, 1983; 1991). Likewise, roles that are important to an individual determine where they allocate resources such as time and emotion (Lobel, 1991; Lobel & St. Claire, 1992). This would be consistent with COR theory that would suggest that people protect and conserve the resources that are most critical to their self-identity. Furthermore, a resource such as self esteem or identity is important not only in itself but to the degree it is instrumental in the acquisition of other resources (Hobfoll, 2001). Finally it is likely that social identity as manifested in role salience is an example of a "resource caravan" (Hobfoll, 2001). A resource caravan is one resource linked with other resources such that over a lifespan the state of a resource at one time tends to carry over to future periods. In other words, salience of a domain allows an individual to build a bank of resources over time that, according to COR theory, are protective and can reduce stress.

Salience of a role generally indicates the personal value of the role to one's identity, as well as the degree to which an individual is invested in and derives resources from a particular role. Hence, COR theory suggests that when faced with a work-family dilemma, people should act in ways to protect highly salient roles. Therefore, we predict

Hypothesis 2a: When faced with simultaneous demands, individuals with higher work salience are more likely to choose work than those with weak work salience.

Hypothesis 2b: When faced with simultaneous demands, individuals with higher family salience are more likely to choose family than those with weak family salience.

Work and Family Importance

Using participants' actual experiences in work-family situations, Powell and Greenhaus (2006) found that an individual's perceived importance of the event influenced his or her response strategy for balancing conflicting work-family events. In fact, importance of the event was a stronger influence on response than was role salience. As with the scenario described above, it seems to reason that the significance or importance of the event (such as a child's vs. friend's birthday) would likely influence event choice. In their scenario study, Greenhaus and Powell (2003) held the importance of the event constant by including conflicting work and family events that were both highly important. In order to build on their work, we wanted to experimentally investigate whether people's choice of event differed based upon whether the event was considered important or not. For example, we expected that people would react to a significant work or family event (such as a once-in-a-lifetime family event of one's parent's 50th wedding anniversary party) differently than to a less significant event (such as a family member's birthday party).

As with the previous predictors reflecting valued resources, COR theory would argue that people would act in a way to protect against resource loss. Further, the protection of this resource is going to be greater to the degree it is valued more by the individual (Hobfoll, 1989). In this case, the value is generated by how important the event is. Thus, the more important the event, the more people will likely choose that event because they value it and will attempt to conserve that resource at all costs. This is consistent with previous research demonstrating that the value an individual attributed to a certain domain played a role in the experience of work-family conflict (Carlson & Kacmar, 2000). Thus, it is reasonable to expect that in order to conserve that valuable resource, they would participate in the event that had the greater importance. Therefore, we predict

Hypothesis 3a: When faced with simultaneous demands, individuals are more likely to choose work when they perceive a high level of importance of the work role activity than a low level of importance.

Hypothesis 3b: When faced with simultaneous demands, individuals are more likely to choose family when they perceive a high level of importance of the family role activity than a low level of importance.

PART 2: WORK-FAMILY CONFLICT

Beyond replicating and extending the work of Greenhaus and Powell (2003) and Powell and Greenhaus (2006), we also consider people's cognitive beliefs following their decision and the impact these beliefs have on people's expected stress. We do so because COR theory suggests the importance of individuals' beliefs regarding resources and the stress that is generated when people believe resources are threatened. Although these beliefs regarding threatened resources are presumed to underlie people's decisions, the actual effect of individuals' beliefs on stress in a work-family situation is untested. Thus, it is important to understand the cognitive beliefs that generate stress while participating in the chosen event.

Beliefs Regarding Threatened Work-Family Relationships

Conservation of Resources theory (Hobfoll, 1989; 2001) rests on the assumption that when people believe that their resources are threatened, they will attempt to conserve or avoid loss of resources in order to minimize stress.

One particular form of loss according to COR theory is not having good relationships at work or with family (Hobfoll, 2001). Applying COR to the work-family decision making context in our study suggests that when individuals believe that their work or family is jeopardized in some way by their decision (that is, a valuable resource is threatened), they are more likely to experience stress. The type of inter-role stress of particular interest to work-family scholars is the degree of inter-role conflict between work and family. Thus, we examine the basic theoretical tenets of COR theory to determine whether beliefs regarding threatened work-family relationships influence anticipated work-family conflict during a chosen event. More specifically, we ask the research question: After people have decided between competing work and family events, do people's beliefs about the degree to which their decision jeopardized their work or family relationships generate anticipated conflict between work and family while at the event?

Beyond the theoretical underpinnings of COR theory, additional empirical evidence, albeit indirect, suggests that when people believe their relationships are threatened, work-to-family conflict is generated. Social support at work and in the family are negatively related to work-to-family conflict (e.g., Bernas & Major, 2000; Carlson & Perrewé, 1999; Edwards, 2007), suggesting that when relationships are believed to be supportive rather than threatened, inter-role conflict is lessened.

From the theoretical basis of COR and empirical evidence, we expect that when people believe that their choice of one event (e.g., work) jeopardized their relationships within another role (e.g., family), they will expect more conflict from that jeopardized role to the other (e.g., anticipated family-to-work conflict). More specifically, we hypothesize that:

Hypothesis 4a: The more that people who chose the work event believe that their doing so jeopardized their family relationships, the more they will anticipate family-to-work conflict while at the event.

Hypothesis 4b: The more that people who chose the family event believe that their doing so jeopardized their work relationships, the more they will anticipate work-to-family conflict while at the event.

Engagement in the Chosen Event

In addition to people's cognitive beliefs, we wanted to examine other resources or behaviors that might influence the degree of anticipated conflict between work and family while at the chosen event. From a practical perspective, we wanted to identify whether there are protective behaviors or resources that might reduce the degree to which people experience cross-role conflict. Conceptually, work-family conflict focuses on the degree of preoccupation, strain, and interference from one role when participating in another. One particular behavior that is likely to reduce cross-role conflict when participating in a chosen activity is the degree of individual's engagement in the event.

Engagement is a concept showing promise for enhancing individual and organizational outcomes and is defined as one's psychological presence in or focus on role activities (Kahn, 1990; Rothbard, 2001). Deep engagement is signified by one's full emotional, cognitive, and physical presence and interest in a role or activity (Grzywacz, Carlson, Kacmar, & Wayne, in press). From a COR framework (Hobfoll, 1989), engagement can be viewed as a resource that has stress resistance potential. In the same way that a good marriage is a resource likely to foster benefits that a poor marriage does not (Rook, 1984; Thoits, 1987), high engagement in a role likely fosters benefits that low engagement does not. Benefits of high role engagement include energy, self-esteem, mental and physical well-being, and other pleasurable experiences (Rothbard, 2001). Such benefits of engagement make it easier to enjoy and be satisfied with a given role rather than being distracted by another role. Further, deeper engagement in a role promotes focus and attention on that role rather than preoccupation with another, reducing inter-role conflict.

It is important to distinguish deep engagement in an isolated event from other constructs such as job and family involvement, which generally promote work-family conflict (e.g., Adams, King, & King, 1996). Involvement is typically conceptualized much like role salience in that it is considered a stable individual characteristic. One would expect that high work and family role salience or involvement are likely to generate great conflict at the time of the decision (because both roles are valued and resources from both need to be conserved). However, our point of interest is on what happens after individuals have chosen the event to attend. Specifically, we examine whether the degree to which individuals are engaged in the event is related to the anticipated experience of work-family conflict at the event. Because of the cognitive and emotional benefits of engagement already described, we expect that active and full engagement at the event should reduce conflict relative to those who are less engaged.

Consider, for example, that one individual chose to attend the parents' anniversary party and expected to be fully engaged (cognitively, emotionally, and physically) in that event. In comparison, another person also chose to attend the party but expected to be less fully engaged in the event. It is reasonable to expect that the latter, not fully cognitively engaged in the family event, would be more distracted and preoccupied with work. That is, she or he would likely be thinking more about work and therefore, report greater work-to-family conflict. In sum, deep cognitive, emotional, and physical engagement in an event should serve to protect individuals from stress generated between competing work-family demands.

Thus, we expect that when individuals who have chosen an event expect to be more fully engaged in that event, they will expect less conflict from another role to that role. More specifically, we hypothesize that:

Hypothesis 5a: For individuals who chose to attend the family event, those who expect to be more fully engaged in the event will anticipate less work-to-family conflict than those who are less engaged.

Hypothesis 5b: For individuals who chose to attend the work event, those who expect to be more fully engaged while at work will anticipate less family-to-work conflict than those who are less engaged.

METHOD

Sample and Procedure

The participants in this study were recruited by undergraduate business students enrolled in upper-level (junior and senior) management courses at a large university in the southeastern United States. Each student was given the opportunity to recruit up to three full-time workers (30 hours or more per week) to complete the survey. The snowball method (Scott, 1991) for data collection has previously been employed in a large number of topical areas with much success (e.g., Liu, Perrewé, Hochwarter, & Kacmar, 2004; Treadway, Hochwarter, Kacmar, & Ferris, 2005). In exchange for recruiting full-time employees to complete the survey, the student received up to three extra credit points (one per survey completed) in the class. Participation was voluntary and the responses were confidential, so as to best ensure participants felt comfortable answering truthfully.

To verify that all responses were from actual, distinct participants, we first asked respondents to provide their business phone numbers. Students were told that respondents would be randomly selected and called to verify that the respondent completed the questionnaire in order for the student to receive extra credit. Finally, we did call randomly selected respondents and we asked innocuous questions (e.g., "What part of the survey was the most difficult to complete?").

We received 174 completed surveys and this sample size was used for our analyses. Our sample was 44% male and 56% female. The average age of the participants was 40.6 years, with a range from 20 to 87 years. The racial composition of our subjects was 68% Caucasian, 17% African-American, 10% Hispanic, and 5% other. On average, the participants in our sample worked 42.2 hours per week.

Scenarios

To frame the situation and give all participants a similar mindset when providing their responses, we used a scenario methodology. Previous research on work and family colliding (Greenhaus & Powell, 2003), as well as other topics that are tough to manipulate in experiments and need a common situational framework to investigate the research questions, have shown this methodology to be appropriate and insightful (e.g., Conlon, Porter, & Parks, 2004; Heilman & Chen, 2005; Naquin & Kurtzberg, 2004).

The variables of work pressure, family pressure, importance of family event, and importance of work event were each manipulated in the scenario. Each manipulated variable had two levels (high and low), resulting in 16 (2x2x2x2) different scenarios. Respondents were instructed to read the short scenario and answer the questions that followed. The scenario that follows is a sample scenario with both domains of pressure and the importance of each event being low. The manipulations are shown in italics, and the high manipulations are in italics in parentheses and the name of the manipulated variable is given in bold.

You have been planning to attend a *surprise family birthday party* (*party for your parents' 50th wedding anniversary*) (i.e., family importance) to be held at your home this Saturday. However, you have been asked to work overtime this Saturday with other project members to meet a deadline for a *project on which you play a role* (*vital project for your organization's most important client*) (i.e., work importance). You cannot participate in both activities. Your manager insists that your participation in this overtime work session on the project is *desirable but not critical* (*critical*) (i.e., work pressure). Your spouse insists that your presence at this party is *desirable but not critical* (*critical*)" (i.e., family pressure).

Participants responded to manipulation checks on each of the four manipulated variables. Results showed that the manipulations were strong enough, as significant differences (at the $p < .05$ level) resulted for each of the domains of pressure as well as the importance of each event.

Measures

Decision event. After reading the questionnaire, participants were asked "Assuming that neither activity could be rescheduled, in which activity would you participate?" The response options were either family party or team project. The family party was coded as 1 and the team project was coded as 2.

Role salience. Work and family salience were each measured with two items developed by Lodahl and Kejner (1965). The two items were "The major satisfaction in my life comes from my work (family)" and "The most important things that happen to me involve my work (family)." The alpha reliability for the work salience items was .74 and for family salience items was .77.

Work-family conflict. We measured work-family conflict in both directions, work-to-family and family-to-work conflict. The items were adapted for the purposes of this scenario study but are based on the items in the established work-family scale developed by Carlson, Kacmar, and Williams (2000). All of these items were measured on a 5-point Likert scale with the anchors being 1 = *Definitely Not* to 5 = *Definitely.*

We measured *family-to-work conflict* with the following three items: "During the team meeting you would be preoccupied with thoughts of the party and unable to concentrate," "Due to the stress of feeling guilty for not attending the party you would have a hard time focusing on work," and "Tension and anxiety from the family demands of the party would weaken your ability to do your job." The alpha reliability for these three items was .78.

We measured *work-to-family conflict* with the following three items: "While at the party, you would be so preoccupied with work you were not able to focus on your parent," "Because of all the stresses of work responsibilities, you would not be able to enjoy the family party," and "By the time you got to the party you would be so emotionally drained that you would not be able to really contribute to the party." The alpha reliability for these three items was .87.

Jeopardize work/family relationship. Regardless of their choice, respondents rated the degree to which their decision jeopardized their relationship at work or in the family by responding to the following questions: "Not attending the work project could jeopardize your career" and "Not attending the party could jeopardize your relationship with family members." The responses for each question were measured on a 5-point Likert scale with the anchors being 1 = *Strongly disagree* to 5 = *Strongly agree.*

Engagement. Regardless of their choice, we measured family and work engagement by asking participants to respond to the questions "If you decided to attend the party, would you" and "If you decided to participate in the work session, would you." The anchors were the degree to which individuals would think about a certain domain with the extreme anchors being constantly thinking about each domain (work or family) with a neutral choice of thinking some about both domains. These items were then given numerical values from 1 to 3 such that a higher score indicated higher engagement in the domain.

Control Variables. In our analyses we controlled for the marital status of participants. This variable has been theoretically suggested and empirically shown to be an important variable to consider when examining work-family issues (e.g., Greenhaus & Powell, 2003).

Analyses

We used the entire sample for part 1 of the study. To analyze hypotheses 1–3, we used logistic regression because the dependent variable (event decision) was dichotomous. In the logistic regression runs marital status, the control variable, was entered in the first step and then the independent variables were entered in the second step.

For part 2 of the study, the sample was split based on response to the event decision in part 1. To analyze hypotheses 4–5, we used hierarchical regression analyses, entering marital status as the control variable in the first step and the predicted engagement and jeopardizing variables in the second step. For these two hypotheses, the dependent variable of conflict was used and the direction of the conflict was based upon the decision that was made in the first half of the study. In other words, if a respondent chose to "go to the party" (i.e., family event) then we examined the factors that influenced their antici- pated work-to-family conflict at the event. Specifically, we investigated whether their family engagement and the degree to which they believe their choice of the family event jeopardized their work relationships influenced the anticipated work-to-family conflict at the party. Likewise, if they chose the "work event," then the dependent variable was anticipated family-to-work conflict and we considered the engagement in the work event and the per- ceived jeopardy to family relationships as predictors.

RESULTS

Part 1— Event Decision

Table 9.1 provides the means, standard deviations, and intercorrelations be- tween study variables. The variables are correlated in the expected manner. It is important to note that some of the variables for part 1 of the study were for the entire sample. Other variables were only measured based on the decision made in part 1 to attend the family or the work event, resulting in a reduced sample size for these analyses. Thus, all the variables in part 2 are for the por- tion of the sample that made that decision.

The logistic regression analysis results are provided in Table 9.2. These re- sults show that marital status was not a significant predictor of the event de- cision. In terms of pressure, neither work pressure nor family pressure was

Table 9.1. Means, Standard Deviations, and Intercorrelations between Study Variables

Variable	Mean	SD	1	2	3	4	5	6	7	8
1. Event to Attend	1.43	.50	-							
2. Work-to-Family Conflict[b]	2.06	.78	.21*	-						
3. Family-to-Work Conflict[c]	2.45	.92	-.10	-	-					
4. Work Salience[a]	2.51	.91	.19*	.20*	-.09	-				
5. Family Salience[a]	4.45	.70	-.18*	.00	.20	-.35**	-			
6. Engagement in Work[a]	3.02	2.75	-.41**	-.08	.20	-.13	.11	-		
7. Engagement in Family[a]	2.26	1.22	-.04	-.51**	-.18	-.13	.03	.11	-	
8. Jeopardizing Work[a]	3.44	.93	.43**	-.01	.15	.16*	-.04	-.21**	.04	-
9. Jeopardizing Family[a]	2.64	1.18	-.27**	-.07	.42**	.00	.03	.24**	-.01	.16*

[a] $n = 174$, [b] $n = 99$, [c] $n = 75$

* $p < .05$, ** $p < .01$

Table 9.2. Results of Logistic Regression Analysis Predicting Choice of Event to Attend

	Step 1	*Step 2*
Marital Status	.02	.1
Work Pressure		
Family Pressure		.30
Work Salience		−.50
Family Salience		.38*
Importance of Work Event		−.45*
Importance of Family Event		.39
		−.82**
ΔR^2		
	.00	.15

Note: Higher scores indicate the choice of the work event.

$N = 174$

$* p < .05, ** p < .01$

significantly related to the event decision. Thus, hypothesis 1a and hypothesis 1b were not supported. The results for salience showed that both work and family salience were significantly ($p < .05$) related to the outcome variable in the predicted directions, thus supporting hypotheses 2a and 2b. The findings for importance of the event were mixed, as the importance of the work event was not significantly related to the event decision, whereas importance of the family event was negatively and significantly ($p < .01$) related to the choice of event. These results do not support hypothesis 3a, but do provide support for hypothesis 3b.

Part 2—Work-Family Conflict

Table 9.3 houses the results with anticipated family-to-work conflict as the outcome variable (for those individuals who chose the work event). As can be seen, individuals' perceptions that their choice of event would jeopardize

Table 9.3. Results of Hierarchical Regression Analysis Predicting Family-to-Work Conflict

	Step 1	Step 2
Marital Status	−.06	−.07
Work Engagement		
Jeopardizing Family		.08
		.34**
ΔR²		
	.01	.19**

$N = 75$

* $p < .05$, ** $p < .01$

their family relationships was a significant, positive predictor ($p < .01$) of family-to-work conflict at the event. This result supports hypothesis 4a. However, being more engaged at work was not significantly associated with family-to-work conflict; thus, hypothesis 5b was not supported.

The results with work-to-family conflict (for those who chose the family event) are provided in Table 9.4. First, individuals' perceptions that choosing

Table 9.4. Results of Hierarchical Regression Analysis Predicting Work-to-Family Conflict

	Step 1	Step 2
Marital Status	−.03	−.01
Family Engagement		
Jeopardizing Work		−.72**
		.01
ΔR²		
	.00	.26**

$N=99$

* $p < .05$, ** $p < .01$

the family event would jeopardize their work relationships did not relate to work-to-family conflict while at the event. This finding does not support hypothesis 4b. On the other hand, the less engaged an individual expected to be at the family event, the more he or she expected work-to-family conflict ($p <$ .01). This result provides support for hypothesis 5a.

DISCUSSION

The purpose of this research was twofold. First, we examined the effect of various resources and their value on the decision to participate in an event when faced with simultaneous work and family demands. Specifically, COR theory suggests that the more valued a resource, the more an individual will behave in a way to protect it. Thus, we expected that when pressure from role senders was great, when a role activity was important, and when an individual highly values a role (that is, resources are of great value and more likely to be threatened), the more an individual will choose that role in order to protect it and minimize stress or conflict. Second, we examined the basic principles of COR theory, which suggests that when individuals believe resources are threatened, they will experience greater stress or inter-role conflict. Thus, we examined whether individuals' beliefs about the degree to which their role relationships, a valued resource, were jeopardized predicted their experience of inter-role conflict at the event they chose. We also examined whether active engagement at the event, as a means of protecting a resource, reduced inter-role conflict.

In terms of factors that influence event choice, we examined two externally generated sources of influence: role pressure and role importance. We considered the effect of role senders' pressure on people's decision to engage in a work or family activity. In particular, an individual's family member and boss exerted either strong or weak pressure to attend the event. We did not find support for the importance of pressure on the decision. However, we found that the importance placed on a *family* event was the most significant predictor of which event individuals chose. That is, regardless of the importance of the work event, if the family event was very important (i.e., the anniversary party), respondents were likely to choose the family event. In contrast, when the family event was relatively unimportant (i.e., birthday party) and a simultaneous work demand was in place (whether it was important or not), respondents were likely to choose the work event. This finding suggests that when individuals are faced with conflicting work and family demands, one primary factor in their decision making process is the importance of the family event. When it is important, they are likely to choose the family event.

When it is unimportant, they are likely to choose work. This finding experimentally confirms the externally valid findings of Powell and Greenhaus (2006), which revealed that event importance was a key factor in individuals' response to work-family demands.

Furthermore, rather than externally generated signals of the value of a resource or role, an internally generated source of role salience was considered. We found that an individual's work and family role salience also influenced event choice. Although externally exerted signs of importance are stronger, the degree to which one values a role influences one's choice of activity. Consistent with COR theory, when employees highly value a role, they will act in ways to protect that role. That is, for those higher in work salience, when faced with competing demands, they are more likely to choose the work activity; the opposite is true for those higher in family salience. In conclusion, our findings are somewhat consistent with those of Greenhaus and Powell (2003) in that we found work salience to be as relevant as they did, but we also found that family salience played a role while they did not. However, they found family salience to interact with self-esteem to affect event choice. Perhaps self-esteem, although unmeasured, operated in such a way in this study, to allow the influence of family salience to be detected. Furthermore, when including two externally generated sources of influence, we found family importance to play a role while pressure did not. This is inconsistent with Greenhaus and Powell (2003), who found work and family pressure to be relevant. Thus, the variable of event importance that was new to this study seemed to be quite relevant to individuals, especially regarding a family event.

In the second part of the study we extended previous research by examining whether, as specified by COR theory, people's beliefs about threatened resources (i.e., relationships) generated greater anticipated conflict. We found that for those who chose the work event and perceived their family relationships would be jeopardized, they expected to have greater experiences of family-to-work conflict while at the work event. For those who chose the family event, however, beliefs about jeopardized work relationships did not relate to anticipated work-to-family conflict at the family event. Rather, expecting to be more actively engaged in the family event was a protective factor that negatively predicted work-to-family conflict at the family event. Thus, the more individuals were engaged in family while at the event, the less conflict they expected to experience.

Although there were some exceptions depending upon the role, the basic tenets of COR theory were supported in event choice in that when salience and importance were greatest, individuals were more likely to choose that role event. Further, when people believed that their choice of work event jeopardized their family relationships, they were more likely to expect family-to-work conflict (although the same was not true of perceived jeopardy of work relationships). Further, in an attempt to conserve resources, high engagement in one's family is a protective factor in reducing work-to-family conflict while at the family event.

From the findings of this study, it seems clear that family is the role that is most critical to the work-family decision. That is, family salience and importance of the family event predicted choice of event. Only work salience predicted choice of work event. Further, when relationships in the family (but not work) were perceived as in jeopardy, inter-role conflict (family-to-work conflict) was generated. Finally, high engagement in one's family (but not work) was a protective factor in reducing inter-role conflict (work-to-family conflict). Thus, factors related to the family role, more so than work, are critical to individuals' choice when faced with competing demands.

Strengths, Limitations, and Future Research

This study has several strengths. First, this study replicated a previous study (Greenhaus & Powell, 2003) and extended it by including the variable of event importance to see what factors play a role in the event an individual chooses when faced with a decision between work and family. This finding suggests that the decision is contingent on the salience of work and family and by how important the event is; also, the acute and chronic experiences of when work and family collide may be different and result in different decisions. Second, this is the first study we know of that examines not only the work-family decision that is made, but also how the decision generates anticipated inter-role conflict while at the event. The different predictors depending on which direction of conflict one is experiencing again suggest that these are conceptually distinct elements of conflict. Third, we investigated whether one's beliefs about threatened relationships is related to the experience of conflict, as expected by COR theory.

As with all research, this study also has several limitations. First, we were using scenarios; individuals were giving their perceptions of the work-family conflict they would experience rather than actual experience. While experimental research provides useful insights into situations and is a helpful start to an investigation, future research should do more event-based studies to understand the critical factors that play a role when an individual's resources are threatened and the factors that are critical to the experience of work-family conflict. Second, we looked at both jeopardy and engagement to understand the experience of conflict but surely there are other variables that would be useful. For example, future research could consider potential resources lost other than relationships, such as time, money, or status.

Practical Implications

In the opening scenario, we asked the reader to consider being faced with the dilemma of attending a child's birthday party or an important project on which the reader is team manager. We asked whether it would matter whether the party was for a child or a friend (varied importance of the family event) or whether one was team leader or a team member (varied importance of the work event). Practically, our findings suggest that the importance of the family event is influential to the decision whereas the importance of the work event is not. Thus, in this scenario and based upon these findings, we would expect that most people would choose to attend their child's birthday. However, if the birthday party is for a friend, most people would choose the work event. Contrary to our expectations, based on these findings, being a team leader vs. a team member would not dictate an individual's choice of the work event. We also asked whether one's individual values and priorities would influence the decision, and clearly, the findings for role salience suggest that individual values do matter. In fact, as we predicted using COR theory, people who highly value each role are likely to act in ways to conserve that role (that is, choose that role when faced with competing demands).

Although these findings suggest some factors relevant to understanding people's choices when faced with competing demands, we are only beginning to scratch the surface. Future research should investigate other role factors that Powell and Greenhaus (2006) have suggested may influence response, such as whether the activity could be held without the focal individual or could be held at a different time. Further, rather than forcing a dichotomous choice between activities, experimental research could investigate other potential response strategies (e.g., staying a short time at both, rescheduling one for the other). Research should continue to investigate and reflect the realities and complexities of people's work and family lives.

NOTE

Dawn S. Carlson, Ph.D., is an associate professor of management in the Department of Management, Hankamer School of Business, Baylor University, Waco, TX 76798-8006. Phone: 254-710-6201. Email: Dawn_Carlson@baylor.edu . Julie Holliday Wayne, Ph.D., is a visiting assistant professor of business in the Calloway School of Business & Accountancy, Wake Forest University, Winston-Salem, NC 27109. Phone: 336-758-5733. Email: waynej@wfu.edu . Kenneth J. Harris, Ph.D., is an assistant professor of management in the School of Business, Indiana University Southeast, 4201 Grant Line Road, New Albany, IN 47150. Phone: 812-941-2501. Email: harriskj@ius.edu.

REFERENCES

Adams, G. A., King, L. A., & King, D. W. (1996). Relationships of job and family involvement, family social support, and work-family conflict with job and life satisfaction. *Journal of Applied Psychology, 81*, 411–420.

Bernas, K. H. & Major, D. A. (2000). Contributors to stress resistance: Testing a model of women's work-family conflict. *Psychology of Women Quarterly, 24*, 170–178.

Carlson, D. S., Kacmar, K. M., & Williams, L. J. (2000). Construction and initial validation of a multidimensional measure of work-family conflict. *Journal of Vocational Behavior, 56*, 249–276.

Carlson, D. S. & Perrewé, P. L. (1999). The role of social support in the stressor-strain relationship: An examination of work-family conflict. *Journal of Management, 25*(4), 513–540.

Conlon, D. E., Porter, C. O. L. H., & McLean-Parks, J. (2004). The fairness of decision rules. *Journal of Management, 30*(3), 329–349.

Edwards, J. R. (2007). The role of husbands' supportive communication practices in the lives of employed mothers. *Marriage and Family Review, 40*(4), 23–46.

Edwards, J. R., & Rothbard, N. P. (2000). Mechanisms linking work and family: Clarifying the relationship between work and family constructs. *Academy of Management Review, 25*, 178–199.

Grandey, A. A., & Cropanzano, R. (1999). The Conservation of Resources model applied to work-family conflict and strain. *Journal of Vocational Behavior, 54*, 350–370.

Greenhaus, J. H., & Powell, G. N. (2003). When work and family collide: Deciding between competing role demands. *Organizational Behavior and Human Decision Processes, 90*, 291–303.

Grzywacz, J. G., Carlson, D. S., Kacmar, K. M., & Wayne, J. H. (in press). Work-family facilitation: A multilevel perspective on the synergies between work and family. *Journal of Organizational and Occupational Psychology.*

Heilman, M. E., and Chen, J. J. (2005). Same behavior, different consequences—Reactions to men's and women's altruistic citizenship behavior. *Journal of Applied Psychology, 90*(3), 431–441.

Hobfoll, S. E. (2001). The influence of culture, community, and the nested-self in the stress process: Advancing Conservation of Resources theory. *Applied Psychology: An International Review, 50*, 337–370.

———. (1989). Conservation of Resources: A new attempt at conceptualizing stress. *American Psychologist, 44*, 513–524.

Kahn, W. A. (1990). Psychological conditions of personal engagement and disengagement at work. *Academy of Management Journal, 33*: 692–724.

Kahn, R. L., Wolfe, D. M., Quinn, R., Snoek, J. D., & Rosenthal, R. A. (1964). *Organizational stress: Studies in role conflict and ambiguity.* New York: Wiley.

Liu, Y., Perrewé, P., Hochwarter, W., & Kacmar, C. (2004). Dispositional antecedents and consequences of emotional labor at work. *Journal of Leadership & Organizational Studies, 10*, 12–26

Lobel, S. A. (1991). Allocation of investment in work and family roles: Alternative theories and implications for research. *Academy of Management Review, 16*, 507–521.

Lobel, S. A., & St. Claire, L. (1992). Effects of family responsibilities, gender and career identity salience on performance outcomes. *Academy of Management Journal, 35*(5), 1057–1069.

Lodahl, T. M., & Kejner, M. (1965). The definition and measurement of job involvement. *Journal of Applied Psychology, 4*, 24–33.

Marks, S. R. (1977). Multiple roles and role strain: Some notes on human energy, time and commitment. *American Sociological Review, 42*, 921–936.

Naquin, C. E., & Kurtzberg, T. R. (2004). Human reactions to technological failure: How accidents rooted in technology vs. human error influence judgments of accountability. *Organizational Behavior and Human Decision Processes, 93*, 129–141.

Powell, G. N. & Greenhaus, J. H. (2006) Managing incidents of work-family conflict: A decision-making perspective. *Human Relations, 59*(9), 1179–1212.

Rook, K. S., (1984). The negative side of social interaction: Impact on psychological well-being. *Journal of Personality and Social Psychology, 46*, 1097–1108.

Rothbard, N. P. (2001). Enriching or depleting? The dynamics of engagement in work and family roles. *Administrative Science Quarterly, 46*, 655–684.

Sieber, S. D. (1974). Toward a theory of role accumulation. *American Sociological Review, 39*, 567–578.

Tajfel, H., & Turner, J.C. (1985). The social identity theory of intergroup behavior. In S. Worchel & W. G. Austin (Eds.), *Psychology of intergroup relations* (pp. 7–24). Chicago: Nelson-Hall.

Thoits, P. A. (1983). Multiple identities and psychological well-being: A reformulation and test of the social isolation hypothesis. *American Sociological Review, 48*, 174–187.

———. (1987). Gender and marital status differences in control and distress: Common stress versus unique stress explanations. *Journal of Health and Social Behavior, 28*, 7–22.

———. (1991). On merging identity theory and stress research. *Social Psychology Quarterly, 54*, 101–112.

Treadway, D. C., Hochwarter, W. A., Kacmar, C. J., & Ferris, G. R. (2005). Political will, political skill, and political behavior. *Journal of Organizational Behavior, 26*, 229–245.

Part 2

FOCUS ON FLEXIBLE
WORK ARRANGEMENTS

Chapter Ten

Workplace Flexibility: Implications for Worker Health and Families

by Joseph G. Grzywacz, Fiona A. Jones,
and Patrick R. Casey

ABSTRACT

There is widespread belief that workplace flexibility contributes to adult health; however, there is surprisingly little direct evidence supporting this belief. In this chapter we outline what is and is not known about the link between workplace flexibility and health, and argue that adult health is a basic resource for optimal family functioning. Then, we examine the effects of one type of flexibility—schedule flexibility—on worker health using longitudinal data from a sample of U.S. workers employed by a large multi-national company. In this analysis we differentiate objective and subjective flexibility, and I examine outcomes in several specific domains of health including morbidity, impairment, and health perceptions. The results of these analyses indicate that there are notable health differences among workers in different types of objective flexible arrangements (e.g., flex-time versus compressed work weeks), and that some of these differences are explained by subjective flexibility. The results also indicate that both objective and subjective flexibility predict changes in health over one year, although the effects are small. These results are interpreted from an enrichment perspective, suggesting that jobs can be designed in ways that are beneficial to organizations as well as workers' families.

The health-related implications of workplace flexibility are drawing substantial interest for diverse constituencies. Employers are interested in the potential health effects of workplace flexibility for utilitarian reasons: if flexibility

219

contributes to enhanced health and well-being, it provides a concrete mechanism for managing and optimizing organizational performance. Social advocates are interested in the health-related implications of workplace flexibility as a means to an end; specifically, if flexibility contributes to employee health it would provide traction for policies encouraging employers to be more family friendly. To others, the potential health implications of workplace flexibility may offer insights into pressing public health problems such as increasing prevalence of depression and obesity. Likewise, to the extent that health is a basic resource that contributes to optimal family functioning through enriching family interactions or by helping the family better respond to external demands placed on it, workplace flexibility may have considerable potential for building resilient and well-functioning families (Halpern, 2005).

Although the link seems obvious, there is little direct evidence that workplace flexibility contributes to individual health. Indeed, most existing research is based on cross-sectional data, thereby undermining any causal inference. Further, the scope of potential health implications for workplace flexibility is not well delineated because most studies focus on a narrow range of health outcomes. Our goal in this chapter is to strengthen understanding of the potential public health impact of workplace flexibility. To achieve this goal we document cross-sectional and longitudinal associations of perceived workplace flexibility with indicators of physical and mental health perceptions, impairment, and morbidity. We also evaluate differences in health among individuals in various flexible work arrangements.

BACKGROUND

Conceptual Foundations

Flexibility. The term *workplace flexibility* is poorly defined in the literature. Workplace flexibility (hereafter referred to as *flexibility*) broadly encompasses a range of working practices that allow employers, employees, or both to adapt ways of working to meet their needs. This includes practices focused around the timing or scheduling of work (e.g., flex-time, compressed or annualized hours, part-time work) and the location of work (e.g., teleworking, home working, hot desking). Within this broad definition it is important to recognize two distinct perspectives on flexibility with diverging foci. The first perspective focuses on the organization and its ability to efficiently and effectively respond to market forces; whereas the second perspective focuses on workers and their ability to exert control over when, where, and how long they work (Costa et al., 2004). The organizational perspective of flexibility may undermine employee health and well-being, in part because it is associated with poorer job security, lower pay, and less favorable job conditions (Benach, Amable, Muntaner, & Benavides, 2002). The individual perspective is believed to empower and benefit workers.

In this chapter we adopt the individual perspective and conceptualize flexibility in terms of the range of working practices that allow employees the scope to meet their own needs and those of their families. These practices are typically introduced with the express intention of helping employees meet their family obligations and enhance work-life balance. Such interventions give employees control over aspects of their work such as scheduling (e.g., flextime, compressed working weeks) or location (e.g., telework). The most recent estimates from the U.S. Department of Labor (2005) indicate that more than one-quarter of workers (27.5%) have flexibility in their work, meaning that they can vary the timing of their work.

Workplace flexibility can be conceptualized as a resource for daily living that can affect individual health through multiple, interrelated pathways. Flexibility, particularly that characterized by high levels of individual control over work, allows workers better to coordinate responsibilities of daily life, thereby reducing exposure to social stressors (Karasek & Theorell, 1990). Consistent with this thinking, Voydanoff (2005) described workplace flexibility as a "boundary-spanning resource" or work-related resource that contributed to positive outcomes because it enabled workers to better meet demands inside and outside the workplace. Reduction in stressor exposure, in turn, is posited to contribute to less illness through several maladaptive coping behaviors (e.g., excessive alcohol consumption) and physiological pathways (e.g., cortisol deregulation) (Cohen & Herbert, 1996). Enhanced ability to coordinate activities of daily life may also contribute to health because it allows individuals to maintain healthier lifestyle habits, like creating opportunities for regular physical activity and periodic health screens. Indeed, it is widely believed that a basic necessity of an effective and sustainable workplace wellness program is that organizations provide flexibility in daily scheduling so that employees can engage in positive lifestyle practices (Allen, 2002; Stokols, Pelletier, & Fielding, 1996). The plausibility of these as well as other linkages contributes to the widely held belief that workplace flexibility contributes to employee health and well-being.

Health. Health is a complex and multifaceted phenomenon. Although there is a wide array of models of health in the literature, there is consistency across these models on at least two primary points. First, it is clear that health is multidimensional, reflecting (minimally) physical and mental health. Important evidence indicates that physical and mental health are distinct, despite the fact that they are bi-directionally interrelated. Indeed, population estimates indicate that approximately 25% of adults have poor physical health yet good mental health, while another 10% of adults have poor mental health yet good physical health (Keyes & Grzywacz, 2002). Second, it is clear that health comprises multiple domains. The health-related quality of life framework, for example, suggests multiple distinct domains of physical and mental health, including health perceptions, impairment, and morbidity (Patrick & Erickson, 1993).

Viewing health multidimensionally has important implications because it raises the possibility that flexibility may affect some domains of health but not others. Whereas flexibility may have clear and direct effects on health perceptions, like overall appraisals of health, it may be only weakly or indirectly related with other domains of health, such as physical or psychiatric morbidity. Likewise, different aspects of flexibility may affect specific domains of health differently. For example, working remotely may contribute to less morbidity because it allows workers to maintain healthy lifestyle habits, but it may be associated with poorer psychological well-being or other indicators of mental health in part because remote workers may feel socially isolated or have difficulty detaching from work. These complexities necessitate examination of the effects of flexibility on a broad set of outcomes reflecting distinct domains of physical and mental health.

Empirical Foundations

Research examining flexibility at work has investigated the effects of a broad spectrum of non-traditional working practices, ranging from enforced irregular hours and temporary insecure employment to schemes that allow employees the flexibility to meet their own needs. Not surprisingly, the findings vary depending on the exact definition and nature of the flexible working practices. Studies have also examined a range of outcomes including sickness absence, psychological well being, and physical well being. These are discussed below.

A number of studies have shown that increased work flexibility is related to reduced absenteeism from work. For example, Dalton and Mesch (1990) found that introduction of a flextime work arrangement, wherein employees were given the discretion to determine when they worked, led to a dramatic reduction in absenteeism compared to a control group. Further, they noted that absenteeism returned to its previous levels after termination of the flextime arrangement. These effects were confirmed in a subsequent meta-analysis (Baltes, Briggs, Huff, Wright, & Neuman, 1999), which concluded that flextime, or giving workers control when work is performed, was associated with reduced employee absenteeism, whereas other forms of flexibility (i.e., compressed work weeks) failed to have any effect. These results are unsurprising as an increase in discretionary time may enable people to cope with family demands without resorting to using sickness absence. Although reduced absenteeism is clearly beneficial for organizational efficiency, it is not necessarily indicative of improved employee health. However, cross-sectional data from the U.S. National Study of the Changing Workforce (Halpern, 2005) indicated that not only did employees with increased flexibility have fewer days' absenteeism, they also reported fewer stress-related health symptoms.

Thomas and Ganster (1995) also found that flexible working practices supportive of family responsibilities were related to better physical and psychological health. Specifically they found that reports of flexible work hours were directly related to fewer somatic complaints. In addition, flexibility had an indirect effect on somatic complaints, depression, and cholesterol levels. These effects were mediated by perceptions of control and (decreasing) work-family conflict. In contrast, Janssen and Nachreiner (2004) found that flexibility is related to poorer health; however, flexibility in their study was operationalized in terms of high variability in work hours. Such variability was related to increased health impairment, particularly where it was controlled by the company. Surprisingly, they found that having autonomy over timing did not entirely compensate for the high variability. However, it is clear that flextime arrangements which may help employees meet family needs do not necessarily imply high variability.

Two studies have looked at differences among those working different types of flexible work schedules. Martens, Nijhuis, Van Boxtel and Knottnerus (1999) found that individuals working compressed work weeks reported greater somatic complaints, poorer psychological well being and poorer sleep quality than those working standard working weeks (8 am to 5 pm, Monday to Friday). No information was given as to whether employees had choice or control over these working hours. In contrast, Almer and Kaplan (2002) found that accountants who had the choice of flexible working hours had lower levels of burnout than employees without these arrangements.

The above studies suggest that control over when or how long work is performed is a critical factor in understanding the potential health effects of workplace flexibility. Consistent with this point, a number of studies have operationalized flexibility in terms of work-time control (e.g., Ala-Mursula, Vahtera, Linna, Pentti, & Kivimaki, 2005; Ala-Mursula, Vahtera, Pentti, & Kivimaki, 2004; Ala-Mursula, Vahtera, Kivimaki, Kevin, & Pentti, 2002; Kauffeld, Jonas, & Frey, 2004). Ala-Mursula and colleagues (2002), in a cross-sectional study, found that low control over timing was linked with poorer health, psychological distress, and increased sickness. These effects were replicated in a longitudinal study (Ala-Mursula et al., 2004) which found that low work control predicted poorer health, more psychological distress, and greater absenteeism in women over a period of 3 years. These effects were particularly strong for women with children. Similar effects were also evident for men with children and male manual workers. Given differences in social programs and cultural norms surrounding work and family between the United States. and Europe, it remains unclear if similar results would emerge from U.S. samples.

Like schedule flexibility, location flexibility is often promoted as a means of helping employees achieve work-life balance (Sullivan & Lewis, 2006), and potentially better health. However, there is little empirical evidence documenting the health and well being implications of location flexibility. Existing research it is not always consistent. For example, Lundberg and Lindfors (2002) found that teleworkers had lower systolic blood pressure while working at home relative to when working in the office, whereas other researchers found that teleworkers may experience more stress and potentially more stress-related illness because of greater feelings of isolation and the omnipresent work demands resulting from the blurring of boundaries between home and work (Montreuil & Lippel, 2003). Conflicting results such as these could result from the diverse types of remote working arrangements examined. Home workers range from professional workers whose remote working is facilitated by new technology to those involved in more traditional forms of unskilled and low-paid manual work. Furthermore, employees may conduct all or only a portion of their work at home. Indeed, approximately one-third of U.S. employers (34%) allow some of their employees to work from home occasionally, while another 30% of employers allow some employees to work from home on a regular basis (Bond, Galinsky, Kim, & Brownfield, 2005). It may be that, for some groups of workers, rather than helping to manage family responsibilities, working at home allows work to impinge more on family life (Sullivan &Lewis, 2006), or home to impinge more on work.

In summary, there is limited available evidence on the health implications of flexible working hours. Much of the existing evidence uses cross-sectional designs, a range of conceptualizations of workplace flexibility ranging from a dominant focus on the ability of the organization to be flexible to those focused on the individual's ability to chose his or her work arrangement, and a narrow set of health outcomes. Nevertheless, evidence suggests that where flexibility is introduced to give employees control over timing to help them manage family needs, it can be beneficial for health. However, employee control appears to be a critical factor. There is a need for more longitudinal research, research that differentiates between different flexible choices for employees, and research that examines a range of more specific outcomes. These will help establish the processes involved and have clear implications for policy.

The Present Study

The goal of this study is to identify the health implications of workplace flexibility over time. We begin by studying cross-sectional associations between flexibility and multiple dimensions of health. These analyses contribute to the existing literature by documenting associations of perceived flexibility with a wider variety of health outcomes in the same study than has been considered previously. Further, these analyses contribute to the literature by delineating differences in health among discrete work arrangements reflecting alternative approaches to flexibility. Then, we shift focus to determine if changes in perceived flexibility are associated with changes in health outcomes over a one-year period.

METHOD

Overview

The data for this study are from U.S. employees of a large multinational corporation who were eligible for benefits. Each year during health insurance open enrollment, employees are invited to participate in a Health Risk Appraisal (HRA) as part of the employee wellness program. Approximately 35% of benefits-eligible employees complete the HRA. In 2005, HRAs were completed by 3,847 employees. Participants were, on average, 42 years of age ($SD = 8.9$), predominantly (58%) female, and non-Hispanic white (78.8%). Nearly three-fourths were currently married, and 50% reported having at least one dependent 21 years of age or younger. Nearly half of the respondents (44.4%) were classified as "low level managers or professionals," while the remainder were "high level managers, executives or officers" (21.0%), "sales" (18.1%), "project leads or administrative" (10.1%), and "production/ manufacturing" (6.4%). Employees from each of five major units in the company, and from 19 business locations across the Midwest and east coast, completed HRAs. Of these employees, 3,188 had also completed an HRA in 2004. The additional 659 employees who completed an HRA only in 2005 did not differ from those with longitudinal data in terms of age, gender, marital status, or presence of dependents. However, the additional employees were disproportionately from the sales and production units of the organization.

Measures: 2005 Cross-Sectional Analyses

Independent Variables. The primary independent variable in this study is perceived flexibility. Perceived flexibility was operationalized from a single item asking, "I have the flexibility I need to meet my work, personal and family commitments." Response options ranged from "disagree strongly" to "agree strongly." Responses were categorized into three mutually exclusive dummy variables reflecting "strongly agree," "agree," and "disagree/strongly disagree," to avoid assumptions of a linear association with outcomes, and because few participants responded "strongly disagree."

Alternative flexible work arrangements were classified into one of the following categories: compressed schedule, part-time, working remotely, or as variable meaning they had the flexibility to determine when they started or stopped working. The data for making these classifications were from the company's human resource system and were originally obtained by voluntary self-reports of employees in response to regular queries by the Human Resources department. Approximately one-third of participants could be classified. The remaining participants were categorized as "Unassigned."

Dependent Variables. Six indicators of health were operationalized to reflect three specific dimensions of health (i.e., health perceptions, impairment, and morbidity) in two health domains (i.e., physical and mental). Self-rated health is used to represent health perceptions in the physical domain. Participants were asked, "Considering your age, how would you describe your overall physical health?" Response options ranged from "poor" to "excellent" with higher values indicating better health. Stress-related symptoms were used to represent health perceptions in the mental health domain. Specifically, participants were asked, "How often do you feel tense, anxious or depressed?" Response options ranged from "never" to "often" with higher scores indicating more frequent stress-related symptoms.

Impairment in the physical health domain was operationalized with an index of six items asking how personal health problems affected work experiences (i.e., "Because of my health problems the stresses of my job were much harder to handle."). Responses ranged from 1 ("Strongly disagree") to 5 ("Strongly agree"), as well as "does not apply." "Does not apply" responses were treated as missing because it is unknown if this response has similar meaning as "strongly disagree." Health impairment was constructed by computing the mean of non-missing responses with higher values indicating greater impairment ($\alpha = .69$). Mental health impairment was operationalized with a single item asking "during the past year, how much effect has stress had on your health?" Response options ranged from "none" to "a lot" with higher values indicating that stress has a greater effect on health.

Morbidity was operationalized with two dichotomous variables. Acid reflux disease or chronic heartburn was used as an indicator of physical morbidity because it is both common and costly: approximately 25% of adults experience acid reflux disease and the direct cost of disease management is $9 billion annually (Moayyedi & Talley, 2006). Individuals were coded 1 if they self-reported having acid reflux/heartburn and also self-reported either currently taking medication or under medical care for acid reflux. Depression was used as indicator of mental morbidity. Individuals were coded 1 if they reported currently having depression and also either taking medication or under medical care for depression.

Measures: Change Scores (2004–2005)

Independent Variables. Responses to an identical flexibility item asked in the 2004 and 2005 HRAs were used to create three mutually exclusive categories of changes in perceived flexibility. *Decline* represents individuals whose flexibility decreased from 2004 to 2005, *stable* represents individuals whose self-reported flexibility remain constant across the two years, and *increased* represents individuals whose flexibility was greater in 2005 than 2004.

Dependent Variables. Again, six indicators of health were operationalized to reflect three specific dimensions and two domains of health. All change indicators are dichotomous variables reflecting health decline from 2004 to 2005. The variables for health perceptions are declines in self-rated health (physical) and increase in frequency of stress symptoms (mental). Variables reflecting impairment are increased or higher scores in the effect of health on work (physical) and an increase in the extent to which stress affects health (mental). Morbidity indicators reflect the development of acid reflux disease (physical) or depression (mental) (i.e., absent in 2004, present in 2005). Our focus on health decline was influenced by practical constraints. First, this is a relatively healthy sample of adults, so our study has greater power looking at health declines than health improvements. We also focused on health declines because some health indicators, specifically indicators of morbidity, are chronic conditions that can be managed but not cured, thereby restricting the number of health domains that could be assessed.

Covariates

In both the cross-sectional and longitudinal analyses several demographic and occupational characteristics were controlled. Demographic characteristics included age, gender, race (white versus nonwhite), marital status (currently married versus not), number of dependents, and yearly earnings. Occupational characteristics included exempt status (salary versus hourly) and employee wage band level as an indicator of status within the organization (e.g., "officer, executive, or senior manager" versus "production lead" or "sales"). Additionally, obesity (BMI > 30) was included in all models because it underlies several physical and mental health problems. In the longitudinal models, health status in 2004 was included as a covariate. For example in predicting declines in self-rated health, self-rated health in 2004 was used to account for potential "floor" and "ceiling" effects.

Analysis

A series of regression models were fit to evaluate the cross-sectional and longitudinal health implications of workplace flexibility. In the cross-sectional models, each health outcome was regressed on perceived flexibility and identified covariates. Ordinary least squares regression models were fit for health perception and impairment outcomes, whereas logistic regression models were fit for the morbidity outcomes. The modeling strategy for the longitudinal analyses focus on health declines because evidence indicates that change scores, in this case dichotomous change, produce less biased results than lagged-dependent models (Johnson, 2005). Each indicator of health decline was regressed on change in perceived flexibility as the independent variables and covariates.

RESULTS

Participants, on average, reported very good self-rated health ($M = 3.89$, $SD = 0.87$), and most participants reported "sometimes" to the item asking about the frequency of feeling tense, anxious, or depressed (Table 10.1). Individuals generally did not believe that their health interfered with their ability to perform their work ($M = 1.89$; $SD = 0.79$), although most employees believed that stress had "some" effect on their health ($M = 2.46$; $SD = .81$). Approximately one in ten participants (9%) had a clinical problem with acid reflux/heartburn that was severe enough for medication or medical oversight. Likewise, 5.8% of participants were depressed.

There was substantial variation across the domains of health in health-related declines. Roughly one-fifth of participants' health perceptions declined. Whereas 17.3% reported poorer self-rated health in 2005 relative to 2004, approximately one in seven participants (13.8%) reported feeling tense, anxious, or depressed more frequently in 2005 than 2004. More than four of ten participants (43.1%) believed more strongly in 2005 than 2004 that health im-

Table 10.1. Descriptive Statistics for Health and Workplace Flexibility

	%	M	SD	Range
Current (2005) health				
Health perceptions				
Self-rated physical health		3.89	0.87	1–5
Depressive symptoms		2.50	0.73	1–4
Health impairment				
Work-related impairment		1.89	0.79	1–5
Stress effect on health		2.46	0.81	1–4
Morbidity				
Acid Reflux/Heartburn	9.0			
Depression	5.8			
Health declines				
Health perceptions				
Decline in self-rated physical health	17.3			
Increased depressive symptoms	13.8			
Health impairment				
Increased work-related impairment	43.1			
Increased belief stress effects health	20.7			
Morbidity				
Developed acid reflux/heartburn	3.0			
Developed depression	3.0			
Flexibility 2005*				
Disagree	6.7			
Agree	50.0			
Strongly Agree	43.2			
Flexibility Change§				
Decline	21.0			
Stable	61.0			
Improved	18.0			
Work arrangement*				
Compressed	4.2			
Part-Time	3.5			
Remote	19.2			
Variable/Flextime	9.8			
Unassigned	63.3			

*Percents may not total 100% because of rounding

paired their ability to work, and one-fifth (20.7%) reported an increase in the extent to which stress affected health. Three percent of individuals reported new cases of acid reflux/heartburn and depression that required medical management either with medications or oversight by a health care provider.

Participants generally agreed that the organization provided sufficient flexibility to meet responsibility inside and outside of work. Indeed, fewer than 10% of participants believed that the company did not provide sufficient flexibility.

Nevertheless, for 21% of participants, appraisals of flexibility declined, whereas 18% of participants' appraisals of flexibility increased between 2004 and 2005. The majority of participants reported no change in the level of perceived flexibility, and the vast majority of these respondents (95%) agreed or strongly agreed in 2004 that the company provided workers with sufficient flexibility.

There is substantial cross-sectional evidence that flexibility is associated with worker health (Table 10.2). In terms of health perceptions, relative to those who disagree that the company provides sufficient flexibility, those who agree and agree strongly report better self-rated health and less frequent feelings of tension, anxiety, and depression. Turning to indicators of health-related impairment, perceptions of the extent to which health undermines the ability to work and the frequency that stress affects health is lower for individuals who agree and strongly agree that the company provides sufficient flexibility, relative to those who disagree. Finally, in terms of physical and mental morbidity, the odds of reporting clinically significant acid reflux/heartburn and depression is 49% and 47% lower, respectively, for individuals who reported "strongly agree" versus "disagree" to the item about flexibility. Additionally, the odds of reporting acid reflex/heartburn was significantly greater for individuals working a compressed work schedule and those with flextime relative to individuals working part time.

Several cross-sectional associations hold in models designed to capture how individuals arrived at their current health status (Table 10.3). Relative to individuals who experienced a decline in perceived flexibility, the odds of reporting poorer self-rated health in 2005 than 2004 was 28% lower for individuals whose level of flexibility increased over the year. The odds of reporting more frequent feelings of tension, anxiety, and depression were lower for individuals with continuous levels of perceived flexibility relative to those whose perceived level of flexibility declined. However, the odds of reporting more frequent feelings of tension and anxiety did not differ between individuals whose perceived flexibility increased and those whose perceived flexibilty decreased. The odds of reporting an increase in the degree to which health impaired the individual's ability to work did not differ by changes in flexibility, although the odds of reporting an increase in effects of stress on health were 45% and 56% lower for workers with stable and increased flexibility, respectively, than individuals whose flexibility declined. Turning to the morbidity outcomes, the results indicate that the odds of developing acid reflux/heartburn are 42% lower for individuals whose flexibility increased relative to those whose flexibility declined. The odds of developing depression were 44% lower for individuals whose flexibility remained stable relative to those whose flexibility declined.

Table 10.2. Cross-Sectional Associations of Workplace Flexibility with Domains of Physical and Mental Health

Health Perceptions

	Self-Rated Health			Frequency of Depressive Symptoms		
	b	β	*SE*	*b*	β	*SE*
Flexibility						
Disagree		Reference			Reference	
Agree	0.28***	0.16	0.05	−0.28***	−0.20	0.05
Strongly Agree	0.50***	0.28	0.05	−0.50***	−0.34	0.05
Arrangement‡						
Compressed	−0.05	−0.01	0.10	−0.11	−0.03	0.09
Part-time		Reference			Reference	
Remote	0.01	0.01	0.08	−0.02	−0.01	0.07
Variable/Flextime	−0.04	−0.02	0.09	−0.03	−0.01	0.07
			0.08			
Adjusted R²	16.6			6.3		

Health-Related Impairment

	Health Impairs Ability to Work			Effect of Stress on Health		
	b	β	*SE*	*b*	β	*SE*
Flexibility						
Disagree						
Agree	−0.27***	−0.17	0.08	−0.39***	−0.24	0.05
Strongly Agree	−0.49***	−0.31	0.08	−0.66***	−0.40	0.05

(continued)

Table 10.2. (continued)

| | Health-Related Impairment | | | | | |
| | Self-Rated Health | | | Frequency of Depressive Symptoms | | |
	b	β	SE	b	β	SE
Arrangement‡						
Compressed	−0.23	−0.07	0.18	−0.12	−0.03	0.10
Part-time		Reference			Reference	
Remote	−0.22	−0.11	0.15	0.01	0.01	0.08
Variable/Flextime	−0.17	−0.07	0.16	−0.09	−0.03	0.08
Adjusted R²		4.1			7.9	

| | Morbidity | | | | | |
| | Acid Reflux/Heartburn | | | Depression | | |
	b	SE	OR	b	SE	OR
Flexibility						
Disagree		Reference			Reference	
Agree	−0.28	0.21	0.75	−0.42†	0.24	0.66
Strongly Agree	−0.68***	0.22	0.51	−0.64**	0.25	0.53
Arrangement‡						
Compressed	1.76**	0.60	5.80	0.11	0.55	1.11
Part-time		Reference			Reference	
Remote	0.95†	0.54	2.58	0.19	0.42	1.21
Variable/Flextime	1.46**	0.57	4.31	0.01	0.48	1.01

† $p < .10$ * $p < .05$ ** $p < .01$ *** $p < .001$ (two-tailed).
Models control for the effects of age, gender, race, marital status, number of dependents, yearly earnings, exempt status (salary versus hourly), and employee wage band level as an indicator of status within the organization. ‡ Models also include a dummy variable reflecting "unassigned" work arrangements; however, parameter estimates are not reported because they do not have any clear meaning.

Table 10.3. Estimated Effect of Changes in Flexibility on Physical and Mental Health Declines over One Year by Domain of Health

Health Perceptions

	Self-Rated Health‡			*Frequency of Depressive Symptoms‡*		
	b	*SE*	*OR*	*b*	*SE*	*OR*
Flexibility						
Decline						
Stable	−0.08	Reference	0.92	−0.31*	Reference	0.74
Increased	−0.33*	0.13	0.72	−0.26	0.13	0.77
Arrangements§						
Compressed	−0.16	0.43	0.86	−0.37	−0.12	0.89
Part-time		Reference			Reference	
Remote	−0.21	0.34	0.81	−0.16	0.32	0.85
Variable/Flextime	−0.33	0.36	0.72	−0.13	0.34	0.88

Health-Related Impairment

	Health Impairs Ability to Work‡			*Effect of Stress on Health‡*		
	b	*SE*	*OR*	*b*	*SE*	*OR*
Flexibility						
Decline						
Stable	−0.30	0.19	0.74	−0.60***	0.12	0.55
Increased	−0.32	0.23	0.72	−0.77***	0.16	0.46

(continued)

Table 10.3. (*continued*)

Health Related Impairment

	Health Impair Ability to Work‡			Effect of Stress on Health‡		
	b	SE	OR	b	SE	OR
Arrangements§						
Compressed	−0.21	0.62	0.81	0.52	0.40	1.68
Part-time		Reference			Reference	
Remote	−0.10	0.49	0.90	0.15	0.32	1.16
Variable/Flextime	−0.15	0.53	0.87	0.56†	0.34	1.75

Morbidity

	Acid Reflux/Heartburn			Depression		
	b	SE	OR	b	SE	OR
Flexibility						
Decline						
Stable	−0.42†	0.24	0.66	−0.58*	0.28	0.56
Increased	−0.74*	0.34	0.58	0.02	0.31	1.02
Arrangements§						
Compressed	1.87†	1.12	6.50	−0.49	0.90	0.62
Part-time		Reference			Reference	
Remote	0.57	1.06	1.76	−0.21	0.68	0.81
Variable/Flextime	1.18	1.09	3.26	−0.68	0.78	0.51

† $p < .10$ * $p < .05$ ** $p < .01$ *** $p < .001$ (two-tailed)
Models control for the effects of age, gender, race, marital status, number of dependents, yearly earnings, exempt status (salary versus hourly), and employee wage band level as an indicator of status within the organization. ‡ Models control for health status in 2004. § Models also include a dummy variable reflecting "unassigned" work arrangements; however, parameter estimates are not reported because they do not have any clear meaning.

DISCUSSION

There are significant gaps in the evidence linking workplace flexibility to individual health, despite widespread claims that flexibility benefits health. Foremost is the virtual absence of longitudinal research that captures how changes in flexibility may contribute to changes in health-related outcomes (cf. Ala-Mursula et al., 2004; Dalton & Mesch, 1990). Research also tends to focus on narrow domains of health in individual studies, thereby undermining a comprehensive and coherent description of the potential health-related consequences of implementing workplace flexibility. These and other gaps in the evidence seriously undermine the ability to use employee health as a leverage point for building enthusiasm for widespread policies advocating expansion of workplace flexibility options. This study begins to address the limitations of previous research and the results make several contributions to the literature.

Results from our cross-sectional analyses expand the scope of previous research linking workplace flexibility with health outcomes in two ways. First, our results indicate that that individuals with greater perceived flexibility have better self-rated physical health, less physical and mental health-related impairment, and lower risk of both physical and mental morbidity. These results, which are consistent with previous research focusing on a narrower range of outcomes (Galinsky, Bond, & Friedman, 1996; Halpern, 2005; Marshall & Barnett, 1994; Thomas & Ganster, 1995), suggest that flexibility may have broad-ranging health implications. The second contribution of the cross-sectional analyses is the general absence of significant health differences among workers in specific types of flexible work arrangements. These results suggest that the way flexibility is structured within an organization is secondary to employees' beliefs that they have the flexibility they need. This conclusion is consistent with growing consensus that workplace flexibility is characterized more by organizational culture than by specific practices within the workplace (Corporate Voices for Working Families, 2005; Galinsky et al., 1996).

Results from our longitudinal analyses also contribute to the literature. We find clear, albeit modest associations between changes in perceived flexibility and health decline across three separate domains of health. Relative to individuals who experience declines in flexibility, individuals whose flexibility increased had lower odds of reporting a decline in overall health, lower odds of reporting an increase in the belief that stress affected personal health, and lower risk of developing acid reflux disorder. Similarly, compared to individuals whose flexibility declined, individuals whose perceived flexibility remained constant (who had relatively high levels in 2004) had lower odds of reporting more frequent feelings of tension, anxiety, and stress. Individuals whose flexibility remained stable also had lower odds of reporting an increase in the effects of stress on health and lower odds of developing depression relative to individuals whose flexibility declined over the year. These results are consistent with the only other longitudinal study of the health effects of workplace flexibility (Ala-Mursula et al., 2004). It is difficult to discern from these panel data whether changes in flexibility preceded changes in health, or vice versa; however, additional sensitivity analyses whereby health change outcomes were regressed on 2004 flexibility levels yielded identical results. Although additional research is needed, these collective results provide needed evidence suggesting that changes in flexibility may contribute to better employee health.

We also conducted additional post-hoc analyses to explore whether the effects of workplace flexibility on health differed among women and men. There is a deep and persistent tendency to argue that workplace arrangements, such as flexibility, may be more important for women than men because women shoulder greater family responsibilities. The results of our supplemental analyses yielded no evidence suggesting that the effects of workplace flexibility differ by gender. These results are consistent with accumulating evidence indicating that the ability to combine work and family is not a women's issue, and they suggest that promoting workplace flexibility will benefit women and men equally.

Before turning to potential implications of our research, it is appropriate to acknowledge the study's limitations. First, although we had a large and diverse sample, they were all employed by a single organization and participants were self-selected into the HRA program; therefore, the results may have limited generalizability. However, it is worth noting that this company is consistently recognized by *Working Mother* magazine as one of the best employers for working families, in large part because of its commitment to flexibility. Observed associations are therefore likely to be conservative estimates of the true associations. Second, many of the constructs in this study were assessed with single items with unknown reliability and validity. Finally, an objective characterization of work arrangements was not available for most participants. Future research should address these limitations by collecting data from more generalizable samples. Future research should also use more comprehensive measures of flexibility, as well as stronger measures of health such as employee sickness absences, validated scales of somatic complaints, or instruments designed to assess specific domains of health (e.g., SF-36) and discrete health problems (e.g., clinical depression).

Limitations notwithstanding, the results of this study have several practical implications. The results of this study provide clear evidence that promoting flexibility in the workplace may contribute to better health of individuals in those workplaces, particularly forms of flexibility that allow workers to control when, where, and how long job-related work is performed. Although the health effects observed in this study are small, advocates should not be discouraged from promoting workplace flexibility because few factors, particularly modifiable social factors, can have profound health effects given its complex etiology (Zapf, Dormann, & Frese, 1996). Indeed, systematic policies that affect large groups of people can have profound effects on population health, even when individual effects are small. Consequently, our results suggest that advocates should continue pressing for expansion of workplace flexibility. However, a note of caution is also required because results from previous research suggest that workplace flexibility is not without risk (Baltes et al., 1999) and care needs to be taken in implementing strategies for promoting flexibility. It is likely that the greatest benefits for workers and their families will be achieved when workers have a high level of control and when the organizational culture and practices ensure support for workers' choices.

The results of this study also have implications for theory development and future research. Our results suggest that health may be an important explanatory mechanism linking work and family. Although emotion has been posited as one way by which work and family shape each other, both positively and negatively (Carlson, Kacmar, Wayne, & Grzywacz, 2006; Edwards & Rothbard, 2000), researchers have given less attention to the way that different domains of health may link work and family. Research examining whether associations between workplace characteristics and family outcomes are mediated by health would be useful for developing comprehensive models of the work-family interface. Similarly, to the extent that individual health enables effective families, the results of this study suggest that workplace characteristics, such as flexibility, may play an important role in understanding optimal family functioning.

In conclusion, this study provides one of the first longitudinal studies of the effects of workplace flexibility on health outcomes. Our results provide clear and consistent evidence indicating that widespread attempts to promote flexibility in the workplace may contribute to enhanced health perceptions, reduced health-related impairment, and less morbidity. Collectively, the results of this study suggest that promoting systematic attempts to build flexibility in the workplace is a viable strategy for promoting health and building strong and resilient families.

NOTE

Joseph G. Grzywacz, Ph.D., is an associate professor of family studies in the Department of Family and Community Medicine, Wake Forest University School of Medicine. Fiona A. Jones, Ph.D., is a senior lecturer of occupational health psychology at the Institute of Psychological Sciences, University of Leeds. Patrick R. Casey, B.S., was a student in the Department of Family and Community Medicine, Wake Forest University School of Medicine. Please address all correspondence to Joseph G. Grzywacz, Ph.D., Department of Family and Community Medicine, Wake Forest University School of Medicine, Medical Center Blvd, Winston-Salem, NC 27157-1084. Phone: 336-716-2237. Fax: 336-716-3206. Email: grzywacz@wfubmc.edu. This research was supported by a grant from the Alfred P. Sloan Foundation (2006-5-22WPF).

REFERENCES

Ala-Mursula, L., Vahtera, J., Kivimaki, M., Kevin, M., & Pentti, J. (2002). Employee control over working times: Associations with subjective health and sickness absences. *Journal of Epidemiology & Community Health, 56*, 272–278.

Ala-Mursula, L., Vahtera, J., Linna, A., Pentti, J., & Kivimaki, M. (2005). Employee worktime control moderates the effects of job strain and effort-reward imbalance on sickness absence: The 10-town study. *Journal of Epidemiology & Community Health, 59*, 851–857.

Ala-Mursula, L., Vahtera, J., Pentti, J., & Kivimaki, M. (2004). Effect of employee worktime control on health: A prospective cohort study. *Occupational and Environmental Medicine, 61*, 254–261.

Allen, J. R. (2002). Building supportive cultural environments. In M. P. O'Donnell (Ed.), *Health promotion in the workplace,* 3rd ed. (pp. 202–217). Albany, NY: Delmar.

Almer, E. D., & Kaplan, S. E. (2002). The effects of flexible work arrangements on stressors, burnout, and behavioral job outcomes in public accounting. *Behavioral Research in Accounting, 14*, 1–34.

Baltes, B. B., Briggs, T. E., Huff, J. W., Wright, J. A., & Neuman, G. A. (1999). Flexible and compressed workweek schedules: A meta-analysis of their effects on work-related criteria. *Journal of Applied Psychology, 84*, 496–513.

Benach, J., Amable, M., Muntaner, C., & Benavides, F. (2002). The consequences of flexible work for health: Are we looking at the right place? *Journal of Epidemiology & Community Health, 56*, 405–406.

Bond, J. T., Galinsky, E., Kim, S. S., & Brownfield, E. (2005, September). *2005 National Study of Employers.* New York: Families and Work Institute. Retrieved April, 12, 2007 from http://familiesandwork.org/eproducts/2005nse.pdf

Carlson, D. S., Kacmar, K. M., Wayne, J. H., & Grzywacz, J. G. (2006). Measuring the positive side of the work-family interface: Development and validation of a work-family enrichment scale. *Journal of Vocational Behavior, 68*, 131–164.

Cohen, S., & Herbert, T. B. (1996). Health psychology: Psychological factors and physical disease from the perspective of human psychoneuroimmunology. *Annual Review of Psychology, 47*, 113–142.

Corporate Voices for Working Families. (2005). *Business impacts of flexibility: An imperative for expansion.* Boston: WFD Consulting.

Costa, G., Akerstedt, T., Nachreiner, F., Baltieri, F., Carvalhais, J., Folkard, S., et al. (2004). Flexible working hours, health, and well-being in Europe: Some considerations from a SALTSA project. *Chronobiology International, 21*, 831–844.

Dalton, D. R., & Mesch, D. J. (1990). The impact of flexible scheduling on employee attendance and turnover. *Administrative Science Quarterly, 35*, 370–387.

Edwards, J. R., & Rothbard, N. P. (2000). Mechanisms linking work and family: Clarifying the relationship between work and family constructs. *Academy of Management Review, 25*, 178–199.

Galinsky, E., Bond, J. T., & Friedman, D. E. (1996). The role of employers in addressing the needs of employed parents. *Journal of Social Issues, 52*, 111–136.

Halpern, D. F. (2005). How time-flexible work policies can reduce stress, improve health and save money. *Stress and Health*, 21, 157–168.

Janssen, D. & Nachreiner, F. (2004). Health and psychosocial effects of flexible working hours. *Revista de Saude Publica, 38*(suppl), 11–18.

Johnson, D. (2005). Two-wave panel analysis: Comparing statistical methods for studying the effects of transitions. *Journal of Marriage and Family, 67*, 1061–1075.

Karasek, R. A., & Theorell, T. (1990). *Healthy work. Stress, productivity and the reconstruction of working life.* New York: Basic Books.

Kauffeld, S., Jonas, E., & Frey, D. (2004). Effects of a flexible work-time design on employee- and company-related aims. *European Journal of Work and Organizational Psychology, 13*, 79–100.

Keyes, C. L., & Grzywacz, J. G. (2002). Complete health: Prevalence and predictors among U.S. adults in 1995. *American Journal of Health Promotion, 17*, 122–131.

Lundberg, U., & Lindfors, P. (2002). Psychophysiological reactions to telework in female and male white-collar workers. *Journal of Occupational Health Psychology, 7*, 354–364.

Marshall, N. L., & Barnett, R. C. (1994). Family-friendly workplaces, work-family interface, and worker health. In G. P. Keita, & J. J. Hurrell (Eds.). *Job stress in a changing workforce: Investigating gender, diversity, and family issues* (pp. 253–264). Washington, DC: American Psychological Association.

Martens, M. F. J., Nijhuis, F. J. N., Van Boxtel, M. P. J., & Knottnerus, J. A. (1999). Flexible work schedules and mental and physical health. A study of a working population with non-traditional working hours. *Journal of Organizational Behavior, 20*, 35–46.

Moayyedi, P., & Talley, N. J. (2006). Gastro-oesophageal reflux disease [see comment]. *Lancet, 367*, 2086–2100.

Montreuil, S., & Lippel, K. (2003). Telework and occupational health: A Quebec empirical study and regulatory implications. *Safety Science, 41*, 339–358.

Patrick, D. L., & Erikson, P. (1993). *Health status and health policy: Quality of life in health care evaluation and resource allocation.* New York: Oxford University Press.

Stokols, D., Pelletier, K. R., & Fielding, J. E. (1996). The ecology of work and health: Research and policy directions for the promotion of employee health. *Health Education Quarterly, 23*, 137–158.

Sullivan, C., & Lewis, S. (2006). Work at home and the work-family interface. In Jones, F., Burke, R. J., & Westman, M. (Eds), *Work-life balance: A psychological perspective* (pp. 143–162). New York: Psychology Press.

Thomas, L. T., & Ganster, D. C. (1995). Impact of family-supportive work variables on work-family conflict and strain: A control perspective. *Journal of Applied Psychology*, 80, 6–15.

U.S. Department of Labor (2005) Flexible work schedules in 2004. Bureau of Labor statistics. Retrieved March 27, 2007, from http://www.bls.gov/opub/ted/2005/jul/wk1/art01.htm

Voydanoff, P. (2005). Toward a conceptualization of perceived work-family fit and balance: A demands and resources approach. *Journal of Marriage and Family*, 67, 822–836.

Zapf, D., Dormann, C., & Frese, M. (1996). Longitudinal studies in organizational stress research: A review of the literature with reference to methodological issues. *Journal of Occupational Health Psychology, 1*, 145–169.

Chapter Eleven

Flexibility and Control: Does One Necessarily Bring the Other?

by Shelley M. MacDermid and Chiung Ya Tang

ABSTRACT

Flexibility in work schedules or locations is frequently promoted as the least costly and most effective way to make it easier for workers to succeed at home and at work. A corollary assumption is that flexibility brings control over work or, on the contrary, control over work allows flexibility, but in practice this may not always be true. For example, workers in high-status occupations such as surgeons or judges may have considerable power and authority, but little ability to control their work schedules because of the demands of medical emergencies or full court dockets. In this chapter we explore the definitions and meaning of flexibility and control at work, examine their overlap and uniqueness, and consider their relevance for workers with different characteristics.

Of all of the policies, programs, and practices developed to make workplaces more family-friendly, job flexibility has become one of the most visible. Touted as a strategy that is inexpensive to implement, feasible in many different kinds of workplaces, and beneficial to many employees, flexible, customized, or alternative work arrangements have become much more common in the United States. For example, the percentage of U.S. workers with the ability to vary the starting or ending times of their work day more than doubled between 1985 and 2000, from 12.4% to 28.8% (Blair-Loy & Wharton, 2004), although almost all of the growth occurred between 1991 and 1997.

Flexible work arrangements, which typically refer to flexibility in schedule (e.g., compressed work weeks, flextime, paid leave) or location (e.g., telecommuting) are often promoted as reducing conflict between work and nonwork life by making it possible for workers to successfully juggle their responsibilities on and off the job. The work-life area of the website for the U.S. Office of Personnel Management, for example, asserts that "Flexible work arrangements . . . give Federal employees more control over when and where they can accomplish their best work. They enable employees to meet their responsibilities at and away from work, while also helping organizations attract and retain a committed, effective workforce" (Office of Personnel Management, 2006).

Empirical evidence for the effectiveness of flexibility has been mixed. A quarter-century ago, the first large-scale evaluation of flextime revealed that while most participants evaluated their arrangements favorably, there were only modest reductions in workers' stress, and generally not for the workers with the greatest need (Bohen & Viveros-Long, 1981). The authors concluded that the flexibility of the program was too modest to provide workers the degrees of freedom they really needed. More recently, a meta-analysis examined 31 quasi-experimental studies with comparison groups that assessed the short- and long-term impact of flexible and compressed workweek schedules on job performance, satisfaction, and absenteeism (Baltes, Briggs, Huff, Wright, & Neuman, 1999). The analyses also took into account the rigor of the methodology of each study. The results showed that workers with more schedule flexibility were more productive and less likely to miss work (based on objective data), and more satisfied with their jobs and their schedules (based on self-report). Effects were strongest for absenteeism and weakest for productivity, and were stronger in more rigorous studies. Two findings deviated from this generally positive pattern: The positive effects of flexibility diminished over time, and—surprisingly—more flexible programs had smaller effects than less flexible ones.

Flexibility also has been distributed quite unevenly across the workforce, seeming to accrue mostly according to status rather than need. Golden (2005) used data from the May 2001 supplement to the U.S. Current Population Survey to examine workers' ability to change when they started or ended work. Workers who were male, older, more educated, or who had higher-status jobs all had more access to flexibility than lower-status workers. Workers in unionized jobs or jobs in local government, K-12 education, health care, other services or retail sales had reduced access to flexibility, as did workers who were members of ethnic minority groups and workers who worked night shifts. In addition, flexibility appeared to carry a price in the form of very long or short work weeks—"it is only workers willing to put in an average of

10 hours per day, or go to part-time status, whose hours afford them greater access to adjusting their daily start and end times" (p. 49).

Golden's findings echoed those from data gathered 10 years earlier. Using the U.S. subset of the 1991 Comparative Project in Class Analysis, McCrate (2005) found that workers with more authority to control the work of others and workers were more likely to be able decide when to begin and end their work days, and to be able to take a day off with pay and without penalty. There also was a striking disadvantage associated with ethnicity, with Black workers having restricted access to flexibility.

In a third nationally representative sample, the 1997 National Study of the Changing Workforce, Swanberg, Pitt-Catsouphes, and Drescher-Burke (2005) again found that less privileged workers had less access to flexible schedule options, including modifying starting and ending times, taking time off for personal or family time, and controlling work hours. Hourly work, lower wages, and lower levels of education all were risk factors for reduced access to flexibility.

While these three large studies make it clear that workers with more power and authority have more latitude to decide when they work, they do not address the degree to which workers feel able to exercise the latitude available to them. Power and authority at work often are accompanied by responsibilities that may limit workers' ability to be away from their jobs. For example, surgeons, judges, and CEOs all must respond to the demands of emergencies, heavy workloads, or accountability to many constituencies that keep them at work even when they have official latitude to leave. Blair-Loy and Wharton (2004) pursued this issue in a study of managers in a firm facing high pressure from global competition, focusing specifically on nonusers of flextime and telecommuting policies to examine the degree to which they felt constrained from using the policies. Workers who felt the most constrained were those with the highest status, income, job demands, and pressure at work, and the lowest control over their jobs. They were also least likely to have a home-making spouse. Workers in work groups with fewer women or fewer parents also felt more constrained.

In addition to high-status workers with power and authority, workers throughout the labor force may face constraints in their use of schedule discretion. Tausig and Fenwick (2001) point out, for example, that most employees working nonstandard or alternate schedules are doing so because it is required by their employers, not by choice. They hypothesized that alternate job schedules would be beneficial only when the schedule was voluntarily chosen. The researchers used data from the 1992 National Study of the Changing Workforce, a survey of a nationally representative sample of U.S. workers, to examine relationships between workers' reports of their ability to balance work, family, personal, and job factors including work schedule and hours, availability of flexible work options, control over schedule, age, race, gender, education, family structure, occupation, industry, union membership, and size of workplace. Regression analyses revealed that work-family balance was positively related to schedule control, but not to the availability of flexible work options.

In the only study found that examined both access to flexibility and the ability to use it, Eaton (2003) surveyed 1,030 workers to test the impact on organizational commitment and self-reported productivity among professional and technical workers in the biotechnology industry. Eaton defined usability as the extent to which workers felt free to use flexibility policies including flextime, part-time work options, telecommuting, job sharing, compressed work weeks, unpaid personal leave beyond that required by the FMLA, or sick leave for ill children. Net of controls for a variety of demographic factors, workers reported stronger commitment when they perceived flexibility policies as more usable, involving greater control over their work, and when they worked in smaller firms. Workers reported being more productive when they had access to more forms of flexibility, either informally or through formal policies, when they perceived those policies as usable, and when they had been at the firm a shorter period of time.

The research reviewed here makes it clear that having the latitude to make decisions about work schedule and being able to exercise that latitude are not synonymous. This distinction is similar to the distinction between decision latitude and job demands drawn by Karasek in demand-control-support theory (1990). and Theorell predicted that workers would experience the greatest strain under conditions of high job demands and low control, and that both of these factors must be taken into account to understand workers' strain (p. 62). A meta-analysis of 63 studies testing this prediction confirmed that the lowest levels of well-being were found among employees working jobs with low control and high demands. Although Karasek and Theorell originally hypothesized an interactive relationship whereby control would moderate the effect of high demands, most studies were consistent with an additive model where both demand and control made independent contributions to well-being (Van Der Doef & Maes, 1999).

A later addition to demand-control theory was the construct of social support, which was hypothesized to offset the negative impact of high demands and low control by facilitating workers' positive sense of identity or efforts to cope with stressors. In the case of flexibility, it is possible that social support in the workplace could affect the amount of discretion that workers are allowed, such as when supportive supervisors permit workers to adjust their work hours without notice. Social support also could affect the opportunities workers have to exercise their latitude, such as when supportive coworkers avoid interrupting one another's work or making it more difficult to meet deadlines.

In this chapter, we conceptualize flexibility as the authority or discretion to control work conditions, including time and pace. We conceptualize control as the degree to which a worker has opportunities to exercise that discretion, similar to Eaton's definition of usability. And we conceptualize support as the supportiveness of coworkers, supervisors, and the organization. Our goal is to extend previous studies by mapping discretion, opportunities, and support among workers who work as full-time employees. Like Golden (2005), Mc-Crate (2005), and Swanberg et al. (2005), we focus on a nationally representative sample of workers. But unlike our colleagues, we exclude workers who are self-employed, who work part-time, or who work multiple jobs because those work arrangements may have been chosen in part as a way to acquire flexibility, making it very difficult to understand flexibility in the context of a full-time position with a single employer. Like Blair-Loy and Wharton (2004) and Eaton (2003), we pay attention to opportunities to use flexibility, but we also include a broader sample of workers extending beyond high-level or high-tech workers. Finally, we pay close attention to differences between hourly and salaried workers because of the requirements of the Fair Labor Standards Act (FLSA). This act requires that workers who are not exempt from its provisions (i.e., hourly workers) be paid overtime pay when they work more than 40 hours in a workweek (U.S. Department of Labor, 2006), and thus provides both employers and workers with a disincentive to prolong the workday.

METHOD

Data Source

Data used in the current study come from the 2002 National Study of the Changing Workforce (NSCW), a nationally representative survey of U.S. workers conducted by the Families and Work Institute (Families and Work Institute, 2004). Data were gathered from 3,504 employed adults using a computer-assisted telephone interview (CATI) that focused on work conditions, personal well-being, and family life. Eligible participants included adults who were at least 18 years old, were in the civilian labor force, and were working for pay at the time of the interview; the response rate was 52%. Since NSCW only surveyed one person per household, the sample was weighted to reflect eligible employed adults per surveyed household.

The sample for this study was intentionally limited in several ways. We concentrated on workers working at least 35 hours per week in a single job as an employee. We excluded workers who were self-employed or worked part-time, and workers with multiple jobs, because our aim was to focus on flexibility within a single job rather than on situations where workers had used part-time work or multiple jobs as flexibility strategies. The final sample for this study, less than half the original sample, consisted of 724 males and 950 females (total $N = 1,674$; weighted $n = 1,647$) with an average age of 42.24 years ($SD = 11.39$), a median family income of $56,100, and an average work week of 46.55 hours.

DEPENDENT VARIABLES

The dependent variables for this study were schedule discretion, opportunities to use that discretion, and support. We conducted factor analyses of 14 indicators that we hypothesized would form three factors corresponding to the dependent variables (because the items had different numbers of response options, we standardized the scores prior to the factor analysis). The analyses revealed that there actually were four factors because formal leave policies for vacations and holidays formed a factor separate from discretion. Table 11.1 presents the final factor loadings and intercorrelations. Scores for each factor were standardized to a mean of 1 and a standard deviation of 0. The components of each factor are described below.

Discretion. This factor comprised indicators of the degree to which workers had the authority to control their work schedule and pace. This factor included three single-item indicators and one three-item scale. One question asking whether the worker could change his or her starting and quitting times daily was a dummy variable ($1 = $ yes and $0 = $ no). Another question stated, "I decide when I take breaks" (responses ranging from $1 = $ strongly agree to $4 = $ strongly disagree). The last item was "overall, how much control would you say you have in scheduling your work?" and responses ranged from 1 meaning complete (control) to 4 meaning a little (control) and 6 meaning none. The autonomy scale consisted of three items regarding whether respondents had a lot of say about what happened on the job or had freedom to decide what they could do on the job and how the job was done. The responses to these three items ranged from 1, representing "strongly agree" to 4, representing "strongly disagree." Cronbach's alpha reliability for the indicators on this factor was 0.61.

Policy. This factor consisted of two single-item indicators concerning whether or not one's benefits included paid vacation or holidays. Respondents

Table 11.1. Factor Loadings and Intercorrelations (Weighted $N = 1647$)

	Factor			
	Discretion	Policy	Opportunity	Support
Overall control in scheduling work	0.295	-0.040	0.015	0.080
Ability to decide start/quit times daily	0.443	0.038	-0.046	-0.030
Ability to decide when to take breaks	0.666	0.042	0.028	-0.079
Job autonomy	0.701	-0.047	-0.034	0.094
Receive paid vacation days	-0.003	1.000	0.010	-0.011
Receive any paid holidays	0.013	0.602	-0.026	0.041
Frequency of feeling overwhelmed	0.013	0.022	0.780	-0.053
Being asked to do excessive amounts of work	0.066	-0.028	0.680	0.079
Having too many tasks per week	-0.090	0.013	0.675	-0.022

(continued)

Table 11.1. (continued)

	Factor			
	Discretion	Policy	Opportunity	Support
Job pressure (reversed)	-0.008	-0.033	0.598	0.011
Supervisor family-related support	-0.005	0.008	-0.031	0.894
Supervisor job-related support	-0.123	0.002	0.018	0.875
Supportiveness of coworkers	0.093	0.000	-0.050	0.582
Supportiveness of workplace culture	0.152	0.045	0.116	0.430
Factor Intercorrelations				
Policy	.161**			
Opportunity	.223**	.023		
Support	.510**	.000	.462**	

NOTE: Maximum likelihood factor extraction with promax rotation was used. Four factors explained 47.96% of the variance. Loadings shown come from the pattern matrix.

received a 1 if the policy was included in their benefits. Cronbach's reliability for this factor was 0.75.

Opportunity. This factor focused on workers' opportunities to use their discretion over work schedule and pace. It consisted of four items associated with the frequency of unexpected work load and pressure (Cronbach's α = .78). Two questions addressed job demands (i.e., "how often in the past three months have you been asked by your supervisor or manager to do excessive amounts of work?" and "during a typical workweek [at your main job], how often do you have to work on too many tasks at the same time?") and one concerned feeling overwhelmed (i.e., "how often you have felt overwhelmed by how much you had to do at work in the last three months?"). Responses to these three questions ranged from 1 meaning "very often" to 5 meaning "never." The fourth indicator was the mean score on three-item job pressure scale, which included respondents' perceptions of having to work very hard, very fast, or never having enough time to complete their work. To be consistent with the focus of the factor, responses to the pressure scale were reversed so that high scores indicated less job pressure or greater opportunity to use schedule discretion.

Support. This factor included scores from four scales comprising workers' ratings of supervisor supportiveness for family and work issues, coworker supportiveness, and supportiveness of the workplace culture. Cronbach's alpha was α = .80. Items in each scale used the same response scale (from 1 indicating "strongly agree" to 4 indicating "strongly disagree"). Except for responses to the index of workplace culture, responses to the other three indexes were all reversed so that for all four indexes, high scores indicated greater support from supervisor, coworker, or workplace culture to manage work and family lives. Sample items included "my supervisor or manager keeps me informed of the things I need to know to do my job well" (supervisor supportiveness for work issues), "my supervisor or manager is fair and doesn't show favoritism in responding to employees' personal or family needs" (supervisor supportiveness for family issues), "I have the support from coworkers that I need to do a good job" (coworker supportiveness) , and "at my place of employment, employees have to choose between advancing in their jobs or devoting attention to their family or personal lives" (supportiveness of workplace culture).

The intercorrelations among the factors are reported at the bottom of Table 11.1. Correlations between the policy factor and the other factors were quite small, never exceeding r = .161. Support was moderately correlated with both discretion (r = .510) and opportunity (r = .462). The correlation between discretion and opportunity was small (r = .223).

Independent Variables

The independent variables were chosen based on prior empirical research and included 15 characteristics of the individual, the family, the job, and the workplace.

Personal and family characteristics. Table 11.2 summarizes the personal and family characteristics used as independent variables. They included age, sex, ethnicity, educational level, family structure, child age, and family income. Age was a continuous variable ranging from 18 to 78 years. *Female* defined female workers. Ethnicity was coded into three dummy variables. With White non-Hispanic as the reference group, variables that were used to denote ethnicity included *Black non-Hispanic, Hispanic origins,* and *other ethnicities. Highest education* defined nine categories of education. Although this was a categorical variable ranging from 1 meaning "less than high school diploma" to 9 meaning "graduate degree," higher scores represented more education. Concerning family structure, we developed five dummy variables based on the information concerning whether participants were living with a spouse/partner, having one or two earners in the same household, or living with at least one child younger than 13 years of age. "Living with a spouse/partner and having no children at home" was the reference group. Similarly, three dummy variables were used to indicate age of the youngest child in the household. The reference group was "having no kid less than 18 years old." Finally, *logged family income* was used due to the skewed data.

Job and workplace characteristics. Table 11.3 summarizes descriptive statistics of the other set of independent variables that were used to represent job and workplace characteristics. They included occupation, work hours, difference between regular and ideal work hours, work shift, exempt/nonexempt status, union membership, supervisory responsibilities, hourly wage, job tenure, work group composition, and establishment size.

Six dummy variables were used to denote participants' occupations with "executive/administrative/manager" as the reference group. The other groups included *professionals, technical, sales, administrative support,* and *service.* Information about respondents' occupations were obtained from an open-ended question and coded based on the 1990 Census's occupational classification system. Work related to transportation, farming, forestry, fishing, and construction was coded as *production/operator/repair,* for it has been recognized as traditional blue collar work.

Participants' *work hours* ranged from 35 to 100 hours per week. Subtracting ideal from regular work hours yielded the difference between regular and ideal work hours per week. A negative score indicated a desire to work longer hours whereas a positive score indicated a desire to work fewer hours than the current regular work hours per week. In addition, four dummy variables were

Table 11.2. Personal and Family Characteristics (Weighted *N* =1647)

Variable	Percentage	Mean (SD)
Age		41.53 (11.67)
Sex		
Female	53.7	
Male	46.3	
Ethnicity		
White non-Hispanic	76.4	
Black non-Hispanic	9.2	
Hispanic	9.1	
Other	4.7	
Educational level		
< High school diploma	9.8	
High school or GED	30.4	
Some college, no degree	19.7	
Associate degree	9.9	
4-yr college degree	21.7	
Graduate or professional degree	8.6	

(*continued*)

Table 11.2. **(continued)**

Variable	Percentage	Mean (SD)
Family Structure		
Single, no kid	23.2	
Single, with kids	7.7	
Married, one earner, no kid	6.2	
Married, one earner, with kids	9.4	
Married, two earners, no kid	25.8	
Married, two earners, with kids	27.3	
Child age		
No kid less than 18	55.3	
Youngest–preschooler	18.9	
Youngest– school aged	15.1	
Youngest–high school	10.6	
Logged Family Income		10.80 (0.81)

Table 11.3. Job and Workplace Characteristics (Weighted *N* =1647)

Variables	Percentage	Mean (SD)
Occupation		
Executive/Administrative/Manager	16.1	
Professionals	19.0	
Technical	4.2	
Sales	9.1	
Administrative support	14.7	
Service	9.4	
Production/Operator/Repair	27.5	
Work hours per week		46.61 (8.49)
Difference between regular and ideal work hours per week		10.63 (15.05)

(continued)

Table 11.3.   (**continued**)

Variables	Percentage	Mean (SD)
Work schedule		
A regular daytime schedule	79.0	
A regular evening shift	3.3	
A regular night shift	3.7	
A rotating shift	6.7	
All others (including on call)	7.3	
Hourly (non-exempt)	62.3	
Union membership	17.7	
Supervisory responsibility	39.7	
Logged hourly wage		2.75 (0.68)
Job tenure		8.5 (8.58)
Composition of work group		4.35 (1.07)
Establishment size		3.93 (2.57)

used to denote ones' working schedule. Those dummy variables included *a regular evening shift, night shift, rotating shift*, and *other types*. A regular daytime schedule was the reference group. *Hourly* represented hourly (non-exempt) workers in contrast to salaried (exempt) workers. *Union* membership defined those who reported themselves as a union member. When one's main job is related to supervising others, his or her score of *supervisory responsibilities* was coded as 1. Respondents' *logged hourly wage* was used due to the skewed data. *Job tenure* indicated the number of years that the participants have worked for their current employers (ranging from 0 to 44 years). The *composition of the work group* was indicated by workers' reports of the percentage of coworkers who were of the same sex as the worker, with answer options ranging from 1 meaning 0% to 6 meaning 100%. Finally, *establishment size* described the number of employees in the workplace where the participants worked.

RESULTS

We conducted four ordinary least squares regressions, one for each of the flexibility factors: discretion, policy, opportunity, and support. Independent variables in each equation were the characteristics of persons, families, jobs, and workplaces listed in Tables 11.2 and 11.3. All independent variables were entered simultaneously.

There were no significant findings for job tenure or composition of work group. There also were no significant differences between workers in "other" ethnic groups compared to Whites, and no differences between the reference group of married single earners with no children and married single or dual earners with children. Finally, there were no differences between the reference category of executive workers and sales or administrative support workers.

Discretion

Three personal and family characteristics were significantly related to discretion. Non-Hispanic Black workers ($t = -2.78$, $p = .005$) and married dual-earner workers without children ($t = -2.50$, $p = .013$) each had less discretion than White workers or married single-earner workers without children. Workers with lower family incomes (logged family income; $t = 3.72$, $p = .000$) also had significantly less discretion. There were no significant relationships between discretion and age, sex, education, or child age.

Eight job and workplace characteristics were significantly related to discretion. Workers in service ($t = -3.13$, $p = .002$), or production, operation, and

Table 11.4. Unstandardized Regression Coefficients (Weighted N=1647)

	Discretion		Policy		Opportunity		Support	
	b	se	b	se	b	se	b	se
(Constant)	-2.08***	0.47	-1.51**	0.50	0.69	0.51	-0.65	0.52
Personal and Family Characteristics								
Age	0.004	0.00	0.002	0.00	0.01**	0.00	0.003	0.00
Female [1]	-0.07	0.05	-0.001	0.06	-0.21***	0.06	0.05	0.06
Ethnicity [2]								
Non-Hispanic Black	-0.23**	0.08	-0.01	0.09	0.01	0.09	-0.10	0.09
Hispanic origins	-0.16	0.08	-0.34***	0.09	-0.09	0.09	-0.06	0.09
Other ethnic groups	-0.01	0.11	0.05	0.12	-0.01	0.12	-0.05	0.12
Highest level of schooling completed	0.02	0.01	-0.01	0.01	0.02	0.02	-0.004	0.02
Family Structure [3]								
Single, 1 earner, no children	-0.20	0.11	0.05	0.12	-0.12	0.12	-0.18	0.12
Married, 2 earners, no children	-0.27*	0.11	0.04	0.11	-0.05	0.12	-0.24*	0.12
Single, 1 earner, with children	-0.13	0.56	0.63	0.60	0.09	0.61	-0.04	0.63
Married, 1 earner, with children	-0.15	0.56	0.44	0.60	0.01	0.62	-0.11	0.63
Married, 2 earners, with children	-0.26	0.56	0.51	0.59	0.23	0.61	-0.05	0.62
Child Age [4]								
Youngest–preschooler	0.12	0.57	-0.36	0.61	-0.13	0.62	0.02	0.64
Youngest–school aged	0.04	0.57	-0.37	0.61	-0.38	0.62	-0.06	0.63
Youngest–high school	0.08	0.56	-0.48	0.60	-0.30	0.61	0.02	0.63
Logged family income	0.16***	0.04	0.08	0.05	-0.05	0.05	0.08	0.05
Job and Workplace Characteristics								
Occupation [5]								
Professionals	-0.09	0.08	-0.39***	0.09	-0.04	0.09	0.09	0.09
Technical	0.05	0.13	-0.01	0.14	-0.32*	0.15	-0.27	0.15

Technical	0.05	0.13	-0.01	0.14	-0.32*	0.15	-0.27	0.15
Sales	-0.16	0.10	0.05	0.11	-0.08	0.11	-0.14	0.11
Administrative support	0.001	0.09	-0.09	0.10	0.06	0.10	0.00	0.10
Service	-0.33**	0.11	-0.53***	0.11	0.002	0.12	-0.06	0.12
Production/Operator/Repair	-0.34***	0.09	-0.28**	0.09	-0.09	0.10	-0.28**	0.10
Total work hours per week	0.01*	0.00	0.004	0.00	-0.01**	0.00	0.002	0.00
Difference b/w regular and ideal work hours/wk	-0.01***	0.00	0.001	0.00	-0.01***	0.00	-0.01***	0.00
Work schedule [6]								
A regular evening shift	0.03	0.13	0.19	0.14	-0.06	0.14	-0.22	0.14
A regular night shift	-0.19	0.12	0.07	0.13	0.25	0.14	-0.13	0.14
Rotating shift	-0.09	0.10	-0.24*	0.10	-0.01	0.11	-0.13	0.11
Other work schedules	-0.08	0.09	-0.22*	0.10	-0.21*	0.10	-0.14	0.11
Hourly worker [7]	-0.14*	0.06	0.21***	0.07	0.23***	0.07	0.10	0.07
Union membership [8]	-0.48***	0.06	-0.21**	0.07	-0.05	0.07	-0.23**	0.07
Supervisory responsibilities [9]	0.26***	0.05	0.01	0.05	-0.15**	0.06	0.05	0.06
Logged hourly wage	0.19***	0.05	0.16***	0.05	0.04	0.05	-0.001	0.05
Job tenure	0.005	0.00	0.01	0.00	-0.01	0.00	-0.001	0.00
Work group composition	-0.01	0.02	-0.04	0.02	0.03	0.02	0.02	0.02
Establishment size	-0.06***	0.01	0.06***	0.01	-0.03**	0.01	-0.05***	0.01
Adjusted r-squared	0.22		0.13		0.07		0.04	
F ratio	13.53***		7.41***		4.11***		3.02***	

* $p < .05$, ** $p < .01$, *** $p < .001$

Note: 1. Ref. group: non-Hispanic White. 2. Ref. group: male. 3. Ref. group: married, one earner, no kid. 4. Ref. group: no child less than 18 years old. 5. Ref. group: Executive/Administrative/Manager. 6. Ref group: a regular day time schedule. 7. Ref. group: salaried worker. 8. Ref. group: no membership. 9. Ref. group: no supervisory responsibilities.

repair occupations (t = −3.87, p = .000) had significantly less discretion than workers in other occupations, as did hourly (t = −2.22, p = .027) and unionized workers (t = −7.38, p = .000). Workers who earned less (logged hourly wage; t = 4.09, p = .000), who did not have supervisory responsibilities (t = 5.17, p = .000), or who worked in larger establishments (t = −6.48, p = .000) also had less discretion. Full-time workers who worked fewer hours (t = 2.08, p = .038), and workers for whom the gap between actual and ideal hours was larger had less discretion (t = −3.63, p = .000). There were no significant relationships between discretion and shift, job tenure, or work group composition. This model accounted for 22% of the variability in discretion.

Policy

Only one personal characteristic was related to policy coverage—Hispanic workers (t = −3.76, p = .000) were significantly less likely to have access to paid vacation or holidays than White workers. Six job and workplace characteristics were related to policy coverage. Professional (t = −4.56, p = .000), service (t = −4.67, p = .000), and production/operation/repair workers (t = −3.04, p = .002) all had less access to paid vacation and holidays than executive workers. Workers on rotating (t = −2.37, p = .018) and other shifts (t = −2.14, p = .033) had less access than workers on day shifts. Hourly workers (t = 3.19, p = .001), workers who earned more (logged hourly wage; t = 3.26, p = .001) and workers who worked in larger establishments (t = 5.91, p = .000) had more access, while unionized workers (t = −3.07, p = .002) had less access. This model accounted for 13% of the variability in policy coverage.

Opportunity

Two personal or family characteristics were related to opportunity. Younger workers (t = 3.15, p = .002) and female workers (t = −3.47, p = .001) had less opportunity to use their schedule discretion than older or male workers. Seven job or workplace characteristics were related to opportunity. Technical workers (t = −2.18, p = .029) had fewer opportunities to use their discretion than executives. Workers who worked more (t = −3.06, p = .002), workers who were working more hours than they wanted to (t = −3.51, p = .000), workers who worked at larger workplaces (t = −2.62, p = .009), workers with supervisory responsibilities (t = −2.64, p = .008), and workers working other work schedules (t = −1.99, p = .047) all had fewer opportunities to use their discretion than others, while hourly workers (t = 3.42, p = .001) had more opportunities. This model accounted for 7% of the variability in opportunity.

Support

The only personal or family characteristic related to support was family structure, where married dual-earners with no children (t = −1.98, p = .047) had less support than married single earners with no children. Production/operation/repair workers (t = −2.90, p = .004) had less support than executives. Workers in larger workplaces (t = −4.62, p = .000), workers working more hours than they wanted to (t = −3.26, p = .001), and unionized workers (t = −3.12, p = .002) all had less support. This model explained only 4% of the variability in support.

DISCUSSION

Job flexibility is currently one of the most-discussed strategies for enabling workers to fulfill their responsibilities at home and at work. Yet research on flexibility has not clearly demonstrated its effectiveness, and only relatively few and relatively privileged workers appear to have access to it. Furthermore, although flexibility is often presumed to increase workers' control over their work circumstances, studies with managers and biotechnology workers indicate that the ability to exercise flexibility options is also unevenly distributed throughout the workforce. In this study, we considered four factors related to flexibility: schedule discretion, access to paid vacation and holidays, opportunities to use discretion, and support for use of discretion from managers/supervisors and co-workers. The goal of our analyses was to map discretion, policies, the ability to use them, and support from others in a nationally representative sample of U.S. employees.

Correlations among the dependent variables offered some clues about the relationships among discretion, policies, opportunities, and support. If flexibility were synonymous with control, we might expect strong positive correlations between schedule discretion and opportunities to exercise it. In reality, the correlation was positive but quite small, suggesting that having and being able to use schedule discretion were distinct. The presence of formal policies also was only minimally correlated with the other dependent variables, indicating that discretion, policy, and opportunity are not usually part of a bundle of flexibility options. Support was moderately correlated with both discretion and opportunity, consistent with the possibility that support is helpful because it acts on the flexibility accorded workers in two ways — increasing both their discretion and their opportunities to use it.

Findings regarding discretion were largely consistent with those of previous studies. Similar to the findings of Golden (2005), McCrate (2005), and Swanberg et al. (2005), more privileged workers appeared to have greater discretion over their schedules than less privileged workers, with privilege indicated by occupational status, hourly earnings, or exempt status. Consistent with McCrate's (2005) findings, Black workers had significantly less discretion than White workers. The personal, family, job, and workplace characteristics we studied explained more of the variability in discretion than any of the other dependent variables.

Policies regarding paid leave for vacations and holidays, which are usually formal, were statistically distinct from other aspects of schedule discretion, which could have been formal or informal (e.g., the ability to choose starting and ending times on a daily basis). As with discretion, access to paid leave was also related to status, with lower-paid workers or workers in lower-status occupations having less access. Unlike schedule discretion, however, hourly workers were more likely to report being covered by these policies than salaried workers.

Like discretion and policy, opportunities to use flexibility also were unevenly distributed throughout the full-time labor force. In a sample of managers, Blair-Loy and Wharton (2004) observed that the most privileged workers felt the most constrained from using flexibility. In this more representative sample, the findings were somewhat different. While it is true that older workers, male workers, and workers with supervisory responsibilities reported fewer opportunities to use their discretion than other workers, we did not find an association with income. Technical workers in our sample also reported fewer opportunities to use their discretion.

The personal, family, job, and workplace characteristics we studied explained a very small proportion of the variability in support and, except for production workers receiving less support than executives, displayed little connection to worker status or privilege. Workers who were union members or who worked in larger workplaces reported receiving less support, perhaps a function of more adversarial or hierarchical relationships in their respective workplaces. In general, there were larger differences among job and workplace characteristics in discretion and policy than in support and opportunity.

Although the results revealed several significant positive correlations among the dependent variables, there were several instances of coefficients for independent variables switching signs across dependent variables. For example, hourly workers had less schedule discretion, but greater access to paid leave and more opportunities to use their discretion than salaried workers (see Figure 11.1). Workers in smaller establishments had more discretion, less ac-

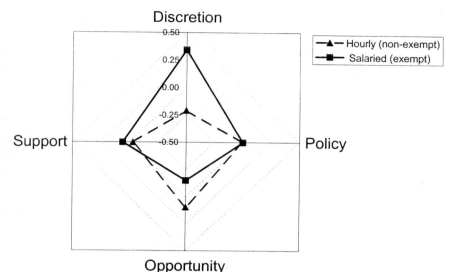

Figure 11.1. Mean Score by Exempt Status.

cess to paid vacation or holidays, but more support and more opportunities to use their discretion than workers in larger establishments (see Figure 11.2). Working more hours or having supervisory responsibilities were positively related to discretion but negatively related to opportunities to use it (see Figures 11.3 and 11.4). These offsetting patterns may help to explain some of the

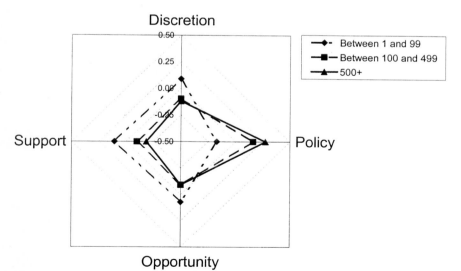

Figure 11.2. Mean Score by Establishment Size.

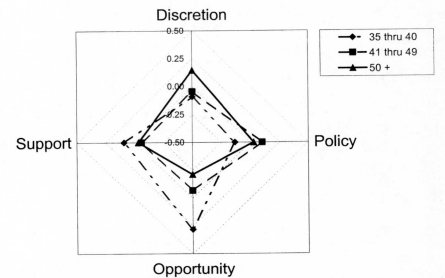

Figure 11.3.   Mean Scores by Work Hours.

weak findings for the effectiveness of flexibility in prior research—it may be necessary to develop measures of true flexibility that correct for constrained opportunities to use it.

So, does job flexibility automatically give workers more control over their schedules? No, not necessarily. Having schedule discretion appears to be only

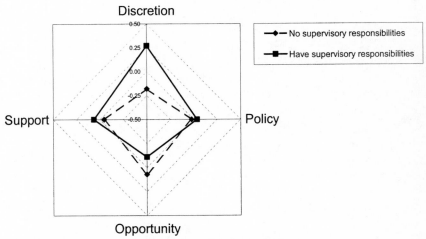

Figure 11.4.   Mean Scores by Supervisory Responsibilities.

modestly related to opportunities to exercise it. While schedule discretion and leave policies appear to be disproportionately available to higher-status workers, access to opportunities and—especially—support for using discretion do not appear to be a function of status.

NOTE

Shelley M. MacDermid, Ph.D., is a professor, director of the Center for Families, and co-director of the Military Family Research Institute at Purdue University. Chiung-Ya Tang, Ph.D., is a research associate in the doctoral program in Public Affairs in the College of Health and Public Affairs at the University of Central Florida. This paper was presented at the Families and Work research conference, Brigham Young University, Provo, Utah, March 2006. We wish to express our appreciation to Ellen Galinsky and James T. Bond for their assistance in using data from the National Study of the Changing Workforce, and to the conference organizers.

REFERENCES

Baltes, B. B., Briggs, T. E., Huff, J. W., Wright, J. A., & Neuman, G. A. (1999). Flexible and compressed workweek schedules: A meta-analysis of their effects of work-related criteria. *Journal of Applied Psychology, 84*(4), 496–513.

Blair-Loy, M., & Wharton, A. S. (2004). Organizational commitment and constraints on work-family policy use: Corporate flexibility policies in a global firm. *Sociological Perspectives, 47*(3), 243–267.

Bohen, H. H. & Viveros-Long, A. (1981). *Balancing jobs and family life: Do flexible schedules help?* Philadelphia: Temple University Press.

Eaton, S. C. (2003). If you can use them: Flexibility policies, organizational commitment, and perceived performance. *Industrial Relations, 42*(2), 145–167.

Families and Work Institute (2004, May). National study of the changing workforce: Guide to public use files. New York: Author.

Golden, L. (2005). The flexibility gap: Employee access to flexibility in work schedules. In I. U. Zeytinoglu (Ed.), *Flexibility in workplaces: Effects on workers, work environment and the unions* (pp. 38–56). Geneva: IIRA/ILO.

Karasek, R. & Theorell, T. (1990). *Healthy work: Stress, productivity, and the reconstruction of working life.* New York: Basic Books.

McCrate, E. (2005). Flexible hours, workplace authority, and compensating wage differentials in the U.S. *Feminist Economics, 11*(1), 11–39.

Swanberg, J. E., Pitt-Catsouphes, M., & Drescher-Burke, K. (2005). A question of justice: Disparities in employees' access to flexible schedule arrangements. *Journal of Family Issues, 26*(6), 866–895.

Tausig, M., & Fenwick, R. (2001). Unbinding time: Alternate work schedules and work-life balance. *Journal of Family and Economic Issues*, 22, 101–119.

U.S. Department of Labor. Retrieved February 21, 2006 from http://www.dol.gov/compliance/laws/comp-flsa.htm

U.S. Office of Personnel Management. Workplace Flexibility. Retrieved February 11, 2006, from http://www.opm.gov/Employment_and_Benefits/worklife/workplace flexibilities/index.asp

Van Der Doef, M., & Maes, Stan. (1999). The job demand-control(-support) model and psychological well-being: A review of 20 years of empirical research. *Work and Stress*, 13(2), 87–114.

Chapter Twelve

Flexible Work Arrangements: Help or Hype?

by Tammy D. Allen and Kristen Shockley

ABSTRACT

Flexible work arrangements have been cited as crucial to helping employees manage work and nonwork responsibilities. Despite the positive press given to flextime work arrangements, research results regarding their efficacy in terms of preventing work-family conflict are inconsistent. Moreover, researchers are beginning to recognize that access to flexible work arrangements (FWA) alone does not create a basis for successful management of work and family roles. The heterogeneity associated with the research findings regarding FWA is underscored by two recent meta-analytic studies. Specifically, one study reported a meta-analytic effect size of −.30 between flexibility and work interference with family (WIF) and of −.17 with family interference with work (FIW). In contrast, the other meta-analytic study reported an effect size of .00 with WIF and .06 with FIW. The inconsistencies found even within meta-analytic research suggest that there is a great deal of variation associated with the effectiveness of FWA. This chapter will review the existing literature regarding the relationship between flexible work arrangements and work-family conflict and present an agenda for future research.

"Flexibility, to me, is the trend that's going to be here and not go away."—Della Delafuente (Carlson, 2005).

"Work-Life is going to be, in some fundamental sense, replaced with something called flexibility. The field literally disappears in the term *flexibility*. I mean it just took over; because corporations were [wondering] what can we do that

265

doesn't cost us money? And flexibility was the answer. It was always the answer, but I don't think people really understood that."—Robert Drago (Harrington, 2007).

Based on the degree of attention given to the topic of flexibility in the workplace at all levels of society recently, one might think that flexibility is the holy grail of mechanisms for helping employees manage work and non-work responsibilities. Initiatives such as "When Work Works" sponsored by the Families and Work Institute and "Workplace Flexibility 2010" at Georgetown Law Center are both designed to promote increased workplace flexibility at a national level. Flexibility has become popular within organizations with flextime being reported as the most commonly offered family-friendly benefit, followed by telework, within the United States and Canada (Comfort, Johnson, & Wallace, 2003; SHRM Foundation, 2001). A substantial proportion of employees at large corporations such as IBM, Sun Microsystems, and Intel are involved in telework arrangements (Conlin, 2005) and a total 100% of the companies that made it to *Working Mother* magazines' list of the 100 best companies to work for allow flextime and telecommuting (Carlson, 2005). Moreover, workers often cite flexibility as a critical desired job feature (e.g., Stone & Lovejoy, 2004).

Despite all the positive attention given to flexible work arrangements (FWA), research results regarding its efficacy in terms of preventing work-family conflict are inconsistent. For example, while some studies indicate that telecommuting relates to less work-family conflict than do standard work arrangements (e.g., Hill, Ferris, & Martinson, 2003; Madsen, 2003), others report no significant differences or mixed results (e.g., Hill, Hawkins, & Miller, 1996; Hill, Miller, Wiener, & Colihan, 1998). Likewise, some research demonstrates that flextime relates to less work-family conflict (e.g., Hammer, Allen, & Grigsby, 1997); Parasuraman, Purohit, Godshalk, & Beutell, 1996), while others do not (e.g., Aryee, 1992; Greenhaus, Parasuraman, Granrose, Rabinowitz, & Beutell, 1989). Such disparities in findings have led some researchers to conclude that access to flexible work arrangements alone are not the way to successful management of work and family roles. For example, Kossek, Lautsch, and Eaton (2004) suggested that access to flexibility is a necessary but insufficient condition for reducing work-family conflict and enhancing employee well-being.

The purpose of the current research is to review the existing literature regarding the relationship between FWA and employee work-family conflict. Our review focuses on empirical results. Following our review of the literature we offer an agenda for future research on FWA and work-family conflict.

DEFINING FLEXIBLE WORK ARRANGEMENTS

Flexible work arrangements can generally be defined as negotiated terms of employment related to the timing and/or place of work (Catalyst, 1997). Flexible work arrangements include those that involve where the work is conducted, typically referred to as telecommuting, and those that involve when work is conducted, typically referred to as flextime (Rau, 2003). Telecommuting primarily involves the ability to work from home. Flextime arrangements generally consist of a set of "core hours" during which employees are expected to be at the workplace, but provide decision latitude regarding the time employees leave and arrive from work, as long as the total daily or weekly number of hours is completed (Baltes, Briggs, Huff, & Wright, 1999). Although there are other forms of FWA such as part-time work, job sharing, and compressed workweeks, this chapter focuses primarily on the two most popular forms, flextime and telecommuting.

REVIEW OF EXISTING RESEARCH

One of the most extensive quantitative reviews of the outcomes associated with FWA is the meta-analysis conducted by Baltes et al. (1999). Baltes et al. examined work-related criteria associated with flextime and with compressed workweek schedules. Importantly, they only included experimental studies to ensure that effects could be attributed to the FWA intervention. The dependent variables examined were productivity, self-rated performance, absenteeism, job satisfaction, and satisfaction with schedule. Of interest in the present chapter are the results regarding flextime. Baltes et al. found that flexible work schedules positively influenced productivity (objective criteria such as number of claims processed), job satisfaction, absenteeism, and satisfaction with work schedule. There was no effect on self-rated performance. The strongest effect was associated with absenteeism. Several moderators were also tested. Managers and professionals were less positively affected by flextime schedules than were employees. Less flexible schedules (fewer core hours) showed stronger effect sizes than did more flexible schedules (greater core hours). Short-interval intervention effects were not significantly different than long-interval effects. Regression analyses controlling for other study characteristics indicated that the effects became smaller as the time after the introduction of flextime increased. Some of the conclusions reached by Baltes et al. include that flextime may be more beneficial in terms of attendance than in terms of worker effectiveness. Additionally, FWA may not benefit those who already have a great degree of autonomy, such as managers and professionals. The finding regarding core hours suggests that too much flexibility may have a negative effect, perhaps because of the difficulty associated with coordinating with other employees. Finally, the positive benefits of flextime may wane over time.

The Baltes et al. (1999) study provided convincing experimental evidence that flextime relates to important work-related criteria. However, work-family conflict was not included in the Baltes et al. review. We now turn our attention to research that has specifically examined WFC.

The inconsistency of results regarding FWA and work-family conflict are highlighted by the findings reported in two recent meta-analyses. With regard to the relationship between flexibility and work interference with family (WIF), Byron (2005) reported a mean effect of $-.30$. With regard to flexibility and family interference with work (FIW), the mean effect reported was $-.17$. Both findings were significant. On the other hand, Mesmer-Magnus and Viswesvaran (2006) found nonsignificant effect sizes of $-.14$ for global work-family conflict, .00 for WIF, and .06 for FIW with flexibility. A closer examination of both studies reveals several potential explanations for the discrepant results. Most telling perhaps is that Byron's analysis was limited to schedule flexibility, while Mesmer-Magnus and Viswesvaran examined studies that included both schedule and location flexibility. Additionally, Byron only included studies in which both WIF and FIW were measured. In both meta-analyses it is uncertain if the distinction was made between research regarding FWA use and research regarding FWA availability. We suspect that a mix of the two may have been included, which might further explain the heterogeneity of results.

Several other findings from the meta-analyses are noteworthy. In both studies, the credibility intervals were large, suggesting a great deal of heterogeneity and accordingly the presence of moderators. Byron (2005) examined the data for moderators and found that flexible schedules were more highly related to work-family conflict when samples more greatly comprised participants with children than participants without children. Additionally, flexible schedules were more highly related to work-family conflict when samples more highly comprised females than males. This suggests that flexible schedules provide more of a protective benefit against work-family conflict for women than for men and for parents than nonparents.

The most recent meta-analysis on flexibility to appear in the published literature focused exclusively on telecommuting (Gajendran & Harrison, 2007). The authors reported an average effect size of $-.13$ between work-family conflict and telecommuting. Examining work-family conflict directionally, the findings indicated a relationship of $-.16$ with WIF and $-.15$ with FIW.

Here again there was enough heterogeneity to suggest the presence of moderators.

We reviewed individual studies in the literature to try and more closely examine the pattern of results and ascertain reasons for inconsistencies. Space constraints prohibit an exhaustive review of this literature, but selected studies were chosen to help illustrate the range of typical findings. Before presenting our review we briefly discuss some important features of the literature.

The flexibility literature is marked by studies that examine the impact of FWA availability and by studies that examine the impact of FWA use. The distinction is an important one. The theory underlying why FWA results in beneficial outcomes differs for availability than for use. Availability is thought to symbolize organizational concern for employees (Batt & Valcour, 2003; Grover & Crooker, 1995). Availability has a positive impact on employee reactions to the workplace based on social-exchange theory. That is, employees appreciate that the organization is providing a valued resource such flexibility and will reciprocate by having more favorable job attitudes. However, it seems less likely that social exchange will impact work-family conflict than it will impact general work-related attitudes. The actual use of FWA should reduce work-family conflict because it gives individuals more control to attend to family responsibilities when needed (Thomas & Ganster, 1995). We also note, however, that the mere availability of FWA can produce perceptions of control, which might help explain why FWA availability would relate to work-family conflict. Additionally, telecommuting use can result in an actual time saving when time that would otherwise be spent commuting to and from the workplace by car or public transportation is considered.

Given that the majority of existing research regarding work-family conflict and FWA is cross-sectional, another important distinction is that the relationships observed between work-family conflict and FWA availability are less likely to be the product of reverse causality than are relationships observed between work-family conflict and FWA use (Batt & Valcour, 2001). Specifically, it seems unlikely that experiencing work-family conflict would increase the likelihood that one would report that FWA is available. On the other hand, experiencing work-family conflict may influence one to use FWA. That is, employees having difficulty managing work and family may be those most likely to use FWA. This is important to keep in mind when interpreting the findings.

Finally, although we think the distinction between availability and use is important, we also note that the two are not mutually exclusive. Specifically, all individuals who report using FWA by definition have FWA available, but not everyone who reports that FWA is available is using FWA. That is, FWA users are a subset of those that have FWA available.

WFC and FWA availability. Studies examining FWA availability include those that have examined flextime exclusively, those that have examined telecommuting availability exclusively, and those that include multiple forms of flexibility within a composite measure. We reviewed each of these groups separately.

Nonsignificant associations between flextime availability and both directions of work-family conflict or an overall measure of work-family conflict were found in a number of studies (e.g., Anderson, Coffey, & Byerly, 2002; Aryee, 1992; Galinsky, Bond, & Friedman, 1996; Greenhaus et al., 1989; Mennino, Rubin, & Brayfield, 2005; Russo & Waters, 2006; Thomas & Ganster, 1995). However, there are also studies reporting significant results. Parasuraman et al. (1996) reported a significant relationship for both WIF and FIW with flextime. Bohen and Viveros-Long (1981) reported less job-family role strain scores among those who reported access to flextime than those who didn't. Based on QES data, Staines and Pleck (1984) reported a significant relationship between flextime and work-family conflict. Also using data QES, Voydanoff (1988) reported a correlation of $-.07$ between work-family conflict and flextime for males and $-.11$ for females, but did not report significance levels. Cao (2006) notes a significant negative correlation between flextime and WIF. Using OLS regression analyses, Blair-Loy and Wharton (2004) found a negative association between scheduling flexibility and work-family conflict ($\beta = -.22$) when controlling for a number of factors, including marital status, gender, weekly hours worked, and supervisory responsibility. The authors did not report the zero-order correlations.

Several studies reported nonsignificant correlations between flextime and FIW, but significant correlations between flextime and WIF in the anticipated direction (Barrah, Shultz, Baltes, Stolz, 2004; Cinamon & Rich, 2002; Neal & Hammer, 2007; Shockley & Allen, 2007). Similarly, one study found a significant correlation between work to family strain but not family to work strain (Hill, Martinson, & Ferris, 2004). Finally, some studies report varying results depending on the sample. Comparing the self-employed with the organizationally employed, Parasuraman and Simmers (2001) found that work-family conflict related to flextime among the self-employed, but not among the organizationally employed. Pal and Saksvik (2006) examined flexibility in working hours and work-family conflict in a Norwegian and Indian sample. No significant relationship emerged in the Norwegian sample, but flexibility related to greater work-family conflict with the Indian participants.

Two studies failed to find a significant association between telecommuting availability and WIF or FIW (Kossek, Lautsch, Eaton, & Bosch,

2004; Shockley & Allen, 2007). However, Kossek and colleagues found that perceptions of job flexibility (the freedom to control where, when, and how one did one's job) were related to both directions of work-family conflict. Conversely, Hill et al. (2004) report a significant negative relationship between spatial flexibility available and WIF, as well as work-to-family strain. The authors did not measure FIW and found a nonsignificant relationship between telecommuting availability and family-to-work strain.

Studies using composite indices of available flexibility also report mixed results. In a study of Spanish employees, Carnicer, Sanchez, and Perez (2004) found a relationship between flexibility and FIW for both men and women, but flexibility was only related to WIF among men. Stevens, Kiger, and Riley (2006) revealed a sizeable correlation of $-.52$ for men and $-.54$ for women between job flexibility and work-to-family spillover. In a study of IBM employees across 48 different countries, Hill, Yang, Hawkins, and Ferris (2004) reported correlations of $-.07$ with FIW and $-.05$ with WIF. Although these correlations are small in magnitude, because of the study's large sample size (25,380), they were significant. Hill, Hawkins, Ferris, and Weitzman (2001) reported a positive relationship between perceived degree of flexibility and work-life balance. Their measure of work-life balance is somewhat distinctive, but similar to existing measures of work-family conflict. Using a single item of overall perceived flexibility, Hammer et al. (1997) found a significant relationship with work-family conflict for both females and males. Based on a study of European managers, Lyness and Kropf (2005) found a small but significant relationship between work-family conflict (referred to as work-family balance) and flexibility that included part-time work, working from home, and flextime. Other studies report no relationship between WIF or overall work-family conflict and FWA availability (Allen, 2001; Batt & Valcour, 2003; Clark, 2001).

Work-family conflict and FWA use. Studies examining FWA use include those that have examined flextime, telecommuting, part-time work, and compressed workweek individually and those that include multiple forms of flexibility as part of a composite measure. We reviewed each of these types of studies separately. Similar to the results regarding FWA availability, the results regarding FWA use are highly variable.

Lapierre and Allen (2006) found that flextime use was not related to either FIW or WIF. Dunham, Pierce, and Casteneda (1987) compared work interference with family and friends before and after the implementation of flextime and found no significant differences. On the other hand, Hicks and Klimoski (1981) found that those on a flextime schedule reported less interrole conflict than did those on a fixed time schedule.

Lapierre and Allen (2006) found that telework users reported more time-based FIW than did non-users. No effects were found between telework use and strain-based FIW, time-based WIF, or strain-based WIF. Using both qualitative and quantitative data, Hill, Miller, Weiner, and Colihan (1998) examined those in a naturally occurring telecommuting situation (i.e., there was no self-selection) and those who worked in a traditional office. With regard to work-life balance, participants wrote a total of 27 favorable (e.g., Mobility enables me to better fulfill household/childcare responsibilities) and 46 unfavorable (e.g., In the mobile environment I feel like I am always working) qualitative comments. The quantitative analysis indicated that mobility was not significantly related to work/life balance. Research by Hill, Ferris, and Martinson (2003) demonstrated the importance knowing more about the place with regard to telecommuting. Individuals who worked from home reported greater work-life balance than did those who worked in traditional offices. However, those who worked virtually; that is those who were on the move and working from a variety of locations, reported experiencing less work-life balance than did those in other work arrangements. Based on the same data set, Madsen (2003, 2006) compared telecommuters (participants teleworked at least two days a week) with nontelecommuters on each form and direction of work-family conflict. She found that those in a telecommuter arrangement reported less overall work-family conflict, WIF, FIW, time-based conflict, and strain-based conflict. No significant differences were found in regards to behavior-based conflict. More specifically, differences also emerged in favor of telecommuting regarding time-based FIW, strain-based WIF, and behavior-based WIF. No differences were found with regard to time-based WIF and behavior-based FIW.

Using more fine-grained measurement, several researchers have examined the relationship between the amount of telecommuting practiced and work-family conflict. Kossek, Lautsch, and Eaton (2006) found that when participants merely reported whether or not they used telework policies (yes or no), use was not significantly related to WIF or FIW. When telework volume was assessed, the negative relationship between telecommuting use and both FIW and WIF increased in magnitude but failed to reach significance. Golden, Veiga, and Simsek (2006) found that the more extensively individuals engaged in telecommuting the lower their WIF, but the higher their FIW.

Two studies have focused exclusively on part-time work with relatively consistent results. Hill et al. (2004) found a significant negative association between part-time work and WIF and work-to-family strain, but no relationship between part-time work and family-to-work strain. Using a sample of Dutch employees, van Rijswijk, Bekker, Rutte, & Croon (2004) also found a negative relationship between part-time work and WIF. Results regarding FIW were not significant.

Only one study has examined compressed work weeks in relation to work-family conflict. Using a quasi-experimental design, Dunham, Pierce, and Casteneda (1987) found that movement from a regular work week to a compressed work week significantly reduced work interference with friends and family. After returning to a regular work week, interference again increased but not a significant amount.

Allen (2001) used a composite measure of flexible benefits options that included flextime, compressed workweek, telecommuting, and part-time work. She found that greater use of FWA was associated with less WIF. In contrast, Blair-Loy and Wharton (2004) used a similar composite (flextime, flexplace, and compressed work week) and did not find a significant association between flexible policy use and WFC. However, it is important to note that zero-order correlations were not reported; thus this statistic is based on regression analyses controlling for the effects of several other variables. In a departure from the cross-sectional studies that typify this area of the literature, Hammer, Neal, Newsome, Brockwood, and Colton (2005) conducted a longitudinal study with a one-year time lag of dual-earner couples with both child and elder care responsibilities. They found that use of FWA (a composite measure of flexible work hours, job-sharing, and telecommuting) was not related to husband reports of WIF or FIW. On the other hand, use of FWA was positively related to wives' FIW over time. That is, greater use of FWA was associated with more FIW one year later. No relationship between FWA and WIF was found for wives. Hammer et al. suggest that use of FWA by wives may allow them to take on more family-related responsibilities, thus resulting in a greater degree of FIW. This is consistent with research by Bohen and Viveros-Long (1981), who found that flextime was associated with more time spent on home chores.

Review summary. Our article title asks if FWA are help or hype. The results of our review of the literature suggest that the common assumption that FWA help employees effectively manage their work and nonwork responsibilities may be wrong at worst, and premature at best. We find no overwhelming, compelling evidence that FWA generally or consistently relates to employee work-family conflict. In fact, we find some evidence consistent with the notion that the use of FWA may exacerbate FIW. Moreover, when significant effects are found, the effect size appears to be small in magnitude. The more moderate positive effects that were observed were associated with psychological perceptions of flexibility.

Taken together, there is some evidence that FWA may more highly relate to WIF than to FIW. This conclusion is consistent with the results of the

Byron (2005) meta-analysis and with several of the individual study results (e.g., Cinamon & Rich, 2002). More research has been conducted regarding benefit availability than benefit use, particularly with regard to flexible scheduling. We now turn our attention to opportunities for future research on FWA.

AN AGENDA FOR FUTURE FLEXIBILITY RESEARCH

The focus of this review has been on the relationship between FWA and work-family conflict. Although it is important to recognize that FWA has been associated with other benefits such as reduced absenteeism (e.g., Baltes et al., 1999) and attraction to the organization (e.g., Rau & Hyland, 2002), our purpose in conducting this review was to highlight the need for placing more research emphasis on outcomes that more squarely represent employee abilities to manage work and nonwork responsibilities.

Many of the same research needs highlighted by Christensen and Staines (1990) in their review of flextime as a viable solution to work-family conflict remain today. They noted that quasi-experimental research designs were needed to make appropriate causal inferences regarding the impact of FWA interventions. They also noted the importance of examining both availability and use of flextime. A third factor they cited as needing additional research was the issue of examining differing levels of flexibility to determine the degree of flexibility that offers positive outcomes. We further discuss these issues and others below.

Place versus time. The research to date suggests that flexibility concerning when work is completed (rather than where) might be more beneficial in terms of reducing or avoiding work-family conflict (e.g., Shockley & Allen, 2007). However, as we discussed with regard to FWA availability and FWA use, flextime and telecommuting are not necessarily mutually exclusive. There may be some telecommuting arrangements that provide limited schedule flexibility. Someone working from home forced to remain chained to the computer from 8 to 5 has little more flexibility than someone sitting in a corporate office chained to a computer from 8 to 5. Therefore, we suggest that in future studies, schedule flexibility may be examined as a moderator of the relationship between telecommuting and work-family conflict. One could expect for telecommuting to be more beneficial under circumstances of greater rather than lesser schedule flexibility. One such study was recently conducted. Golden et al. (2006) found that scheduling flexibility moderated the relationship between extent of telecommuting and WIF such that the relationship between telecommuting and WIF was stronger for telecommuters with higher perceived scheduling flexibility than for those with lesser perceived scheduling flexibility. However, no moderation was found for FIW as the dependent variable. More research looking at how different combinations of time and place flexibility interact to predict work-family conflict is needed to determine what forms of flexibility are more or less helpful in reducing work-family conflict.

More sophisticated designs and analyses. Baltes et al. (1999) found that the positive effects of FWA appear to wane over time. Most of the research regarding FWA and WFC has been cross-sectional and correlational in nature. We did not find any studies that used an experimental design with pre- and post-measures of work-family conflict compared against a control group. Moreover, there are few longitudinal studies (see Hammer et al., 2005 for an exception). Generally a greater consideration of the role of time is needed. As noted by Hill et al. (1998) positive results soon after the start of FWA may be due to a honeymoon effect. On the other hand, after a longer time period, outcomes may improve as the individual becomes comfortable and learns to adjust to the new work arrangements. For example, an individual who begins a telecommuting arrangement and initially has difficulty disengaging from work may develop ways to adapt to the new work situation after a period of time.

There is also a need to consider curvilinear effects. Golden and Veiga (2005) found that among a sample of professional-level employees, there was a curvilinear relationship between extent of telecommuting and job satisfaction. Specifically, job satisfaction appears to plateau at more extensive levels of telecommuting. This relationship was moderated by task interdependence and job discretion. It would not be surprising to find similar results for work-family conflict. For example, telecommuting several days a week may be better than full-time telecommuting.

Boundary management and the role of rituals for telecommuters. Problems with telecommuting are thought to exist primarily because workers have trouble preserving work and family boundaries. Boundary theory assumes that humans create boundaries in order to better cope with and understand their environments (Nippert-Eng, 1996). Boundaries are constructed to better comprehend a variety of things, such as geography, history, ethnicity, and even our personal lives. As family and work are important facets of most individuals' personal lives, they naturally create boundaries between the two; these abstract borders advise individuals when to fulfill the family role vs. the worker role (Ashforth, Kreiner, & Fugate, 2000). Moreover, individuals often use outside clues to help differentiate between work and home borders. For instance, the externally imposed physical barrier of location is an important cue as to when one is inside a home or a work boundary (Hill et al., 2003;

Sullivan & Lewis, 2001). Telework removes the physical separation between work and family roles, thus making it potentially more difficult to maintain a boundary between both roles (Eckenrode & Gore, 1990; Lapierre & Allen, 2006). When the boundaries between work and home become blurred, a worker is forced to enact dual roles and may experience interrole strain and conflict (Ashforth et al. 2000).

Additional research designed to identify successful boundary management strategies may be useful. For example, Ahrentzen (1990) and Gurstein (1991) found that many successful telecommuters practice boundary maintenance by creating a space in the home that is solely designated for work. Hill et al. (1998) suggested that telecommuters may need to establish rituals to help them learn how to disengage from work. For example, at the end of the work-day a telecommuter may close and lock the door to his or her home office. It would be interesting to examine other habits associated with telecommuting. For example, does it make a difference if a telecommuter is working in his or her pajamas or in slacks and a button-down shirt? Does wearing office attire make it easier to segment the work role from the family role? Or does the ability to forgo the trappings of appearance associated with typical corporate office decorum have benefits? Women in particular may benefit from this aspect of telecommuting in that they are typically held to more exacting standards concerning appearance (Jackson, Hunter, & Hodge, 1995).

Consideration of individual differences. Generally speaking, individual differences have received less research attention than have organizational situational factors within the work and family literature. There may be certain dispositional variables that better enable individuals to effectively take advantage of flexible work options. Hill (1995) as cited in Hill et al. (1998) made the astute observation that giving a workaholic an electronic briefcase may be like giving an alcoholic a bottle of gin. Individuals who are prone to overwork may find that FWA acts as an enabler. Other individual attributes that may make a difference include conscientiousness and self-discipline. A certain degree of control may be needed by those working at home in a telecommuting arrangement to stay focused on work rather than become distracted by household obligations. Time management skills may become even more important without the typical signals and cues regarding work that come from coworkers. Recent research has shown that individuals who use selection, optimization, and compensation strategies report fewer job and family stressors, and subsequent less work-family conflict (Baltes & Heydens-Gahir, 2003). It may be useful to use a person-environment approach to better understand the circumstances under which FWA will reduce work-family conflict. Once we acknowledge that there are individual differences in people's abilities to use FWA effectively, we can focus on developing strategies that might better prepare individuals for the challenges FWA can pose.

What happens at home when individuals use FWA? Hammer et al. (2005) suggested that women who use FWA take on more family-related responsibilities and accordingly increase their level of FIW. This is consistent with Silver and Goldscheider (1994) who found that women with more flexible jobs spent more time on housework. Individuals with greater flexibility may be expected to take on more of the domestic obligations. It may be easier for the spouse with greater flexibility to assume household tasks such as running errands, attending children's school-related functions, taking children to the doctor, dealing with home deliveries and repairs, etc. Research is needed to understand how FWA use relates to changes in household work, which in turn relates to work-family conflict. Further, family members may also have difficulty with the blurring of work and nonwork boundaries when individuals work from home. Research examining support from family members in the form of respecting the telecommuters' physical workspace and minimizing interruptions could shed additional light on the conditions under which telecommuting is more or less effective.

Other forms of support within the organization. The inconsistent positive results for flextime may not be based on flexibility per se, but on the lack of support surrounding it within the organization. As suggested by Sutton and Noe (2005), organizations may adopt family-supportive policies for reasons such as to gain legitimacy among peers, but fail to consider how the programs should be operated within their particular organization. In a qualitative study, Nord, Fox, Phoenix, and Viano (2002) found that employees reported negative experiences associated with flexible schedules and telecommuting that affected their levels of productivity and stress. Specifically, employees indicated that factors such as inadequate technological infrastructure, lack of technical support, poorly defined policies and procedures for participating in telecommuting, failure of the organization to adjust selection, appraisal, project management, and motivational systems for consistency with work performed under new scheduling options, and lack of work schedule fit were obstacles associated FWA use. Hill et al. (2003) has also discussed the importance of providing technological support to individuals who telecommute. This research highlights the need for organizations to conduct a thorough evaluation of current human resource systems when implementing FWA practices. Without an integrated change implementation process, the stress created by the type of problems noted above may offset any flexibility advantages.

Future research may also consider the interaction between FWA and informal forms of support within the organization. A number of studies have supported the point of view that organizational policies and benefits will not be successful without support from supervisors and a family-supportive work environment (e.g., Allen, 2001; Anderson et al., 2002; Thompson et al., 1999). It may be that under conditions of poor supervisor support FWA will have no or even negative effects on work-family conflict.

Too much of a good thing? Work and family researchers have seemingly assumed that giving workers more choice regarding when and where work will be completed is beneficial. However, one of the findings of the Baltes et al. (1999) meta-analysis was that less flexible schedules were more highly related to work-related criteria than were more flexible schedules, suggesting that too much flexibility may have a negative effect. Greater flexibility in the timing and location of work means workers have to make a greater number of choices. This is potentially problematic in that research has shown that "choice overload" can undermine satisfaction and motivation (Iyengar & Lepper, 2000). For example, consumer research has shown that when individuals have a variety of products from which to choose, they are more likely to worry if they have made a poor selection. Iyengar and Lepper also found that the same choice selected from a limited-choice set resulted in better performance than that selected from a larger choice set. Similarly, Schwartz (2000) has argued that freedom, autonomy, and self-determination can become excessive. Schwartz suggests that unconstrained freedom can result in paralysis and even chaos. Other research has shown that adding options can make the choices that have to be made less attractive (Beattie, Baron, Hershey, & Spranca, 1994).

Having too many choices can become overwhelming. Participating in a FWA places greater responsibility for getting the work done on the individual. Iyengar and Lepper (2000) suggest that if freedom of choice passes a manageable boundary, people will actually experience a loss of control. Thus, some individuals with a great deal of schedule control may feel as though that have lost all boundaries between their work and nonwork lives. Although having choices regarding where and when work is to be done may initially appear appealing to workers, too much choice can ultimately be demotivating. These issues may also be moderated by culture. For example, research has shown that the availability of choice is more important for European Americans than for Asian Americans, who place more value on interdependence (Iyengar & Lepper, 1999). In sum, we need to take into consideration that giving workers a greater variety of options regarding when and where work can completed has the potential to overwhelm rather than empower. As noted by Sullivan and Lewis (2001), giving a certain amount of flexibility to employees may be useful, but too much flexibility provides the opportunity for the loss of control of overzealous work tendencies.

There is a great deal of variability in the usage of FWA. More specifically, individuals may telecommute a few days a month or every day. With regard to flextime, there can be a considerable range in the number of core hours. Start and stop times may be able to be changed from day to day or considered stable. A more nuanced approach to how we assess FWA use may help us discover what amount of use works best.

CONCLUSION

A major impetus for FWA has been the desire to help employees manage work and family, yet the outcomes more thoroughly studied have been oriented toward the organization. In an effort to provide organizations with data on how FWA can increase productivity and profits we have given less attention to systematically examining the impact of FWA on the individual outcomes that we are most interested in affecting—the employee's ability to effectively manage work and nonwork responsibilities. That is, by focusing on the business case in order to lure organizations to implement FWA, we may have neglected the human case. It appears that FWA may be more beneficial as a tool to increase productivity than as a tool to decrease work-family conflict (cf., Hill et al., 1998). FWA appears to hold promise as a means for helping employees manage their work and nonwork lives. However, we believe the current state of research is such that we need to know much more about the impact of FWA on outcomes associated with individual well-being.

NOTE

Tammy D. Allen is professor of psychology at the University of South Florida. She received her doctorate in industrial and organizational psychology from the University of Tennessee. Her research interests include work-family issues, mentoring relationships, occupational health psychology, and organizational citizenship behavior. Her work has appeared in *Journal of Applied Psychology*, *Personnel Psychology*, *Organizational Behavior and Human Decision Processes*, and *Journal of Vocational Behavior*, among others. She is currently Associate Editor of the *Journal of Applied Psychology* and of the *Journal of Occupational Health Psychology*.

Kristen M. Shockley is a doctoral student in the industrial and organizational psychology program at the University of South Florida. She completed her undergraduate degree in psychology at the University of Georgia.

Her primary research interest is work/family issues. She is also interested in
and has conducted research on workplace mentoring relationships.

Address correspondence to Tammy D. Allen, University of South Florida,
Department of Psychology, 4202 E. Fowler Ave., PCD4118, Tampa, FL
33620-7200; Phone: 813.974.0484; Fax: 813.974.4617; Email: tallen@shell
.cas.usf.edu

REFERENCES

Ahrentzen, S. B. (1990). Managing conflict by managing boundaries: How professional homeworkers cope with multiple roles at home. *Environment and Behavior,
22*, 723–752.

Allen, T. D. (2001). Family supportive work environments: The role of organizational
perceptions. *Journal of Vocational Behavior, 58*, 414–435.

Aryee, S. (1992). Antecedents and outcomes of work-family conflict among married
professional women: Evidence from Singapore. *Human Relations, 45*, 813–837.

Anderson, S. E., Coffey, B. S., & Byerly, R. T. (2002). Formal organizational initiatives and informal workplace practices: Links to work-family conflict and job-related outcomes. *Journal of Management, 28*(6), 787–810.

Ashforth, B. E., Kreiner, G. E., & Fugate, M. (2000). All in a day's work: Boundaries
in micro role transitions. *Academy of Management Review, 25*(3), 472–490.

Baltes, B. B., Briggs, T. E., Huff, J. W., Wright, J. A. (1999). Flexible and compressed
workweek schedules: A meta-analysis of their effects on work-related criteria.
Journal of Applied Psychology, 84, 496–513.

Baltes, B. B., & Heydens-Gahir, H. A. (2003). Reduction of work-family conflict
through the use of selection, optimization, and compensation behaviors. *Journal of
Applied Psychology, 88*, 1005–1018.

Barrah, J. L., Shultz, K. S., Baltes, B., & Stolz, H. E. (2004). Men's and women's el-
dercare-based work-family conflict: Antecedents and work-related outcomes. *Fathering, 2*(3), 305–330.

Batt, R., & Valcour, P. M. (2003). Human resource practices as predictors of work-
family outcomes and employee turnover. *Industrial Relations, 42*, 189–220.

Beattie, J., Baron, J., Hershey, J. C., & Spranca, M. D. (1994). Psychological determinants of decision attitude. *Journal of Behavioral Decision Making, 7*, 129–144.

Blair-Loy, M., & Wharton, A. S. (2004). Mothers in finance: Surviving and thriving.
The ANNALS of the American Academy of Political and Social Science, 596,
151–171.

Bohen H. H. & Viveros-Long, A. (1981). *Balancing jobs and family life: Do flexible
schedules help?* Philadelphia: Temple University Press.

Byron, K. (2005). A meta-analytic review of work-family conflict and its antecedents.
Journal of Vocational Behavior, 67(2), 169–198.

Carlson, L. (2005, December 1). Benefits that meet moms' needs—then and now. *Employee Benefit News*, 19. http://ebn.benefitnews.com. Retrieved 26 May 2008.

Cao, F. (2006). Exploring the relations among availability of temporal flexibility at work, work-to-family conflict, and job satisfaction. *Dissertation Abstracts International 67*, 585B.

Carnicer, M. P., Sanchez, A. M., & Perez, M. P. (2004) Work-family conflict in a southern European country. *Journal of Managerial Psychology, 19*(5), 466–489

Catalyst (1997). *A new approach to flexibility: Managing the work/time equation.* New York: Catalyst.

Christensen, K., & Staines, G. L. (1990). Flextime: A viable solution to work/family conflict? *Journal of Family Issues, 11*, 455–476.

Cinamon, R. G. & Rich, Y. (2002). Profiles of attribution of importance of life roles and their implications for the work-family conflict. *Journal of Counseling Psychology, 49*(2), 212–220.

Clark, S. C. (2001). Work cultures and work/family balance. *Journal of Vocational Behavior, 58*, 348–365

Comfort, D., Johnson, K., & Wallace, D. (2003). *Part-time work and family-friendly practices in Canadian workplaces* (The Evolving Workplace Series, No. 71-584-MIE No. 6). Ottawa, Canada: Statistics Canada/Human Resources Development Canada.

Conlin, M. (2005, December 12). The easiest commute of all. *Business Week*, Retrieved March 5, 2009 from http://www.businessweek.com/magazine/content/05_50/63963137.htm.

Dunham, R. B., Pierce, J. L., & Casteneda, M. B. (1987). Alternative work schedules: Two field quasi experiments. *Personnel Psychology, 40*, 215–242.

Eckenrode, J., & Gore, S. (1990). Stress and coping at the boundary of work and family. In J. Echenrode & S. Gore (Eds.), *Stress between work and family* (pp. 1–16). New York: Plenum.

Galinsky, E., Bond, J. T., & Friedman, D. E. (1996). The role of employers in addressing the needs of employed parents. *Journal of Social Issues, 52*(3), 111–136.

Golden, T. D., & Veiga, J. F. (2005). The impact of extent of telecommuting on job satisfaction: Resolving inconsistent findings. *Journal of Management, 31*, 301–318.

Golden, T. D., Veiga, J. F., Simsek, Z. (2006). Telecommuting's differential impact on work-family conflict: Is there no place like home? *Journal of Applied Psychology, 91*(6), 1340–1350.

Greenhaus, J. H., Parasuraman, S., Granrose, C. S., Rabinowitz, S. & Beutell, N. J. (1989). Sources of work family conflict among two-career couples. *Journal of Vocational Behavior, 34*, 133–153.

Grover, S. L., & Crooker, K. J. (1995). Who appreciates family-responsive human resource policies: The impact of family-friendly policies on the organizational attachment of parents and non-parents. *Personnel Psychology, 48*(2), 271–288.

Gurstein, P. (1991) Working at home and living at home: emerging scenarios. *The Journal of Architectural and Planning Research, 8*(2), 164–80.

Hammer, L. B., Allen, E., & Grigsby, T. D. (1997). Work-family conflict in dual-earner couples: Within-individual and crossover effects of work and family. *Journal of Vocational Behavior, 50*, 185–203.

Hammer, L. B., & Neal, M. B. (2007). *Working couples caring for children and aging parents: Effects on work and well-being.* Mahwah, NJ: Lawrence Erlbaum.

Hammer, L. B., Neal, M. B., Newsome, J. T., Brockwood, K. J., & Colton, C. L. (2005). A longitudinal study of the effects of dual-earner couples' utilization of family-friendly workplace supports on work and family outcomes. *Journal of Applied Psychology, 90*, 799–810.

Harrington, B. (2007). The work-life evolution study. Boston College Center for Work & Family.

Hicks, W. D. & Klimoski, R .J. (1981). The impact of flextime on employee attitudes. *Academy of Management Journal, 24*(2), 333.

Hill, E. J., Ferris, M., & Martinson, V. (2003). Does it matter where you work? A comparison of how three work venues (traditional office, virtual office, and home office) influence aspects of work and personal/family life. *Journal of Vocational Behavior, 63*, 220–241.

Hill, E. J., Hawkins, A. J., Ferris, M., & Weitzman, M. (2001). Finding an extra day a week: The positive influence of perceived job flexibility and work family life balance. *Family Relations, 50*, 49–58.

Hill, E. J., Hawkins, A. J., Miller, B. C. (1996). Work and family in the virtual office: perceived influences of mobile telework. *Family Relations, 45*(3), 293–301.

Hill, E.J., Martinson, V., & Ferris, M. (2004). New-concept part-time employment as a work-family adaptive strategy for women professionals with small children. *Family Relations, 53*, 282–292.

Hill, E. J., Miller, B. C., Weiner, S. P. & Colihan, J. (1998). Influences of the virtual office on aspects of work and work/life balance. *Personnel Psychology, 51*, 667–683.

Hill, E. J., Yang, C., Hawkins, A. J., & Ferris, M. (2004). A cross-cultural test of the work-family interface in 48 countries. *Journal of Marriage and Family, 66*, 1300–1316.

Iyengar, S. S., & Lepper, M. R. (1999). Rethinking the value of choice: A cultural perspective on intrinsic motivation. *Journal of Personality and Social Psychology, 76*, 349–366.

Iyengar, S. S., & Lepper, M. R. (2000). When choice is demotivating: Can one desire too much of a good thing? *Journal of Personality and Social Psychology, 79*, 995–1006.

Jackson, L. A., Hunter, J. E., & Hodge, C. N. (1995). Physical attractiveness and intellectual competence: A meta-analytic review. *Social Psychological Quarterly, 58*, 108–122.

Kossek, E. E., Lautsch, B. A., Eaton, S. C., & Bosch, K. L. V. (2004, April). Managing work-home boundaries, performance and well-being: The effects of formal access to telework and flexibility enactment. Paper presented at the annual meeting of the Society for Industrial and Organizational Psychology, Chicago, Illinois.

Kossek, E. E., Lautsch, B. A., & Eaton, S. C. (2005). Flexibility enactment theory: Implications of flexibility type, control, and boundary management for work and family effectiveness. In E. E. Kossek & S. Lambert (Eds.), *Work and life integration: Organizational, cultural, and individual perspectives* (pp. 243–262). Mahwah, NJ: Lawrence Erlbaum.

Kossek, E. E., Lautsch, B. A., & Eaton, S. C. (2006). Telecommuting, control, and boundary management: Correlates of policy use and practice, job control, and work-family effectiveness. *Journal of Vocational Behavior, 68*(2), 347–367

Lapierre, L. M., & Allen, T. D. (2006). Work supportive family, family-supportive supervision, use of organizational benefits, and problem-focused coping: Implications for work-family conflict and employee well-being. *Journal of Occupational Health Psychology, 11*, 169–181.

Lyness, K. S., & Kropf, M. B. (2005). The relationships of national gender equality and organizational support with work-family balance: A study of European managers. *Human Relations, 58*, 33–60.

Madsen, S. R. (2003). The effects of home-based teleworking on work-family conflict. *Human Resource Development Quarterly, 14*(1), 35–58.

Madsen, S. R. (2006). Work and family conflict: Can home-based teleworking make a difference? *International Journal of Organization Theory and Behavior, 9*, 307–350.

Mennino, S. F., Rubin, B. A., & Brayfield, A. (2005). Home-to-job and job-to-home spillover: The impact of company policies and workplace culture. *Sociological Quarterly, 46*(1), 107–135.

Mesmer-Magnus, J. R., & Viswesvaran, C. (2006). How family-friendly work environments affect work/family conflict: A meta-analytic examination. *Journal of Labor Research, 4*, 555–574.

Nippert-Eng, C. (1996). Calendars and keys: The classification of "home" and "work." *Sociological Forum, 11*, 563–582.

Nord, W. R., Fox, S., Phoenix, A., & Viano, K. (2002). Real-world reactions to work-life balance programs: Lessons for effective implementation. *Organizational Dynamics, 30*, 223–238.

Pal, S., & Saksvik, P. O. (2006). A comparative study of work and family conflict in Norwegian and Indian hospitals. *Nordic Psychology, 58*(4), 298–314.

Parasuraman, S., Purohit, Y. S., Godshalk, V. M., & Beutell, N. J. (1996). Work and family variables, entrepreneurial career success, and psychological well-being. *Journal of Vocational Behavior, 48*, 275–300.

Parasuraman, S., & Simmers, C. A. (2001). Type of employment, work-family conflict and well-being: a comparative study. *Journal of Organizational Behavior, 22*, 551–568.

Rau, B. L. (2003). Flexible work arrangements. *Sloan Online Work and Family Encyclopedia.* http://wfnetwork.bc.edu/encyclopedia_entry.php?id=240&area=All

Rau, B. L., & Hyland, M. M. (2002). Role conflict and flexible work arrangements: The effects on applicant attraction. *Personnel Psychology, 55*, 111–136.

Russo, J. A., & Waters, L. E. (2006). Workaholic worker type differences in work-family conflict: The moderating role of supervisor support and flexible work scheduling. *Career Development International, 11*(5), 418–439.

Schwartz, B. (2000). Self-determination: The tyranny of freedom. *American Psychologist, 55*, 79–88.

Shockley, K. M., & Allen, T. D. (2007). When flexibility helps: Another look at the availability of flexible work arrangements and work-family conflict. *Journal of Vocational Behavior, 71*, 479–493.

SHRM Foundation. (2001). *SHRM 2001 benefits survey*. [city, state]: Society for Human Resource Management.

Silver, H., & Goldscheider, F. (1994). Flexible work and housework: Work and family constraints on women's domestic labor. *Social Forces, 72*, 1103–1119.

Staines G. L. & Pleck, J. H. (1984). Nonstandard work schedules and family life. *Journal of Applied Psychology, 69*, 515–523.

Stevens, D. P., Kiger, G., Riley, P. J. (2006). His, hers, or ours? Work-to-family spillover, crossover, and family cohesion. *Social Science Journal, 43*(3), 425–436.

Stone, P., & Lovejoy, M. (2004). Fast-track women and the "choice" to stay home. *Annals, 596*, 62–83.

Sullivan, C. & Lewis, S. (2001). Home-based telework, gender, and the synchronization of work and family: perspectives of teleworkers and their co-residents. *Gender, Work, and Organizations, 8*(2), 123–145.

Sutton, K. L., & Noe, R. A. (2005). Family-friendly programs and work-life integration: More myth than magic? In E. E. Kossek & S. Lambert (Eds.), *Work and life integration: Organizational, cultural, and individual perspectives* (pp. 151–169). Mahwah, NJ: Lawrence Erlbaum.

Thomas, L. T. & Ganster, D. C. (1995) Impact of family-supportive work variables on work-family conflict and strain: a control perspective. *Journal of Applied Psychology, 80*(1), 6–15.

Thompson, C. A., Beauvais, L. L., & Lyness, K. S. (1999). When work-family benefits are not enough: The influence of work-family culture on benefit utilization, organizational attachment, and work-family conflict. *Journal of Vocational Behavior, 54*, 392–415.

van Rijswijk, K., Bekker, M. H. J., Rutte, C G, & Croon, M. A.(2004). The relationships among part-time work, work-family interference, and well-being. *Journal of Occupational Health Psychology, 9*, 286–295.

Voydanoff, P. (1988). Work role characteristics, family structure demands, and work/family conflict. *Journal of Marriage and the Family, 50*, 749–761.

Part 3

WORKING FATHERS, WORKING MOTHERS, WORKING SPOUSES, WORKING GRANDPARENTS

Chapter Thirteen

Work and Family Conditions that Give Rise to Fathers' Knowledge of Children's Daily Activities

by Ann C. Crouter and W. Benjamin Goodman

ABSTRACT

Compared to the literature on maternal employment and mothers' work circumstances, much less is known about how fathers' work is related to their behavior as parents and to the quality of their relationships with their children. In this chapter, we identify paternal occupational conditions that are associated with the quality of father-child relationships, drawing upon several ongoing, longitudinal studies that focus on the work-family interface during the childrearing years. We will provide illustrations that highlight different strategies for learning about the work-family interface for fathers. These strategies include person-oriented approaches (e.g., creating typologies of fathers who share multi-faceted work or parenting profiles) and variable-oriented approaches that examine work or family phenomena one at a time. Although the focus of the chapter will be on fathers, not mothers, we will review some evidence that suggests that the links between occupational conditions and parenting may be stronger for fathers than for mothers and make the argument that this reflects the less scripted nature of the father role.

As children enter school and become actively engaged in peer groups, extracurricular activities, and neighborhood life, the role of parents undergoes a subtle shift. Although much of mothers' and fathers' time continues to be in direct, face-to-face interaction with their offspring in the context of meals, supervision, transportation, homework assistance, television viewing, religious activities, and other day-to-day events, it is also important that parents now also stay abreast of children's experiences that occur when parents are not physically present. Over the past 50 years, a host of studies from the fields of developmental and clinical psychology, family sociology, criminology, and public health have documented that when parents are well informed about their children's activities, whereabouts, and companions, children and youth fare better on a wide range of academic and psychosocial outcomes (see reviews by Crouter & Head, 2002; Dishion & McMahon, 1998).

Early research on this aspect of parenting referred to it as *parental monitoring,* taking the stance that it was parent-driven, involving active surveillance, tracking, and supervision on the part of mothers and fathers. Increasingly, however, in recognition of the active role that children and youth play in revealing or withholding information to parents, researchers are reconceptualizing this dimension of parenting. Some investigators now refer to this construct as *parental knowledge,* a term that leaves open the possibility that knowledge can be acquired in many different ways, including from children self-disclosing to parents (Crouter, Bumpus, Davis, & McHale, 2005; Kerr & Stattin, 2000; Stattin & Kerr, 2000; Waizenhofer, Buchanan, & Jackson-Newsom, 2004).

Parental knowledge is a fascinating window through which to study dynamics in dual-earner families. In this chapter, we use our ongoing program of research on parental knowledge to show how parenting is shaped by the demands and challenges imposed by parents' jobs, as well as how it reflects coordination by fathers and mothers. Because so much of the literature on parental monitoring and parental knowledge either focuses only on mothers or, of even greater concern, blurs the identities of mothers and fathers by asking generically about "parents," we focus here on fathers. As we will show, understanding the conditions under which dual-earner fathers are knowledgeable about what their children are experiencing at school, on the athletic field, and with their friends illuminates more general principles about work-family dynamics in dual-earner families raising school-aged and adolescent offspring.

We first provide some background on how parental knowledge has been conceptualized in the literature, including the ongoing debate about how to define, measure, and interpret this construct. We then review some of our own work on day-to-day processes in dual-earner families, setting the stage with a brief description of our research design and methods. We address three questions. First, how is fathers' knowledge shaped by the time and timing of their own jobs, as well as the time and timing of mothers' jobs? Second, how are the pressures and demands of parents' jobs related to how much fathers know about their children's daily experiences? Third, how do fathers acquire their knowledge?

PARENTAL KNOWLEDGE: A CONCEPTUAL PRIMER

A sizeable body of research has accumulated showing that children and adolescents fare better on a host of psychosocial outcomes if their parents are better informed about how they spend their time (see review by Crouter & Head, 2002). Many of these investigations conceptualize this construct as *parental monitoring*. Dishion and McMahon (1998, p. 61), for example, defined parental monitoring as "a set of correlated parenting behaviors involving attention to and tracking of the child's whereabouts, activities, and adaptations." This view of parental knowledge has seeped into the public's consciousness. For example, a series of public service announcements by the Partnership for a Drug Free America (see public service banners at: http://www.drugfree.org/banners/questions.html) extrapolated from these parental monitoring findings and urged parents to ask their children questions, arguing that asking questions will help steer youth away from drugs.

Asking children questions is not the only route to acquiring knowledge of their daily lives, however. Stattin and Kerr (2000; Kerr & Stattin, 2000), using data on a large Swedish sample of adolescents, made a powerful argument that the strongest correlate of how much parents know about their children's activities, whereabouts, and companions is not parents' own behavior, such as questioning the child or instituting firm rules that control youth's discretionary time and make it easier for parents to stay informed, but, rather, is the child's tendency to self-disclose to the parent. In their view, at least by adolescence, parents' knowledge depends in large part on what children choose for them to know. Building on this idea, Kerr, Stattin, and Trost (1999) emphasized the importance of trust in the parent-adolescent relationship; they found that the more youth trusted their parents, the more they self-disclosed to them, which, in turn, was linked to higher levels of parental knowledge. One way to integrate the parent- and child-driven perspectives on parental monitoring and knowledge is to put this family construct into a relationship framework. As Crouter, MacDermid, McHale, and Perry-Jenkins (1990, p. 656) explained:

> Parents who are good monitors have made the effort to establish channels of communication with their child, and as a result of their relationship with the

child, they are knowledgeable about the child's daily experiences. In order to be an effective monitor, however, parental interest is not enough: A child must be willing to share his or her experiences and activities with the parent. Seen in this light, parental monitoring is a relationship property.

THE PENN STATE FAMILY RELATIONSHIPS PROJECT

Sample and Design

In the Family Relationships Project (Crouter, Helms-Erikson, Updegraff, & McHale, 1999; McHale, Crouter, & Tucker, 1999), we have been interested in the conditions under which parents in dual-earner families are able to stay informed about what their children are doing on a daily basis. In the mid-1990s, we recruited 201 families through school districts throughout central Pennsylvania. In recruiting the sample, we sought two-parent, non-divorced families in which both parents were working at least part-time, the eldest child was a fourth- or fifth-grade student, and there was at least one sibling one to four years younger. We began studying these families when the two eldest offspring in each family were approximately 10 and 8 years of age.

At the time we began this work, fathers were still somewhat neglected in family research. Moreover the typical investigation in child development or family studies focused on a single target child in each family; studies of siblings were rare (McHale & Crouter, 1996). A notable feature of our design was that we paid equal attention to mothers and fathers and to two target children, an approach that enabled us to focus not only on between-family comparisons of unrelated men vs. women and boys vs. girls, so often the focus of families studies research, but also on within-family comparisons of mothers vs. fathers and of sons vs. daughters. We have recently completed 10 years of annual longitudinal data collection on these families, concluding when the firstborns were one year post–high school. Thus, the data set captures much of the sweep of middle childhood and adolescence.

The sample, drawn from small cities, towns, and rural areas, is working and middle class and, reflecting the racial composition of central Pennsylvania, almost entirely White. Throughout the study we were able to minimize attrition, although over the course of the five years several families separated and divorced and five fathers died. We are now collaborating on research on African American and Mexican American families, using similar designs. In these studies we continue to investigate parental knowledge in some depth, so we hope soon to be able to contribute new knowledge to the literature on how this family process looks in other cultural contexts.

Measuring Parental Knowledge

Typically, researchers measure parental monitoring or knowledge using self reports. Parents are asked how much they really know about their child's leisure activities, friends, involvement in risky behavior and so on, or youth are asked to assess how much their parents really know about these issues (e.g., Pettit, Laird, Dodge, Bates, & Criss, 2001; Steinberg, Fletcher, & Darling, 1994). This approach is problematic for several reasons. First, there is no way to assess accuracy; parents likely do not have a full account of what they should know, particularly if the child deliberately withholds information, and children have no way of accurately knowing of what their parents actually are and are not aware. Second, these self report measures are general in nature whereas, conceptually, parental monitoring or parental knowledge is a family process that is likely to ebb and flow. On some days, parents are likely to be well aware of what their children have been doing, and on other days such information may be elusive. Global measures that ask parents to generalize how much they usually know do not do justice to this phenomenon.

We went to special lengths to try to accurately assess, on a daily basis, how much mothers and fathers knew about important aspects of their children's experiences that might not involve the parent directly (see Crouter, et al. 1990; Crouter, Helms-Erikson, et al., 1999 for details). In Years 1, 2, 3, 6, and 7 of the study, in addition to home interviews with mothers, fathers, and the two target offspring, we conducted a series of seven telephone interviews with each family. These short telephone calls (5 weekdays, 2 weekends) were designed to find out how children had spent their out-of-school time on that specific day, as well as how informed parents were about what their children had been doing that day. We called from about 7 to 10 p.m. to try to capture as much of the day as we could, spending about 10–20 minutes talking with each family member. We talked to the two youth during each of the seven calls and to mothers and fathers during four telephone interviews each.

To measure parental knowledge, each evening we asked the parent and each child a set of six questions about the child's day (parents answered the questions twice, once about each child, at different times in the interview). These questions, which were different each night to minimize practice effects, tapped everyday phenomena in four domains: leisure activities, school, peer relations, and problem behavior. Questions included what homework the child was assigned that night, what programs he or she had been watching on TV, school grades the child had received that day, upcoming tests or long-term school projects the child was preparing for, purchases the child might have made, misbehavior that may have occurred, places the child had gone, friends the child had talked to, and so on. Each question had a first part that was answered in yes/no format ("Did *child* make any purchases today?"). If the parent or child indicated "yes," there was a follow-up question to learn about details ("What did *child* buy?"). During the telephone interview, we first interviewed the parent and then the child, making sure first that they were out of earshot of one another. We operationalized parental knowledge as the match between the parent and child's answers. If a parent answered all 24 questions (4 days x 6 questions), including the follow-up questions, in the same way as the child had, the parent received a score of 100%. More often, parents knew the answers to some questions but not others or knew the broad outlines of children's experiences but not the details; these patterns were reflected in their final scores. As might be expected, mothers were more knowledgeable overall than fathers were (Crouter, Helms-Erikson, et al., 1999). In addition, when families included a boy and a girl, parents specialized in children of the same sex, with mothers knowing somewhat more about girls than boys and fathers knowing considerably more about boys than girls. These gendered patterns were only apparent because our design enabled us to make within-family comparisons of sons and daughters growing up in the same families.

FATHERS' KNOWLEDGE: THE ROLE OF WORK CONDITIONS

What does fathers' knowledge look like in dual-earner families? How is fathers' knowledge related to fathers' work conditions and circumstances and to those of mothers?

Time and Timing of Work

In an analysis of the first wave of data, gathered when the target children were ages 10 and 8, we found that fathers' work hours were not related to either their own levels of knowledge about their school-aged children's activities, whereabouts, or companions or to mothers' levels of knowledge (Crouter, Helms-Erikson et al., 1999). In contrast, although mothers' work hours were not related to mothers' own knowledge levels, fathers whose wives worked longer hours knew significantly more about their children's activities than other fathers did. Putting the mother and father findings together, when mothers worked longer hours, children actually had better informed parents overall because mothers' knowledge did not suffer and fathers knew more. This pattern suggests that, in dual-earner families, mothers' longer work hours may pull fathers into a more active parenting role, with the result that they are better informed about their children on a daily basis.

We examined this issue from another angle using another sample of two-parent, single- and dual-earner families with school-aged children for whom we had gathered short-term longitudinal data during two school years and the summer in between, using the same data collection strategies (Crouter & McHale, 1993). Examining fathers' knowledge scores over the three occasions of measurement, we found that when mothers maintained a high level of involvement in paid employment across the school years and the summer months, fathers maintained a consistent and reasonably high level of knowledge about their children's daily activities across those three time points. In those families in which mothers worked during both school year times of measurement but cut back their level of involvement in work significantly over the summer, however, fathers' pattern of knowledge mirrored mothers' work involvement: Fathers' knowledge was high during the school year, dropped significantly during the summer months, and then rebounded again the following school year.

Given the debate about what parental knowledge means, several processes could explain the connection between mothers' involvement in employment and fathers' levels of knowledge. First, if mothers are spending more time away from home, fathers may increase monitoring of their children by keeping track more carefully of where they are and who they are with and asking questions about their day. Alternatively, a child effects explanation would be that when mothers work longer hours, fathers are more likely to be the ones who are available at home for children to report to about the day's events or to confide in about problems, disappointments, and concerns. Anecdotally, our parents remarked that they frequently learned more about their children's ongoing peer relationships and school issues when driving them to and from activities than in the context of direct conversations. When mothers work longer hours, fathers may handle more of the routine driving and other shared activities that encourage naturally occurring conversations and confidences.

More recently, we have explored parents' shift work and parental knowledge. Using a combined sample of more than 350 offspring who averaged about 14 years of age, Davis, Crouter, and McHale (2006) found no differences in mothers' knowledge for mothers working nonstandard shifts versus day shifts, but fathers working nonstandard shifts were less knowledgeable about their children's daily experiences compared to their counterparts working day shifts. Indeed, mothers who worked nonstandard shifts managed to be more knowledgeable than fathers who worked day shifts, a testimony perhaps to how well mothers manage to cope with parenting demands even when their days do not conform to a 9-to-5 schedule.

Work Demands and Challenges

Parents' work involves more than just time away from the family. The conditions that parents experience doing their particular job and in their particular work group and workplace have implications for their psychosocial functioning (see review by Perry-Jenkins, Repetti, & Crouter, 2000), the quality of the home environment they provide for their children (Parcel & Menaghan, 1994), and the nature of their relationships with their children (e.g., Crouter, Bumpus, Maguire, & McHale, 1999). We have examined the stresses and demands that parents experience on the job in relation to their parental knowledge from several different angles.

We recently investigated the connections between mothers' and fathers' perceptions of negative work-to-family spillover and their level of knowledge about their children's daily experiences (Bumpus, Crouter, & McHale, 2006). Mothers and fathers did not differ significantly in their reports of negative work-to-family spillover. Mirroring the prior findings about work time, however, mothers' perceptions of negative spillover were not connected to their levels of knowledge; mothers managed to be highly knowledgeable regardless of how much they felt their work created problems for them at home. In contrast, for fathers, higher perceived negative work-to-family spillover was related to significantly lower levels of knowledge.

We next explored three possible pathways connecting negative spillover to fathers' knowledge: marital love, shared father-adolescent activities, and perceptions of warmth and acceptance in the father-child relationship. We reasoned that fathers who perceived that their work caused problems for them at home might be less happy in their marriages, more withdrawn and less involved in terms of their levels of shared activities with offspring, or less emotionally engaged with their sons and daughters, reflecting the withdrawal processes that Repetti (1994) has documented in studies of fathers' daily work stress and family interaction.

Marital love emerged as an independent predictor of fathers' knowledge but it did not mediate the connections between fathers' perceptions of negative work-to-family spillover and paternal knowledge. In other words, when partners perceived their marriage to be a loving one, fathers were better informed, but this did not account for the connection between negative spillover and knowledge. The association between negative spillover and knowledge remained significant even when marital love was included in the model.

Evidence for mediation emerged for shared activities and warmth and acceptance, however. First, using children's reports of time spent in different activities and in different social contexts, data gathered in the seven daily telephone interviews, fathers reporting higher levels of negative spillover spent less time with their offspring overall. Spending less time in shared activities, in turn, translated into fathers being less informed about children's daily experiences; a test of mediation revealed that time in joint activities partially mediated the association between fathers' perceptions of negative spillover and fathers' knowledge. Second, fathers experiencing higher levels of negative spillover reported having less accepting and less warm relationships with their adolescent offspring, and, in turn, fathers knew less about their children's daily experiences when the relationship was less accepting and warm. Relationship warmth and acceptance fully mediated the connection between negative spillover and paternal knowledge. In a final model that included all three possible mediators, marital love dropped out as an independent correlate of knowledge, but shared father-adolescent time and relationship warmth both remained significant predictors of paternal knowledge, suggesting that there may be at least two independent paths linking fathers' perceptions of negative work-to-family spillover to their ongoing daily knowledge about their children's experiences, one involving shared activity involvement on the part of fathers and youth and one involving emotional connectedness.

Although we examined the implications of mothers' negative work-to-family spillover for fathers' knowledge as well as the implications of fathers' negative work-to-family spillover for mothers, we found no evidence of crossover effects. Thus, at least for this aspect of the work-family interface and this dimension of the parent-child relationship, fathers' perceptions of work-to-family spillover matter, albeit only for fathers themselves, and mothers' do not.

Thus far, our examples have all taken a variable-oriented approach to understanding the correlates of fathers' knowledge. That is, constructs such as negative work-to-family spillover or work hours were operationalized as continuous, linear phenomena, and attention was focused on understanding how much of the variance in fathers' knowledge could be explained by these variables, alone and in combination. Another strategy for understanding these links is to take a "pattern-analytic" or "person-centered" approach (Bergman, Magnusson, & El-Khouri, 2003). Here, the goal is to use multiple pieces of information to identify groups that share certain profiles. Cluster analysis, latent classification analysis, or mixture modeling can be used to uncover shared profiles, and, once the groups that share features in common are identified, other information can be used to describe the groups and to compare them to one another.

Interested in variations among dual-earner couples in the work demands mothers and fathers experience, Bumpus, Crouter, and McHale (1999) cluster analyzed indicators of fathers' and mothers' work demands to typologize dual-earner families with adolescent offspring. Specifically, they cluster analyzed six variables—mothers' and fathers' weekly work hours and their reports of pressure on the job (e.g., fast pace, deadlines) and role overload. The analysis yielded three groups: a group characterized by high father work demands; a group characterized by high mother work demands; and a group in which both parents scored quite low on all three indicators of work demands. Compared to other parents, both mothers and fathers in the group characterized by high father work demands were significantly less knowledgeable about their children, but only when their marriages were less harmonious. Mothers and fathers in the high father demands group who reported strong marital relationships were as knowledgeable as other parents.

Bumpus et al. (1999) speculated that the combination of a highly demanding work situation for fathers, coupled with a less positive marital dynamic, may make it more difficult for parents to keep abreast of their children's ongoing experiences. This may happen for several reasons. First, marital tension and demanding jobs may distract parents from the task of supervising and monitoring their children, a parenting explanation. Second, children may be less comfortable confiding in parents whose work and marital circumstances may make them less accessible and harder to talk to, a child effects explanation. Alternatively, an explanation focused on the marriage is that parents in happy marriages may be more adept at keeping one another informed about what their children are doing. Smooth marital communication about children's daily experiences gives each partner in a well-functioning marriage the benefit of the other spouse's information. Thus, a mother who drives her son to baseball practice and learns about the poor grade on his math homework may explain to her husband why the son is feeling down. Without this extra help, the father may not have ever learned about the disappointing math grade. Indeed, all of three of these explanations may hold, and they may have differential explanatory value in different families and, within families, for different children.

It is somewhat puzzling that parents in the group in which fathers held demanding jobs had lower knowledge, but that this did not hold for parents in the group in which mothers reported high work demands. Indeed, parents in the latter group were as knowledgeable as parents in the low work-demands group. There are several possible reasons for this pattern. First, in other research we have noted that fathers' work pressure seems to have a more powerful effect on the family than is the case for mothers' work pressure. Crouter, Bumpus, et al., (1999), using structural equation modeling, found that fathers' pressure was linked both to fathers' own reports of role overload and to mothers' reports of overload, but that mothers' work pressure was connected only to mothers' own reports of overload. Thus mothers, often thought of as the emotional managers and kin keepers in families, may be more attentive to (and reactive to) fathers' work strain than fathers are to mothers' work pressure. A second and related point is that in this sample, and in dual-earner families more generally, fathers typically earned more than mothers did, giving their work perhaps more influence in the family at large. Third, mothers often take the lead in terms of organizing family life and thus may have to become better at compartmentalizing work and family than fathers are. To the extent that they are able to do this, their families may be buffered from the effects of high demands. Mothers may accomplish this at some personal cost, however. Bianchi (2000) noted that one reason why there are minimal differences in time investments in children on the part of employed vs. nonemployed mothers is that employed mothers appear to cut back their time in personal care, leisure activities, and sleep.

SOURCES OF KNOWLEDGE

The controversy about whether parental knowledge taps parental monitoring and surveillance or children's disclosure, coupled with our findings about marriage, shared time, and relationship quality serving as mediators or moderators of the connections between parental work and parental knowledge, made us wish we knew more about mothers' and fathers' strategies and methods for acquiring knowledge about their adolescent children's daily experiences. At wave 7, when firstborn children were about age 16, we asked mothers and fathers to rate how much they relied on each of six different strategies for acquiring knowledge (Crouter, Bumpus, Davis, & McHale, 2005; see also Waizenhofer, Buchanan, & Jackson-Newsom, 2004). Three strategies were relationship-oriented because they involved the parent interacting with the child: parent asked questions of the child, the child voluntarily self-disclosed to the parent, and the parent listened to and observed the child (e.g., paid attention to child's signals). The other three sources of knowledge involved relying on other people for information. These included the spouse, other children in the family, or people outside the family such as teachers, coaches, and parents of the child's friends.

On average, the most common strategy for fathers was to rely on mothers, followed by asking questions, child self-disclosure, listening and observing, relying on siblings, and relying on others outside the family. For mothers, in contrast, asking questions was the most endorsed strategy, followed by child self-disclosure, listening and observing, relying on siblings, relying on spouse, and relying on others. Note that the most striking difference between fathers and mothers was that fathers relied heavily on their partners whereas mothers' first approach was to ask questions of the child.

Using cluster analysis, we clustered fathers' six sources of knowledge and identified three groups of fathers that shared similar profiles. The first group we referred to as the relational group, because these fathers relied heavily on asking their child questions, the child self-disclosing, and the father listening to and observing the child in the course of everyday life. The second group stood out because they relied primarily on mothers for information about the child's day. The third group relied primarily on other siblings and on people outside the family.

Interestingly, the only aspect of fathers' jobs that discriminated among the groups was fathers' work hours. Fathers who relied on their wives to keep them informed worked longer hours than other fathers. In addition, families in that group had a preponderance of daughters. In contrast, the group that relied primarily on other siblings and people outside the family had a preponderance of sons and, three years earlier, had described their children as more difficult to supervise. The relational fathers were equally likely to have sons and daughters and reported enjoying harmonious relationships with them. Although our earlier findings had led us to wonder whether the groups would vary as a function of the quality of the marital relationship, there were no group differences in this regard, but fathers who relied on other children and people outside the family for information reported the highest levels of conflict with their offspring.

Does one profile or another have better implications for adolescents' psychosocial functioning? To answer this question we examined our longitudinal data. There is an inherent risk of circularity in studies of parental knowledge and child outcomes. Do children exhibit more problems because their parents are less informed, or do children with more problems keep their parents in the dark? Indeed, longitudinal analyses have revealed complex, reciprocal linkages between knowledge and problem behavior (Laird, Pettit, Bates, & Dodge, 2003). Only an intervention study with random assignment to treatment (e.g., training program in parenting or communication) and control conditions is capable of satisfactorily disentangling these messy associations, but longitudinal data are a helpful first step in piecing together a logical causal scenario. Using path analysis, we examined the connections between offspring's risky behavior (i.e., externalizing problems such as substance use, delinquency, lying, disciplinary problems at school, etc.), assessed when youth were about age 13, sources of knowledge assessed when youth were about age 16, fathers' knowledge assessed at age 16, and adolescents' subsequent risky behavior at about age 17.

As can be seen in Figure 13.1, we found that earlier levels of risky behavior did not predict fathers' sources of knowledge but that fathers whose offspring engaged in more risky behavior at age 13 were significantly less

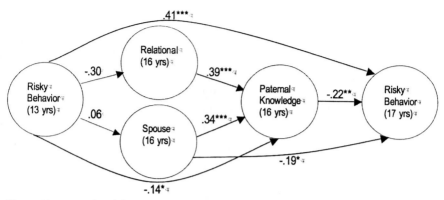

Figure 13.1. Paths Linking Adolescents' Risky Behavior in Early Adolescence, Fathers' Sources of Knowledge, Levels of Knowledge, and Adolescents' Subsequent Risky Behavior (Figure from Crouter, Bumpus, Davis, & McHale, 2005).

knowledgeable three years later. In addition, the sources groups were related to fathers' knowledge: Fathers in the relational group and fathers in the group that relied on mothers for information knew significantly more than fathers who relied on other children or people outside the family for information (the latter group served as the reference group in the analyses and thus is not depicted on the figure). Controlling for prior levels of risky behavior, fathers' knowledge mediated the effects of fathers' sources of knowledge on subsequent risky behavior. Increases in risky behavior were attenuated when fathers were better informed either through direct interaction with the adolescent or via the mother, and youth fared considerably worse in terms of risky behavior when their fathers relied on other children or people outside the family, the constellation of strategies we have come to see as a last resort.

Fathers who acquire their knowledge through relational means and those who rely on mothers have very different source profiles and yet both yield positive results as far as the child is concerned. For us, this signifies that in dual-earner families parental knowledge can be conceptualized as a task for the marital dyad. There are multiple ways in which a couple can pool together its resources to stay on top of their children's fast-paced lives. Particularly when fathers work long hours, and when they have daughters, relying heavily on mothers for information appears to be as effective as directly relying on questions, self-disclosure, and listening and observing. Interestingly, when we performed the same cluster analysis on mothers' sources of knowledge, a group in which mothers relied heavily on fathers for information was not found. This asymmetry says a lot about gender roles in dual-earner families. Although undoubtedly couples do exist in which the father is the primary parent who acquires information about his children's daily experiences and passes that knowledge along to the mother when she returns from work, this pattern was not apparent in sufficient numbers to emerge in our analyses.

CONCLUSIONS

In this chapter, we focused on fathers' ongoing daily knowledge about the activities and experiences of their child and adolescent offspring, with an eye to how fathers' and mothers' work conditions may be connected to fathers' parenting. In focusing on one dimension of parenting—knowledge of children's daily activities—our goal was to illuminate more general principles about how dual-earner families work. In our concluding comments we review some of these principles and suggest directions for future research.

A theme of this review is that fathers' levels of knowledge seem to be calibrated to how involved mothers are in employment. When mothers worked longer hours, fathers knew more. The reverse was not apparent; neither mothers' nor fathers' knowledge appeared to be connected to how much time fathers spend working. Why are we able to predict fathers' knowledge but not mothers'? One explanation is that there is a strong cultural script for mothers, part of which calls for mothers to stay informed about what their children are doing. Heeding the cues from this script, mothers do what it takes to stay informed even when they are working long hours or a nonstandard shift. As we have seen, one way they may be able to accomplish this is that parental knowledge is a two-way street. To the extent that mothers have developed a trusting relationship with their children, a process that begins early in childhood, their children may keep them informed even when they are working longer hours or have nonstandard schedules.

In contrast, the cultural script gives fathers more options. Although one route to being a good father is to be actively involved in children's lives, including direct supervision and communication, fathers can also be seen as capably fulfilling the role of the good father by being a supportive back-up for the mother or by providing well for the family. Fathers have choices. Seen in this light, a father who might ordinarily not choose to be heavily involved in childrearing might rise to the occasion when his wife works longer hours. In doing so, he acquires more day-to-day knowledge about what his children are doing. Without the extra push, however, he might not extend himself to be involved, knowing that the mother is playing that role. Thus, one way to think about these findings is that, relative to mothers, there is more variability in what fathers do, and that greater variability means that it may be easier for researchers to predict fathers' knowledge than it is for them to predict mothers'.

We have also seen some evidence that fathers' job demands are related not only to fathers' knowledge but to mothers' knowledge as well. Thus, mothers' knowledge is not immune to the effects of work but, at least in our data, the emotional tenor of work appears to matter more than the hours involved. Moreover, mothers' knowledge is linked to the emotional tenor of fathers' work demands, but not to their own work demands. As discussed above, we suspect that the emotional tenor of fathers' jobs may be a particularly important source of influence on families (Crouter, Bumpus, et al., 1999). Why? Fathers work longer hours and thus may have less time to recover from work-related affect than mothers do. In addition, fathers earn more than mothers, and their greater economic contributions may give their work, including their work-related stress, special status in the family.

A hypothesis for future research is that the connections between fathers' and mothers' work time and their knowledge about their children's daily experiences may vary as a function of the dual-earner couple's ethos about parenting and provider roles. In couples in which parenting and providing are seen by both partners as equally shared, we may see similar linkages between work time and knowledge, for both mothers and fathers. That is, fathers may step in and become more knowledgeable when mothers work longer hours, and, in like manner, mothers may be more knowledgeable when fathers work longer hours. In families in which mothers' job is seen as secondary to that of fathers, however, mothers may maintain high levels of knowledge no matter how many hours they work and fathers' knowledge may be depend upon how much the mother presses for greater participation in childrearing.

We have also seen that parents' work is only one of several important factors that are related to how knowledgeable mothers and fathers are about their offspring's daily experiences. The quality of the marriage, warmth and acceptance in the parent-child relationship, and shared time together between parents and offspring also play important roles. Indeed, we argued that in dual-earner families, parental knowledge can be thought of as a marital construct because sharing information between them is one way in which mothers and fathers can become knowledgeable. At least for fathers, this sharing is more likely to happen when they work longer hours and when they have daughters. In future research, we will be interested in the conditions under which mothers rely on fathers for knowledge. We may see such a pattern in families with sons, particularly when fathers engage in high levels of shared activities with their sons. Thus, a final principle to be gleaned from our review is that, seen as a parenting task for the marital dyad, parental knowledge becomes part of the repertoire of co-parenting, the teamwork that fathers and mothers engage in together to raise their children. Although there has been a surge of research on co-parenting in the last decade, almost all of the research in this area has focused on parents raising young children. Few studies have examined how mothers and fathers work as a team during their children's school-aged and adolescent years. We see our own research moving in that direction and hope that parental knowledge and strategies for its acquisition will be part of the research agendas of child and adolescent development, parenting, and marital scholars in the years to come.

NOTE

Ann C. Crouter, Ph.D., is the Raymond E. and Erin Stuart Schultz Dean of the College of Health and Human Development at The Pennsylvania State University. W. Benjamin Goodman, M.S., is a graduate student in the Department of Human Development and Family Studies at The Pennsylvania State University. Address correspondence to Ann Crouter, 201 Henderson Building, The Pennsylvania State University, University Park, PA 16802, USA. Phone: 814-865-1420; FAX: 814-865-3282; Email: ac1@psu.edu). This research was supported by a grant from the National Institute for Child Health and Human Development (R01-HD32336), Susan McHale and Ann Crouter, Co-PIs.

REFERENCES

Bergman, L., Magnusson, D., & El-Khouri, B. M. (2003). *Studying individual development in an interindividual context: A person-oriented approach (Paths through life, Vol. 4)*. Mahwah, NJ: Lawrence Erlbaum.

Bianchi, S. M. (2000). Maternal employment and time with children: Dramatic change or surprising continuity? *Demography, 37*, 401–414.

Bumpus, M. F., Crouter, A. C., & McHale, S. M. (2006). Linkages between negative work-to-family spillover and mothers' and fathers' knowledge of their young adolescents' daily lives. *Journal of Early Adolescence, 26*, 36–59.

Bumpus, M. F., Crouter, A. C., & McHale, S. M. (1999). Work demands of dual-earner couples: Implications for parents' knowledge about children's daily lives in middle childhood. *Journal of Marriage and the Family, 61*, 465–475.

Crouter, A. C., Bumpus, M. F., Davis, K. D., & McHale, S. M. (2005). How do parents learn about adolescents' experiences? Implications for parental knowledge and adolescent risky behavior. *Child Development, 76*, 869–882.

Crouter, A. C., Bumpus, M. F., Maguire, M. C., & McHale, S. M. (1999). Linking parents' work pressure and adolescents' well being: Insights into dynamics in dual earner families. *Developmental Psychology, 35*, 1453–1461.

Crouter, A. C., & Head, M. R. (2002). Parental monitoring and knowledge of children. In M. Bornstein (Ed.), *Handbook on parenting* (2nd ed.) (pp. 461–484). Mahwah, NJ: Lawrence Erlbaum.

Crouter, A. C., Helms-Erikson, H., Updegraff, K., & McHale, S. M. (1999). Conditions underlying parents' knowledge about children's daily lives in middle childhood: Between- and within-family comparisons. *Child Development, 70,* 246–259.

Crouter, A. C., MacDermid, S., McHale, S. M., & Perry-Jenkins, M. (1990). Parental monitoring and perceptions of children's school performance and conduct in dual- and single-earner families. *Developmental Psychology, 26,* 649–657.

Crouter, A. C., & McHale, S. M. (1993). Temporal rhythms in family life: Seasonal variation in the relation between parental work and family process. *Developmental Psychology, 29,* 198–205.

Davis, K., Crouter, A. C., & McHale, S. M. (2006). Implications of shift work for parent-adolescent relationships in dual-earner families. *Family Relations, 55,* 450–460.

Dishion, T. J., & McMahon, R. J. (1998). Parental monitoring and the prevention of child and adolescent problem behavior: A conceptual and empirical formulation. *Clinical Child and Family Psychology Review, 1,* 61–75.

Kerr, M., & Stattin, H. (2000). What parents know, how they know it, and several forms of adolescent adjustment: Further support for reinterpretation of monitoring. *Developmental Psychology, 36,* 366–380.

Kerr, M., Stattin, H., & Trost, K. (1999). To know you is to trust you: Parents' trust is rooted in child disclosure of information. *Journal of Adolescence, 22,* 737–752.

Laird, R. D., Pettit, G. S., Bates, J. E., & Dodge, K. A. (2003). Parents' monitoring-relevant knowledge and adolescents' delinquent behavior: Evidence of correlated developmental changes and reciprocal influences. *Child Development, 74,* 752–768.

McHale, S. M., & Crouter, A. C. (1996). The family contexts of children's sibling relationships. In G. Brody (Ed.), *Sibling relationships: Their causes and consequences* (pp. 173–196). Norwood, NJ: Ablex.

McHale, S. M, Crouter, A. C., & Tucker, C. J. (1999). Family context and gender socialization in middle childhood: Comparing girls to boys and sisters to brothers. *Child Development, 70,* 990–1004.

Parcel, T. L. & Menaghan, E. G. (1994). *Parents' jobs and children's lives.* Hawthorne, NY: Aldine de Gruyter.

Perry-Jenkins, M., Repetti, R. L., & Crouter, A. C. (2000). Work and family in the 1990s. *Journal of Marriage and the Family, 64,* 981–998.

Pettit, G. S., Laird, R. D., Dodge, K. A., Bates, J., E., & Criss, M. M. (2001). Antecedents and behavior-problem outcomes of parental monitoring and psychological control in early adolescence. *Child Development, 72,* 583–598.

Repetti, R. L. (1994). Short-term and long-term processes linking job stressors to father-child interaction. *Social Development, 3,* 1–15.

Stattin, H., & Kerr, M. (2000). Parental monitoring: A reinterpretation. *Child Development, 71,* 1072–1085.

Steinberg, L., Fletcher, A., and Darling, N. (1994). Parental monitoring and peer influences on adolescent substance use. *Pediatrics*, *93,* 1060–1063.

Waizenhofer, R. N., Buchanan, C. M., & Jackson-Newsom, J. (2004). Mothers' and fathers' knowledge of adolescents' daily activities: Its sources and its links with adolescent adjustment. *Journal of Family Psychology*, *18*, 348–360.

Chapter Fourteen

What Gives When Mothers Are Employed? Parental Time Allocation in Dual-Earner and Single-Earner Two-Parent Families

by Suzanne M. Bianchi

ABSTRACT

If the increase in maternal employment had been the only change in the family in the past few decades, mother's time with children would have decreased significantly. Yet mothers' average time with children was as high in 1998 as it was in 1965. This paper will review forces that keep investments in childrearing high even among employed mothers, such as the changing selection into and timing of parenthood; changing norms about what children need from parents; and increased fear for children's safety, especially in urban environments. Then, using recently collected time diary data, the paper will focus on the trends and differentials in maternal time with children by mothers' employment status. Examination of the time diaries seeks to answer three questions: (1) How large are differences in time with children between employed and nonemployed mothers? (2) What, in addition to time with children, does market work seem to crowd out of mothers' days? Are the activities that get squeezed out consistent with the idea that employed mothers go to great lengths to protect time with children? (3) If so, are there subjective costs to trying to do it all? That is, are there differences in subjective assessments of time pressures and the quality or adequacy of time with children and spouse between employed and nonemployed mothers?

One of the most important trends to alter family life in the latter half of the 20th century was the increase in women's labor market opportunities and mothers' employment outside the home. In the United States, the employment of mothers with children under age 18 increased from 45% to 78% between 1965 and 2000 with the increase in full-year employment (50 + weeks) rising from 19% to 57% during the same period (Bianchi and Raley, 2005: Table 14.2). The transformation of mothers' time was in many ways revolutionary and remains at the heart of current debates about the adequacy or inadequacy of state supports for families and children (see, for example, Gornick & Meyers, 2003; Jacobs & Gerson, 2004).

To understand change in the family and inform policy debates on reconciling work and family obligations, we need a more complete picture of time use patterns in families where mothers are employed and where they are not. Although qualitative research provides rich descriptions of the competing claims on mothers' time and their feelings of stress and work overload, it is difficult to gauge from this literature how representative the findings are for all mothers, including those who opt for full-time mothering when their children are young. At the same time, the quantitative research on time pressures and the "second shift" of employed mothers is also incomplete: Time allocated to housework is studied separately from time allocated to child care or market work. Few assessments provide an overall picture of time allocation using data that allow the examination of all types of time use.

This chapter's goal is to paint a comprehensive picture of what mothers do less of—or do not do at all—when they allocate time to paid employment. Mothers likely develop a sense of what market work will crowd out of their days, in terms of foregone leisure and other valued activities such as time with their children. Given the set of labor market opportunities and income constraints that they face, mothers make calculations about what is too much to give up and what they, their partners, and their children can tolerate. At any given point in time, mothers are in different labor market positions, with their location influenced in part by their beliefs about what their children need, what they think they need to have a satisfying life, and what they think they can manage all at once.

This paper focuses on the time use of married mothers because much of the literature has either explicitly or implicitly compared what mothers do to what fathers do and argued that mothers more than fathers are (over)burdened with work in the home. In two-parent families, activities in the home that mothers forego to work outside the home can at least theoretically be reallocated to their partner. Much of the current debate about gender equity is about how much, if any, reallocation is taking place in dual-earner families.

Time diary data captures the full array of daily activities leading to questions on five topics—mothers' overall workloads, time with children, individual health and well-being, marriages, and connections to others. Specifically:

(1) Total workloads. How long is the workweek of an employed mother? How long is the "second shift" of unpaid family caregiving and housework that a mother adds to her paid workweek? Is the workweek of employed mothers far longer than that of fathers who do less of the unpaid work in the home?

(2) Children. How much less time do mothers who are employed spend with their children? Does time with children become a casualty of overloaded, time-pressed schedules in dual-earner families? Do fathers with an employed spouse spend more time with children than fathers whose spouse is a full-time homemaker, perhaps to compensate for reduced maternal time in the home?

(3) Individual rest and relaxation. Do employed mothers forego rest, relaxation, and sleep to accomplish all they must, risking their own health and well-being? How large is any sleep or leisure deficit of employed mothers compared with nonemployed mothers? Are mothers much more likely than fathers to sacrifice their rest and relaxation to accommodate paid work and childrearing?

(4) Marriage. What is the association between a mother's employment and the time she spends with her spouse or her feelings of adequacy of time with her spouse? Are investments of time in the marriage, in the couple relationship, sacrificed to the pressures of work and family?

(5) Connections to others. Finally, do busy lifestyles seem to crowd out involvement with a wider group of others? Is there evidence that time socializing with family and friends falls by the wayside in busy working families? What about civic engagement—time spent on the PTA and other organizational activities? Do activities with and for others in one's community become casualties of increased employment of mothers outside the home?

BACKGROUND

James Coleman (1988) suggested that the increase in the number of employed mothers might be leading to declining "social capital" in the family and in neighborhoods. Paid work removed mothers from day-to-day interactions with their children and also resulted in neighborhoods where there were far fewer adults present during the day to monitor children's behavior.

Another body of literature on the "second shift" of employed women suggested a somewhat different picture of the cost of maternal employment. Here, it was argued, the brunt of the impact was most likely on women themselves because women added market work to their commitment to family work. In the classic study, *The Second Shift,* Arlie Hochschild (1989) estimated that employed mothers devoted an extra month a year of workdays to the family, and that mothers experienced a much greater emotional toll of trying to do it all than did fathers. Marital relationships also suffered as women came to resent the lack of assistance from their husbands with the demands of the home.

Still other evidence suggested that mothers did not exhaust themselves by doing it all. Rather, they mortgaged their future economic security by curtailing labor force participation when childrearing demands were greatest. For example, the majority (54%) of married women ages 25–54 with preschool-age children in the home do not work full-time, year-round (Cohen & Bianchi, 1999) and mothers' employment hours (but not fathers' hours) remain highly responsive to the age of the youngest child (Bianchi & Raley, 2005). Some mothers exit the labor force for the first year or few years of their children's lives, while others may reduce their labor force status to part time (Klerman & Liebowitz, 1999). When mothers return to market work, or return to full-time employment, they often structure their employment hours so that they overlap with children's school schedules (Crouter & McHale, 2005). An extensive literature documents the economic costs to women of curtailing market work to spend more time in the home (e.g., Budig and England's (2001) finding of a motherhood wage penalty, Waldfogel's (1997) documentation of a "family gap," Crittenden's (2001) assertion of a "mommy tax," Williams's (2000) arguments about the cost to mothers of the "ideal worker" norm).

Still other research suggested that those mothers who successfully combined paid work and family caregiving did it by protecting the most important or "most precious" uses of time in the home while either foregoing other activities or outsourcing them to others. For example, the historical U.S. time-use data show that across the 1965–2000 period, as mothers increased market work, they reduced their time in housework but not childcare (Bianchi, Robinson, & Milkie, 2006). As market work rose, mothers' average time in childcare activities declined between 1965 and 1975 but then rose. Most studies in the United States and other developed countries suggest that the amount of time parents are directly engaged in caring for children may be on the increase, despite trends (more maternal employment, more single parenting) that should have led to the declining investment in children (Bianchi, 2000; Bianchi, Robinson, & Milkie, 2006; Gauthier, Smeeding, & Furstenberg, 2004; Sandberg & Hofferth, 2001; Sayer, Bianchi, & Robinson, 2004).

Qualitative work suggests reasons why it may be difficult to cut back on family caregiving, even as women expand their hours of employment. Modern-day mothers face "competing devotions" to market and family work

(Blair-Loy, 2003) and strong social expectations to engage in "intensive mothering" even in the face of increased labor market demands (Hays, 1996). The cultural script of intensive mothering suggests that mothers are compelled to devote themselves totally to the project of childrearing and are likely to feel uncomfortable outsourcing this task to other caregivers (Hattery, 2001). Developing the capacities of children through an array of structured activities is also on the rise, particularly in the middle class (Lareau, 2003) and is perhaps partly an outcome of the shift in focus toward "child quality" in smaller families (Gauthier et al., 2004). Fear for children's safety may also have increased, encouraging greater parental vigilance of children and children's activities (Sayer et al., 2004; Warr & Ellison, 2000).

Finally, although the "second shift" literature is skeptical that fathers have adjusted their behavior in response to greater maternal employment, there is some evidence that fathers may be increasing their investment in the home. Fathers more than doubled their housework hours between 1965 and 1985 and fathers' primary childcare time increased sharply after 1985. By 2000, fathers had nearly tripled their primary childcare time, reporting almost 7 hours per week of childcare in time diary data collections (Bianchi, Robinson, & Milkie, 2006).

To summarize, mothers (and fathers) facing a 24-hour time constraint must make difficult day-to-day decisions about how to allocate time to market and family work. There are a number of competing claims about how mothers (and fathers) have responded to the challenge of balancing work and family demands. Time is finite and, although it can be stretched somewhat by multitasking, there are limits. The goal of this paper is to provide a rich description of the activities that differ in the households of employed and nonemployed mothers. There is, of course, a "zero-sum" or accounting aspect to this approach: more hours in one activity of necessity mean less in others, although mothers' engagement in simultaneous activities are considered for some measures.

Mothers differ on more than employment, and the analysis standardizes on demographic characteristics that can be measured in order to estimate an "employment difference" or "employment effect." However, one cannot assess the unmeasured differences in tastes or motivations of the two groups of mothers (or their partners). Hence, the associations with employment are suggestive, they hint at what might be cause and effect relationships. One cannot know with certainty, for example, whether the nonemployed mother would make the same tradeoffs as the employed mother were she to become employed. However, rich description seems the right starting point for trying to enlarge understanding of the array of factors that influence a family's calculations about the costs and benefits of mother's market work.

DATA

Data for this study come from two nationally representative time diary collections undertaken at the University of Maryland: the 2000–01 National Survey of Parents (NSP), funded by the Alfred P. Sloan Foundation's Workplace, Work Force, and Working Families Program, and the slightly earlier 1998–99 Family Interaction, Social Capital, and Time Use Study (FISCT) funded by the National Science Foundation.

The National Survey of Parents (NSP). With funding from the Alfred P. Sloan Foundation's Workplace, Work Force, and Working Families Program, we interviewed a national sample of 1,200 parents living with children under age eighteen in 2000–2001. Parents were asked an array of attitudinal questions about their activities with children and their feelings about the time they spent alone, with children, and with a spouse. Embedded in the study was a one-day, yesterday diary of time expenditures. The data were collected in computer-assisted telephone interviews, with a 64% response rate. For more information, see Bianchi, Robinson, and Milkie (2006; Chapter 2).

1998–1999 Family Interaction, Social Capital, and Trends in Time Use Study (FISCT). In 1998–99, we conducted a national study of adults, age 18 and over, in which 1,151 adults were interviewed. Respondents were interviewed by telephone and completed a one-day, yesterday diary. The overall response rate was 56%. The study, conducted with funding from the National Science Foundation (NSF) (and supplementary funding from the National Institute on Aging for interviews with the population age 65 and older), was designed to be comparable to earlier national time-diary data collections. For the analyses based on the time diary, the sample of parents from the NSF study is combined with the Sloan sample of 1,200 parents to augment the sample sizes; examination of the differences between mothers and fathers in the two studies suggested minimal differences.

The sample was restricted to married or cohabitating parents aged 18 to 64 with an employed husband (given that paternal employment is normative in most American couples with children under age 18; indeed, over 90% of fathers were employed in both samples). The total sample is 647 married mothers with employed spouses, aged 18 to 64, and 525 married employed fathers aged 18 to 64. It should be noted that both studies interviewed one person per household so there are no time diaries from couples, although we do have the respondent's report of the employment status and hours worked per week of his or her spouse. This information is used to classify fathers by a wife's employment status.

The 2000–01 time diaries were embedded in a survey with an array of questions about parenting practices and feelings about time pressure. Hence, most of the subjective indicators examined are only available in the 2000–01 NSP and tabulations exclude parents from the 1998–1999 survey.

Time diary data assess all types of activities, not just market work. Because diaries cover a full twenty-four hour period, they provide information on paid work outside the household and time spent in productive activity in and for the household—the "second shift" of interest to family researchers. Diaries also allow one to examine all of the personal care and discretionary pursuits that could be affected by the busy schedules in working families.

Estimates from time diaries seem superior to survey-estimate questions for assessing individuals' time expenditures for a number of reasons. Activities like housework and childcare often occur in snippets throughout the day and may be difficult to recall and calculate precisely in response to a survey question asking about time spent in these activities. Time diary data are collected in a way that guides respondents through their days, starting with the question "What were you doing yesterday at midnight?" The interviewer follows the respondent through the day until the entire day's main activities, or primary activities, are recounted. This structure of data collection helps the respondent sequentially report activities and forces the respondent to adhere to a 24-hour constraint.

The report of secondary activities, or what else the respondent was doing, as well as "with whom" data are also available in both data sets. This information is useful in developing several parenting and leisure measures. For example, a substantial amount of child care is provided in conjunction with other activities, or as a "secondary activity." Estimates of time caring for children often increase by 30%–40% percent when secondary child care is added to primary child care time. Also, parents spend time in activities where the child may be present but child care is not the focal activity. Much of this time is also time parents are caring for children, even though the care is not focused on the child and may be somewhat passive (Folbre, Yoon, Finnoff, & Fuligni, 2005). Not considering this time may give a misleading picture of childcare foregone by employed mothers.

A NOTE ON MEASUREMENT

One issue with the comparison of mothers who are and are not employed—as well as with the comparison of fathers whose wives are and are not employed—is that the nonemployed face overall higher childcare demands. Women with the heaviest workloads—those with young children—often curtail employment to ease the burden of combining work and family. This suggests heterogeneity across mothers and within the individual lives of mothers as their children age. Indeed, Table 14.1 shows that the group of employed mothers have slightly fewer children and are much less likely to have a child under age 6 in the home. Employed mothers are also older and

Table 14.1 Means and Percentage Distributions of Married Parents' Demographic Characteristics by Maternal Employment

	Mothers					Fathers		
	Total	Employed	Nonemployed		Total	Fathers with Employed Wives	Fathers with Nonemployed Wives	
Maternal Employment	68.8%				74.7%			
Family Characteristics								
Number of Children	2.0	2.0	2.2	*	2.0	2.0	2.2	*
Children < 6	56.8%	48.9%	74.1%	***	52.0%	47.0%	66.9%	***
Education								
Less Than High School	10.9%	8.7%	15.7%	**	15.0%	14.5%	16.6%	
High School Grad	33.4%	36.2%	27.4%	*	30.9%	30.8%	31.1%	
Some College	27.8%	25.1%	33.6%	*	22.5%	22.7%	21.6%	
College Grad, Plus	27.9%	30.0%	23.3%		31.7%	32.0%	30.7%	
Age								
Aged 18 to 24	14.4%	12.2%	19.3%	*	8.2%	11.0%	0.0%	***
Aged 25 to 34	34.1%	33.7%	35.1%		22.7%	20.2%	29.9%	*
Aged 35 to 44	37.6%	39.3%	33.8%		41.7%	41.3%	42.9%	
Aged 45 to 64	13.9%	14.9%	11.8%		27.4%	27.4%	27.2%	
Diary Characteristics								
Weekend diary	26.4%	27.2%	24.6%		31.3%	31.1%	32.0%	
N	647	471	176		525	393	132	

Source: Authors Calculations from the combined file of the 1998–99 Family Interaction, Social Capital, and Trends in Time Use Study and the 2000 National Survey of Parents.

Note: Analysis is restricted to married parents aged 18 to 64. All fathers are employed.

***p < .001, ** p < .01 level, * p < 0.05, # p < .10 level

somewhat better educated than non-employed mothers. Age and education do not distinguish fathers in dual-earner and single-earner families, but there are parallel differences by age of children.

The following presents estimates of the time use of mothers and fathers in single-earner and dual-earner families along with the unadjusted difference between the two groups. Also used are OLS regression models that include age, education, number of children, the presence of children under age 6, and a control for whether the diary day was a weekend day to estimate the cost of employment that is net of the effect associated with number of children, presence of a preschooler, and the respondent's age and educational attainment.

MATERNAL EMPLOYMENT, TOTAL WORKLOADS, AND THE SECOND SHIFT

Time diary evidence allows one to estimate workloads of mothers that combine hours of market work or paid work activity with hours spent working in the home—doing housework, childcare, and shopping to obtain goods and services for the household. Hence, the first questions posed are:

- If we combine paid and unpaid work hours, what is the average weekly workload of employed mothers and how does it compare with nonemployed mothers and (employed) fathers?
- Does the employed mother add a "second shift" of unpaid household work that makes her far more overworked than others—not only nonemployed mothers but also fathers?

Figure 14.1 provides estimates of weekly workloads for married mothers and fathers in single-earner and dual-earner couples. Overall, workloads are large and average 65+ hours per week for both mothers and fathers. Workloads are gender-specialized, with paid work hours constituting a much greater share of fathers' total hours and unpaid work hours a much greater share of mothers' total hours. These estimates are only based on reports of the respondent's main activity—and hence observe the 24-hour constraint.

Nonemployed mothers, who account for about 30% of all married mothers, put in far more hours of unpaid work than employed mothers (56 hours per week of childcare and other unpaid family work compared with 36 hours for employed mothers). However, when employed mothers' 36 hours of unpaid work are added to their average of 34 hours of paid work per week, they average 70 hours per week, the highest of any group. That is, the employed mother does add a second shift that makes her overall work week much

Chapter Fourteen

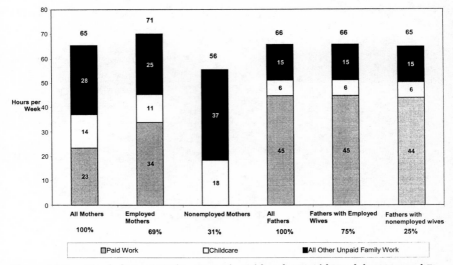

Figure 14.1. Married Parents' Time Spent in Paid and .Unpaid Work by Maternal Employment.

longer than a nonemployed mother's work week, yet only a little longer than a father's work week.

Table 14.2 shows that, after adjustment for the effects associated with other variables, employed mothers average 16 more hours per week of work than nonemployed mothers. They do almost 11 fewer hours of housework and spend 6 fewer hours with their children. That is, the main family activity that is omitted when mothers are employed is housework, but childcare is also omitted.

Adjusted estimates for fathers show no statistically significant differences in the amounts of housework and child care of fathers with employed and nonemployed wives, although the adjusted estimate of maternal employment on father's childcare is positive (and almost 3 hours). The overall picture, however, is that spousal employment is not associated with an increase in the domestic workloads of married fathers. That is, spousal employment is not statistically significantly associated with any kind of unpaid work among fathers—childcare, housework, or other unpaid family work.

CHILDCARE ACTIVITIES AND TIME WITH CHILDREN

Not only for Coleman (1988) but for many social observers, one of the greatest concerns about increased maternal employment is that children might not

Table 14.2. Married Parents' Hours Per Week Spent in Paid and Unpaid Work Activities by Maternal Employment

	Total	Mother/Wife Employed	Mother/Wife Not Employed	Difference	Effect of Maternal Employment OLS Regression Coefficient
Mothers					
Total Paid + Unpaid Work	65.5	69.9	55.7	14.3 ***	16.3 ***
Total Paid Work	23.4	34.0	-	-	-
Work	21.0	30.5	-	-	-
Commute	2.4	3.4	-	-	-
Total Unpaid Work	42.0	36.0	55.4	-19.5 ***	-12.1 ***
Housework	19.6	16.4	26.7	-10.3 ***	-10.0 ***
Childcare	13.6	11.4	18.5	-7.1 ***	-4.9 ***
Shopping	8.8	8.2	10.3	-2.1 ***	-2.1
Fathers					
Total Paid + Unpaid Work	65.5	65.8	64.7	1.1	0.4
Total Paid Work	44.6	44.8	43.9	0.9	-1.7
Work	39.6	39.8	38.8	1.0	-1.4
Commute	5.0	5.0	5.1	-0.1	-0.4
Total Unpaid Work	21.0	21.0	20.9	0.1	0.5
Housework	9.6	9.3	10.5	-1.2	-1.0
Childcare	6.4	6.4	6.3	0.1	1.7
Shopping	5.0	5.3	4.0	1.2	1.0

Source: Authors Calculations from the combined file of the 1998-99 Family Interaction, Social Capital, and Trends in Time Use Study and the 2000 National Survey of Parents.

Note: Analysis is restricted to married parents aged 18 to 64. All fathers are employed. Regression models control for number of children, presence of preschooler, educational attainment, age, and whether the diary was collected on a weekend.

***p-value < .001, **p-value < .01, *p-value < .05.

receive the time and attention they need from a working mother. In terms of primary activity time, Table 14.2 shows that employed mothers average 6 fewer hours per week in primary childcare activities.

Primary child care time is the measure that is most consistently available, both across time in the United States and in time diary studies from other countries. Some make compelling arguments that the activity focus of time diary data collection and the heavy reliance on assessments of primary activity time provide only a partial picture at best. Historical estimates of childcare collected in time diaries may miss changes in mothers' overall availability to children as more mothers spend more hours away from home in employment (see Budig & Folbre, 2004). Hence, we consider not only trends in mothers' primary childcare activities but also expanded measures of investment in childrearing through the following questions:

- How much less time do employed than nonemployed mothers spend with their children—either directly attending to their children's needs or in terms of the total amount of time with their children?
- Is the quality of time with children eroded in families with employed mothers? For example, do dual-earner families find it more difficult to have the time-honored family meal together? Do activities like reading to children and helping with homework get squeezed out or are these types of quality activities protected even when overall time is in short supply?
- Finally, do fathers participate more in childrearing when mothers are employed?

Table 14.3 repeats the estimate of primary childcare time from Table 14.2 but adds estimates of secondary time and all (total) time a parent spends with the child. A working mother's time with children expands from 11 hours per week to almost 16 hours per week when secondary time is included and to 44 hours per week when all time with children is included. However, the adjusted gap in her time with children compared with a mother who is not employed doubles from a 6 hour to a 12 hour gap and increases to a 22 hour gap in total time with children. Fathers' time with children also increases as the measures become more expansive, is always less than mothers' time, and shows little difference in homes where the mother is or is not employed.

Table 14.3 also shows one subjective measure of time with children—the percentage who feel they have too little time with their youngest child. Here there is also a large gap between employed and nonemployed mothers, with 44 percent of the former compared with 20 percent of the latter feeling they spend too little time with their youngest child. Fathers are more likely than

Table 14.3. Married Parents' Hours Per Week Spent in Child Care Activities and Feelings about Time with Children by Maternal Employment

	Total	Mother/Wife Employed	Mother/Wife Not Employed	Difference	Effect of Maternal Employment	
					OLS Regression Coefficient	Odds Ratio
Mothers						
Primary Childcare	13.6	11.4	18.5	-7.1 ***	-4.9 ***	
Secondary Child Care	6.4	4.1	11.4	-7.2 ***	-6.0 ***	
Primary + Secondary Child Care	20.0	15.5	29.9	-14.4 ***	-1.1 ***	
All Time with Children	52.4	44.1	70.8	-26.7 ***	-21.7 ***	
Percent with "Too Little" Time with Youngest (only) Child[A]	36.0%	43.5%	20.3%	23.2% ***		3.5 ***
Percent "Completely" Satisfied with Time with Children[A]	28.7%	17.8%	51.4%	-33.7% ***		0.2 ***
Fathers						
Primary Childcare	6.4	6.4	6.3	0.1	1.7	
Secondary Child Care	1.6	1.4	2.2	-0.7	1.7	
Primary + Secondary Child Care	8.0	7.8	8.5	-0.7	1.4	
All Time with Children	32.3	31.4	35.0	-3.6	0.1	
Percent with "Too Little" Time with Youngest (only) Child[A]	55.9%	55.4%	57.3%	-1.9%		1.0
Percent "Completely" Satisfied with Time with Children[A]	16.6%	15.5%	19.4%	-3.9%		0.7

Source: Authors Calculations from the combined file of the 1998-99 Family Interaction, Social Capital, and Trends in Time Use Study and the 2000 National Survey of Parents.

Note: Analysis is restricted to married parents aged 18 to 64. All fathers are employed. Regression models control for number of children, presence of preschooler, educational attainment, age, and whether the diary was collected on a weekend.

either group of mothers to feel they have too little time with their youngest child, but there is no statistically significant difference between the two groups of fathers, with 55%–57% reporting they feel they have too little time with their youngest child.

What about quality interactions between parents and children in dual-earner and single-earner homes? On the one hand, homemaker mothers have more overall time available to spend on certain activities like reading to children and preparing time and space for the family to eat together. However, these quality activities may be the least likely to be forgone, if employed mothers recognize their value and shift out of other activities to make room for what are perceived to be quality kinds of child time.

Table 14.4 shows estimates of the average number of days per week that married mothers and fathers report engaging in selected child care activities as well as the odds that parents report certain behaviors with their children on a daily basis. In only two cases are there statistically significant differences of parents' engagement in specific child-related activities once demographic characteristics are controlled. Employed mothers report about 1.0 fewer days per week on which they read to their children and 0.8 fewer days per week where the family eats their main meal together. These differences are mirrored for fathers: those with employed spouses read less often to their children and eat together as a family less often. There are no significant differences in the extent to which employed and nonemployed mothers report helping their children with homework, driving their children to activities, supervising their children's activities, or involving their children in household chores.

Table 14.4 also shows the extent to which families with an employed mother differ from families with a stay-at-home mother in their reports of raising their voices, laughing, showing physical affection, and praising their children. Few differences emerge, save one. Both mothers and fathers are less likely to report that they laugh with their children every day when there is an employed mother in the home rather than a mother who does not participate in market work. Further, fathers with an employed spouse may be somewhat more likely to raise their voice or yell at their children on a daily basis than those with a stay-at-home wife. Both of these might be taken as an indication of a little more stress in dual-earner homes.

MOTHERS' TIME FOR SLEEP, REST, AND RELAXATION

Some time expenditures, like sleep, may be more central to mothers' health and well-being than others. The second shift literature would suggest that

Table 14.4 Survey Measures of Married Parents' Mean Days Per Week Spent in Selected Child-related Activities

	Total	Mother/ Wife Employed	Mother/ Wife Not Employed	Difference	Effect of Maternal Employment OLS Regression Coefficient	Odds Ratio
Mothers						
Mean days/week read to child[A]	4.2	3.8	5.0	-1.2 ***	-1.0 **	
Mean days/week helped with homework[B]	3.3	3.1	3.8	-0.7 *	-0.3	
Mean days/week drove child to activities[B]	2.6	2.7	2.5	0.1	0.1	
Mean days/week supervised child's activities[B]	2.2	2.1	1.9	0.2	0.1	
Mean days/week had child help with chores[B]	4.8	4.8	4.8	0.0	0.0	
Mean days/week family ate main meal together	4.5	4.3	4.8	-0.5 **	-0.8 ***	
Percent who raise voice with children "daily"	36.5%	33.6%	42.7%	-9.1 #		0.8
Percent who laugh with children "daily"	87.0%	84.0%	93.0%	-9.0 ***		0.4 *
Percent who hug and kiss children "daily"	88.9%	87.5%	91.8%	-4.3		0.8
Percent who praise children "daily"	75.5%	74.5%	77.6%	-3.2		1.0

(continued)

Table 14.4 (Continued)

| | | Mother/Wife Employed | Mother/Wife Not Employed | | Effect of Maternal Employment | |
	Total			Difference	OLS Regression Coefficient	Odds Ratio
Fathers						
Mean days/week read to child[A]	2.6	2.3	3.5	-1.2 ***	-0.8 *	
Mean days/week helped with homework[B]	2.7	2.8	2.5	0.3	0.4	
Mean days/week drove child to activities[B]	2.0	2.1	1.8	0.3	0.5	
Mean days/week supervised child's activities[B]	1.8	1.9	1.5	0.4	0.2	
Mean days/week had child help with chores[B]	4.6	4.7	4.3	0.4	0.3	
Mean days/week family ate main meal together	4.8	4.6	5.1	-0.5 *	-0.6 *	
Percent who raise voice with children "daily"	27.2%	24.0%	35.4%	-11.4 *		0.7 #
Percent who laugh with children "daily"	84.3%	80.7%	93.9%	-13.1 **		0.3
Percent who hug and kiss children "daily"	82.2%	79.7%	88.8%	-9.0 *		0.6
Percent who praise children "daily"	67.0%	64.0%	75.0%	-11.1 *		0.7

Source: Authors Calculations from the 2000 National Survey of Parents.

Note: Analysis is restricted to married parents aged 18 to 64. All fathers are employed. Regression models control for number of children, presence of preschooler, educational attainment, age, and whether the diary was collected on a weekend.

[A]asked only of mothers with children aged 3-12, [B]asked only of mothers with children aged 5-17.

***p-value < .001, **p-value < .01, *p-value< .05.

men do not pick up the slack when women are employed and hence, although we might find employed mothers foregoing sleep or leisure activities, we will not find similar adjustments on the part of their husbands (Hochschild, 1989). On the other hand, if mothers have more bargaining power when they become earners, husbands of employed wives more so than husbands of nonemployed wives should face greater pressures to take reductions in rest and relaxation. Both husbands and wives should have less time for themselves in dual-earner than in single-earner households, all other things being equal.

Hence, we investigate the following:

- Do employed women aim to do it all by sacrificing sleep to accommodate paid work and family caregiving? That is, does rest and relaxation fall by the wayside for the employed mother?
- If employed women forego leisure and sleep to attend to responsibilities in the home, do their husbands also reduce these activities to accommodate the harried pace of family life?

In Table 14.5 we document employed and personal care, sleep, and leisure, as well as mothers' and fathers' subjective sense of not enough time for themselves, always feeling rushed and multitasking most of the time.

Do employed mothers get less sleep? The answer is yes—about four hours less per week, although it is not clear that they spend any less time on other personal care activities. Because time is finite, they also have about 12 hours less free time, including almost 8 fewer hours of arguably the most relaxing of free time—what we label "pure" child-free time; i.e., free time not spent in charge of children and not spent combining some unpaid domestic activity with leisure. Employed mothers also spend about 6 hours less per week watching television. Once again, there are no differences in the schedules of fathers with employed and nonemployed spouses.

In order to investigate the subjective aspect of family life, our data are examined for indicators of feeling rushed, feeling like one is multitasking all the time, and an indicator of feeling that one has too little time for oneself. As shown in Table 14.5, employed mothers are nearly three times as likely to report always feeling rushed and are almost twice as likely to report that they multitask most of the time. They are not necessarily more likely to say they have too little time for themselves: around 71% of both groups of mothers feel they do not have enough time for themselves.

Fathers' reports of feeling rushed are intermediate; lower than employed mothers but a little higher than nonemployed mothers. The two groups of fathers are similar in their reports of feeling rushed and in reports of multitasking and they report much lower levels of multitasking most of the time (a little

Table 14.5. Married Parents' Hours Per Week Spent in Personal Care and Rest and Relaxation Activities and Feelings about Time Use by Maternal Employment

	Total	Mother/Wife Employed	Mother/Wife Not Employed	Difference	Effect of Maternal Employment	
					OLS Regression Coefficient	Odds Ratio
Mothers						
Personal Care	16.2	16.0	16.7	-0.7	-0.8	
Sleep	54.6	53.5	57.1	-3.5 **	-3.5 **	
Free Time	31.7	28.5	38.6	-10.0 ***	-12.1 ***	
Watching Television	10.7	9.1	14.0	-4.9 ***	-4.9 ***	
"Always" Feeling Rushed[A]	40.1	46.4	27.1	19.3 **		2.8 ***
Multitasking "Most of the time"[A]	66.8	70.5	59.1	11.4 *		1.7 *
"Too Little" Time to Oneself[A]	71.4	71.1	71.9	-0.8		1.2
Fathers						
Personal Care	15.6	15.3	16.5	-1.2	-1.8	
Sleep	54.0	54.8	51.6	3.2	3.2 *	
Free Time	32.9	32.1	35.2	-3.1	-2.1	
Watching Television	13.9	14.2	13.0	1.1	1.8	
"Always" Feeling Rushed[A]	32.9	32.6	33.9	-1.3		1.0
Multitasking "Most of the time"[A]	41.2	40.8	42.4	-1.7		1.0
"Too Little" Time to Oneself[A]	57.4	54.4	65.4	-11.1 *		0.8

Source: Authors Calculations from the combined file of the 1998-99 Family Interaction, Social Capital, and Trends in Time Use Study and the 2000 National Survey of Parents.
Note: Analysis is restricted to married parents aged 18 to 64. All fathers are employed. Regression models control for number of children, presence of preschooler, educational attainment, age, and whether the diary was collected on a weekend.

more than 40%) than either group of mothers. The one difference by maternal employment status is that fathers who are sole breadwinners are more likely to report "too little time" for themselves than are fathers in dual-earner families.

EMPLOYMENT AND TIME WITH SPOUSE

Does maternal employment cut into time that a couple spends together? The feeling that one does not have enough time with one's spouse seems ubiquitous—perhaps more related to having children than to the employment status of parents. As shown in Table 14.6, two-thirds of mothers (employed and nonemployed) report too little time with a spouse. The percentages for fathers are in the range of 55–60 percent.

As far as actual time with a spouse reported in the time diary, time alone with the spouse is not significantly different for families with and without an employed mother but in couples with a full-time homemaker, the overall amount of time the couple spends together is greater. The adjusted estimate is that single-earner couples average 9 more hours together per week than do dual-earner couples.

BEYOND THE COUPLE AND THE FAMILY: SOCIALIZING AND CIVIC ENGAGEMENT

A final set of activities to be investigated are those that connect the family to a wider circle of friends and organizations. A set of activities that receives attention from social scientists of various disciplines, particularly in light of its political ramifications, are civic leisure pursuits (Putman, 2000). Most recent accounts indicate employment reduces a woman's time available for volunteering, although trends over time are unclear (see Bianchi, 2000, for a review).

To expand our categorization of leisure to activities of concern to some social observers—for example, the supposed decline in community or civic connection in society documented in Robert Putnam's (2000) *Bowling Alone*—we examine a category of leisure activities that Sayer (2001) labels "civic leisure." Civic leisure includes organizational activities such as PTA meetings and the like. As shown in Table 14.7, estimates of weekly hours in this type of activity are relatively low. Employed mothers do about 1.3 hours of this type of activity compared with 2.8 hours by nonemployed mothers. The adjusted difference is 1.8 fewer hours of this type of engaged leisure on

Table 14.6. Married Parents' Hours Per Week Spent with Spouse and Feelings about Time with Spouse by Maternal Employment

	Total	Mother/Wife Employed	Mother/Wife Not Employed	Difference	Effect of Maternal Employment	
					OLS Regression Coefficient	Odds Ratio
Mothers						
Any Time with Spouse	26.3	23.8	31.9	-8.1 ***	-8.6 ***	
Time with Spouse Only	7.9	7.8	8.3	-0.6	-1.3	
"Too Little" Time with Spouse[A]	67.7	68.2	66.8	1.4 **		1.5
Fathers						
Any Time with Spouse	30.32	29.00	34.20	-5.2 *	-2.7	
Time with Spouse Only	9.76	10.07	8.84	1.2	2.5	
"Too Little" Time with Spouse[A]	59.3	61.0	55.0	6.0 **		1.4

Source: Authors Calculations from the combined file of the 1998-99 Family Interaction, Social Capital, and Trends in Time Use Study and the 2000 National Survey of Parents.

Note: Analysis is restricted to married parents aged 18 to 64. All fathers are employed. Regression models control for number of children, presence of preschooler, educational attainment, age, and whether the diary was collected on a weekend.

[A]Source is 2000 National Survey of Parents only.

***p-value < .001, **p-value < .01, *p-value < .05.

the part of employed mothers and no difference for fathers in the two types of households.

Two other categories in Table 14.7 have to do with the "glue" of relationships—activities that Sayer (2001) includes in a category labeled "social leisure"—socializing, attending events with others, and doing hobbies with others. Overall, all groups report a significant number of hours in such activities (see Table 14.8 for the activities included)—as many as 20 hours per week for nonemployed mothers. Employed mothers engage in four fewer hours of social leisure than nonemployed mothers. There is a parallel difference among fathers, with those married to employed wives spending about 4 hours less per week in social pursuits than those married to a mother at home full time.

Finally, an alternative estimate is the time the respondent reports in the time diary that he or she spends with friends and relatives. Here there is no significant difference between mothers or fathers depending on a mother's employment status. Hence, the picture is mixed in this area. Dual-earner families spend less time socializing than single-earner families but still spend a sizable number of hours per week in these activities. They spend just as much time with friends and relatives but employed mothers do seem to curtail their time in voluntary organizations.

DISCUSSION AND CONCLUSION

This paper provides a snapshot of the objective and subjective time-use differences between employed and nonemployed mothers: employed mothers experience time deficits in an array of activities and experience greater time pressures than nonemployed mothers. Employed mothers' houses are probably less clean, they get less sleep, they do not spend as much time with their children, and seem to feel guilty about it. They relax less, do not spend as much time with their spouses, and they more often report always feeling rushed.

Perhaps this begins to shed light on why, some 40 years after the gender revolution—and despite increased educational, occupational, and early career opportunities for women—once children arrive, mothers reduce market employment in favor of more time in the home. Although attitudes toward maternal employment have become more accepting and many couples espouse an ideal of gender egalitarianism in work and family life (Casper & Bianchi, 2002), this ideal has proven quite difficult to realize. The continued high rate of temporary labor-force exits by mothers when children are young and the reduction in women's labor market hours throughout the childrearing years

Table 14.7. Married Parents' Hours Per Week Spent in Community and Social Activities and Feelings about Time spent with Family by
Maternal Employment

	Total	Mother/Wife Employed	Mother/Wife Not Employed	Difference	Effect of Maternal Employment OLS Regression Coefficient	Odds Ratio
Mothers						
Civic Leisure	1.8	1.3	2.8	−1.5**	−1.8***	
Social Leisure	18.0	16.9	20.4	−3.5*	−0.4**	
Time with Friends and Relatives	10.9	11.1	10.3	0.8	1.4	
"Completely" Satisfied with Time with Family^A	12.1%	8.9%	18.8%	−9.9% **		0.3***
Fathers						
Civic Leisure	2.1	2.2	1.8	0.4	0.3	
Social Leisure	14.8	13.7	18.3	−4.6**	−4.2*	
Time with Friends and Relatives	9.3	8.9	10.5	−1.6	−1.9	
"Completely" Satisfied with Time with Family^A	12.1%	9.2%	19.7%	−0.1 **		0.3 ***

Source: Authors Calculations from the combined file of the 1998-99 Family Interaction, Social Capital, and Trends in Time Use Study and the 2000 National Survey of Parents.
Note: Analysis is restricted to married parents aged 18 to 64. All fathers are employed. Regression models control for number of children, presence of preschooler, educational attainment, age, and whether the diary was collected on a weekend.
^A Source is 2000 National Survey of Parents only
***p-value < .001, **p-value < .01, *p-value < .05.

Table. 14.8. Mothers' and Fathers' Hours Per Week Spent in Primary Activities by Maternal Employment Status: 2000

	All Mothers	Employed Mothers	Nonemployed Mothers	All Fathers	Fathers with Employed Wives	Fathers with Nonemployed Wives
Paid Work	23	34	18	45	45	44
Childcare	14	11		6	6	6
All Other Unpaid Family Work	28	25	37	15	15	15
Total Paid + Unpaid Work	65	70	56	66	66	65

Note: All mother differences are significant, fathers are not.

partially explain why it has been difficult for women, even highly educated women, to achieve labor market parity with men. The picture I present of what constitutes the status quo when these exits do not happen helps make clear why they persist.

One important caveat to what I have presented is that the data I use do not capture the substantial financial and emotional sacrifices nonemployed mothers may make in order to stay at home with their children full time. Even nonemployed mothers who find stay-at-home motherhood satisfying may miss the intellectual stimulation they received when employed. Employed mothers may experience higher levels of time pressure, but they also may be enjoying the activities they pack into their day. Larson, Richards, and Perry-Jenkins (1994) find that although nonemployed mothers have lower total workloads than their employed counterparts, their average hourly level of happiness during reported activities is significantly lower than that of employed mothers.

In some sense I view this paper as a corrective. We have had far more empirical work on what happens to women economically when they take time out of the labor force. Equally important is to ask what happens to them when they do not. We need the answer to both questions to understand why mothers (and fathers) make the decisions they do and to assess what has and has not changed in work and family life. The lifetime costs and benefits of different work and family pathways is a fruitful area for further research.

NOTES

Suzanne M. Bianchi, Ph.D., is a professor in the Department of Sociology and Maryland Population Research Center (MPRC), University of Maryland, College Park. Please send correspondence to the author at 2112 Art-Sociology Building, Department of Sociology, University of Maryland, College Park, MD 20742; email bianchi@umd.edu. This paper was prepared for "The Families and Work Research Conference," Brigham Young University, Provo, Utah, March 20–22, 2006.

There is a long history of time diary studies showing that employed mothers do not spend as much time with children as nonemployed mothers, but some estimates suggest that the gap is not large. For example, Nock and Kingston (1988) found nonemployed mothers spent relatively little time in direct child care. Sandberg and Hofferth (2001) estimated that children 12 and under spent 86% as much time with an employed as a nonemployed mother (27 vs. 31 hours per week). Zick and Bryant (1996) estimated that a mother employed throughout her children's life would spend 82% as many hours directly caring for children as a stay-at-home mother. Time diary studies conducted in other industrialized countries in Western Europe, as well as Canada and Australia, also indicated that employed mothers devoted less time to their children than their nonemployed counterparts, but that the difference was small relative to the time devoted to paid work (Gauthier et al., 2004).

REFERENCES

Bianchi, S. M. (2000). Maternal employment and time with children: Dramatic change or surprising continuity? *Demography, 37*(4), 401–414.

Bianchi, S. M., & Raley, S. (2005). Time allocation in families. In S. M. Bianchi, L. M. Casper, & R. B. King (Eds.). *Work, family, health, and well-being* (pp. 21–42). Mahwah, NJ: Lawrence Erlbaum and Associates.

Bianchi, S. M., Robinson, J. P., & Milkie, M. A. (2006). *Changing rhythms of American family life.* New York: Russell Sage.

Blair-Loy, M. (2003). *Competing devotions: Career and family among women executives.* Cambridge, MA: Harvard University Press.

Budig, M. J., & England, P. (2001). The wage penalty for motherhood. *American Sociological Review, 66*, 204–225.

Budig, M., & Folbre, N. (2004). Activity, proximity, or responsibility: Measuring parental childcare time. In N. Folbre & M. Bittman (Eds.). *Family time: The social organization of care* (pp. 51–68). New York: Routledge.

Casper, L. M., & Bianchi, S. M. (2002). *Continuity and change in the American family.* Thousand Oaks, CA: Sage.

Cohen, P. S., & Bianchi, S. M. (1999). Marriage, children, and women's employment: What do we know? *Monthly Labor Review, 122*(12), 22–31.

Coleman, J. (1988). Social capital in the creation of human capital. *American Journal of Sociology, 94* (supplement), 95–121.

Crittenden, A. (2001). *The price of motherhood: Why the most important job in the world is still the least valued.* New York: Owl Books.

Crouter, A. C., & McHale, S. M. (2005). Work, family, and children's time: Implications for youth. In S. M. Bianchi, L. M. Casper, & R. B. King (Eds.), *Work, family, health, and well-being* (pp. 49–66). Mahwah, NJ: Lawrence Erlbaum and Associates.

Folbre, N., Yoon, J., Finnoff, K., & Fuligni, A. S. (2005). By what measure? Family time devoted to children in the U.S. *Demography, 42*(2), 373–390.

Gauthier, A. H., Smeeding, T. M., & Furstenberg, Jr., F. F. (2004). Are parents investing less time in children? Trends in selected industrialized countries. *Population and Development Review, 30*(4), 647–671.

Goldin, C. (2006, January). *The quiet revolution that transformed women's employment, education, and family.* Paper presented at the 2006 meeting of the American Economic Association, Boston, MA.

Gornick, J. C., & Meyers, M. K. (2003). *Families that work: Policies for reconciling parenthood and employment.* New York: Russell Sage Foundation.

Hattery, A. J. (2001). Tag-team parenting: Costs and benefits of utilizing nonoverlapping shift work patterns in families with young children. *Families in Society, 82*(4), 419–427.

Hays, S. (1996). *The cultural contradictions of motherhood.* New Haven, CT: Yale University Press.

Hochschild, A. (1989). *The second shift: Working parents and the revolution at home.* New York: Viking.

Jacobs, J. A., & Gerson, K. (2004). *The time divide: Work, family, and gender inequality.* Cambridge, MA: Harvard University Press.

Klerman, J. A., & Leibowitz, A. (1999). Job continuity among new mothers. *Demography, 36,* 145–55.

Larson, R. W., Richards, M. H., & Perry-Jenkins, M. (1994). Divergent worlds: The daily emotional experience of mothers and fathers in the domestic and public spheres. *Journal of Personality & Social Psychology, 94,* 1034–1046.

Nock, S. L., & Kingston, P. W. (1988). Time with children: The impact of couples' work-time commitments. *Social Forces, 67,* 59–85.

Putnam, R. D. (2000). *Bowling alone: The collapse and revival of American community.* New York: Simon and Schuster.

Sandberg, J., & Hofferth, S. (2001). Changes in children's time with parents, United States, 1981–1997. *Demography, 38,* 423–436.

Sayer, L. (2001). *Time use, gender and inequality: Differences in men's and women's market, nonmarket, and leisure time.* Unpublished doctoral dissertation, University of Maryland, College Park.

Sayer, L. C., Bianchi, S. M., & Robinson, J. P. (2004). Are parents investing less in children: Trends in mothers' and fathers' time with children. *American Journal of Sociology, 110*(1), 1–43.

Waldfogel, J. (1997). The effect of children on women's wages. *American Sociological Review, 62,* 209–217.

Warr, M., & Ellison, C. (2000). Rethinking social reactions to crime: Personal and altruistic fear in family households. *American Journal of Sociology, 106,* 551–578.

Williams, J. (2000). *Unbending gender: Why family and work conflict and what to do about it.* New York: Oxford University Press.

Zick, C. D., & Bryant, W. K. (1996). A new look at parents' time spent in child care: Primary and secondary time use. *Social Science Research, 25,* 260–280.

Chapter Fifteen

Maternal Employment and Child Development

by Christopher J. Ruhm

ABSTRACT

This chapter summarizes recent research examining how maternal employment affects child outcomes. It begins with descriptive information on patterns of maternal employment. This is followed by discussions of the mechanisms through which parental employment might affect children and the difficulties encountered by researchers in attempting to measure the causal effects of such employment. Next, it summarizes what recent research reveals about the consequences of maternal employment, as well as emphasizing the many questions that currently remain unanswered. The chapter concludes by discussing implications for policy.

The labor force participation rate (LFPR) of mothers with non-adult children grew 54% (from 47% to 73 %) between 1975 and 2000 (U.S. Department of Labor, 2005).[1] One implication is that most mothers now work, raising the question of how maternal employment affects child development. This issue is even more salient when considering job-holding during the first years of the child's life, since participation rates for women with children under six rose 67% (from 39% to 65%) between 1975 and 2000, while those of mothers with children under the age of three increased 78% (from 34% to 61%).[2]

Women with young children are also now much less likely to have a spouse available to help with household responsibilities. In 1960, just 8% of children lived with only their mothers and fully 88% were in two-parent households; the corresponding figures in 2003 were 23% and 68% (U.S. Bureau of the Census, 2004).[3] Parents in single-parent households are likely to have a particularly difficult time balancing the conflicting demands of work and family. Moreover the participation rates in the workforce of single mothers with children under six grew 44% (from 49% to 70%) between 1990 and 2003, whereas those of their married counterparts barely changed (from 59% to 60%) over this period (U.S. Bureau of the Census, 2005).[4]

Increases both in mothers' market employment and in the proportion of children in single-parent households suggest that families have less time available for their children. However, there are at least two mitigating factors. First, fertility rates have fallen—from 3.09 to 1.93 children per family between 1975 and 2002 (Downs, 2003)—implying that, all else being equal, there is more time for each child. Second, mothers have significantly decreased time spent on housework—from 32 to 19 hours per week between 1965 and 2000 (Bianchi & Raley, 2005).[5]

The rise in female labor force participation and changing family structure have motivated a large body of research examining how maternal employment (and much less frequently work by fathers) affects children. Yet, methodological difficulties make it difficult to have confidence in our answers to this question. Even when reasonable estimates of the effects have been obtained, mechanisms for the relationships are often unclear and it is not obvious how much has been learned about the outcomes of ultimate interest.

The focus of this paper is on how maternal employment during the earliest years affects children. This is motivated by a widely held belief that the first years of life are a particularly important period (Carnegie Task Force on Meeting the Needs of Young Children, 1994; U.S. Council of Economic Advisers, 1997), which partially reflects research emphasizing the effects of early influences on brain development (Shore, 1997) and of investments during young childhood on the growth of learning skills, self-esteem, and emotional security (Heckman, 2000).[6] The primary outcomes discussed are cognitive or socioemotional development measured around or prior to the time of school entry.[7] Due to space constraints, this review is restricted to studies conducted in the United States, although these issues are also increasingly being investigated in other countries (e.g. Horwood & Fergusson, 1999; Gregg, Washbrook, Propper, & Burgess, 2005; Verropoulou & Joshi, 2005).[8]

HOW MIGHT PARENTAL EMPLOYMENT AFFECT CHILDREN?

Two aspects characterize most economic approaches to maternal employment's effects on children. First, households produce outputs, such as child outcomes, using purchased inputs like food, books, and medical care, as well as nonmarket time spent in household activities (Becker, 1981; Blau, Guilkey & Popkin, 1996). Second, parents attempt to maximize utility, which is a function of many factors including but not limited to child development. This framework implies that there is a tradeoff between the gains of spending time at home with children and the income foregone by reducing market employment. Parents attempt to balance the benefits associated with income and time to reach the highest level of household utility.[9]

This framework yields ambiguous predictions about the consequences of parental employment. Specifically, labor supply may benefit children by raising incomes but could have deleterious consequences because parents have less time available to spend with their offspring. These effects could vary with the timing and intensity of employment, and with characteristics of the institutional environment. For example, differences in the quality of parental and nonparental care may matter. Thus, maternal employment might have negative effects in the United States, because the average quality of nonparental day care is typically quite low (e.g., Helburn & Howes, 1996; NICHD EC-CRN, 1997a), but less detrimental or more beneficial consequences in countries offering higher quality care.

The psychology, sociology, and child development literatures suggest complementary pathways through which parental employment may affect children. For instance, a great deal of research has been conducted examining whether labor supply early in the child's life harms child-mother attachment relationships (e.g., Belsky & Rovine, 1988; NICHD ECCRN, 1997b). Maternal employment might also affect children by reducing the duration or frequency of breastfeeding (Roe, Whittington, Fein, & Teisl, 1999), or through its effects on parent-child interactions (Hoffman, 1980) and social capital (Coleman, 1988). Similarly, the stress of market employment may negatively affect children by increasing parents' feelings of overload and strain, leading to higher levels of parent-child conflict and lower levels of parental acceptance (Crouter & Bumpus, 2001). In each case, the potential benefits resulting from market-employment provided income may be partially or fully offset by deleterious consequences of reduced parental time investments in children.

Maternal Employment and Time with Children

One remarkable research finding is that, despite rapid increases in market work by mothers, parents spent almost exactly the same amount of time with children in 2000 as they did in 1975 (Sandberg & Hofferth, 2001; Bianchi & Raley, 2005). This was partially possible because mothers economized on the time spent on household chores, with some compensating rise in the contribution of fathers. Fathers also provide increasing amounts of child care, although still only around half as much as mothers, and many parents made other accommodations, such as synchronizing work schedules, to increase the time available for children.

Despite these efforts, virtually all available time-diary evidence confirms that working mothers spend less time with children than their nonemployed peers (e.g. Bryant & Zick, 1996; Bianchi, 2000; Gershuny, 2000; Sandberg & Hofferth, 2001; Apps & Rees, 2005; Ichino & Sanz de Galdeano, 2005). Long work hours are also likely to impose other costs. For instance, working parents engage in more multitasking while caring for children and are likely to cut back on valued activities such as sleep, leisure pursuits, and personal care (Bianchi, 2000).[10] One consequence is that an increasing proportion of parents report feeling rushed and having too little time available to spend with their children, spouse, and alone (Bianchi & Raley, 2005). This evidence is consistent with the concern that reductions in time with children may have negative consequences, but we know relatively little about how big any such effects may be, the marginal returns to time investments, or how the impacts vary with age of the child.

How Much Does Additional Income Help?

There is wide agreement that extreme poverty has negative effects on children (e.g., Duncan & Brooks-Gunn, 1997), but less consensus on the impact of additional income for the non-poor. Most studies find either modest positive income effects or negligible consequences (e.g. Mayer, 1997; Blau, 1999; Shea, 2000; Aughinbaugh & Gittleman, 2003). Even when beneficial, the estimated income effects are small relative to the consequences of other family background variables. One reason for this may be because a greater portion of total income is devoted to children in poor than wealthy families (Lazear & Michael, 1988).

Once again, it is unclear if the timing of the income receipt matters or the extent to which the benefits of additional income diminish at higher levels. The amount of extra income provided by maternal employment also depends on a variety of factors that have probably changed over time. For example, earnings of the mother (in two-adult households) may be partially offset by reductions in the labor supply or wage rates of fathers. The policy environment also matters, since many transfer payments phase out at higher incomes and tax rates vary with the distribution if earnings across spouses.

MEASURING THE CAUSAL EFFECT
OF PARENTAL EMPLOYMENT

Researchers face many difficulties when attempting to determine how parental employment affects child outcomes. To illustrate, if children with mothers working full-time score higher on a series of cognitive assessments than their peers with nonworking mothers, does this mean that the maternal labor supply is the cause of better test scores? Not necessarily. One reason is that mothers with high levels of measured ability tend to have high employment rates (e.g., see Vandell & Ramanan, 1992, Han, Waldfogel, & Brooks-Gunn, 2001; Waldfogel, Han & Brooks-Gunn, 2002; Ruhm, 2004). This is referred to as selection bias in the economics literature and implies that methodological approaches insufficiently accounting for these sources of heterogeneity will overstate the benefits or understate the costs of maternal job-holding. Many previous studies, particularly those conducted more than a few years ago, contain only rudimentary controls and the estimates obtained from them are likely to be severely biased.

A similar problem will often occur if the mother's work decisions are affected by child characteristics. For example, most evidence suggests that child health or developmental problems are associated with reductions in maternal employment (Berhman, Pollack, & Taubman, 1982; Norberg, 1998; Neidell, 2000; Ermisch & Francesconi, 2001). Failure to account for this reverse causation will therefore result in overly optimistic estimates of the effects of job-holding.

Two other methodological issues deserve mention. First, since work hours tend to be highly correlated across time periods, it is important to control for employment occurring throughout the child's life (from birth until the assessment date). If this is not done, the labor supply coefficients are likely to partially reflect the effects of working in other periods and yield misleading estimates. Consider the case where employment has harmful effects if it occurs during the infancy period but benefits if undertaken later in the child's life. Models that control for employment during the first year only will average together these offsetting impacts and may yield estimates of no effect or even positive consequences. This potential problem becomes more severe when looking at outcomes for adolescents if, as mentioned above, the mother's labor supply is partially determined by status of children at younger ages.

Second, biased estimates will be obtained if the control variables include factors that result from maternal employment. For example, child care choices are dictated by work decisions and so, if held constant, are likely to absorb a portion of the total employment effect. Similar problems occur when controlling for household incomes and some dimensions of the home environment. On the other hand, these factors may have an independent effect on the child outcomes, suggesting that one prudent strategy is to test the sensitivity of the results obtained with and without their inclusion in the set of independent variables in the regression equation.

Selection bias would not be an issue if mothers could be randomly assigned into workers and nonworkers: in this case a simple comparison of the average outcomes of children in the two groups would often be sufficient.[11] Such randomization is not an option, however, since mothers choose whether, when, and how much to work.[12] Economists and other social scientists have developed a variety of nonexperimental methods for dealing with these issues.

The most common procedure is to include covariates in a regression framework that, it is to be hoped, directly control for the heterogeneity between working and nonworking mothers (and their children). To illustrate, assume that the outcome for child i at age t (C_{it}) is estimated by:

$$(1) C_{it} = a + E_i\beta + X_i\gamma + \mu_{it},$$

where E_i refers to maternal employment, X_i is a vector of additional covariates, and μ_{it} is the regression error term. The effect of maternal employment will be consistently estimated if the supplementary regressors (X) sufficiently control for other determinants of child development such that the error term is uncorrelated with the maternal employment variable.[13] The problem is that few data sets contain sufficiently rich information on potential confounding factors to fulfill this condition. One potentially useful approach is to examine how the estimates of interest change when including successively more complete sets of covariates (e.g., see Ruhm, 2004, 2008). This will indicate the direction (although not necessarily the size) of remaining omitted variables bias, provided that the observed and unobserved components of the selection process vary in similar ways. Another helpful strategy is to include specification tests. For instance, Ruhm (2004) shows that a statistically significant coefficient on maternal employment prior to childbirth or after the assessment date often suggests the presence of remaining selection bias.

A second, and increasingly common, strategy is to exploit variations in maternal labor supply across children in the same family (e.g., see Neidell, 2000; Ermisch & Francesconi, 2001; Waldfogel et al., 2002; James-Burdumy, 2005). These are called *fixed-effect* models and have the advantage of automatically accounting for factors that remain constant within the families over time. However, they also have several potential shortcomings. First, some family-specific factors vary over time. Second, restricting the analysis to siblings decreases the size of the sample analyzed and may make it less representative. Third, and most serious, the fixed-effect models do not account for child-specific factors that influence maternal employment. A consequence is that overly favorable estimates will be obtained if child health or developmental problems cause mothers to cut back on work.

A third approach is to use instrumental variables (IV) techniques (e.g. Blau & Grossberg, 1992; Baum, 2003; James-Burdumy, 2005). A good instrument is strongly correlated with maternal employment but does not have an independent impact on child outcomes. However, even when using plausible instruments, the previous research provides little evidence that the IV estimates improve on those obtained using ordinary least squares. Moreover, the values of most potential instruments (such as measures of local labor market conditions) will be highly correlated over time, implying that it will be difficult to assess the impact of maternal employment occurring at different points in the child's life.

A final possibility is to use propensity score methods. These provide a flexible procedure for matching mothers in the treatment and control groups, facilitating relatively simple comparisons of child outcomes. Matching methods have only recently been used to assess the effects of maternal employment (e.g. Berger, Hill, & Waldfogel, 2005; Hill, Waldfogel, Brooks-Gunn, & Han, 2005; Ruhm, 2008) and have potential disadvantages. First, the definition of the treatment to be examined is somewhat arbitrary. For instance, when considering maternal employment, should the treatment group consist of all children with working mothers or only those where maternal labor supply exceeds a threshold (e.g., 30 hours per week)? Similarly, should the control group contain all remaining children or just those whose mothers work less than a specified amount? Second, the results obtained using propensity score methods are sometimes sensitive to specific details of the estimation method (e.g., the type of matching used) and to the choice of model covariates required to meet a technical condition known as "balancing."[14]

RESULTS OF PREVIOUS RESEARCH

The preceding discussion generally used the terms *parental* and *maternal* employment interchangeably. Thus it did not distinguish the consequences of labor supply provided by mothers from that of fathers. This was intentional. Although the mothers and fathers may well provide different inputs—for instance, only mothers can breastfeed—previous research provides, at most, a rudimentary understanding of these issues. Few studies (e.g., Parcel & Menaghan, 1994; Harvey, 1999; Ermisch & Francesconi, 2001; Ruhm, 2004) have explicitly examined paternal employment, in large part because of inadequate data.[15] At this point, we simply do not know whether or how inputs of mothers and fathers differ. Until better information is obtained, my view is that the results of previous research on maternal employment should be interpreted as applying equally to the time contributions of fathers.

Effects of Early Maternal Employment

Table 15.1 summarizes 23 studies examining the effects of maternal (and occasionally paternal) employment. This should not be viewed as a comprehensive list of previous research, but I am confident that most major investigations have been included and that these provide a representative sample of prior analyses.

Perusal of the table reveals several points. First, researchers have examined cognitive development more frequently (21 studies) than behavioral or other socioemotional outcomes (11 studies). Second, a large fraction of analyses (18 out of 23) use data from a single source—the National Longitudinal Survey of Youth (NLSY). The NLSY contains many strengths, including comprehensive information on family background characteristics and detailed information on maternal employment. However, it is less complete in other areas (such as the measurement of child health) and it would be desirable to have research conducted on more diverse sources of data. Third, the analytical methods vary considerably, with earlier research generally controlling less adequately for confounding factors. Fourth, the results vary. A few investigations find positive effects of maternal employment, others obtain negative impacts, and many uncover variation depending on the timing of work or the group analyzed.

Useful information can be obtained by examining how the findings differ with the timing of the studies, under the assumption that the increasingly sophisticated methods used in recent analyses are likely to provide more accurate results. When this is done, a reasonably strong consensus emerges that long hours of maternal employment during the child's first year have deleterious effects on cognitive development: full-time jobs are predicted to have negative effects in each of the 11 studies dated 1999 or later, contrasting with more mixed results for earlier work. Several investigations (e.g., Moore & Driscoll, 1997; Neidell, 2000; Baum, 2003; Ruhm, 2004; Berger et al., 2005) explicitly examine how the estimates change with the addition of more complete controls for nonrandom selection into maternal employment. Each shows that doing so reveals more adverse effects on cognitive development. One implication is that earlier studies, particularly those with limited covariates, are likely to understate the negative consequences of job-holding. That said, part-time employment is predicted to have weaker deleterious effects or no adverse consequences in much recent research, with similarly mixed results obtained for market labor supplied during the child's second or third year.

Consensus is also lacking on other important questions. As mentioned, socioemotional development has been less widely researched than cognitive

Table 15.1.   The Effects of Parental Employment On Cognitive and Socioemotional Development

Study	Data/Sample	Results	Comments
Leibowitz (1977)	Sesame data, 805 3–5 year olds (in 1969)	Full-time maternal employment negatively (but not quite significantly) associated with PPVT. No effect of part-time employment. Positive effect of labor-saving devices (dishwashers) in home and of reading to children/self, but negative effects of other activities. Negative relationship between number of children & PPVT.	Controls for parent's education, race/ethnicity, native language, home environment, childcare arrangements, number of children.
Stafford (1987)	SRC Time Use Study, 77 elem. school students (in 1981/2)	Cognitive skills (measured by 7 indicators and a composite) fall with the number of siblings (particularly males), rise with family income, and decline with mother's market work hours in the pre-school years.	Detailed teacher evaluations of cognitive development. Maternal employment refers to various ages prior to start of school.
Desai, Chase-Lansdale, & Michael (1989)	NLSY, 503 4-year-olds (in 1986)	Negative effect of maternal employment on PPVT scores, particularly for continuous employment in first 4 years. Strong negative effect of continuous maternal employment and job-holding in the first year for boys in high-income families. Possible positive effect beginning in the second year for girls.	Controls for maternal characteristics (age, verbal ability, education, marital history, race/ethnicity), household income, birth order, sibling age, number of childcare arrangements.
Baydar & Brooks-Gunn (1991)	NLSY, 572 white 3–4 year olds (in 1986)	Maternal employment during the first year has negative effects on PPVT and BPI. No negative effects for working in second or third year. Some evidence of bigger negative effects for entering work earlier in the first year.	Other controls limited to maternal AFQT score, child gender, parity, poverty status. Nonlinear "effect" of work in first year.

(continued)

Table 15.1 (*continued*)

Study	Data/Sample	Results	Comments
Belsky & Eggebeen (1991)	NLSY, 1248 Nonhispanic 4–6 year olds (in 1986)	Employment in the first two years of the child's life unrelated to shyness but positively correlated with adjustment problems and levels of noncompliance. No statistically significant effect on attachment security.	Controls for age, race, sex, parity, birth weight, maternal characteristics, & household size.
Mott (1991)	NLSY, 2387 1–4 year olds (in 1986)	Maternal employment averaging more than 20 hours per week in second quarter of child's life negatively related to PPVT scores (ages 3–4); no effect on MFL or MSD scores (ages 1–3). No effect of lower work hours. Employment in first quarter insignificantly negatively related to MFL and MSD scores. Nonmaternal child care in first year (particularly non-home based care and for girls) positively related to PPVT scores.	Comprehensive controls for child & family characteristics including early health problems and substance use during pregnancy. Collinearity between maternal employment and childcare arrangements makes results difficult to interpret.
Blau & Grossberg (1992)	NLSY, 874 3–4 year olds (in 1986)	Maternal employment in the first (second & third) years of life associated with lower (higher) PPVT scores. No net effect of working in all three years. Much of second & third year benefit is due to higher incomes. Larger negative first year effects for high income households.	Controls for parent's education, household incomes, race/ethnicity, gender, parity, % of life in female-headed household. IV models estimated, but few plausible instruments.
Vandell & Ramanan (1992)	NLSY, 189 low income non-Hispanic second-graders (in 1986)	Maternal employment in first 3 years (and subsequently) positively correlated with the mothers' education, AFQT score, family income, and quality of home environment. Employment in first three years correlated	Controls for the child's race, gender; mother's age, education, marital status, family income, attitudes, AFQT and Rosenberg self-esteem scores, and HOME scale. Sample selection criteria are not specified.

		Findings	Controls / Comments
		with higher PIAT-math and insignificantly lower PPVT scores. Employment after first three years correlated with higher PIAT-reading and PPVT scores.	Comprehensive controls for child and parent characteristics, the home environment, and working conditions. Results are difficult to interpret because of potential endogeneity (e.g., home environment and work hours) and collinearity (e.g., wage, occupational complexity, and work hours) of regressors.
Parcel & Menaghan (1994)	NLSY, 768 3–6 year olds with employed mothers (in 1986)	Maternal employment during the first year or first three years positively (insignificantly negatively) correlated with PPVT (BPI) scores. Effect not monotonic in hours. Subsequent full-time maternal work correlated with higher PPVT and BPI, compared to working part-time. Early (current) full-time paternal employment associated with lower BPI and insignificantly lower PPVT (higher PPVT & lower BPI) scores. Some evidence that maternal employment is more problematic for less well-off women.	
Greenstein (1995)	NLSY, 2040 4–6 year olds (in 1986, 1988, or 1990)	Little relationship between maternal employment and PPVT score. Interactions between maternal employment and family income or cognitive stimulation insignificant. No evidence of more detrimental effects for high-income households.	Controls for child and maternal characteristics and family environment. Results difficult to interpret because of potential collinearity between regressors.
Moore & Driscoll (1997)	NLSY, 1154 5–14 year olds (in 1992); with mothers on AFDC during 1986–1990	Maternal employment in 1991 associated with higher PIAT Reading and Math scores and lower BPI scores. Most effects eliminated after controlling for child, maternal, & household characteristics, although fewer behavioral problems and higher math scores persist for daughters of higher-earning women.	Controls for sex, age, birth order, health, birth weight, maternal characteristics & attitudes, family employment & AFDC history. Omitted variable bias probably persists.

(continued)

Table 15.1. (*continued*)

Study	Data/Sample	Results	Comments
Barglow, Contreras, Kavesh, & Vaughn (1998)	92 6–7 year olds (in 1992) born to intact middle-class families	High levels of maternal employment in first year of life associated with increased maternal reports of problem behaviors but also some positive correlations with social problem solving and quality of play interactions.	Few controls. Collinearity between maternal employment & attachment security makes findings difficult to interpret. Results combine effects of working in first and later years.
Harvey (1999)	NLSY, 3–12 year olds in 1986, 1988, 1990, 1992, or 1994 (variable sample sizes)	Negative effect of maternal work hours on PPVT and PIAT scores at young ages, which weakens or disappears at later ages. No consistent relationship between early employment and BPI, compliance, or self-esteem scores. Some differences with marital status, income, or paternal employment.	Individual, maternal, and household characteristics controlled for; however, the regressors and samples vary across models making the results difficult to interpret and often subject to omitted variables bias.
Neidell (2000)	NLSY, 1681–4581 children (age and survey date not specified)	Delaying resuming maternal employment until the 6th through 12th months of child's life has a marginally significant (insignificant) positive effect on PPVT (PIAT) scores and a larger positive impact on SPS and SPW scales. Ambiguous impacts of returning to jobs at late ages. Models that less adequately control for heterogeneity imply less harmful effects of early maternal employment.	Controls for child age, birth weight, breastfeeding, maternal/family characteristics, and sibling fixed-effect. Maternal employment limited to dichotomous measures of weeks after birth until return to work.
Ermisch & Francesconi (2001)	BHPS, 591 siblings born in 1970–1979	Negative effect of full-time maternal employment during first five years of life on probability of subsequently completing A level exams in sibling fixed-effect models. No effect of part-time jobs or paternal employment.	Controls for age, gender, parity, household structure, maternal and paternal characteristics. Small sample sizes and parental labor supply crudely measured.

Han, et al. (2001)	NLSY, 412 children born in 1982 or 1983	Negative effects of first year employment on PPVT scores of 3–4 year olds and PIAT scores of 5–8 year olds. Larger negative impact of full-time than part-time work but some offsetting benefits of working in years 2 and 3. Higher BPI scores at ages 7–8 (but not younger ages) when mother worked in first year.	Controls for sex, parity, family poverty status, and maternal characteristics and household characteristics. Small sample sizes reduce statistical power. Deleterious effects restricted to white children.
Brooks-Gunn, et al. (2002)	NICHD, 900 non-Hispanic whites born in 1991	Employment in first 9 months of child's life negatively associated with Bracken School Readiness scores at age 3. Bigger effect for full-time work (>30 hours per week), low maternal sensitivity, boys, and married women. Smaller effects on MDI scores at 15 or 24 months of age.	Controls for home environment, maternal sensitivity, childcare mode and quality, maternal characteristics. Pattern of employment effects suggests presence of selection bias.
Waldfogel, et al. (2002)	NLSY, 1872 children born in 1982–89, assessed at ages 3–8	Negative effects of maternal employment in the first year on PPVT and PIAT scores for white or Hispanic children (particularly for girls), which increase with the number of hours worked. Ambiguous results for work in the second or third year and little impact on African-American children. Smaller deleterious employment effects in sibling fixed-effect models	Controls for sex, parity, family income, maternal characteristics, breast feeding, day care arrangements. Maternal employment mostly measured by dichotomous variables for any work versus no work.
Baum (2003)	NLSY, 2022 children born in 1988–1993	Negative effects of maternal employment during first year on PPVT and PIAT scores. Mixed (usually insignificant) effects of employment in second and third year. Mixed evidence on whether employment in first quarter of child's life has more negative	Controls for gender, birth order, race, child age, birth weight, maternal & family characteristics. Some models use IV methods or restrict sample to mothers employed before birth. Labor supply distinguished from periods mother is employed but on leave.

(continued)

Table 15.1. (*continued*)

Study	Data/Sample	Results	Comments
Baum (2003) (continued)		effects than work during the next three quarters. Estimate effects generally become more negative with more complete controls for heterogeneity.	
Ruhm (2004)	NLSY, 3042 children born from 1980–1992, assessed at ages 3–6.	Maternal employment during the first (second and third) years of life negatively related to PPVT (PIAT) scores. Larger deleterious consequences in models with more completely controls for heterogeneity, for full-time than part-time work, and for two-parent versus female-headed households. Some indication of negative effects of long work hours by fathers.	Extensive controls for child, maternal, and household characteristics. Maternal employment in the year prior to childbirth included as a specification check for remaining unobserved heterogeneity.
Berger, et al. (2005)	NLSY, 1907 children born from 1988–1996, assessed at ages 3–4.	Returning to work during first 12 weeks of child's life is associated with lower PPVT and higher externalizing BPI scores. Generally stronger deleterious effects when mothers hold full-time jobs and in propensity score than OLS models.	Controls for child and maternal characteristics and location variables. Analysis limited to cases where mother was employed in quarter before birth.

Hill, et al. (2005)	NLSY, 6114 children born from 1982–1993, assessed at ages 3–8	Negative effects of full-time maternal employment in first year on PPVT scores of 3–4 year olds and PIAT scores of 5–8 year olds; positive effects on externalizing BPI scores. Generally no impact of part-time work in first year or employment in second or third year. Few differences by race or sex but stronger deleterious effects for advantaged children.	Propensity score matching methods used to account for heterogeneity, with multiple imputation for missing values. Sample sizes are sometimes small. Children with missing values tend to be less advantaged.
James-Burdumy (2005)	NLSY, 2119 3–5 year olds (in 1986 or 1988)	OLS estimates indicate negative (positive) effects of maternal employment during first (second) year on PPVT scores. FE estimates are small and insignificant, except for negative effect of work in first year on PIAT–math scores. OLS results not reported for PIAT scores.	Controls for individual, maternal, and household characteristics. FE and IV techniques used to control for heterogeneity but with small samples (498 siblings) and weak instruments.

Abbreviations: BHPS: British Household Panel Survey; BPI: Behavioral Problems Index; DS: Digital Span Subscale of WISC-R; MDI: Bayley Mental Development Index; MFL: Memory for Location score; MSD: Motor and Social Development Scale; NICHD: NICHD Study of Early Child Care; NLSY: National Longitudinal Survey of Youth; PIAT: Peabody Individual Achievement Test; PPVT: Peabody Picture Vocabulary Test; SPS: scholastic competence scale; SPW: global self-worth scale; SRC: Survey Research Center.

outcomes, particularly in recent years. Three recent studies (Han et al., 2001; Berger et al., 2005; Hill et al., 2005) suggest that maternal labor supply during the child's infancy increases future behavior problems, but the results often vary with assessment age and we know little about the effects of employment occurring after the first year.

Do Adverse Effects of Maternal Employment Matter?

Even if we were sure that maternal employment during the child's infancy has negative effects on cognitive development around the time of school entry (which is not the case), the implications would be far from clear. There are at least three sources of uncertainty. First, we know relatively little about the extent to which such initial differences persist. Second, even if sustained, we need to better understand whether the impacts are large or small relative to other determinants of cognitive development, as well as the extent to which they may be offset by other advantages associated with maternal employment. For instance, working mothers may save some of their earnings to pay for a child's college education. Third, even if the effects are large, it is not obvious that cognitive skills are of key importance for the outcomes of ultimate interest (e.g., the child's future employment and life satisfaction).

Limited previous research provides conflicting evidence on the persistence of the initial cognitive disadvantages associated with early maternal employment. An influential paper by Harvey (1999) indicates that the negative effects weaken or disappear by the beginning of adolescence, but Han et al. (2001) and Waldfogel et al. (2002) suggest that the effects are more sustained. Ruhm (2008) finds small average negative impacts of maternal employment on the cognitive development of 10- and 11-year-olds, suggesting that most of the initial penalty quickly dissipates, but much stronger deleterious consequences were found for children in high socioeconomic status households. These issues are complicated. For instance, research on related topics, such as the long-run effects of Head Start or child care, indicates that initial effects may be moderated or amplified by the child's later environment. Generally, it seems likely that the negative effects of maternal employment are of small or moderate size, relative to other determinants of child outcomes like parental education, household structure, and overall economic advantage.

Even less is known about whether the outcomes examined (e.g., cognitive test scores and measures of behavior problems) are the ones that we should care about. One response is that this is the best we can do with the available data, and that these have been long studied by child development experts. A second is that there is at least some evidence that early test performance is related to future educational and labor market outcomes (e.g., Currie &

Thomas, 2001). However, enormous uncertainty remains, requiring considerable caution when designing policies based on such imperfect information.

IMPLICATIONS FOR POLICY

As just mentioned, policies designed to influence patterns of parental employment should reflect our lack of answers to many key research questions. Further caution is engendered by the fundamental principle of economics that agents (in this case parents) attempt to achieve optimal outcomes given existing constraints. An important consequence is that interventions constraining or distorting these choices often leave participants worse off. Such a conclusion is not absolute, however, particularly if there are sources of market failure (e.g., if decision-makers do not bear the full costs or benefits of their actions), information is imperfect or the constraints themselves (such as the difficulty of borrowing against future income) lead to undesirable outcomes.

An emerging consensus that maternal employment during a child's infancy harms cognitive development suggests the potential efficacy of measures making it easier for parents to take time off work or reduce hours when their children are very young. The United States took one step in this direction in 1993, by enacting the Family and Medical Leave Act (FMLA), which mandates entitlements to a 12-week period of leave for many new parents. However, the leaves are brief by international standards, unpaid, and exempt a large fraction of employees. There is currently active discussion about the desirability of extending these policies and incorporating income replacement during the leave period.

One often hears that both parents in a household must work to afford a decent standard of living, or that having two working parents is now a necessity rather than a luxury. At first glance such arguments seem strange. The United States is much wealthier than in the past, so it would seem to have become easier for parents to reduce employment hours or stop working altogether during some of their children's earliest years.[16]

There are several reasons, however, why the situation is complicated. Consider two-adult households. (The same principles generalize to single-parent families.) If well being is determined by relative rather than absolute status, households with a stay-at-home parent will often feel worse off than their counterparts in previous cohorts, because their family incomes have declined compared to those where both parents work. Moreover, when employment becomes the norm, a greater proportion of social interactions may revolve around the workplace, leaving stay-at-home parents feeling isolated.[17] Single-income households may also bear a financial cost that exceeds the direct loss of earnings. For example, employers are raising employee contributions for health insurance in an effort to encourage workers to obtain family coverage through their spouse's plan (e.g., Dranove, Spier & Baker, 2000), with particularly deleterious financial consequences for single-earner households. Similarly, the growth of two-income families is likely to bid up housing prices in areas with constrained land availability, which will generally be especially costly to single-income families. Finally, reductions in the fraction of families with a stay-at-home parent may increase the time children spend in organized activities (e.g., in after-school care or recreational sports teams) versus neighborhood settings. To the extent that these require parents to provide financial rather than time inputs, they will again worsen the status of households with a stay-at-home parent.

One implication is that the desirability and perceived (or actual) need for parents to engage in market employment may depend in part on the activities of their peers. Specifically, mothers may feel greater pressure to work when others become more likely to do so. A similar constraint is imposed on fathers who would otherwise like to reduce their labor supply when their children are young. Such discussion takes us well beyond the confines of conventional economic models and poses significant challenges for efforts to design policies that increase labor market options while simultaneously supporting the diverse needs of working families.

NOTES

Christopher J. Ruhm, Ph.D., is a professor of economics at the University of North Carolina, Greensboro, and research associate at the National Bureau of Economic Research. Address correspondence to the author, Department of Economics, University of North Carolina at Greensboro, 444 Bryan School, UNCG, P.O. Box 26165, Greensboro, NC 27402-6165. Phone: (336)334-5148. Fax: (336)334-4089. E-Mail: CHRISRUHM@UNCG.EDU. This paper was prepared for presentation at the 2006 Families and Work Conference, sponsored by Brigham Young University Family Studies Center.

1. This partially reflects a more general rise in female labor force participation, from 43% in 1970 to a peak of 60% in 1999. By contrast, participation rates of males fell (mainly due to earlier retirement) from 80% to 73% between 1970 and 2004.

2 Participation rates declined slightly after 2000. In 2004, 59% of women were in the labor force, as were 71% of mothers with nonadult children and 62(57)% of those with children under 6(3).

3. The percentage of children living only with fathers rose from 1.1% to 4.6% between 1960 and 2003, while the share living with nonparent relatives changed little (from 2.5% to 3.0%).

4. Meyer and Rosenbaum (2001) indicate that the increase for single women can largely be attributed to changes in the Earned Income Tax Credit (EITC) and other tax policies, as well as welfare reform. Conversely, Eissa and Hoynes (2004) estimate that the EITC marginally reduced the employment rates of married women.

5. Time fathers devoted to housework increased from 4 to 10 hours per week over the same period.

6. However, the mechanisms for these effects are poorly understood and the relationship between early brain development and future outcomes remains controversial (Bruer, 1999).

7. A more limited, but growing, body of research examines how maternal employment affects adolescents (e.g., Richards & Duckett, 1994; Vander Ven, Cullen, Carrozza, & Wright, 2001; Aughinbaugh & Gittleman, 2004; Ruhm, 2005) or other outcomes such as child health or nutrition (e.g., Coreil, Wilson, Wood, & Liller, K., 1998; Crepinseck & Burstein, 2004; Currie & Hotz, 2004).

8. Nor do I discuss the extensive literature examining how nonparent day care affects child outcomes, although this is related since maternal employment is one of the major determinants of the use of day care. Examples of recent studies focusing on these issues include: National Institute of Child Health and Human Development Early Child Care Research Network (NICHD ECCRN) & Duncan (2003); Magnuson, Meyers, Ruhm, & Waldfogel, (2004); Loeb, Bridges, Bassok, Fuller, & Rumberger. (2005, December); and Blau & Currie (in press).

9. In a strict optimizing framework, they will work to the point where the utility from the income provided by the last hour of employment is equal to loss of utility from spending one less hour on home activities. More complicated formulations allow for choices of the distribution of work hours between parents (in two-adult households) and the possibility that multiple decision makers place different value on the various outcomes in the utility function.

10. Thus, working mothers sleep 6 hours (10 percent) less per week than their nonemployed counterparts. The U.S. Council of Economic Advisers (1999) estimates that parents had 22 hours (14 percent) less time available for children in 1969 than in 1999.

11. The remainder of this section draws heavily on the excellent, and detailed, description of these issues in Currie (2005), as well as the methodological discussion in Ruhm (2004).

12. One exception is that random assignment has been used in a number of experimental studies of welfare reform, where increases in maternal employment are often one of the key initiatives (e.g., see Zaslow et al., 2002, and Gennetian, Duncan, Knox, Vargas, Clark-Kauffman, & London (2004). However, it is not clear how generalizable these results are, since they refer to mandated employment among a disadvantaged population.

13. More specifically, the required condition is $cov(X_{imit}) = cov(E_{i,mit}) = 0$.

14. Intuitively, balancing requires that the treatment and control groups have the same distribution of observable characteristics (i.e., that they are, on average, observationally identical).

15. There are at least two challenges. First, major data sets often limit information on fathers to those living with the child's mother and, even in this case, often supply much less comprehensive data for fathers. Second, most nonemployment by fathers does not appear to reflect choices to spend more time with children but rather occurs for other reasons, such as involuntary unemployment (Hofferth, 2001; Ruhm, 2004).

16. This statement is true despite rising income inequality. Some households are worse off than their previous counterparts but the vast majority are not. However, it is reasonable to characterize working as a necessity in most single-parent households, particularly given reductions in government income support provided to them.

17. Anecdotal evidence suggests this has long been a significant issue for stay-at-home fathers.

REFERENCES

Apps, P., & Rees, R. (2005). Time use and costs of child care over the lifecyle. In D. S. Hammermesh & G. A. Pfann (Eds.), *The economics of time use* (pp. 205–235). Amsterdam: Elsevier B.V.

Aughinbaugh, A., & Gittleman, M. (2004). Maternal employment and adolescent risky behavior. *Journal of Health Economics, 23*(4), 815–838.

Barglow, P., Contreras, J., Kavesh, L., & Vaughn, B. E. (1998). Developmental follow-up of 6–7 year old children of mothers employed during their infancies. *Child Psychiatry and Human Development, 29*(1), 3–20.

Baum, C. L. (2003). Does early maternal employment harm child development? An analysis of the potential benefits of leave taking. *Journal of Labor Economics, 21*(2), 409–448.

Baydar, N., & Brooks-Gunn, J. (1991). Effects of maternal employment and child-care arrangements on preschoolers' cognitive and behavioral outcomes: Evidence from the children of the National Longitudinal Survey of Youth. *Developmental Psychology, 27*(6), 932–945.

Becker, G. S. (1981). *A treatise on the family*. Cambridge, MA: Harvard University Press.

Behrman, J. R., Pollack, R. A., & Taubman, P. (1982). Parental preferences and provision for progeny. *Journal of Political Economy, 90*(1), 52–73.

Belsky, J., & Eggebeen, D. (1991). Early and extensive maternal employment and young children's socioemotional development: Children of the National Longitudinal Survey of Youth. *Journal of Marriage and Family, 53*(4), 1081–1110.

Belsky, J., & Rovine, M. J. (1988). Nonmaternal care in the first year of life and the security of infant-parent attachment. *Child Development, 59*(1), 157–167.

Berger, L. M., Hill, J., & Waldfogel, J. (2005). Maternity leave, early maternal employment and child health and development in the US. *Economic Journal, 115*(501), F29–F47.

Bianchi, S. (2000). Maternal employment and time with children: Dramatic change or surprising continuity. *Demography, 37*(4), 401–414.

Bianchi, S. M., & Raley, S. B. (2005). Time allocation in families. In S. M. Bianchi, L. M. Casper & R. B. King (Eds.), *Work, family, health, and wellbeing* (pp. 21–42). Mahwah, NJ: Lawrence Erlbaum Associates.

Blau, D. M. (1999). The effect of income on child development. *Review of Economics and Statistics, 82*(2), 261–276.

Blau, D. M., Guilkey, D. K., & Popkin, B. M. (1996). Infant health and the labor supply of mothers. *Journal of Human Resources, 31*(1), 90–139.

Blau, D., & Currie, J. (in press). Who's minding the kids?: Preschool, day care, and after school care. In F. Welch & E. Hanushek (Eds.), *The handbook of the economics of education.* New York: North Holland.

Blau, F. B., & Grossberg, A. J. (1992). Maternal labor supply and children's cognitive development. *The Review of Economics and Statistics, 74*(3), 474–481.

Bryant, W. K. & Zick, C. D. (1996). An examination of parent-child shared time. *Journal of Marriage and the Family, 58*(1), 227–237.

Brooks-Gunn, J., Han, W-J., & Waldfogel, J. (2002). Maternal employment and child cognitive outcomes in the first two years of life: The NICHD Study of Early Child Care. *Child Development, 73*(4), 1052–1072.

Bruer, J. T. (1999). *The myth of the first three years: A new understanding of early brain development and lifelong learning.* New York: The Free Press.

Carnegie Task Force on Meeting the Needs of Young Children. (1994). *Starting points: Meeting the needs of our youngest children.* New York: Carnegie Corporation.

Coleman, J. S. (1988). Social capital and the creation of human capital. *American Journal of Sociology, 94*(supplement), s95–s120.

Coreil, J., Wilson, F., Wood, D., & Liller, K. (1998). Maternal employment and child preventive health practices. *Preventive Medicine 27,* 488–492.

Crouter, A. C., & Bumpus, M. F. (2001). Linking parents' work stress to children's and adolescents' psychological adjustment. *Current Directions in Psychological Science, 10*(5), 156–159.

Crepinseck, M. K & Burstein, N. R. (2004). *Maternal employment and children's nutrition.* Economic Research Service, U.S. Department of Agriculture. Retrieved July 27, 2006 from http://www.ers.usda.gov/publications/efan04006

Currie, J. (2005). When do we know what we think we know? Determining causality. In S. M. Bianchi, L. M. Casper, & R. B. King (Eds.), *Work, family, health, and wellbeing* (pp. 279–296). Mahwah, NJ: Lawrence Erlbaum Associates.

Currie, J. & Hotz, V. J. (2004). Accidents will happen? Unintentional injury, maternal employment and child care policy. *Journal of Health Economics, 23*(1), 25–59.

Currie, J. & Thomas, D. (2001). Early test scores, school quality and SES: Long-run effects on wage and employment outcomes. In S. Polachek (Ed.), *Research in Labor Economics,* vol. 20 (pp. 103–132). Amsterdam: Elsevier Science Ltd.

Desai, S., Chase-Lansdale, P. L, & Michael, R. T. (1989). Mother or market? Effects of maternal employment on the intellectual ability of 4-year old children. *Demography, 26*(4), 545–561.

Downs, B. (2003). *Fertility of American women: June 2002.* U.S. Census Bureau, Current Population Reports, P20–548. Washington DC: U.S. Census Bureau.

Dranove, D., Spier, K. E., & Baker, L. (2000). Competition among employers offering health insurance. *Journal of Health Economics*, *19*(1), 121–40.

Duncan, G. J., & Brooks-Gunn, J. (1997). Income effects across the life span: Integration and interpretation. In G. J. Duncan & J. Brooks-Gunn (Eds.), *Consequences of growing up poor* (pp. 596–610). New York: Russell Sage Foundation.

Eissa, N., & Hoynes, H. W. (2004). Taxes and the labor market participation of married couples: The earned income tax credit. *Journal of Public Economics*, *88*(9–10), 1931–1958.

Ermisch, J., & Francesconi, M. (2001, June). *The effects of parents' employment on children's educational attainment*, Unpublished working paper, University of Essex, UK.

Gennetian, L. A., Duncan, G., Knox, V., Vargas, W., Clark-Kauffman, E., & London, A. S. (2004). How welfare policies affect adolescents' school outcomes: A synthesis of evidence from experimental studies. *Journal of Research on Adolescence*, *14*(4), 399–423.

Gershuny, J. (2000). *Changing times: Work and leisure in postindustrial society*. New York: Oxford University Press.

Gregg, P., Washbrook, E., Propper, C., & Burgess, S. (2005). The effects of a mother's return to work decision on child development in the UK. *Economic Journal, 115*, F48–F80.

Greenstein, T. N. (1995). Are the most disadvantaged children truly disadvantaged by early maternal employment? *Journal of Family Issues, 16*(2), 149–169.

Han, W. J., Waldfogel, J., & Brooks-Gunn, J. (2001). The effects of early maternal employment on later cognitive and behavioral outcomes. *Journal of Marriage and Family, 63*(1), 336–354.

Harvey, E. (1999). Short-term and long-term effects of early parental employment on children of the National Longitudinal Survey of Youth. *Developmental Psychology, 35*(2), 445–459.

Heckman, J. J. (2000). Policies to foster human capital. *Research in Economics*, *54*(1), 3–56.

Helburn, S. W., & Howes, C. (1996). Child care cost and quality. *The Future of Children, 63*(2), 62–82.

Hill, J., Waldfogel, J., Brooks-Gunn, J., & Han, W. (2005). Maternal employment and child development: A fresh look using newer methods. *Developmental Psychology*, *41*(6), 833–850.

Hofferth, S. L. (2001). Women's employment and care of children in the United States. In T. van der Lippe & L. van Dijk (Eds.), *Women's employment in a comparative perspective* (pp. 151–174). New York: Aldine de Gruyter.

Hoffman, L.W. (1980). The effects of maternal employment on the academic studies and performance of school-age children. *School Psychology Review, 9*(4), 319–335.

Horwood, L. J., & Fergusson, D. M. (1999). A longitudinal study of maternal labour force participation and child academic achievement. *Journal of Child Psychology and Psychiatry, 40*(7), 1013–1024.

Ichino, A., & Sanz de Galdeano, A. (2005). Reconciling motherhood and work: Evidence from time-use data in three countries. In D. S. Hammermesh & G. A. Pfann (Eds.), *The economics of time use* (pp. 263–288). Amsterdam: Elsevier B.V.

James-Burdumy, S. (2005). The effect of maternal labor force participation on child development. *Journal of Labor Economics, 23*(1), 177–211.

Lazear, E., & Michael, R. (1988). *Allocation of income within the household.* Chicago: University of Chicago Press.

Leibowitz, A. (1977). Parental inputs and children's achievement. *Journal of Human Resources, 12*(2), 242–251.

Loeb, S., Bridges, M., Bassok, D., Fuller B., & Rumberger, R. (2005, December). *How much is too much? The influence of preschool centers on children's social and cognitive development* (Working Paper No. 11812). National Bureau of Economic Research.

Magnuson, K. A., Meyers, M., Ruhm, C. J., & Waldfogel, J. (2004). Inequality in preschool education and school readiness. *American Educational Research Journal, 41*(1), 115–157.

Mayer, S. E. (1997). Indicators of children's economic well-being and parental employment. In R. M. Hauser, B. V. Brown & W. R. Prosser (Eds.), *Indicators of children's well-being* (pp. 237–257). New York: Russell Sage Foundation.

Moore, K. A., & Driscoll, A. K. (1997). Low-wage maternal employment and outcomes for children: A study. *The Future of Children, 7*(1), 122–127.

Mott, F. L. (1991). Developmental effects of infant care: The mediating role of gender and health. *Journal of Social Issues, 47*(2), 139–58.

National Institute of Child Health and Human Development Early Child Care Research Network. (1997a). Child care in the first year of life. *Merrill Palmer Quarterly, 43*(3), 340–60.

National Institute of Child Health and Human Development Early Child Care Research Network. (1997b). The effects of infant child care on infant-mother attachment security: Results of the NICHD Study of Child Care. *Child Development, 68*(5), 860–879.

National Institute of Child Health and Human Development Early Child Care Research Network & Duncan, G. J. (2003). Modeling the impacts of child care quality on children's preschool cognitive development. *Child Development, 74*(5), 1454–1475.

Neidell, M. J. (2000, August). *Early parental time investments in children's human capital development: Effects of time in the first year on cognitive and non-cognitive outcomes.* Unpublished working paper. University of California at Los Angeles.

Norberg, K. (1998, October). *The effects of daycare reconsidered.* (Working Paper No. 6769). National Bureau of Economic Research.

Parcel, T. L., & Menaghan, E. G. (1994). Early parental work, family social capital, and early childhood outcomes. *American Journal of Sociology, 99*(4), 972–1009.

Richards, M. H., & Duckett, E. (1994). The relationship of maternal employment to early adolescent experience with and without parents. *Child Development, 65,* 225–236.

Roe, B., Whittington, L. A., Fein, S. B., & Teisl, M. F. (1999). Is there competition between breast-feeding and maternal employment? *Demography, 36*(2), 157–171.

Ruhm, C. J. (2004). Parental employment and child cognitive development. *Journal of Human Resources, 39*(1), 155–192.

Ruhm, C. J. (in press). Maternal employment and adolescent development. *Labour Economics.*

Sandberg, J. F., & Hofferth, S. L. (2001). Changes in children's time with parents: United States, 1981–1997. *Demography, 38*(3), 423–436.

Shea, J. (2000). Does parents' money matter? *Journal of Public Economics, 77*(2), 155–184.

Shore, R. (1997). *Rethinking the brain: New insights into early development.* New York: Families and Work Institute.

Stafford, F. P. (1987). Women's work, sibling competition, and children's school performance. *American Economic Review, 77*(5), 972–980.

U.S. Bureau of the Census. (2004). *Living arrangements of children under 18 years old: 1960 to present.* Retrieved August 10, 2006 from http://www.census.gov/population/socdemo/hh-fam/tabCH-1.pdf

U.S. Bureau of the Census. (2005). *Statistical abstract of the United States: 2004–2005* (124th Edition). Washington DC: U.S. Government Printing Office.

U.S. Council of Economic Advisers. (1997). *The first three years: Investments that pay.* Washington, DC: Executive Office of the President.

U.S. Council of Economic Advisers. (1999). *Families and the labor market, 1969–1999: Analyzing the time crunch.* Washington, DC: Executive Office of the President.

U.S. Department of Labor, Bureau of Labor Statistics. (2005). *Women in the labor force: A databook* (Report No. 985). Retrieved August 10, 2006 from http://www.bls.gov/cps/wlf-databook-2005.pdf

Vandell, D. L., & Ramanan, J. (1992). Effects of early and recent maternal employment on children from low-income families. *Child Development, 63*(4), 938–949.

Vander Ven, T. M., Cullen, F. T., Carrozza, M. A., & Wright, J. P. (2001). Home alone: The impact of maternal employment on delinquency. *Social Problems, 48*(2), 236–257.

Verropoulou, G., & Joshi, H. (2005, January). *Does mothers' employment conflict with child development? Multilevel analysis of British mothers born in 1958.* Unpublished working paper. University of London.

Waldfogel, J., Han, W., & Brooks-Gunn, J. (2002). The effects of early maternal employment on child cognitive development. *Demography, 39*(2), 369–392.

Zaslow, M. J., Moore, K. A., Brooks, J. L., Morris, P. A., Tout, K., Redd, Z. A., & Emig, C. A. (2002). Experimental studies of welfare reform and children. *The Future of Children, 12*(1), 79–95.

Chapter Sixteen

Mothers' Shiftwork: Effects on Mothers, Fathers, and Children

by Rosalind Chait Barnett and Karen C. Gareis

INTRODUCTION

Major demographic trends are affecting the work schedules of U.S. employees. Among workers in the U.S. and increasingly in other countries, nonstandard schedules have become normative (Presser, 2003; Strazdins, Korda, Lim, Broom, & D'Souza, 2004). In the United States, an astonishing 70% of employees work other than standard hours; that is, other than 35 to 40 hours per week on weekdays during the daytime (Presser, 2003). Fewer than half of dual-earner couples in the United States—45.7% of all dual-earner couples and 48.1% of full-time dual-earner couples—are "traditional" dual-earner couples with both spouses working standard weekday hours (Presser, 2003). In 27% of married couples, the wife is employed full time on a nonstandard schedule and the couple has at least one child under 14 (Presser, 2003, p. 70).

Moreover, the percentage of employees working nonstandard shifts is likely to increase. Future job growth in the United States is projected to be disproportionately high in occupations in which shiftwork is common, such as cashier, truck driver, commodities sales worker in retail and personal services, and wait staff (Presser, 2003). In addition to service-sector occupations, shiftwork is normative among health-care workers, especially nurses working in hospitals or other 24-hour settings. Because many of these jobs are dominated by female employees, this anticipated job growth will disproportionately involve more women (Presser, 2003). Yet little empirical attention has been paid to the relationship between maternal shiftwork, mothers' and fathers' parenting behaviors, and children's socioemotional well-being (for an exception, see Davis, Crouter, & McHale, 2006). Much of the literature linking work conditions to outcomes focuses on the number of hours employees work (Jacobs & Gerson, 2004). In contrast, this chapter focuses on the distribution of mothers' work hours; that is, when during a 24-hour day she is at work and, in the case of the parent outcomes, the number of hours she works.

We pose two sets of questions: (1) What is the impact of wives' work schedules on their and their husbands' mental health and quality-of-life outcomes? and (2) What is the linkage between maternal work schedules, parenting behaviors, and children's socioemotional well-being? We address these questions in two separate analyses of data collected from the same sample—mothers, fathers, and children in 55 families in which the mothers are registered nurses who regularly work either day (typically 7:00 a.m. to 3:00 p.m.) or evening (typically 3:00 p.m. to 11:00 p.m.) shifts and had worked that schedule for at least one year prior to being interviewed, the fathers are employed full-time (two-thirds work either 9-to-5 or the day shift), and they have at least one child who is at least 8 years old but has not yet started high school.

In the first analysis we ask whether wives' day vs. evening work shift is related to husbands' and wives' reports of work-family conflict, psychological distress, and marital-role conflict. We collected data from both husbands and wives and employed a within-couple analysis strategy. We ask whether wives' work schedule variables (i.e., shift, hours worked, and the interaction between shift and work hours) are related to wives' own outcomes and, in a crossover effect, to their husbands' outcomes.

In the second analysis, using a within-family strategy, we ask whether various aspects of mothers' and fathers' parenting (i.e., time spent directly involved with children, parental knowledge of children's activities, spontaneous disclosure by children, and parenting skills as rated by both parents and children) differ by mothers' day vs. evening work shift and whether those aspects of parenting are linked to children's socioemotional well-being (i.e., internalizing, externalizing, and risky behaviors).

We selected mothers who worked day and evening shifts and not night or rotating shifts because previous research suggests that the evening shift is the hardest schedule for mothers with school-age children and the day shift is the easiest (Heymann, 2000). Thus, these two groups represent extremes in terms of their regular availability to supervise their children after school. (Mothers who work nights, typically 11:00 p.m. to 7:00 a.m., are also available after school, but are a much smaller and more atypical group than mothers who work days; they also pay a price in terms of sleep disruption and physical health consequences for such availability.)

Families in which the mother works days rather than evenings more closely resemble typical families in which parents and children do things together, including socializing and recreation (Presser, 2003), and in which mothers take on a much larger role in child-rearing than do fathers. Therefore, when mothers work days, both parents incur fewer violations of gendered expectations and potentially fewer stressful adjustments than families in which the mothers work evenings. Overall, these two groups present the greatest contrast with respect to potential strains on the individual spouses and on their marital relationship.

We sampled children aged 8<high school because: (1) In order to collect closed-ended survey data from children on their risky behaviors and perceptions of parents, the children had to be old enough to understand the questions and provide reliable data; and (2) Although younger children require more supervision after school than older ones, few after-school programs are available for tweens and early teens who still require supervision.

Data were collected separately from mothers, fathers, and children. For the analyses reported in this paper, we rely on data from both parents on their work-family conflict, psychological distress, marital-role quality, and perceptions of their own parenting skills. We rely on data from mothers on parents' time directly involved with the child and the child's internalizing and externalizing behaviors. Finally, children provided data on their own risky behaviors as well as on their mothers' and fathers' parental knowledge, parenting skills, and the extent to which the children spontaneously disclosed information to each parent. Adult outcome analyses control for husband's work hours, years of marriage, number of children in the home, household income, negative affectivity, and percentage of the wife's work hours that fall into her typical (day or evening) shift. Child outcome analyses control for child's age and gender.

Registered nurses, it is important to note, are atypical shiftworkers. In contrast to most of their counterparts, registered nurses have more control over their work schedules. Whereas most shiftworkers work nonstandard hours because their jobs require them to do so (Bogen & Cherlin, 2004; Presser, 2003), registered nurses can often choose their own schedules. In addition, nurses have the option of working in non-24/7 environments (e.g., doctors' offices, clinics, schools) if they cannot obtain their preferred shift or if the burden of shiftwork becomes too great. Most other shiftworkers do not have such flexibility.

Given the well-publicized shortage of nurses and the associated control nurses have over their work schedules, why would nurses chose to work evening hours, especially when they have school-age children? In a preliminary qualitative phase of the current study, we found that both day-shift and evening-shift nurses indicated that their primary reason for working their shift was to have a parent available to supervise children after school. In the case of the day-shift nurses, that parent was the mother; in the case of the evening-shift nurses, that parent was the father.

The sample was drawn randomly from the registry of the Board of Certification in Nursing, which licenses all nurses practicing in the Commonwealth of Massachusetts. Potential participants first received letters describing the study and eligibility criteria; screeners followed up by telephone to determine whether the family was eligible and whether all eligible family members were willing to participate in the study.

Data were collected during the school year between December 2002 and February 2004 in face-to-face quantitative interviews scheduled at a time and place convenient to participants. Most families were interviewed in a single visit to their home, with each member interviewed privately. Some families had more than one child in the target age range; all were interviewed. Because only 16 families had more than one age-eligible child, only data from the oldest age-eligible participating child in each family are presented here. Interviews took approximately 45 minutes for the mothers, 35 minutes for the fathers, and 15 minutes for the children. Before the interview, mothers and fathers also filled out a brief (20 minutes for mothers; 5 minutes for fathers) mailed questionnaire about the child. Families received $100 for their participation, plus $25 for each additional participating child.

The remainder of this chapter consists of three sections: (1) what we have learned about the within-couple relationship between wives' work schedules and their own and their husbands' outcomes; (2) what we have learned about the within-family relationships among wives' work schedules, mothers' and fathers' parenting behaviors (i.e., parental knowledge, children's spontaneous disclosures, and parenting skills), and child outcomes; and (3) overall conclusions.

PARENT OUTCOMES

Literature Review

Work-family conflict. When mothers and fathers work during daytime hours, family life is what many would consider "Traditional." Both parents are home during at least some of the after-school hours to supervise children, attend school functions, participate in parent-teacher conferences, and so forth. Moreover, the whole family is home on work nights to eat dinner together. Both parents are able to check on the children's homework, share daily happenings, and get the children ready for bed.

In sharp contrast, families in which the mothers regularly work evenings face many challenges in their nontraditional family life. Critically, the family as a whole is not typically together during dinner, nor are they all together for such afternoon or evening social events as workday school performances (Staines & Pleck, 1984). Previous studies of shiftworking couples found that when wives work non-day compared to day shifts, husbands spend more time on housework and child care (Presser, 2003). Compared to day-shift couples, couples in which one spouse works a nonstandard schedule report more work-family conflict, often linked to scheduling problems (Staines & Pleck, 1983). More recently, La Valle and her colleagues (La Valle, Arthur, Millward, Scott, & Clayden, 2002) found that all types of nonstandard work schedules can disrupt family life, resulting in heightened work-family conflict.

Being away from the family during after-school hours and traditional family times is thought to be stressful for mothers, especially those who work long hours; that is, the more time away from family during these hours, the more conflict mothers will experience. For example, these mothers may experience work-family conflict when their work schedules preclude them from sharing family dinners, "an especially important day-to-day ritual" (Presser, 2003, p. 16; see also Hertz & Charlton, 1989).

Moreover, many husbands in these families assume primary responsibility for preparing dinner for their children, supervising homework for school-age children, and supervising bedtime preparations for younger children. Some men may find these activities especially stressful or undesirable, increasing the likelihood of negative outcomes; others may find special pleasure in their greater involvement with their children (Coltrane, 2000; Risman, 1986).

In general, the more hours husbands are not at work while their wives are at work, the more likely they are to do housework that is traditionally done by women, thereby violating gender stereotypes. This conclusion was also drawn in a recent Australian study of shiftworking nurses. Moorehead (2003) coined the phrase "the power of absence" to reflect the fact that shiftwork enables some women to be absent from the home in the late afternoon and early evening, during peak periods of domestic work. Husbands and fathers are often therefore required to take up a much larger than usual domestic workload (Probert, 2005). In contrast, when wives are not at work and husbands are, wives tend to spend more hours on traditionally female tasks, thereby reinforcing gender stereotypes (Barnett & Shen, 1997). Presser (2003) reported similar findings. Thus, evening-shift wives and their husbands may experience more work-family conflict than their day-shift counterparts, especially when the wives work long hours. Alternatively, fathers whose wives work evenings rather than days may experience less work-family conflict because of the pleasure they obtain from the time they are able to spend alone with their children.

Psychological distress. Previous studies indicate that the absolute number of hours women work is unrelated (Barnett & Gareis, 2000) or even inversely related (Baruch, Barnett, & Rivers, 1985) to their psychological distress. However, no previous studies have addressed the relationship between maternal shiftwork and psychological distress. Yet mothers who work evenings, especially those who work long hours, may experience more psychological distress than their day-shift counterparts because they are unable to be home at dinnertime or to engage with their children after school. Although they know that their children are being cared for by their husbands, they may feel that they should still be there to help children with homework, accompany them to after-school activities, be there when they play with friends, and get them ready for bed (Deutsch, 1999).

Alternatively, in couples who have chosen to have the mother work an evening schedule in order to maximize parental child care, mothers may view not being home during the after-school hours or not being able to participate in family dinners as a minor price to pay and may therefore not be adversely affected by working nonstandard schedules (Thompson & Bunderson, 2001). Indeed, it may be that evening-shift mothers are relieved to know their children are being cared for by their fathers and may therefore experience low psychological distress, perhaps especially when they work long hours. By the same reasoning, fathers whose wives work evenings may also experience high work-schedule fit and therefore low distress. Previous research lends indirect support to this speculation: Work-schedule fit, defined as the degree to which one's own and one's spouse's work arrangements meet one's own and one's family's needs, was found to mediate the relationship between work hours and burnout (Barnett, Gareis, & Brennan, 1999). That is, long work hours alone did not predict burnout; instead, the relationship between work hours and burnout depended upon the extent to which spouses' work schedules met family needs.

Importantly, the couples in the present study have had at least one year to work out the child care and other issues raised by the wife's evening work schedule and for the wives to develop trust in their husbands' ability to care for the children. On balance, we expect that evening-shift mothers, even if they work long hours, will not differ in their experience of psychological distress from day-shift mothers. Previous research indicates that fathers actively participate with their wives in making the decision for the wife to work her particular schedule (Barnett & Gareis, 2005; Deutsch, 1999). Thus, men whose wives work evening shifts may not report higher psychological distress, even if their wives work long hours, than men whose wives work day shifts.

Marital-role quality. Previous research suggests that marital dissatisfaction is greater among dual-earner parents when one spouse works a non-day shift compared with couples in which both spouses work day shifts (Deutsch, 1999; Grosswald, 2004; Han, 2004; Jacobs & Gerson, 2004; Presser, 2000, 2003; White & Keith, 1990). In Presser's (2003) comprehensive study of the quality and stability of marriages in dual-earner couples working nonstandard shifts, she found that the greater risk of marital instability was especially marked among night-shift and rotating-shift workers with children and did not apply to evening-shift workers. However, Presser notes that it is difficult to generalize her findings because the results varied with the specific measure of marital instability and the specific shift schedule. Importantly, most employees in Presser's analyses had little opportunity to change their work schedules.

Findings from a previous within-couple longitudinal analysis of the relationship between work hours and marital-role quality were that none of the time-invariant work hours variables was significantly associated with marital-role quality. However, change over time in work hours was related to change over time in marital-role quality (Barnett, Gareis, & Brennan, in press). One implication of these findings may be that spouses adapt to each other's typical work hours, whatever those may be, with no significant effect on their evaluations of the quality of their marriages. However, change over time in work hours seems to require adjustments, with associated effects on marital-role quality. Thus, in this cross-sectional study, we do not expect wives' work schedules to affect either their own or their spouses' marital-role quality.

Results

Overall, the significant findings differed for husbands and wives and depended on the particular outcome. Women who regularly work evening shifts, regardless of the number of hours they work, report significantly higher work-family conflict than women who regularly work days. It appears that even after working evening shifts for at least a year, mothers of school-age children continue to report higher work-family conflict than their counterparts who work days, although one must assume that if the level of work-family conflict were too high, mothers would have changed their schedules or left their positions. Thus, even among this select group of registered nurses who have regularly worked evening shifts for a year or more, there is still a price to pay for not being with their families in the evening, albeit not a catastrophic or pervasive one. Not surprisingly, men showed a trend to report more work-family conflict when their wives worked evenings vs.days, but only if their wives worked long hours in the evenings. Thus, with respect to work-family conflict, it appears that regardless of how many hours they work, it is hard for women who work evening shifts to adapt to being away from their families during the after-school hours. In contrast, men whose wives work evenings seem to pay little price in terms of work-family conflict for assuming nontraditional household and childcare tasks, unless their wives work long hours in the evenings.

There was no significant difference between day- and evening-shift wives with respect to psychological distress. However, there was a significant interaction effect such that the longer the hours the wives worked during the evening shift, the lower was their psychological distress. It appears that these wives trust that their children are being well cared for by their husbands and can therefore work long hours without experiencing high levels of distress. Alternatively, it may be that they feel free to work long hours because they have confidence in their husbands' parenting skills.

Notably, husbands' distress was not related to wife's shift, wife's work hours, nor the interaction of wife's shift with wife's work hours. Apparently, the non-normative division of child care and household tasks is not a source of distress for these fathers. Moreover, as discussed below, these fathers spend more time alone with their children than do fathers whose wives work days and, as a result, they may derive benefits that offset any feelings of distress. Previous research suggests that the more time fathers are alone with their children, the more they report feeling competent as parents (Baruch & Barnett, 1986; Barnett & Gareis, 2007). Such feelings of competence may, in turn, offset feelings of distress.

As expected, there were no significant differences in marital-role quality between day- and evening-shift wives, even taking work hours into consideration. Similarly, men's marital-role quality was unrelated to their wives' work shift or work hours, or to the interaction between the two. These findings are consistent with Presser's (2003) conclusion that the effects of nonstandard work schedules on marital quality and stability were limited to night- and rotating-shift workers with children. Further, in our sample, it may be that if the evening shift were taking too big a toll on the marriage, the wife would probably have changed her schedule or left that job.

CHILD OUTCOMES

Literature Review

Our within-family approach to understanding the complex relationships among parents' work schedules, mothers' and fathers' parenting behaviors, and children's socioemotional outcomes is consistent with Bronfenbrenner's (1979) ecological theory and with family-systems theory. In Bronfenbrenner's view, child outcomes need to be understood in the context of the child's family situation, important components of which are the parents' work schedules and their parenting behaviors. The general assumption is that greater parental involvement will be associated with better child outcomes. This assumption receives considerable support in the empirical literature (e.g., Aldous & Mulligan, 2002; Updegraff, McHale, Crouter, Kupanoff, 2001; Zick, Bryant, & Osterbacka, 2001). This approach is also consistent with family systems theory (see Cox & Paley, 1997, for a review), which emphasizes the interdependence among all family members.

Parenting Behaviors

Parents' time with children. Considerable research has been done on the linkages between maternal employment and the amount of time mothers spend with children. Several studies suggest that regardless of their employment status and their work schedules, mothers do not sacrifice time with their children (Bianchi, 2000; Bogen & Cherlin, 2004; Davis et al., 2006). Rather, they may sleep fewer hours and forgo leisure activities (Bianchi, 2000; Kingston & Nock, 1985). Bogen and Cherlin (2004) found that nonstandard maternal work schedules did not affect the amount of time mothers spend with their children. Similarly, in a study of dual-earner families with adolescent children, Davis et al. (2006) found no significant differences between parents' shift schedules and they time they spent with their children. Based on these findings, we do not expect a direct effect of maternal day versus evening shift schedules on mother's time with the child.

In contrast, fathers' caregiving has been associated with mothers' work schedules (Brayfield, 1995; Presser, 2003). In dual-earner families, the likelihood that fathers would be caregivers to their children varied with the mother's but not the father's work schedule (Brayfield, 1995). Instead, a key factor in fathers' caregiving appears to be the degree of non-overlap in parental work schedules (Brayfield, 1995; Presser, 2000). In the present study, the majority (69%) of fathers worked either a standard 9-to-5 schedule or a day shift. Thus, in our sample, non-overlap would be lowest if both parents worked the day shift and highest if the mother worked evenings and the father worked days. (Because so few fathers worked non-day hours, we excluded fathers' work schedule as a variable in our analyses.) Building on the work of Brayfield (1995), which focused only on whether the father was a caregiver at all, we expect that fathers whose wives regularly work evenings vs. days will spend more time directly involved with their children.

In addition, previous research suggests that fathers' time with children might mediate the effects of maternal shiftwork on child outcomes (e.g., Han, 2005).

Parental knowledge. Previous research has established a link between parents' time with children and parental knowledge (Crouter, Helms-Erikson, Updegraff, & McHale, 1999; Crouter & McHale, 1993; Davis et al., 2006; Kerr & Stattin, 2000). In a series of studies, Crouter and her team found that mothers' knowledge about their children's activities is unrelated to their own work schedules, but among fathers, parental knowledge is related to the mother's work schedule: The more time mothers spend at work, the greater is the fathers' parental knowledge (Crouter et al., 1999). Crouter and McHale (1993) were even able to link seasonal variations in mothers' work schedules with changes in fathers' parental knowledge, indicating that "fathers may calibrate the extent to which they monitor their school-aged children in part as a function of mothers' availability" (p. 203). Based on these findings, we expect that mothers' parental knowledge will not differ depending on her work shift, but that fathers whose wives regularly work evenings vs. days will know more about their children's activities.

In addition, children who have close relations with their parents may volunteer information about the day's events, thereby increasing parental knowledge (Crouter et al., 1999). It appears that children's spontaneous disclosures are more strongly related to children's outcomes than is parental solicitation (Kerr & Stattin, 2000). Because of the greater opportunity to spend time with their fathers in the evenings, children whose mothers work evening vs. day shifts are likely to disclose more to their fathers. In contrast, we do not expect child disclosure to mothers to differ by maternal work schedule.

Parenting skills. Previous research has shown that the more time fathers spend in child care, the higher they rate their competence as parents (Baruch & Barnett, 1986). Thus, if fathers whose wives regularly work evening vs. day shifts spend more time directly involved with their children, we expect them to also rate their own parenting skills higher. However, we do not expect mothers' ratings of their own parenting skills to differ by work shift. We also expect that children whose mothers work evenings vs. days will grade their fathers higher on parenting skills. Again, we do not expect children's ratings of their mothers' parenting skills to be related to maternal shift.

Effects on Children

Different shiftwork schedules seem to have different effects on child outcomes. With respect to maternal shiftwork, research has linked mothers' non-standard work schedules to poor physical and cognitive outcomes in their children (Han, 2005; Heymann, 2000). At present, however, there is scant systematic research on the association between parents' work shifts and their children's socioemotional outcomes, including internalizing, externalizing, and risky behaviors (for exceptions, see La Valle et al., 2002 and Strazdins et al., 2004).

In the present study, we operationalize socioemotional well-being as low levels of internalizing (anxious, depressed, withdrawn) and externalizing (rule-breaking, aggressive) behaviors and engagement in risky behaviors. Strazdins et al. (2004) found that children in dual-earner families with at least one parent working a nonstandard schedule were more likely to have at least one emotional or behavioral difficulty than when both parents worked standard schedules. Importantly, these findings provide no insight into the possible mechanisms—for example, parents' time and engagement with the children—linking parents' shiftwork to their children's socioemotional well-being.

A large body of literature links parental time with children and parental knowledge with such child outcomes as internalizing, externalizing, and risky behaviors (Aldous & Mulligan, 2002; Crouter, Head, McHale, & Tucker, 2004; Kerr & Stattin, 2000; Ozer, Park, Paul, Brindis, & Irwin, 2003). Research shows that parents' perceptions of their own efficacy are also related to better child outcomes, including lower levels of risky behaviors (Elder, Eccles, Ardelt, & Lord, 1995; Ozer, 2004). Thus, we expect that fathers' and mother's time with children, parental knowledge, and ratings of their own parenting skills will be similarly associated with better socioemotional outcomes in school-age children.

Results

The major findings of this study are that, controlling for child's age and gender: (1) Mothers' work schedules do not affect the amount of time they spend directly involved with their children, their knowledge of their children's activities, their receipt of spontaneous disclosures from their children, or their children's or their own ratings of their parenting skills; (2) Mothers' work schedules do affect fathers' parenting behaviors and ratings of their own parenting skills. Specifically, in families with evening- vs. day-shift mothers, fathers spend more time directly involved with children, children report that their fathers know more about their activities and that they spontaneously disclose more to their fathers, and both children and fathers rate the fathers' parenting skills higher; (3) Fathers' and mothers' parenting behaviors are related to a number of socioemotional outcomes in their children, with the strongest results found for risk-taking behaviors; and (4) There is some suggestive evidence that the effects of maternal work shifts on child outcomes may be mediated by fathers' parenting behaviors.

Specifically, for fathers, the amount of time involved with children is associated with fewer internalizing and externalizing behaviors in the children. Further, fathers' time with children shows a trend to mediate the relationship between maternal work shift and children's internalizing behaviors and is a significant mediator of the relationship between maternal work shift and children's externalizing behaviors. For mothers, the amount of time they spend directly involved with their child is unrelated to any of the three child outcomes. Children whose fathers know more about their activities and who disclose more to their fathers show significantly fewer risk-taking behaviors; and children who rate their fathers' parenting skills higher show significantly fewer externalizing and risk-taking behaviors. Further, we found trends for fathers' knowledge of children's activities, children's disclosure to fathers, and children's ratings of father's parenting skills to mediate the relationship between maternal work shift and children's risky behaviors. The pattern of results is similar for mothers, with children whose mothers know more about their activities, who disclose more to their mothers, and who rate their mothers' parenting skills higher reporting engaging in fewer risk-taking behaviors. Given the small sample size, these results, particularly the mediation findings, are encouraging and warrant further study.

These results support those of previous research in suggesting that working mothers do not reduce their time with their children (Bianchi, 2000). We now have evidence that this conclusion holds true even when mothers work during nonstandard times of the day. Apparently these mothers compensate for the time they spend at work during the after-school and evening hours by spending more time with their children before school and on days when they are not at work.

Confirming Bronfenbrenner's insight (1979), these results emphasize the need to take the family as the unit of analysis in studies of child outcomes. Without children's reports of parenting behaviors and mothers' reports of parental time with children, we would have drawn the erroneous conclusion that maternal shift schedule was unrelated to child outcomes simply because there is no direct relationship between these two variables. In fact, the context of family life appears to be different in families in which the mother works the day vs. the evening shift, and these differing contexts affect child outcomes. Specifically, fathers in families with evening- vs. day-shift mothers behave more like their wives vis-à-vis their children in terms of time spent with children, knowledge about children's activities, receipt of spontaneous disclosures by children, and parenting skills as rated by themselves and by their children.

The findings appear to conflict with those of Brayfield (1995) indicating that mothers' work hours, but not their shift schedules, were associated with the likelihood of fathers being caregivers to their school-age children. It is not clear how Brayfield's findings would have differed if fathers' time with children had been included as an outcome variable. Conceptually, however, our findings are consistent with those of Brayfield (1995) and Presser (2000) that non-overlap in parents' hours predicted fathers' caregiving to children. In our study, when mothers work evening shifts, there is more non-overlap with their husbands' work schedules, and fathers spend more time directly involved with children in those families. As discussed above, we also found suggestive evidence to support a plausible mediating link between maternal shiftwork, father's parenting behaviors, and child outcomes.

Do fathers of evening-shift wives self-select into a more involved parenting role, or do they adapt to it out of necessity? With cross-sectional data, we cannot answer this question definitively; either or both of these processes may be at work. Perhaps fathers who want to be more engaged with their children encourage their wives to work the evening shift, or wives who trust their husbands to take on an active parenting role feel freer to work evening shifts. Or, consistent with work by Risman (1986) and Coltrane (2000), perhaps fathers whose wives work evenings respond to increased caretaking responsibilities by developing good parenting skills.

Preliminary interviews conducted in preparation for the present study provide some evidence supporting the last interpretation. Several husbands whose wives worked evenings reported initial concerns about their increased caretaking role but reported that they had been able to adapt. For example, one father of three whose wife worked evening shifts said: "When we are both here, it's really easy to manage. In her absence, I find it difficult, but I'm learning through trial and error." These qualitative data suggest that fathers whose wives work evenings learn on the job. Their parenting skills seem to be a consequence rather than a cause of their wives' shift schedule choice. However, prospective longitudinal studies are needed to clarify these causal linkages.

The data suggest that in order for mothers to be able to work evening shifts, fathers must be flexible. It may also be that in cases where the fathers were unable to take on these traditionally female tasks, the wives changed to a day shift or a job in a 9-to-5 setting (e.g., a doctor's office), left nursing, took a leave from work, or perhaps even divorced their husbands. In any case, the sample of couples with wives working evening shifts consisted of those who, whether by nature or by adaptation, adjusted well to the demands of the wife's nonstandard work schedule.

Most of the research on the effects of maternal shiftwork on child outcomes focuses on negative outcomes. The evening shift has been singled out as particularly problematic when the children are school-aged (Heymann, 2000). The argument is that mothers who work nonstandard shifts experience adverse well-being outcomes that may have direct or indirect negative impacts on their children's well-being (Han, 2005). While this portrayal may be accurate among families headed by single mothers, it does not seem to be true among dual-earner families. Based on the findings of the present study, it appears that fathers in families with mothers who regularly work evening vs. day shifts are more involved with their children in various ways. To the extent that father involvement predicts positive child outcomes, then children in these families are advantaged. However, as we have seen, evening-shift mothers may pay a price in terms of work-family conflict (and perhaps in such other unmeasured outcomes as sleep deprivation, inadequate leisure, strained friendships, and so on).

Among the positive outcomes of shiftwork that should be included in future studies are support, cooperation, and fathers' increased time and engagement with school-aged children. As we and others have shown, father involvement has beneficial effects on child outcomes. Previous research has shown that it also has positive effects on fathers (Baruch & Barnett, 1981). Other studies suggest another possible benefit: When fathers are more involved in childrearing, their wives evaluate their marriages more positively (Ozer, Barnett, Brennan, & Sperling, 1998), and their marriages are also more stable (Kalmijn, 1999).

CONCLUSIONS

Although evening-shift work is associated with a dramatically different home life than day-shift work, we find relatively few effects—negative or positive—on the parents, but a number of positive effects on fathers' parenting behaviors which are, in turn, associated with positive effects on children. The results might be quite different in a more heterogeneous sample of nonstandard-schedule workers given registered nurses' high degree of control over their work schedules. Moreover, the women in our sample have been working their schedules for at least a year, allowing them and their families either to adapt or to change to a more amenable work schedule. Because of the relatively favorable work situation of this sample, our findings should be considered optimistic. In a more typical sample of nonstandard-schedule workers, there might be more negative outcomes for all family members given employees' lesser ability to control their work schedules.

Most striking, wives' evening vs. day work results in a regendering of the division of household and child-care tasks, with fathers spending much more time involved with children and, as Presser (2003) found, in more traditionally feminine household tasks. Yet men whose wives work evening vs. day shifts are no less positive about their marriages, nor do these men report greater psychological distress. However, there was a trend for men whose wives who work long evening hours to report more work-family conflict than their counterparts whose wives work day shifts.

Our findings suggest that mothers who regularly work evening shifts, but not their children, pay a price. These mothers do not differ from their day-shift counterparts in any of the parenting behaviors we studied. However, even though they have been working evenings for over a year, they still experience conflict in managing their work and family lives.

In contrast, with respect to psychological distress, mothers seem to derive a benefit, with those who work long evening hours reporting lower psychological distress. It appears that these mothers trust that their husbands will take good care of the children in their absence, or perhaps their decreased distress is attributable to Moorehead's (2003) power of absence; that is, being away at work during the hours when many stress-related household tasks (e.g., dinner preparation and cleanup; Barnett & Shen, 1997) are typically done. Longitudinal data would shed light on which processes operate to produce this finding.

The school-age children of mothers who work evenings vs. days seem to reap particular benefits. There is no evidence that these children react or feel any differently toward their mothers as a function of their mothers' work schedules, or that their mothers behave any differently toward them; instead, the difference appears to lie in the father-child relationships in these families. Compared to children whose mothers work days, children whose mothers work evenings are equally engaged with their mothers, but significantly more engaged with their fathers. Further, children who are more closely engaged with their fathers in various ways exhibit lower levels of internalizing, externalizing, and risky behaviors. In short, the socioemotional well-being of children whose mothers work evenings is not compromised.

Overall, the findings of this study support Presser's (2003) observation that the consequences of nonstandard work schedules on the family "are complex, since they depend not only on the type of family but on the particular work schedule and on the gender of the person working this schedule; moreover . . . there are positive as well as negative family consequences of employment at nonstandard times" (pp. 215–216).

Like other studies, this study has several limitations. Most important, in contrast to most mothers who work nonstandard shifts, the mothers in this study were older, better educated, and married, whereas the typical nonstandard-schedule worker is young, low-income, less educated, and more likely to be a single mother (Presser & Cox, 1997). Moreover, we limited our sample to mothers who were working either days or evenings. We excluded mothers working nights because that schedule is less disruptive of parent-child interactions. We also excluded mothers working rotating shifts because of the complexity of those schedules and the difficulty of locating a sample of mothers who worked the same rotating schedule. Future research should include mothers who work these other nonstandard schedules.

Future research should also estimate the relationship between fathers' nonstandard shift schedules, mothers' and fathers' parenting behaviors, and children's socioemotional outcomes. In the present 24/7 economy, mothers and fathers will increasingly work nonstandard shifts, and it is crucial that we understand the effects on children's socioemotional well-being, regardless of which parent is the nonstandard-shift worker. In addition, we need to study these linkages among single parents who work nonstandard shifts; single parents are a fast-growing segment of the population and of the workforce. Finally, due to our sample size, we had only limited ability to estimate mediating effects. A larger sample would be desirable in future studies.

Possibly, had we assessed different outcomes and had a more heterogeneous sample of nonstandard workers, our results might have been quite different. However, considering that this is the first study of its kind, there is virtue in keeping the sample homogenous and minimizing the effect of confounding variables. Thus, although our results may not generalize to a more heterogeneous sample, they do provide a solid base for future research on the within-family effects of wives' shiftwork on the mental health and quality-of-life outcomes of both spouses and on their children's socioemotional well-being.

NOTE

Rosalind Chait Barnett, Ph.D., is a Senior Scientist and Director of the Community, Families & Work Program at the Women's Studies Research Center, Brandeis University. Karen C. Gareis, Ph.D. is a senior research associate and program director of the Community, Families & Work Program at Brandeis University. Data for this analysis were gathered under a grant from the Alfred P. Sloan Foundation (2001-10-12) to the first author. We gratefully acknowledge the contributions of our HLM consultant, Robert T. Brennan, our research assistant, Jema Turk, and our interviewers, Joyce Buni, Patti Cassidy, Connie Festo, Carol Genovese, Michele Meagher, Jennifer Ginsburg Richard, and Jeri Silverman. Correspondence concerning this analysis should be addressed to Rosalind Chait Barnett, Brandeis University, Women's Studies Research Center, Mailstop 079, 515 South Street, Waltham, MA 02453-2720, rbarnett@brandeis.edu, (781) 736-2287, FAX (781) 736-4881

REFERENCES

Aldous, J., & Mulligan, G. M. (2002). Fathers' child care and children's behavior problems: A longitudinal study. *Journal of Family Issues, 23*(5), 624–647.

Barnett, R. C., & Gareis, K. C. (2000). Reduced-hours employment: The relationship between difficulty of trade-offs and quality of life. *Work and Occupations, 27*, 168–187.

Barnett, R. C., & Gareis, K. C. (2005). *How and why registered nurses decide to work their schedules: Views of RNs and their husbands.* (Final report on qualitative data to the Alfred P. Sloan Foundation). Waltham, MA: Brandeis University.

Barnett, R. C., & Gareis, K. C. (2007). Shift work, parenting behaviors, and children's socioemotional well-being: A within-family study. *Journal of Family Issues, 28*(6), 727–748.

Barnett, R. C., Gareis, K. C., & Brennan, R. T. (1999). Fit as a mediator of the relationship between work hours and burnout. *Journal of Occupational Health Psychology, 4*, 307–317.

Barnett, R. C., Gareis, K. C., & Brennan, R. T. (under review). *Time to consider time: A longitudinal within-couple analysis of total family work hours.* Manuscript submitted.

Barnett, R. C., Gareis, K. C., & Brennan, R. T. (in press). *Reconsidering worktime: A longitudinal within-couple analysis of total family work hours. Community, Work & Family.*

Barnett, R. C., & Shen, Y.-C. (1997). Gender, high- and low-schedule-control housework tasks, and psychological distress. *Journal of Family Issues, 18*, 403–428.

Baruch, G. K., & Barnett, R. C. (1981). Fathers' participation in the care of their preschool children. *Sex Roles, 7*(10), 1043–1055.

Baruch, G. K., & Barnett, R. C. (1986). Consequences of fathers' participation in family work: Parents' role strain and well-being. *Journal of Personality and Social Psychology, 51*, 983–992.

Baruch, G., Barnett, R., & Rivers, C. (1985). *Lifeprints: New patterns of love and work for today's women.* New York: Signet.

Bianchi, S. M. (2000). Maternal employment and time with children: Dramatic change or surprising continuity? *Demography, 37*(4), 401–414.

Bogen, K., & Cherlin, A. (2004, April). *Jobs and parenting 24-7: Work schedules and parenting of the working poor.* Paper presented at the 2004 Annual Meeting of the Population Association of America, Boston.

Brayfield, A. (1995). Juggling jobs and kids: The impact of employment schedules on fathers' caring for children. *Journal of Marriage and the Family, 57*, 321–332.

Bronfenbrenner, U. (1979). *The ecology of human development: Experiments by nature and design.* Cambridge, MA: Harvard University Press.

Coltrane, S. (2000). *Gender and families.* Walnut Creek, CA: AltaMira Press.

Cox, M. J., & Paley, B. (1997). Families as systems. *Annual Review of Psychology, 48*, 243–267.

Crouter, A. C., Head, M. R., McHale, S. M., & Tucker, C. J. (2004). Family time and the psychosocial adjustment of adolescent siblings and their parents. *Journal of Marriage and Family, 66*, 147–162.

Crouter, A. C., Helms-Erikson, H., Updegraff, K., & McHale, S. M. (1999). Conditions underlying parents' knowledge about children's daily lives in middle childhood: Between-and within-family comparisons. *Child Development, 70*(1), 246–259.

Crouter, A. C., & McHale, S. M. (1993). Temporal rhythms in family life: Seasonal variation in the relation between parental work and family processes. *Developmental Psychology, 29*(2), 198–205.

Davis, K. D., Crouter, A. C., & McHale, S. M. (2006). Implications of shift work for parent-adolescent relationships in dual-earner families. *Family Relations, 55*(4), 450–460.

Deutsch, F. M. (1999). *Halving it all: How equally shared parenting works.* Cambridge: Harvard University Press.

Elder, G. H., Jr., Eccles, J. S., Ardelt, M., & Lord. S. (1995). Inner-city parents under economic pressure: Perspectives on the strategies of parenting. *Journal of Marriage and the Family, 57*, 771–784.

Grosswald, B. (2004). The effects of shift work on family satisfaction. *The Journal of Contemporary Human Services, 85*, 413–423.

Han, W. J. (2004). Nonstandard work schedules and child care decisions: Evidence from the NICHD Study of Early Child Care. *Early Childhood Research Quarterly, 19*, 231–256.

Han, W.-J. (2005). Maternal nonstandard work schedules and child cognitive outcomes. *Child Development, 76*, 137–154.

Hertz, R., & Charlton, J. (1989). Making family under a shiftwork schedule: Air Force security guards and their wives. *Social Problems, 36*, 491–507.

Heymann, J. (2000). *The widening gap: Why America's working families are in jeopardy—and what can be done about it.* New York: Basic Books.

Jacobs, J. A., & Gerson, K. (2004). *The time divide: Work, family and gender inequality.* Cambridge, MA: Harvard University Press.

Kalmijn, M. (1999). Father involvement in childrearing and the perceived stability of marriage. *Journal of Marriage and the Family, 61*, 409–421.

Kerr, M., & Stattin, H. (2000). What parents know, how they know it, and several forms of adolescent adjustment: Further support for a reinterpretation of monitoring. *Developmental Psychology, 36*(3), 366–380.

Kingston, P. W., & Nock, S. L. (1985). Consequences of the family work day. *Journal of Marriage and the Family, 47*, 619–629.

La Valle, I., Arthur, S., Millward, C., Scott, J., & Clayden, M. (2002). *Happy families? Atypical work and its influence on family life.* Bristol, UK: The Policy Press.

Moorehead, A. (2003). *How employed mothers allocate time for work and family.* Unpublished doctoral dissertation, University of Sydney, Australia.

Ozer, E. M. (2004, July). *Work hours, parental efficacy, and adolescent risky behavior.* Paper presented at the annual meeting of the American Psychological Association, Honolulu, HI.

Ozer, E. M., Barnett, R. C., Brennan, R. T., & Sperling, J. (1998). Does child care involvement increase or decrease distress among dual-earner couples? *Women's Health: Research on Gender, Behavior, and Policy, 4*, 285–311.

Ozer, E. M., Park, M. J., Paul, T., Brindis, C. D., & Irwin, C. E., Jr. (2003). *America's adolescents: Are they healthy?* San Francisco: University of California, National Adolescent Health Information Center.

Presser, H. B. (2000). Nonstandard work schedules and marital instability. *Journal of Marriage and the Family, 62*, 93–110.

Presser, H. B. (2003). *Working in a 24/7 economy* (hardcover ed.). New York: Russell Sage Foundation.

Presser, H. B., & Cox, A. G. (1997, April). The work schedules of low-educated American women and welfare reform. *Monthly Labor Review*, 25–34.

Probert, B. (2005). 'I just couldn't fit it in': Gender and unequal outcomes in academic careers. *Gender, Work and Organization, 12*, 50–72.

Risman, B. A. (1986). Can men "mother"? Life as a single father. *Family Relations, 35*, 95–102.

Staines, G. L., & Pleck, J. H. (1983). *The impact of work schedules on the family.* Ann Arbor: Institute for Social Research, The University of Michigan.

Staines, G. L., & Pleck, J. H. (1984). Nonstandard work schedules and family life. *Journal of Applied Psychology, 69*, 515–523.

Strazdins, L., Korda, R. J., Lim, L. L.-Y., Broom, D. H., & D'Souza, R. M. (2004). Around-the-clock: Parent work schedules and children's well-being in a 24-hr economy. *Social Science & Medicine, 59*, 1517–1527.

Thompson, J. A., & Bunderson, J. S. (2001). Work-nonwork conflict and the phenomenology of time: Beyond the balance metaphor. *Work and Occupations, 28*, 17–39.

Updegraff, K. A., McHale, S. M., Crouter, A. C., & Kupanoff, K. (2001). Parents' involvement in adolescents' peer relationships: A comparison of mothers' and fathers' roles. *Journal of Marriage and Family, 63*, 655–668.

White, L., & Keith, B. (1990). The effect of shift work on the quality and stability of marital relations. *Journal of Marriage and the Family, 52*, 453–462.

Zick, C. D., Bryant, W. K., & Osterbacka, E. (2001). Mothers' employment, parental involvement, and the implications for intermediate child outcomes. *Social Science Research, 30*, 25–49.

Chapter Seventeen

To Work and To Love: Bi-directional Relationships between Job Conditions and Marriage

by Maureen Perry-Jenkins, Amy Claxton, JuliAnna Smith & Mark Manning

ABSTRACT

Increasingly, over the past three decades, pressures associated with parental employment, work conditions, work schedules, and child care have become growing concerns of new parents, due to the sharp rise in women's employment rates (Bachu & O'Connell, 2000). Despite the fact that the majority of new mothers return to paid employment within 6 months of their child's birth, the transition to parenthood literature has paid little attention to the effects of this second transition back to work on the mental health of mothers, fathers, and infants. In addition, we know even less about how social and cultural factors, such as race, ethnicity, social class, and family structure, shape how parents and children cope and develop across these multiple transitions. The goal of this presentation is twofold. The first aim is to describe both the formal and informal workplace policies and work conditions (e.g., control, autonomy) experienced by working-class parents as they cope with the transition to parenthood. A second aim is to examine how multiple dimensions of new parents' lives including social support, marital quality, gender ideology, work conditions and workplace policies predict levels and rates of change in new parents' mental health across the first year of parenthood. Data for this project will come from a longitudinal study of 153 working-class, dual-earner couples who were interviewed multiple times across the first year of parenthood.

Love and work have been identified as two of the most salient aspects of adults' lives. Not surprisingly, it is the rare article on work and family research that does not make reference to the importance of the bi-directional relationships between these two spheres of influence. Despite the acknowledgement of the interconnection of work and family, the empirical findings focus far more on the effects of work on individual and family well-being than on the influences of family on work (Crouter, 1984; Perry-Jenkins, Repetti, & Crouter, 2000; Rogers & May, 2003). Due to a lack of experimental research designs and longitudinal data on work-family interconnections, researchers are rarely able to make definitive statements about the direction of effects between work and family. Nevertheless, policy makers at workplaces and at both the state and federal levels of government continually make important assumptions about directionality in the work-family interface as they debate family leave policies or the Healthy Marriage Initiative proposed by the federal government.

For example, over the past decade much research has examined how conditions of employment, namely flextime, leave benefits, supportive work places, and work complexity, affect workers' and their families' well-being (Hyde, Essex, Clark, & Klein, 2001; O'Driscoll et al., 2003). In contrast, the Healthy Marriage Initiative funded by the federal government provides $1.5 billion—$200 million a year for five years from the federal government, the rest from state matching funds—for programs to promote marriage. One assumption of this legislation is that healthy marriages will lead to more financially stable families, and presumably more stable relationships. So, are we better off creating flexible, supportive, jobs that provide a livable wage so as to enhance the stability and happiness of workers' close relationships, or are we better off enhancing marital relationships and in turn building more financially stable and working families? In an attempt to answer this question, we will review past research as well as introduce some new findings uncovered with our sample of dual-earner, working-class couples.

SPILLOVER FROM WORK TO FAMILY

A large body of literature examines spillover between work and family life in general, and to a lesser extent, work and marriage. One line of research in this area assesses workers' perceptions of both work-to-family spillover and family-to-work spillover. An assumption of this research is that the ways in which work conditions affect family life are mediated through perceptions of work-to-family conflict; and conversely, family affects work life as mediated through perceptions of family-to-work conflict (Frone, 2003; Grzywacz & Butler, 2005). This has been an important line of inquiry in the work-family literature; however, questions arise as to how accurately respondents can assess the effects of these two spheres on one another. Another approach is to examine underlying relationships between separate assessments of work and family life in order to uncover links that the workers may not even recognize.

Direct comparisons between work and family life have emerged from both diary data, documenting daily patterns of influence, as well as longitudinal studies designed to track patterns of influence over broader time frames. For example, diary studies that have focused on variation in work experiences and marital interactions across days have found that work stress is related to subsequent marital conflict (Crouter, Perry-Jenkins, Huston, & Crawford, 1989) and marital withdrawal (Repetti, 1989). Using diary data, Bolger, DeLongis, Kessler, & Wethington (1989) found work conflict on a given day predicted a higher likelihood of subsequent marital conflict for both spouses in a couple. Heller and Watson (2005) examined the lagged and concurrent associations between job and marital satisfaction using a diary study of 76 employed individuals. They found evidence for both job to marriage and marriage to job spillover; however, they did not address gender differences in these relationships.

In a large cross-sectional study of white-collar workers, Hughes, Galinsky and Morris (1992) found that both structural (i.e., hours, flexibility) and psychosocial characteristics (i.e., pressure, enrichment) of work predicted marital quality. Interesting findings from this study point to different work predictors of marital arguments versus marital companionship. Specifically, high work pressure was related to higher reports of marital conflict, but this relationship was mediated through perceptions of work-family interference, such that work pressure predicted more work-family competition, which in turn predicted conflict. In contrast, an enriching job was directly related to more marital companionship, suggesting a positive spillover process.

Matthews, Conger, and Wickrama (1996), in a longitudinal analysis of 337 couples, found that work–related distress predicted more psychological distress, which in turn was associated with more hostility and decreased marital warmth and supportiveness. These researchers did not examine the effects of marriage on work.

SPILLOVER FROM FAMILY TO WORK

More than twenty years ago, Crouter (1984) stated that family-to-work spillover models represented the neglected side of the work-family interface. It appears that, by and large, her observation still holds true. Although a search of the work-family literature over the past decade reveals far more studies linking work to family than family to work, there is evidence to suggest that scholars have begun to pay more attention to family life as it affects work. Moreover, a review of the studies that have examined the effects of family life on work reveals a fairly consistent pattern of significant results. Crouter found that negative spillover from home to work occurred most often for women with young children. In addition, positive spillover focused on the supportive nature of relationships at home and useful skills and attitudes developed at home that could be used at work. Bolger et al. (1989) found that home-to-work stress spillover occurred more often for husbands than wives. Moreover, it was found that the "work-to-home stress contagion occurs for both men and women, although it is less consistent and powerful than the home-to-work contagion found among men" (p. 181). Frone, Yardley, and Markel (1997) found that workers perceived that difficult family circumstances made work conditions more difficult. Barnett, Marshall, Raudenbush, and Brennan (1993), examining work-family spillover models for a sample of full-time employed women and men in dual-earner couples, found evidence of home-to-work and work-to-home effects. Specifically, links between work experiences and psychological distress were moderated by family life such that positive family experiences buffered the effects of job stress. Thus, despite our one-sided focus in much of the empirical research on the work-to-family direction of effects, research examining family-to-work effects has highlighted some consistent and intriguing relationships.

A few studies have focused specifically on the bi-directional relationships between work and marriage. Early work in this area documented gender differences in effects, finding that women experienced more family-to-work spillover than men (Crouter, 1984; MacEwen & Barling, 1994; Voydanoff, 1988). Others have found similar effects of work on family for women and men (Eagle, Miles, Icenogle, 1997; Duxbury, Higgins & Lee, 1994) as well as family on work (Bolger et al., 1989). Rogers and May (2003), using data from a 12-year panel survey of a nationally representative sample of married individuals (not couples), investigated whether the influence flowed primarily from work to marriage or from marriage to work. In addition, they explored whether job and marriage were related in similar ways for men and women. In short, they found that over time marital quality was more influential than job satisfaction. Specifically, increases in marital satisfaction contributed significantly to increases in job satisfaction over time. There was also evidence that increases in marital discord predicted declines in job satisfaction over time. In addition, it was found that these spillover processes operated the same for men and women.

The work and family literature just reviewed may be examined from an ecological perspective (Bronfenbrenner, 1979; 1992); and, in so doing, a number of challenges to our current knowledge base emerge. First, from a developmental perspective, relatively few studies have questioned whether work and family spillover processes function in the same way and with similar magnitude across the life course. For example, would we expect the relationship between work and marriage to function similarly for newly married couples, couples with young children, couples with school-aged children, or empty nest couples? Are there times in the life course when marriage may bear stronger effects than work and vice versa?

Second, there has been a lack of attention to the role of social context as it moderates work-family spillover processes. Macrosystem influences, such as race, ethnicity, religion, and social class, as well as exosystem factors, such as welfare policies and health care, can all affect conditions of employment and marriage. In fact, a symposium on marriage held at the National Council on Family Relations annual conference in 2003 highlighted a consistent theme reiterated by sociologists, historians, and psychologists alike; all pointed to the importance of social structures and inequalities as they serve to support or undermine marriage. These scholars looked beyond the interiors of marital functioning and pointed to economic development, job training, safe neighborhoods, reliable child care, and affordable housing as key factors affecting marital quality and stability (Bradbury & Karney, 2004; Huston & Melz, 2004; Smock, 2004). By extension, we can also ask how these factors affect the nature of the relationship between work and marriage.

The current debate over the Healthy Marriage Initiative highlights the importance of social class issues as they shape experiences of work and marriage. Often in our efforts to understand the charcteristic problems and concerns that face families at different levels of the social strata, namely the poor, the working poor, the working class, the middle class, and upper middle-class families, we oversimplify distinctions among groups. We may inflate differences between social classes and overlook the variability within groups. In the following discussion, we highlight the value of studying the range of experiences within differing "ecological niches," while not overlooking some of the common challenges and opportunities that all experience.

BLUE-COLLAR WORK AND MARRIAGE

Both marriage and work have been explored with attention to the characteristic aspects of the working class. More than 50 years ago, Komarovsky and Philips (1962) wrote their classic book, *Blue-Collar Marriage*, where they highlighted the gendered and patriarchal structure of working-class marriages with their unmistakably segregated marital roles. In the 1970s, Rubin's (1976) book titled *Worlds of Pain* painted a picture of silent despair and unfulfilled dreams for men and women in blue-collar marriages. Similarly, LeMasters's (1976) qualitative research with construction workers and their families presented a picture of husbands' and wives' separate lives, due in large part to the separation of labor with men working outside of the home and women working in the home. It is important to note that in these rather bleak portrayals of married life in the working class, the majority of women in these studies were homemakers. In stark contrast, the statistics on women's employment in the 21st century indicate that the majority of married women at all social class levels are employed, even those with young children.

More than 20 years after writing *Worlds of Pain*, Rubin (1994) updated her story on blue-collar families in her book *Families on the Fault Line*. Although noting significant changes in family roles and structure over the previous two decades, Rubin highlighted familiar themes of work instability, financial stress, and the precarious nature of employment. These stories of financial struggle, lost opportunities, and discouragement leave one feeling that little has changed for low-income families during the past 50 years.

Thus, it is not surprising that as we re-examined these books in light of the data we are currently collecting from working-class families, we were struck by some of the similarities between couples' stories of marriage and work across generations. We were also struck by the range of experiences described by families in our study that are not reflected in past research. To be blunt, we have interviewed many men and women over the past eight years who love their jobs and their spouses. In fact, what stands out dramatically in our data is the range of experiences and stories about marriage and work that emerge in stark contrast to the fairly homogenous experiences described in much of literature on working-class families.

Similar to the images of marriage reflected in previous literature, working-class jobs are often described in negative terms, characterized as boring, monotonous, and mind-numbing. Our data don't deny that some blue-collar workers would characterize their jobs with these same adjectives; yet others view their work as challenging, satisfying, and important. For example, one woman in our study who rated her job among the highest in terms of autonomy, challenge, and organizational support worked in a candle-packing factory. She prided herself on getting the orders right, on sending personal notes to her customers, and meeting deadlines. She also talked about her coworkers as her family. Perhaps the most important observation to be made about our data is the great variability that exists for working-class men and women in perceptions of both work and marriage.

Moreover, even when our participants seem to fit into some stereotypical image of the "working class," they continually challenge us to think beyond the category as we hear their stories. Often, it is only through the qualitative data that we can really see beyond the numbers and stereotypes.

This point was brought home to us in one of the most eye-opening interviews conducted for this study. The story allows a description of what precipitated this cognitive change. One Saturday morning the primary researcher and a graduate student interviewed Jake and Amanda, who were expecting their first baby in about a month. Jake and Amanda both worked at a supermarket chain in a nearby town, Jake in the butcher shop and Amanda in bookkeeping. We drove up to their small ranch located in a subdivision just off a major interstate. Jake was interviewed separately in "his room," as he called it. The most prominent items of decor were a huge Budweiser neon light glowing over framed NASCAR race pictures. On the opposite wall were two sets of antlers and a bear's head. Jake proudly showed off the new bar he had just built and talked about his plans to some day teach his new son to hunt with him. At that point, Jake looked at the interviewer and said, "I am guessing you don't hunt?" Although it was left unspoken, we both knew we were treading into each other's different worlds. The interviewer sat down, pulled out her notebooks, pens, piles of paper and tape recorder, and thought that this was going to be one long interview. As a brief aside, while the interviewer's own working-class background led to her profound interest in blue-collar families, it does not always protect her against stereotyping the experiences of those families. In fact, at times her roots may serve to reify images of the working class. Thus, despite all her best intentions, she was already predicting what Jake would tell about his work, his marriage, and his life because, in the interviewer's mind, he fit into some working-class mold. He knew better.

As the interview began, the interviewer asked Jake about his expectations for the pregnancy and birth. It was at this point that her stereotypes were first challenged. Jake began with the following statement, "Well, to me, pregnancy and all it entails is really just a theory. They tell you what it is like and you have to believe it but you will never really know and there is no proof since I can't ever give birth." Jake then pulled out a diary he had been keeping filled with messages and poetry to his unborn baby as well as his theory of pregnancy. He went on during the interview to talk about his respect and awe of his wife's ability to manage the pregnancy so well. He talked about the importance of couple time even after the baby came to keep the spark alive in their marriage. As the interviewer reflected on his response, she didn't remember any men like Jake in Komarovsky's, Rubin's, or LeMasters's work.

Of course, there was also the other extreme of couples who seemed to live parallel lives; he hung out with his friends, went to work, had his own hobbies, and she had her friends and work and was often far more focused on the baby. We offer these examples to make an important point: there is no "working-class experience." Rather, there are the experiences of working-class couples. Our aim is to understand how these experiences of work and of marriage influence each other as these young couples become first-time parents.

The goal of the current study is to examine the flow of influence between work and marriage within a specific social context and at a specific life cycle stage for families. Data for this study come from a sample of 153 working-class parents experiencing the transition to parenthood for the first time. By controlling for social class in this project, we can look at the variability within working-class families as they juggle the demands of work and family life. Moreover, by focusing on a specific life transition, the transition to parenthood, we can examine the effects of a significant life stressor on couples' ability to maintain both marital and work commitments.

THE WORK AND FAMILY TRANSITIONS PROJECT

Data for this project come from a longitudinal study of 153 working-class, dual-earner couples experiencing the transition to parenthood for the first time. Heterosexual couples in their third trimester of pregnancy were recruited from various prenatal classes at hospitals in the New England area. Criteria for eligibility included the following: (a) both members of the couple were employed full-time (32+ hours per week) prior to the baby's birth, (b) both members of the couple planned to return to full-time work within six months of the baby's birth, (c) both members of the couple were "working-class" (educational level restricted to an associate's degree or less), (d) both members of the couple were expecting their first child, and (e) the couple was either married or cohabiting for at least one year at the time of inclusion in the study.

Both partners participated in four in-home interviews across the transition to parenthood and completed one mail survey. They were interviewed at the following time points: (1) during the couples' third trimester of pregnancy, (2) approximately one month after the baby's birth but before mother had returned to full-time employment, (3) one month after mothers returned to full-time employment (12 weeks postpartum, on average), (4) six months postpartum, and (5) one year after the baby was born. At phases 1, 2, 3 and 5, interviews were conducted separately with both partners in their homes and were between two and three hours long; phase 4 was a mail interview. For the purpose of this study, respondents completed standardized questionnaires that assessed work conditions, job satisfaction, supervisor and coworker support, and marital love and conflict at Time 1, the prenatal interview, and Time 2, the one-year postnatal interview. The following analyses use Time 1 and Time 2 data to examine the direction of effects between work and marriage.

Sample Characteristics

The average age of parents at the first prenatal visit was 28.9 years for fathers (range 18.6 to 41.3) and 27.0 years for mothers (range 17.7 to 40.8). Although

Table 17.1. Descriptive Statistics

	Husbands' Scores		Wives' Scores	
Time 1:	*Mean*	*Standard Deviation*	*Mean*	*Standard Deviation*
Love	7.99	0.70	8.15	0.54
Conflict	3.26	1.03	3.45	1.03
Job Satisfaction	1.66	0.71	1.70	0.73
Supervisor Support	3.82	0.96	3.99	0.94
Supervisor Flexibility	2.32	0.52	2.41	0.47
Coworker Support	3.93	0.63	4.13	0.83
Organizational Support	2.86	0.67	2.86	0.58
Time 2:				
Love	7.85	0.84	7.80	1.04
Conflict	3.39	1.28	3.81	1.29
Job Satisfaction	1.73	0.77	1.78	0.77
Supervisor Support	3.59	0.99	3.90	0.93
Supervisor Flexibility	2.42	0.56	2.47	0.54
Coworker Support	3.71	0.67	3.93	0.82
Organizational Support	2.82	0.57	2.78	0.66

we use the words *husbands* and *wives* to describe the gender of the participants, both married (77.8%) and cohabiting (22.2%) couples were included. Couples had been married for an average of 3.0 years, and this was a first marriage for 90.8% of the men and 97.7% of the women. Cohabiting couples had lived together for an average of 1.6 years. Most participants identified as White (90.2% of men and 94.8% of women).

Whereas only 1.3% of men and 3.3% of women did not complete high school, the highest educational attainment of 31.4% of the men and 19.0% of the women was a high school diploma or GED. About half of all participants (52.3 % of men and 50.3% of women) had some additional type of schooling (e.g., some college courses, cosmetology license, EMT certification) but no associate's degree, whereas 15.0% of men and 27.5% of women had completed an associate's degree; none had college degrees.

Income ranged from $0 to $58,900 for mothers and from $4,000 to $70,000 for fathers. Median incomes for men and women were $31,000 and $22,000 respectively, and the median family income was $54,768. Thus, it is clear that these families are far from poverty; however, it is important to note that if one parent chose to step out of the work force to care for their child, their financial situation would be much more precarious. Fathers worked an average of 45.9 hours per week and mothers worked an average of 36.3 hours. About one-third of couples (34.6%) worked alternating shifts.

MEASURES

Work relationship. In terms of demographic variables, all participants reported on age, income, and years married or cohabiting. In terms of work characteristics, we assessed five key aspects of work: Organizational Support, Supervisor Flexibility, Supervisor Support, Coworker Support, and Job Satisfaction. *Organizational Support* (Lambert & Hopkins, 1995) is a 10-item scale that tapped into individuals' sense that work appreciates their efforts and looks out for their interests. *Supervisor Flexibility* assessed the degree to which respondents perceived their supervisor as allowing scheduling flexibility and other latitude when family needs arose (Greenberger, Goldberg, Hamill, O'Neil, & Payne, 1989). *Supervisor and Coworker Support* (Caplan, Cobb, & French, 1975) were assessed from a 10-item scale in which respondents rated their perceptions of their supervisors' and coworkers' flexibility, reliability, and overall supportiveness. *Job Satisfaction* was measured on a four-point scale with 1 indicating low satisfaction and 4 indicating high satisfaction.

Marital relationship. Braiker and Kelley's (1979) 25-item Personal Relationship Scale was administered to each couple member. The responses gathered prenatally (Time 1) and when the child was one year old (Time 2) were used in these analyses. We used two scales from this measure. The *Love* subscale has 10 items that tap into attitudes and beliefs about the relationship by assessing respondents' feelings of closeness or belonging toward their spouse with questions such as, "To what extent do you have a sense of 'belonging' with your partner?" The *Conflict-Negativity* subscale has 5 items assessing the interpersonal character of the relationship by indicating the amount of conflict and negativity with questions such as, "How often do you and your partner argue with each other?" Responses range from 1, "not at all" or "very infrequently" to 9, "very much" or "very frequently."

Scale reliability alphas for the love items for men and women, respectively, were .73 and .61 at Time 1, and .83 and .89 at Time 2. For the conflict-negativity subscale, alphas were .53 for husbands and .64 for wives at Time 1 and .78 and .76 at Time 2.

RESULTS

Descriptive analyses were run on all of the work and marriage measures. Turning first to marriage, husbands' and wives' reports of love were above average on the scale indicating relatively high levels of love and below average on conflict indicating low levels of conflict. In addition, there was wide variability on both husbands' and wives' reports of love and conflict. There

was even greater variability on the work scales indicating mean levels lean-
ing more to positive assessments of support and satisfaction. Tables of these
data at both phases are available from the authors.

Next we turned to our primary question, namely what is the flow of influence between work and marriage across the first year of parenthood. We used
structural equation modeling to analyze our data as it provided a way of looking at multiple predictors and outcomes in a single model. At a basic level,
our measurement model specified a relationship between two latent constructs: work and marriage. We hypothesized that positive spillover from
work at Time 1 to marriage at Time 2 as well as positive spillover from marriage to work would emerge. Although the past research findings related to
gender are equivocal, we hypothesized that stronger spillover would exist for
women, given the demands of returning to work soon after the baby's birth;
on average mothers took 12 weeks of leave. We chose to fit separate models
for husbands and wives because preliminary analyses pointed to different patterns of the relationship between work and marriage for husbands and wives,
suggesting that work had different effects on men than women.

Our initial model consisted of a single Time 1 work factor and a single
Time 1 marriage factor predicting a Time 2 work factor and a Time 2 marriage factor. To measure marriage we used the two scales in Braiker and
Kelly's (1979) Personal Relationship Scale, which represented stable factors:
love and conflict. The indicators of work consisted of measures of job satisfaction, supervisor support, supervisor flexibility, coworker support, and organizational support.

Our first model was a poor fit to the data, indicating that we had a problem
in the measurement component of the model. In addition, we failed to find
any effect of work on marriage or vice versa for husbands and wives.

We began to wonder if lumping all of these disparate aspects of work and
marriage together in one factor made sense. In fact, an examination of the bi-
variate correlations among work and marriage characteristics revealed that
perceptions of greater coworker support were associated with more negative
marriage ratings for men, while all other supportive aspects of work were
positively related to marriage. In addition, job satisfaction seemed to tap into
a general sense of liking one's job while the other measures tapped into how
supported one felt at work, two different constructs. Theoretically, it made
more sense to remove job satisfaction and create a job support factor. In addition to supervisor support and supervisor flexibility, we added organizational support as an indicator of this factor.

In addition, we re-examined our assumptions about marriage. Past research had found different predictors of marital love and marital conflict in
testing spillover models (Hughes et al., 1992). Thus, we decided to examine

love and conflict as separate factors with single-item indicators in subsequent structural regression models. These structural regression models tested whether new fathers' or mothers' perceptions of job support (as assessed through organizational support, supervisor support, and supervisor flexibility), marital love, and marital conflict in the third trimester of pregnancy predicted perceptions of job support, love, and conflict when the baby was one year old.

We fit a series of structural regression models for mothers looking at the bi-directional relationships between job support and marital love and conflict. Our final model, depicted in Figure 17.1, included both paths within marriage and work and paths between marriage and work. Results indicated that mothers who perceived more job support at Time 1 reported more marital love one year later (γ (standardized coefficient) = .55), while mothers who reported more marital conflict in their third trimester of pregnancy perceived less job support when their child was one year old ($\gamma = -0.24$). Comparing models with and without paths between work and marriage showed that inclusion of the paths between work and marriage significantly improved the fit of the model ($\Delta\chi^2 = 35.927$, df = 2, $p < .001$).

As shown in Figure 17.2, less support was found for the same model when examined for fathers. When we fit the model for fathers, one path emerged at the level of a trend between marriage and work. Specifically, fathers who perceived more marital conflict at Time 1 perceived less job support at Time 2 ($\gamma = -0.17$). Comparing the model with and without this path, however,

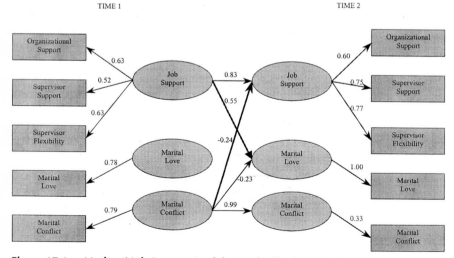

Figure 17.1.   Mothers' Job Support Model (Standardized Solution).

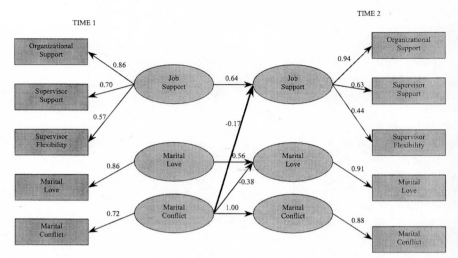

Figure 17.2.   Fathers' Job Support Model (Standardized Solution).

showed that the model with the marriage-to-work path was a better fit only at the level of a trend ($\Delta\chi^2 = 2.728$, df $= 1, p < .10$).

Although we had cut job satisfaction and coworker support from our support models, we reasoned that they could still be important components of the work-marriage interface. Therefore, we conducted path analyses of the relationship between job satisfaction, coworker support, marital love, and marital conflict before the birth of the child and one year after.

Turning first to the results for mothers, we found that mothers who perceived more coworker support in their third trimester of pregnancy perceived more marital love ($\gamma = .14$) and less marital conflict ($\gamma = -.20$) when the child was one year old (see Figure 17.3). Conversely, more marital conflict in the third trimester predicted greater perceptions of coworker support ($\gamma = .19$) when the child was one year old. A comparison of models with and without the work-marriage paths showed that their inclusion resulted in a significantly better fit ($\Delta\chi^2 = 9.449$, df $= 2, p < .01$).

The best-fitting path analysis for fathers showed that higher love before the birth of the child predicted higher job satisfaction one year after birth ($\gamma = .21$) (see Figure 17.4). An examination of the work-to-marriage paths revealed that greater coworker support before the birth predicted less marital love when the child was one year old ($\gamma = -0.15$). Inclusion of these work-marriage paths led to a significantly better model fit ($\Delta\chi^2 = 8.162$, df $= 2$, $p < .05$).

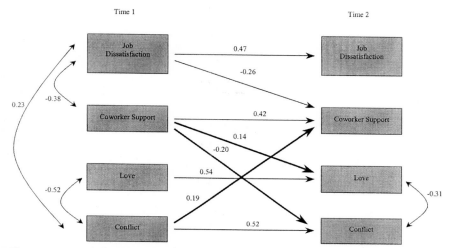

Figure 17.3. Work and Marriage Path Analysis for Mothers (Standardized Solution).

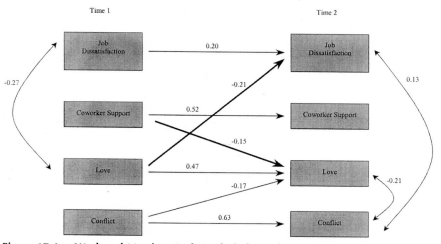

Figure 17.4. Work and Marriage Path Analysis for Fathers (Standardized Solution).

CONCLUSIONS

Our findings highlight bidirectional spillover from both marriage to work and work to marriage. For both husbands and wives more marital conflict before the baby was born predicted lower perceptions of job support one year later. More specifically, higher conflict predicted less supervisor support, less supervisor flexibility, and lower organizational support; although for husbands, this finding was only supported at the level of a trend. These results are consistent with the research of Rogers and May (2003), who found marriage to have stronger effects on work than vice versa. Rogers and May suggest marriage is a more influential domain in individuals' lives than work and thus has a stronger influence on other domains. Especially given that couples in our sample are becoming new parents across the course of the study, it is likely that parenting and spousal roles are more meaningful aspects of one's life than work. In contrast, only one effect of job support on marriage was found and it only emerged for women. Job support prior to the baby's birth predicted more marital love one year later. Job support, especially as new mothers are negotiating parenthood, marriage, and work roles, may be especially important for women who tend to take on more responsibility for parenting than men. A supportive workplace may not only make life easier to manage for new mothers but also contribute to their overall well-being which, in turn, enhances their marriages.

Gender differences were even more apparent, in our analyses of the interplay between coworker support and marriage. For women, more coworker support prior to the baby's birth predicted more love and less conflict one year later. Moreover, higher conflict reported by mothers prenatally predicted more coworker support when their child was one year. Clearly, supportive coworkers not only enhance mothers' perceptions of their marriage but may also serve as supports when marriages are conflictual.

In direct contrast, higher levels of coworker support for fathers prior to the baby's birth predicted less marital love one year later. The reason why coworker support negatively affects marriage for men may be related to the nature of coworker friendships that extend beyond the workplace. In other analyses, we have found that husbands who report high levels of leisure with friends have wives who report higher levels of marital conflict (Claxton & Perry-Jenkins, 2008). Especially during the transition to parenthood, mothers may have higher expectations for father involvement and expect fathers to pull back from some leisure activities away from home. For example, one father in our study spent much of his free time attending car racing events with his buddies from work. Once the baby was born his wife fully expected that his attention would shift towards home and the baby; however, this was not the case and it became a continual source of distress for this couple.

Finally, results also revealed that fathers' reports of more love prior to the baby's birth predicted higher job satisfaction one year later. Again, this finding is consistent with those of Rogers and May (2003), indicating positive spillover from home to work.

In returning to the question posed at the outset of this paper, we asked: *are we better off creating flexible, supportive jobs that provide a livable wage so as to enhance the stability and happiness of workers' close relationships, or are we better off enhancing marital relationships and in turn building more financially stable and working families?* From our data it appears that both endeavors are important. Work and marriage are likely to influence each other over time with varying degrees of saliency depending on life stage and life circumstances. Our study focused on a select group of families, namely the working class, experiencing a significant life transition of becoming new parents. At this time point, although we found mutual levels of influence between work and marriage, the strongest path was between job support and mothers' assessment of marriage. Job support during this life-changing experience may be critical for mothers' ability to cope and manage their marital relationship. Future work would benefit from attention to how the flow of work to family life and family life to work changes in intensity and direction as workers and their families travel through the life course.

NOTE

Maureen Perry-Jenkins, Ph.D., is a professor of psychology (mpj@psych.umass.edu); Amy Claxton is a graduate student (email: amyclaxton@psych.umass.edu); JuliAnna Smith is a research associate; and Mark Manning is a graduate student (email: mmanning@psych.umass.edu), all in the Department of Psychology, Tobin Hall, University of Massachusetts Amherst, Amherst, MA 01003. This research is supported by grants from the National Institute of Mental Health to Maureen Perry-Jenkins (FIRST Award, R29-MH56777; R01-MH56777). We gratefully acknowledge Abbie Goldberg, Courtney Pierce, Elizabeth Turner, Karen Meteyer, and Jade Logan for their assistance on this project. Correspondence for this article should be addressed to Maureen Perry-Jenkins, 608 Tobin Hall, University of Massachusetts, Amherst, MA 01003 Phone: (413) 545-0258 email: mpj@psych.umass.edu

REFERENCES

Barnett, R. C., Marshall, N. L., Raudenbush, S. W., & Brennan, R. T. (1993). Gender and the relationship between job experiences and psychological distress: A study of dual-earner couples. *Journal of Personality and Social Psychology, 64(5)*, 794–806.

Bolger, N., DeLongis, A., Kessler, R. C., & Wethington, E. (1989). The contagion of stress across multiple roles. *Journal of Marriage and the Family, 51*, 175–183.

Bradbury, T. N., & Karney, B. R. (2004). Understanding and altering the longitudinal course of marriage. *Journal of Marriage and Family, 66(4)*, 862–879.

Braiker, H. B., & Kelley, H. H. (1979). Conflict in the development of close relationships. In R. L. Burgess & T. L. Huston (Eds.), *Social change in developing relationships* (pp. 15–168). New York: Academic Press.

Bronfenbrenner, U. (1979). Contexts of child rearing: Problems and prospects. *American Psychologist, 34*(10), 844–850.

Bronfenbrenner, U. (1992). Ecological systems theory. In R. Vasta (Ed.), *Six theories of child development: Revised formulations and current issues* (pp. 187–249). Philadelphia: Jessica Kingsley Publishers.

Caplan, R. D., Cobb, S., & French, J. R. (1975). *Relationships of cessation of smoking with job stress, personality, and social support.* Journal of Applied Psychology, *60(2), 211–19.*

Claxton, A., & Perry-Jenkins, M. (2008). No fun anymore: Leisure and marital quality across the transition to parenthood. *Journal of Marriage and Family, 70*, 28–43.

Crouter, A. C. (1984). Spillover from family to work: The neglected side of the work-family interface. *Human Relations, 37*, 425–442.

Crouter, A. C., Perry-Jenkins, M., Huston, T. L., & Crawford, D. W. (1989). The influence of work induced psychological states on behavior at home. *Basic and Applied Social Psychology, 10,* 273–292.

Duxbury, L. E., Higgins, C., & Lee, C. (1994). Work-family conflict: A comparison by gender, family type, and perceived control. *Journal of Family Issues, 15,* 449–466.

Eagle, B. W., Miles, E. W., & Icenogle, M. L. (1997). Interrole conflicts and the permeability of work and family domains: Are there gender differences? *Journal of Vocational Behavior, 50,* 168–184.

Frone, M. R. (2003). Work-family balance. In J. C. Quick & L. E. Tetrick (Eds.), *Handbook of occupational health psychology* (pp. 143–162). Washington, DC: American Psychological Association.

Frone, M. R., Yardley, J. K., & Markel, K. S. (1997). Developing and testing an integrative model of the work-family interface. *Journal of Vocational Behavior, 50,* 145–167.

Greenberger, E., Goldberg, W. A., Hamill, S., O'Neil, R., & Payne, C. K. (1989). Contributions of a supportive work environment to parents' well-being and orientation to work. *American Journal of Community Psychology, 17*, 755–783.

Grzywacz, J. G., & Butler, A. B. (2005). The impact of job characteristics on work-to-family facilitation: Testing a theory and distinguishing a construct. *Journal of Occupational Health, 10*(2), 97–109.

Heller, D., & Watson, D. (2005). The dynamic spillover of satisfaction between work and marriage: The role of time and mood. *Journal of Applied Psychology, 90*(6), 1273–1279.

Hughes, D., Galinsky, E., & Morris, A. (1992). The effects of job characteristics on marital quality: Specifying linking mechanisms. *Journal of Marriage and the Family, 54,* 31–42.

Huston, T. L., & Melz, H. (2004). The case for (promoting) marriage: The devil is in the details. *Journal of Marriage and Family, 66*(4), 943–958.

Hyde, J. S., Essex, M. J., Clark, R., & Klein, M. H. (2001). Maternity leave, women's employment, and marital incompatibility. *Journal of Family Psychology, 15*(3), 476–491.

Komarovsky, M., & Philips, J. H. (1962). *Blue-collar marriage*. New Haven, CT: Yale University Press.

Lambert, S. J., & Hopkins, K. (1995). Occupational conditions and workers' sense of community: Variations by gender and race. *American Journal of Community Psychology, 25*, 151–179.

LeMasters, E. E., (1976). *Blue-collar aristocrats: Life styles at a working-class tavern*. Madison, WI: University of Wisconsin Press.

MacEwen, K. E., & Barling, J. (1994). Daily consequences of work interference with family and family interference with work. *Work & Stress, 8*, 244–254.

Matthews, L. S., Conger, R. D., & Wickrama, K. A. S. (1996). Work-family conflict and marital quality: Mediating processes. *Social Psychology Quarterly, 59*, 62–79.

O'Driscoll, M. P., Poelmans, S., Spector, P. E., Kalliath, T., Allen, T. D., Cooper, C. L., & Sanchez, J. I. (2003). Family-responsive interventions, perceived organizational and supervisor support, work-family conflict, and psychological strain. *International Journal of Stress Management, 10*(4), 326–344.

Perry-Jenkins, M., Repetti, R., & Crouter, A. C. (2000). Work and family in the 1990s. *Journal of Marriage and the Family, 62*, 981–998.

Repetti, R. L. (1989). Effects of daily workload on subsequent behavior during marital interaction: The roles of social withdrawal and spouse support. *Journal of Personality and Social Psychology, 57*, 651–659.

Rogers, S. J., & May, D. C. (2003). Spillover between marital quality and job satisfaction: Long-term patterns and gender differences. *Journal of Marriage and the Family, 85*, 482–495.

Rubin, L. B. (1976). *Worlds of pain: Life in the working-class family*. New York: HarperCollins.

Rubin, L. B. (1994). *Families on the fault line*. New York: HarperCollins.

Smock, P. J. (2004). The wax and wane of marriage: Prospects for marriage in the 21st century. *Journal of Marriage and Family, 66*(4), 966–973.

Voydanoff, P. (1988). Work role characteristics, family structure demands, and work/family conflict. *Journal of Marriage & the Family, 50*(3), 749–761.

Chapter Eighteen

The Interaction between Marital Relationships and Retirement

by Richard B. Miller and Jeremy B. Yorgason

ABSTRACT

In recent decades, retirement has become an institutionalized part of culture in developed countries and an expected phase of adulthood. Since 1950, the proportion of men over the age of 65 in the U.S. workforce has declined from 50% to 18% (Rix, 2004), with many of those still in the workforce having retired from their primary career and currently engaged in part-time or secondary full-time jobs. Moreover, the age of retirement has declined substantially in recent decades. In 1950, the median age of male and female retirees in the United States was 67 years old, while 50 years later, at the beginning of the 21st century, it was 62 years old (Gendell, 2001). This decrease in the age of retirement, combined with increased longevity of older adults, has created a substantial period of retirement. The average expected years of retirement for men has increased 50%, from 12 to 18 years since 1950, while it has increased 62% for women, from 14 to 22 years (Gendell, 2001). Consequently, older adults can expect to spend a considerable portion of their adulthood in retirement.

Retirement as we now know it is basically a post–World War II phenomenon. Before then, leaving the workforce was usually involuntary, with poor health or unemployment being the main reasons for not working in later life (Hardy, 2002), and the status of being retired was similar to being unemployed or disabled and unable to work. Widespread unemployment that disproportionately affected older workers led to the passage of the Social Security Act of 1935, which created financial payments to unemployed older adults. By 1960, 80% of workers were covered by Social Security. In addition, the Revenue Act of 1942 encouraged companies to provide pensions to their employees, and the passage of Medicare in the 1960s provided health insurance for older adults. The availability of retirement income through Social Security and pensions, along with health insurance through Medicare, made it possible for older adults to retire without becoming dependent upon family members or others for support (Hardy, 2002). Financial security, combined with improved health and a new emphasis on leisure and travel in later life, transformed retirement from an unwelcome state of unemployment to a positive stage of life filled with freedom and leisure activities.

The history of retirement is really a story of men's exit from the workforce. However, demographic changes during the latter part of the 20th century have seen the majority of middle-aged women in the workforce and subsequently retiring (Szinovacz & Ekerdt, 1996). The percentage of women between the ages of 55 and 64 in the workforce increased from 28% in 1950 to 55% in 2000. Currently, 63% of women between the ages of 55 and 59 are in the labor force (U.S. Department of Labor, 2005). Consequently, with nearly as many women as men approaching retirement, issues of retirement have become relevant to women, as well.

Research indicates that retirement is a positive experience for most people, with a high percentage of retired workers reporting satisfaction with retirement. Moreover, being retired, as opposed to still being in the labor force, is related to higher levels of happiness and enjoyment, as well as lower levels of anxiety and psychological distress (Drentea, 2002; Vaillant, DiRago, & Mukamal, 2006).

Marriage interacts with retirement in important ways. With both spouses typically in the labor force, there are marital dynamics that influence when each will retire, as well as their levels of retirement satisfaction. Moreover, it is important to examine the influence that retirement has on marital relationships. With the substantial changes in daily routine and lifestyles during the transition to retirement, it is likely that couples must make significant adjustments in their relationships. This chapter addresses two primary questions: First, how does marriage influence the timing of retirement and retirement satisfaction, and second, how does retirement influence marital relationships?

MARITAL INFLUENCES ON RETIREMENT

Family Structure and Retirement

Family structures and relationship histories leading up to retirement have diversified greatly during the last century. These varying relationship histories and family structures are likely to influence the timing of and satisfaction following retirement. In addition to the growing diversity of family structures, there is an acknowledgement of within-group differences (Demo, Aquilino, & Fine, 2005). A growing body of research examining spousal relationships around retirement has contributed to a better understanding of differences within the retirement of married couples. Gender differences are particularly salient, as illustrated in workforce participation and histories, family obligations, and timing of retirement. Interacting together, these factors can influence individual and couple well-being around retirement.

Gender within marriage. Gender plays a paramount role in couples' retirement decision-making processes. Being a husband or wife often influences labor force participation (current and past patterns), family obligations, and retirement timing, each of which can be associated with relationship satisfaction for couples. These gender-related retirement trends often occur within the context of couple relationships, as most individuals who retire are married (Mock & Cornelius, 2007; Szinovacz, 1996).

In general, retirement for husbands has been described as following an institutionalized pattern, being influenced by such factors as age, education, occupation, health, and pension status (Blau & Gilleskie, 2006; Pienta & Hayward, 2002; Pienta, 2003; Szinovacz & DeViney, 1999). In other words, having worked throughout their lives, husbands expect to retire in their early or mid 60s, depending on whether their occupation status provides the availability of a retirement pension.

In contrast, retirement timing for wives generally involves the complex interactions of spousal and familial factors, in addition to things such as age, social and economic status, and health (Pienta, 2003). Some have suggested that women spend approximately 12 years out of the workforce throughout their lives to provide family caregiving (Kutza, 2005). Women also are more than twice as likely to be employed part-time, rather than full-time (U.S. Department of Labor, 2003). For those women who maintain continued workforce participation during child- rearing years, early retirement is more common (especially if the husband has retired; Henretta, O'Rand, & Chan, 1993). Thus, the intermittent work patterns of women in and outside of the home influence decisions around retirement, with women often working beyond the retirement of their husbands in order to qualify for needed or wanted benefits.

Marital status can also influence retirement decision making differently for men and women. Workforce participation patterns show that married men are more likely to be working than those who are single, but that single women (divorced, widowed, single–never married) are more likely than their married counterparts to work and often delay retirement to meet financial needs (Fethke, 1989; Ogg & Renaut, 2007; Szinovacz & Ekerdt, 1996). Research findings that further elaborate on the influence of marital status suggest that unmarried women are less likely to report retirement forced by their circumstances, except in the case where a marriage recently ended, wherein married women reported higher perceptions of forced retirement (Szinovacz & Davey, 2005). In addition, Szinovacz and DeViney (1999) found that widows were more likely to identify themselves as either being fully retired or not retired (as opposed to partially retired), that women who remarried after widowhood more often reported being fully retired as opposed to not retired, and that never-married individuals were more likely to report not being retired before receiving benefits. As these findings indicate, the complexity of retirement decision making is compounded by interactions between gender, workforce participation, and marital histories.

Spousal health. Around retirement age, a number of family factors influence wives' retirement decisions, including spousal health limitations, caring for children and parents, and family financial need (Szinovacz & DeViney, 2000; Szinovacz, DeViney, & Davey, 2001). The health of a spouse is a particularly relevant marital variable related to retirement timing. Research examining the relationship between spousal health and retirement status has produced inconsistent results (Honig, 1996; Szinovacz & DeViney, 2000; Talaga & Beehr, 1995). Szinovacz and DeViney (2000) found that, although husbands were at greater risk for retirement when their wives had poor health, wives' retirement was not related to husbands' health. In contrast, a number of studies have found that wives were more likely to retire when their husbands had poor health or were disabled (Detinger & Clarkberg, 2002; Pienta & Hayward, 2002). These inconsistent findings may represent competing health-related demands, such as the need for caregiving (predictive of early retirement) and the need for medical insurance and financial support to pay for medical care (predictive of prolonged workforce involvement). More research is needed to better understand the mechanisms associated with earlier versus later retirement when spousal health is poor.

Marital quality. Only two studies were found that explored links between marital quality and retirement decision making. Although structural family qualities may seem more intuitively linked to retirement decision making, Szinovacz and DeViney (2000) found that higher marital quality was associated with earlier retirement for husbands and wives, even after controlling for obvious influences, such as years in the workforce. Offering an interpretation, the researchers hypothesized that happily married couples might seek retirement in order to spend more time together, while less happily married couples may prefer to remain in the workforce where they can avoid unpleasant marital interactions. In another study, Mock and Cornelius (2007) reported that relationship satisfaction among heterosexual married, heterosexual cohabiting, and lesbian couples was predictive of planning for retirement. More research is need in this area to understand the underlying motivations for more satisfied couples to plan for and retire early.

Cultural influences. The majority of studies examining marital relationships and retirement do not explore racial differences. Most studies either employ data that includes only Caucasian participants, or race is "controlled" in analyses. The few exceptions either included or exclusively examined retirement experiences of African American couples. Research by Szinovacz and colleagues (2001) suggested that retirement decisions of African American individuals were based on a complex interaction of "care obligations, financial obligations, and financial contributions by resident kin" (p. S20). In addition, cultural norms apparently influence definitions of retirement, with disabled status, lifetime work continuity, and financial security all being associated with whether or not older African Americans consider themselves retired (Gibson, 1991, 1987; Szinovacz & DeViney, 1999). Further work is needed in this area to better understand cultural influences in relation to retirement experiences.

Pre-retirement Marital Relationships and Retirement Adjustment

In contrast to family structure, aspects of couple relationships seem to be more naturally associated with adjustment during and following the retirement process. Gender roles carried out by husbands and wives, and the balance of power or influence within those roles, seem linked to adjustment during retirement. Also, pre-retirement marital qualities are associated with post-retirement satisfaction.

Spousal influence. Studies suggest that spouses have some influence in the decision of when a person retires (Moen, Juang, Plassmann, & Dentinger, 2006; Smith & Moen, 1998; Szinovacz & DeViney, 1999). Although spouses influence each others' retirement decisions, Smith and Moen (2004) reported a moderating effect of gender in this relationship. Specifically, they found greater retirement satisfaction for husbands when their wives were influential in the decision to retire. In stark contrast, lower retirement satisfaction was reported by wives whose husbands were influential in their decision to retire. One interpretation of these findings is that wives' influence is seen by husbands as supportive, while husbands' influence is perceived by wives as coercive or intrusive. In a later study, Moen and colleagues (2006) found that cohort moderated the link between husbands' and wives' planning for retirement. Specifically, they indicated that in their overall sample husbands' planning predicted wives' planning. However, in smaller groups of their sample, planning had different effects. For example, wives' planning predicted husbands' planning (among couples without children at home, and among the leading-edge baby boomers), and planning among spouses was reciprocal (among couples with children at home).

Additional studies shed further light on gender role power balances. Szinovacz and Davey (2005) reported that lower retirement satisfaction was linked to situations where husbands or wives lost power or authority in the marital relationship upon their own or their spouses' retirement. For example, retirement satisfaction was lower for husbands when they historically had greater influence in decision making, but that influence was diminished when they retired and their wives stayed in the workforce. The same was true for wives that retired and lost power in the relationship, while their husbands stayed in the workforce. The complex interaction between retirement timing and power within relationships is further illustrated by findings from a study of early/forced retirement and depression. Szinovacz and Davey (2004) indicated that higher levels of depression were reported by women who were forced to retire early and whose husbands had health care needs (health care needs were defined as being unable to perform activities of daily living). This finding was not replicated for husbands that were forced to retire early and whose wives had health care needs. These trends support typical gender-related motivations for leaving the workforce (Kutza, 2005). In summary, these findings suggest that gender-related power and influence, coupled with retirement timing, are linked with retirement satisfaction.

Marital quality. Within a family stress and adaptation framework (McCubbin & Patterson, 1982), marital quality can be viewed as a resource or buffer during retirement transitions. Although few studies have examined this relationship directly, one longitudinal study suggested that husbands who interacted with their wives in relaxed and positive ways prior to retirement reported greater retirement satisfaction (Kupperbusch, Levenson, & Ebling, 2003). Further research linking marital and retirement quality is needed to better understand the extent and power of the buffering effects of marital quality during the retirement transition.

THE EFFECT OF RETIREMENT ON MARITAL QUALITY

The transition to retirement represents a significant alteration in the lives of couples. Whether couples have a dual-career arrangement or only one spouse has worked over the years, unless it is a family business, the couple has spent a substantial part of each day apart from each other. A considerable daily part of each working spouse's time and energy has been spent pursuing a career. However, retirement changes this routine that has been part of their lives for decades. Suddenly placed in a new lifestyle where they no longer need to go away for the day (or evening) to work, they must adjust to a new routine of spending most of their time together.

In addition to spending more time together, retired couples experience a change in lifestyle focus. Whereas their preretirement years had included a large focus on their careers and the stresses, commitments, and concerns that accompany them, retirement brings a release from these career strains. Even if a retired person returns to the workforce as a paid worker, these part-time jobs, or secondary full-time jobs, do not carry the same time and emotional commitment that accompany careers. Instead, the attention of retired couples often turns to leisure activities, such as recreation and travel (Henry, Miller, & Giarrusso, 2005). Thus, a major focus of retired couples changes from work and careers to leisure activities.

How do these significant changes in routine and lifestyle affect the quality of couples' relationships? Although early research suggested that retirement creates a relationship crisis for many couples, more recent studies that use more rigorous research methodologies provide substantial evidence that marital relationships during the pre- and post-retirement years are best characterized by continuity (Szinovacz, 1996). In other words, the bulk of the research indicates that retirement does not seem to have a negative or a positive effect on most couples. However, there are some contextual issues, such as the timing of retirement, that influence the impact of retirement on marital quality.

Continuity of Marital Quality

There is substantial evidence that retirement, per se, does not have a significant effect on the marital quality of retired couples. Cross-sectional studies that compare marital quality between working and retired couples have found few, if any differences in mean levels of marital quality between the two groups (Atchley, 1992; Lee & Shehan, 1989; Szinovacz, 1996). After comparing working and retired couples from the Normative Aging Study, Ekerdt and Vinick concluded that "retirement appears . . . as neither boon or bane for the marital relationship" (1991, p. 378). Using a measure of marital complaints, they found that working and retired couples generally have similar complaints about their spouses' behavior.

Longitudinal research has found similar results. Longitudinal studies are powerful assessments of the effect of retirement on marital quality because they can track the effect of change in work status on change in subsequent marital quality. Szinovacz and Schaffer concluded, after analyzing longitudinal data from the National Study of Families and Households, that "for most marriages, retirement has little lasting impact on the relationship" (2000, p.

386). Another longitudinal study (Myers & Booth, 1996) found that the transition to retirement between two points of data collection did not have a significant effect on change in either positive or negative marital quality. Another study collected data on married adults over 17 years. The authors found that retirement did not have a significant effect on the trajectory of marital happiness (Van Laningham, Johnson, & Amato, 2001).

One reason for the general nonsignificance of retirement for marital quality in longitudinal research is the high level of stability in marital quality from one data collection point to the next. For example, in the study by Myers and Booth (1996), the correlation between Time-1 marital quality and Time-2 marital quality was .64 and .66 for positive and negative marital quality, respectively, which indicates substantial stability in marital quality scores over time. Results from another longitudinal study indicated that the correlation of preretirement marital quality and postretirement marital quality was .75 (Fitzpatrick & Vinick, 2003). Expanding on earlier research, Davey and Szinovacz (2004) examined the stability of marital quality scores over time using Structural Equation Modeling. They found "considerable continuity in marital relations over the retirement transition" (2004, p. 458).

There is some evidence that retirement reinforces the quality of the marital relationship (Davey & Szinovacz, 2004; Myers & Booth, 1996). Couples generally spend more time together after retirement, which intensifies their interaction. Consequently, positive interactions will increase after retirement, which will increase positive sentiment in the relationship; conversely, more frequent negative interaction will increase the level of negativity in the relationship. Hence, couples who had high quality relationships before retirement will likely have a modest increase in their marital quality, while couples who were unhappy in their relationships before retirement will probably become less happy after retirement.

Most couples, then, experience considerable continuity in the quality of their marriages from their years of being in the workforce to their retirement years. These findings are consistent with other research on mid- and later-life couples that indicate that marital relationships are relatively stable in the second half of life (Johnson, Amoloza, & Booth, 1992; Miller, 2000). For example, VanLaningham and colleagues (2001) found in their analysis of 17 years of data a modest decline in marital happiness in the early years of marriage, followed by few changes in mid- and later life. After finding few differences between marital relations at mid- and later life in her study, Ade-Ridder (1985, p. 233) concluded that "patterns established during the middle years are likely to persist in the later years."

After being married for many years, it is not surprising that patterns of interaction and subjective appraisal of the relationship that couples establish early in their relationships do not alter substantially over decades of marriage. From a theoretical perspective, the concept of homeostasis from family systems theory suggests that relationships are characterized by considerable continuity (Miller, 2000; Miller, Yorgason, Sandberg, & White, 2003). During the establishment of a new family system, patterns of interaction and subjective appraisals of the relationship are developed. Once these patterns are organized, the system develops a sense of equilibrium, or homeostasis (Broderick & Smith, 1979). Thereafter, even when stresses and new circumstances are introduced into the system, the basic patterns of interaction and appraisal remain remarkably unyielding to substantial change. The introduction of significant transitions, such as retirement, may create some fluctuation in the system, but after a period of adjustment, the system will generally return back to its homeostatic patterns.

While the process of retirement introduces substantial change into the marital system as the lifestyle and daily routine are altered significantly, the basic, core dynamics of the relationship remain relatively unchanged. The patterns of communication, including long-held habits of listening and speaking styles, will probably remain unchanged. Styles of managing relationship conflict that have been honed for decades will also remain unchanged. Patterns and styles of expressing affection and appreciation, as well as disappointment and anger, will remain unchanged. All of these patterns of interacting are governed by rules of interaction that have been established in the early years of marriage. Consequently, it is reasonable to understand why there is relative stability and continuity in marital quality in later life, with major transitions having minimal impact on the marital interaction and subjective appraisals of relationship satisfaction.

Adjustment to Retirement

Although there is general continuity in marital quality through the retirement years, there is some evidence that the transition to retirement is associated with a temporary, modest decrease in the quality of the relationship. Whereas other longitudinal studies have looked at the effect of the transition to retirement over a 3- to 5-year interval, Moen, Kim, and Hofmeister (2001) used longitudinal data that had only a 2-year span. They found that those couples that retired between the two waves of data collection experienced an increase in marital conflict and a decrease in marital satisfaction. However, those who had been continuously retired (retired before the first wave of data collection) experienced no changes in marital quality. Consequently, the state of being retired is not related to changes in marital quality, but the transition to retirement is associated with a temporary decrease in marital quality. These findings suggest that once the couple has made the adjustment to their new routine and lifestyle that is associated with retirement, their marital quality returns to preretirement levels.

Wives of newly retired husbands often struggle with the "husband underfoot syndrome" (Szinovacz & Schaffer, 2000, p. 369). Several researchers have found that some wives become annoyed with their newly retired husbands' impingement on their household domain, getting in their way as they try to perform their household tasks (Hill & Dorfman, 1982; Keating & Cole, 1980, Szinovacz & Ekerdt, 1996; Ekerdt & Vinick, 1991). This annoyance was usually minor and subsided over time. Interestingly, it was typically resolved by wives getting used to the situation, rather than the couple negotiating new rules about personal space and privacy (Vinick & Ekerdt, 1991).

The Timing of Retirement

An important exception to the general finding that marital quality is not influenced by retirement is consistent evidence that marital quality suffers when the husband is retired while the wife is still working (Davey & Szinovacz, 2004; Ekerdt & Vinick, 1991; Lee & Shehan, 1989). The pattern of a retired husband and a wife still in the labor force creates status incongruence between husbands and wives (Moen et al., 2001) and is inconsistent with traditional gender roles. Myers and Booth (1996) found that role reversals during the transition to retirement are associated with lower marital quality, and Szinovacz (1996) reported that the negative effect of nonsynchronous retirement on marital quality is most pronounced among couples who espouse traditional gender roles.

Household Labor

One factor that plays a role in the adjustment of couples to retirement is the division of household labor. Research indicates that the inequitable division of household labor in retirement is related to decreased marital quality, especially among wives (Myers & Booth, 1996; Szinovacz & Ekerdt, 1996). There are a number of possible reasons for the association between husband's postretirement housework and wives' marital quality. The results of one study indicated that the division of household labor affected wives' marital quality because greater help from husbands with housework led wives to perceive that their husbands provided more emotional and instrumental support (Piña & Bengtson, 1993). However, this was true only among wives who had egalitarian beliefs about marital roles. Findings from another study suggested that perceived fairness, rather than the actual of number of hours that husbands spent performing household labor, was a significant predictor of marital quality among older wives, but not husbands (Ward, 1993). A third study found that husbands' attitudes toward division of household labor, not the amount of housework that they performed, were related to wives' marital quality (Szinovacz, 1986).

Retirement does, indeed, have an impact on household labor. Following retirement, both husbands and wives spend more time doing housework (Szinovacz, 2000; Szinovacz & Harpster, 1994). This increase includes both traditionally female and traditionally male household tasks. Husbands spend the most time doing housework, including traditionally female tasks, when their wives are still in the labor force. However, although the working wives still do more housework than retired husbands, the discrepancy is less than when they are both working or both retired. When working wives retire, though, the amount of traditionally female housework that husbands perform decreases.

DIRECTIONS FOR FUTURE RESEARCH

Recent research has considerably advanced our understanding of the interaction between retirement and marital relationships. Although certain trends have been uncovered, several issues warrant further study. The examination of complex interactions between and among retirement-related relationship structures, processes, and qualities can be framed within a life-course perspective (Elder, 1995; also see Smith & Moen, 1998). Within this framework appear several areas of future research, providing policy makers, educators, and practitioners with more complete information regarding retiring families. Our suggestions fit within two categories: marital relations and societal trends.

Marital Relations

Research has examined the links between family structure and retirement decision making, between family structure and retirement adjustment, and between family relationship quality and retirement adjustment. Interestingly, few have explored links between family relationship quality and retirement decision making. Although not previously explored, there may be subtle reasons why relationship quality could be related to decisions that seem more intuitively associated with structural and institutionalized influences. For example, do spouses in less satisfied relationships find refuge at work, potentially leading to later retirement? Might spouses hang on to workforce involvement in order to maintain power within the couple relationship? Alternatively, might spouses who have spent a great deal of time in the work-place, at the expense of family relationship quality, retire early in an effort to spend more time with family? These and other questions related to relation-ship quality merit exploration.

In addition, research on postretirement couples needs to examine the influ-ence of leisure activities on marital quality. When couples retire, they typi-cally engage in more leisure activities, such as golf and traveling. Many also participate in volunteer activities, where they provide service to others. Re-search suggests that leisure activities are a major source of disagreements among couples after retirement (Henry et al., 2005). Similar to the writing of Szinovacz (2000) regarding the role of metarules that couples develop to gov-ern their division of household labor, it is important to understand the metarules that couples develop about leisure activities. With leisure activities becoming more salient after retirement, it is important for researchers to study how couples conform to and violate these metarules of leisure activities. In so doing, they will be able to better understand how leisure activities influence postretirement marital quality.

Societal Trends

A number of changes at the societal level have and will likely continue to in-fluence marital relations around retirement. First, as family structures are transforming and diversifying, research will need to accommodate the ac-companying complexity of retirement experiences. One growing trend in U.S. society is the increase in custodial grandparent households (Hayslip & Kaminski, 2005). Retirement patterns among this group are relatively unex-plored. Trends related to custodial grandparents become relevant as compet-ing financial pressures and time demands influence workforce participation.

Second, it is important for future research to explore postretirement labor force activities among couples. The transition to retirement is becoming "blurred or fuzzy" (Moen et al., 2001, p. 68), with retirees increasingly work-ing part-time jobs or secondary full-time jobs. Thus, the exit from the work-force is becoming less often a single event and more often a phased process that can take years to complete (Hardy, 2002). Little research has addressed the influence of going back to work after officially retiring from one's pri-mary career. One study examined the impact of postretirement employment on marital quality, with results stratified by gender. Wives who worked after retirement reported higher levels of marital quality than retired wives, while re-employed husbands reported lower marital quality (Moen et al., 2001). More research is needed to better understand the influence of postretirement employment on marital quality.

Third, the interplay between family and life-course experiences around retirement needs to be further explored, with a specific focus on cultural meanings and attitudes in various racial and ethnic groups. This focus will be increasingly important as older minority adult populations are anticipated to increase in the coming years, while Caucasian percentages are anticipated to decrease (Federal Interagency Forum on Aging-related Statistics, 2004). Furthermore, minority groups are more likely to be employed in work that does not allow them to qualify for Social Security benefits or pension plans, and they may be forced into early retirement more often than Caucasian persons due to inadequate job opportunities and greater health problems in later life (Kutza, 2005). As an important step towards closing the gap in racial disparities in later life, future research needs to address family-related retirement influences in various minority groups.

Fourth, the approaching retirement of the baby boom generation signals probable changes in the timing of retirement and its effect on marital quality. Research that has been done on marriage and retirement has been based on couples who came of age during World War II and the Korean War, representing couples who typically had traditional beliefs about marital roles. The baby boomers represent a very different generation. Female baby boomers are generally more highly educated, more likely to have professional careers, and more likely to have egalitarian beliefs about marital roles (Henretta et al., 1993; U.S. Department of Labor). Men of this generation are also more likely to have egalitarian beliefs about marital roles. Consequently, the research showing that husband retired/wife working patterns have a negative influence on marital quality (Szinovacz & Ekerdt, 1996) may become obsolete as the baby boomers begin to retire. Szinovacz's research (1996) shows that this pattern of retirement has a negative influence on marital quality, primarily among couples who have traditional beliefs about marital roles. As the norms of gender roles change in future generations, the effect of the husband retired/wife working pattern on marital quality may be different. It is also possible that the issue of division of household labor during retirement will become more pronounced. With this issue being more salient to women who espouse egalitarian marital roles (Piña & Bengtson, 2003), perceived lack of support and inequity may well play a larger role in the marital quality of wives in the future.

In conclusion, the availability of large, longitudinal datasets has enabled researchers to provide more reliable and valid inferences about retirement and marital quality. The findings of these studies are providing a clearer picture of the influence of marital relationships on the timing of and adjustment to retirement. For example, the negative impact of the pattern of a retired husband and a working wife on marital quality is becoming a robust finding, and the role of perceived equity in household labor on wives' postretirement marital quality is becoming increasingly clear. In addition, studies provide significant evidence of the stability of marital relationships in later life, with retirement generally having a minimal long-term impact on marital relationships. In contrast to this stability, changes at the societal level continue to present challenges to couples around retirement. Some of these macro-influences include the retirement of members of the baby boomer cohort, fluidity of expected age at retirement and how retired persons spend their time, and growing diversity in the ethnic and cultural makeup of our society. Findings from future studies surrounding these trends will lead to a better understanding of the interface between work and family in later life.

NOTE

Richard B. Miller, Ph.D., is a professor in the School of Family Life at Brigham Young University. Contact Richard B. Miller, Brigham Young University, 1041E JFSB, Provo, UT 84602; phone: 801-422-2860; email: rick_miller@byu.edu. Jeremy B. Yorgason, Ph.D., is an assistant professor of Marriage, Family, and Human Development in the School of Family Life at Brigham Young University. Contact Jeremy B. Yorgason, Brigham Young University, 2079 JFSB, Provo, UT 84602; phone: 801-422-3515; email: jeremy_yorgason@byu.edu

REFERENCES

Ade-Ridder, L. (1985). Quality of marriage: A comparison between golden wedding couples and couples married less than fifty years. *Lifestyles, 7*, 224–237.

Atchley, R. C. (1992). Retirement and marital satisfaction. In M. Szinovacz, D. J. Ekerdt, & B. H. Vinick (Eds.), *Families and retirement* (pp. 145–158). Newbury Park, CA: Sage.

Blau, D. M., & Gilleskie, D. B. (2006). Health insurance and retirement of married couples. *Journal of Applied Econometrics, 21*, 935–953.

Broderick, C., & Smith, J., (1979). The general systems approach to the family. In W. R. Burr, R. Hill, F. I. Nye, & I. L. Reiss (Eds.), *Contemporary theories about the family* (pp. 112–129). New York: Free Press.

Davey, A. & Szinovacz, M. E. (2004). Dimensions of marital quality and retirement. *Journal of Family Issues, 25,* 431–464.

Demo, D. H., Aquilino, W. S., & Fine, M. A. (2005). Family composition and family transitions. In V. L. Bengtson, A. C. Acock, K. R. Allen, P. Dilworth-Anderson, & D. M. Klein (Eds.), *Sourcebook of family theory and research* (pp. 119–142). Thousand Oaks, CA: Sage.

Detinger, E., & Clarkberg, M. (2002). Informal caregiving and retirement timing among men and women. *Journal of Family Issues, 23*(7), 857–879.

Drentea, P. (2002). Retirement and mental health. *Journal of Aging and Health, 14,* 167–194.

Ekerdt, D. J., & Vinick, B. (1991). Marital complaints in husband-working and husband-retired couples. *Research on Aging, 13,* 364–382.

Elder, G., Jr., (1995). The life course paradigm: Social change and individual development. In P. Moen, G. Elder, Jr., & K. Lüscher (Eds.), *Examining lives in context: Perspectives on the ecology of human development* (pp. 101–140). Washington, DC: American Psychological Association.

Federal Interagency Forum on Aging-Related Statistics. (2004). *Older Americans 2004: Key Indicators of well-being.* Washington, DC: U.S. Government Printing Office.

Fethke, C. C. (1989). Life-cycle models of saving and the effect of the timing of divorce on retirement economic well-being. *Journal of Gerontology: Social Sciences, 44,* S121–S128.

Fitzpatrick, T. R., & Vinick, B. (2003). The impact of husbands' retirement on wives' marital quality. *Journal of Family Social Work, 7,* 83–100.

Gendell, M. (2001). Retirement age declines again in 1990s. *Monthly Labor Review, 124,* 12–21.

Gibson, R. C. (1991). The subjective retirement of Black Americans. *Journal of Gerontology: Social Sciences, 46*(4), S204–S209.

Gibson, R. C. (1987). Reconceptualizing retirement for Black Americans. *The Gerontologist, 27,* 691–698.

Hardy, M. A. (2002). The transformation of retirement in twentieth-century America: From discontent to satisfaction. *Generations, 26,* 9–16.

Hayslip, B., Jr., & Kaminski, P. L. (2005). Grandparents raising their grandchildren: A review of the literature and suggestions for practice. *The Gerontologist, 45*(2), 262–269.

Henretta, J. C., O'Rand, A. M., & Chan, C. G. (1993). Joint role investments and synchronization of retirement: A sequential approach to couples' retirement timing. *Social Forces, 71*(4), 981–1000.

Henry, R. G., Miller, R. B., & Giarrusso, R. (2005). Difficulties, disagreements, and disappointments in late-life marriages. *International Journal of Aging and Human Development, 61*(3), 243–264.

Hill, E. A., & Dorfman, L. T. (1982). Reactions of housewives to the retirement of their husbands. *Family Relations, 31,* 195–200.

Honig, M. (1996). Retirement expectations: Differences by race, ethnicity, and gender. *The Gerontologist, 36,* 373–382.

Johnson, D. R., Amoloza, T. O., and Booth, A. (1992). Stability and developmental change in marital quality: A three-wave panel analysis. *Journal of Marriage and the Family, 54,* 582–594.

Keating, N. C., & Cole, P. (1980). What do I do with him 24 hours a day? Changes in the housewife role after retirement. *The Gerontologist, 20,* 84–89.

Kupperbusch, C., Levenson, R. W., & Ebling, R. (2003). Predicting husbands' and wives' retirement satisfaction from the emotional qualities of marital interaction. *Journal of Social and Personal Relationships, 20*(3), 335–354.

Kutza, E. A. (2005). The intersection of economics and family status in late life: Implications for the future. *Marriage and Family Review, 37*(1/2), 9–26.

Lee, G. R. & Shehan, C. L. (1989) Retirement and marital satisfaction. *Journal of Gerontology, 44*, 5226–5230.

McCubbin, H., & Patterson, J. (1982). Family adaptation to crisis. In H. McCubbin, A. Cauble, & J. Patterson (Eds.), *Family stress, coping and social support* (pp. 000–000). Springfield, IL: C.C. Thomas.

Miller, R. B. (2000). Misconceptions about the U-shaped curve of marital satisfaction over the life course. *Family Science Review, 13*, 60–73.

Miller, R. B., Yorgason, J., Sandberg, J. G., & White, M. B. (2003). Problems that couples bring to therapy: A view across the family life cycle. *American Journal of Family Therapy, 31*, 395–407.

Mock, S. E., & Cornelius, S. W. (2007). Profiles of interdependence: The retirement planning of married, cohabiting, and lesbian couples. *Sex Roles, 56*, 793–800.

Moen, P., Huang, Q., Plassmann, V., & Dentinger, E. (2006). Deciding the future: Do dual-earner couples plan together for retirement? *The American Behavioral Scientist, 49*, 1422–1443.

Moen, P., Kim, J. E., & Hofmeister, H. (2001). Couples' work/retirement transitions, gender, and marital quality. *Social Psychology Quarterly, 64*, 55–71

Myers, S. & Booth, A. (1996). Men's retirement and marital quality. *Journal of Family Issues, 17*, 336–357.

Ogg, J., & Renaut, S. (2007). The influence of living arrangements, marital patterns and family configuration on employment rates among the 1945–1954 birth cohort: Evidence from ten European countries. *European Journal of Ageing, 4*, 155–169.

Pienta, A. M., & Hayward, M. D. (2002). Who expects to continue working after age 62? The retirement plans of couples. *The Journals of Gerontology, 57B*, S199–S208.

Pienta, A. M. (2003). Partners in marriage: An analysis of husbands' and wives' retirement behavior. *The Journal of Applied Gerontology, 22*(3), 340–358.

Piña, D. L. & Bengtson, V. L. (1993) The division of household labor and wives' happiness: Ideology, employment, and perceptions of support. *Journal of Marriage and Family, 55*, 901–912.

———. (1995). Division of household labor and the well-being of retirement-aged wives. *The Gerontologist, 35*(3), 308–317.

Rix, S. E. (2004). *Aging and work: A view from the United States* (Report #2004-02). Washington, DC: AARP Public Policy Institute.

Smith, D. B., & Moen, P. (2004). Retirement satisfaction for retirees and their spouses: Do gender and the retirement decision-making process matter? *Journal of Family Issues, 25*(2), 262–285.

Smith, D. B. & Moen, P. (1998) Spousal influence on retirement: His, her, and their perceptions. *Journal of Marriage and the Family, 60*(3), 734–744.

Szinovacz, M. (1996). Couples' employment/retirement patterns and perceptions of marital quality. *Research of Aging, 18*, 243–268.

Szinovacz, M. (2000). Changes in housework after retirement: A panel analysis. *Journal of Marriage and Family, 62*, 78–92.

Szinovacz, M. E., & Davey, A. (2005). Retirement and marital decision making: Effects on retirement satisfaction. *Journal of Marriage and Family, 6,* 387–398.

Szinovacz, M. E., & Davey, A. (2004). Retirement transitions and spouse disability: Effects on depressive symptoms. *The Journal of Gerontology, 59B*(6), S333–S342.

Szinovacz, M. E., & DeViney, S. (1999). The retiree identity: Gender and race differences. *Journal of Gerontology: Social Sciences, 54B,* S207–S218.

Szinovacz, M. E., & DeViney, S. (2000). Marital characteristics and retirement decisions. *Research on Aging, 22*(5), 470–498.

Szinovacz, M. E., DeViney, S., & Davey, A. (2001). Influences of family obligations and relationships on retirement: Variations by gender, race, and marital status. *The Journals of Gerontology, 56B*(1), S20–S27.

Szinovacz, M. E., & Ekerdt, D. J. (1996). Families and retirement. In R. Blieszner & V. H. Bedford (Eds.) *Aging and the family: Theory and research* (pp. 375–400). Westport, CT: Praeger .

Szinovacz, M. & Harpster, P. (1994). Couples' employment/retirement status and the division of household tasks. *Journal of Gerontology: Social Sciences, 49,* 125–136.

Szinovacz, M. & Schaffer, A. (2000). Effects of retirement on marital conflict tactics. *Journal of Family Issues, 21,* 367–389.

Talaga, J. T., & Beehr, T. A. (1995). Are there gender differences in predicting retirement decisions? *Journal of Applied Psychology, 80,* 16–28.

U.S. Department of Labor (2005). *Women in the labor force: A databook.* (Report 985). Washington, DC: U.S. Bureau of Labor Statistics.

Vaillant, G. E., DiRago, A. C., & Mukamal, K. (2006). Natural history of male psychological health, XV: Retirement satisfaction. *American Journal of Psychiatry, 163,* 682–688.

Van Laningham, J., Johnson, D. R., & Amato, P. (2001). Marital happiness, marital duration, and the U-shaped curve: Evidence from a five-wave panel study. *Social Forces, 78,* 1313–1341.

Ward, R. A. (1993). Marital happiness and household equity in later life. *Journal of Marriage and the Family, 55,* 427–438.

Chapter Nineteen

Parental Employment and Child Development: Variation by Child, Family, and Job Characteristics

by Wen-Jui Han and Jane Waldfogel

ABSTRACT

An extensive literature documents associations between parental employment and child developmental outcomes. A common finding in this literature is that these associations vary a good deal by child, family, and job characteristics. We review this literature focusing on what we know about such variation and what more remains to be learned.

INTRODUCTION

The literature concerning associations between parental employment and child developmental outcomes has drawn on theory from various disciplines and made use of rich data on child developmental outcomes from sources such as the National Longitudinal Survey of Youth—Child Supplement (NLSY–CS) and the NICHD Study of Early Child Care (NICHD SECC) (see review in Ruhm, (in press). Studies by sociologists and economists, as well as psychologists, have commonly found that the associations between parental employment and child outcomes are not uniform, but rather vary a good deal by child, family, and job characteristics (what psychologists refer to as *moderators)* (see Shonkoff & Phillips, 2000; Smolensky & Gootman, 2003; Waldfogel, 2006). In this chapter, we review this literature focusing on what we know about such variation and what more remains to be learned.

Variation by Child Characteristics

Age. The first child characteristic that we consider is child age. It has been acknowledged for quite some time that the effects of parental employment on child development will likely depend on the age of the child at the time that employment is undertaken (see review in Waldfogel, 2006). Studies of children who were infants at the time their mothers began work have been particularly emphasized and have consistently found that children score more poorly on cognitive tests, measures of behavior problems, or both if their mothers work during the first year of their lives, particularly if that work is full time (Bates, Marvinney, Kelly, Dodge, Bennett, & Pettit, 1994; Baum, 2003; Baydar & Brooks-Gunn, 1991; Belsky & Eggebeen, 1991; Blau & Grossberg, 1992; Brooks-Gunn, Han, & Waldfogel, 2002, 2007; Desai, Chase-Lansdale, & Michael, 1989; Han, Waldfogel, & Brooks-Gunn, 2001; Haskins, 1985; Hill, Waldfogel, Brooks-Gunn, & Han 2005; James-Burdumy, 2005; Neidell, 2000; Ruhm, 2004; Waldfogel, Han, & Brooks-Gunn, 2002).

We know much less about the effects of paternal employment in the first year of life, because paternal employment has been less studied. When it is studied, datasets contain few fathers who are in the home and not working, and these fathers tend to be a select group (see Ruhm, 2004).

Only a few studies to date have examined how the timing of parental employment in the first year of life affects child outcomes. Such studies are beginning to provide evidence of the importance of timing of employment within the first year. A study of health effects using data from the NLSY-CS (Berger et al., 2006) finds that when mothers work by 3 months, children are less likely to be breastfed, less likely to be fully immunized, and less likely to be taken to well-baby visits. Although that study finds no significant effects of maternal work by 3 months on child behavior outcomes, other research using the NICHD-SECC provides some evidence that children have more behavioral problems if their mothers work earlier in the first year (i.e., work by 3 months or 6 months) (Brooks-Gunn et al., 2002, 2007). The effect of timing in the first year of life on cognitive outcomes has also been studied and here the evidence suggests that maternal work begun earlier (e.g., before 6th month) in the first year does not have greater adverse effects than maternal employment begun later that year (e.g., between the 9th and 12th months) although the evidence also suggests that women who go back to work earlier are more likely to go back to the same job and are more likely to be from more advantaged family backgrounds (see, e.g., Brooks-Gunn et al., 2007). Knowing whether and how much timing matters in the first year, and for which outcomes, is of great importance for public policy around family leave and child care, and this is therefore an area where more research would be helpful.

Results for employment after the first year of life are quite different from the results for first-year employment. When studies have estimated a separate effect of maternal employment in the second or third year of life, typically that effect has been neutral or positive (see, for example, Brooks-Gunn et al., 2002, 2007; Han et al., 2001; Waldfogel et al., 2002; although see also Ruhm, 2004, who finds negative effects of maternal employment in the second or third years of life on later child cognitive development).

What of older children? In general, the literature finds neutral effects of parental employment on child outcomes when that employment occurs during the older preschool or school-age years (see review in Hoffman & Young-blade, 1999; Waldfogel, 2006). It is not until adolescence that there begins to be a hint again of some possible adverse effects of parental employment, although even here these effects are not consistently present. In experimental studies of low-income welfare recipients, for instance, MDRC evaluators find that the same welfare-to-work reforms that have neutral or even positive effects for school-age children result in some adverse outcomes for adolescents (Gennetian et al., 2002). However, in the Three City Study of low-income families, mental health outcomes for adolescents improve when their mothers go to work (Chase-Lansdale et al., 2003). The answer to the seeming discrepancy between the two studies may lie in differences in how employment affects the family. In the MDRC studies, it appears that adolescents are taking on more household responsibilities when their mothers go to work, and their school performance suffers. In the Three City Study, in contrast, when mothers go to work, adolescents report less financial stress and worry, and also report spending as much time as before with their mothers.

Gender. The second child characteristic that has been extensively studied in this literature is gender. A recurrent theme is that, where maternal employment is found to have adverse effects, the group most strongly affected tends to be boys. For example, in the many studies of first-year maternal employment, several studies have analyzed children separately by gender and reported some evidence that boys are more strongly affected than girls (see, e.g., Brooks-Gunn et al., 2002, 2007; Han et al., 2001; Waldfogel et al., 2002). The differences by gender are, if anything, more pronounced for school-age children and adolescents. Several studies of school-age children and adolescents have reported no overall effects of parental employment, but find significant effects for boys (and not for girls) when they are analyzed separately, or positive effects for girls alongside negative effects for boys (see review in Waldfogel, 2006).

What explains these differential effects by gender? Several hypotheses have been advanced. One is that boys are simply more sensitive to many types of external influences, particularly in early childhood, and thus boys are more upset by the disruption to their routine when their mothers go to work than are girls (Rutter, 1979; Zaslow & Hayes, 1986). Another hypothesis has to do with child care, again particularly in early childhood, when boys may be less likely than girls to bond with predominantly female child care providers and may be more likely than girls to get involved in rough-and-tumble play with other boys that puts them on a path toward more aggressive subsequent behavior (Maccoby & Lewis, 2003). For older children, another hypothesis has to do with the influence of mothers as role models. By this reasoning, when a mother is working, her school-age or adolescent daughter may lose out in terms of monitoring or support but will also likely gain in terms of role modeling, thus promoting more effort in school or better social functioning; for boys, in contrast, the role model aspect may be less important, leaving only the net loss due to less monitoring or support (Hoffman & Youngblade, 1999).

Other characteristics. Of course, many other child characteristics are likely to matter in influencing how parental employment affects children. Factors such as the child's temperament and health are likely to be particularly consequential (Crockenberg, 2003; Shonkoff & Phillips, 2000), but have been little studied to date. A recent study (Brooks-Gunn et al., 2007) examined whether children with more difficult temperaments are more affected by first-year maternal employment than are children with less difficult temperaments and found no striking differences. But other studies have found that the effects of child care differ a good deal by child temperament (see, e.g., Watamura, Donzella, Alwin, & Gunnar, 2003); this is an area that would benefit from more research.

Variation by Family Characteristics

Parental education or family income. The early literature on the effects of parental employment on child outcomes tended to make use of small samples of mainly White and middle-class families. As larger and more nationally representative samples of families became available for study in datasets such as the NLSY-CS, researchers began to explore whether the effects of parental employment on child outcomes were constant across families or whether such effects varied by family characteristics such as parental education or income. Overall, no clear pattern emerged, as some studies found more adverse effects of parental employment when parents had more education or higher incomes while others did not (Desai et al., 1989; Greenstein, 1995; Han et al., 2001).

Race and ethnicity. The availability of larger-scale datasets also made it possible to consider whether the effects of parental employment varied across families of different race or ethnicity. The NLSY-CS, unlike earlier small-scale studies, did include Black families (it also included Hispanic and other racial/ethnic minority families, but the numbers were small). When researchers analyzed White and Black families separately, they discovered that the effects of parental employment that were typically seen in White families were not always present in Black families. Most notably, although numerous studies (as discussed above) had found associations between first-year maternal employment and poorer child cognitive and behavioral outcomes in non-Hispanic White families, studies that carried out the same analyses for Black families did not find the same pattern of results.

In an early study with the NLSY-CS, Baydar and Brooks-Gunn (1991) found significant negative effects of first-year maternal employment on child cognitive outcomes in White families, but not in Black families (this study did not examine Hispanic families as the numbers were too small). A later analysis of the NLSY-CS, by Han et al. (2001), found significant negative effects of first-year maternal employment on both cognitive and behavioral outcomes in White families, but not in Black families (this study, like the earlier one, did not examine Hispanic families due to small sample sizes). Subsequent studies (Hill et al., 2005; Waldfogel et al., 2002) found the same pattern of results: significant negative effects of first-year maternal employment on child outcomes in White families, but not Black or Hispanic families (although see also Han, Waldfogel, & Brooks-Gunn, 2002, who found adverse effects of full-time first-year maternal employment on child behavior problems in Hispanic families). However, at least one study (Hill et al., 2005) cautioned that small sample sizes hampered the estimation for Black and Hispanic families and that effects for such families could not be conclusively ruled out with the NLSY-CS data. Nor could the NICHD-SECC data shed much light on this question, as that dataset contained very small numbers of Black or Hispanic families (only 174 combined vs. 900 White families) and analyses of them were inconclusive (Brooks-Gunn et al., 2002, 2007).

Only recently has a dataset had large enough numbers of Black and Hispanic families to allow researchers to analyze effects for them with confidence. The dataset in question—the Fragile Families and Child Wellbeing Study (FFCW)—is a birth cohort study of children born to predominantly low-income and single mothers (although some higher-income and married couple families are included) in 20 medium-to-large U.S. cities. The sample is racially and ethnically diverse: just over half of the sample is (non-Hispanic) Black, one fifth is Hispanic, and the other fifth is (non-Hispanic) White.

A recent study (Berger et al., in press) uses data from FFCW to analyze differences in the associations between first-year maternal employment and child outcomes across these three racial and ethnic groups. The study examines two child outcomes: the child's score on the PPVT-R, a commonly used measure of cognitive development; and the child's score on an abridged version of the Child Behavior Checklist (containing items from the anxious/withdrawn and aggressive subscales), a commonly used measure of social and emotional development. Both outcomes were assessed when the child was age 3.

Berger and co-authors examine two possible explanations for variation in the associations between first-year maternal employment and child outcomes across racial and ethnic groups. The first explanation is differential selection into employment. If, for example, White women who do not work in the first year after a birth tend to be primarily affluent married women, then those who do work by 12 months post-birth may be negatively selected. This might contrast with the situation for Black families, where those who do not work may disproportionately be low-income single mothers, in which case those who worked by 12 months post-birth would be positively selected. To address this possibility, they include extensive controls for work history and maternal characteristics, including a measure of the mother's cognitive development, in all their regression models. They also estimate propensity score matching models as another way to address selection (although such models can not address selection on unobservable factors).

The second explanation they examine is that racial and ethnic differences in associations between first-year maternal employment and child outcomes are related to differences in the child care experiences or in-home experiences of children of different races or ethnicities. They test this hypothesis by estimating associations between first-year maternal employment and child outcomes, including interaction terms that test whether these associations differ by racial or ethnic group, while holding constant measures of non-parental child care, maternal depressive symptoms and stress, and selected aspects of parenting. They estimate these associations using both standard regressions and propensity score matching models.

Consistent with prior research, Berger and co-authors (in press) find that there is a significant negative association between first-year maternal employment and the child's PPVT-R score for White, but not Black or Hispanic children. The magnitude of the effect is .24 of a standard deviation in the standard regression model and .50 of a standard deviation in the propensity score matching model. These results suggest that, if anything, selection bias might lead to under-estimating the negative association between first-year maternal employment and PPVT-R scores for White children. Adding controls for potential in-home or child care mediators does not alter these findings.

In similar models for child behavior problems, the group where significant effects are found is Hispanic families. Hispanic children whose mothers worked by 12 months have .19 of a standard deviation more behavior problems at 36 months than comparable children whose mothers did not work by 12 months in the standard regression models, and this effect rises to .45 of a standard deviation in the propensity score models. In addition, in the propensity score models, first-year maternal employment is associated with significantly lower levels of behavior problems for Black children (the reduction is nearly .20 of a standard deviation). (The results for White children point to a nonsignificant increase in behavior problems.) Again, these results are robust to including controls for potential in-home and child care mediators.

The Berger et al. (in press) results indicate that, as suggested by prior research, the associations between first-year maternal employment and child outcomes are not uniform across racial and ethnic groups. They suggest that maternal employment in the first year after birth is associated with lower PPVT-R scores for White children, but not Black or Hispanic children, and that there are significant associations between first-year maternal employment and elevated levels of child behavior problems for Hispanic children, but not White or Black children. These results do not seem to be explained by differential selection or by differences in home or child care experiences. What then might explain them? Berger and co-authors speculate that the results for the PPVT-R might reflect that the White mothers had significantly higher PPVT-R scores themselves and also were providing significantly more cognitively stimulating materials than Black mothers or Hispanic mothers. They note that it is also possible that White mothers are more likely to engage in activities such as book-reading with their infants (see, e.g., Raikes et al., 2006). If so, such differences might help explain why working by 12 months is associated with lower levels of vocabulary for White children but not the other two groups. With regard to the behavior problem results, the Hispanic women in the FFCW sample may hold jobs that are more stressful or less rewarding than those held by the other mothers, perhaps because they are less-educated and some among them are immigrants and thus have less experience in the U.S. labor market. If so, the stress in the workplace may spill over to the children, resulting in more behavior problems (see, e.g., Parke et al., 2004). It may also be that the meaning of work, and the mother's satisfaction with work, differs for the Hispanic mothers. Another possibility is that the differential associations reflect differences in how Hispanic mothers engage with their children (Carlson & Harwood, 2003; Ispa et al., 2004). It may be that, due to these differences, the disruption to an infant's social and emotional development when a Hispanic mother works is greater than when a comparable White or Black mother works.

And what of the absence of negative effects in Black families? Berger at al. (in press) note that Black women have historically had higher levels of employment than White or Hispanic women, and therefore working by 12 months may be seen as more normative in Black families than it is in White or Hispanic families. It is also possible that maternal employment leads to fewer changes for the typical Black child than it does for the typical White or Hispanic child, given the more extensive involvement of kin in the rearing of Black children (see, e.g., Stack, 1974).

But this too is an area where further research would be useful. The FFCW study (Berger et al., in press) uses data on a sample that is primarily low-income and not married. It would be useful to examine racial/ethnic differences in the effects of parental employment in a more heterogeneous sample. It would also be useful to examine differences in the effects of parental employment within racial/ethnic groups. Hispanic families, in particular, vary greatly (by factors such as country of origin, immigration status, and length of time in the United States), and it would be important to examine how the effects of parental employment vary by those factors.

Variation by Job Characteristics

The literature on parental employment and child outcomes has also considered the role of parents' job characteristics. It has been long argued that the meaning of a parent's job, and the satisfaction that he or she takes in it, will have an effect on how that job affects his or her family life (Galinsky, 1999; Menaghan & Parcel, 1995; Parcel & Menaghan, 1994, 1997). When jobs are more satisfying and rewarding, parents may come home and be more nurturing and supportive of their children's development. Conversely, when jobs are less satisfying and more stressful, parents may come home and be harsher or more neglectful of their child's development. Several studies have confirmed these expectations (see review in Repetti, 2005). For instance, a classic study of air traffic controllers found that on days when their work was more stressful, they were harsher or more detached with their children than on days when their work was less stressful (Repetti, 1994).

Another job characteristic that has received a great deal of attention in this literature is parents' working hours; i.e., the distinction between full-time and part-time employment. As Ruhm (in press) points out in his review, studies of early parental employment have typically found larger associations between employment and child outcomes when that employment is full-time, rather than part-time.

However, parental work schedules have received little attention to date. As a growing share of the workforce is employed at non-standard hours (i.e., at hours that are not between 6 am and 6 pm), increasing attention is now turning to the impact that non-standard, as opposed to standard, work schedules might have on child outcomes. Currently, about 15% of the U.S. workforce (approximately 15 million people) work evenings, nights, rotating shifts, or irregular schedules or hours (U.S. Bureau of Labor Statistics, 2005). Those who are male, young, African American, low educated, and/or low skilled are more likely than others to work nonstandard hours; in addition, parent(s) in married-couple families, families with young children (under age 6), and single-mother families are also more likely to work nonstandard hours (Presser, 2003). Occupations that are the most likely to require nonstandard hours (service jobs such as janitors, waitresses, nurses, and sales jobs such as sales, retail, and personal services workers) are among those projected to be the fastest growing in the United States for at least the next 10 years (Presser, 2001).

Children may benefit or suffer from parent(s) working nonstandard hours. For instance, some mothers may choose to work nonstandard hours in order to spend the days with their young children (Garey, 1999), whereas for others working nonstandard hours is a job requirement (Presser & Cox, 1997). In the former case, any physical or mental stress from working nonstandard hours might be overridden by the mother's satisfaction with her ability to spend time with and take care of her child (Garey, 1999). In the latter case, children's wellbeing could be adversely affected by factors such as parental stress, marital instability, or parental fatigue or depression (Bohle & Tilley, 1998; Booth et al., 1984; Hertz & Charlton, 1989; Heymann, 2000; Presser, 2000; Tapp & Holloway, 1981; White & Keith, 1990).

We know relatively little about the association between parental shift work and child development. To date, only a small number of studies have examined how nonstandard work schedules affect child outcomes. Six find negative associations between mothers' nonstandard schedules and children's cognitive or behavioral outcomes (Bogen & Joshi, 2002; Dosa, Auinger, Olson, & Weitzman, 2002; Han, 2005; Heymann, 2000; Strazdins, Clements, Korda, Broom, & D'Souza, 2006; Strazdins, Korda, Lim, Broom, & D'Souza, 2004), whereas two find no significant effects (Dunifon, Kalil, & Bajrachaya, 2005; Ross Phillips, 2002). Two of these studies were limited to pre-school age children (Bogen & Joshi, 2002; Han, 2005), one was primarily qualitative (Heymann, 2000), three focused primarily on low-income families (Bogen & Joshi, 2002; Dunifon et al., 2005; Ross Phillips, 2002), and two were based on samples from Canada (Strazdins et al., 2004; Strazdins et al., 2006). (The rest used samples from the United States.)

With regard to cognitive outcomes, using longitudinal data from the NICHD SECC, Han (2005) finds that both the timing and duration of maternal nonstandard work schedules are important to children's later well-being. Specifically, the effects of mothers working nonstandard schedules tend to be negative, particularly if these schedules begin in the first year of the child's life, and particularly for the child's cognitive development at 24 months and expressive language at 36 months. These negative effects may be due to the type of child care used, since children whose mothers work nonstandard hours are less likely to be enrolled in center care (Han, 2005). Similar findings are reported in a qualitative study (Heymann, 2000), which finds that children are more likely to have poor educational outcomes if their mothers have worked evenings or nights over a 6-year period during childhood.

Among studies focusing on children's social and emotional outcomes, an analysis of survey data from Welfare, Children, and Families study (a low-income sample) reveals that the higher the propensity for nonstandard work schedules, the more likely mothers are to report high levels of problem behavior and low levels of positive behavior in their 2- to 4-year-olds (Bogen & Joshi, 2002). Han (in press), using data from the NLSY-CS, finds that maternal nonstandard work schedules may contribute to more behavior problems for children age 4 to 10, particularly if the mother is single, a welfare recipient, or low income, works in a cashier or services occupation, and works a non-day shift full-time. In addition, children in two-parent families whose mothers and fathers both work non-day shifts on a full-time basis have the most behavioral problems (Han, in press). Stradzins and her colleagues (2006, 2004), using a sample from Canada, find a strong negative association between parents working non-day shifts and measures of child socioemotional well-being (e.g., property offenses for children between age 4 and 11; physical and conduct aggression for 2- or 3-year-old children). Heightened parental depression and ineffective parenting behaviors due to working non-day shifts may account, at least partially, for these negative associations (Stradzins et al., 2006). Dosa and her colleagues (2002), using a sample from the United States, also find that children aged 4–12 are more likely to have behaviors that require counseling if both parents work split shifts.

In a study of early adolescents, Han and Waldfogel (2007), using data from the NLSY-CS, find that parental work schedules have complex links with home life and socioemotional outcomes for 13- and 14-year-olds. Parental nonstandard schedules are associated with some improvements in home life (e.g., teens whose parents work nights report being more likely to have an adult home in the afternoon after school) but also have some downsides (e.g., teens whose parents work rotating shifts are more likely to say their parents miss important events at school); as a result, overall, the effects of parental nonstandard work schedules on adolescent outcomes tend to be neutral. Further evidence about the impacts on adolescents comes from a recent study using a small local sample (Davis, Crouter, & McHale, 2006) which finds that while adolescents whose mothers work nonstandard hours report a closer relationship with her than those with daytime working mothers, adolescents whose fathers work nonstandard shifts say their fathers know significantly less about their daily activities than those whose fathers work daytime shifts. Also, adolescents report significantly less closeness with their parents when their fathers work nonstandard shifts, as well as when their parents have a high level of marital conflict.

As this review indicates, the impact of parents' shift work on their children's well-being has only just begun to be explored. We concur with Harriet Presser (2003, p. 226) that "we need to better understand how employment that is mostly at nonstandard times or rotating around the clock affects America's families—particularly those with children. It is time that we embrace the complexities of this issue by putting it on center stage, both in public discourse and in our research." As noted earlier, nonstandard work hours affect a sizable and growing share of American families. We have much more to learn about how these work hours are affecting our children.

CONCLUSION

A common complaint about social scientists is their reluctance to give firm answers to questions about their research, tending instead to fall back on phrases that begin with "it depends." However, we hope we have shown in this chapter that when it comes to answering questions as to how children are affected by parental employment, the correct answer really is "it depends." The evidence is clear that how a child is affected by maternal employment depends crucially on how old the child is at the time. Factors such as the child's gender, health, and temperament are also likely to be important, but we know less about them at this time. We also know relatively little about how the effects of parental employment vary by factors such as parental education or income. But a growing body of evidence suggests that how young children are affected by maternal employment varies a good deal by race/ethnicity. The evidence also indicates that how parental work affects children depends on the nature of that work, and in particular on the hours during which that work is undertaken.

Although the literature we reviewed here is quite large, we still have a great deal more to learn about how parental employment affects children. The single biggest gap in knowledge has to do with fathers and how their employment affects child well-being. For too long, the literature has focused on how mothers' employment affects children, taking fathers' employment for granted. As fathers become more involved in the home (and mothers become more involved in the labor market), research in this area will have to shift accordingly and will have to pay more attention to fathers. There is also a need for more research on many of the child, family, and job factors examined above. Because of their policy relevance, we would highlight as particular priorities further work on how the timing of work in the first year of life affects child health and development, how parental work affects child outcomes in immigrant families, and how the characteristics of jobs influence how parental employment affects child well-being.

A further aspect of parental employment's relationship to child development has to do with the pathways through which the effects of parental employment on child outcomes, where present, come about (what psychologists call *mediators*). Parental employment is likely to affect parents' time and interactions with children, income and other resources available to the family, and children's placement into and time spent in non-parental child care, among other factors. We have not considered such pathways here (for a recent extensive discussion, see Brooks-Gunn et al., 2007) but note that these too are a fertile area for further research.

NOTE

Wen-Jui Han, Ph.D., is an associate professor of social work and Jane Waldfogel, Ph.D., is a professor of social work and public affairs, both at Columbia University. Address correspondence to Wen-Jui Han, Columbia University School of Social Work, 1255 Amsterdam Avenue, New York, NY 10027. Email: wh41@columbia.edu. Note: We gratefully acknowledge funding support from NICHDR01 HD04721501A2.

REFERENCES

Bates, J. E., Marvinney, D., Kelly, T., Dodge, K. A., Bennett, D. S., & Pettit, G. S. (1994). Child-care history and kindergarten adjustment. *Developmental Psychology, 30,* 690–700.

Baum, C. L. (2003). Does early maternal employment harm child development? An analysis of the potential benefits of leave-taking. *Journal of Labor Economics, 21*(2), 409–448.

Baydar, N., & Brooks-Gunn, J. (1991). Effects of maternal employment and child care arrangements in infancy on preschoolers' cognitive and behavioral outcomes: Evidence from the children of the NLSY. *Developmental Psychology, 27,* 918–931.

Belsky, J., & Eggebeen, D. (1991). Early and extensive maternal employment and young children's socioemotional development: Children of the National Longitudinal Survey of Youth. *Journal of Marriage and the Family, 53,* 1083–1099.

Berger, L. M., Brooks-Gunn, J., Paxson, C., & Waldfogel, J. (in press). First-year maternal employment and child outcomes: Differences across racial and ethnic groups. *Children and Youth Services Review.*

Blau, F. D., & Grossberg, A. J. (1992). Maternal labor supply and children's cognitive development. *Review of Economics and Statistics, 74*(3), 474–481.

Bogen, K. & Joshi, P. (2002). *Bad work or good work: The relationship of part-time and non-standard work schedules to parenting and child behavior in working poor families.* Paper presented at NICHD conference on Working Poor Families: Coping as Parents and Workers.

Bohle, P., & Tilley, A. J. (1998). Early experience of shiftwork: Influences on attitudes. *Journal of Occupational & Organizational Psychology, 71*, 61–79.

Booth, A., Johnson, D. R., White, L., & Edwards, J. (1984). Women, outside employment, and marital instability. *American Journal of Sociology, 90*, 567–583.

Brooks-Gunn, J., Han, W.-J., & Waldfogel, J. (2002). Maternal employment and child cognitive outcomes in the first three years of life: The NICHD Study of Early Child Care. *Child Development, 73*, 1052–1072.

Brooks-Gunn, J., Han, W.-J., & Waldfogel, J. (2007). *First-year maternal employment and child development in the first seven years.* Unpublished working paper, Columbia University.

Carlson, V., & Harwood, R. (2003). Attachment, culture, and the caregiving system: The cultural patterning of everyday experiences among Anglo and Puerto Rican mother-infant pairs. *Infant Mental Health Journal, 24*, 53–73.

Chase-Lansdale, P. L., Moffitt, R. A., Lohman, B. J, Cherlin, A. J., Coley, R. L., Pittman, L. D., et al. (2003). Mothers' transitions from welfare to work and the well-being of preschoolers and adolescents. *Science, 299*, 1548–52.

Crockenberg, S. C. (2003). Rescuing the baby from the bathwater: How gender and temperament (may) influence how child care affects child development. *Child Development, 74*(4), 1034–1038.

Davis, K. D., Crouter, A. C., & McHale, S. M. (2006). Implications of shift work for parent-adolescent relationships in dual-earner families. *Family Relations, 55*, 450–460.

Desai, S., Chase-Lansdale, L., & Michael, R. (1989). Mother or market? Effects of maternal employment on cognitive development of four year old children. *Demography, 26*, 545–561.

Dosa, N. P., Auinger, P., Olson, B., & Weitzman, M. (2002, May). Parents' workshift and attention and behavior problems in school aged children. Paper presented at the Pediatric Academic Societies' Annual Meeting, Baltimore, MD.

Dunifon, R., Kalil, A., & Bajrachaya, A. (2005). Maternal working conditions and child well-being in welfare-leaving families. *Developmental Psychology, 41*(6), 851–859.

Galinsky, E. (1999). *Ask the children: What America's children really think about working parents.* New York: William Morrow.

Garey, A. I. (1999). Motherhood on the night shift. In A.I. Garey (Ed.) *Weaving work and motherhood* (pp. 108–139). Philadelphia: Temple University Press.

Gennetian, L. A., Duncan, G. J., Knox, V. W., Vargas, W. G., Clark-Kauffman, E., & London, A. S. (2002). *How welfare and work policies for parents affect adolescents: A synthesis of research.* Technical Resources. New York: Manpower Demonstration Research Corporation.

Greenstein, T. N. (1995). Are the "most advantaged" children truly disadvantaged by early maternal employment? Effects on child cognitive outcomes. *Journal of Family Issues, 16*(2), 149–169.

Han, W.-J. (2004). Nonstandard work schedules and child care choices: Evidence from the NICHD Study of Early Child Care. *Early Childhood Research Quarterly, 19*(2), 231–256.

———. (2005). Maternal nonstandard work schedules and child cognitive outcomes. *Child Development, 76*(1), 137–154.

———. (in press). Shift work and child behavioral outcomes. *Work, Employment, and Society.*

Han, W.-J, & Waldfogel, J. (2007). Parental work schedules, family process, and early adolescents' risky behavior. *Children and Youth Services Review, 29*, 1249–1266.

Han, W.-J., Waldfogel, J., & Brooks-Gunn, J. (2001). The effects of early maternal employment on later cognitive and behavioral outcomes. *Journal of Marriage and the Family 63*, 336–354.

———. (2002, May). Early maternal employment and child behavior outcomes: What do we know? Evidence from two longitudinal studies. Paper presented at the Population Association of American Annual Meeting, Atlanta, Georgia.

Haskins, R. (1985). Public school aggression among children with varying day care experience. *Child Development, 56*, 689–703.

Hertz, R., & Charlton, J. (1989). Making family under a shiftwork schedule: Air Force security guards and their wives. *Social Problems, 36*(5), 491–507.

Heymann, J. (2000). *The widening gap: Why America's working families are in jeopardy and what can be done about it.* New York: Basic Books.

Hoffman, L. W. & Youngblade, L. M. (with Coley, R. L., Fuligni, A. S., & Kovacs, D. D.). (1999). *Mothers at work: Effects on children's well-being.* Cambridge, UK: Cambridge University Press.

Hill, J., Waldfogel, J., Brooks-Gunn, J., & Han, W.-J. (2005). Maternal employment and child development: A fresh look using newer methods. *Developmental Psychology, 41*, 833–850.

Ispa, J. M., Fine, M., Halgunseth, L. C., Harper, S., Robinson, J., Boyce, L., Brooks-Gunn, J., & Brady-Smith, C. (2004). Maternal intrusiveness, maternal warmth, and mother-toddler relationship outcomes: Variations across low-income ethnic and language groups. *Child Development, 75*, 1613–1631.

James-Burdumy, S. (2005). The effect of maternal labor force participation on child development. *Journal of Labor Economics, 25*(1), 177–211.

Maccoby, E. E. & Lewis, C. C. (2003). Less day care or different day care. *Child Development, 74*, 1069–1075.

Menaghan, E. G., & Parcel, T. L. (1995). Social sources of change in children's home environments: Effects of parental occupational experiences and family conditions over time. *Journal of Marriage and the Family, 57*, 69–84.

Neidell, M. (2000). Early parental time investments in children's human capital development: Effects of time in the first year on cognitive and non-cognitive outcomes. Unpublished working paper, University of California at Los Angeles.

Parcel, T. L., & Menaghan, E. G. (1994). Early parental work, family social capital, and early childhood outcomes. *American Journal of Sociology*, *99*, 972–1009.

———. (1997). Effects of low-wage employment on family well-being. *The Future of Children*, *7*, 116–121.

Parke, R., Coltrane, S., Duffy, S., Buriel, R., Dennis, J., Powers, J., et al. (2004). Economic stress, parenting, and child adjustment in Mexican American and Euro-American families. *Child Development, 75,* 1632–1656.

Presser, H. B. (2000). Nonstandard work schedules and marital instability. *Journal of Marriage and the Family*, *62*, 93–110.

———. (2001). Race-ethnic and gender differences in nonstandard work shifts. *Work and Occupations*, *30*, 412–439.

———. (2003). *Working in a 24/7 economy: Challenges for American families.* New York: Russell Sage Foundation.

Presser, H. B., & Cox, A. G. (1997). The work schedules of low-educated American women and the welfare reform. *Monthly Labor Review* (April), 25–34.

Raikes, H., Luze, G., Brooks-Gunn, J., Raikes, H. A., Pan, B. A., Tamis-LeMonda, C. S., et al., (2006). Mother-child bookreading in low-income families: Correlates and outcomes during the first three years of life. *Child Development, 77,* 924–953.

Repetti, R. (2005). A psychological perspective on the health and well-being consequences of employment experiences for children and families. In S. Bianchi, L. Capser, & R. King (Eds). *Work, family, health, and well-being.* Mahwah, NJ: Lawrence Erlbaum Associates.

Repetti, R. (1994). Short-term and long-term processes linking job stressors to father-child interaction. *Social Development, 3,* 1–15.

Ross Phillips, K. (2002). *Parent work and child well-being in low-income families.* Assessing the New Federalism Occasional Paper Number 56. Washington, DC: Urban Institute.

Ruhm, C. (2004). Parental employment and child cognitive development. *Journal of Human Resources, 39*(1), 155–192.

Ruhm, C. J. (in press). Maternal employment and child development. In D. R. Crane & E. J. Hill. *Handbook of families and work: Interdisciplinary perspectives.* Lanham, MD: University Press of America.

Rutter, M. (1979). Protective factors in children's responses to stress and disadvantage. In W.W. Dent & J. E. Rolf (Eds.). *Primary prevention of psychopathology: Vol. 3. Social competence in children* (pp. 49–74). Hanover, NH: University Press of New England.

Shonkoff, J. P., & Phillips, D. A. (Eds.). (2000). *From neurons to neighborhoods: The science of early childhood development.* Washington, DC: National Academy Press.

Smolensky, E. & Gootman, J.(Eds.). (2003). *Working families and growing kids: Caring for children and adolescents.* Washington, DC: National Academy Press.

Stack, C. (1974). *All our kin.* New York: Basic Books.

Strazdins, L., Clements, M. S., Korda, R. J., Broom, D. H., & D'Souza, R. M. (2006). Unsociable work?: Non-standard work schedules, family relationships, and children's well-being. *Journal of Marriage and Family, 68*(2), 394–410.

Strazdins, L., Korda, R. J., Lim, L. Y., Broom, D. H., & D'Souza, R. M. (2004). Around-the-clock: Parent work schedules and children's well-being in a 24-hr economy. *Social Science and Medicine, 59*(7), 1517–1527.

Tapp, W. N., & Holloway, F. A. (1981). Phase shifting and circadian rhythms produces retrograde amnesia. *Science, 211,* 1056–1058.

U.S. Bureau of Labor Statistics. (2005). *Workers on flexible and shift schedules in May 2004*. United States Department of Labor. Retrieved January 5, 2007, from http://www.bls.gov/news.release/flex.toc.htm

Waldfogel, J. (2006). *What children need*. Cambridge, MA: Harvard University Press.

Waldfogel, J., Han, W.-J., & Brooks-Gunn, J. (2002). The effects of early maternal employment on child cognitive development. *Demography, 39*(2), 369–392.

Watamura, S. E., Donzella, B., Alwin, J., & Gunnar, M. R. (2003). Morning-to-afternoon increases in cortisol concentrations for infants and toddlers at child care: Age differences and behavioral correlates. *Child Development, 74*(4), 1006–1020.

White, L., & Keith, B. (1990). The effect of shift work on the quality and stability of marital relations. *Journal of Marriage & the Family, 52,* 453–462.

Zaslow, M. S., & Hayes, C. D. (1986). Sex differences in children's responses to psychosocial stress: Toward a cross-context analysis. In M. Lamb & B. Rogoff (Eds.), *Advances in developmental psychology,* vol. 4, pp. 289–337. Hillsdale, NJ: Erlbaum.

Chapter Twenty

Generation and Gender in the Workplace: A New Generation at Work

by Ellen Galinsky and James T. Bond

ABSTRACT

There has been a great deal of speculation, based on anecdotal data, about generational and gender differences in the U.S. workforce and the implications of these differences for business. The National Study of the Changing Workforce (NSCW), conducted in 1992, 1997, and 2002 by the Families and Work Institute (FWI), together with comparable information collected in the 1977 Quality of Employment Survey (QES) conducted by the U.S. Department of Labor, provide data from representative samples of the U.S. workforce. These data shed new light upon the current importance of generational and gender differences as well as changes over the past 25 years (1977–2002). The topics addressed in this chapter include: (1) Are members of the Baby Boomer generation more "work-centric" than members of Generation X?; (2) Are today's younger male workers with children assuming greater responsibility for child care than their predecessors?; (3) Have men's attitudes toward women's/wives' employment changed over the past 25 years?; (4) Are today's younger workers more or less likely to want jobs with more responsibility (and greater rewards) than their predecessors—in light of the sacrifices required for advancement?; (5) Are companies in danger of having their "management pipelines" dry up because of the increasing demands of the workplace and because workers are simultaneously placing greater emphasis on the quality of personal and family life?

INTRODUCTION

A great deal of speculation concerns generational and gender differences in the workforce. However, until now, many of these assertions have been based on intuition or relatively limited data. The National Study of the Changing Workforce (NSCW), conducted in 1992 (Galinsky, Bond, & Freeman, 1993), 1997 (Bond, Galinsky, & Swanberg, 1998), and 2002 (Bond, Thompson, Galinsky, & Prottas, 2003) by the Families and Work Institute (FWI), and the Quality of Employment Survey (QES), conducted in 1977 by the U.S. Department of Labor (Quinn & Staines, 1979), offer an opportunity to bring hard data into this discussion. Because we have information about the workforce during the past 25 years, we can test some of the most current assumptions. Using rigorous research analyses, we can look at how today's workers differ from workers of the same age a generation ago as well as how workers of different generations have changed over time.

This chapter was initially prepared as an Issue Brief by the Families and Work Institute for the American Business Collaboration (ABC), a groundbreaking collaboration of leading U.S. companies ("Champions") to inform their work together to help their employees manage their work and personal responsibilities. At the time of this report, ABC Champion companies were: Abbott Laboratories, Deloitte & Touche USA LLP, Exxon Mobil Corporation, General Electric, IBM Corporation, Johnson & Johnson, PricewaterhouseCoopers, and Texas Instruments. The basic principle guiding the ABC is the belief that companies can accomplish more by working together than by working alone.

FINDINGS

This chapter, originally prepared as an issue brief prepared by the Families and Work Institute (FWI) for the American Business Collaboration (ABC) explores generation and gender, beginning with a focus on younger employees. When data for this study were collected in 2002, members of Generation Y were 18 through 22 years old, and members of Generation X were 23 through 37 years old, compared with Baby Boomers, who were 38 through 57, and Matures, who were 58 or older. This brief moves beyond speculation and hype by bringing a rigorous analysis to the debates and discussions, using data from the Families and Work Institute's 1992, 1997, and 2002 National Study of the Changing Workforce (NSCW) and the U.S. Department of Labor's 1977 Quality of Employment Survey (QES). In this chapter, we explore how today's employees differ from employees of the same age a generation ago as well as how employees of different generations have changed over time. We use a question and answer format to explore what has changed and what has stayed the same.

What Are the Demographic Characteristics of the Different Generations?

Employees in the Boomer (post-war 38–57 year olds) and Mature (58 or more year olds) generations are more likely to be women (52% and 53%, respectively) than men (48% and 47%, respectively). In contrast, employees in Gen-X (23–37 year olds) and Gen-Y (18–22 year olds) are more likely to be men (57% in both generations) than women (43%). Why this pattern? Men tend to retire earlier and women are more likely to take time off for childbearing and childrearing.

- As everyone knows from firsthand observation, the workforce has become more racially and ethnically diverse. The proportion of white, non-Hispanic employees varies significantly by generation. While 80% of Matures and 79% of Boomers are white, non-Hispanic, only 70% of Gen-X and 68 percent of Gen-Y are.
- Perhaps less well known is that each generation is becoming much better educated as judged by the rate of high school and college completion. Statistics on college completion at any given point in time are difficult to interpret because many members of younger generations of employees—Gen-X (21%) and Gen-Y (fully 48%)—are still in school. Continuing education among Gen-Y and Gen-X employees obviously places constraints upon their workforce participation. However, many need employment to cover educational costs and also seek quality employment to obtain valuable work experience.
- Marital status also varies significantly by generation. Matures (64%) and Boomers (70%) are most likely to be legally married, followed by Gen-X (53%) and Gen-Y (only 11%). Members of Gen-Y (12%) and Gen-X (11%) are much more likely to be living with someone as a couple—that is, to have a domestic partner—than older employees (4%). Matures are much more likely (19%) than others (1%) to be widowed. And Mature women are much more likely (30%) than Mature men (5%) to be widowed. Partly because their husbands have died and partly because of divorce not followed by remarriage, Mature women are also less likely (47%) than Mature men (82%) to live in a couple. Among married employees, Boomers are most likely (82%) to have spouses who are employed for pay versus 61% of Matures, 79% of Gen-Y and 74% of Gen-X.

- Partly as a function of differences in marital status, household composition also varies by generation. Only 6% of Gen-Y employees live with any family members (spouse, partner, children, and/or other relatives) at home versus 84% of Gen-X, 88% of Boomers, and 77% of Matures. Parental status also varies by generation: only 7% of Mature and 15% of Gen-Y employees have children under 18 at home compared with 55% of Gen-X and 48% of Boomer employees.

Are Younger Employees Less Work-Centric than Older Employees?

From two questions—"how often do you feel you put your job before your family?" and "how often do you feel you put your family before your job?"—we derived a single index of the degree to which respondents prioritize job versus family. Those placing a higher priority on work than family are considered work-centric, those placing higher priority on family than work are considered family-centric, and those placing an equivalent priority on their job and family are considered dual-centric.

- Boomers are more likely to be work-centric than other generations. Gen-X and Gen-Y are more likely to be dual-centric or family-centric. Twenty-two percent of Boomers are work-centric, compared with 12% to 13% of other generations.
- In contrast, 50% of Gen-Y and 52% of Gen-X are family-centric—putting family first—compared with 41% of Boomers.
- Interestingly, employees 58 and older (Matures) are most likely (54%) to be dual-centric compared with an average of 36% of employees in younger generations.

One could argue that the relative emphasis on work versus family is a function of employees' lifestyles. That is, of course Boomers are more work-centric because they have older children. To explore this issue, we conducted two sets of analyses. First we asked:

Table 20.1.   Work Priorities Across the Generations

Relative Priority Placed on Work vs. Family	Gen-Y (under 23) n = 250	Gen-X (23–37) n = 855	Boomer (38–57) n = 404	Mature (58 or older) n = 276
Work-centric	13%	13%	22%	12%
Dual-centric	37%	35%	37%	54%
Family-centric	50%	52%	41%	34%

Table 20.2.   Male Employees with Children of Any Age (N = 368) and Living in Families

Relative Emphasis on Work and Family	Age of Youngest Child			
	under 6	*6–12 years*	*13–17 years*	*18 or older*
Family-centric	46%	44%	43%	36%
Dual-centric	37%	38%	40%	41%
Work-centric	18%	19%	17%	23%

No statistically significant difference.

Does having children change one's priorities? Our analysis includes employees with children of any age, whether or not they still live at home. We find that as women move through the life cycle their relative priorities on work and family change, while this is not the case for men. Employed mothers are significantly less likely to be family-centric and significantly more likely to be dual-centric or work-centric when their children are older, but this is not the case for fathers. These findings support the view that having younger children constrains the commitment that women, but not men, make to paid work.

Then we asked a second question:

Are Boomers with children under 18 at home more work-centric and less family-centric than Gen-X parents who have children under 18? When we compare the priorities of Boomer parents with Gen-X parents who have children under 18 living at home with them, we find that Boomers are more work-centric. This finding suggests that there is a generational difference between Boomers and Gen-X rather than a life cycle–difference related to parental responsibilities.

Moreover, if we control (using multiple linear regression) for the age of the employee's youngest child (1–17 years) who resides at home, we still find that Boomers are significantly more likely (p < .001) than members of Gen-X to

Table 20.3.   Female Employees with Children of Any Age (N = 435) and Living in Families

Relative Emphasis on Work and Family	Age of Youngest Child			
	under 6	*6–12 years*	*13–17 years*	*18 or older*
Family-centric	60%	53%	51%	37%
Dual-centric	28%	30%	33%	41%
Work-centric	12%	17%	16%	22%

Difference is statistically significant at p <.001.

Table 20.4. Relative Emphasis on Work and Family among Parents with Children under 18 Years Old: Boomers versus Members of Gen-X

Relative Emphasis on Work and Family	2002 Ages	
	Gen-X (23–37)	Boomers (38–57)
Family-centric	55%	46%
Dual-centric	33%	35%
Work-centric	13%	20%

p = .001

be work-centric. This reinforces our hypothesis that the observed difference is generational rather than life cycle–related.

There are many possible reasons why Gen-X and Gen-Y employees might be more family- or dual-centric than Boomers. These generations are more likely to know firsthand what it's like to have a working mother. They also know what it's like to have seen their parents or other adults put everything into work only to lose their jobs as wave after wave of downsizing hit the economy during their growing-up years. In fact, in FWI's 1992 NSCW, we found that 42% of all U.S. employees worked for companies (including large, mid-sized, and small companies) that had downsized over the past year. The Gen-X and Gen-Y employees have seen the notion of a job-for-life replaced by the notion of job insecurity, where employers are less loyal to employees whom they see as free agents responsible for their own employability. Furthermore, today's younger employees have seen work become more and more demanding as the 24/7 global economy has taken hold. Finally, they have been shaped by September 11, 2001, which has caused many people to step back and ask themselves what is truly important in their lives.

Arguably, employees who are dual-centric manage work and family demands in a way that serves both their employers and their families well. This prioritization is, of course, dynamic, with work demands taking priority on some days or even hours and family responsibility on others.

- It is important to note that employees who are dual-centric or family-centric exhibit significantly better mental health, greater satisfaction with their lives, and higher levels of job satisfaction than employees who are work-centric. Although employers may want their employees to be work-centric—focusing on work to the exclusion of the rest of their lives—actually achieving this goal could be a pyrrhic victory, especially in light of escalating work stress and its potential cost in health care.

Do Employees Spend More Time on Their Family Lives Than They Did 25 Years Ago?

It is one thing for employees to say that they are focused on their families and other aspects of their lives, but quite another to see if they "walk the talk." Mothers have traditionally taken the greatest responsibility for family life. We wondered, however, whether fathers' time on household chores and caring for and doing things with their children had changed over the past 25 years as some have speculated. To explore this issue, we compared married employees of all ages in 2002 with married employees of all ages in 1977.

- In 2002, married men spent significantly more time on workdays (1.9 hours) doing household chores than married men did 25 years ago (1.2 hours).
- Although married women are spending significantly less time doing household chores on days when they are working—down from 3.3 hours in 1977 to 2.7 hours in 2002—the reduction in women's time doing chores (approximately 42 minutes less) is made up by their spouses, who are spending approximately 42 minutes more on chores.
- Among married couples with children, mothers are spending the same amount of time doing things with and taking care of their children on days when they are working as they did 25 years ago (3.3 to 3.4 hours).
- On the other hand, fathers' time with children has increased dramatically—from 1.8 hours to 2.7 hours.
- Women's sustained levels of attention to their children, when complemented by the growing amount of time spent by spouses or partners, means that children in couple families are actually receiving more combined attention from their parents today than children did 25 years ago—6 hours per workday in 2002 versus 5 hours in 1977. This finding does not reveal whether the nature of parent-child interaction has changed or stayed the same over the years. For example, although parents are spending more time with their children, they may also be doing more multi-tasking during that time or feeling more stressed and less able to focus on their children than in times past.

It is important to state that despite changes in the behavior of married men, employed married women still spend significantly more time than their husbands doing chores and caring for children, which is to say they are much more likely than their husbands to work "two shifts" (Hochschild, 1989)— one at their paid job and one at home. Nevertheless, employers should take

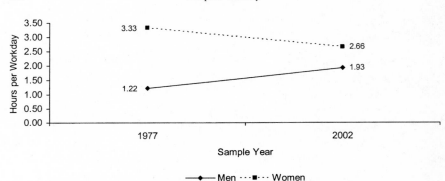

Figure 20.1. Workday Hours Spent Doing Household Chores Comparing Married Employees in 1977 and 2002.

note of the rather dramatic changes in men's responsibility and behavior off the job. As men take more responsibility for family work, they may want to have more reasonable hours, avoid taking on additional responsibility at work, resist demands for overtime work that is unscheduled or last minute, take time off for child-related reasons, and so forth—behaviors that have traditionally been associated with female employees. Work-family issues are clearly family issues, not just women's issues.

Do Single Mothers Spend More or Less Time with Their Children Than Married Mothers?

In 2002, single mothers spent an average of 3.3 hours caring for and doing things with their children on workdays—the same amount of time as married

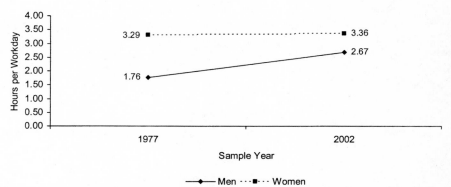

Figure 20.2. Workday Hours Spent Caring for and Doing Things with Children Comparing Married Employees in 1977 and 2002.

mothers. There is no statistically significant difference in the amount of time single mothers spend caring for and doing things with their children on workdays in 1977 and 2002—despite the fact that single moms in 2002 were working nearly 5 more hours per week on average (44 hours) than their counterparts in 1977 (39 hours).

Do Today's Gen-X Fathers Spend More Time Caring For and Doing Things with Their Children Than Boomer Fathers?

It is assumed by some and hoped by others that with each generation, fathers are becoming more involved in the lives and care of their children. The previous findings suggest that this is happening, but here we address the question more directly.

- When we compare the workday hours Gen-X and Boomer fathers spend caring for and doing things with their children in 2002, we find that Gen-X fathers spend significantly more time—an average of 3.4 hours per workday versus an average of 2.2 hours for Boomer fathers—an average difference of more than 1 hour. Because Gen-X fathers have younger children on average than Boomer fathers, we then made the previous comparison with adjustments for the age of youngest child and found the same significant difference favoring Gen-X.

Although the number of Gen-Y fathers (under 23 years old when the 2002 NSCW was conducted) in our sample is very small, it appears Gen-Y will continue this trend—with Gen-Y fathers spending more time with their children than fathers in Gen-X, who in turn spend more time than fathers in the Boomer generation.

How Do Members of the Boomer Generation (38–57 Years Old in 2002) Feel About Women's Participation in the Paid Labor Force? Have the Attitudes of Men and Women Changed over the Past 25 Years?

Obviously, fathers' increased involvement in family life is affected by the increase in the number of mothers who are employed, so we wondered if men and women in the Boomer age group have become more accepting of maternal employment. In the National Study of the Changing Workforce, employees were asked whether they agreed or disagreed with the following statement: "It is much better for everyone involved if the man earns the money and the woman takes care of the home and children." We find that over the course of 25 years and in the face of societal and economic changes, including the fact that the majority of male Boomers now have employed wives, both male and female members of the Boomer generation were significantly more likely in 2002 (61%) to disagree with this statement than they were when they were 25 years younger in 1977 (36%). This overall change reflects the fact that men, but not women, have changed their views about maternal employment.

- The views of employed women have not changed significantly over this period, remaining steady at about 61%.
- The views of men, however, have changed dramatically. In 1977, only 34% of male Boomers (then under 32 years old) disagreed with the notion that it is better for all involved for men to bring home the bacon and for women to take care of the home and children. In contrast, 58% of this same generation disagree in 2002—a large difference of 24 percentage points. Today's reality is that most employed married men of all ages (68%) have employed wives.

Are Younger Workers in 2002 Less Likely to Support Traditional Gender Roles Than Older Workers?

Yes, the new generation is less likely to support traditional gender roles.

- Sixty-three percent of Gen-Y employees disagree that it is much better for everyone involved if the man earns the money and the woman takes care of the home and children, compared with 49% of Matures. On the other hand, there is no statistically significant difference between Gen-X and all Boomer employees, with about 60% disagreeing with the notion that it is better for all concerned if the man earns the money and the woman takes care of the home and children.

In 2002, Gen-X and Boomer women were equally likely (62%) to disagree with the statement that it is better for all concerned if the man earns the money and the woman takes care of the home and children. However, Gen-Y women were significantly more likely (73%) to disagree, while Mature women (54%) were less likely to disagree. In this era, when maternal employment is much more prevalent, one might wonder why only 63% of Gen-Y employees disagree with this statement. Rather than seeing this primarily as an indictment of employed mothers, it may more nearly reflect the family focus of today's workforce—a belief that it would be good if one parent (typically the mother) could remain at home with children.

Although there is this support for the notion of having one parent at home, there is also an widespread acceptance that employment doesn't necessarily harm the relationship between mother and child:

- Eighty-two percent of Gen-Y employees agree that "a mother who works outside the home can have just as good a relationship with her children as a mother who is not employed" compared with 60% of Matures. The very high percentage of young employees who agree that employed mothers can have just as good a relationship with their children as their stay-at-home counterparts may well reflect their positive firsthand experiences having employed mothers as they were growing up.

Do the Generations Differ in Their Desire to Advance?

Given the family focus of today's workforce, particularly among younger employees, we next explore the issue of advancement, looking at generational differences in who wants to move to jobs with more responsibility, who wants to stay at the same level of responsibility, and who wants jobs with decreased responsibility.

- Not surprisingly, the proportion of employees who want jobs with more responsibility is highest for Gen-Y (60%), which has lower-status and lower-paying jobs on average, and lowest for Matures (15%), who are nearing retirement.
- Mature employees (58–64 years old) are most likely (70%) to want to stay in jobs with the same level of responsibility.
- Regarding gender, men are more likely (45%) than women (32%) to want jobs with greater responsibility, while women are more likely (59%) than men (47%) to prefer staying in jobs at the same level of responsibility.
- It's interesting and possibly disconcerting that only 40% of the total wage and salaried workforce under age 65 in 2002 wanted jobs with greater responsibility.

Have U.S. Workers Become Less Eager to Advance in Recent Years?

Through our conversations with senior managers, we have seen growing concern that fewer employees today seem to be interested in job/career advancement than was the case as recently as 10 years ago. Fortunately, FWI's National Study of the Changing Workforce enables us to test the validity of this concern by making comparisons between 1992 and 2002. We find that

Table 20.5.   Advancement Across the Generations

Group in 2002	% Wanting Job with Less, Same, or More Responsibility		
	Less	*Same*	*More*
Gen-Y (under 23)	7%	33%	60%
Gen-X (23–37 years)	7%	40%	54%***
Boomer (38–57 years)	10%	60%	31%
Mature (58–64 years)	15%	70%	15%
Gender:			
Men	9%	47%	45%***
Women	9%	59%	32%

Significance: ns = not significant; ** = p < .01; *** = p < .001.

the desire to move into jobs with greater responsibility has, in fact, declined from 1992 to 2002 for all age groups—from 54% in 1992 to 40% in
2002. Comparisons of different age groups are presented in Table 20.6.
The most dramatic decline is seen among the youngest workers (under 23
years old, who were members of Gen-Y in 2002). In 1992, only 16 years
ago, 80% of employees under 23 years old wanted to move into jobs with
more responsibility; in 2002, that proportion had dropped to 60%, a decline of 20 percentage points. Less dramatic but still statistically significant declines also occurred for employees 23–27 years old (Gen-X in
2002), and employees 38–57 years old (Boomers in 2002). Only Mature
employees (defined as those 58–64 years of age in this analysis) in 1992
and 2002 exhibited no change in their desires to move into jobs with
greater responsibility (14% and 15%, respectively).

Management concern is probably greatest when it comes to Gen-Y, Gen-X,
and Boomer college- and graduate-level educated hires upon whom many

Table 20.6.   Desire for Job Advancement by Generations in 2002

Age Group/Generation	Employees Wanting Jobs with Greater Responsibility	
Under 23 years old (Gen-Y in 2002	80%	60%**
23–37 years old (Gen-X in 2002)	69%	54%***
38–57 years old (Boomers in 2002)	41%	31%***
58 or more years old (2002)*	14%	15%ns

Statistical significance: ** = p < .01; *** = p < .001; ns = not significant.
* These percentages refer only to employees

companies count to gradually replace current managers. When we looked only at these employees, we found:

- Among college-educated men of Gen-Y, Gen-X, and Boomer ages in 1992 and 2002, 68% wanted to move into jobs with more responsibility in 1992 versus only 52% in 2002—a decline of 16 percentage points.
- Among college-educated women of Gen-Y, Gen-X, and Boomer ages in 1992 and 2002, 57% wanted to move into jobs with more responsibility in 1992 versus only 36% in 2002—a decline of 21 percentage points.

One might wonder if these changes in the desire to advance reflect the aging workforce and the fact that there are more Boomers who might skew the results. To test for this, we conducted a generation by generation analysis and found that with the exception of employees 58 or more years old, employees' ambitions to move into jobs with greater responsibility have declined (on average) over the past decade, controlling for age.

Although there has been a lot of press about the "Opt-Out Revolution," defined as employed women leaving the workforce when they have very young children, we see the apparent downtrend in career ambition as the real revolution, where very sizeable numbers of women and men are working hard, but not willing to make the trade-offs required by advancing into jobs with more responsibility.

For organizations particularly concerned about moving college-educated women—and men—into managerial ranks, these findings should give pause. Adjustments to workplaces and jobs may well be necessary to respond younger women and men and motivate them to pursue higher-level jobs.

Who Wants to Move into Jobs with Greater Responsibility?

Overall, only 40% of today's total wage and salaried workforce under 65 years of age would like to have jobs with greater responsibility versus 54% a decade ago. This decline is not due to aging of the workforce, as is clear from findings presented in Table 20.6 indicating that the decline in ambition is greater for the youngest workers.

Examining data for 2002, the main explanatory variables for this trend are demographic: younger employees, employees with lower incomes, employees in lower-status occupations, men, employees with an education beyond high school, unmarried employees, and employees who have children are more likely than other employees to want to move into jobs with more responsibility. It is obvious why many of these employees would want to better their situation.

In addition, several non-demographic factors make a difference:

- Employees who would like to work fewer paid and unpaid hours per week are much less likely than those who would like to work more hours to want to move into jobs with greater responsibility.
- Curiously, employees who place a higher priority on work than family—that is are work-centric—are less likely than employees who are family-centric to want jobs with greater responsibility. This finding may be explained by the fact that employees who are work-centric have significantly more difficulty managing the demands of their work, personal, and family lives. Having a job with greater responsibility would perhaps only exacerbate this problem.
- Employees who experience high levels of negative spillover from their jobs into their home lives are less likely to want jobs with greater responsibility.
- Employees who more frequently feel overwhelmed by all they have to do at work are less likely to want jobs with greater responsibility.

It appears that when evaluating whether or not they want a job with more responsibility, a significant number of employees may consider its impact on their personal and family lives.

Who Among College-Educated Employees Wants to Advance?

College-educated Gen-Y, Gen-X, and Boomer employees represent the employees that many companies count on to replace current managers as they retire. Only 43% of these prime candidates for promotion—46% of four-year college graduates and 39% of employees with graduate and professional degrees—want to move into jobs with greater responsibility. Because this is a much smaller proportion than one might expect and employers might hope for, we conducted a series of analyses to explain these findings. Note that these analyses are restricted to college-educated employees who are Boomers or younger and thus the findings differ from those reported above that include employees of all ages.

As with employees in general, the main explanatory variables for the desire to advance or not to advance are demographic—age, gender, occupation, marital status, parental status, earnings, and family income (Table 20.7):

- Employees who are younger and have not yet advanced very far in their careers, employees in lower-status occupations who earn less, and those in families with lower incomes are significantly more interested in getting ahead—and presumably earning more money.

- Men are more likely (52%) than women (36%) to have career advancement ambitions.
- As with employees in general, we find that college-educated Gen-Y, Gen-X, and Boomer employees who would prefer to work fewer paid and unpaid hours than they currently do are much less likely (40%) to want jobs with more responsibility than those who would like to work longer hours (75%).

Table 20.7. Demographic Factors Predicting Ambition among College-Educated Gen-Y, Gen-X, and Boomer Employees

Group in 2002	% Wanting Job with Less, Same, or More Responsibility		
	Less	Same	More
Generation:			
Gen-Y	0%	36%	64%
Gen-X	4%	37%	58%***
Boomer	9%	56%	34%
Gender:			
Men	6%	41%	52%***
Women	8%	56%	36%
Marital Status			
Married/living with partner	8%	51%	41%*
Not married or partnered	6%	44%	50%
Spouse/Partner Employed:			
Yes	8%	54%	39%ns
No	8%	41%	51%
Parental Status—Children Under 18 at Home			
Yes	9%	51%	40%*
No	6%	48%	47%
Occupation:			
Manager/Professional	9%	53%	38%***
Other occupation	5%	40%	55%
Respondent Earnings in Quartiles			
Less than $20,600	3%	39%	59%:
$20,600–$34,314	6%	50%	44%*
$34,315–$53,000	8%	56%	37%
More than $53,000	10%	45%	45%
Family Income in Quartiles			
Less than $28,000	3%	32%	65%
$28,000–$49,999	6%	51%	44%**
$50,000–$79,000	6%	49%	45%
$80,000 or more	10%	52%	38%

Significance: ns = not significant; * p < .05;** p < .01; *** p < .001. Percentages total to 100% from left to right except when there is rounding error.
Other factors predicting ambition are examined in Table 20.8.

It is striking that 80% of these prime candidates for promotion would like to work fewer hours than they currently work. Because we have found that workplace flexibility is critical to an effective workplace in other studies, we wondered if having access to workplace flexibility makes a difference in the desire to advance. We have found in other studies (see FWI's When Work Works, www.whenworkworks.org) that employees with access to flexibility are more likely to be engaged and committed, to be satisfied with their jobs, to want to remain with their employers, and to have better mental health. However, flexibility is not related to the desire to advance. Perhaps some forms of flexibility today actually encourage employees to work longer hours, as some employers hope. At some point, work hours on the job, however flexible, so reduce available waking hours off the job that employees' personal and family lives are negatively affected and that affects the desire to advance (or not).

We also wondered if the other ingredients that we have identified as part of effective workplaces make a difference. They are job autonomy, learning opportunities and challenges on the job, supervisor support for job success, coworker team support for job success, and involvement in management decision-making (Jacob, Bond, Galinsky & Hill, in press). Although all of these factors, like flexibility, are linked with positive job outcomes, they are not linked to the desire to advance. It may be that stressful jobs with long hours negate the good things that employers do to create effective and productive workplaces. On the other hand, feeling overworked and multi-tasking are linked in negative ways with the desire to move ahead:

- Among college-educated Gen-Y, Gen-X, and Boomer employees, only 30% of those who very often feel overwhelmed by how much they have to do at work want jobs with more responsibility, versus 53% of those who rarely or never feel overwhelmed.
- Similarly, only 41% of those who very often have to work on too many tasks at the same time want to move into jobs with more responsibility, versus 65% of employees who never have this experience.
- While only 40% of those who are interrupted very often, making it difficult for them to get their work done, want jobs with more responsibility; 59% of employees who are never interrupted want to advance.

In addition, we find that the ambitions of potentially promotable employees are diminished by experiences of negative spillover from their jobs into their family lives. Negative spillover includes not having enough time or enough energy for family or other important people in one's life because of one's job, not being able to do as good a job as one would like at home, not being able to concentrate on important things in personal or family life because of work, and not being in as good a mood as one would like to be at home because of one's job.

- Although fully 60% of college-educated Gen-Y, Gen-X, and Boomer employees who experience low levels of negative spillover from job to home would like to have jobs with more responsibility; only 39% (21 percentage points less) who experience high levels of negative spillover want jobs with more responsibility. Findings are the same for men and women.
  In addition,
- Fifty percent of those who find it easy or very easy to manage their work, personal, and family lives want jobs with more responsibility, versus 44% who find it difficult or very difficult and 39% who find it sometimes easy and sometimes difficult.

It is clear that the way we work today is having an impact on the advancement aspirations of employees. Managers and professionals and higher-earning employees in the workplace may not present particularly attractive role models for those employees that companies are hoping to move into the management pipeline. They report significantly higher levels of negative job-to-home spillover, more often feel overwhelmed by how much they have to do at work, more often report that they have to work on too many tasks at the same time, more often report that they are interrupted on the job making it difficult for them to get their work done, and have greater difficulty managing their work, personal, and family lives. As one employer recently put it, the "bad mood meter" among managers is obvious to those in the pipeline.

Why Are Women Less Likely to Want to Advance Than Men?

We have noted that women are less likely than men to desire jobs with greater responsibility. Some of the factors we have explored relate directly to women. For example, women are more likely than men to have jobs where they are multi-tasking, which in turn is strongly linked to feeling more overwhelmed by how much they have to do at work. Both of these factors are associated with ambitions to advance (Table 20.8).

Does the fact that women are more likely than men to engage in family work, as reported above, make a difference? In fact, this does not appear to be the case. Women who currently spend more time on family work or take more responsibility for family work are no less likely than other women to want jobs with more responsibility.

Table 20.8.   Other Factors Predicting Ambition among College-Educated Gen-Y, Gen-X, and Boomer Employees

	% Wanting Job with Less, Same, or More Responsibility		
Other Explanatory Factors	*Less*	*Same*	*More*
Desired work hours:			
fewer hours	9%	51%	40%
same hours	2%	50%	47%***
more hours	2%	23%	75%
Negative spillover from job to home:			
low	4%	37%	60%
moderate	5%	53%	41%**
high	14%	48%	39%
Frequency felt overwhelmed by how much you had to do at work in the past 3 months:			
very often	16%	54%	30%
often	11%	49%	40%***
sometimes	4%	51%	45%
rarely	5%	43%	53%
never	0%	48%	53%
During a typical workweek, how often have to work on too many tasks at the same time?			
very often	11%	47%	41%
often	11%	53%	36%***
sometimes	5%	46%	49%
rarely	3%	55%	42%
never	2%	33%	65%
During a typical workweek, how often interrupted during the workday making it difficult to get work done?			
very often	10%	51%	40%
often	9%	49%	42%**
sometimes	6%	50%	44%
rarely	4%	45%	51%
never	0%	41%	59%
Difficulty managing work, personal, and family life:			
Easy/very easy	5%	45%	50%**
Sometimes easy/ sometimes difficult	8%	53%	39%
Difficult/very difficult	15%	40%	44%

Significance: ns = not significant; * p < .05;** p < .01; *** p < .001. Percentages total to 100% from left to right except when there is rounding error.

Differences related to gender role attitudes among women, however, are significant:

- Thirty-three percent of women who strongly agree that men should earn the money and women should take care of the home and children do not want

jobs with greater responsibility versus 41% of women who strongly disagree with this statement.

Gender role attitudes among men have no bearing on their ambitions. As
some have observed from interviews and focus groups, it may also be the case
(1) that women tend to be more future-oriented than men, thinking about the
potentially negative future consequences of taking a job with greater responsibility and (2) that women have broader concerns about the way in which
more demanding jobs might disrupt not only their immediate personal and
family lives but also other primary social relationships with friends and extended family that they highly value. These are factors that this study did not
include but we suspect might make a difference.

The decreasing desire to advance should be of concern to all those who
care about leadership and the economy and calls for further study and action.
Employers might think about providing ways for women—and men—to step
off and on the fast track and about re-defining the fast track all together.

ARE AMERICANS WORKING LONGER HOURS?

Given our finding that employees who work longer paid and unpaid hours
than they desire are less likely to want to advance, we next explored the issue
of work hours. Remember that fully 61% of the total U.S. workforce and 80%
of college-educated employees in Gen-Y and Gen-X, as well as Boomers,
would like to work fewer hours.

There is no question that work hours have increased for many Americans
over the past 25 years. In comparing the 2002 NSCW with the 1977 Quality
of Employment Survey for employees who work 20 or more hours per week
we find that:

- In 2002, men worked 49 paid and unpaid hours per week on average at all
  jobs or the only job they had, an average of 2 more hours than the 47 hours
  men worked in 1977.
- The increase in hours worked by women is even larger. Women worked an
  average of 43.5 paid and unpaid hours per week in 2002 at all jobs, compared with 39 hours in 1977.

In 2002, 72% of men and 55% of women report that their regularly scheduled workweek in their main jobs was 40 hours, with the average being 39.3
hours per week for men and 35 hours for women. In reality, most people work
much longer hours because unscheduled hours have been climbing [source?].

- In 2002, men worked an average of 46 paid and unpaid hours at their main job (5 hours more than their regularly scheduled hours) and women worked 39.8 hours (3.8 hours more than their regularly scheduled hours).

When asked about how many hours employees would prefer to work, we find:

- Men would like to work an average of 38.5 hours, women, an average of 32.5—in other words, more closely paralleling the hours they are scheduled to work than the total hours they actually put in.

Do Managers, Professionals, and Higher Earners Work Longer Hours and Have More Stressful Jobs Than Those in Other Occupations?

Within the context of increasing hours, the desire to advance has declined. Employees are well aware that taking on more responsibility means taking on longer work hours. They have only to look around them, at managers and professionals, to reach that conclusion.

- On average, managers and professionals work 45.3 hours per week at their main/only jobs while employees in other occupations work 41.9 hours.
- Even more striking, employees in the top quartile of the earnings distribution (more than $53,000 per year) work an average of 49.7 hours per week, 15 hours per week more than those in the bottom quartile of the earnings distribution (less than $20,600 per year).

There are not only greater time demands associated with job advancement, but often additional stresses and disruptions. For example:

- Half as many managers and professionals (24%) as employees in other occupations (48%) report that they are never contacted about work matters outside normal work hours by coworkers, managers/supervisors, or customers/clients. The findings are the same when we compare low- and high-earning employees.
- Overnight business trips can also be disruptive of personal and family life, and higher-level jobs frequently require more business travel. While 87% of non-managers and non-professionals said they had not traveled overnight on business in the past three months, only 70% of managers and professionals reported no travel.

- The difference by earnings is even more striking: 91% of employees in the bottom quartile of earnings (less than $20,600 per year) reported that they had not engaged in overnight business travel in the past three months versus 62% of employees in the top earnings quartile—a difference of nearly 30 percentage points. The visible personal and family downsides to job or career advancement discourage many employees from wanting to get ahead.

Were Gen-Y and Gen-X Employees in 2002 Less Willing to Work Hard Than Employees in Other Generations or Than Employees of Comparable Ages in 1977?

Because Gen-X and Gen-Y employees are more likely to be dual- or family-centric than Boomers, the question arises: Are they less willing to work hard? In fact, the popular press has frequently characterized the younger generations as "slackers." To explore whether this characterization is accurate, we first compared the work hours of members of different generations. We found:

- Employees in the Boomer and Gen-X generations work the longest (paid and unpaid) hours at their main or only jobs—an average of 45 and 44 hours per week, respectively. There is no statistically significant difference in the hours members of these two generations work.
- Matures and Gen-Y employees work significantly fewer hours—an average of 39 and 35 hours, respectively. It should be remembered that 48% of Gen-Y employees are still enrolled in school.

When we compare Gen-Y and Gen-X employees in 2002 with their age counterparts in 1977 to investigate whether younger employees today work shorter hours than employees their age 25 years ago, we find:

- There is no statistically significant difference between Gen-Y in 2002 and their age counterparts (18–22 year olds) in 1977 with respect to the total paid and unpaid hours they work per week.
- In 2002, Gen-X employees actually work about three more paid and unpaid hours per week than employees of comparable ages in 1977.

Clearly, members of Gen-Y and Gen-X are not averse to hard work. It is important to note that working long hours is not necessarily undesirable, distasteful, or stressful. Indeed, employees who really like their jobs tend to work longer hours (paid and unpaid) because they want to. But when hours consistently exceed personally acceptable levels, problems arise.

Were Gen-Y and Gen-X Employees in 2002 Any More Likely to Leave Their Current Employers within the Next Year to Seek Employment Elsewhere Than Employees of Comparable Ages in 1977?

Both Gen-Y and Gen-X employees have also been portrayed as "job hoppers" with little allegiance to their employers.

- We find that Gen-X employees in 2002 are no more likely than their age counterparts (23–37 years old) in 1977 to plan to leave their current employers within the next year (43% somewhat or very likely).
- In contrast, Gen-Y employees in 2002 were significantly more likely (70% somewhat or very likely) to plan to leave their current employers in the next year than their age counterparts (under 23 years old) in 1977 (52% somewhat or very likely).

This appears to be a generational difference—perhaps related to the fact that employees of Gen-Y age today are more likely to be attending college or junior college while moving in and out of the labor force than their counterparts 25 years ago, perhaps due to lowered expectations of long-term jobs with the same employer because of the downsizing experiences of their parents, but perhaps also to higher expectations on the part of Gen-Y employees about the kinds of jobs they find acceptable. Gen-Y appears to be a choosier generation posing more challenges for retention.

Do Employees Who Want Jobs with More or Less Responsibility Feel That They Can Find These Jobs with Their Current Employers?

Not necessarily.

- More than half (52%) of employees who would like to have jobs with greater responsibility are "somewhat" or "very" likely to seek employment elsewhere in the coming year, suggesting that these employees feel that their current employers do not or cannot offer desirable opportunities for advancement.
- Interestingly, 44% of employees who would like to move into jobs with less responsibility are also "somewhat" or "very" likely to seek employment

elsewhere in the coming year. While promotion opportunities may be limited, it is not clear why employers cannot accommodate employees who for whatever reason want to have jobs with less responsibility—assuming they provide added value. Among employees who want to stay in jobs at the same level of responsibility, the majority (73%) are satisfied staying with their current employers.

CONCLUSION

Today's workplace is a far different workplace than in the past. Work has become faster paced, 24/7, and fiercely competitive in this global economy. Findings from generation and gender make it clear that the workforce has also changed. Nowhere is this trend more evident than in the dramatic decrease in the numbers of employees, especially those who are college educated, who want to advance. Especially important are the findings revealing that the large numbers of those who want to work fewer hours and those who are experiencing feelings of overwork are much less likely to want to advance than other employees. As a result, the way we work today is taking a toll on the pipeline of talent for American business. The findings of this study are a clarion call for rethinking work and rethinking advancement.

NOTE

Ellen Galinsky and James T. Bond are affiliated with the Families and Work Institute. Address correspondence to Ellen Galinsky, Families and Work Institute, 267 Fifth Avenue, Second Floor, New York, NY 10016; Phone: 212-465-2044; FAX: 212-465-8637; Email: egalinsky@familiesandwork.org. The 2002 National Study of the Changing Workforce would not have been possible without the generous financial support of the following Sponsors: Alfred P. Sloan Foundation, IBM Corporation, Johnson & Johnson, Motorola; Contributors: The Ford Foundation, KPMG LLP, Ceridian, Citigroup Foundation, Xerox Corporation; Donors: Salt River Project, and the survey respondents who donated their honoraria in order that we might continue this kind of research.

REFERENCES

Bond, J. T., Galinsky, E., & Swanberg, J. E. (1998). *The 1997 National Study of the Changing Workforce.* New York: Families and Work Institute.

Bond, J. T. (with Thompson, C., Galinsky, E., and Prottas, D.). (2003). *Highlights of the [2002] National Study of the Changing Workforce.* New York: Families and Work Institute.

Galinsky, E., Bond, J. T., & Friedman, D. E. (1993). *The changing workforce: Highlights of the [1992] national study.* New York: Families and Work Institute.

Galinsky, E., Bond, J. T., & Hill, E. J. (2004). *When work works: A status report on workplace flexibility.* New York: Families and Work Institute.

Hochschild, A. (with Anne Machung). (1989). *The Second Shift: Working Parents and the Revolution at Home.* New York: Viking/Penguin.

Jacob, J., Bond, J. T., Galinsky, E. and Hill, E. J. (2008). Flexibility: A critical ingredient in creating an effective workplace. *The Psychologist-Manager Journal*, 11, 141–162.

Quinn, R. P. & Staines, G. L. (1979). *The 1977 Quality of Employment Survey.* Ann Arbor: Institute for Social Research, University of Michigan.

Chapter Twenty-One

Living through Work; Working through Life

by Graeme Russell

ABSTRACT

The focus in this paper is on the current and expected future issues associated with enabling both women and men to meet their employment (e.g., career) and caring aspirations (e.g., to have children) and responsibilities. It takes a life span perspective—both in terms of the pathways for individuals and in terms of issues for different cohorts of carers (e.g., those who have their children in their mid- to late thirties, those who have elderly parents when they have retired, grandparents). Caring is defined broadly to include: children (at all ages), disability, elderly, and partners (where intimacy is included as part of caring), and self. The paper is based on an analysis of available research data, and it takes account both of employment and demographic trends, and options for change (e.g., for work redesign to enable different patterns of work and care).

The arguments developed in this paper are derived from three perspectives. First, the ongoing academic research on work and family; second, the developing debate on work and caring as it has been framed in Australia within a business context; and third, my experiences in organizations, both in conducting action research and in developing more effective approaches to work and caring (especially for men). Each of these perspectives has the potential to contribute to the development of theory, research, policy, and practice. The initial impetus for the approach taken here derives from a dialogue within the National Diversity Think Tank (NDTT)—representatives of major private sector organizations in Australia, formed with the intention of leading and shaping debates on a range of key workplace issues associated with diversity and work/family/life. The questions posed by this group and other social commentators are challenging for researchers, organizational decision-makers, and public policy makers. The intention here is to outline the framing of this discussion and then review the various components of the debate as they have been played out.

FRAMING THE ANALYSIS

At the heart of this analysis is a fundamental challenge posed about work and care—a challenge that is experienced at all levels of society—from children, the elderly, couples, parents, schools, child care centers, aged-care centers, non-government organizations, agencies that support the work of carers, public and private sector organizations, public policy, the economy, political parties, etc. The challenge is: How can we give and receive care across our lifespan in ways that are based on informed choice in how we arrange our work and care responsibilities, and that enable sustainable well-being for individuals, relationships, families, the community, business organizations, and the economy. Further, how can this be done while enabling people to achieve their aspirations and satisfy their needs for a sense of purpose, generosity, social identity, and security.

Recognizing both that these two aspects of life, work and care, are fundamentally connected and that addressing the life-span work/care challenge has relevance at all levels of society is a key starting point for this analysis. Sometimes an argument is made within a business context that how you provide and receive care is a private matter and that how individuals negotiate their work and caring responsibilities is a matter of individual choice (e.g., it is a matter of choice to work 80 hours a week and have a low level of participation in giving and receiving care; it is a matter of choice to work or not work for an organization that requires you to fly in and out of remote work sites on a weekly basis—"if you can't stand the heat, get out of the kitchen," it is a matter of choice if a couple are both employed and their child is cared for by a paid carer; it is a matter of choice if a person is unemployed and provides the full-time care for an elderly parent). Decisions are influenced by a complex set of personal and social circumstances, as well as government and organizational policies. Increasingly, too, research findings, such as research into child outcomes and the impact of child care, are being used to shape these complex personal decisions.

What is usually missing in the discussion, however, is the consideration of two key aspects of choice: informed choice and supported choice. For example, what are the potential personal, family, relationship, organizational, societal, and economic risks associated with working long hours, working unsociable hours, or working on a fly-in/fly-out basis? These are not questions that can be dismissed lightly by business and government, nor dismissed on the basis that they become irrelevant in the context of heightened economic prosperity. Although decision makers and those they affect may assume decisions are being made in the context of a high level of knowledge and resources, and with a capacity to take into account all potential risks and opportunities, no evidence confirms those assumptions.

At issue here is the well-being of individuals, relationships, families, society, and organizations, and social and economic productivity and prosperity. Further, it can be argued that the risks of not responding are high indeed. At one level, there are risks associated with economic prosperity (e.g., not having a skilled and motivated workforce) and at another level there are risks associated with individual and family well-being.

Stanley, Richardson, and Prior (2005) argue that despite Australia's increasing economic prosperity and technological advancement, many of our children are not benefiting from these improvements. Indeed, their data show that for many children there has been a significant decline in physical and psychological outcomes. They also argue that changes in the economy, such as increased competitiveness and workplace demands, have made it harder for workers to be effective parents, or to be parents at all. They draw particular attention to the increased number of mothers who are employed in workplaces that are often unresponsive to the needs of parents, and to the impact on family well-being of long working hours, the high intensity of work required, and the increasing number of so-called bad jobs (low pay, low security, and poor quality work).

What is not at issue in the business discussion is that a different approach is needed to work and care, and one that emphasizes both informed and supported choice. It is here that theoretical models and research findings have particular relevance, as much of the debate and decision-making in business organizations occurs within a research vacuum.

The discussion of choice also needs take account of (1) the different aspirations people have; (2) the fact that these change across the life span, and (3) that they are influenced by the social, economic, employment, and policy context we experience during our life course. To illustrate, changes in technology and the nature of work during the past 20 years (e.g., more knowledge-based as opposed to production-based work) means that there are more options to conduct our work in different places, such as at home or while travelling). In some organizations in the Australian mining industry moving from a wage-based/hours system to annualized salaries has also reduced the demand for overtime and increased opportunities for involvement in family life.

It can be argued (see Edgar, 2005) that many organizations pay lip service to the work and care needs of their employees, and that there is a considerable distance to go before most organizations demonstrate genuine care about the work and caring responsibilities of their employees. On the other hand, it is the case that many Australian organizations cared more about these issues in 2005 than they did in 1985. Further, many more workplaces in 2005 were more open to flexible work options than was the case in 1985. Evidence to support this can be obtained from various sources, including historical analyses of specific organizations and from the sustained interest in and quality of policies in organizations that continue to nominate for the Corporate Work and Family Awards.

This openness to flexibility has changed the expectations of employees, and provides a very different workplace context for both the emerging workforce, for those who seek to phase into retirement, and for those with a diversity of work and caring challenges. Many of the current discussions of assumed generational differences operate from the perspective that workplaces have remained constant and that what has changed are the characteristics of the emerging workforce (Sheahan, 2005). Workplaces have changed; the economic and social context is very different today compared with 20 or 30 years ago. Decisions are now being made in a different reality, with different aspirations in mind.

Consideration also needs to be given to whether and how these aspirations are reflected in the available policies and opportunities. The current pattern of work and care might not represent preferred options, nor indeed the options needed to ensure social and economic well-being. With different enabling strategies (e.g., taxation, employment policies, organizational work and caring strategies), the patterns of work and care people will choose, or have the option to choose, could be very different. These are all themes that have been taken up by various Australian authors in the past few years (e.g., Edgar, 2005; Pocock, 2003; Stanley et al., 2005).

This analysis is based on two fundamental propositions, that:

(1) a society should be built on the assumption that we have rights and responsibilities to both work and to provide and receive care (Haas, 1992).
(2) our involvement in, and capacity to provide and receive care are intimately connected to our own well-being, those that we are closely connected to (our families and friends), the community—community capacity and social capital, and to the broader society.

These are essential elements of any debate about the intersection between work and family/personal lives, yet they are aspects that are often overlooked, or de-emphasized in business discourses about work and care. These are issues taken up by Colegate (2004). Of major interest to this paper are the work of Tronto (1993) and the four phases of caring:

1. *Caring about and attentiveness:* The process whereby we recognize and pay attention to others' or our own need for care. In this context this could relate to our own acknowledgment or the acknowledgment of employers, governments, and policy makers of our need for care or our need to care for others (e.g., a disabled parent). This is neither about behavior nor acting on our recognition of the need for care.
2. *Taking care of and acting responsibly:* "The focus here is on accepting the responsibility to act in order to meet a need for care, without actually providing any the direct care." In a business policy context, it might mean supporting paid parental leave or providing a child-care center for its employees.
3. *Caregiving and competence:* Providing the direct caregiving in a competent way, e.g., childcare—where a person is resourced and competent to do this. For employers this might mean providing flexibility to enable people to be competent caregivers.
4. *Care receiving and responsiveness:* This relates to care being appropriate to the needs of those being cared for and the capacity of someone to provide the necessary care to those they have responsibility for—e.g., a parent being able to provide the necessary supervision of an adolescent during school vacations. The focus is on responsiveness rather than reciprocity. "Responsiveness suggests that we consider the other's position as that other expresses it. Thus, one is engaged from the standpoint of the other, but not simply by presuming that the other is exactly like the self" (Colegate, 2004).

What need to be considered, therefore, are the current and expected future issues associated with enabling people to meet their work and caring responsibilities (e.g., to provide care for an elderly parent) and aspirations (e.g., aspirations to have children, to have a satisfying relationship). Further, a life-span perspective is suggested—both in terms of the pathways for individuals and in terms of the issues experienced by different cohorts of carers (e.g., those who have their children in their mid- to late thirties, those who have retired and have caring responsibilities for elderly parents). The often-held assumption that current or likely future patterns are fixed and that there are clear and fixed generational differences (e.g., based on a particular age cohort) also need to be questioned.

Caring for and about can be defined broadly to include (but not limited to) children (at all ages), siblings, disabled people, people with ill health, the elderly, partners/spouses, friends, the communities we live in, and ourselves. The addition of the final aspect of caring—caring for yourself—is also aligned with Colegate (2004), where she argues for the importance of this aspect of caring.

Expectations and aspirations for combining work and care over the lifespan will also be influenced by the particular cultural context. For example, cultural values and expectations have the potential to influence gender-based patterns of care and who is assumed to have the responsibility for caring at different stages of life (e.g., who is assumed to have the responsibility for caring for elderly parents). In the case of indigenous Australians there are several issues that need to be included in the debate, e.g., self-care and life expectancy and sustainable employment, as well as alternative models of care.

A SUMMARY OF THE EVIDENCE AND THE ARGUMENTS

At the same time there has been heightened business interest in the challenges of work and care, there has been an upsurge in academic and public debate on these issues in Australia (Bittman & Pixley, 1997; Cannold, 2005; Cost of Care Task Force, *Creating Choice: Employment and the Cost of Care*; Cox, "ABC Boyer Lectures: A Truly Civil Society"; "Defining the Role of the State: New Matilda"; Edgar (2005); Human Rights and Equal Opportunity Commission, *Striking the Balance*, 2005; Hamilton & Denniss, 2005; Macken, 2005; Pocock, 2003; Russell & Bowman (2000); Summers (2003); Stanley et al., 2005; de Vaus, 2004). These issues have also been of major concern to various commissions (e.g., Productivity Commission), governments, industry bodies, NGOs (e.g., carers' organizations), unions, and various advocate groups.

Following is a summary of the data and the conclusions drawn by these authors:

—if things stay the same, Australia will have a workforce shortage as well as shortages in particular skills in the future
—if things stay the same, Australia will have difficulty in financially supporting its aging population
—workforce participation rates for prime age males in Australia are low in comparison with OECD countries (Banks, 2005)
—difficulties are currently experienced in recruiting and retaining older workers and in providing a workplace free of age discrimination

—concern has been expressed about Australia's fertility rate being too low — however, recent analyses suggest otherwise (McDonald, 2005; Banks, 2005)

—many people who aspire to have children are not doing so

—women currently provide more of the care for dependents than men do (for all aspects of care: children, disabled, the elderly, etc.),

—there is considerable diversity in caring arrangements and responsibilities

—there have been increases in the number of people both in and out of the paid workforce who have multiple caring responsibilities (e.g., for children and elderly parents; for grandchildren and elderly parents, etc.), and this trend is likely to increase in the future

—those who work and care for dependents report that they have difficulties in meeting these dual responsibilities

—there is a shortage in the availability of paid care for dependents and many people experience financial difficulties in providing this care

—there is gender inequity both in paid work (pay, power, nature of work) and in caring for dependents (more likely to be the responsibility of women); this also means that many people are not able to be in the paid workforce (e.g., workforce participation rates for women over 45 are relatively low)

—low value is placed on the work involved in both paid and unpaid care

—a significant number of women do not have adequate financial provision for retirement

—many people experience difficulties with both overwork (working long hours; work intensification) and underwork (not being able to work the number of hours they would like)

—many people experience high levels of workforce insecurity

—child health outcomes are declining

—parents are experiencing difficulties in providing the type of care that leads to positive child development outcomes

—rates of separation and divorce are high, and there is an absence of equity in the nature of financial support and caring for children after separation and divorce

—suicide rates are high, especially for men in specific demographic groups (e.g., 35 to 44 years) and men who live in rural areas

—many people experience a gap between an organizations' espoused policies on work and caring and what they feel would be effective in enabling them to meet their work and caring responsibilities

—mindsets and frameworks that influence debates and policies in relation to work and caring have not shifted to match the current and likely future demographics of patterns of work and caring

—many people experience low levels of quality in their work

—social, government, and organizational policies are generally not supportive of people with work and caring responsibilities, and represent significant barriers to choice (where choice takes into account the diversity of
work/care patterns, current needs, and aspirations)

The above analyses also establishes a potential gap between levels of understanding and acceptance of the evidence associated with the various identified work and caring challenges, on the one hand, and what would be the
most effective solutions, on the other hand. Further, based on their own in-
terpretations, most commentators provide their own blueprints for change,
e.g., Cannold, 2005, chapter 7: "Solving circumstantial childlessness: On the
road to parenthood together"; Edgar, 2005, chapter 9: "A framework for future work and family policy"; Hamilton and Denniss, 2005, chapter 11, "A
political manifesto for wellbeing"; Pocock, 2003, chapter 10, "Countering the
collision: what we can do now"; Stanley et al., 2005, chapter 9: "Creating a
civil society." These analyses will be returned to later in the chapter.

Additionally, there is often a mindset that things will stay the same and that
we are stuck with the current predictions. Two commentators present alternative viewpoints. McDonald (2005), in his recent paper argues that among other
things (p. 5): "the apparent fall in fertility in the 1990s may have been exaggerated by the apparent increasing under-registration of births across the
decade" and "recent policy changes (increasing family payments in 2004 and
the decisions of the Australian Industrial Relations Commission in the Family
Provisions Case—that an employee has the right to request (1) a period of simultaneous unpaid parental leave for up to 8 weeks; (2) unpaid parental leave
for a period up to 104 weeks; and (3) to return to work, from parental leave,
on a part-time basis until the child reaches school age) and the recent widespread public discussion of the risks of waiting too long are likely to maintain
Australian fertility at least at 1.8 births per woman for the next decade.

Banks (2005), in a Productivity Commission presentation, argues that there
is no ageing crisis: "Aging does not represent a crisis. Nor should it be viewed
just as a negative phenomenon for Australia. It is important to put it into perspective" (p. 8). Further, it is argued that the debate needs to be conducted
within a framework of projections rather than forecasts, in the sense that projections take account of present trends and policies and that it is highly likely
that behavioral and policy responses will result in changes.

REFRAMING THE CURRENT DEBATES

The fundamental work and caring challenge occurs at three levels—(1) the
individual, (2) social relationships and families, and (3) at the community/

societal level (including work organizations). The challenge, however, takes place within a broader social and economic context. There are many current and highly topical social debates and discourses in Australia that are central to the work/care challenge, e.g., gender equity; a crisis in masculinity; parental leave; child care; a crisis in fertility; parenting; relationship breakdown; separation and custody disputes; productivity and labor flexibility; aging workforce and inter-generational conflict; stress and work/life balance; employee engagement.

The next aim of this paper is to describe and analyze the essential elements of a sample of these debates in the context of the work and care challenge. Each has been reframed to take account of the link with the work and care challenge. (Some of this reframing has already been incorporated into the recent central commentaries listed above.)

From Gender Equity to Equal Opportunities and Responsibilities to Care and Work

The ongoing gender equity debate underlies many of the other debates discussed below. This debate is more commonly framed within the context of addressing inequities in outcomes for women in the public domain, e.g., in power, employment and financial well-being, and the inequities in the inputs women make to caring. The argument is that women and men should have equal rights to paid employment, to all the opportunities available in the range of employment options, and that there should be pay equity (both within and between job categories). This approach is highlighted in the recent book by Summers (2003). Summers argues that the economic, political, and social well-being of Australian women has been steadily and systematically undermined over the past 10 years. Key points of evidence presented include the statistics that women's total average earnings are 66% of men's (May, 2004); more than 160,000 women are prevented from working because they are unable to find childcare; 10.2% of senior executives in Australian private sector companies are women (EOWA, 2004); and only 8.6% of company board directors in ASX200 companies are women (EOWA, 2004). Although Summers mentions the lack of gender equity in childcare and housework, these are not key parts of her analysis.

A lack of gender equity in providing care is a key part of the analysis of the recent project initiated by the Sex Discrimination Unit in HREOC, titled *Striking the Balance: Women, Men, Work and Family.* The intention here was to spark a public debate about gender equity issues in relation to participation in the paid work and contributions to unpaid caring. Critically, a major purpose is to reframe this debate away from the common emphasis on women to include men—it is recognised that if change is to occur, men's experiences and attitudes towards paid work and family issues need to be considered. This argument about the need to include men has been made in many different forms and contexts over the past 20 to 30 years (e.g., Russell, 1983; Russell, James & Watson, 1988). Of particular note are the extensive academic and research literature and the public campaign conducted in the early 1990s "Sharing the Load."

It can be argued, however, that there have been considerable changes in the recent years in the policies and practices in relation to men. Importantly, the HREOC paper includes a comprehensive analysis of research and programs in relation to men's health, fatherhood, and early childhood development, and fatherhood and family separation. The paper also provides an extensive analysis of available research on both women's and men's participation in paid work and unpaid caring.

For gender equity to occur the opportunities for both women and men to care will need to achieve the same status in society as the opportunity for paid employment. Some have argued that equal employment opportunities for women in paid work is a prerequisite for men's opportunities to provide care (e.g., to develop close relationships with their children, to contribute to family care and child socialization). Because mothers do not have equal access to the full range of jobs at the same rate of pay as fathers, for example, it could mean that couples decide rationally that fathers should spend more time in the paid workforce than mothers. The assumed gender contract also needs to be considered in a more open way. This contract is usually based on three key assumptions (Haas & Hwang, 2002): (1) men should have more power than women; (2) the roles of men and women are different—and that mothers should be the primary caregivers of children; and (3) men's roles and ways of thinking should have greater value than women's.

Addressing all aspects of this assumed contract is essential if women and men are to achieve equity in the work and care challenge. Greater emphasis also needs to be given to the role of fathers in society. Research in the industrialized world indicates that fatherhood is, by and large, invisible in the workplace. Very little consideration is given to children's relations with their fathers and the need to place a priority on these relationships—the research evidence is clear that fathers make an independent contribution to children's outcomes. Work organizations in most societies are structured as if people have no other life and as if no fathers work there (Haas, 2002). Rather than focusing on fathers and their involvement in care, the public debate in Australia in relation to men has focused more on the crisis of masculinity and on the family work burden currently experienced by women, especially women who are in the paid workforce.

From the Crisis in Masculinity to Men as Active Partners in Gender Equity

An emerging debate in Australia is that men and boys are in crisis—there is a crisis in masculinity with men being confused (and part of the problem is assumed to be associated with the changing role of women in society), with assumptions that boys suffer from a lack of role models and mentors. The data to support these various propositions—both the nature of the problem and the nature of the solutions are scant indeed. There is often an assumption that many (most?) boys do not have close relationships with their fathers, or might not have any contact at all. Yet research findings indicate a positive shift in the past 20 years for fathers to be more involved with their children and to spend more time alone with them (Russell et al., 1999).

In the debate about the crisis in masculinity there has been very little mention of gender equity issues in the paid workforce, nor about the involvement of men and women in parenting and child care. An argument that there are potential positive outcomes for men who are involved in caring, however, could hardly be disputed—where positive outcomes are framed to include the potential benefits for the well-being of men themselves (a change here might also have an impact on the lowering of male suicide rates, especially following separation and divorce).

This argument might better be framed as men taking responsibility for the care of their children. Again, this could be reflected at the individual level and the policy level. The key to this is to question approaches at all levels (and in framing our research models) to assume and presume that men have equal roles and responsibilities in caring for children—where caring is meant to include all aspects from the very beginning stages. Another argument that can probably be sustained here is the impact that unemployment, or underemployment, can have on men given the fact that men are still by and large expected to construct their self-identities through involvement in paid work and career success.

More generally, though, more analysis is needed of the position of men in society, and of men as participants in the solutions, and to begin from the assumption that many men are active participants in care (see Carers NSW: "The Social and Emotional Circumstances of Male Carers"). Overall, there is a need for more focus on examining the actual and potential active contribution men make to gender equity outcomes. The United Nations has recently recognised this and has released the following statement:

> "The Commission on the Status of Women recalls and reiterates that the Beijing Declaration and Platform for Action[1] encouraged men to participate fully in all actions towards gender equality and urged the establishment of the principle of

shared power and responsibility between women and men at home, in the community, in the workplace and in the wider national and international communities. The Commission also recalls and reiterates the outcome document adopted at the twenty-third special session of the General Assembly entitled 'Gender equality, development and peace in the twenty-first century' which emphasised that men must take joint responsibility with women for the promotion of gender equality." (Commission on the Status of Women, 12 March 2004).

From Paid Maternity Leave to Paternity and Parental Leave

The recent framing of this debate in Australia has primarily focused on addressing the challenges for mothers to meet their work and child-care commitments/aspirations when they have young children. The reason for this is the increased rate of employment for mothers of young children. As is reported by de Vaus (2004, p. 301), 48.7% of mothers with preschool-aged children (who were in couple arrangements) were employed in 2002, compared with 37.2% in 1986. Even though the employment rate for mothers of young children in Australia is low by international comparisons, there has been a significant increase, and this increase has contributed to the defined individual and public need for paid maternity leave. Overall, 64.3% of full-time employed women (and 24.5% of women employed part time) have access to paid maternity leave. Fewer women have this entitlement in the private sector (36%) than in the public sector (71.3%). In contrast, 50.4% of full-time employed men have access to paid paternity leave (compared to 7% of those employed part-time), and 36.8% in the private sector (compared to 73% in the public sector) have access to paid paternity leave (ABS, 2004).[2]

Many leading private sector organizations have responded to the increased demand for parental leave for both women and men with the number of weeks provided being regularly cited as an indicator of an employer of choice. This paid leave has been provided on the expectation that return rates for women (men are rarely considered) will be higher—that talented women will be attracted and retained. Despite this, data show that a key enabling strategy for retention for women with young children involves having access to part-time work with career flexibility.

In essence, though, this debate and the policy recommendations have been somewhat narrow in perspective, ignoring broader gender equity issues and the need to consider providing both paid parental and paternity leave. Missing from this debate are the consideration of fathers and their work and caring commitments/aspirations—to also provide paid parental leave that could be taken by either a mother or a father; recognizing the potential impact parental leave policies can have on gender equity outcomes—and the potential that exists to improve gender equity outcomes through parental leave policies (e.g., to implement strategies adopted in some European countries where some of the parental leave entitlement is lost if fathers do not access it).

While mandatory unpaid paternity leave is now widely available in many countries (Haas, Hwang, & Russell, 2000; Wilkinson, Radley, Christie, Lawson, & Sainsbury, 1997), mandatory paid paternity leave is much less common. Deven and Moss (2002) have conducted a comprehensive review of statutory leave arrangements—maternity, paternity and parental leave—in the European Union (15), Norway, Central European countries (4), and Australia, Canada, New Zealand and the United States. The authors argue that the most striking recent developments are the emerging emphasis on fatherhood and increased flexibility in taking leave (e.g., working part-time and extending the period of leave; having choice about when the leave is taken in relation to the age of the child). In terms of fatherhood, this has involved either the introduction or enhancement of paternity leave, or by providing inducements to fathers to take parental leave (Sweden, Italy and Norway). Ten of the 24 countries have entitlements for paternity leave (for 8 the leave is paid), ranging from 2 days to 3 weeks. All countries included in the study provide some form of parental leave which theoretically could be taken by fathers, and in 17 of these there is some form of payment. In Italy, the total period of parental leave is extended from 10 to 11 months if the father takes at least 3 months of the leave; in Sweden, 2 months are specifically designated for fathers, and in Norway (where one month is designated for fathers), fathers have an independent right to obtain a financial benefit if they take parental leave, irrespective of the mother's employment status.

In countries where paid paternity leave is not mandated, very few organizations offer it to their employees. For example, in the United States only 1% of fathers in either the public or private sectors are eligible for at least some paid paternity leave (Tamis-LeMonda & Cabrera, 1999). In Australia, the figure has remained relatively constant over the past 5 years. Morehead, Steele, Alexander, Stephen & Duffin (1997) reported the figure to be 18% in 1995, whereas in 2002 it was 19% ABS, 2002).

A major reason why this has not shifted is because of the lack of importance placed on the needs for men to take such leave, such as the opportunity for men to provide care for their newborns, and the lack of emphasis on the needs of children to be connected to their fathers. Greater consideration needs to be given to the potential impact paid paternity leave and men taking parental leave could have on the connections men make with children. Further, children need to have this direct caring experience with their fathers. There is almost an absence of a recognition of the needs of children in relation to their fathers (see White & Russell, 2005), although this appears to be changing with the recent industrial relations case (see below).

From the Childcare Debate to the Caring Debate

This is a highly contentious debate with varying perspectives being presented, in part because of different positions that are adopted in relation to who should provide the care, and the expected consequences if they don't. This is more likely to be an issue in relation to preschool-aged children, where debates often revolve around questions to do with the impact of children being cared for outside versus inside their homes—and the proposition that children benefit from being cared for by their mothers within their homes. Recent reviews of the research (see Halpern, 2005) indicate that maternal employment per se does not have a detrimental effect on child development outcomes. Commonly, too, this discussion has been associated with providing increased opportunities for women to participate in the paid workforce. Lower female participation rates and reduced choices for women to participate in the paid workforce have been associated with various aspects of providing care, e.g., caring for preschool-aged children, being available in the afternoons for school-aged children, caring for disabled children, caring for their dependent partners/spouses (either because of disability or ill health) and caring for both their own and their partner's elderly parents.

The data, as reviewed in *Striking the Balance,* are clear in showing both that (1) women provide the majority of this care (and this is maintained when both partners in a household are in the paid workforce) and (2) that there are clear links between the lower workforce participation rates for women and higher caring demands (e.g., the relatively low participation rates for women in the 45 to 55 years age range). In the recent paper on "Men as Carers" from Carers NSW it is reported (ABS, 2005) that men make up nearly 50% of those classified as carers. Also recent U.S. data as reviewed in Halpern (2005) indicate that a significant number of men are caring for older adults, and that "the relational nature of adult caregiving, especially spousal caregiving, has different meanings and psychological consequences for adult women and men").

These data also highlight the different demands for different generations, e.g., having expectations (and aspirations?) to care for grandchildren as well as expectations (but not necessarily aspirations?) to care for frail elderly parents or a partner (e.g., with dementia); having teenage children and frail elderly parents; being in poor health yourself in retirement and having to care for frail elderly parents, etc. Those who are in the paid workforce with these different patterns of caring responsibilities potentially will also experience heightened demands with potential negative impact on personal and relationship well-being.

The recently formed Taskforce on Care Costs has also taken up these issues. This taskforce was established by key Australian business and non-government stakeholders to investigate the financial cost of care and how it impacts workforce participation, and to promote reforms within a policy framework of financial sustainability, equity, and choice. Findings included:

1. Affordability of care is a key issue for employees with caring responsibilities and strategies to reduce the financial cost of care will increase workforce participation levels.
2. The Australian government's current financial support for workers with caring responsibilities is minimal, and below best practice internationally.
3. Current strategies to reduce the cost of care focus on child-care and neglect workers with elder and disability caring arrangements. This is particularly critical given the ageing demographic.
4. Caring responsibilities have a direct impact on workforce participation. For workers with caring responsibilities:
    a. 1 in 4 has already reduced their hours of work because the cost of care is too high, and
    b. 1 in 4 is likely to leave the workforce because the cost of care is too high (and these results are amplified for workers with elder care responsibilities—40% of whom are likely to leave the workforce because of the cost of care).
5. The relationship between the cost of care and employment choices affects employees at all income levels (i.e., from low to high).
6. For every $1 spent by government on child-care there is a direct return to the government of $1.8 in terms of increased tax contributions and reduced government outlays.

From a Crisis in Fertility and Women Not Having Children to the Factors That Influence Couples to Have Children

A common argument made is that Australia's birth rate is too low at the present time—1.75 children per woman. Too low in the sense that if it continues at this rate, difficulties will be experienced in the future because Australia will have an inadequate labor force, and an increasing tax burden will fall on a smaller, younger generation in comparison to an aging population. This debate has been rather narrow in its perspective (overly pessimistic) and has often been conducted with static rather than a dynamic mindset. This is amply demonstrated by the recent report of the ABS (2005) that there was a significant increase in the birth rates for women in the 35 to 39 age group in 2003 and by the more recent paper of McDonald (2005).

The debate needs to be broadened to take account of the work and care aspirations of women and men who potentially could have children (see Cannold, 2005)—who focuses on "women who don't have children not because they are childless by choice or infertile, but because circumstances have limited their freedom to choose motherhood" and McDonald, who reports that of the 25% of women who are predicted to remain childless, only 7% will actually choose to remain childless). Whether or not people have children, when they have children, and whether they have more than one child are all dependent on a complex mix of factors (see Cannold's analysis). Research also shows that fertility rates have changed over different time periods (Björklund, 2002).

Research across a range of countries (see McDonald, 2005; de Vaus, 2004), conducted in different historical contexts, show that fertility rates are dependent upon: the economic context (availability and cost of housing, taxation regimes, capacity to split incomes, tax benefits to support family care), the labor market (high vs. low needs for workers), type of job a person is in, organizational policies/practices (flexibility in how, when, and where work is completed, availability of maternity leave, availability of part-time work, as well as flexibility in career options), perceived risks to longer term financial security, individual aspirations/expectations (about having children, about the value of children, centrality to their lives—for both women and men), availability of support (availability of child care, availability of other carers in the community, how equitable the gender division of household labor is following childbirth.). It has been found that couples are more likely to have children if there is a grandparent available to support the care of the child, and couples are more likely to have a second child if the father takes parental leave to care for the first.

In the most recent update of this research, McDonald (2005) argues that "the Australian total fertility rate has stopped falling and it is likely in 2004 it rose." Further, he argues that the current fertility rate of 1.8 births is "perfectly acceptable from a demographic perspective" and that "recent policy changes (such as increases in family payments last year) are very likely to maintain fertility at least 1.8 births per woman for the next decade."

In Australia, there have been a growing number of research studies focusing on the decision-making process involved in having children (Cannold, 2005). As is argued by Parker & Alexander (2004), the fertility literature is replete with reasons for delayed childbearing and the decline in large families. But what shapes men's and women's thinking about whether or not to have children?

From Parenting Is a Problem to Parenting As a Team

Parenting forms another dimension of care as defined in this paper. The nature of parenting, especially for older children, has become a key issue in public and political debates, with, at one time, a suggestion being made that all parents should be forced to attend parent education classes as a way of increasing the quality of parenting. This is based on the concern expressed by some that many parents are not currently meeting their responsibilities. In this context, though, the care debate has been framed slightly differently. Parental care has been discussed in terms of providing the necessary nurturance and love, ensuring children have appropriate supervision (e.g., before and after school), and that parents provide the necessary boundaries and discipline to their children.

The recent analysis by Stanley et al. (2005) provides a new and potentially startling perspective on these issues. The title indicates the essence of their argument: "Children of the Lucky Country? How Australian society has turned its back on children and why children matter." They summarize child health and well-being statistics that show that despite our economic prosperity, there have been significant increases in children with obesity, diabetes, asthma, literacy difficulties, mental health disorders, violent behavior, and substance abuse, and increases in children who are abused and neglected. They also argue that "the present generation of children may be the first in the history of the world to have lower life expectancy than their parents" (p. 52). In terms of solutions to these issues, Stanley et al. argue that caring for children and parenting is a community responsibility—recognising that an extended team approach is essential to ensure the well-being of children and of our society.

There is of course, a fundamental work and care challenge here. This can be expressed in two ways. First, a person having aspirations for either engagement in, or a particular level of engagement in the workforce (e.g., full-time hours or some variation less than this) but not being able to achieve it because of their expectations about providing care for their children, or because of the lack of availability of options to share this care (e.g., lack of finances to pay for care, lack of access to vacation care, not having a partner available to share the day-to-day care—e.g., single parent households). Second, a person who is engaged in the workforce (with a range of responsibilities and commitments), may have the basic care covered (e.g., can afford it and it is available), however, is challenged to provide the basic nurturance, boundaries and discipline.

This is sometimes referred to as the spillover effect of work demands onto family life, where because of work demands a person either lacks the physical or emotional energy and will to be the kind of parent they aspire to be (see

Galinsky, 1999), or that their children would like them to be (see Pocock, 2003), who reported that children would prefer to spend more time with their fathers, irrespective of the actual amount of time they currently spend with their mothers). Under these circumstances, parents find it difficult to provide the boundaries and to be engaged with their children. Recent research has addressed this issue, especially from the point of view of the impact of fathers' work demands.

Workplace demands. In many industrialized countries the norm of a 35–44 hour week has given way to either a part-time working week or longer hours in the full-time working week. Parents who are not so threatened by the possibility of job insecurity, unemployment, or underemployment might experience difficulties on another front—that of negative impacts from working intensively for longer hours. Working smarter and longer hours against a background of high unemployment means that for many parents the need to earn an adequate income takes an overwhelming priority in their lives. In Australia, the average number of hours worked by full-time employed persons has risen from 38.7 in 1983–1984 to 41.2 in 2003–2004. The relevant figures for women and men in 2003–2004 were 37.5 and 41.9 (ABS, 2005, pp. 174–175). Further, of those who worked 45 hours and more, 13% were women and 36% were men. The percentage of full-time employees working 50 hours or more a week has increased from 22.4% in 1993 to 24.7% in 2003 (Social Trends, 2004, p. 102).

The demise of standard working hours for full-time work—working harder and longer—is likely to have an impact on the opportunities for employed parents, and particularly men (given the current patterns of paid work), to be involved in family life. Many children, therefore, are likely to see less and less of their parents in daylight hours and on the weekends. The time demands of the workplace cut across all job sectors and indeed may be most keenly felt at the highly skilled end of the job market. Advances in information technology, while providing much needed flexibility for many parents (e.g., telecommuting), also have the potential to increase the number of hours worked (especially for managers and professionals) by enabling them to more easily conduct work from home and to be more independent of traditional support staff (e.g., e-mails and memos can be typed from home late at night).

A limited number of studies have examined the impact of job demands on parental involvement—both in terms of qualitative and quantitative involvement. In what is probably the most cited study, Repetti (1994) examined the impact of daily job stressors on parent-child interaction for a sample of 15 air traffic controllers (in a major international airport in the United States) who had school-aged children. The parents described their job stressors (e.g., workload, negative workplace social interactions) and parent-child interaction (emotional tone and quality of interactions, and their parenting behavior and state of mind during these interactions) on three consecutive days. Objective measures of daily workload were also obtained from the workplace. Repetti (1994) reported that after a demanding day at work parents were more behaviorally and emotionally withdrawn during their interactions with their children. She also reported evidence for there being direct spillover from negative feelings associated with distressing experiences at work to parents' expressions of anger and greater use of discipline.

Crouter, Bumpus, Head, and McHale (2001) examined the implications of men's long work hours and role overload (feelings of being overwhelmed by multiple work commitments and not having enough time for themselves) for the quality of their relationships with both their firstborn and second-born adolescents. The study included 190 dual-earner families from the central region of a northeastern state in the United States (both working and middle-class families were included). Data were collected both from face-to-face family interviews and from telephone interviews of parents and adolescents conducted on seven different evenings, asking about how family members spent their time. In contrast with previous findings, work hours and role overload did not have an effect on fathers' temporal involvement with either his firstborn or second-born adolescent. The authors suggest that this finding might be attributed to the fact that "adolescents typically share so few activities with their fathers that even fathers' very long work hours do not make an impact on the amount of time they share, a sobering thought" (p. 414). In contrast, it was found that the combination of working long hours and feeling overloaded predicted the quality of the relationships fathers had with both children. Fathers were seen as being less accepting and the relationship was characterised by less effective perspective taking when fathers both worked long hours and felt overloaded.

Working unsociable hours. For some in the paid workforce, work demands such as working unsociable hours at night or on weekends or because of travel demands, has a dual impact—both in terms of availability and in terms of being able to connect emotionally when at home. Although it very rarely gets into the debate, this issue is being highlighted more in terms of fathers' contribution to family life. An assumption about the importance of fathers was addressed recently by the Australian Industrial Relations Commission in a ruling (in relation to shift workers on a Bass Strait oil-rig) where it was accepted that keeping fathers away from their families for extended periods of time is not in the public interest.

Bittman (2003) provides a summary of findings from the comprehensive time use study conducted by ABS in 1997. It is clear from this analysis that family and social interactions occur much more frequently on weekends, and

especially on Sundays. This is especially the case for time spent with immediate family members (70% higher on Sundays than midweek), time spent
having family meals together, the engagement in family leisure activities, and
especially the engagement in leisure activities with children. Time use data,
of course, cannot provide information on differences in the family and relationship salience of family meals and social interactions that occur at different times of the week. It would be expected, though, that given current social
norms, salient family activities and meals (e.g., celebrations, extended family
gatherings) would be more likely to occur on Sundays. Although data are not
available, Sunday is also likely to be a more salient day for parent-child interaction in the context of family separation and divorce. It is much more
likely that access is given on weekends rather than on weekdays (e.g., to reduce the potential level of disruption to a child's weekly activities, such as
school).

Bittman also reports that 2.5 times more playing with children occurs on
Sundays in comparison with weekdays. Although data have not been broken
down as a function of gender, it would be expected that Sundays would provide the greatest opportunities for fathers to engage in play with their children, especially school-aged children, who are more likely to have sporting
commitments on Saturdays. (Research shows that this is a highly significant
aspect of father-child interaction and has consequences for the development
of children, see Lamb, 1997.)

Bittman (2003) has also examined the impact that working on Sundays has
on time spent on salient family activities. In summary, he found that those
who worked on Sundays spent two hours less on family leisure time and for
parents, it reduced their time with children by two hours. Those who work on
Sundays, therefore, have reduced opportunities to engage in critical family
activities. Bittman has also considered the possibility that those who work on
Sundays make up for the reduction of family and social interaction on this
day on other days during the week when they are not working. The findings,
though, do not support this hypothesis. Therefore, there appears to something
particularly salient about family and social interactions on Sundays. After
controlling for the effects of gender, family, household composition, occupation, and industry, Bittman's analysis did not reveal any pattern of compensation in time spent in activities associated with family togetherness and
broader social contacts.

These analyses show that those who work on Sunday have fewer opportunities to engage in significant family and social interactions. These analyses,
of course, cannot address the potential psychological impact that the absence
of a family member from key family activities has on other family members
or on the quality of long-term relationships. It would be expected, though,

that a continuing pattern of absence from significant family activities would increase the risks to family and personal well-being.

Numerous research studies have examined the impact of working unsocial hours and shift work on family and individual well-being. The consistent pattern of findings from both large-scale and small-scale qualitative studies, and from studies conducted in a range of different countries is that working nonstandard/atypical/unsocial hours does have a significant impact on family, couple, and child well-being. The summary below provides key findings from the most recent of these. Definitions and measures of non-standard hours and of shift work patterns vary considerably from one study to another. It is therefore difficult to provide a summary of relevant research findings from different types of working patterns. In a more recent review, Presser (2004) also highlights additional issues in interpreting this complex and under-researched area.

Impact on childcare arrangements. Le Bihan & Martin (2004) highlight the impact that working atypical hours can have on parents having access to childcare. Childcare is mostly provided during what can be considered "traditional" working times, 8 am to 6 or 7 pm, Mondays to Fridays. Parents who work atypical hours find it much more difficult to find suitable long-term arrangements for the care of their children. This impact can be reduced, however, if the atypical work arrangements are both predictable and negotiable. Also, some parents choose to work atypical hours in order to cover the care of their children. In Australia it has been found that 9% of employed parents work atypical hours specifically so that they can care for their children (Australian Bureau of Statistics, 2002).

Impact on family and child well-being. Le Bihan & Martin (2004, p. 570) report findings from a study by Rochette (2003) where it was concluded that: "Not only do they (working atypical hours) disrupt the biological clock of workers and that of their children, but they also disrupt their social and parental roles. In addition they cause numerous conjugal tensions, due to the difficulties of reconciling family and work." Grosswald (2004) in her study of 3,552 U.S. workers found that working a nonstandard, nonflexible shift was significantly associated with lower levels of self-reported family satisfaction.

Strazdins, Korda, Lim, Broom, and D'Souza (2004) have carried on the few comprehensive studies of the impact of parent work schedules on children's well-being. Their study involved the analysis of data from 4,433 dual earner families with children aged 2 to 11 years (6,361 children). They compared child outcomes for families where both parents worked standard hours with families where one or both parents regularly worked nonstandard hours (defined as working evenings, nights, or weekends). They found that "compared with households where both parents work standard times, children whose parents work non-standard times are more likely to have emotional or behavioural difficulties, indicative of child stress. This association persists after adjustment for a range of other influences, including SES (socioeconomic status) and patterns of child-care" (p. 1524). These findings were even stronger in families where there were younger children.

FROM RELATIONSHIP BREAKDOWN TO RELATIONSHIPS ARE THE HEART OF THE MATTER

A common community and policy discussion occurs around problems associated with relationship stability and divorce or separation rates. This is a key work and care challenge. Critical to this analysis is the assumption that caring is central to the development and maintenance of intimate relationships. Research evidence indicates that the quality of intimate relationships matters to individuals, to families, and to organizations. A focus on providing better opportunities for people to both establish and maintain intimate relationships will have a positive impact on personal and family well-being as well as on a person's effectiveness at the workplace.

In a recent comprehensive review of research findings, it was pointed out that close or intimate relationships (involving passion, mutual trust, and commitment) are a major part of the lives of most people. There is growing evidence from longitudinal studies that the presence of supportiveness of a close relationship is related to living longer and being less psychologically distressed. Further, it has been found that for full-time employed men and women in dual-earner couples, having higher-quality couple relationships can buffer the negative effects of job demands on psychological distress.

Research has also shown that work/family conflict and job stress are associated with lower levels of couple satisfaction for women and men, and withdrawal from couple interactions by both women and men. Working unsociable and long hours has also been found to have an impact on intimate relationships. In a large-scale longitudinal study, long working hours were found to reduce marital quality and increase the probability of divorce.

Similar outcomes would be expected in relation to some of the current workplace demands that reduce the capacity of employees (both women and men) to either establish or maintain quality intimate relationships. Two work demands that are especially likely to have this impact are extended hours of work and working at unsocial times.

Impact on relationship well-being. Studies (e.g., White & Keith, 1990) have been conducted that show that working atypical hours has a negative impact on the quality of couple relationships. Rochette (2003) (cited in Le Bihan & Martin, 2004) report that they cause numerous conjugal tensions, due to the difficulties of reconciling family and work. Jekielek (2003) examined the impact of non-standard work hours on the relationship quality of 1,016 dual-earner parents. She found that people who worked non-standard work schedules were more likely to experience higher levels of conflict and lower levels of positive interaction. Further, she did not find that this impact varied according to whether people worked evening compared to night shifts or regular compared to irregular shifts.

Marcil-Gratton & Lebourdais (2000) (cited in Le Bihan & Martin, 2004) found that in those families where both parents worked at atypical times they had twice as many separations as other families. In her study of 3,476 married couples, Presser (2000) found that: (1) among men with children, married less than 5 years, working fixed nights made it six times more likely they would separate or divorce than those who worked days; and (2) among women with children, married more than five years, working fixed nights increased their odds of separating or divorcing by three times.

From Separation, Custody Disputes to Staying Connected

A common policy and social discourse relates to issues associated with divorce and separation, and custody, child maintenance, and access disputes. This is clearly a work and caring issue, not the least of all because the workplace is involved in the collection of child support payments (linked to the child support agency). It is also an issue because there are significantly more parents in the paid workforce who either do not live with their children on a day-to-day basis, but have contact visits, or who have the sole responsibility for the day-to-day care of their children (single-parent households). Data also show that the proportion of single parents who are in the paid workforce has increased in recent years. These situations present different challenges for work and caring. This is also critical in the context of Welfare to Work policies and their impact on the work and care challenges of single parents.

Of marriages that began in 1975–1976, 17.1% had ended in divorce within 10 years. Of marriages that began in 1989–1990, 20.4% had ended in divorce 10 years later. It is expected (de Vaus, 2004, p. 211) that of marriages begun in 1999, 20% will end in divorce 10 years later, and that eventually 46% of these will end in divorce. In terms of the total population, in 1999, 7.4% of those over 15 were currently divorced.

In terms of families with children, approximately 10% of children are not with both biological parents by the time they turn 5 years of age, whereas approximately 17% are not with both biological parents when they turn 10, and close to 25% are not with their biological parents when they turn 15. Of all families with a child under 18 (de Vaus, 2004), 4% are blended families and 5.5% are stepfamilies.

In terms of employment (see de Vaus, 2004, p. 301), in couple households with a child under 15, 93% of men are employed, compared to 64.5% of women; in single-parent households with a child under 15, 72.6% of the men are employed compared with only 53.8% of women. Employment data do not appear to be available for blended and stepparent households.

The work and caring challenge for one group of parents—the non-custodial parent's challenge is one of staying connected and having the flexibility to do this, while for the custodial parent who lives in a single-parent household, the challenge is one of managing day-to-day care and the nurturance and support required when they return from paid work. Financial support is also a key issue for both parents following separation, and particularly so for the vast majority of women who are in single-parent households. Additional challenges would be expected to occur for employed parents who have children from more than one relationship and where some of these children do not currently live with the parent.

As is pointed out by Stanley et al. (2005), it is "the ongoing parent relationship and management styles that most strongly influence outcomes for children, rather than the separation and divorce" (p. 126). Research also indicates that, taking account of the needs of children in arrangements, child outcomes following parental separation are also influenced by the extent of and nature of involvement (having regular contact in the context of day-to-day family interactions) of both parents. Workplace policies clearly have the potential to enable parents to stay connected with their children or a potential barrier to this.

From Stress and Work/Life Balance to Caring for Yourself

Caring for yourself and having a high sense of well-being is probably the most significant building block of the work/care challenge (see also Edgar, 2005, p. 40). In this context, caring for yourself has commonly covered the following areas (see also Loehr & Schwartz, 2001).

Physical well-being. There is also good reason to examine these issues through the perspective of gender. Findings from the Australian Longitudinal Study on Women's Health indicate some trends in women's health that give reason for concern, e.g., increasing rates of obesity, increasing difficulties in balancing work, family, and personal health, and the particular pressures experienced by younger women. There is not a comparable study of men's health; however, there has been increasing attention given to men's health and the risks associated with their lifestyles (e.g., the 6th National Men's Health Conference). Particular emphasis has been given to the high suicide rates for men—reducing these rates has also been an issue addressed by several federal government initiatives.

Mental or psychological well-being. In a statement released by the World Federation for Mental Health, it was argued:

> The stage is set for a global business agenda on mental health starting with the proposition that mental health is an important productivity weapon in an intensely competitive data-based world economy. In this environment, organizations that promote employee well-being enhance their own competitive position by promoting the mental output of skilled workers. That being true, it is easy to see that management practices—by definition—can either promote or impair emotional stability and functioning in the modern workforce.
>
> In the information economy, more than ever, corporate success will depend on resilient, well-adjusted, and motivated employees—those with the skills and mindsets that will sustain the competitive edge of companies in the new economy of sustainable mental performance.

Emotional well-being. Essential to our emotional resilience is having quality personal (e.g., friendships) and intimate (with spouses/partners) relationships.

Spiritual well-being. Having purpose and meaning in life, our values and a strong sense of direction and identity in what we do, are all crucial to spiritual well-being. Having children and nurturing and caring for them are a central aspect of purpose for many people.

Financial well-being (including both quantity and the security). Financial well-being is a key component of our ability to care for ourselves. Taking a life-span perspective, the data show quite clearly that as a group, women are much less likely to have longer-term financial well-being and therefore they have a reduced capacity to provide care for themselves. Data from several analyses of the provision of superannuation provides a clear example. In a recent survey summarized in the Australian Financial Review (September 14, 2005, p. 30) conducted by the BT Financial Group, it was reported that 56% of women aged over 55 indicated they did not have enough funds to live comfortably after retirement.

Business organizations rarely adopt a highly integrated and strategic approach by including broader issues of self-care at all levels. Neither do they critically evaluate work practices and remuneration and employee bonus systems that operate as significant barriers to self-care.

CONCLUSIONS

Several commentators have covered parts of the above analysis, some using similar, others using different, frameworks. It makes sense, though, to capture the essence of the conclusions and recommendations from the various commentators. A key underlying theme is to build a society that permits greater diversity in choice—from the perspective of this paper would be added the need to focus more on both informed and supported choice. Suggestions made by the various academics to enable greater choice and opportunities for a diversity of people to address their work/care challenges include:

Pocock (2003) argues for reduced hours of work, secure part-time jobs, leave to care for others (more and more flexible), care (universal right to publicly provided care), workplace arrangements to facilitate work/care, government payments to families, change the gendered pattern of domestic work and unpaid care (focus on men), liberation from the cultures of intensive mothering, greater expectations of fathers, and greater valuation of care itself, revitalizing community—strengthen local communities, rethink consumption.

Stanley et al. (2005) make various recommendations for different groups of people and, social institutions: families and parents, local governments, communities, councils, and local non-government organizations, local clubs and organisations, politicians, policy makers, and those influencing policy (such as the media), schools, the workplace, employers, state and federal , and unions. In terms of the workplace, their suggestions include more workers rather than more work (ensure there is full employment and quality work); make paid maternity and paternity leave universal; cut down the hours; workplace provisions for high quality child care on or near the site of work; offer flexibility for working parent in their options for working hours; universal paid parental leave of at least six months on near full pay or 12 months on half pay, half of the cost to be paid by government; insist on a maximum average number of hours of 40 per week; firms recognize that their employees have home lives and important work to do in raising their children, and it must take some responsibility for making it possible for their workers to do this as well; firms must be encouraged in every forum to offer more secure forms of work, especially when they are employing people of parenting age.

Striking the Balance (2005). This comprehensive analysis leads to many different recommendations for change. Amongst these are law reform, e.g., the right to, or the right to request, part-time work; legislated paid maternity and paternity leave; social policy, e.g.,,, changes to assistance to families to encourage greater engagement of men as carers by better supporting families with two part-time incomes; changes in family assistance to encourage women to maintain workforce attachment; greater assistance to families to access affordable, quality care for children or other family members; cultural change in the workplace, e.g.,, encouraging employers to consider flexible arrangements tailored for both men and women; government support for parenting programs for men in the workplace; attitudinal change, e.g., strong leadership in equality and sharing of unpaid work by role models and national leaders.

Banks (2005), from the Productivity Commission argues that there are four areas of policy that need to be addressed to increase workforce participation rates across the life span (it is critical to point out that the argument here is that the focus should be on increasing participation rates for all age groups, not just older workers). (1) Increased skill levels through education and training. Also: "But we should be aware that there are limits to its likely benefits for labor participation and ensure that policy approaches take account of heterogeneity of people and policy does not focus overly on education duration." (2) Financial incentives to work (over leisure, home duties, welfare). It is recognized that this is a complex area (e.g., in determining eligibility age for pension) and needs to take account of implications for government revenue and equity. (3) Support systems (rehabilitation, childcare, and job search/training). It is argued that a focus on rehabilitation could have the effect of reducing the number of males on the Disability Support Pension. Although not discussed in this paper, there is also a possible link between the availability of childcare and workforce participation rates for grandparents. It is possible that some grandparents currently caring for grandchildren would be more likely to be in paid work if quality, affordable child care was available to their children. (4) Flexible workplaces. Banks argues that workplace design is likely to be less important than flexibility in work arrangements as a tool to increase workforce participation. Included in this conception is part-time work as well as sporadic work (e.g., offering jobs to those who have left full-time employment during peaks in demand). It is not clear what the basis of Banks' argument is about the lesser importance of workplace design, as there seem to be some clear opportunities here in terms of increasing the quality of work for all employees and therefore increasing the attractiveness of full-time employment for those who are not interested in working long hours.

Banks also argues (2005) that: "productivity improvements in the health sector greater than the economy-wide average *would* have direct benefits for the fiscal bottom line. Health reform should be a key part of the aging agenda." Not mentioned directly here is the possible impact of better health outcomes for all. This not only would help reduce health costs, it would have a direct impact on the productivity of those in the paid workforce. This further underlies the importance given to self-care in the present paper.

All of these debates/discourses are related, but often occur in different contexts and are considered in different policy domains or activity areas. There has been a tendency to demarcate and divide and not to consider work and care issues within a lifespan perspective. It also needs to be recognized, though, that there have been recent concerns about the problems between generations—inter-generational conflict—and assumed problems of resourcing and providing economically for an aging population. What is often missing, however, is the consideration of the right and responsibility to give care, or a person's right (and indeed need) to care for their aging parents.

There is obviously an individual choice component here, whether the individual wants to and will provide the care. But it is also clear that policies, the social discourse, and workplaces all combine to enable or restrict opportunity and aspirations. The social context creates an additional layer of meaning, for this issue is one of cultural, social and individual diversity.

The dilemmas and challenges faced by the diversity of people are many and they will vary at different life stages. Questions to be answered are: "What are the options that will work best in different contexts, and what evidence do we have to guide different initiatives?" "What is the basis for enabling people to make informed choices and what is the available evidence base?" These are questions that are equally relevant to individuals, families, policy makers, researchers, and employers.

NOTE

Graeme Russell, Ph.D., was formerly an associate professor in the Department of Psychology, Division of Linguistics and Psychology, Macquarie University, Sydney, Australia. He is currently working for Aequus Partners. Address correspondence to Graeme Russell, P.O. Box 681, Rozelle, NSW 2039, Australia.

1. An earlier version of this paper was presented to the National Diversity Think Tank.
2. Report of the Fourth World Conference on Women, Beijing 4–15 September 1995 (United Nations publication, Sales No. E.96.IV.13).

REFERENCES

ABS (1997) *Time Use Survey 1997.* Canberra: ABS
ABS (2002) *Australian social trends 2002.* Canberra: ABS.
ABS (2004) *Australian social trends 2004.* Canberra: ABS.
ABS (2005). *2005 year book Australia.* Canberra: ABS.

ACCI (2003). *Workplace relationships and family life: ACCI work and family policy.*

Australian Council of Trade Unions (2003). *The future of work: Working hours and work intensification policy.* Melbourne: ACTU Congress.

Banks, G. (2005, September). *Policy implications of an ageing Australia: an illustrated guide.* Paper presented to the *Financial Review* Ageing Summit, Sydney.

Barnham, L. J., Gottlieb, B. H., & Kelloway, E. K. (1998). Variables affecting managers' willingness to grant alternative work arrangements. *The Journal of Social Psychology, 138*(3), 291–302.

Bittman, M. (2003). A report on the effects working on Sundays has on other family activities. Unpublished manuscript, University of New South Wales, Sydney, Australia.

Bittman, M., & Pixley, J. (1997). *The double life of the family.* Sydney: Allen & Unwin.

Burgess, A., & Russell, G. (2004). Fatherhood and public policy. In *Supporting fathers: Contributions from the International Fatherhood Summit 2003.* The Hague: Bernard van Leer Foundation.

Burud, S., & Tumolo, M. (2004). *Leveraging the new human capital.* Palo Alto, CA: Davies-Black.

Cannold, L. (2005). *What, no baby? Why women are losing the freedom to mother, and how they can get it back.* Fremantle: Fremantle Arts Centre Press.

Colegate, C. (2004). *Just between you and me: The art of ethical relationships.* Sydney: Pan Macmillan.

Crouter, A. C., Bumpus, M. E., Head, M. R., & McHale, S. M. (2001). Implications of overwork and overload for the quality of men's family relationships. *Journal of Marriage and the Family, 63*(2), 404–417.

de Vaus, D. (2004). *Diversity and change in Australian families: Statistical profiles.* Melbourne: Australian Institute of Family Studies.

Deven, F., & Moss, P. (2002). Leave arrangements for parents: overview and future outlook. *Community, Work & Family, 5*(3), 237–256.

Edgar, D. (2005). *The war over work: The future of work and family.* Melbourne: University Press.

Eisenberg, M. E., Olson, R. E., Newmark-Sztainer, D., Story, M., & Bearinger, L. H. (2004). Correlations between family meals and psychological well-being among adolescents. *Arch Pediatr Adolesc Med, 158,* 792–796.

Gottman, J. (1997). *Why marriages succeed or fail: And how you can make yours last.* London: Bloomsbury.

Grosswald, B. (2004). The effects of shift work on family satisfaction. *Families in Society: The Journal of Contemporary Social Services, 85*(3), 413–423.

Haas, L. (1992). *Equal parenthood and social policy.* Albany: State University of New York Press.

Haas, L. (2002). Parental leave and gender equality: Lessons from the European Union. *Policy Studies Review, 20,* 89–114.

Haas, L., Allard, K., & Hwang, P. (2002). The impact of organizational culture on men's use of parental leave in Sweden. *Community, Work & Family, 5*(2), 319–342.

Haas, L., Hwang, P., & Russell, G. (Eds.) (2000). *Organizational change and gender equity: International perspectives on fathers and mothers at the workplace.* Thousand Oaks: Sage.

Halpern, D. (2005, July/August). Psychology at the intersection of work and family: Recommendations for employers, working families, and policymakers. *American Psychologist, 60*(5), pp. 397–409.

Hamilton, C., & Denniss, R. (2005). *Affluenza: When too much is never enough.* Sydney: Allen & Unwin.

Jekielek, S. M. (2003). Non-standard work hours and the relationship quality of dual earner parents. Unpublished dissertation, The Ohio State University.

Kaufman, G., & Uhlenberg, P. (2000). The influence of parenthood on the work effort of married men and women. *Social Forces, 78*(3), 931–947.

Le Bihan, B., & Martin, C. (2004). Atypical working hours: Consequences for childcare arrangements. *Social Policy & Administration, 38*(6), 565–590.

Macken, D. (2005). *Oh no, we forgot to have children.* Sydney: Allen & Unwin.

McDonald, P. (2005). Has the Australian fertility rate stopped falling? *People and Place, 13*(3), 1–5.

Parker, R. and Alexander, M. (2004), 'Factors influencing men's and women's decisions about having children.' *Family Matters,* 69(Spring/Summer), 24–31.

Parker, R. (2002). *Why marriages last: A discussion of the literature.* Melbourne: Australian Institute of Family Studies, Research Paper No. 28.

Pocock, B. (2003). *The work/life collision.* Sydney: The Federation Press.

Presser, H. B. (2000). Nonstandard work hours and marital instability. *Journal of Marriage and Family, 62,* 93–110.

Presser, H. B. (2004). Employment in a 24/7 economy: Challenges for the family. In A. C. Crouter & A. Booth (Eds.). *Work-family challenges for low-income parents and their children.* Mahwah, New Jersey: Lawrence Erlbaum Associates.

Repetti, R. L. (1994). Short-term and long-term processes linking job stressors to father-child interaction. *Social Development, 3*(1), 1–15.

Rostgaard, T. (2002). Setting time aside for the father: Father's leave in Scandinavia. *Community, Work & Family, 5*(3), 343–364.

Russell, G. (1983). *The changing role of fathers?* Brisbane: University of Queensland Press.

Russell, G., Barclay, L., Edgecombe, G., Donnovan, J., Habib, G., Callaghan, H., & Pawson, Q. (1999). *Fitting Fathers Into Families.* Canberra: Commonwealth Department of Family and Community Services.

Russell, G., & Bowman, L. (2000). *Work and family: Current thinking, research and practice.* Canberra: Department of Family and Community Services.

Seligman, M. (2002). *Authentic happiness.* Sydney: Random House.

Sex Discrimination Unit, HREOC (2005). *Striking the balance: Women, men, work and family.* Sydney: HREOC.

Sheahan, P. (2005). *Generation Y: Thriving and Surviving with Generation Y at Work.* Prahan, Victoria: Hardie Grant Books.

Stanley, F., Richardson, S., & Prior, M. (2005). *Children of the lucky country: How Australian society has turned its back on children and why children matter*. Sydney: Pan Macmillan.

Strazdins, L., Korda, R. J., Lim, L. L.-Y., Broom, D., & D'Souza, R. M. (2004). Around-the-clock: parent work schedules and children's well-being in a 24-h economy. *Social Science & Medicine, 59,* 1517–1527.

Summers, A. (2003). *The end of equality*. Sydney: Random House.

Tamis-LeMonda, C. S,, & Cabrera, N. (1999). Perspectives on father involvement: Research and policy. *Social Policy Report: Society for Research in Child Development, XIII* (2), 1–26.

Monthly Labor Review, September, 17–23.

Thew, P., Eastman, K., & Bourke, J. (2005). *Age discrimination: Mitigating risk in the workplace*. Sydney: CCH.

Trinca, H., & Fox, C. (2004). *Better than sex*. Sydney: Random House.

Voydanoff, P. (2002). Linkages between the work-family interface and work, family, and individual outcomes. *Journal of Family Issues, 23*(1), 138–164.

Waldfogel, J. (2001). *Family and medical leave: Evidence from the 2000 surveys*.

Warin, J., Solomon, Y., Lewis, C., & Langford, W. (1999). *Fathers, work and family life*. London: Family Policy Study Centre.

Wilkinson, H., Radley, S., Christie, I., Lawson, G. & Sainsbury, J. (1997). *Time out: The costs and benefits of paid parental leave*. London: Demos.

White, L., & Keith, B. (1990). The effect of shift work on the quality and stability of marital relations. *Journal of Marriage and the Family, 52,* 453–462.

White, T., & Russell, G. (2005). *First-time father*. Sydney: Finch Publishing.

Chapter Twenty-Two

Work-Family Facilitation: What Does It Look Like?

by E. Jeffrey Hill, Sarah Allen, Jenet I. Jacob,
Ashley Ferrin Bair, Sacha Leah Bikhazi,
Alisa Van Langeveld, Guiseppe Martinengo,
Taralyn Trost Palmer, and Eric Walker

ABSTRACT

This study uses qualitative research methods to enhance understanding of work-to-family and family-to-work facilitation by identifying key themes in free-response comments by employees of a large multinational corporation. Data come from an IBM work-life survey in 79 countries. Employees were asked to describe the positive influences of their work life on their home life and vice versa. The comments of a sub-sample (n = 22,064) in 13 countries were analyzed using N-Vivo to identify key themes and frequencies. Participants most frequently mentioned workplace flexibility, financial benefits, and the ability to keep family commitments as important components of work-to home facilitation. Supportive family relationships, psychological benefits of home, and psychological aspects of work were most frequently identified as important components of family-to-work facilitation. Gaps in the current research literature and suggestions for future work-family facilitation research are identified.

Work is often seen as the irreconcilable nemesis of home and family life. When *work* is used in the same sentence as *family,* words like *conflict, stress, strain, interference, balance* and *juggling* are often closely associated. All of these presuppose that the way for work to optimally intersect with home and family life is to limit each and to find an appropriate balance between the two. Certainly this perspective has salience. The preponderance of 30 years of work and family research has yielded a great harvest of theory and knowledge.

In this volume many chapters embrace this perspective. Butler, Bass, and Grzywacz (in press) use the metaphor of balance to examine work and family resources. Moen and Kelly (in press) describe the stresses of gendered working families in socially toxic job ecologies. Perry-Jenkins, Claxton, Smith, and Manning (in press) inspect the stresses experienced by fathers, mothers, and children as mothers transition back to work after the birth of a child. Repetti and Saxbe (in press) contribute to our understanding of the daily job stresses and their deleterious influence on family life, especially for women. Heymann and Simmons (in press) report that the conflicts and challenges of working parents are universal whether in the United States, Botswana, Mexico, or Vietnam. Carlson, Wayne, & Harris (in press) examine the decision processes people use when faced with conflicting work and family demands. Ruhm (in press) summarizes how maternal employment may sometime conflict with desired child outcomes. Waldfogel and Han (in press) also examine how variations in parental employment arrangements differentially and sometimes conflictually relate to child outcomes. Bianchi (in press) explicitly explores what happens to mothers' scarce resource of time at home when they choose to work longer hours outside of the home. Barnett (in press) looks at the effects of maternal shift work on mothers', fathers', and children's well-being, especially work-family conflict. All of these articles help us understand better the interface between work and home and family life.

However, in this final chapter of the *Handbook of Families and Work: Interdisciplinary Perspectives,* we make the case for using a different perspective, a perspective that looks for the ways in which work and family life benefit one another. After two decades of work-family literature dominated by a conflict perspective, there is increasing impetus for exploring the positive interaction between work and family roles (Barnett, 1998; Frone, 2003; Grzywacz, 2002; Hill, 2005). Several contributions to this volume also acknowledge this perspective. Wayne (in press) departs from the zero-sum conflict metaphor to examine the positive side of the work-family interface and offer a framework to differentiate constructs such as enhancement, positive spillover, enrichment, integration, and facilitation. Grzywacz (in press) finds beneficial health effects of schedule flexibility and frames them from an enrichment perspective, suggesting that jobs can be designed in ways that are beneficial to organizations and families. van Steenbergen, Ellemers, and Mooijaart (in press) also examine how supportiveness at work and home appear to stimulate work-family facilitation.

This growing body of studies demonstrates positive relationships be-tween paid work and family life that challenge scarcity-based assumptions that these roles are inherently incompatible. But research has been hindered by limited theoretical frameworks and methodological approaches from ex-ploring these positive relationships (Greenhaus & Powell, 2006). Grzywacz's (2002) theory of the positive interdependencies between work and family roles and Greenhaus and Powell's (2006) proposed model of the process of work-family enrichment contribute significantly to theoretical understanding, but need to be tested and refined. Studies incorporating methodologies beyond self-report scales and observed correlations are also needed to expand understanding of what defines positive interdependencies in the work-family interface and how they are experienced (Greenhaus & Powell, 2006).

In an effort to further that pursuit, we use qualitative research methods to explore employees' perceptions of how work life is enhanced by the experi-ence of family life and how family life is enhanced by the experience of work life. Qualitative research is particularly well adapted to reveal perceptions and attributions of meaning to phenomena (Bryman, 1988). As a result, it has the potential to contribute to theoretical understanding of positive interde-pendencies between work and family in several specific ways. First, qualita-tive methods will facilitate development of theoretical frameworks and mea-sures based on concepts emerging from the voices of those experiencing the work-family interface. Second, concepts emerging from qualitative analyses can be compared with those from theory-driven quantitative analyses to ad-just and deepen what is currently understood about facilitative work-family processes.

RELATED RESEARCH

Research on the positive side of the work-family interface began nearly two decades ago when Crouter (1984) identified positive spillover between work and family as the neglected side of the work-family interface. After this cri-tique, however, relatively little scholarly attention was paid to work-family facilitation during the 1980s and 1990s (Bidyadhar & Sahoo, 1997; Kirch-meyer, 1992; Pittman & Orthner 1988; Zedeck & Mosier, 1990). That trend changed during the 2000s when there was a clear shift in focus toward work-family facilitation. Since that time there has been a burgeoning interest in the positive influences of work on the home, and of the home on work (Butler, Grzywacz, Bass, & Linney, 2005; Hill, 2005; Mellor, Mathieu, Barnes-Far-rell, & Rogelberg, 2001; Voydanoff, 2004).

Extant literature conceptualizes this positive reciprocal relationship using four different terms: (1) *positive work-family spillover* (Crouter, 1984; Butler et al., 2005; Glass & Estes, 1997; Grzywacz, 2000; Grzywacz, Almeida, & McDonald, 2002; Stephens, Franks, & Atienza, 1997; and Zedeck & Mosier, 1990), (2) *work-family facilitation* (Butler et al., 2005; Frone, 2003; Grzywacz & Butler, 2005; Hill, 2005; and Voydanoff, 2005), (3) *work-family enrichment* (Friedman & Greenhaus, 2000), and (4) *work-family enhancement.* (Voydanoff, 2002). These positive processes have been associated with individualized experiences of *work-family compatibility* (Grzywacz & Bass, 2003), *work-family fit* (Barnett, 1998; Edwards & Rothbard, 1999; Grzywacz & Bass, 2003; and Voydanoff, 2002), and *balance* (Frone 2003; Butler et al., 2005). These studies have contributed to identifying aspects of work life that lead to positive outcomes in family life and aspects of family life that lead to positive outcomes in work life. In this study, we anticipate finding evidence to corroborate these findings. The use of open-ended responses and qualitative analysis, however, will enable further exploration of how family and work contribute to one another in the eyes of the worker.

The current analysis uses the term *work-family facilitation,* defined as "the extent to which participation at work [or home] is made easier by virtue of the experiences, skills, and opportunities gained or developed at home [or work]" (Frone, 2003, p. 145). For the purposes of this paper we focus on work to home and home to work facilitation but do not draw distinctions between the terms *work-home* and *work-family* facilitation (and vice versa), although they may be conceptually distinct in some cases. Work-home facilitation does not contain prohibitive restrictions on family structure and recognizes that work-family facilitation may occur with family members who are not co-resident with the worker. The research questions center on the ways in which paid work positively benefits family life and the ways in which family life positively benefits paid work as perceived by employees of a large company.

RESEARCH DESIGN AND METHODOLOGY

Survey and sample description. Data come from the *IBM 2004 Global Work and Life Issues Survey.* This survey was translated into 12 languages and was administered over the Internet to IBM employees in 79 countries. The sample was representative of IBM's employee distribution globally and included employees from Europe, North America, Asia/Pacific, South America, and Africa. The sample was also stratified by country and by gender. Altogether 97,644 employees (31% of the IBM population) were invited to participate and 41,769 responded, for a participation rate of 43%. A sub-sample of respondents

($n = 22,064$) from 13 countries was selected from the larger sample to match the language capabilities of our research team. Response coding was completed in English, Spanish, Portuguese, and Italian for the following countries (% of overall sample): Argentina (2.8%), Australia (6.9%), Brazil (6.2 %), Canada (9.5%), Hong Kong (1.9%), Israel (1%), Italy (5.8%), Mexico (3%), Portugal (1.7%), South Africa (1.6%), Spain (5.1%), the United Kingdom (10.1%), and the United States (44.3%). This selection of countries maintained the global diversity of the overall sample with representation from each continent.

The sample was 50.5% female and 49.5% male. Participants were on average 41 years old, but a wide range of ages were represented (less than 25 to more than 70 years). For description purposes, the sample was broken down into three age categories: (a) young (less than 35 years), (b) middle-aged (ages 35 to 54 years), and (c) mature (ages 55 years and more). The majority were in non-managerial positions (83%) but manager (12.2%) and executive (4.7%) positions were also represented. Employees had worked an average of 12 years for IBM and an average of 55 hours per week. Married employees comprised 68.5% of the sample and 57.2% had at least one child. Most employees (51.1%) had a spouse who worked full time. However, 17.7% had a spouse who had no paid work and 11.9% had a spouse who worked part time. Employees who had no spouse or partner represented 19.3% of the sample.

Data analysis. We analyzed the written responses to two open-ended questions: (a) In what ways does your work at IBM positively influence your home life? And (b) In what ways does your home life positively influence your work at IBM? In total, 13,315 comments were coded and analyzed using N-Vivo software. A generic qualitative approach (Rossman & Rallis, 2003) was used to analyze the data, which involved organizing the data, familiarizing oneself with the data, generating categories and themes, coding the data, interpreting, and writing.

Responses to the two open-ended questions were first analyzed by a small coding team on a line-by-line basis using open coding to discover, name, and identify as many potentially relevant categories as possible. After coding several transcripts in this manner, it became apparent that some categories were more salient than others because they kept appearing in the responses. The small coding team worked collaboratively to create a working list of common themes and categories found in the data and then joint coded with members of a larger coding team to train them on the coding scheme. The progress of this larger coding group was periodically reviewed in order to ensure consistent coding. Using the constant comparative method (Strauss & Corbin, 1998), categories were compared with other incidents coded for those categories from other transcripts. This helped to generate theoretical properties and dimensions for each category and suggested potential relationships to other categories. Further coding helped to relate categories to their sub-categories and began to hypothesize the relationships among the core categories (Strauss & Corbin, 1998). In order to preserve the confidentiality of each participant, a pseudonym was used in reporting the data.

RESULTS

The process of coding revealed that participants were identifying not only aspects of paid work that were facilitators of home life and vice versa, but also specific aspects of home life that were facilitators of work life and vice versa. Consequently, the coding team organized the data into four large core categories (see Figure 22.1). These included: (1) Aspects of work most frequently

Work-to-Home Facilitation

(1) In what ways does your work at IBM positively influence your home life?

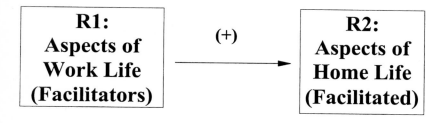

Home-to-Work Facilitation

(2) In what ways does your home life positively influence your work at IBM?

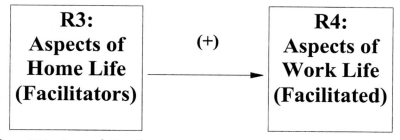

Figure 22.1   Research Questions.

identified as positively influencing home life; (2) Aspects of home life most frequently identified as being positively influenced by work life; (3) Aspects of home life most frequently identified as positively influencing work life; and (4) Aspects of work life most frequently identified as being positively influenced by home life.

Work aspects positively influencing home life. Participants identified six aspects of work that positively influenced home life: (a) flexibility, (b) employee benefits, (c) psychological benefits, (d) skills and resources, (e) relationships at work, and (f) work itself. (Please see Table 22.1 for the frequency of each category). Job flexibility in the place or time work was done was consistently identified as the most important component of work that positively influenced participants' home life. As Mary, a middle-aged mother living in the United States said about working from home:

> The ability to work at home and have flexible hours when needed enables me to pick up my children if they get sick at school, pick them up after school if needed, attend school events during the day, etc. This has been very positive and has decreased the stress related to my family life.

Employee benefits such as salary, vacation time, and leave were also frequently cited by participants as having a positive influence on their home life. Emily, a middle-aged mother living in the United States, said, "Working for IBM allows me to provide for my family due to a nice salary and the availability of benefits needed to ensure my family's health." Participant responses also indicated that psychological benefits from working including a sense of accomplishment, job satisfaction, job security, or having pride in IBM and their work positively influenced their home life. For example, Mandela, a young father from South Africa, said, "I enjoy my work, which means that I am happy, which means that I am positive and happy at home."

Resources obtained through work, such as access to technology, travel, and skills also emerged as important aspects of work that could benefit home. Benjamin, a father of mature age from Israel, said, "The skills I have acquired at IBM have helped me handle or manage personal planning and financial matters and handle or manage out of office projects and problem solving issues." Relationships with managers and co-workers were also an important feature of work that benefited home. Tom, a father of mature age from the United States, said:

> My manager values and respects the individual and his/her necessary commitment to self and family. Personal situations involving family members over the last four to five years have been able to be tended to by me because of IBM's environment and managers' understanding and commitment to flexibility.

Table 22.1. Aspects of Work that Benefit Home

Main Categories	Subcategories		Frequency Mentioned
Flexibility	Flex-place		945
	Work at home		3067
	Commute		414
	Flex-time		1538
	Part Time		266
	Convenient Work Hours		159
	Longer Work Hours		60
	Compressed Work Week		53
	Job Flexibility		862
	Autonomy		128
		TOTAL	7492
Employee Benefits	Salary		1748
	Benefits		587
	Compensation		237
	Vacation		113
	Leave		57
		TOTAL	2472
Psychological Benefits	Sense of Accomplishment		497
	Job Satisfaction		390
	Pride in Work		293
	Job Security		267
	Psychological State at Work		213
	Pride in IBM		58
		TOTAL	1720
Skills and Resources	Access to Technology		97
	Travel		112
	Skills learned at work		496
		TOTAL	705
Relationships at Work	Relationships with managers		175
	Relationships with coworkers		181
	Relationships at work		181
	Support of Spouse who works at IBM		95
		TOTAL	632
Work Itself	Job Productivity		226
	Challenging Work		160
		TOTAL	386
Other		TOTAL	122

Having challenging and productive work was also mentioned as a feature of work that positively affected family life. Lachlan, a middle-aged man with children from Australia said, "Work at IBM is a good balance to some of the more mundane tasks of family life. Work problem solving keeps my brain challenged, which is good for my health and keeps me up to the challenges of raising children."

Home aspects positively influenced by work life. Participants identified seven aspects of home life that were benefited by work: (a) ability to make family commitments, (b) individual well-being (c) material well-being (d) home and family time, (e) relationships with family, (f) home-management skills, and (g) access to technology. (Please see Table 22.2 for the frequency of each category). But a sizeable number of responses (*n* = 746) specified that there were no aspects of their home life that were benefited by their work.

Many workers indicated that flexible work options facilitated not only their ability to meet and make commitments to themselves, their children, and family but also increased their ability to participate in family activities. Jane, a middle-aged mother from Australia, said:

> I am a part-time employee, working 2 days per week. This part-time arrangement allows me to spend considerable time with my 3-year-old daughter. I am actively involved in her life now, and participate in such things as playgroup, swimming lessons, ice skating, picnics, playing at the beach. Bliss!

Table 22.2.   Feature of Home that are Benefited by Work

Main Categories	Subcategories		Frequency Mentioned
Ability to make Family Commitments	Commitments to Children & Child Care		638
	Commitments to Family		306
	Participate in Family Activities		440
	Flexibility at Home		165
	Home Commitments		247
	Personal Commitments		361
		TOTAL 2157	
Individual Well-Being	Balance		410
	Personal Psych Benefits		741
	Physical Health		67
	Personal time		77
		TOTAL 1295	
Financial Well-Being	Financial Stability		694
	Household Expenses		285
		TOTAL 979	
Home/Family Time		TOTAL 642	
Relationships with Family	Relationship with Family, Spouse, Children		208
	Role Model		104
		TOTAL 312	
Home Management Skills		TOTAL 128	
Access to Technology		TOTAL 124	
Cycle of Benefits		TOTAL 98	
None		TOTAL 746	

Workers also identified increased personal well-being, personal time, and psychological and physical wellness as features of their home life that were benefited by work. Sophie, a mother of mature age from the United Kingdom, said:

> Being able to work from home saves me 2 hours of transport every day. It enables me to get a bit more sleep in the morning and avoid the stress of traveling by the packed tube to and from work. I feel less stressed and less tired that way, which has a positive influence on my health (less colds and flues).

Work also benefited home life by enabling families to meet household expenses and have financial stability. Lesley, a middle-aged mother from the United Kingdom, said, "By having a fulfilling job that is adequately remunerated my family and I can enjoy a good standard of living."

Participants also identified work as facilitating home and family time and benefiting relationships with their family, spouse, and children. Mia, a young mother living in the United States, said that work "gives me more confidence in the my ability to accomplish difficult tasks, helps me and the family feel more secure, and improves communication and family relationships when I bring what I learn about teaming home." In some cases, such positive effects circled around back to work indicating pathways through which benefits are experienced. For example, David, a mature father living in the United States, said, "When I do have the opportunity to work from home remotely, I can better balance time with my family. This provides me a more positive attitude which, in turn, motivates me to do more work on IBM assignments."

Some skills learned at work benefited home and family life because they were transferable and acted to increase participants' home management skills. Jane, a mother of mature age living in the United States, said:

> The skills I've learned at IBM have positively affected my home life. Time management, project management, negotiations, decision making, situation analysis and communication are a few skills used on a daily basis at IBM that are transferred over to my home life making it easier/faster to get things done in an efficient manner.

In some cases, work facilitated an increase in the home's access to technology in the form of software, hardware, and internet connections that would not have been available otherwise. Ryan, a mature man living in Australia, said, "Having cable modem at home lets me spend the evening at home with the family rather than in the office, which is simply wonderful."

Home aspects positively influencing work life. Participants identified six aspects of home life that positively influenced work: (a) physical and psychological benefits, (b) relationships with family members, (c) flexibility, (d) interaction with family members, (e) resources, and (f) stability. (Please see Table 22.3 for the frequency of each category). Many physical and psychological benefits rooted in home life were identified as benefiting work life. Participants talked about how their home and family life helped to keep the

Table 22.3. Aspects of Home that Benefit Work

Main Categories	Subcategories	Frequency Mentioned	
Physical and Psychological Benefits	Balance		301
	Positive Attitude		15
	Personal Psychological Benefits		507
	Spirituality		49
	Mental		126
	Emotional		98
	Physical		236
		TOTAL 1418	
Relationship with family members	Family Relationships		92
	Children Relationships		42
	Spouse Relationships		57
	Family Harmony		204
	Children Support		26
	Family Support		681
	Spouse Support		343
		TOTAL 1445	
Flexibility	Work at Home		355
	Flexi Family Time		134
	Flexibility		269
		TOTAL 758	
Interaction with Family Members	Family Commitments		90
	Childcare		58
	Personal Commitments		32
	Lack of Home Commitments		138
	Recreational Activities		36
	Family Time		140
		TOTAL 494	
Stability	Family Stability		196
	Financial Stability		39
	General Stability		71
		TOTAL 306	
Skills		TOTAL 228	
Household Expenses	Household Expenses		11
	Financial Stability		39
	Financial Motivation		126
		TOTAL 176	
Separate Time and Space	Time away from work		86
	Time at home		32
	Personal Time		40
		TOTAL 158	

pressures experienced at work in perspective. Rachel, a mature woman living in the United States, said, "My family helps me keep things in perspective when IBM work issues can otherwise seem overwhelming and take over your life." Chung, a young father living in China, talked about home as a place of physical renewal where he "Reliev[ed] work pressure by exercising every week and eating healthily." Xiu, a middle-aged woman living in Hong Kong, spoke about home as a place of psychological renewal. "A good home life provides emotional support to help relieve and regulate the work pressure." Speaking more dramatically of home as a place of renewal, Sam, a mature father living in the United States, said:

> My home is a glorious place of renewal. I may come home after a hard day at work feeling like I have been chewed up and spit out. But then at the [door] I'm greeted like a conquering hero by my children and a miracle occurs. I am restored. I have clarity of vision. My energy returns. By the next morning and I am full of energy ready for work again.

Supportive family relationships were also identified as benefiting work life. Kristine, a mature mother living in Australia, talked about how her relationship with her spouse helped her succeed at work. She said, "My husband is my confidant and sounding board. My manager is remote (different state and sector) but helpful. The person with the most control over me is not interested in the type of work that I do, so my husband is my saving grace." Having a supportive partner also facilitated optimal work situations. Samora, a mature woman living in South Africa, said, "My partner allows me the flexibility to work at home after hours and supports me in my job as he knows that I love doing what I do." The facilitative role of positive relationships in the responses was nicely summarized by Nicole, a young mother living in Australia, who said, "It's all a circle . . . happy family, happy employee who's able to focus on work when they're here."

Flexibility was also frequently mentioned as an aspect of home that positively influenced work. This was interesting to note, as flexibility is often thought of as a work-based dimension that facilitates home. It is, however, possible for flexibility to work in the other direction. Carrie, a young mother from Australia, said, "Flexibility works both ways. A flexible home life and family enables me to meet deadlines, put in extra hours, and travel for work when needed."

Spending time together by participating in a variety of family activities with family members and being able to meet one's commitments to them were also aspects of home that facilitated work. Jia Li, a middle-aged woman living in Hong Kong said that "spending more time with the family can balance out the stress on number chasing." Chloe, a mature mother from South

Africa spoke about how her ability to meet her commitments to family helped her at work. She said, "My availability to my children when they need me has provided tremendous harmony and peace for my family life that makes me a more productive and dedicated employee."

Home-based skills were also identified as beneficial at work. Katherine, a middle-aged mother living in the United States said, "I'm able to use the same skills I use to manage my household to manage my projects at work. Negotiation skills I use with my children help me to negotiate with my team members."

Home also benefited work by providing a space and time away from work. Describing the benefit of having time with family away from co-workers, Alba, a middle-aged mother from Spain, said, "It helps me tolerate the bosses, the unscrupulous employees, the intrigues, and the injustices. Without my family I wouldn't be able to stand it." Workers also identified the space and time of home as important in enabling them to fulfill personal interests and forget about office politics. When they returned to work, they could work more effectively. As Joan, a middle-aged woman living in the United States said, "Having a little more time for my hobbies helps me to handle the stress of trying to meet deadlines and to deal with other job-related pressures."

The desire to provide for a family and have financial stability were aspects of home that also benefited work by enhancing work motivation. William, a middle-aged father living in the United Kingdom, said, "Fiscal requirements of mortgage and children means commitment and dedication to work is not optional." Diego, a young father from Argentina, further explained, "The harmony in my family and the knowledge that my responsibilities to my family as a father are met, whether material or affective, allows me to work with greater dedication and efficiency."

Participant responses also identified family, home, and marital stability as aspects of home that facilitated optimal work performance. Jenny, a middle-aged mother living in Australia, said, "I am in a stable family/marriage relationship. Therefore, there are really no great concerns I bring to work. Balancing family and work has increased my management and relationship skills." In a similar vein, Ari, a mature father living in Israel, said, "My overall home life stability helps me concentrate on my work at IBM without distractions."

Work aspects positively influenced by home life. Participants identified six aspects of work that were positively influenced by home: (a) psychological aspects, (b) flexibility in work, (c) job productivity, (d) relationships at work, (e) skills and resources, and (f) travel. (Please see Table 22.4 for the frequency of each category). Participants identified numerous ways in which their home life helped them to feel they were a better employee at work.

Table 22.4. Features of Work that are Benefited by Home

Main Categories	Subcategories		Frequency Mentioned
Psychological aspects	Sense of Accomplishment		59
	Psychological State		484
	Motivation		747
	Balance		72
		TOTAL 1362	
Flexibility in Work	Flexi-time		417
	Flexi-place		57
	Job Flexibility		75
	Part-time		20
	Commute		136
		TOTAL 705	
Job Productivity	Job Productivity		498
	Can meet work commitments		177
		TOTAL 675	
Relationships at Work		TOTAL 429	
Travel		TOTAL 115	
Skills and Resources		TOTAL 65	

Tracy, a middle aged mother living in Australia said, "By having a break from the work environment I'm able to approach my work with a fresh mind and a willingness to achieve." Many other participants talked about how time at home helped them to "have a more enthusiastic attitude toward work," "excel at work," be "more motivated and focused at work," have a "desire to go that extra mile" at work, or be "more motivated to meet and exceed work commitments." John, a middle-aged father living in the United States, said:

> I believe that a "happy employee" is a "good employee" and although job satisfaction can contribute to happiness, our home life is the primary motivation behind our happiness. The ability to nurture one's personal life is important to maintaining a strong motivation to work.

Participants also identified ways in which their home life increased their ability to experience more flexibility in the time and place they did their work. Olivia, a young mother living in Australia, wanted to be able to spend more time at home with her children. Commitment to home and family enabled her to experience more flexible job arrangements with IBM. She said, "I work after hours and can therefore pick up any work not done by the office during the day in readiness for start of business the next day." Having supportive family members also enabled employees to have the flexibility needed to get their work completed. Javier, a young father living in Mexico, said, "The support of my family allows me to work non-regular hours" while

Alejandro, a middle aged father from Spain, said, "My family really allows me the time necessary for work that includes travel."

Participants also described how aspects of their home life enabled them to be more productive at work. Charlotte, a young mother from Australia, said, "I feel very motivated to achieve and perform well at work as I have a family to be a role model for and to provide for." Likewise, Simon, a mature father living in the United Kingdom, said that "A flexible home life enables one to work out of normal hours on urgent tasks or large pieces of work." In some cases, employee skills at work were enhanced because of a personal interest or hobby done at home. Jack, a young man from the United Kingdom, said, "Computing hobbies at home give me the increased knowledge that is useful for work."

Some participant responses suggested that their home and personal life facilitated positive relationships at work. Juan, a young father from Argentina, said, "My own personal happiness improves the working relationships among my team members at work." Likewise, Francisca, a young woman in Chile, said, "My personal life has really enabled me to demonstrate more professionalism at work and make my work environment friendlier."

CONCLUSION

Summary and discussion. The current study used qualitative research methods to explore employees' perceptions of how work life is enhanced by the experience of family life and how family life is enhanced by the experience of work life. The findings revealed aspects of paid work that facilitate, and are facilitated by, specific aspects of home life as well as aspects of home life that facilitate, and are facilitated by, specific aspects of paid work. The finding that flexibility was the most frequently mentioned work factor benefiting home corroborates with previous studies identifying flexibility of employment and work hours as key features of work-family facilitation (Clark, 2000; Glass & Estes, 1997; Hill, Hawkins, Ferris, & Weitzman 2001). This finding also fits well with Grzywacz & Butler's (2005) theory of work-family facilitation which found that jobs with more variety in time and place, that required greater complexity and social skills, enabled greater work-family facilitation.

Of the nine aspects of home life that were benefited by work, the ability of individuals to meet their family commitments and gain personal, psychological, and physical benefits were reported more often than the benefit of salary. This finding indicates that non-monetary aspects of work are beneficial at home although current research often cites salary as the most important benefit (Pittman & Orthner, 1988). Of the eight aspects of home that positively influenced work, psychological, non-monetary, and non-skill based themes were most prevalent. This suggests that relational and psychological aspects of home life can be important resources in both personal and professional arenas. Previous findings similarly found that interpersonal strengths such as empathy and helping others (Ruderman, Ohlott, Panzer, & King, 2002) and emotional or practical support received through family relationships (Pearson, 2001; Frame & Shehan, 1994; Pittman & Orthner, 1988; Ruderman et al., 2002; and Sinacore & Akcali, 2000) benefited work life. Statements on the benefits of home on work life in this analysis also support Greenhaus & Powell's (2006) theoretical premise that psychological benefits obtained in Role A (family) can enhance cognitive functioning, motivation, interpersonal activity, and commitment in Role B (work).

Of the six aspects of work that were positively influenced by home, psychological, non-monetary, and non-tangible benefits emerged as being most important. Previous research similarly identified benefits from home life on job satisfaction (Sinacore & Akcali, 2000), productivity (Masuo, Fong, Ynagida, & Cabal, 2001); work commitment (Sinacore & Akcali, 2000), and social connections (Scott, 2001). Although responses relating to the ways in which home facilitates work were lower in frequency than the ways in which work facilitates home, the number and variation in responses related to both domains supports research that work and family are allies in specific and identifiable ways.

Through listening to the voices of those engaged in the work-family interface, this analysis highlighted insights that support and extend the existing theoretical work relating to the facilitative relationship between paid work and family life. First, the facilitative work and home aspects identified in this analysis are largely consistent with Greenhaus & Powell's (2006) theoretical discussion of five categories of role-generated resources (skills and perspectives, psychological and physical resources, social-capital resources, flexibility and material resources) in that many of the specific categories that emerged in our data could fit into their broad theoretical categories. The facilitative processes Greenhaus and Powell describe are also similar to the processes we noted in our data. For example, our analysis found, as did Greenhaus and Powell's theorizing, that positive aspects (or resources) generated in one role (paid work), such as organizational skills or access to technology, may be transferred directly to the other role (home life), thereby enhancing experience in that role (home life). Alternatively, a positive aspect (or resource) in one role (paid work), such as a sense of accomplishment may generate positive affect in the same role that then produces high performance and positive affect in the other role (home life).

Second, our analysis has expanded on Greenhaus and Powell's theoretical framework by identifying specific categories or aspects of paid work and home life that facilitate and are facilitated by each of the resource categories identified. Identifying the specific aspect of paid work or home life that was benefited revealed possible pathways for the process of work-family facilitation. This provides a rationale for further exploration of Greenhaus and Powell's (2006) discussion of moderators of instrumental and affective pathways between home and work and points to the exploration of other mechanisms of facilitation between the two, such as a cycling of benefits within a positive amplifying feedback loop.

Limitations and future research. Although this research has identified aspects of work and home life that facilitate each other as well as aspects that are facilitated, future research should further explore the pathways through which this process occurs. Evidence was found for a cycling of benefits that amplifies as it passes from work to home and back to work. Future research that explores how these pathways of cyclical interaction operate and the variety of relationships between the facilitators and the facilitated may provide further clues as to the processes and mechanisms of work-family facilitation (Frone, Yardley, & Markel, 1997; Glass & Estes, 1997; Pittman & Orthner, 1988). Future research could also benefit from exploring differences in work-family facilitation based on demographic position. Research indicates that variance may occur based on nationality, culture, race, age, gender, family structure/stage, personality type, gender role perception, and employment structure. Paying attention to individual shifts in demographic features may help explain why employees experience facilitation differently and vary in the identification of specific benefits.

Using the words, language, and expressions of IBM employees located around the globe, this research has captured the experience of work-family facilitation as it is described and grounded within everyday life. This contributes to existing theorizing because it not only provides evidence for the hypothesized pathways and directions of effect but also is able to demonstrate a goodness of fit between the theories we have about work-family facilitation and the experience of the specific ways in which work and family life facilitate each other. Future research can build on the existing theoretical work with confidence, knowing that it is congruent with, and reflective of the everyday family experience.

NOTE

E. Jeffrey Hill, Ph.D., is an associate professor; Sarah Allen, Ph.D., is an adjunct research professor; and Jenet I. Jacob, Ph.D., is an assistant professor in the School of Family Life, Brigham Young University. Ashley Ferrin Bair, B.S., Sacha Leah Bikhazi, M.S., Alisa Van Langeveld, Ph.D., Guiseppe Martinengo, Ph.D., Taralyn Trost Palmer, M.S., and Eric Walker, Ph.D., recently completed degrees in the School of

Family Life, Brigham Young University. Address correspondence to E. Jeffrey Hill, School of Family Life, Brigham Young University, 2052 JFSB, Provo, UT 84602; FAX 801-422-0230; Email jeff_hill@byu.edu.

The authors would like to thank International Business Machines Corporation (IBM) for providing the support and cooperation needed to collect the data used in this article. Ideas expressed are the opinions of the authors, not necessarily of IBM. We also thank the Family Studies Center of the BYU School of Family Life for its support of this project. Finally, we would especially like to thank our research assistants, Rachael Mae Baugley, Sarah June Carroll, Robb Clawson, Marissa Gutierrez, Brittany Harvey, Chelsi Kizerian, Rachel Norris, and Janet Tiempos for coding thousands of comments.

REFERENCES

Barnett, R. C. (1998). Toward a review and reconceptualization of the work/family literature. *Genetic, Social, and General Psychology Monographs, 124*(2), 125–182.

Barnett, R. C. (in press). Effects of maternal shift work on mothers', fathers', and children's well-being outcomes. In D. R. Crane & E. J. Hill (Eds.), *Handbook of families and work: Interdisciplinary perspectives.* Lanham, MD: University Press of America.

Bianchi, S. M. (in press). "What gives" when mothers are employed? In D. R. Crane & E. J. Hill (Eds.), *Handbook of families and work: Interdisciplinary perspectives.* Lanham, MD: University Press of America.

Bidyadhar, S., & Sahoo, F. M. (1997). Psychosocial factors of work-family linkage. *Psychological Studies, 42*(2&3), 49–60.

Bryman, A. (1988). *Quantity and quality in social research.* London: Unwin Hyman.

Butler, A. B., Grzywacz, J. G., Bass, B. L., & Linney, K. D. (2005). Extending the demands-control model: A daily diary study of job characteristics, work-family conflict and work-family facilitation. *Journal of Occupational and Organizational Psychology, 78*(2), 155–169.

Butler, A. B., Bass, B. L., & Grzywacz, J. G. (in press). Work-family balance in nonprofessional couples: An examination of work and family resources. In D. R. Crane & E. J. Hill (Eds.), *Handbook of families and work: Interdisciplinary perspectives.* Lanham, MD: University Press of America.

Carlson, D. S., Wayne, J. H., & Harris, K. J. (in press). Resource allocation decisions: Resources that play a role when choosing between work and family. In D. R. Crane & E. J. Hill (Eds.), *Handbook of families and work: Interdisciplinary perspectives.* Lanham, MD: University Press of America.

Clark, S. C. (2000). Work/family border theory: A new theory of work/family balance. *Human Relations, 53*(6), 747–770.

Crouter, A. C. (1984). Spillover from family to work: The neglected side of the work-family interface. *Human Relations, 37*(6), 425–442.

Edwards, J. R., & Rothbard, N. P. (1999). Work and family stress and well-being: An examination of person-environment fit in the work and family domains. *Organizational Behavior and Human Decision Processes, 77*(2), 85–129.

Frame, M. W., & Shehan, C. L. (1994). Work and well-being in the two-person career: Relocation stress and coping among clergy husbands and wives. *Family Relations: Interdisciplinary Journal of Applied Family Studies, 43*(2), 196–205.

Friedman, S. D., & Greenhaus, J. H. (2000). *Work and family—allies or enemies? What happens when business professionals confront life choices.* New York: Oxford University Press.

Frone, M. R. (2003). Work-family balance. In Quick, J. C. & Tetrick, L. E. (Eds.), *Handbook of occupational health psychology.* Washington, DC: American Psychological Association.

Frone, M. R., Yardley, J. K., & Markel, K. S. (1997). Developing and testing an integrative model of the work family interface. *Journal of Vocational Behavior, 50*(2), 145–167.

Glass, J. L., & Estes, S. B. (1997). The family responsive workplace. *Annual Review of Sociology, 23*, 289–313.

Greenhaus, J. H., & Powell, G. N. (2006). When work and family are allies: A theory of work-family enrichment. *Academy of Management Review, 31*(1), 72–92.

Grzywacz, J. G. (2000). Work-family spillover and health during midlife: Is managing conflict everything? *American Journal of Health Promotion, 14*(4), 236–243.

Grzywacz, J. G. (2002, February). Toward a theory of work-family faciltation. Paper presented at the 2002 Persons, Processes and Places: Research on Families, Workplaces and Commmunities Conference, San Francisco, CA.

Grzywacz, J. G. (in press). Workplace flexibility: Implications for worker health and families. In D. R. Crane & E. J. Hill (Eds.), *Handbook of families and work: Interdisciplinary perspectives.* Lanham, MD: University Press of America.

Grzywacz, J. G., Almeida, D. M., & McDonald, D. A. (2002). Work-family spillover and daily reports of work and family stress in the adult labor force. *Family Relations, 51*(1), 28–36.

Grzywacz, J. G., & Bass, B. L. (2003). Work, family, and mental health: Testing different models of work-family fit. *Journal of Marriage and Family, 65*(1), 248–262.

Grzywacz, J. G., & Butler, A. B. (2005). The impact of job characteristics on work-to-family facilitation: Testing a theory and distinguishing a construct. *Journal of Occupational and Organizational Psychology, 10*(2), 97–109.

Grzwacz, J. G., & Butler, A. B. (2005). The impact of job characteristics on work-to-family facilitation: Testing a theory and distinguishing a construct. *Journal of Occupational Health Psychology, 10*(2), 97–109.

Heymann, J., & Simmons, S. (in press).Work and family in the global context. In D. R. Crane & E. J. Hill (Eds.), *Handbook of families and work: Interdisciplinary perspectives.* Lanham, MD: University Press of America.

Hill, E. J. (2005). Work-family facilitation and conflict, working fathers and mothers, work-family stressors and support. *Journal of Family Issues, 26*(6), 793–819.

Hill, E. J., Hawkins, A. J., Ferris, M., & Weitzman, M. (2001). Finding an extra day a week: The positive influence of perceived job flexibility on work and family life balance. *Family Relations, 50*(1), 49–54.

Kirchmeyer, C. (1992). Perceptions of work-to-work spillover: challenging the common view of conflict-ridden domain relationships. *Basic and Applied Social Psychology, 13*, 231–249.

Masuo, D., Fong, G., Yanagida, J., & Cabal, C. (2001). Factors associated with business and family success: A comparison of single manager and dual manager family business households. *Journal of Family and Economic Issues, 22*(1), 55–73.

Mellor, S., Mathieu, J. E., Barnes-Farrell, J. L., & Rogelberg, S. G. (2001). Employees' nonwork obligations and organizational commitments: A new way to look at the relationship. *Human Resource Management, 40*(2), 171–184.

Moen, P., & Kelly, E. L. (in press). Working families under stress: Socially toxic job ecologies and time. In D. R. Crane & E. J. Hill (Eds.), *Handbook of families and work: Interdisciplinary perspectives*. Lanham, MD: University Press of America.

Perry-Jenkins, M., Claxton, A., Smith, J., & Manning, M. (in press). Linkages between job conditions and the well-being of working-class parents. In D. R. Crane & E. J. Hill (Eds.), *Handbook of families and work: Interdisciplinary perspectives*. Lanham, MD: University Press of America.

Repetti, R., & Saxbe, D. (in press). The effects of job stress on family: One size does not fit all. In D. R. Crane & E. J. Hill (Eds.), *Handbook of families and work: Interdisciplinary perspectives*. Lanham, MD: University Press of America.

Ruhm, C. J. (in press). Maternal employment and child outcomes. In D. R. Crane & E. J. Hill (Eds.), *Handbook of families and work: Interdisciplinary perspectives*. Lanham, MD: University Press of America.

van Steenbergen, E., Ellemers, N., & Mooijaart, A. (in press). Combining work and family: How family supportive work environments and work supportive home environments can reduce conflict and enhance facilitation. In D. R. Crane & E. J. Hill (Eds.), *Handbook of families and work: Interdisciplinary perspectives*. Lanham, MD: University Press of America.

Voydanoff, P. (2002). Linkages between the work-family interface and work, family, and individual outcomes: An integrative model. *Journal of Family Issues, 23*(1), 138–164.

———. (2004). The effects of work demands and resources on work-to-family conflict and facilitation. *Journal of Marriage and Family, 66*(2), 398–412.

———. (2005). Social integration: Work-family conflict and facilitation, and job and marital quality. *Journal of Marriage and Family, 67*(3), 666–679.

Waldfogel, J., & Han, W. (in press). Variation in the effects of parental employment on child outcomes. In D. R. Crane & E. J. Hill (Eds.), *Handbook of families and work: Interdisciplinary perspectives*. Lanham, MD: University Press of America.

Wayne, J. H. (in press). Cleaning up the constructs on the positive side of the work-family interface. In D. R. Crane & E. J. Hill (Eds.), *Handbook of families and work: Interdisciplinary perspectives*. Lanham, MD: University Press of America.

Zedeck, S., & Mosier, K. L. (1990). Work in the family and employing organization. *American Psychologist, 45*(2), 240–251.

Index

Note to index: An *f* after a page number denotes a figure on that page. An *n* following a page number denotes a note on that page. A *t* following a page number denotes a table on that page.